EXPLOITATION
CONSERVATION
PRESERVATION
A Geographic Perspective on Natural Resource Use

EXPLOITATION
CONSERVATION
PRESERVATION

A Geographic Perspective on Natural Resource Use

Second Edition

SUSAN L. CUTTER
Rutgers University

HILARY LAMBERT RENWICK
American Geographical Society

WILLIAM H. RENWICK
Miami University

WILEY

JOHN WILEY & SONS, INC.

New York   Chichester   Brisbane   Toronto   Singapore

Library of Congress Cataloging in Publication Data:

ACQUISITIONS EDITOR   /   Barry Harmon
PRODUCTION MANAGER   /   Katharine Rubin
DESIGNER   /   Laura Nicholls
PRODUCTION SUPERVISOR   /   Sandra Russell
MANUFACTURING MANAGER   /   Lorraine Fumoso
COPY EDITOR   /   Richard Blander
PHOTO RESEARCHER   /   Jennifer Atkins
PHOTO RESEARCH MANAGER   /   Stella Kupferberg
ILLUSTRATION   /   Sigmund Malinowski

Cover Photo Courtesy of National Park Service
INSET Photo Courtesy of USDA

Recognizing the importance of preserving what has been written, it
is a policy of John Wiley & Sons, Inc. to have books of enduring
value published in the United States printed on acid-free paper, and
we exert our best efforts to that end.

Library of Congress Cataloging-in-Publication Data
Cutter, Susan L.
    Exploitation, conservation, preservation : a geographic
perspective on natural resource use / Susan L. Cutter, William H.
Renwick, Hilary L. Renwick.—2nd ed.
   Includes bibliographical references and indexes.
   ISBN 0-471-50077-1 (cloth)
   1. Natural resources.   2. Environmental policy.
3. Conservation of natural resources.   I. Renwick, William H.
II. Renwick, Hilary Lambert.   III. Title.
HC21.C96   1991
333.7′2—dc20   90-24653
                                                                CIP

Printed in the United States of America

10   9   8   7   6   5   4   3   2

Preface to the Second Edition

Natural resource conservation has been an important college-level course for several decades, and many good texts have been written on the subject. Moreover, in the 20 years since the first Earth Day, students' interest in environmental issues has been high. The textbooks most often used in these latter years have reflected the ideals of the recent environmental movement, with its concern for natural environmental processes, pollution control, the population explosion, and depletion of mineral and other resources.

The environmental movement of the 1960s and 1970s was one of idealism. Throughout the 1970s and 1980s those ideals became incorporated into many aspects of government policy, business practice, and the everyday concerns of the general population. In the late 1980s we have seen a renewal of the idealism that sparked the movement in the 1960s. Today natural resource issues have great emotional and political significance, and form one of the most central elements of our economic and social lives. We must therefore examine many and diverse facets of these issues.

In this book, we have integrated physical, economic, social, and political considerations in our examination of the major natural resource issues facing the world today. We take the view that none of these four factors alone determines the suitability of a resource for any particular use at any time. Rather a dynamic interplay between these factors causes continuing changes in methods and rates of resource exploitation. The title, *Exploitation, Conservation, Preservation,* includes three value-laden and politically charged words that have been at the heart of the natural resources debate over the last century. The subtitle, *A Geographic Perspective on Natural Resource Use,* reflects the traditional use of geography, which integrates studies of physical and human phenomena to understand human use of the earth.

Although the authors share this approach to the subject, we come from diverse scientific, philosophical, and cultural backgrounds. Accordingly, with the exception of the epilogue, we have avoided, as much as possible, taking any one point of view. Instead, we have attempted in most cases to include a wide range of opinions and interpretations of natural resource issues, in the hope that this will provide both a balanced review and a basis for discussion. At the same time, no commentary on natural resources can be free of political content, and we recognize that this book must inevitably be influenced by its authors' personal views. We hope that students reading this book will learn to recognize and understand the political contents of our discussions as well as others' presentations and arguments on these issues.

This book was first prepared in 1983 and 1984, at a time when governmental efforts to better understand and manage the environment had recently produced a substantial amount of statistical information about natural resources in the United States. In the 1980s, however, collection and publication of environmental information by the U.S. government was significantly reduced. As a result, it is much more difficult now to assemble reliable data that uses widely applicable definitions and standards of data quality. Instead, we must rely much more on diverse nongovernmental sources of information. We have made every attempt to overcome these problems, but there are several instances where comprehensive data on natural resources were not available. We encourage students and instructors to supplement the information in the text with additional data whenever possible.

Those familiar with the first edition will recognize many changes, most immediately two additional chapters. A chapter has been added on land resources, in recognition of the importance of land-use issues to a wide range of environmental problems. Also, the chapter on air resources has been split into two parts —the first covering local and urban air pollution problems, and the second focusing on large-scale regional and global problems. We have also added a section on toxic substance issues to each of the relevant chapters. The chapter on global modeling has also been substantially reoriented to focus on global modeling and data resources important to modern work on global environmental change.

A glossary has been included for students' use. The definitions given are not universal, but specific to usage in this text. An Instructor's Manual for this book is available from the publisher.

In the early stages of preparing the first edition, several chapters at a time were assigned primarily to one or two of the authors. In its current form, however, each of us has written at least part of each chapter. We have shared these responsibilities equally, and our names are listed alphabetically.

During the preparation of the manuscript, many people aided us by providing reference materials, illustrations, critical reviews, and moral support for our efforts. Stephanie Happer originally brought us to Wiley, and Barry Harmon saw the project through to fruition. For their help with the second edition, we thank the anonymous reviewers of various drafts; we also thank Dale J. Blahna, Northeastern Illinois University; Brian Brodeur, Rutgers University; Carol P. Harden, University of Tennessee-Knoxville; Cheryl Lougeay, State University of New York at Geneseo; Kenneth Martis, West Virginia University; Jonathan D. Phillips, East Carolina University; John Tiefenbacher, Rutgers University; Stanley W. Trimble, UCLA; Charles I. Zinser, SUNY Plattsburgh; and the students in the Rutgers University classes on conservation of natural resources (Fall 1988 and Fall 1989). The comments of these supporters have provided invaluable feedback.

And of course, we thank Penelope, Barbara, Margaret, Daisy, Donna, Nathaniel, Oliver, and Megan, who each contributed in their own special way. The three authors accept all responsibility for any errors, and we share credit with everyone who helped us for any praise this book may receive.

Susan L. Cutter
Hilary Lambert Renwick
William H. Renwick

Contents

8 Rangelands: Food Resources for Animals   152

9 Forests: A Multiple-Use Resource   172

10   Water Resources: Supply and Demand   199

11   Water Quality: Everybody's Problem   229

13   The Air Resource and Urban Air Quality   282

14   Regional and Global Atmospheric Change   307

15   Minerals: Finite or Infinite?   328

16   Energy Resources   350

17   Potential and Amenity Resources   383

18   Preparing for the Future: Information Gathering, Planning, and Action   415

Photo Credits

Chapter 1 Fig. 1.2: Calvin Larsen/Photo Researchers. Fig. 1.4: Grant Heilman/Grant Heilman Photography.

Chapter 2 Fig. 2.1a: Courtesy Wal-Mart. Fig. 2.1b: Courtesy Photo Research Dept., John Wiley & Sons, Inc.

Chapter 3 Fig. 3.1: Courtesy National Park Service. Fig. 3.2a: Courtesy Japan National Tourist Organization. Fig. 3.2b: Courtesy French Government Tourist Office. Fig. 3.3: Courtesy Bureau of Reclamation. Fig. 3.4: Reprinted by permission, Tribune Media Services. Fig. 3.6a: Courtesy U.S.F.S. Fig. 3.6b: Pat & Tom Leeson/Photo Researchers.

Chapter 4 Fig. 4.1: Courtesy National Park Service. Fig. 4.9: Courtesy National Weather Service.

Chapter 5 Fig. 5.3: Photograph by John Isaac, courtesy of United Nations. Fig. 5.5: Photograph by Ray Witlin, courtesy of United Nations. Fig. 5.8: Photograph by John Isaac, courtesy of United Nations.

Chapter 6 Fig. 6.2: Courtesy National Park Service. Fig. 6.3: Courtesy U.S.F.S. Fig. 6.6: Photograph by J. Clark, courtesy of U.S.D.A. Fig. 6.9: Courtesy E.P.A. Fig. 6.10: Courtesy Tennessee Valley Authority.

Chapter 7 Fig. 7.7a: Grant Heilman/Grant Heilman Photography. Fig. 7.7b: Courtesy U.S.D.A., Soil Conservation Service. Fig. 7.9: Joe Munroe/Photo Researchers. Fig. 7.10: Photograph by Doug Wilson, courtesy of U.S.D.A. Fig. 7.11: Photograph by Tim McCabe, courtesy of U.S.D.A. Fig. 7.15a: Courtesy U.S.D.A., Soil Conservation Service. Fig. 7.15b and c: Courtesy U.S.D.A. Fig. 7.15d: Courtesy U.S.D.A., Soil Conservation Service.

Chapter 8 Fig. 8.3: Photograph by E. Boubat, courtesy of WHO. Fig. 8.4: Photograph by John McConnell, courtesy of U.S.D.A., Soil Conservation Service. Fig. 8.5: Courtesy U.S.D.A., Forest Service.

Chapter 9 Fig. 9.1: Photograph by P.S. Sudhkaran, courtesy of United Nations. Fig. 9.3: Neil A. Palumbo/Gamma-Liaison. Fig. 9.4: Courtesy U.S.F.S Fig. 9.9: Bob Daemmrich/Stock Boston. Fig. 9.10a: Earl Roberge/Photo Researchers. Fig. 9.10b: Courtesy U.S.F.S.

Chapter 10 Fig. 10.12: Dion Ogust/The Image Works. Fig. 10.13: Courtesy Department of Water Resources. Fig. 10.17: Kathy Tarantola/The Picture Cube. Fig. 10.18: Kim Newton/ Woodfin Camp.

Chapter 11 Fig. 11.4: Kirk Condyles/Impact Visuals. Fig. 11.5: Grant Heilman/Grant Heilman Photography. Fig. 11.7: Daniel S. Brody/Stock Boston.

Chapter 12 Fig. 12.5: Steve Morgan/Greenpeace. Fig. 12.7: Twilly Cannon/Greenpeace. Fig. 12.10: Sygma. Fig. 12.13: Dennis Capolongo/Black Star.

Chapter 13 Fig. 13.1: Anthony Suau/Black Star. Fig. 13.4: Joel W. Rogers/Earth Images.

Chapter 14 Fig. 14.4: Runk/Schoenberger/Grant Heilman Photography. Fig. 14.6: Courtesy Landesdenkmalamt Westfalen-Lippe.

Chapter 15   Fig. 15.5: Photograph by Don Green, courtesy of Kennecott Cooper Corp. Fig. 15.6: Courtesy U.S.F.S. Fig. 15.7: Courtesy State of Tennessee, Department of Conservation. Fig. 15.9: Courtesy Reynolds Aluminum Recycling Company.

Chapter 16   Fig. 16.8: Grant Heilman/Grant Heilman Photography. Fig. 16.10: Courtesy Nuclear Regulatory Commission. Fig. 16.11: Stig Stasig/2 Maj/Impact Visuals. Fig. 16.13: Courtesy State of New Mexico, Energy Conservation and Management Division. Fig. 16.14: Courtesy Pacific Gas & Electric.

Chapter 17   Fig. 17.1: Courtesy Wyoming Travel Commission. Fig. 17.3: Grant Heilman/Grant Heilman Photography. Fig. 17.4: Courtesy Tennessee Valley Authority. Fig. 17.7: Courtesy Vermont Travel Division. Fig. 17.9: James Higgins. Fig. 17.12: Courtesy Lurray Caverns.

EXPLOITATION
CONSERVATION
PRESERVATION
A Geographic Perspective on Natural Resource Use

1

Natural Resources: Thoughts, Words, and Deeds

INTRODUCTION

Have you ever wondered what went into the manufacture of the pencil you are now using? A seed germinated and consumed soil nutrients, sprouted and was warmed by the sun, breathed the air, was watered by the rain, and grew into a beautiful straight tree. The tree was cut down. It rode a river's current, was stacked in a lumberyard, and was sawed into small pieces. This wood was transported to a factory, where it was dried, polished, cut, drilled, inserted with graphite (which is made from coal), and painted. Then consider how the pencil made its way to you. It has been packaged attractively with appealing letters painted down its side, shipped via truck, and stored in a warehouse. Your pencil's active life will not end with you, as it may be used by many other hands and minds, if you lose or discard it.

Where are the natural resources in that description? *Resources* are things that have utility. *Natural resources* are resources that are derived from the earth and/or biosphere or atmosphere and that exist independently of human activity. The seed, the tree, the soil, air, water, sun, and river are all natural resources. They are out there, regardless of whether or not human beings choose to use them. They are the *"neutral stuff"* (Zimmerman, 1951) that makes up the world, but they become resources when we find utility in them.

Now, consider the role of human effort in the creation, sale, and use of that pencil. First, in addition to natural resources, there are non-natural resources that are needed, such as saws, labor, and the intelligence to create the pencil. But what motivates people to select and use some portions of the neutral stuff so they become resources while other things are neglected? It is here that we are able to isolate the subject matter of this book. Geographers examine the interactions between human beings and the neutral stuff—the earth and its working parts. When geographers focus on natural resources, we are asking: What portions of the earth's whole have people found of value? Why? How do these values arise? How do conflicts arise, and how are they resolved? Neutral stuff may exist outside of our use, but it becomes resources only within the context of politics, culture, and economics. Let us begin, then, to try to understand how and why resources emerge and are used and fought over.

RESOURCE COGNITION AND VALUE

A resource does not exist without someone to use it. Resources are by their very nature human-centered. To complicate the picture, different groups of people value resources differently. Let's look at the role of environmental cognition in the emergence of resource use.

Environmental cognition is the mental process of making sense out of the environment that surrounds us. To cognize, or think, about the environment leads to the formation of images and attitudes about the environment and its parts. Because we constantly think and react to the environment, our cognition of it is constantly changing on some levels. Nonetheless, certain elements of environmental cognition will remain stable through our lives. There are a number of factors that influence our cognition of resources and thus how they will be used. These can be grouped into five broad categories: (1) cultural background; (2) view of nature; (3) social change; (4) scarcity; and (5) technological and economic factors (see Fig. 1.1).

There are many different cultures in the world, and each has a different system of values. What has value and meaning in one culture may be regarded as a nuisance in another. The mesquite, a deep-rooted drylands shrub, is a good example. Ranchers in West Texas feel the need to fight the thirsty mesquite because they perceive that it dictates what will flourish and what will wither and die in the semiarid environment. Range grasses are shallow rooted and do not compete well with mesquite, which thus deprives range animals of a source of food. As one popular magazine reported, "the rancher enjoys with his mesquite the same relationship that Wile E. Coyote maintains with the Roadrunner in the children's cartoon; the rancher will try anything short of nuclear weapons to conquer mesquite" (*Time*, March 1, 1982). Yet, not too long ago, the Indians of the American Southwest lived quite harmoniously with the now pesky mesquite. The mesquite was used for fuel and shade, while the bush's annual crop of highly nutritious beans was a staple resource. Even diapers were fashioned from the bark. Today mesquite is popular as a fuel for gourmet barbecues.

A society's view of itself relative to its natural environment is a second indicator of how it will ultimately use natural resources. On an idealized spectrum, different worldviews range from fear of or domination by nature to trying to live in harmony with nature to a desire to have control of nature (Kluckhohn *et al.*, 1961). Of course, there is variation within any one group; not all members will agree on their view of nature (Fig. 1.2).

Social change influences the value and use of resources. The composition of societies is constantly changing. People grow older, richer, and poorer, and the cultural makeup of societies changes. All of these factors, particularly ethnicity, sex or gender, education, and income, influence how societies cognize and use resources. For example, higher-income house-

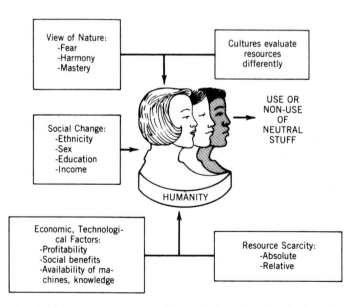

Figure 1.1   Factors involved in resource use cognition include cultural evaluation, view of nature, social change, economic and technological factors, and resource scarcity.

Figure 1.2 Society's view of nature. Nature can be viewed as wild, hostile, and in need of taming, or it can be viewed as a scenic wonder in need of preservation, such as this scene along the McDonald River in Glacier National Park, Montana.

holds in the United States use more water than do lower-income households. Lobsters in colonial New England were fed to indentured servants as a cheap food resource. It was not until the late nineteenth century and the influx of southern European immigrants, who regarded the lobster highly, that it became a valuable culinary delicacy.

Cognition of future resources is colored by historical and current use. Cognitions also change over time. Because of this, planning for natural resource use in the future must take account of these changes. Economists, politicians, and industrialists find it difficult to forecast accurately future resource uses. We may overlook today a resource that will become invaluable in twenty years.

The fourth factor influencing natural resource cognition and use is resource scarcity. As a natural resource becomes scarce or is cognized as becoming scarce, its value may increase. This scarcity may be of two different types. *Absolute scarcity* occurs when the supplies of that resource are insufficient to meet present and future demand. The exhaustibility of all supplies and known reserves of some resources is possible, if improbable. The dwindling supply of certain land resources such as wilderness could conceivably lead to an absolute scarcity of these. *Relative scarcity* occurs when there are imbalances in the distribution of a resource rather than the insufficiency of the total supply. This can be either short or long term. Climatic fluctuations resulting in floods, droughts, or frost routinely cause relative shortages of fresh produce. Open space was not considered a resource until it became relatively scarce in urban areas. Then it became something to be valued, protected, and incorporated into urban redevelopment plans. Relative scarcity also results from one group being able to control the ownership or distribution of resources at the expense of another group. In the energy crises of the mid-1970s, Americans were told by both environmental and industry experts that the supply of oil and gas was dwindling—and that it would be impossible to meet future demand because of the absolute scarcity of the resource. Yet, twenty years later, we see moderately higher prices and a more than adequate supply, suggesting that relative scarcity was in fact the cause of the energy crisis.

Finally, the fifth set of factors that influence resource cognition and use are technological and economic, both basic to understanding the role of scarcity. Technological factors relate to our knowledge and skills in exploiting resources. Groundwater is not a resource until it is made available by drilling a well and installing pumps or other means to bring it to the surface. Desert lands have little agricultural value unless we possess the technical capability to collect and distribute irrigation water, at which time they become very valuable. Deuterium in the oceans is not at present a resource, except for its use in weapons. However, if we learn how to control the fusion reaction for energy production in the future, it will become a resource.

Economic factors combine technology and cognition, as reflected in our pricing system. That is, the value or price of a good is determined by its physical characteristics plus our ability and desire to exploit those characteristics. In a capitalist economy, a commodity will not be exploited unless this can be done at a profit. Therefore, as prices change, things become (or cease to be) resources. A deposit of iron ore in a remote location may be too expensive to exploit today, but if prices rise substantially it may become profitable to exploit and sell that ore; at that time it becomes a resource.

Rarely is the status of a resource determined by technological, cognitive, or economic factors alone; usually it is a combination of these. The nuclear power industry is a good example. The development of fission reactors and related technology was of course necessary for uranium to become a valuable energy resource. But rapid expansion of nuclear generating capacity depends on this energy source being economically competitive with other sources, such as coal and oil. Coal has become costly to use, in part because of concerns about the negative environmental ef-

fects of air pollution. This high cost of coal-generated electricity helped make nuclear power competitive. But the belief that nuclear power is unsafe necessitated modifications in plants that drove up the cost of nuclear power to the point where it is no longer economically attractive. In addition, many people, citing environmental and health fears, reject nuclear energy at any price. The interplay of these forces will continue to affect the choice of nuclear power relative to other energy sources for some time.

KINDS OF RESOURCES

There are various ways to classify resources. We can ask how renewable they are and who benefits from them. *Perpetual resources* (Fig. 1.3) are resources that will always exist in relatively constant supply regardless of how or whether we exploit them. Solar energy is a good example of a perpetual resource; it will

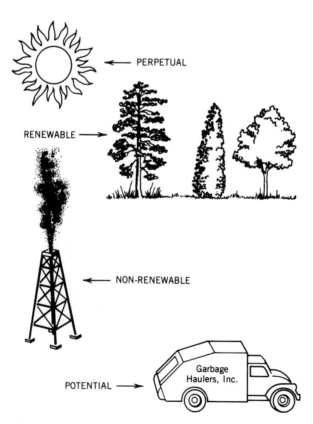

Figure 1.3   The four traditional resource classifications. In reality, a resource can shift from one category to another.

continue to arrive at the earth at a reasonably constant rate for the foreseeable future. In the past the atmosphere and precipitation were regarded as perpetual resources. Recently, however, their quality and the absolute supply of rainfall in some locations have been questioned.

Resources that can be depleted in the short run but that replace themselves in the long run are called *renewable* or *flow resources*. Forests, most groundwater, and fisheries are good examples. Although they can be depleted by harvesting in excess of the replacement rate, if given sufficient time and the right conditions, natural processes will replace them. The key to maintaining the availability of renewable resources is keeping our rate of use at or below the rate of natural replacement.

Nonrenewable or *stock resources* exist in finite supply and are not being generated at a significant rate in comparison to our use of them. Once they are used up that is the end of them. Most geologic resources, such as fossil fuels and mineral ores, are of this type, as is wilderness.

Finally, *potential resources* are not resources at present, but may become resources in the future depending on cognitive, technological, and economic developments. Their potential depends in part on decisions made about them today. Should we make decisions that eliminate them from consideration (such as allowing a plant or animal species to become extinct), then there is no chance of our discovering a resource value in them. Some contemporary examples of potential resources that have recently come into use are solid waste as an alternative fuel source and the use of treated wastewater for irrigation and industrial cooling.

CLASSIFYING RESOURCES: HOW USEFUL A TASK?

Although it may seem that these definitions are relatively clear, to a large extent the status of any resource as perpetual, renewable, or nonrenewable depends on the time scale in which we view it and on how we manage the resource. Even though rainfall on the global level is reasonably constant from year to year,

in many areas the quality of that water has been changed by industrial and auto emissions that produce acid rain. On a longer time scale, there is evidence that we may be causing global climatic changes, resulting in increases or decreases in rainfall at the regional level if not worldwide. Soil, generally regarded as a renewable resource, will restore some degree of its natural fertility if left fallow for a few years. But if accelerated erosion removes a substantial portion of the soil profile, the ability of that soil to support plants that restore nutrients and organic matter may be impaired. It may be centuries before the soil is again productive. That time period is probably too long to consider the soil renewable in human terms.

Similarly, groundwater is generally considered a renewable resource, but in many areas, particularly desert areas where it is so important, the natural rate of recharge is very low, and in some cases there is presently little or no recharge. In these cases the groundwater is effectively a stock resource; once it is used it is lost forever. For these reasons the traditional definitions of resources tell us little about the true nature of particular resources. In fact, they may be harmful, leading us to think that a renewable resource will always be available regardless of how we exploit it. These classifications illustrate, however, that not all resources are equal to the demands put on them. They also indicate the importance of examining the detailed characteristics of resources, and their ability to meet our needs under varying conditions.

CONSERVING RESOURCES: WHAT DOES IT MEAN?

Certainly, few politicians would ever admit to being opposed to the conservation of natural resources, but just as certainly people disagree on what that phrase means. Some believe that it means limited or no use of certain resources. A person with this point of view might maintain that no air pollution is acceptable, and that wilderness cannot be wilderness if there are any people in it. Others feel that conservation means efficient use. They argue that a resource should be used to produce the greatest possible human good. Resources are beneficial, but only if they are used; disuse is seen as waste. Some of the history of the development of these two viewpoints in the United States is discussed in Chapter 3.

The disagreement, however, is even more complex than this. There are many definitions of the meaning of efficient, because few agree on what is truly beneficial. Is profit the highest benefit? Or is spiritual renewal the best use? If a beautiful valley is filled with four houses to the acre, each resident has a home and a quarter acre of land. Is this a more efficient and beneficial use than making the valley into a park, so that many more can enjoy it, albeit less often?

Also, how much time should be considered for use of a resource? Should its beneficial use be spread over many years, in small amounts? Or should we gain all the benefits we can now and use other resources in the future? In some cases these questions are answerable in rational terms, but often they are philosophical or political in nature. As suggested by the title, this book will present many viewpoints regarding resource use along a spectrum from those who advocate full use (or exploitation), to those who would conserve (or balance efficient use with protection), to those who would preserve (or remove from use those resources in need of full protection). *Exploitation* is the complete or maximum use of a resource for individual profit or societal gain. *Conservation* is the wise utilization of a resource so that use is tempered by protection to enhance the resource's continued availability. *Preservation* is the nonuse of a resource by which it is fully protected and left unimpaired for future generations.

NATURE, ECONOMICS, AND THE POLITICS OF NATURAL RESOURCE USE

We believe that a combination of natural, economic, and political factors determines resource use (see Issue 1–1). This means that the study of natural resources must be interdisciplinary and integrative. Integrative approaches must also rely on increasingly specialized work on particular aspects of resource problems, and so we must be able to think in

both specific and integrative ways (Clawson, 1986). Most modern views of natural resources use *systems thinking* to achieve this integration, and that approach will be used here. To illustrate this view, consider the availability of a basic mineral commodity, such as a metal ore (Fig. 1.4). What determines how much of the mineral we will use?

Ores exist in rocks in a wide range of conditions and with a wide range of qualities. This means that some deposits might be mined relatively cheaply, whereas others are costly to mine. There are also deposits that are as yet undiscovered, but that might be found if one made a careful effort to do so (which is more likely if substantial profits are to be gained from mining the ore).

From the standpoint of a consumer of a mineral, availability depends on whether someone is able and willing to sell at a price the consumer is willing to pay. Willingness to sell usually depends on ability to do so profitably, which depends on a combination of the costs of mining and processing and the market price. Economic factors affecting both costs of mining and consumer willingness to pay include

Figure 1.4 Ore mine. The mining of iron ore in northern Minnesota provided the backbone of the regional economy for over a century.

general levels of wealth and economic activity and many more specific aspects of a national or world economy. Social goals and policies also come into play in that they affect both consumer preferences and environmental policies relating to mining activities, for example.

Figure 1.5 is a simplified representation of how all of these factors interact in determining how much of a mineral is used. Clearly there are advantages to being able to consider economics, geology, environmental regulation, marketing, and technology simultaneously. We also must rely on specialists who can analyze the details of individual components of that system. This book will examine both integrative and specific problems.

THE SYSTEMS APPROACH

In the fourth century B.C., the Greek philosopher Aristotle stated that the whole is greater than the sum of its parts. This view, more fully developed over the centuries, argues that we should understand the entire world by examining all of it at once, rather than looking at each of its constituent parts and then adding them up. During the twentieth century this holistic view has gained acceptance in many fields of study. It was formalized in the scientific community in the 1950s under the heading of *general systems theory* (von Bertalanffy, 1950).

Systems thinking is a way of viewing the world. The focus is on the comprehensive treatment of a whole by a simultaneous treatment of all parts. A systems approach not only examines the parts individually, but also looks at how they interact both with each other and as part of the entire system. Geographers use the systems approach to make sense of both natural and human systems, and to better understand why the two types interact as they do.

As we saw with the example of the pencil, natural resource use involves elements of both human and physical systems. Examples of natural systems are forest ecosystems, the hydrologic cycle, and atmospheric circulation. Human systems include technological, economic,

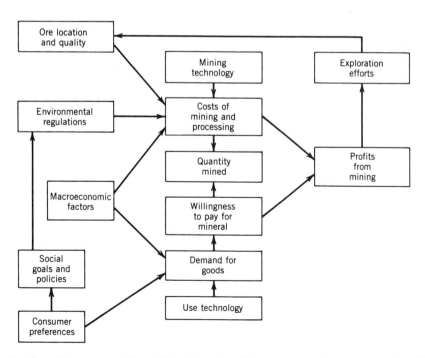

Figure 1.5 A schematic representation of the interaction between natural, economic, and political factors in determining mineral availability and use. Quantity mined is most immediately determined by mining costs and market price, but these are in turn affected by a wide range of economic, technological, and social factors.

and social systems. Figure 1.5 is a highly simplified illustration of these systems as they apply to mineral resources. The complexity and interrelatedness of human and natural systems make the systems approach particularly important. Natural resources cannot be viewed simply as parts of the physical environment, nor as commodities that are bought and sold. Instead, they must be considered in the context of the many natural and human factors that affect them, and with concern for the potentially far-reaching impacts of changes in resource use.

The need for an integrated, systems approach to natural resource use was made abundantly clear in the late 1980s when it appeared that the "spaceship earth" was rapidly deteriorating. Droughts plagued the northern Plains states, raw sewage and medical waste fouled the nation's beaches, the depletion of the ozone layer became fact, not conjecture, and unprecedented tropical deforestation continued. As Senator Albert Gore stated, "humankind has suddenly entered into a brand new relationship with our planet. Unless we quickly and profoundly change the course of our civilization, we face an immediate and grave danger of destroying the worldwide ecological system that sustains life as we know it" (Gore, 1989). This dire prediction, and others like it, has echoed throughout the world. Environmental disasters so dominated the news that in their annual Woman or Man of the Year Issue, *Time* magazine selected the "Endangered Earth as Planet of the Year" for 1988.

As we progress through the 1990s, environmental concerns will influence every aspect of our lives. The halcyon days of rapid

---

ISSUE 1–1   European Integration and the Environment

Europe has undergone rapid changes in recent years, and this can be expected to continue in the 1990s. It has become more prosperous than at any other time since before World War I, and its economy is more fully integrated today than it has ever been. With the recent democratization movements, this trend will continue. Economic integration and prosperity are in large part attributable to the establishment of the European Economic Community, or as it is commonly referred to today, the European Community (EC).

The EC began in the 1950s as an economic association with the aim of improving the standard of living in member states through elimination of internal trade barriers, while economically linking nations so as to reduce the likelihood of war. Since then it has grown and become a political as well as economic association, for as economic cooperation has expanded it has been necessary and desirable for the member nations to act in concert on other matters as well. For example, social policy is often carried out through taxation and subsidies: taxing alcoholic beverages and tobacco or subsidizing rail systems. Social policies are thus linked to economic ones. The EC is still far from becoming a "United States of Europe," however, as the member states retain much of their political independence.

The EC is working toward a 1992 goal of an internal market with no barriers to the movement of goods, labor, or capital. This means the complete removal of any import restrictions, taxes, or regulations that could interfere with business across the international boundaries of the member nations. Many of the less contentious steps that must be taken, for example, elimination of import tariffs and standardization of product safety requirements and similar specifications, have already been achieved. More difficult matters, such as elimination of barriers to international movements of labor, still remain. It is possible that a completely integrated and barrier-free internal market may not be achieved by 1992 or in this century for that matter, but certainly the degree of integration is increasing steadily and most of the important barriers are likely to be significantly lowered, if not removed altogether.

Europeans have been aware of problems of pollution and environmental degradation for decades, but until recently actions to deal with these problems have been uneven at best. Several major events galvanized public concern and governmental support for environmental protection. In 1986 the nuclear reactor accident at Chernobyl, in the USSR, spread radioactive fallout across Europe, contaminating ecosystems

exploitation are over and are being replaced by more conservation-oriented strategies that emphasize sustainable development, less resource use, and more awareness of the longer-term consequences of resource use (Fig. 1.6). Understanding the complexities of these human and physical systems and their interaction is essential as we fulfill our stewardship of the planet. You can make a difference, and we hope that this book will help you realize that.

GENERAL OUTLINE OF THE BOOK

In this book, the analysis of natural resources and management policies has both physical and human foci. We stress the interrelations among the physical attributes of resources, their role in economic systems, and the political and social factors that govern decision-making about their use. We take the view that, even though resources can be classified as perpetual, renewable, nonrenewable, or potential at any given time, they are dynamic and subject to modification or redefinition. Human activity has as much effect on the nature of resources as do natural processes.

Part I focuses on the basic human and natural components of resource use. Chapter 2 provides an overview of the economics of natural resource use, including pricing systems, demand elasticities, externalities, and the relationship between economic growth and resource use. In Chapter 3 the decision-making processes governing resource use and the historical origins of current conservation philosophies in the United States are discussed. Chapter 4 provides a review of the ecological bases

and food supplies. Later that year a fire in Basel, Switzerland, resulted in a massive spill of pesticides and other toxic substances in the Rhine River, poisoning fish along the river's course through Germany, France, and the Netherlands. In 1988 an outbreak of canine distemper virus killed about two-thirds of the seal population in the North Sea, and although the cause of this epidemic is uncertain, environmental pollution was a prime suspect. These and other events, along with the growing awareness of global issues such as deforestation, climate change, and ozone depletion, have stimulated a new drive for environmental protection in Europe.

One aspect of this increased environmental awareness is the growth of the Green Parties. The Greens are a group of political parties with an environmentalist viewpoint. The Greens are a diverse coalition, but most believe in preserving natural ecological systems, protecting the environment for the benefit of all people rather than a wealthy elite, the use of nonviolence, and grassroots democracy. They have nominated candidates for a wide range of local, regional, and national offices and have had their greatest successes in Germany, France, and Denmark. More recently, the Greens have become a viable political force in Eastern Europe as well.

Many European nations elect governments in a proportional representation system, in which a party that wins, say, 20 percent of the vote would be awarded 20 percent of the seats in parliament. Such a system allows representation for minority parties, such as the Greens, even though they may never win a majority of the votes in any one area. Obviously a system of proportional representation is very favorable for a minor party like the Greens, and in the 1989 elections for the European Parliament the Greens won 25 of 518 seats. In Germany and France, the Greens won 8.6 and 10.6 percent of the vote, respectively. They did best in Britain, where they won 15 percent of the vote. Representatives to the European Parliament are elected according to different procedures in each nation, and if Britain had proportional representation, which it does not, the Greens would have won considerably more seats.

The rise in the political power of the Greens coupled with the move toward economic integration has helped to institutionalize environmental policy throughout Europe and accelerate common efforts at reducing pollution. The EC first established an environmental policy in 1972, with an idealistic declaration of environmental goals by a summit of the heads of state. This was followed in the late 1970s and early 1980s by

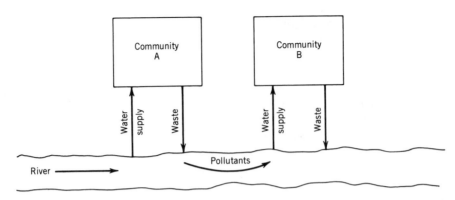

Figure 1.6 The external effects of one system on another. Communities A and B rely on the river as a source of drinking water and a receptacle for their waste. Unfortunately, Community B must use the water after it has been polluted by Community A's waste because of its downstream location.

of natural resources. Chapter 5 examines the human population system, and Chapter 6 describes the land resource base.

Part II deals with specific resource issues. These include agriculture (Chapter 7), grazing (Chapter 8), forests (Chapter 9), water quantity and quality (Chapters 10 and 11), oceans (Chapter 12), air resources and regional/global air issues (Chapters 13 and 14), minerals (Chapter 15), energy resources (Chapter 16), potential and amenity resources (Chapter 17), and lastly a chapter on predicting the fu-

ture (Chapter 18). We conclude with an epilogue that provides each author's own personal view of the future.

REFERENCES AND ADDITIONAL READING

Bertalanffy, L. von. 1950. An outline of general systems theory. *Brit. J. Philos. Sci.* 1(2):134–165.

Clawson, M. 1986. Integrative concepts in natural resource development and policy. In R.W. Kates

environmental quality standards relating to such matters as drinking water quality, air quality, lead and sulfur content in motor fuels and heating oil, noise pollution, and similar problems. Although the EC established pollution reduction policies and standards, each member nation had to implement them according to their own needs and procedures. The goal was laudable, but the results were uneven. For example, in countries like Germany, where there is very strong public desire for improved air quality, major achievements were made. But in Britain, where the government is less concerned about this problem, there was considerable resistance to the EC policies and accordingly very little reduction in emissions occurred.

But as economic and political integration increases, there is less and less room for variation in environmental standards from one country to the next. One important factor is the recognition that many European environmental problems, such as acid rain, waste disposal in the

North Sea, and pollution in the Rhine and major rivers, are international problems that cannot be effectively handled by individual governments. Perhaps more important is the interaction between environmental regulations and economic policy. If automobiles in one country, for example, must be fitted with catalytic converters, and if automobiles are to be traded freely within the EC, then all automobiles sold in the EC must have catalytic converters. Because catalytic converters require lead-free fuel, if one country requires catalytic converters then other countries must make lead-free fuel available, otherwise one could not drive a car with a catalytic converter in those countries. Or if paper manufacturers in one country are required to reduce their discharges of pollutants to rivers, then other countries must adopt similar rules. If they do not, paper manufacturing would cease in the countries with more stringent rules and the pollution (and income) would be transferred to the countries with less regulation. Such problems

and I. Burton (Eds.), *Geography, Resources, and Environment*, Vol. II, pp. 69–82. Chicago: University of Chicago Press.

Gore, A. 1989. An ecological Krystallnacht. Listen. *The New York Times*, March 19, p. E27.

Hardin, G. 1985. *Filters against Folly.* New York: Basic Books.

Kates, R.W., and I. Burton (Eds.). 1986. *Geography, Resources, and Environment*, Vol. I. Chicago: University of Chicago Press.

Kluckhohn, F.R., *et al.* 1961. *Variations in Value Orientations.* Evanston, IL: Row, Peterson & Co.

O'Riordan, T. 1986. Coping with environmental hazards. In R.W. Kates and I. Burton (Eds.). *Geography, Resources, and Environment*, Vol. II, pp. 272–309. Chicago: University of Chicago Press.

Smil, V. 1987. *Energy, Food, Environment.* Oxford: Clarendon Press.

Southwick, C.H. (Ed.). 1985. *Global Ecology.* Sunderland, MA: Sinauer Associates.

Welch, S., and R. Miewald (Eds.). 1983. *Scarce Natural Resources: The Challenge to Public Policy-making.* Beverly Hills, CA: Sage Publications.

White, G.F., 1969, *Strategies of American Water Management.* Ann Arbor, Univ. of Michigan Press.

Zimmerman, E.W. 1951. *World Resources and Industries.* New York: Harper & Brothers.

TERMS TO KNOW

Absolute Scarcity
Conservation
Environmental Cognition
Exploitation
Flow Resource
General Systems Theory
Natural Resource
Neutral Stuff
Nonrenewable Resource
Perpetual Resource
Potential Resource
Preservation
Relative Scarcity
Renewable Resource
Resource
Stock Resource
System

STUDY QUESTIONS

1. What is a natural resource?
2. What are the five categories of factors that influence resource cognition?

have made economic integration more difficult, as it obviously requires detailed negotiations among several nations with widely differing economic and environmental situations. But they also serve to encourage environmental improvement, as the desire for economic integration forces the establishment of uniform environmental legislation throughout the EC.

The European Community has also combined its goal of economic improvement with environmental action through a policy of stimulating investment in the business of environmental protection. If stricter environmental standards are to be met, then money must be spent in modifying industrial processes. Industry will need equipment to remove sulfur from power plant emissions, processes to remove impurities from wastewater, and instruments for detecting and monitoring pollution. This is potentially a major area for economic and industrial growth, and Europe is in a position to become an impor-

tant exporter of environmental technology. The political liberalization of Eastern Europe, along with the recognition of severe environmental problems there, provides an obvious opportunity to expand the business of environmental protection. It will also challenge the EC as it moves toward its 1992 goals.

And so the environmental movement in Europe today is subject to a wide range of pressures. There are many nations involved, with diverse cultural and political systems. The desire to improve living standards and stimulate trade provides the stimulus for economic cooperation, but because environmental and economic policies are closely intertwined, any improvement in economic conditions cannot be achieved without environmental improvement. Political systems also become involved, as the proportional representation system allows the growth of environmentally focused political parties, and democratization allows more freedom of expression.

3. Is the list of resources unchanging through time? Why or why not?

4. What are the four major categories of resources?

5. How is it that soil can be both a renewable and a nonrenewable resource?

6. What is meant by "the whole is greater than the sum of its parts"?

7. How does systems theory help us to understand natural resource use?

2

Economics of Natural Resources

INTRODUCTION

Decisions on the exploitation, conservation, and preservation of natural resources are always made within the context of a particular culture, with its own economic system. This can be a centrally planned Marxist society, or at the other extreme an unregulated capitalist system based exclusively on the pressures of the marketplace. Most countries today have economies somewhere in between these two. No matter what the political or social system, a mechanism must exist for the exchange of goods and services. In most societies this mechanism is price—the value society places on an item.

The price of a good or service is usually represented by its monetary equivalent. In some cases, however, the price of a good or service can include less tangible values. For example, although many in the United States consider clean water and free-flowing streams valuable, it is difficult to place a monetary value on such a resource. Today, resource economists have begun to view natural resources differently from other commodities, and suggest ways in which economies can include an accounting of the degradation or conservation of natural resources. This will lead to a more realistic look at how well we are taking care of our resources for future use (Krutilla and Fisher, 1975).

William D. Ruckelshaus, first administrator of the U.S. EPA, calls for the development of a "sustainability consciousness"—toward a way of living that does not destroy the environment but keeps it healthy for future use. Ruck-

elshaus says that such a consciousness requires the following beliefs:

- The human species is part of nature. Its existence depends on its ability to draw sustenance from a finite natural world; its continuance depends on its ability to abstain from destroying the natural systems that regenerate this world.

- Economic activity must account for the environmental costs of production.

- The maintenance of a livable global environment depends on the sustainable development of the entire human family. (Ruckleshaus, 1989)

Ruckelshaus and others (Stavins, 1989; Group of Seven, 1989; MacNeill, 1989) feel that it is time to make environment and economics work together instead of being continually pitted against one another. In the past, a clean and healthy environment was seen by industry and development as "too expensive" in the face of economic reality. This chapter provides a look at the evolution of thought on the dilemma of economics and environment, as they have moved from being natural enemies to being natural allies. It remains to be seen if legislation can move effective environmental regulation from being punitive to being profitable, or whether market forces (including consumer demand) can initiate better environmental protection (see Issue 2–1 and Figure 2.1).

This sustainability consciousness is illustrated in the following example. In the past when calculating a country's lumber supplies, an economist would simply add up all the woodland acreage as supplied by the govern-

(a)

(b)

Figure 2.1 Retailing and the environment. The retail industry has recently developed its own environmental consciousness by touting its "greenness," by taking pro-environmental positions (a), and by using environmental terms, such as "degradable," to sell products (b).

ment and by private companies and state: "this country has these many acres/hectares in forest, and this many people are employed in the industry, and the country earns this dollar amount from its lumber interests." The resource economist adds some new information to this assessment: How much soil erosion is occurring in areas where timber has been harvested? This will affect future forests planted and the water quality of streams in the area. How much clear-cutting is practiced? How much replanting is being done? Is the company and country cutting virgin forests or newly planted ones? What kinds of air and water pollutants are being produced by the lumber and pulp mills that handle the lumber? All of these questions, when answered, tell a country what the environmental costs of lumbering are, as well as the monetary benefits of the lumbering. With this additional information, we can plan for an environmentally stable future.

As discussed in the previous chapter, a natural resource is defined by a society's cognition of that resource and its technical ability to extract the resource. This means that the value and price of a resource can change over time. Since the cognition of a resource can also vary from person to person, different user groups will place a different price on the resource.

To further complicate matters, the resource value held by some user groups will be dictated by easily defined market forces, whereas others will have a more intangible system of determining price. A forester, for example, will determine the value of a woodlot based on prevailing market prices for lumber. But would the county wildlife manager be willing to use the supermarket price of meat or poultry in deciding the natural habitat value of that same woodlot? No, because the value of wild animals in our American society today is far greater than the simple price of pelts or meat. The study of natural resource economics requires an understanding of how the cognition of natural resources is reflected in the world's various economic systems.

This chapter looks at the role of economics in natural resource management. Three questions are examined.

1. How do economic forces influence our use of resources? Natural resources are commodities regulated in part by supply, demand, and price, but several unique characteristics of natural resources alter the economic use that we make of them.

2. How do we place a value on a natural resource? To operate within an economic system, a value or price of a resource must be determined. Yet, there are many values of a resource that may not be reflected in price. Deciding on the value of a resource is the key to understanding how economic pressures influence both the use and the management of a resource.

3. How do economic forces influence the management of a resource? Short-term pricing mechanisms might dictate the use and management of a resource quite differently than pricing systems based on long-term social needs.

ECONOMICS AND THE USE OF RESOURCES

CHARACTERISTICS OF NATURAL RESOURCES

In most societies, natural resources are the basic building blocks in the production system. They are raw materials. Little of their value is derived from human inputs such as labor, so they generally have a lower value per unit than other commodities. The value of a standing forest, for example, is rarely more than the cost of owning the land for a period of time, and usually it is much less. When the trees are cut they are somewhat more valuable, but milling and drying add much more value. By the time the wood is made into a house or a piece of furniture, the price of the standing tree accounts for a very small portion of the value of the finished product. In other words, most of the value of the finished product was added after the tree was grown. There are cases where natural resources have a high value "in the ground," but in such cases it is the consumer that drives the price up, if demand is greater than the amount of the resource available.

A second important characteristic of natural resources is that over short periods of time supply is relatively inelastic. Most natural resources require substantial capital investment and planning to bring them into production. For example, suppose the demand for a particular metal increases significantly. To a certain extent existing mines can step up activity by hiring more miners and buying more equipment. But a large increase in production will probably require that new mines be opened. This may require geologic exploration, but even if the deposits are known and owned by mining companies they must still build roads and other facilities to allow extraction, sink the initial mine shafts, and build housing for labor, before extraction can actually begin. All of these things take time, generally years, and so in the short run the supply cannot keep up with increased demand. This means that the supply cannot be stretched quickly: supply is inelastic.

The inelastic nature of many resources can encourage wide fluctuations in price. A notorious example is the price of gasoline at the pump. During the "energy crisis" of the early 1970s, when imports from the Middle East were dramatically reduced, the cost of gas quadrupled in a matter of months. In the years since then, gas prices have become very sensitive to real and apparent shortages in the supply. In 1989, for example, when the Exxon Valdez spilled its oil cargo along the Alaska shoreline, the price at the pump rose overnight in both the United States and Great Britain, even though the spill was irrelevant to the supply of gasoline. Simultaneously, the intangible value of pristine coastline and healthy wildlife rose incalculably across the nation within a period of days (see Issue 2–2). "Price-gouging" was an issue again in 1990, when gas prices soared following Iraq's invasion of Kuwait.

Sudden changes in demand as well as supply can cause a dramatic rise or fall in price, yet there is little that the producers can do in the short run to assure a steady, long-term trend. To illustrate, a bitter cold snap in December 1989 hit the eastern half of the United States. Consumer demand for fuel oil and propane supplies reduced existing supplies to perilously low levels. Almost overnight, prices for fuel oil and propane skyrocketed to double and triple what they were earlier in the month. When warmer weather returned in January, consumer demand slackened, and prices fell once again.

Whenever possible, it is desirable to have a relatively high degree of substitutability among raw materials. Not only can one metal be substituted for another in, say, an automobile, but recently plastics, fiberglass, carbon fibers, and other synthetic materials have begun to replace metals for many purposes. Beet sugar can substitute for cane sugar; coal can substitute for natural gas. Although this substitutability contributes to stability for the makers of finished products, it often leads to considerable volatility in natural resources markets. The endless pattern of boom and bust cycles in one-employer mining towns is one of the sadder human consequences of this volatility.

For some natural resources, particularly minerals, supply is theoretically infinite, assuming we are able to pay a high enough price. Most metals exist in the earth's crust in much greater total quantities than we have need for; the problem is that in only a limited number of locations are they found in high enough concentrations or close enough to the surface to allow them to be extracted at a profit. But as long as we are willing to pay a little more to obtain them, then we can dig a little deeper, or refine less concentrated ores, and still obtain the desired commodity. At some point, we will find that it is cheaper to recycle used metals than to mine new ores, and at that point we will be able to supply much of our new requirements by recycling. When we also consider the substitutability of most substances, then it seems unlikely that we will encounter a situation in which we run out of raw materials. On the other hand, the theoretical supply of energy may or may not be infinite, depending on what technologies are available to us, and activities such as mining and recycling may very well be limited by shortages of energy.

PRICING SYSTEMS

Natural resources are commodities and we value them for their ability to provide the basic needs of life: food, clothing, shelter, and happiness. As commodities they are exchanged among individuals, groups, and nations using some sort of pricing system as a medium of exchange. This pricing system can have a major impact on how resources are used. Resource price is dictated both by a society's determination of resource value (discussed in the next section) and by the economic system in use.

Economic Systems

Although there are three major types of world economic systems—commercial, centrally planned, and subsistence—only commercial and centrally planned economies produce a surplus of goods. In a commercial economy, prices are set by the producers who sell goods and services. Producers are characterized by a profit motivation and pressure to produce at low cost. This usually leads to specialization, thus allowing more efficient production. A producer will try to do one thing well instead of many things in a mediocre way: there is greater profit in the former. Profit and efficiency are balanced by market forces, where supply and demand govern the price and quantity of goods exchanged. In other words, a producer can be efficient and offer a high-quality product, but once he or she enters the world market, there are economic forces at work that are beyond the control of the individual company, and dreamed-of profits are not guaranteed. In a commercial economy the use and allocation of natural resources are governed by many forces, especially market competition and profit maximization. Producers respond to these forces to protect their own best interests. Examples of commercial economies include the United States, Western European countries, most Latin American countries, India, and South Africa.

In a centrally planned economic system, the government controls the resources. Producers market goods and services to the central government, which in turn controls the supply and price according to its own objectives. These can range from monetary gain to social and economic equality, goals not normally found in a commercial economy. The Soviet Union and China are examples of centrally planned economies, although the Soviet economic system is changing rapidly. The failure of socialist governments in eastern Europe to consider environmental values in their planning, and the difficulty of recognizing amenity values in a materialist society have clearly contributed to the severe environmental problems evident there.

Regardless of the type of economic system in place, a price is placed on a resource, thus permitting exchange and use by the society. There are different approaches to the determination of price. For example, Marxists follow the *labor theory* of value, which states that the price of a good is determined by the amount of labor required to produce it. An alternative approach is the *consumer theory* of value, which says that value is determined by how much a consumer is willing to pay. Still another view is the *cost theory*, which says that in a competitive system different producers will compete by reducing prices until they equal the cost of production. Finally, the *production theory* emphasizes the inputs of some critical commodity, for example, energy. That is, the value of goods is a function of the energy required to produce them and thus they are priced accordingly. Although each of these theories addresses at least one aspect of the value of resources, in the final analysis it is the interaction of supply and demand that determines both the price of a good and the quantity sold at that price.

Supply and Demand

The laws of supply and demand tell us that the amount of a good demanded by consumers and the amount the producers are willing to supply vary depending on price. As price increases, the amount consumers are willing to buy decreases. Conversely, as price increases, the amount that producers are willing to sell increases. The intersection of these two functions determines the equilibrium price and quantity sold. If there is a change in conditions, say, increasing scarcity of a commodity, then it will cost producers more to supply that commodity and they will either require a higher price to produce the same amount or they will supply less at the same price.

In either case the supply function shifts up and to the left, with the result that price increases and quantity sold decreases. Similarly, a change in the value consumers place on a commodity will change the demand function,

with appropriate changes in price and quantity sold. This process assumes perfect competition, which exists only when no individual consumer or producer can exert influence on the market, and when all producers and consumers have full information and access to the market. Obviously, perfect competition does not exist in the real world, so these assumptions are violated in many cases.

Market Imperfections

Unfair competition causes price to be determined by factors other than supply and demand, and this situation results in an imperfect market. A *monopoly* exists when a single buyer or seller dominates the market. Monopolistic or *oligopolistic competition* describes what happens when a few buyers or sellers either follow a price leader in fixing the price of a commodity or engage in discriminatory practices to set prices so as to maximize their own profits. Their purpose is to restrain competition by keeping prices artificially high.

There are many resource oligopolies in the world today, and these are normally referred to as cartels. A *cartel* is a consortium of commercial enterprises that work together to limit competition. These cartels can either be similar industries (such as refineries) or resource-rich exporting countries. In the latter case, these countries band together for economic advantage to fix the world prices of their commodity. The Organization of Petroleum Exporting Countries (OPEC) is a good example of a cartel. OPEC consists of 13 member nations: Algeria, Ecuador, Gabon, Indonesia, Iran, Iraq, Kuwait, Libya, Nigeria, Qatar, Saudi Arabia, United Arab Emirates, and Venezuela. OPEC nations supply a little more than half of the noncommunist world's supply of crude oil. There are many other examples of cartels, including those controlling copper and bauxite.

DETERMINING RESOURCE VALUE: QUANTIFYING THE INTANGIBLES

Not all resources have a value that can be quantified and expressed in monetary terms. Clean air is one example; an unobstructed view of the landscape is another. Yet these resources are increasingly part of the picture in determining the use we make of our earth. As mentioned in the chapter introduction, only in the past few years have economists begun to look for ways that the environment and the marketplace can work together instead of being pitted against each other. Let us look at the historical development of the marketing of the environment.

The techniques that are most widely used to determine the value of intangibles such as clean air and scenic views have been cost-effectiveness analysis and benefit–cost analysis. *Cost-effectiveness analysis* simply involves summing all the costs and monetary returns involved in a single plan to determine the expected return on investment. *Benefit–cost analysis*, on the other hand, compares all the costs and benefits of several different plans. It requires an understanding of the social context—the alternative values placed on a resource by different sectors of the society—within which the balancing of costs and benefits is made.

Cost-effectiveness analysis aids the decisionmaker in determining the least costly and most efficient strategy for carrying out a project or exploiting a resource once the decision has been made to proceed. Benefit–cost analysis is a tool for helping society make choices on the allocation of resources, whereas cost-effectiveness analysis aids the individual firm or agency in implementing that decision. Benefit–cost analysis evaluates alternative uses of a resource within a particular social context, and it usually seeks to find the alternative that has the greatest ratio of total benefits to total costs.

BENEFIT–COST ANALYSIS

Because benefit–cost analysis has been the building block of both environmental protection and exploitation in the era since 1970, we will examine it in greater detail. When a shopper goes to the supermarket, he or she is constantly making choices of what and how much to buy. How long will that small jar of peanut butter last? Is it worth it to me to buy a larger jar at a lower unit price? Do I really need prime rib or should I settle for hamburger? Economic theory tells us that making such decisions usually involves thinking about the costs and benefits of each item, and purchasing those items whose benefits appear to outweigh costs. Intangibles enter the picture even here, however, if the consumer considers the health aspects of cholesterol, fiber, and fats when choosing foods.

The balancing process observed in the supermarket can also be found in natural resource economics. Decisions on whether or not to build a dam, invest in new timberland, or clean up a polluted river usually involve some sort of benefit–cost analysis. This analysis can range from the elaborate accounting used to justify large government water projects to simple judgments made by individual farmers, foresters, or fisherfolk. In either case, some sort of value is placed upon expected costs and benefits and the two values are then compared within a particular time frame. Some sort of price must be placed on all the factors in the resource decision: the price of the resource in question and the price of improvements or costs of damages to resources and society expected to result from a project.

Benefit–cost analysis involves a number of factors, including price, interest rate, and time. Since the analysis frequently must take into account nonmonetary variables, the value chosen for these factors can have a major impact on the outcome of the analysis and the resulting decision on how the resource is to be used. For example, in the American Northwest, debate has been raging over what is of greater value: trees as lumber and as a source of employment or trees as habitat for an endangered species, the spotted owl (Mitchell, 1990).

Frequently the organization conducting a benefit–cost analysis has a vested interest in some particular outcome, leading to a bias in estimates of resource values that favor that outcome. This is especially true for estimates of amenity resources such as recreation or a scenic view.

One common approach to applying the result of a benefit–cost analysis is to determine the ratio by separately summing the costs and benefits over time, then dividing benefits by costs. A B : C ratio greater than 1 indicates that benefits are greater than costs and the project should go forward. A B : C ratio can be very misleading when the analysis includes potential environmental impacts. Any project will presumably have some environmental impacts, regardless of benefits or costs. These impacts should be applied to either the calculation of costs (by addition) or the calculation of benefits (by subtraction) and must be used consistently. Another problem is that the present value of future costs or benefits depends on the interest or discount rate used in the calculations. Small changes in interest rates can result in very large differences in project costs. Despite these problems, B : C ratios are frequently used to justify many public works projects.

QUANTIFYING PRICE

When faced with a decision whether or not to permit lumbering in a National Forest, a resource manager seeks various types of information to include in an analysis of benefits and costs. Some of this information, like the value of standing timber, the cost of replanting trees after harvest, or the increased water yield as a result of cutting the forest, can be expressed in monetary terms. Other information is more speculative, such as the value of wildlife habitat lost and the resulting decline in the numbers of hunters and fisherfolk. These so-called incommensurables and intangibles can frustrate benefit–cost analysis, forcing the decisionmaker to create an artificial or *shadow price* for that resource.

Incommensurables are effects (both benefits and costs) that cannot readily be translated into a monetary value or price. *Intangibles* are incommensurables that cannot be measured at all—they are truly outside the analysis. The trick in benefit–cost analysis is to separate the incommensurable effects from the intangible effects (see Issue 2–2). Although it is impossible to assign a value to intangibles, it is possible to assign a value or shadow price to incommensurables. In any assessment of the benefits and costs of resource exploitation, it is necessary to clearly define the limitations of such methods to quantify these incommensurable effects.

Economists employ a broad range of techniques to establish the shadow price of incommensurable resources. Three of the most commonly used techniques are discussed here.

Willingness to pay is a method in which potential users of a resource are asked how much they are willing to pay for access to the resource. Conversely, one could ask how much society would have to pay the individual not to use the resource. An example would be a survey of beach users to determine how much they are willing to pay to use the beach or how much they would have to be paid not to go to the beach. The value of the latter could be used to estimate the value of recreation losses caused by an oil spill on the beach. The former could be used to justify importing beach sand to keep an eroding beach the way it is.

Another technique is determining *proxy value* or the value of similar resources elsewhere. This technique estimates the value of a day's hunting, for example, by summarizing the hunter's investment in supplies, time, and travel and dividing this figure by the number of days of hunting. This is an estimate of the value that would have resulted if the project or exploitation did not occur in the first place. Another example would be estimating the decline in commercial fish harvest due to the destruction of their habitat by an oil spill.

The third technique is called *replacement cost*. This is simply the cost of replacing the resource that is being used, such as substitution of clean sand for polluted sand on a beach fouled by an offshore oil spill. Often there is no market for the replacement of extramarket goods as the resources are not substitutable.

The accuracy varies when using these and other methods of estimating the shadow prices of resources. It is important to recognize the limitations of such techniques as well as their ability to provide the necessary data for a benefit–cost analysis. They are useful in placing a comparable value (price) on those resources that normally do not have one, but only within the limitations discussed.

MANAGEMENT AND ALLOCATION OF RESOURCES

Economic forces shape the price and utility of a resource. That is, oil shale in western

Colorado and Wyoming was valuable enough to extract and process when the world's oil price was high, but when that price dropped, oil shale became too expensive as a source of oil. Economic forces also affect who gets to use a resource and how it is managed. When the North American deserts were seen as valueless a century ago, they became a dumping ground for Native American tribes, who were displaced from more valuable lands elsewhere. Recently, however, rich mineral deposits have been found on many of these "valueless" tribal lands. In some cases, tribal corporations and private industry have agreed on mutually beneficial business deals. Overall, the influence of economics on management decisions can best be classified into three categories. These are ownership of the resource, social costs, and the economics of the individual company or firm.

OWNERSHIP

Many natural resources are held in communal, rather than private, ownership. This is true both for resources that are government owned, such as national forests and offshore mineral rights, and for resources for which no formal ownership is designated, such as air or the water in the oceans. Although these resources are commonly owned, that is, owned by everyone, they are exploited by private individuals and corporations for their own profit. This discrepancy between ownership and management responsibility causes problems. These types of resources are called *common property resources* because they are owned by everyone, even though they may only be used by a few who have the technical and economic means to do so (see Chapter 12).

This conflict was first described by Garrett Hardin (1968) in his classic article entitled "The Tragedy of the Commons." Hardin argued that commonly owned resources are nearly always overexploited. The reason for this is that while the costs of exploitation are shared among all the owners of the resource, the benefits accrue to the individual, and so it is always in the individual's interest to increase exploitation, even to the point of overexploitation of the resource. Hardin concludes that there must be some institutional arrangement that prohibits overuse and encourages conservation.

For example, if a group of people all dump sewage into the same water body, they all suffer, but for any one person to not dump sewage would be foolish from a purely economic standpoint. This person would still suffer everyone else's sewage and would not reap the full benefit of his or her reduction in pollution. The consequence of this is that some governing body may step in, and through that body all agree to regulate their exploitation of the resource for mutual benefit.

In some cases this is relatively easy, and in others not. When large corporations are both exploiters and employers and thus politically powerful, or when enforcement of restrictions is difficult, then overuse and degradation of commonly held resources can result. For example, the debate over acid rain and what to do about it has been raging between Canada and the United States for well over a decade, with no end in sight. Canada claims that the United States is hurting Canadian forests and water with air pollution, but the American government is reluctant to bring any pressure to bear on the steel mills and power plants that are the basic components of the United States' midwestern economy. The responsibility for management of these common property resources is a major issue in air, water, and ocean resources as we shall see in later chapters.

In the last few years a new approach to the commons problem has emerged: How can government make it profitable to the individual to protect the commons? We can call this approach "the opportunity of the commons," in which government creates economic incentives that promise increased profits to a company that decreases its pollution output.

How might this work? In the case of acid rain, Stavins (1989) reports on a plan that would give pollution credits to companies that contribute to the acid rain problem. If a company lowered its emissions below the level required by law, it could make deals with the difference—to delay compliance with another regulation, or by selling accumulated pollution-compliance points to a company that remains in violation of the law. This would earn a profit for the first company and a delay for the second. Pollution credits could thus be bought and sold among companies to allow the marketplace to decide the cheapest way to reduce smokestack emissions, but why restrict this to companies? Why shouldn't environmentalists be allowed to buy pollution rights (or credits) from publicly owned utilities and then retire the facility? In 1989, the going rate for the right to discharge a ton of pollutants per year in this case was between $1000 and $2000 per ton (Hershey, 1989). The air quality would improve via a direct financial action on the part of the environmental community rather than through a long and protracted political process.

But can we trust the bottom line, a purely market-oriented approach to environmental protection? Even advocates for this approach warn that the market is limited as a tool for protection: while companies wheel and deal for points and profits, pollutants are still produced, and the commons continues to absorb them. Government remains a necessary tool to force industry to internalize the cost of pollution (MacNeill, 1989). However, government has its own problems to address, as government-owned enterprises such as the Tennessee Valley Authority and nuclear weapons facilities have been among the nation's most notorious and prolonged polluters and have voiced opposition to increased pollution abatement measures. How can industry be required to produce fewer pollutants? Let's look at economic concepts that, if made into law, would encourage industry to create fewer pollutants.

SOCIAL COSTS

In commercial economies both the producer and consumer bear the costs of production. These production systems are termed efficient if they maximize output (finished goods or services) per unit cost of production. Economists today recognize that not all production systems are truly efficient. There are certain spillover effects from the production system that enter the environment and affect consumers disproportionately. These spillover effects are called *externalities.* Externalities are the unwanted by-products from modern industrial processes and usually consist of pollutants such as heat, toxic chemicals, or sediment.

These pollutants or *residuals,* as they are sometimes called, are normally discharged into one of the many common property resources—air, water, and public land—and this is where conflict arises.

The problem with externalities is that they have clear environmental and social impacts. A private or government-operated producer wants to minimize costs and maximize profits, which ultimately forces the local community where the factory or plant is located to absorb the externality (Seneca and Taussig, 1974). In most cases, the conflict is between a private company and a community, as the following example shows. Chemsweet Inc. is located upstream from Farmer Green. Chemsweet routinely discharges chemicals into the stream that Green uses to irrigate her crops. Eventually, the crop is damaged as a result of the contaminated water. Any costs that are attributed to these spillover effects or residuals are called external costs. Chemsweet Inc. does not incur any cost for polluting the stream, yet costs are imposed on neighbors like Farmer Green. Not only does Farmer Green bear the costs of a reduced harvest (and less profit), but she must also pay for a new source of water or lose her crop entirely. These external costs are outside the market system and are not reflected in the price of the manufactured good that Chemsweet Inc. produces.

Social costs are those costs to society that not only involve externalities but also include the cost of producing the good in the first place. In most cases, natural resource use does not fully embrace this in the pricing structure and we are thus left with the problem of managing and coping with these externalities or residuals.

Residuals management is a major part of natural resource economics. There have been several techniques developed for understanding and managing residuals, and these usually involve economic or pricing mechanisms and/or government intervention in the form of pollution regulations. Residuals management is the term used to describe the first technique.

Residuals management (or materials/energy balance as it is also known) is a process used to describe and quantify the inputs and outputs of a production system including the residuals. The economic model that first described this process was developed by Kneese, Ayers, d'Arge (1971), and their colleagues at Resources for the Future, a Washington, D.C. think tank. Residuals management advocates a steady-state production system where inputs and outputs are balanced. The residuals, or waste products, are either fed back into the production system (recycling) or released into the environment. Specific techniques have been developed to manage residuals. A *residuals tax* or effluent charge was first proposed by Kneese and Bower (1971) as a method of controlling residuals. This can also be called the *polluter pays principle*. Producers of goods would pay for the residuals they discharge, with taxes levied against firms in relation to how much pollution they release to the environment. A residuals tax would force the polluter to bear the true social costs of production and contamination of common property resources by internalizing the externalities. It would encourage the polluter to reduce the quantity of residuals, as the tax would be in direct proportion to the amount discharged. This fee would then be used to either clean up the environment or compensate those consumers adversely affected by the pollution.

Another technique of residuals manage-ment is the *throughput tax* or disposal charge. Producers of goods would be charged a materials fee that would reflect the social costs of the disposal of the residuals. This tax would of course be passed on to the consumer in the form of increased prices for the commodity. Although a throughput tax might provide an incentive to recycle and make products last longer, many of the disposal charges currently used, such as deposits on beverage containers, are discriminatory against consumers. These types of taxes influence the price of a commodity beyond the simple demand and supply accounting.

ECONOMICS OF THE INDIVIDUAL FIRM

Microeconomics refers to the economics of the firm or individual company. In a commercial system, resource exploitation is undertaken by the firm rather than by society as a whole, and so it is worthwhile to examine some microeconomic activities that affect natural resource decisions.

The primary goal of a firm is to earn money. This is done by investing money (capital) in the physical plant needed for production (land, machinery, etc.) and in other pro-

---

ISSUE 2–1   Madison Avenue Markets the Environment

It was just a matter of time before retailers and their advertising firms on Madison Avenue discovered the environment. The use of environmental marketing to sell products ranging from disposable diapers to trash bags has increased dramatically since 1989. Advertisers are clearly taking advantage of the renewed environmental consciousness of the public and are preying on environmental sympathies to sell consumer goods (Fig. 2.1).

Environmental marketing takes many forms. For example, Wal-Mart Stores Inc. and K Mart Corporation publicly tout their efforts to get manufacturers to produce products and packaging that are environmentally safe. Full-page ads publicize their concern, and tags on shelves in their stores highlight packaging made from recycled paperboard or fibers, or products that no longer contain CFCs. A coalition of up-scale department stores (Macy's and Lord & Taylor) took out full-page ads in *The New York Times* and other newspapers to proclaim that ivory was out of fashion in an effort to help the declining African elephant population. These stores also refused to carry ivory products. Although this is a beginning to the greening of America's retailers, it does not cost them very much. The demand for ivory jewelry has declined in recent years, and the sales of such items are a minuscule percentage of total jewelry sales, so most stores will not incur any loss of sales by the anti-ivory campaign. The amount of consumer confidence and good will, however, is enormous and this is precisely what these stores are banking on.

Another form of marketing is the use of environmental terms like degradable and recyclable to enhance a product's image. The use of

duction inputs (energy and labor) in order to produce an output that can be sold for more money than was invested. The producer's costs in producing a given output can be divided into two categories, fixed costs and variable costs. *Fixed costs* are bills that must be paid regardless of how much of a product is made in a given time. Fixed costs are primarily the costs of owning the means of production (the physical plant). If the money needed to set up a plant was borrowed, then the fixed costs are the interest expenses on that loan. *Variable costs* consist of labor, energy, transportation, and similar inputs in the production process itself, and these vary according to the rate of production. Variable costs are a relatively constant fraction of the selling price of the goods produced, although there are some levels of output that are more efficient than others.

Let us assume there is a given investment required to open up a particular mine. Afterward, variable costs vary in direct proportion to the rate of extraction of minerals. The faster the minerals are extracted, the greater the profit will be, as the fixed costs need be borne for a shorter period of time. In practice, variable costs per unit output are high at low rates

of production because of economies of scale. However, variable costs increase again at still higher rates of production because of the need for greater capital and labor inputs to maintain high rates of production.

The optimal rate of production is of course determined by a combination of fixed and variable costs. Fixed costs always have the effect of making the optimal rate of output higher. As interest rates go up, the need to recover the initial investment in a short time period increases, hence the need to increase rates of production.

As a result of these pressures, demands are made on the firm to maximize the rate of production, regardless of whether it is good conservation policy in the long run. This generalization strictly applies only to a single facility, such as a single mine or a single forest unit. A large corporation owning many mines will vary its total output not by varying output at every mine simultaneously, but by closing or opening mines. That is how it keeps its fixed costs as low as possible. But in most cases there will be pressure on the extracting firm to maximize rate of extraction to recover fixed costs, often at the expense of the environment.

Another important aspect of the firm rela-

these terms is increasing, as is the level of scientific skepticism regarding the claims. Plastic trash bags and disposable diapers are the two products that have come under federal scrutiny for false claims in advertising. Many consumer and environmental advocates feel that such claims are false and simply a new marketing gimmick. Glad and Hefty trash bags proclaim they are degradable, suggesting that in the presence of sunlight the bag will break down over time. What they don't mention is that if the bags are left in the sun long enough to break down, the contents will be strewn all over. Furthermore, if the bags are hauled away to a landfill, sunlight will never penetrate, thus leaving the trash bag and its contents intact. Nowhere is the debate more heated than with disposable diapers. These so-called biodegradable diapers contain corn starch, which is designed to decompose in the landfills through the actions of microorganisms.

All too often, however, landfills are too dry and too tightly packed, and thus even organic matter such as banana peels do not readily decompose. Newspapers printed twenty or thirty years ago were found intact by an Arizona archeologist who excavated landfills throughout the country.

Concern for truth in advertising has become so critical that the Federal Trade Commission, which regulates advertising practices, is looking into the issue of the degradable and recyclable claims. Even other manufacturers are questioning the claims. Procter and Gamble, manufacturers of Luvs and Pampers disposable diapers, ran a full-page ad attacking their competition for false advertising by explaining "why we don't call our diapers biodegradable." What they failed to mention was their marketing of a corn starch diaper in Europe, lest they fall behind in the diaper wars (Luoma, 1990; Meier, 1990; Schwadel, 1989).

tive to natural resources is the degree of liquidity of its assets, or how easily the firm can sell out if it needs to. Remember that the goal of any company is to turn a monetary investment into monetary return, and production of a particular commodity is simply a means to that end. An oil company consists of a group of people who have particular expertise in finding, extracting, and selling oil, and who also own the equipment needed to do those things. If that oil company has an opportunity to invest its capital in a housing development or a soft drink bottling plant and receive a greater return on investment than it would in drilling for oil, then it will do so. Only the existing investment in oil-related equipment and experience prevent an oil company from taking its money elsewhere if the financial opportunities are more attractive in some other business.

BUSINESS AND THE ENVIRONMENT: RECENT TRENDS

One significant trend in business in the 1970s and 1980s was toward *diversification* of large corporations. Tobacco companies buy soap companies; oil companies buy electronics companies; and steel companies buy oil companies. Among other things, this diversification serves to protect large companies from unfavorable market conditions in particular sectors of the economy. It also serves to weaken the commitment of a company to the long-term stability of a particular enterprise or resource.

For example, in the 1970s there was a major increase in corporate ownership of farms. This was a result of rapidly rising land prices that have attracted speculative investments. In several areas of the United States, large diversified corporations have become major holders of agricultural land. If they carry on a policy of maximizing return on investment, then they may adopt farming practices that lead to excessive soil erosion. In this instance, as in many others, the best interests of business are not the best interests of society as a whole.

The large forest product (lumber and paper) companies are an exception to this tendency of corporations to be interested only in short-term returns. Although many of the for-

---

ISSUE 2–2 Acts of God and Human Beings: The Exxon Valdez Affair

What is a sea otter worth? How do you put a price on the purity of Alaska's wilderness? What is the dollar value of clean air in the Los Angeles basin? How many thousands of dollars are equal to the good health lost to cancer by a petroleum industry worker? And finally, if price could be calculated for these commodities, how will it affect the price we pay at the pump per gallon of gas?

Americans, by and large, accept that their prosperity and high standard of living are due to benign rule by the marketplace. Capitalism, competition, and the almighty dollar are the standards by which success has been measured in the United States, at least until the 1970s turn toward environmentalism. One of the basic arguments made by environmentalists is that there are values other than monetary ones, and that intangibles are just as important as dollars and cents. When the Exxon Valdez struck a reef at Bligh Island in Alaska's Prince William Sound on March 24, 1989, and dumped 240,000 barrels of oil into pristine waters, the debate over dollars, intangibles, and the American way of life rose to a new crescendo, where it has since remained.

The United States is a big country, and its citizens feel that cheap gasoline is not only a necessity but a right, enabling us to support our suburbanized, motorized way of life. When we were threatened with higher oil and gas prices during the energy crisis of the early 1970s there were two alternatives: use less oil and gas or find new supplies. The latter has obvious tangible benefits in the form of income to the oil industry. The former has more intangible benefits, primarily in environmental and health matters. Although there was some conservation, for the most part the second option triumphed. The energy crisis led the government to give oil companies permission to extract oil and gas from Alaska's North Slope, and the American way of life was saved from the clutches of OPEC. Oil and

est products companies are diversified, they also own large tracts of land that require decades to produce harvestable trees. This creates a tendency for these companies to maintain a long-term, environmentally healthy commitment to their land.

Another important trend of the last few decades has been the formation and growth of *multinational corporations* (MNCs). These are companies that operate in several countries or own or collaborate with companies in several countries. They have the ability to shift resources, production, and marketing activities from one country to another depending on where potential profits are greatest. They are generally large enough to have major control over markets in individual nations, if not at the world level. Their ability to move money and commodities internationally greatly limits the controls that individual governments have over them, and thus it is more difficult to force consideration of social costs in decision-making.

The environmental record and corporate role of MNCs in environmental management is subject to intense debate. Some advocates feel that the MNCs are industry innovators and that with advanced technology and an enhanced environmental ethos they will make significant contributions to upgrade plants to meet environmental standards. The investment in pollution control (in the absence of strict environmental regulation) will ultimately be based on minimizing the MNCs present and future investment costs while offsetting any potential political or social conflict, including adverse public opinion (Roysten, 1985). That pollution prevention pays is not only the anthem of environmentalists, but also the rallying cry of 3M Corporation, which cleaned up its operations and saved money in the process.

Industry detractors feel that many MNCs deliberately seek pollution havens in developing countries to reduce their pollution control costs or their residuals costs. An example of this is multinational behavior and the disposal of hazardous wastes. In recent years new controls have been established on the disposal of hazardous wastes in the United States and other wealthy nations. Between 1979 and 1989, landfill space in the United States

gas prospecting and pumping also flourished along other U.S. coastlines.

Throughout, however, environmentalists and scientists have struggled to force the oil industry and the American public to realize the inevitable consequences of rule by the marketplace. A litany of social and environmental ills includes the greenhouse effect to which vehicle emissions are an important contributor; the health effects of vehicle emissions, which are partly responsible for a 25 percent increase in childhood asthma during the mid-1980s and a 36 percent rise in chronic lung cancer since 1970; health effects on workers in the petroleum and chemical industries; damages to agriculture, forests, wildlife, and water by air pollution; and finally, the direct effects of oil prospecting, extraction, and transport both on land and in the sea.

Almost as much as the dollar, wilderness and the great out-of-doors are dear to the American psyche. Simultaneously, with the 1970s oil and gas exploration and development in Alaska, legislators and environmentalists worked to set aside vast areas of the state as national parks, wilderness areas, and wildlife refuges. Oil companies had to promise to protect the wildlife and environment in which they worked, and the state of Alaska found itself in the paradoxical position of having the nation's largest acreage of protected lands, with 85 percent of the state's economy supported by the oil industry. Tangibles and intangibles were the state's two masters. A 1972 environmental impact statement warned that a collision between the two was inevitable and would come in the form of an offshore tanker breakup in the remote waters off the oil-shipping port of Valdez. "Not to worry!" responded the industry, promising that state-of-the-art cleanup technology and crews would be on the ready, 24 hours a day, and that any spill could be quickly contained.

Americans believed the oil industry's assur-

dropped by 70 percent as full landfills have closed and not been replaced by new ones as a result of environmental concerns. Thus many U.S.-based producers of hazardous wastes find it economically advantageous to export wastes to other countries rather than incur extremely high costs for domestic disposal.

The U.S. EPA is required by law to fully inform waste recipients of what they are getting. However, government officials are lax in providing host countries with the opportunity to turn down a waste shipment or to list the wastes that the country was about to receive. Poorer countries, for whom the fees paid by polluters are very tempting, are uniting to combat "toxic terrorism" (Deery Uva and Bloom, 1989). As a result, waste minimization

(the reduction of waste at its source) is now a major issue for industry. It is also helping to focus attention on conservation and recycling efforts at the individual firm level. A global pollution consciousness is in the making, with the understanding that a pollutant produced on one side of the globe can affect life on the other side.

Multinational corporations have also had the effect of greatly increasing the degree of worldwide economic integration. Markets for resources are controlled by world supply and demand rather than at the national level. A shortage of a commodity in one country causes increases in prices in other countries.

Economists have been debating for de-

---

ances and so their horror was all the more intense when they were television witnesses to the total failure of technology and planning as Exxon, the local fishing industry, the environmental science community, and the U.S. Armed Forces were unable to control the ravages of the Exxon Valdez spill during the brief Alaskan summer of 1989. As the thick mousse—an emulsified mix of seawater and oil—spread out of the Sound into the Gulf of Alaska and along ever-larger stretches of pristine coastline, recriminations and accusations flew furiously. America wanted a scapegoat, it wanted a dollar value on the damage, and it wanted a dollar value on the cleanup. Drunk driving, an oil-greedy economy, a slipshod industry response, an unwillingness to pay the environmental price of prosperity: Which was the culprit? Who would pay? How much?

Exxon maintains that the cleanup is just "another cost of doing business," thus reducing the catastrophe to a simple dollar value. The Wilderness Society pointed out how the oil companies assured the American public that they could drill without harming the environment and, in the unlikely event of a spill, that they could handle that quickly and responsibly. Of course, the oil industry was wrong on both counts.

Obviously, the dollar value of a pristine Alaskan coastline is incalculable, and the cost will be borne by four groups. The American public will pay in that its last remaining untouched wilderness is now besmirched. Alaska, for Americans, is irrevocably tarnished. The oil companies will pay by having to adhere more closely—at least for a while—to the rules and regulations that they promised to uphold. The U.S. government will pay—the politically conservative Bush administration will have to split the bill with the oil industry for the failed cleanup operation and will have a more difficult political fight ahead to obtain access for offshore drilling along the U.S. coasts. Finally, Alaska and its residents will pay. The salmon industry was hit hard, the future of coastal and offshore fishing is in doubt, and even tourism will struggle to regain the visitors who once flocked on pilgrimages to pure and untouched places. Each of these four groups will bear both tangible and intangible costs of the spill.

Puffins, terns, cormorants, sea lions, sea otters, plankton, bald eagles, deer, porpoises, whales, marine biota large to microscopic, and the food chain from bottom to top have been hit hard in the short term and will be paying the environmental price over decades as the oil sludge slowly degrades into its toxic components on the rocks, beaches, and sea bottom. On the other hand, the American life-style is unaffected, and Americans continue to pay low prices for oil and gas in comparison to most other countries in the developed world. We get what we pay for, and the price is measured in both tangible and intangible ways (Barinaga 1989a, 1989b; Epstein, 1989; Marshall, 1989; Roberts, 1989).

cades on the nature of economic systems and the relationship between economic growth and environmental quality. The neoclassical view of economics as open systems unrestrained by environmental limits (either natural resources or residuals disposal) is seriously being questioned in the 1990s. Nearly 30 years ago, a lone voice in the economic wilderness dubbed this neoclassical view "*cowboy economics.*" Boulding (1966) advocated that cowboy economics be replaced by a more sensible perspective in which economic systems are closed systems with economic processes constrained by negative feedback effects. This "spaceship earth" view of ecologic–economic interaction was later utilized by Kneese and Ayres in their materials balance approach described earlier. Further refinements were made calling for steady-state economic systems (Daly, 1973) in which the objective is to establish the lowest rate of throughput of

energy and matter, not to maximize the output of goods and services. Finally, the entropy concept (a measure of disorder in a system) was used to explain how economies will decline as predicted by the second law of thermodynamics. Georgescu-Roegen (1976) proposed a bioeconomic program based on the flow of solar energy and the minimal depletion of terrestrial matter (resources).

During 1988, a series of environmental traumas—extreme weather, reports of atmospheric holes, death of rainforests from overuse and the Black Forest from acid rain—impressed upon even the most cynical of business minds that maybe we are consuming our natural resource capital when we should be living frugally off its interest (MacNeill, 1989). At the same time, the developing countries began to think that "development" is not so great if it means overuse of natural resources to the point where they cannot recover. Earth

---

ISSUE 2–3 The Greening of Big Business

Cleaning up the environment is a profit-making enterprise. The environmental control industry (solid waste companies, consulting companies, hazardous treatment firms, and so on) generates over $100 billion a year in revenues, with many companies growing by 20–25 percent per year (Schiffres, 1990). The companies that are involved in cleaning up environmental pollution (oil spills, hazardous waste, solid waste, medical waste, asbestos, and so on) constitute one of the fastest-growing industrial sectors of the economy and will surely be the growth industries of the 1990s. Manufacturers and distributors of environmentally safe consumer products such as Seventh Generation in Burlington, Vermont, will also increase their sales and clout in the marketplace. Firms that specialize in environmental analysis and testing will also experience rapid growth during the decade (Mackerron, 1989).

Investor interest in environmental stocks is also growing as environmentally concerned citizens put their money where their mouths are. Just as socially responsive investing was important during the 1980s (no military weapons contracts or business in South Africa), environmentally responsive investing will be important during the 1990s. Already, four mutual funds

specialize in environmental stocks: Fidelity Select Environmental Services Portfolio, Freedom Environmental Fund, New Alternatives Fund, and SFT Environmental Awareness Fund. Consumers can even choose among a variety of different bank cards with the logo of their favorite environmental group emblazoned across their Visa or Master Charge card, with a small percentage of the proceeds donated to the group.

Finally, business schools have also joined the environmental bandwagon. Environmental management courses are now being added to business curricula across the country at the behest of corporate sponsors who felt that students were totally ignorant about the business impact of environmental issues. Environmental issues can have far-reaching implications, ranging from capital expenditures, to cash flow, to redesign of manufacturing processes. The litany of recent disasters such as the oil spill by the Exxon Valdez in 1989 and the release of a toxic gas used by Union Carbide to manufacture pesticides in Bhopal, India, in 1984 illustrate the financial impact of environmental issues on business. The greening of American business is beginning, but it still has a long way to go (Fowler, 1990).

Day 1990 helped to publicize that message (see Issue 2–3).

Today the popular idea is *sustainability*—a concept that suggests that economic growth should take place within a framework of environmental responsibility to ensure the continued viability of our habitat (Ruckelshaus, 1989; MacNeill, 1989). This concept has made its way even into the highly pragmatic thinking of the Group of Seven—the top seven industrial democracies, including Canada, Japan, the United Kingdom, the United States, Italy, France, and West Germany, who released a joint communique during their 1989 summit meeting that embraced the notion of the interrelationship of environment and economics:

> *Environmental protection is integral to issues such as trade, development, energy, transport, agriculture and economic planning. Therefore, environmental considerations must be taken into account into economic decision-making. . . .*
>
> *In order to achieve sustainable development, we shall ensure the compatibility of economic growth and development with protection of the environment. Environmental protection and related investment should contribute to economic growth. . . . (The New York Times, July 17, 1989, p. 5)*

It will be a long time before sustainability becomes international policy. In the meantime, and in the aftermath of the 1989 Exxon Valdez oil spill in Alaska, a coalition of environmental and religious groups and investors has formulated the ten-point Valdez Principles, which will be used to judge which corporations are environmentally responsible (Feder, 1989). In the absence of effective environmental law, embarrassment and shame can work wonders when the bottom line is at stake.

CONCLUSIONS

The business of natural resource use is no different from any other business. It is governed by the same need to turn investment into profit as quickly as possible and is subject to the same vagaries of economics caused by fluctuating interest rates, inflation, and the ups and downs of business cycles. Although we often blame our government, big corporations, foreign governments, or natural calamities for problems related to natural resource supply or prices, in almost all instances the real causes of the problem can be traced to the economic constraints on the businesses involved and the simple desire of companies to make as much profit as possible. In centrally planned economies, economic development has always been favored over environmental protection. This has been made exceedingly clear in the past few years as Eastern and Central European countries have been found to have some of the worst air and water pollution in the world. Environmental degradation is extensive in many of these countries, and as a result of the pro-democracy movements the rest of the world is slowly becoming informed of the disastrous level of pollution. It is hoped that the greening of Eastern and Central Europe will continue.

Natural resources are of fundamental importance to us all, not least because many of them are commonly owned. Decisions involving natural resources are therefore very likely to have external costs and social effects that businesses do not normally consider. Government intervention is necessary to modify the management process, so that intangible resources, long-term needs, and social costs can be managed along with the commodities that move through our economic system.

REFERENCES AND ADDITIONAL READING

Barinaga, M. 1989a. Shipwreck fouls the water. *Nature* 338: 451.

———. 1989b. Fisheries first to suffer. *Nature* 338: 533.

Boulding, K.E. 1966. The economics of the coming spaceship Earth. In H. Jarrett (Ed.), *Environmental Quality in a Growing Economy*. Baltimore: Johns Hopkins University Press.

Daly, H.E. 1973. *Towards a Steady State Economy*. San Francisco: W.H. Freeman.

Deery Uva, M., and J. Bloom. 1989. Exporting pollution: The international waste trade. *Environment* 31(5): 4–5, 43–44.

Epstein, S.S. 1989. The real cost of petroleum. *Ecologist* 19: 137–138.

Feder, B.J. 1989. Group sets corporate code on environmental conduct. *The New York Times*, Sept. 8, p. D1.

Fowler, E. 1990. Careers: Environment courses in M.B.A. study. *The New York Times*, March 13, p. D22.

Friends of the Earth. 1981. *Progress as if Survival Mattered.* San Francisco: Friends of the Earth.

Georgescu-Roegen, N. 1976. *Energy and Economic Myths.* New York: Pergamon Press.

Group of Seven. 1989. Paris communique by the Group of Seven. *The New York Times*, July 17, p. A7.

Hardin, G. 1968. The tragedy of the commons. *Science* 162: 1243–1248.

————. 1972. *Exploring New Ethics for Survival: The Voyage of the Spaceship Beagle.* New York: Viking.

Hershey, R.D., Jr. 1989. New market is seen for "pollution rights." *The New York Times*, June 14, p. D1.

Kneese, A.V., R.V. Ayres, and R.C. d'Arge. 1971. *Economics and the Environment: A Materials Balance Approach.* Baltimore: Johns Hopkins University Press.

Kneese, A.V., and B.T. Bower (Eds.). 1971. *Environmental Quality Analysis: Theory and Method in the Social Sciences.* Baltimore: Johns Hopkins University Press.

Krutilla, J.V., and A. Fisher. 1975. *The Economics of Natural Environments.* Baltimore: Resources for the Future/Johns Hopkins University Press.

Luoma, J.R. 1990. Trash can realities. *Audubon* 92(2) (March): 86–97.

Mackerron, C.B. 1989. Special report on cleaning up: Lucrative markets abound in environmental services. *Chem. Week*, October 11, pp. 21–26.

MacNeill, J. 1989. Strategies for sustainable economic development. *Sci. Amer.* 261(3): 154–165.

Markham, J.M. 1989. Paris group urges "decisive action" for environment. *The New York Times*, July 17, p. A1.

Marshall, E. 1989. Valdez: The predicted oil spill. *Science* 244: 20–21.

Meier, B. 1990. Is degradability a throwaway claim? *The New York Times*, February 17, p. A52.

Mitchell, J.G. 1990. War in the woods II: West Side story. *Audubon* 92(1) (January): 82–121.

O'Riordan, T., and R.K. Turner. 1983. *An Annotated Reader in Environmental Planning and Management.* Oxford: Pergamon Press.

Rees, J. 1985. *Natural Resources: Allocation, Economics, and Policy.* London: Methuen.

Roberts, L. 1989. Long, slow recovery period predicted for Alaska. *Science* 244: 22–24.

Roysten, M.G. 1985. Local and multinational corporations: Reappraising environmental management. *Environment* 27(1): 12–20, 39–43.

Ruckelshaus, W.D. 1989. Toward a sustainable world. *Sci. Amer.* 261(3): 166–175.

Schiffres, M. 1990. A cleaner environment: Where to invest. *Changing Times* 44(2) (February): 33–39.

Schwadel, F. 1989. Retailers latch on to the environment. *Wall Street Journal*, November 13, p. B1.

Seneca, J.J., and M.K. Taussig. 1974. *Environmental Economics.* Englewood Cliffs, NJ: Prentice–Hall.

Stavins, R.N. 1989. Harnessing market forces to protect the environment. *Environment* 31(1): 5–7, 28–35.

TERMS TO KNOW

Benefit–Cost Analysis
Cartel
Common Property Resource
Cost-Effectiveness Analysis
Cowboy Economics
Diversification
Externalities
Fixed Costs
Incommensurables
Intangibles
Monopoly
Multinational Corporation
Oligopolistic Competition
Proxy Value
Replacement Cost
Residuals Management
Shadow Price
Social Cost
Sustainability
Throughput Tax
Variable Costs
Willingness to Pay

STUDY QUESTIONS

1. What are the four characteristics of natural resources?

2. Do the laws of supply and demand work perfectly? Why or why not?

3. What is the difference between benefit–cost analysis and cost-effectiveness analysis? Between incommensurables and intangibles?

4. What are the three ways in which economic considerations influence natural resource decisions?

5. What are the different theories for the determination of price?

6. How are residuals managed?

7. Is business becoming more environmentally aware? If so, what might account for this new attitude toward the environment?

3

Environmental Ideology, Politics, and Decisionmaking

INTRODUCTION

Government policy is a fundamental determinant of how natural resources are exploited and conserved. In the United States, the policies that control natural resource use have been developed over three centuries by both governmental and private actions. Governmental policy is a product of the political process, constrained by history and precedent. The political process in turn is essentially one of confrontation and compromise among many disparate interests, both economic and ideological. This chapter examines the history of human impact on the environment worldwide, and the development of natural resource policy in the United States. The decision-making process is described, along with the various ideological and economic interest groups that are the major forces in the national political arena today.

NATURAL RESOURCE USE: A HISTORICAL PERSPECTIVE

Conservationist Max Nicholson sees human history as a process of increasing ability to manipulate and alter usable aspects of the physical environment. He suggests (1970) that in the early stages of human evolution, at least 2 million years ago, the natural environment was largely unaffected by humans. Small numbers of protohumans in their hunting bands,

using simple technology (bone, stone, and wood tools and hunting pits), were generally capable of competing with animal species. Like animals, protohumans were also at the mercy of climate and topography and did not have the technological skills to master the earth's more difficult climates. Thus they were best able to utilize the food and shelter resources of open and coastal lands, locations that were far more vulnerable to natural hazards such as floods than to any alteration by people.

Nicholson and others agree that the first human tool to have a major environmental impact was fire. Early humans used it to drive animals into traps; when agriculture was developed between 10,000 and 7000 B.C., fire was used to clear land for crops and to create grazing areas for livestock. Fire is the only example in which the capacity of modern technology to alter the environment is matched by that of the pretechnological humans. The deliberate use of fire introduced three types of environmental effects: (1) it was widespread, affecting a large area; (2) it was a repetitive process and could cover the same areas at frequent intervals; and (3) it was highly selective in its effects on animal and plant species, having a negative effect on some, while encouraging those with rapid powers of recovery or resistance to fire (Nicholson, 1970). The environmental result was to improve the yield of certain species for human use and to modify the vegetation cover. These early effects were confined largely to tropical, subtropical, and temperate forests and grasslands, and some wetlands.

At least 10,000 years ago the human race had spread to all continents except Antarctica. With the shift from hunting and gathering to agriculture, human culture developed more sophisticated food production tools for planting, harvesting, and transporting. Also, in drier areas in the Middle East and later elsewhere, large-scale irrigation works were built. The sedentary life of the agriculturalist went hand-in-hand with the development of cities. These two developments, agriculture and urbanization, led for the first time to a substantial change in land use, from natural to human-made forms of productivity, in the form of fields, streets, homes, and irrigation ditches. The development of cities led to large-scale environmental disruption and change because of the concentration of large populations and the wide areas in which land was cultivated, grazed, cleared of trees, and subjected to erosion to support the urban population. Also, through the domestication of plants and animals, people were able to direct the energy and nutrients of an ecosystem to produce more of certain foods than the environment would naturally. This in turn permitted the growth of human populations beyond the limits set by their preagricultural patterns. Thus agriculture raised the *carrying capacity* of the earth to support human beings.

Since about 1000 B.C., humans began to move freely around the world, and rulers began to dominate large regions from a distance. Settlements and their impacts were no longer necessarily small in scale or localized in effect. The era of colonialism that began in the fifteenth century A.D. placed the environments and resources of far-distant lands under European control. These colonial powers were interested in removing and using resources, with little regard for environmental consequences either abroad or close to home. The advent of industrialization led to a global-scale use of fuel and mineral resources that altered or destroyed local and regional ecosystems, perhaps ultimately affecting global climate and other environmental patterns.

The last three millennia, and particularly the last 500 years, have seen a transformation in the kinds and scales of natural resource use in the world. Early societies depended primarily on locally available resources with rela-

tively little trade, whereas now most of the goods we consume come from quite far away. Resource use systems have become complex, with a wide variety of goods utilized in everyday life. This increasing complexity has isolated us somewhat from the basic raw materials provided by the environment and made us more dependent on human systems of resource manipulation and distribution. There clearly are innumerable ways of making a living in the world today. No single commodity or geographic area is indispensable, and resource management has become a task of selecting which resource utilization techniques are most appropriate for our needs at any given time.

DEVELOPMENT OF U.S. NATURAL RESOURCE POLICY

The history of natural resource policy in the United States from the seventeenth century to the present can be divided into six phases. In most cases these do not have distinct beginning and ending dates and overlap considerably. However, they are useful in distinguishing important historical trends, and so approximate dates are indicated. The discussion here is not intended to be exhaustive, but rather a summary of some of the major actions and events that form the basis of much of current U.S. conservation philosophy and policy.

PHASE I: EXPLOITATION AND EXPANSION (1600–1870)

When the early European settlers arrived in North America they found a vast continent with natural resources in apparently limitless supply, particularly in comparison to urbanized and developed Europe. Their goal was to establish stable and profitable colonies. To accomplish this, the European landholders who controlled settlement promoted population growth and resource extraction to maximize their security and prosperity. The colonial economy was, by design, based on exporting raw materials to industrial Europe, with agriculture for domestic food production. The enormous land area of North America was the primary resource for this economic development, and exploitation of its natural resources was the means to the desired end.

The forests that covered most of the eastern third of the continent were seen partly as a resource and partly as a nuisance. Wood was needed for fuel and construction purposes, but the vast amount of forest compared to productive agricultural land meant that timber cutting was a low-value land use. The forests, then, were cleared as rapidly as possible to make room for agriculture. In addition, the prevailing aesthetic attitudes toward forests were different. Forests were seen as unproductive, undesirable, and dangerous, whereas agricultural land was productive, attractive, and secure (Fig. 3.1). Except in a very few cases, regulations limiting the clearing of forests were unknown, as was the notion of natural resource conservation. This exploitative attitude toward the land prevailed for about the first 250 years of European occupation of North America, until the middle or late 1800s. The growth of an industrial economy in the nineteenth century had little effect on this, except perhaps to increase the demands of urban populations for food, timber, and, later, coal. Forests were first culled of the most valuable trees, and later the remaining timber was

generally clear-cut and often burned. Agriculture in many areas was largely cash cropping of a very few crop types, and except for liming soils in some areas, little was done to maintain, let alone enhance, soil fertility. As a result, soil erosion was rapid, and declines in fertility forced abandonment of land after only a few years, particularly in the southeastern United States.

As the nation expanded westward, political as well as economic goals required rapid settlement and development of the Great Plains. With each major territorial expansion from the Louisiana Purchase to the Alaska Purchase (the annexation of Texas excepted), the federal government acquired possession of vast acreages. In the early nineteenth century, much government land was sold to provide income to the fledgling republic as well as to promote settlement. Several laws were passed in the mid-1800s to promote settlement, largely by transferring government-owned lands to private ownership either for free or at a nominal cost. The most notable among these laws were the *Homestead Act* of 1862, the *Railroad Acts* of the 1850s and 1860s, the *Timber Culture Act* of 1873, and the *Mining Act* of 1872.

Figure 3.1 Backpacking in Isle Royale National Park, Michigan. Today, Americans enjoy the wilderness, but in previous centuries it was a place to be feared.

The Homestead Act and the Railroad Acts were specifically designed to encourage settlement, especially in the Great Plains. The Homestead Act gave any qualified settler 160 acres free of charge, and the Railroad Acts granted large rights of way to the railroad companies to finance construction of transcontinental and other rail lines that would further accelerate settlement of the west. Most of the land granted to the railroads was sold to other private interests, but substantial acreages remain in railroad ownership today, particularly in California. The Timber Culture and Mining Acts granted free access to forests and minerals to anyone willing to exploit them. There were widespread abuses of these privileges, which resulted in land companies and speculators acquiring vast acreages at nominal expense. Although these laws were successful in stimulating settlement and economic development, in many cases they encouraged excessive exploitation by artificially depressing the price of resources. Environmental degradation usually followed, as with the forests of the upper Midwest (Michigan, Wisconsin, and Minnesota) in which much timber was lost to wasteful logging practices and fires, and soil was lost to accelerated erosion.

The primary themes of this era included resource exploitation for economic prosperity and land transfers from public to private ownership. In fact, this era is best characterized by the massive land transfers from federal to private ownership, be it the individual, developers, or selected industries such as the railroads.

Near the end of this phase, the practice of promoting exploitation of resources for economic growth was limited somewhat by the growth of the conservation movement. Exploitative policies continued into the twentieth century, however, with legislation such as the Reclamation Act of 1902, which provided for development of water at public expense for crop irrigation in the arid west. Today, natural resource exploitation for economic prosperity is still the basis of government management of mineral resources such as coal and oil, as well as being an important consideration in other areas such as water and rangelands.

PHASE II: EARLY WARNINGS AND A CONSERVATION ETHIC (1840–1910)

As the westward expansion continued, Americans escalated their efforts to exploit the environment for their own needs, and with improved technology, settlers had a much easier job of "taming the land." For example, the mechanization of farming certainly enhanced the settlement of the Great Plains. McCormick's grain reaper allowed the timely harvest of wheat. Iron and steel plows developed by John Deere helped to break up the prairie soil for cultivation. The cotton gin provided a mechanical means to sort lint from the cotton, and of course barbed wire allowed farmers and ranchers to demarcate property. As a result of many of these mechanical inventions, wildlife populations were particularly hard hit as they were either displaced from their ecosystem, outcompeted by the domesticated animals (cows and sheep), or succumbed to harsh winters and the rifle.

During the time when settlement was rapidly advancing westward with the stimulation and encouragement of the government, a few individuals were suggesting that the exploitation of resources was too rapid and too destructive. In general these persons were intellectuals and academics who did not enjoy popular audiences for their criticisms, thus the effects of their writings were limited at the time. Eventually, however, their warnings were heard by decisionmakers in government and this led to a new concern for conserving and preserving resources.

Among the early American writers advocating wilderness preservation were Ralph Waldo Emerson and Henry David Thoreau, who argued on philosophical grounds in the 1840s and 1850s against continued destruction of natural areas by logging and similar activities. George Perkins Marsh's *Man and Nature, or Physical Geography as Modified by Human Action*, published in 1864, was perhaps more influential in the conservation versus exploitation debate. Marsh was both a public servant and a scientist, which led him to advocate government action to protect natural resources. Although a native of Vermont, Marsh traveled widely in the Mediterranean lands, areas long damaged by overgrazing. He saw a parallel between the Mediterranean situation and the damage done by sheep grazing in the Green Mountains in his home state. In *Man and Nature,* Marsh argued that humans should attempt to live in harmony rather than in competition with nature (Fig. 3.2). More important, Marsh argued that natural resources were far from inexhaustible. This book was widely read and had considerable influence on Carl Schurz, who later became Secretary of the Interior under Rutherford Hayes in 1877.

Phase II included a series of developments in the late nineteenth century, when many of the basic doctrines of government natural resource conservation policy were established. The primary tenet was that land resources should be managed for long-term rather than short-term benefits to the general population. This phase, dominated by concern for forest resources and to a lesser extent wilderness preservation, began in the 1860s and was marked by the first significant government action aimed at restricting exploitation of natural resources. One important governmental action was the formation, in 1862, of the Department of Agriculture's Land Grant College System, which was designed to help improve the management and productivity of agriculture and forestry through improved education (Council on Environmental Quality, 1986). The establishment of the Cooperative Extension Service by the Smith–Lever Act of 1914 also helped to improve conservation education by linking the local farmer to agricultural experts in the state universities.

By the late nineteenth century, the forests of much of the eastern United States were either entirely cut over or were rapidly disappearing. Thus it is not surprising that the forest resource was the first focus of the emerging conservation efforts in the 1870s. Carl Schurz launched an attack on corrupt and wasteful practices in timber harvesting on federal lands and brought the severity of the problem to the public eye. In 1872, the Adirondack Forest Reserve Act halted the sale of state forest lands, an action that eventually led to the creation of the Adirondack Forest Preserve (now Adirondack State Park). The most significant development during this period was the passage, in 1891, of a rider on a public lands bill that gave the President the authority to set aside forested lands by proclamation, thus reserving them from timber cutting. President Benjamin Harrison quickly began withdrawing land from timber cutting, and in 1897 additional reservations by Grover Cleveland brought the total forest reserves to about 40 million acres (16 million ha). The federal government thus had established what would later become the National Forest System, but at the time it had no real management policy for these lands. In 1898, Gifford Pinchot was appointed as the first Chief Forester. Pinchot was trained as a forester in Europe, where the field was well established. He brought with him a knowledge of the scientific basis for land management, in particular the notion of *sustained yield* forestry. The principle of sustained yield management of renewable resources has since been

(a)

(b)

Figure 3.2   Formal gardens. Formal gardens like those in Tofukuji Temple, Kyoto, Japan (*a*) and Versailles, France (*b*) show our love for nature's forms, but more important, our domination over it.

firmly incorporated into all aspects of official federal policy, although there is some debate as to whether the principle is truly followed in practice.

In 1901, Theodore Roosevelt became president, and his administration represented the culmination of this phase of American natural resource history. Roosevelt was an adventurer and an outdoorsman, and thus had a personal appreciation for the values of undeveloped land, particularly the still untouched wilderness areas of the western United States. Pinchot was one of his key advisors, and with the forester's advice, Roosevelt added large acreages to the nation's forest reserves. In 1905, the U.S. Forest Service was established with Gifford Pinchot as its first chief and "forest reserves" became national forests. By the end of Roosevelt's administration these reserves totaled 172 million acres (70 million ha). Later, large acreages were added to the National Forests in the eastern United States after the passage of the Weeks Act in 1911, which provided for federal acquisition of tax-delinquent cutover lands.

Theodore Roosevelt was also instrumental in expanding what would later become the National Park System. Yellowstone was reserved as a national park in 1872, and several other parks were created in this period. Roosevelt protected the Grand Canyon from development by invoking the Antiquities Act. Passed in 1906, this act was primarily intended to allow the President to preserve national historic sites such as buildings and battlefields. Roosevelt, however, used it to create the Grand Canyon National Monument, which later became a National Park. Some 78 years later, Jimmy Carter was to use this same act to temporarily preserve hundreds of millions of acres in Alaska while Congress debated the Alaska Lands Bill. Finally, near the end of his presidency, Roosevelt sponsored the first White House Conference on Conservation, further bringing the issue to public attention and concern.

Another important figure during this period was John Muir, who founded the Sierra Club in 1892. Muir was a strong preservationist and wilderness advocate, whose primary area of interest was the Sierra Nevada Range of California. The Yosemite region was one of his favorite spots, and he led the battle to protect the area from damage by sheep grazing by establishing what would later become Yosemite National Park.

One of the most significant battles of Muir's life was fought over the preservation of Hetch-Hetchy Valley. This valley is adjacent to Yosemite Valley and was very similar in scenic beauty. Hetch-Hetchy was, however, a convenient source of water for the growing city of San Francisco and an excellent dam site. Muir fought hard to prevent the damming of the Tuolumne River, but eventually lost in a battle with a former ally in the conservation movement, Gifford Pinchot. Pinchot was of course a conservationist, but he believed in conservation for maintenance of the productive capacity of natural resources. To prevent development was contrary to the notion that resources could be used for general benefit of the population, and Pinchot opposed Muir in the debate over Hetch-Hetchy. In the end, the development interests prevailed, and today the valley is a reservoir providing water and electricity to the cities of northern California. Almost a century later, there is now talk of draining Hetch Hetchy and restoring the valley to its original state.

The Hetch-Hetchy controversy made clear the distinction between conservationists, who encourage careful husbanding of resources yet do not condemn their use, and preservationists, who would stop all use or development on the basis that some areas and resources are too valuable to be used. This second phase ushered in major achievements in resource conservation and saw the establishment of the principles of both sustained yield management and preservation of outstanding natural features for future generations. This period also witnessed the emergence of two of the major ideological camps, the preservationists and the conservationists, which still dominate the debates over natural resources today.

PHASE III: CONSERVATION FOR ECONOMIC RECOVERY (1930–1940)

The Great Depression of 1929–1941 and Franklin Roosevelt's New Deal of the 1930s had more impact on all aspects of modern domestic policy than in any other period in American history, and natural resource use was no exception. The depression provided the impetus for massive programs aimed at relief, recovery, and prevention of similar problems in the future. Most of the major programs of this period were primarily economic rather than conservation-oriented in emphasis. The Civilian Conservation Corps, for example, did not represent a major new policy, but rather was a make-work program that put many of the unemployed to work on conservation projects, principally planting trees and maintaining or constructing park facilities. In contrast, two major agencies established by the New Deal, the Tennessee Valley Authority (TVA) and the Soil Conservation Service (SCS), were aimed at correcting problems that, if not major contributors to the depression, were very much worsened by it.

The Appalachian region of the Southeast had long been economically depressed and was among the areas hardest hit by the depression. The forests were largely cut over, farms were not competitive with those in the Midwest, soil erosion and flooding were particularly severe, and there was no significant industrial employment available. The TVA was the first major effort to address this wide range of problems in an integrated regional resource management and economic development program. The major elements of the program were the construction of dams for hydroelectric power generation and flood control, with the power generated being used to support new industries, particularly fertilizer and later munitions production. Forests were replanted to control erosion, and many smaller erosion control measures were instituted, in part to protect the newly created reservoirs from sedimentation. The TVA today is mostly an electric power generating authority, but its important legacy in natural resources is that it represents the recognition that good natural resource management and economic vitality are interdependent, and both must be undertaken together for long-term economic stability.

In addition to dam construction in the Tennessee Valley, many large dams were completed in the arid western states, including the Hoover Dam on the Colorado River and several dams in the Columbia River basin (Fig. 3.3). These were seen as important government investments in agriculture and electric power generation, which would help revitalize agriculture and provide new sources of energy for industry.

The agricultural expansion in the Midwest and Great Plains during the late nineteenth and early twentieth centuries took advantage of the naturally fertile soils of that region, and farming was successful without significant inputs of fertilizers or other means to maintain soil fertility. Severe soil erosion was widespread, but it took the economic collapse of the 1930s and the ensuing dust bowl conditions in portions of the Midwest and Great Plains to focus attention on the problem. Several dry years on land that was marginal for farming, combined with economic hardship brought on by low farm prices, led to severe wind erosion in Oklahoma, Colorado, and nearby areas, forcing thousands off the land.

The Soil Erosion Service, created in 1933, was established in response to these problems. Hugh Hammond Bennett became the first director of the newly renamed Soil Conservation Service in 1935. He led an extensive research effort to determine the causes of soil erosion and to devise means to prevent it. This effort resulted in the development and implementation of many important soil conservation techniques, which yielded dramatic reductions in soil erosion in much of the nation. The Agricultural Adjustment Administration, forerunner to the present Agricultural Stabilization and Conservation Service, was established to provide payments to farmers who reduced crop acreage. This not only reduced farm surpluses, but also helped support prices and reduced the rate of soil erosion.

Another significant piece of legislation of this period was the *Taylor Grazing Act* of 1934, which established a system of fees for grazing on federal lands, with limitations on the numbers of animals that could be grazed. This was a partial response to the widespread accelerated erosion caused by overgrazing. The act also closed most of the public lands to homesteading, effectively ending the large-scale transfer of public lands to private ownership that had begun in 1862. Today, these public lands are administered by the Bureau of

Figure 3.3   Hoover Dam. This 1938 Bureau of Reclamation photo shows the multi-purpose dam that spans the Colorado River at the Nevada–Arizona border. Hoover Dam and its reservoir, Lake Mead, provide flood protection, water storage, hydroelectric power, and recreation. These benefits typify the goals of the governmental public works projects during the 1930s and 1940s.

Land Management. The Natural Resources Planning Board was another milestone of resource management in the FDR years and was a major step toward establishing long-term comprehensive natural resources planning.

In summary, the FDR years saw important advances in federal resource management and conservation activities. Most of the new programs were conceived as a result of the depression and were designed to alleviate the problems of the time as well as prevent future mismanagement of resources. The need for careful management of renewable resources, particularly soil and water, was recognized, and the close relation between economic and resource problems became clear.

PHASE IV: THE ENVIRONMENTAL MOVEMENT (1962–1976)

The years 1940 to 1960 saw relatively few new developments in conservation policy. The 1940s were dominated by war, and the economic recovery and ensuing prosperity of the 1950s diverted attention from natural re-

sources. There was, however, considerable progress in soil, water, and forest conservation, expanding on the achievements made under FDR. The major federal actions of this period were largely in the area of recreational activities, with the expansion of the national parks and similar recreational areas in response to increased use by the American public.

By the 1960s, attention was being focused on the quality of life available to Americans, and natural resources became more broadly defined. Two significant books published in 1962 and 1963 called attention to this broader view of natural resources and signaled the beginning of a new era in which environmental pollution was recognized as a major threat to natural resources and the quality of life.

One of these was *The Quiet Crisis*, by Stewart Udall, Secretary of the Interior under John F. Kennedy. In this book Udall presented much of the history of natural resource use in the United States, particularly focusing on the destruction of natural environments and wildlife. He called for renewed attention to the human effects on the environment, echoing many of the sentiments of G.P. Marsh 100 years earlier. The second book was Rachel Carson's *Silent Spring,* which described the effects of pesticides on the ecosystem and predicted drastic environmental consequences of continued pollution.

Throughout the 1960s, a popular movement for pollution control grew, led largely by scientists, student activists, and a few government officials such as Stewart Udall. Many influential authors argued that the environment had already been severely damaged and that urgent action was needed to restore its health and prevent further damage to both natural and managed ecosystems. A major focus of the movement was the disparity between a limited resource base on "spaceship earth" and a rapidly growing world population that already faced severe shortages of food and raw materials. A long list of laws was passed in the late 1960s and early 1970s aimed at reducing pollution, preserving wilderness and endangered species, and promoting ecological considerations in resource development. Some of the more important of these are the Wilderness Act of 1964, the Clean Air Act of 1963 and its amendments of 1970 and 1977, the Federal Water Pollution Control Act of 1964 and its amendments of 1972, the Coastal Zone Management Act of 1972, the Endangered Species Act of 1973, and the National Environmental Policy Act of 1970 (NEPA). The laws relating to specific resource problems such as air and water pollution have been the most important in terms of improving environmental quality, and they are discussed in more detail later in this and other chapters.

The National Environmental Policy Act (NEPA) represents the first comprehensive statement of U.S. environmental policy, and it is illustrative of the character of this phase of American natural resources history. Section 101 of NEPA contains a statement of the federal government's environmental responsibilities. These are to:

1. fulfill the responsibilities of each generation as trustee of the environment for succeeding generations;

2. assure for all Americans safe, healthful, productive, and aesthetically and culturally pleasing surroundings;

3. attain the widest range of beneficial uses of the environment without degradation, risk to health or safety, or other undesirable and unintended consequences;

4. preserve important historic, cultural, and natural aspects of our national heritage, and maintain, wherever possible, an environment which supports diversity and variety of individual choice;

5. achieve a balance between population and resource use which will permit high standards of living and a wide sharing of life's amenities; and

6. enhance the quality of renewable resources and approach the maximum attainable recycling of depletable resources. (CEQ, 1980, pp. 426–427)

These are lofty goals, but they reflect the idealism of the time as well as the far-reaching concerns of the environmental movement. They emphasize quality of life, preservation or maintenance rather than exploitation, and the concern with a limited and finite resource base supporting a rapidly growing population. NEPA also established the requirement for environmental impact statements in order to ensure compliance with its policies.

PHASE V: PRAGMATISM AND RISK REDUCTION (1976–1988)

By the late 1970s a complex set of laws, regulations, and procedures was in place along with a bureaucracy to administer them. The mass of environmental legislation generated in the preceding decade was being translated into everyday action, and the energy crises of the mid-1970s emphasized the need for resource conservation. Substantial improvements in environmental quality were being made, particularly in the areas of air and water pollution. With an upsurge of public concern about the effects of pollution and toxic chemicals on health, the Toxic Substances Control Act and the Resource Conservation and Recovery Act were signed into law in 1975 and 1976, respectively. The Comprehensive Environmental Responsibility and Liability Act (Superfund) was signed into law in 1980, whose purpose was to reduce the toxicity, mobility, and volume of hazardous wastes and clean up existing hazardous waste sites. The Superfund Amendments and Reauthorization Act (SARA), passed in 1986, further clarified the goals of the Superfund program to enhance the long-term prevention of health effects through waste reduction and better treatment and incineration of wastes. Land disposal of hazardous wastes was not considered a viable policy option. Risk reduction as environmental policy placed the Environmental Protection Agency in the leading role. However, scientific uncertainty regarding the nature of toxic risk, coupled with the scale and complexity of abandoned waste sites and 5000 known toxic chemicals, resulted in very little cleanup and standard setting during this phase. Inadequate funding for enforcement and cleanup, compounded by a lack of agency and governmental priorities, exacerbated the situation.

At the same time, public debate shifted away from the rather abstract issues of ecological stability and environmental quality and began focusing more on economic problems. With a downturn in the national and world economy, the costs of improving environmental quality began to be seen by some as contributing to economic problems, and by others as simply too expensive for the benefits derived. When President Reagan took office in 1980, he rode a tide of political conservatism that turned away from the idealism of the 1960s and focused more on stimulating economic development (see Issue 3–1). Public lands policy shifted from federal management and conservation to state or private control of resources and exploitation to improve supplies of raw materials, especially energy. Federally owned coal, which had not been sold during earlier administrations because of an oversupply of minable coal, was once again made available to the industry. In its rush to divest the federal government of its holdings, the Interior Department sold coal leasing rights in many areas at below market value. Pollution abatement efforts by the federal government were

---

ISSUE 3–1   The Reagan Legacy

When Ronald Reagan first took office in January 1981, no one expected him to become the "environmental President," yet no other Presidency since Franklin D. Roosevelt's has had more profound impacts on environmental decisionmaking. Perhaps the most enduring aspect of the Reagan legacy was his dismantling of the federal bureaucracy for resource management. Reagan filled many of the subcabinet and lower echelons of agencies with political cronies who were often not well-suited for their new roles as stewards of the nation's national resources. Many career managers simply left government service at that time, preferring not to be involved in the great natural resource giveaway. Thus, the professional staff at key agencies like the Department of Interior or the Environmental Protection Agency were often subject to enormous pressure to conform to the new administrative policies that favored industry and less government.

A second major legacy was the shift in environmental responsibility from the federal government to the state governments. This was coupled with a decline in funding for natural resource protection and pollution control. The consequences included very few additions to preservation systems (e.g., the Wilderness System and Wild and Scenic Rivers) and a virtual decimation of the EPA, particularly its environmental enforcement branch. The result was relatively lax enforcement of pollution laws at the federal level. States were free to act, of course, but were provided little financial assistance or encouragement from the federal government to do so.

Another feature of the Reagan years was a dramatic reduction in the collection and dissemination of information about environmental quality. Data-collection programs and planning studies were eliminated or reduced in scope, and even when the data were still being collected they were no longer published or distributed widely. The effects of these cutbacks were to make it much more difficult for citizens to learn about the quality of the nation's environment and to force the authors of this book to rely much more heavily on late-1970s and early-1980s data than they would have liked! Private organizations such as the Conservation Foundation, the

reduced in favor of state and local control over these policies. Attention was also turned toward reducing the costs of pollution control to industry. Clearly resource conservation has entered a new phase that considers the economic aspects of resource decisions along with the ecological goals established in the 1960s and 1970s.

PHASE VI: THE NEW GLOBAL ENVIRONMENTAL CONSCIOUSNESS (1988–)

During the late 1980s, a new awareness of global environmental issues reemerged. The spaceship earth philosophy, which had been popular 20 years earlier, fell out of favor in the intervening years as predicted catastrophes (widespread famines, climate change, and species extinctions) failed to materialize, and environmentalists who voiced these fears were regarded as alarmist. But a number of dramatic events, including the environmental catastro-

phes at Chernobyl, the Rhine chemical spill, and the canine distemper epidemic of North Sea seals, brought new credibility and attention to concerns about the stability of the global environment. In the United States, a short but severe summer drought in 1988 and marine pollution problems on both coasts heightened concern. These events came at a time when there was increasing evidence that earlier predictions of global climate change and stratospheric ozone depletion were in fact occurring. Beginning in 1986, data on the Antarctic ozone "hole" were widely publicized, and consensus emerged among scientists that this was probably attributable to pollution by chlorofluorocarbons (CFCs) and other substances. Evidence of measurable climate warming was also growing and public opinion was further swayed by the extreme weather conditions in 1988 (drought and heat in the central United States) and 1990 (severe storms in Europe). Throughout this period, concern was also increasing about acid pre-

Wilderness Society, Sierra Club, and Greenpeace have been important in reporting environmental data in the absence of government documentation. The data-collection issue continues to be important in the 1990s, and was a factor in the defeat of 1990 legislation to establish a cabinet-level Department of the Environment.

The Reagan Presidency made it very clear that an overriding goal was to ease the effect of natural resource decisions on industry. This was accomplished with great fervor and ranged from the lowering of fuel efficiency standards on cars (thus protecting the auto industry), to lack of acid rain controls (protecting utilities), to lax enforcement of hazardous waste regulations. In light of this "free-market economy approach," the Reagan era was also characterized by the increased privatization of natural resources for individual profit. During his eight years in office, there was increased leasing of national forest lands and outer continental shelf areas for resource exploitation, largely timber and mineral resources. Concessions in the national parks (hotels, restaurants, and gift shops) were turned over to private concerns, and fees at all national

parks and recreation areas were increased, thus placing the costs of running these national parks partially on the users.

Finally, in an age of global concern and awareness, the Reagan administration was particularly remiss in its lack of attention to transboundary and international environmental issues. The avoidance of any legislative movement on the acid rain issue despite its known impacts in both the United States and Canada is one glaring example. Although the Bush administration may view some of these problems differently, in many respects the damage has already been done. It will take decades, for example, for the environmental infrastructure within the government to recover, assuming of course that budgetary restraints are lifted. There is hope, however, in that the Bush administration has shown some scientific and policy interest in international environmental issues such as global warming. Time will tell the true impacts of the Reagan years on the conservation of natural resources and the protection of environmental quality in this country (Lamm and Barron, 1988).

cipitation, tropical deforestation, and a host of other global ills.

It remains to be seen how long this new awareness will last, or how important it will be in changing policies and behavior. The concern has already generated numerous proposals for international efforts to reduce carbon dioxide emissions, chlorofluorocarbon production, marine pollution, and tropical deforestation. These are global problems and most of the pressure for solving them is coming from industrialized nations, where the technical, political, and socioeconomic barriers are enormous.

CURRENT NATURAL RESOURCE POLICY

The history of policy development for natural resource use reviewed in the previous section shows that many important goals have motivated government decisionmaking at one time or another, and many of these are embodied in present policy. These goals can be grouped into four general categories: to promote economic development; to conserve resources for the future; to protect public health; and to preserve important natural features.

Clearly the most frequent motivation for government actions with respect to natural resources has been to promote economic development. This began with the land divestitures of the eighteenth and nineteenth centuries and continues today in the management of our national forests, offshore oil resources, rivers, and grazing land. The construction of major dams and reservoirs on rivers for hydroelectric power generation, irrigation, or flood control addresses this goal. Economic development is clearly the motivation in the recent increases in federal mineral lease sales, with development rights being sold at below market value to stimulate production. It is also the primary justification for one of the basic tenets of public land management policy, that of *multiple use*. The concept of multiple use was incorporated into the Multiple Use and Sustained Yield Act of 1960 and restated in NEPA, but it originated much earlier.

In encouraging economic development, the companion to the multiple use concept is

the idea of sustained yield, which aids in achieving the second goal, to conserve resources for future generations. This of course is the fundamental principle of renewable resource management established by Pinchot in forest management, but it applies equally to the mission of the Soil Conservation Service and indeed to every agency managing natural resources.

The third goal, to promote public health, is the basis for most pollution control legislation. Many of the early laws regulating potential health hazards in the environment were enacted at the state level, and major federal actions in this area did not appear until the late nineteenth and early twentieth centuries. Today most of the water and air quality standards established by the government are based on health criteria and risk assessments (Chapters 11 and 13).

The fourth major goal of natural resource policy is to preserve significant natural features that are valuable for aesthetic or scientific reasons, if not for economic ones. This is the aim of the extensive legislation enacted regarding wilderness preservation and protection of endangered species, and it is the principal mission of the National Park Service. This goal also forms the basis of some water quality criteria, and it is considered one of the uses of public lands incorporated in multiple use planning.

Many natural resource policies combine these different goals. An example of this is water pollution control, which not only protects the public health but also provides recreational, aesthetic, and economic benefits to fisheries. All the agencies involved in resource management address these multiple goals in devising management strategies, and this combination of purposes also plays an important role in creating political coalitions to enact new laws. Together they form the basis of sound resource management.

In the late 1980s, after a decade of polarization and politicization, environmental issues again garnered bipartisan support. Conservation and environmental issues became part of the national and international agenda in such diverse areas as national security, international trade, and population policies. International concerns over acid rain, global warm-

APRIL						
SUNDAY	MONDAY	TUESDAY	WEDNESDAY	THURSDAY	FRIDAY	SATURDAY
1 CFC DAY	**2** TOXIC WASTE DAY	**3** NUCLEAR DUMP DAY	**4** OZONE DEPLETION DAY	**5** DRIFT-NETTING DAY	**6** EXTINCT SPECIES DAY	**7** DISPOSABLE DIAPER DAY
8 SPOTTED OWL DAY	**9** CLEAR-CUTTING DAY	**10** BURNING RAIN FOREST DAY	**11** AUTO EMISSION DAY	**12** OIL SPILL DAY	**13** WATER POLLUTION DAY	**14** POLLUTED STREAM DAY
15 ACID RAIN DAY	**16** FISH KILL DAY	**17** STRIP MINING DAY	**18** SOIL EROSION DAY	**19** CARBON MONOXIDE DAY	**20** LEAKING CHEMICAL DAY	**21** GREENHOUSE EFFECT DAY
22 EARTH DAY !!!	**23** GAS HOG DAY	**24** INSECTICIDE DAY	**25** DDT DAY	**26** ALAR DAY	**27** FAMINE DAY	**28** WHALE KILL DAY
29 SEAL KILL DAY	**30** SMOKESTACK DAY					

Figure 3.4 Celebrating Earth Day. Despite two decades of environmental concern and activism, we still have a long way to go.

ing, and tropical deforestation, to name but a few, fueled the international debate on how to best manage these resources. Earth Day 1990 was celebrated by millions of people worldwide (Fig. 3.4) and helped to heighten global awareness of environmental issues.

HOW DECISIONS ARE MADE

Several different groups are involved in any decision over the use of natural resources: re-source managers, social agents, and interest groups. Membership in these groups is not constant, as any individual may shift from one role to another as the decisionmaking process unfolds (Fig. 3.5).

A resource manager is the individual or agency in immediate contact with the resource and who has a direct stake in how that re-source is used or misused. Examples of re-source managers include an individual farmer concerned with soil erosion, a forest ranger charged with managing a particular national forest, or the Secretary of the Interior, who manages the resources under his or her juris-diction—parks, public lands, and so on.

Resource managers are subject to outside influences, or social agents. These range from the forest rangers' superiors in the Depart-ment of Agriculture to the U.S. President, who oversees the Secretary of the Interior. These social agents provide technical expertise and direction to the individual managers in the field. The goals, objectives, and responsibilities of the social agents are broader than those of the resource manager. Social agents are thus influenced by interest groups who have a stake in how a resource is eventually used. Special interests range from timber companies seek-

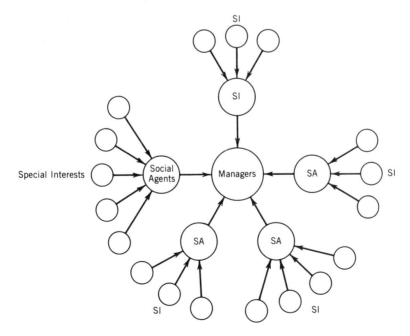

Figure 3.5 Participants in the resource use decision-making process. Individuals may shift roles, depending on the resource issue under consideration.

ing access to a national forest, to supermarket chains buying farm produce, to environmental groups seeking to preserve a piece of nature.

Conflicts between participants inevitably lead to disagreement over management policies (Fig. 3.6). One example is whether to manage forests for water yield, timber harvesting or species habitat. These disagreements are further complicated by *goal-oriented* and *mitigation-oriented* management strategies. Some governmental bodies are charged with the management of a resource, that is, they are goal-directed, and others are charged with regulation and protection of environmental quality, or mitigation-oriented. Often there are conflicts between the two, even when they are in the same agency. Decisionmaking then becomes very difficult and usually involves conflict, cooperation, and compromise between the resource manager, social agents, and interest groups. In addition, conflicting environmental ideologies complicate the matter further (Pepper, 1986) (see Issue 3–2).

THE POLITICS OF ENVIRONMENTAL LEGISLATION

At the national level, the fundamental decisionmaking process is of course the congressional legislative process. Laws are initially drafted by individual legislators, or more commonly groups of legislators and their staffs. They are discussed before the various congressional committees that have responsibility for particular areas of government policy. These committees modify the proposals and, if approved, forward them to the full Senate or House of Representatives for amendment and approval. When, usually after much debate and revision, they are passed by both houses of Congress, they are forwarded to the President for signing into law. At each stage of the process, resource managers, social agents, and interest groups make their positions known, and their opinions may be either incorporated or ignored in the proposed legislation.

Each law is unique, and each one is subjected to different forces depending on the course the process takes from initial proposal to final enactment. An example of the politics of environmental legislation is the Alaska National Interest Lands Conservation Act

(a)

(b)

Figure 3.6   Conflicts in resource management. The harvesting of timber in the old growth forests of the Pacific Northwest (*a*) compete with the habitat of the spotted owl (*b*), now considered an endangered species.

(ANILCA) passed in 1980. This act, better known as the Alaska Lands Bill, is a good example because the battles over it were particularly intense and involved many different actors. Few environmental laws in recent decades have been so controversial as this one.

Alaska has an area of about 375 million acres (152 million ha), and virtually all of this was in federal ownership when Alaska became a state in 1959. The terms of the Statehood Act required, however, that 104 million acres (42 million ha) eventually be turned over to the state. In 1971, the Alaska Native Claims Act was passed, which paved the way for construction of the Alaska pipeline by providing a settlement of the land claims of the native peoples. This act called for 44 million acres (18 million ha) to be turned over to the natives. But before these lands could be transferred, it was necessary for the federal government to decide, by the end of 1978, which lands it would retain in federal ownership, and of these which would be preserved as wilderness and which would be open to development. The Alaska lands issue was thus a classic battle of preservation versus development, and the stakes were high: spectacular and unique natural areas containing potentially very valuable mineral and timber resources. The battle took much longer than was expected, and to prevent development of some areas while Congress debated, President Carter proclaimed about 44 million acres (18 million ha) as national monuments.

The House of Representatives was the first to take up the Alaska lands issue, in 1977. Morris Udall, a leading environmentalist in congress, introduced a bill that would place nearly 170 million acres (69 million ha) in the "four systems": the national parks, wildlife refuges, forests, and wild and scenic rivers. In contrast, a proposal introduced by Alaska representative Don Young would place only 25 million acres (10 million ha) in the four systems, and another 57 million acres (23 million ha) in a joint state–federal management area to be managed for multiple uses. The battle lines were drawn, and the special interests went to work. One of the most effective of these was the Alaska Coalition, a group of conservation organizations that banded together to press for a preservation-oriented bill. On the other side were the state of Alaska, which wanted as much development potential as possible, and industry groups like the American Mining Congress and the Western Oil and Gas

Association. In the numerous negotiations the various proposals were modified, and eventually they were narrowed to two: the Udall bill and another that would have preserved much less land. Public sentiment for preservation was mobilized by the Alaska Coalition, which produced and distributed literature and films depicting the spectacular wilderness. In the end this sentiment was very important, and the Udall bill passed by a wide margin.

Once the House had passed its bill, the Senate began deliberations on its own versions of the bill. In general the Senate was less conservation-minded than the House, though there was a powerful group supporting a bill very similar to the House-passed bill. But the bill that finally emerged from committee in the Senate was rather different, including substantial reductions in areas designated as wilderness and more access for development in other areas. This was far from acceptable to the two Alaskan Senators, Ted Stevens and Mike Gravel, who vowed to filibuster to prevent passage of a bill that would not meet the desires of the state. The debate was a heated one, and at one point the Senate went into closed session after a shouting match between Stevens and Colorado Senator Gary Hart. Eventually Stevens and Gravel's attempts at a filibuster failed as the Senate voted to cut off debate. The Senate version finally passed and placed 104 million acres (42 million ha) in the four systems, substantially less than the 127 million acres (51 million ha) in the House bill. Wilderness designation was made for 67 million acres (27 million ha) in the House bill, but only 57 million acres (23 million ha) in the Senate version, and mineral exploration was permitted in some wildlife refuges.

After Senate passage of its bill, the House again took up the issue under threats of a filibuster if it failed to agree to the Senate version. It did accept the Senate version of the bill, and finally in late 1980 the bill was signed by President Carter. It was most certainly a compromise, but not an entirely happy one. Morris Udall said that he got most of what he wanted, but that there were still provisions that were unacceptable to him and that he hoped would be modified in the next Congress. Alaska Representative Don Young was pleased that the bill did allow for more mineral exploration than the original House bill, but he too said he wanted to change things in the next Congress to allow for even more exploration and development.

Throughout the debate on the Alaska Lands Bill, the changing strengths and fortunes of the actors could be seen. Conservationists were buoyed by support from the Carter administration, particularly Interior Secretary Cecil Andrus. In the midst of the debate, the Alaska legislature was repealing income taxes and rebating millions of dollars to its citizens as a result of accumulating oil revenues, actions that earned no extra sympathy for their demands for resource development. Carter and most environmental groups hailed the bill as the most significant environmental achievement of the Carter administration. Mike Gravel was defeated in a primary election during the height of the debate, and one of the major issues was his inability to force the Senate to recognize Alaska's interests. But at the same time, industry won some crucial battles, and most of the valuable mineral and timber resources are open to development.

ISSUE 3-2   Ideologies of Natural Resource Management

Most political debates are defined by the ideological viewpoints of the participants, and natural resource decisionmaking is no exception. Ideology generally refers to adherence to broad, comprehensive bodies of thought such as capitalism or Marxism. Ideology thus affects opinions on issues by determining the information used in decisionmaking and the ways in which problems are defined. If the same body of information on some particular topic is put before people with differing ideologies, their interpretations of the information will differ, as will their recommendations for appropriate action. However, in an open political system there can be as many ideological variations as there are participants, and two people may agree on most issues yet be worlds apart on some specific topic. It is therefore impossible to describe all the viewpoints that enter into the natural resources debate, but sketches are provided of a few common viewpoints to give an idea of the ideological frameworks that people adhere to today.

For example, there is a fairly well defined body of data that is used to estimate how much recoverable petroleum remains in the United States. One would think that experts would have little trouble in agreeing on a procedure for analyzing those data, and hence on the conclusion that is reached. But in fact, reasonable estimates made by competent analysts vary by as much as a factor of 10. The key word here is "recoverable." The choice of which method to use to calculate recoverable petroleum resources is affected by ideological outlook. A capitalist would tend to think in terms of economic recoverability and conclude that because oil will become too expensive to extract, it will be replaced by other energy sources and hence oil companies will in fact only be able to recover a portion of what is in the ground. A socialist, on the other hand, would be more inclined to think in terms of technical recoverability and conclude that there is a lot of recoverable oil, by using the drilling and pumping technology likely to be available over the next few decades, and that if the recovery is worth our labor we will get it.

In recent years many environmental experts have presented their viewpoints on the issue of the major causes of the present environmental crises. From these, we have constructed a few examples of important ideological approaches. Each includes an example of how an adherent to the viewpoint would answer the following question: "What are the major causes of the environmental crisis?" This question itself shows the ideological bias of the inquirer, as not all persons would agree that there is a crisis. We will call the adherents a conservative capitalist, a capitalist environmentalist, a Marxist, a socialist environmentalist, and a spaceship earth ecologist. These labels are as descriptive as possible, but given the nature of ideology, those who adhere to these ideas would probably object to the terms we use to describe them.

The conservative capitalist believes that the free market system is the best means to allocate resources, and the less government interference in that system the better. An adherent of this

The congressional process is one of compromise, and the most effective means for compromise is to make sure everyone gets something they want. Each actor, and each interest group, is given at least token recognition of its interests in an attempt to gain support for the final outcome. The particular characteristics of that outcome—which interests get more of what they want and which get less— is of course dependent on the strengths of their various power bases. In the case of the Alaska Lands Bill, the environmentalists had much more popular support than their opponents, and that resulted in a bill that is generally regarded as a significant achievement for conservation.

THE DECISIONMAKING PROCESS

The legislative process is not the only way in which environmental law is decided. There are over 50 federal entities involved in natural resources policy and decisionmaking (Table 3.1). Many times overlapping jurisdictions, different goals, and antagonistic staffs result in interagency squabbling over the management

---

viewpoint believes that the consumer and the producer will, through the mechanism of supply and demand, determine how much of a given resource is used and at what price. Every commodity has a price associated with it, or would have if someone were concerned enough to want to control it. For example, the question of how much forest to cut and how much to leave as wilderness should be answered by the price people are willing to pay to have either lumber or wilderness. If wilderness is indeed a desirable commodity then a price will be offered for it, and if this price is greater than the price bid for the lumber, then wilderness it will be. The intervention of government in preserving wilderness represents a misallocation of resources. According to the conservative capitalist, there is no environmental crisis. Rather, there is a group of selfish people (environmentalists) who are trying to get something for nothing. They are trying to get the government to force industries to provide them with a commodity (clean water) without their having to pay for it directly, and as a result they are demanding cleaner water than they would really want if they had to pay the cost of pollution control. The crisis is one of nonmarket forces (government) trying to do what the market should be allowed to do, and as a result a few environmentalists are getting what they want at the expense of the majority of the population.

The capitalist environmentalist recognizes that there are certain resources that simply cannot be traded properly on the open market. Pollution is a good example. Smoke from a factory's chimney represents a commodity exchanged between the factory owner and those who breathe the air polluted by it, and yet no price is bid for the exchange, by either the factory or the population, and so the population has no way of economically choosing whether or not to receive that smoke. The exchange represents an externality, or an exchange outside the market system, and this must be eliminated. Externalities may be eliminated in any of several ways as discussed in Chapter 2. According to the capitalist environmentalist, the cause of the environmental crisis is the existence of market externalities. Government action is necessary to correct these imperfections of the capitalist system, but if that action is taken according to the basic capitalist principles then there should be no problem with the pollution—either it is there and people don't mind or it is not there. In a few cases the government may have been a little overzealous in its application of pollution controls, and the result has been a cleanup that is more costly than we are willing to pay. Careful benefit cost analyses of pollution controls in the future will correct this problem.

The Marxist believes that natural resources have no intrinsic value; the value of goods is derived solely from the labor that goes into producing them. Like the conservative capitalist, the Marxist believes there is no environmental crisis. Production decisions are made by the population as a whole through the state. The desirability of any particular environmental condition (polluted or not polluted; high consumption or low

of specific resources. There are also intra-agency conflicts between temporary political appointees who head the agencies and their professional civil servant staffs. How these agencies go about making decisions and implementing policy is crucial to our understanding of natural resources management in the United States.

Organizations

There are few differences between how organizations make decisions and how you do. Their decisions differ from yours only in scale and complexity. Governmental and other public organizations are similar in at least four ways in the types of decisions that are made and how they are made. Publicly oriented decisions are usually in response to human need and require government efforts for implementation. Second, government agencies are influenced by the opinions of others such as lobby groups or political action committees. In addition, these decisions can be influenced by the motivations and political philosophy that underlie the decisionmakers' choices (see Issue 3–2). Finally, decisions will often be

---

consumption) is culturally defined rather than dictated by any absolute principles. Therefore, if it is decided to extract a certain natural resource, or discharge certain pollutants, then that is the wish of the people and there is no problem. If there is an environmental crisis, because the state is not a truly socialist one, then obviously decisions are made in the interests of a few rather than for the entire population.

The socialist environmentalist believes in collective decisionmaking, but also believes that natural resource decisions must take into consideration the inherent limitations of the environment's ability to supply raw materials and absorb waste. If the population as a whole had more control over the decisionmaking process, then they would certainly choose a cleaner environment. The environmental crisis is a result of the fact that production is controlled by an elite few, who waste resources and pollute the environment without regard for the welfare of the general population. Multinational corporations are particularly to blame, for not only are they in control of vast natural resources but they are largely outside governmental regulation, and so there is virtually no way for the people to influence their activities.

The spaceship earth ecologist feels that regardless of what economic or decisionmaking system is used, the ability of the earth to supply living space, raw materials, and waste disposal is very limited. Industrialized societies consume vast amounts of natural resources, and not only are they rapidly running out of nonrenewable resources but renewable ones are being damaged beyond repair. The poorer nations consume nonrenewables at a lower rate than rich nations,

but deforestation and soil erosion are rampant in the Third World. Most importantly, worldwide population is growing much more rapidly than technological abilities to produce basic goods for those people, and population growth is most rapid in those countries that have the least ability to accommodate it. The spaceship earth ecologist believes that worldwide crisis is around the corner, with famines, plagues, and resource wars. What is immediately necessary is the reduction of population growth to zero-growth levels and the complete restructuring of systems of production of goods and disposal of wastes. The new production system must be one that mirrors nature by using such techniques as solar energy harvesting, mixed cropping systems using organic fertilizer and biological control of pests, and total waste recycling. To the spaceship earth ecologist, the environmental crisis is an acute one, and it is a result of a Malthusian imbalance between finite resource availability and exponentially growing population, made worse by a production system that damages the ability of the earth to provide for its inhabitants by over-exploitation of resources and pollution of the environment.

To some extent the viewpoints above represent extremes, but they are by no means so extreme that one would not hear them espoused in the halls of government or in respected academic journals. They are viewpoints held by many responsible and powerful people. It should be recognized, however, that most individuals have opinions that are variations on the ones presented, or more likely combinations of two or more of them. Can you name some individuals who fit any of these descriptions? Do you fit any of them?

TABLE 3.1   Federal Agencies with Major Responsibility for Environmental Policy or Management

Department of Interior
  National Park Service
  Bureau of Land Management
  Fisheries and Wildlife Service
  Geological Survey
  Mineral Management Service
  Bureau of Reclamation
  Surface Mining Reclamation and Enforcement
  Bureau of Mines
Department of Agriculture
  Forest Service
  Soil Conservation Service
  Agricultural Conservation and Stabilization
    Service
Department of Commerce
  National Oceanographic and Atmospheric
    Administration
  U.S. Coast Guard
Department of Energy
  Federal Energy Regulatory Commission
  National Center for Appropriate Technology
  Nuclear Waste Policy Act Project Office
Department of Defense
  Army Corps of Engineers
  Departments of Army, Navy, Air Force
Department of Transportation
Department of Labor
  Occupational Safety and Health Administration
Department of Health and Human Services
  Food and Drug Administration
Environmental Protection Agency
Executive Office of the President
  Council on Environmental Quality
Independent Agencies
  Tennessee Valley Authority
  Bonneville Power Commission
  Water Resources Council
  National Science Foundation/National Research
    Council
  Nuclear Regulatory Commission
  Great Lakes Basin Commission
  Federal Emergency Management Agency

avoided because they are painful in terms of conflict between the governmental entity and the other groups or individuals. This results in nondecisions, which in fact becomes a form of decisionmaking. Non-decisionmaking is more pervasive in the United States than most people realize (O'Riordan, 1976). For example, Environmental Protection Agency administrators under Ronald Reagan in the early 1980s were often directed to avoid making environmentally oriented decisions that would be harmful to business interests.

There are several ideal procedures that if followed would assure good decisionmaking (Janis and Mann, 1977). The decisionmakers should thoroughly investigate a wide range of alternative courses of action and objectives to be met. All available information should be gathered, including expert opinions. The positive and negative aspects of each alternative should also be considered before taking any action.

In theory, responsible, objective decisions are possible, but in practice many factors bias both decisionmakers and their conclusions, resulting in less than perfect decisions. One of these is the constraint imposed by organizational tradition—we have always done things this way, and there is a tradition to maintain. Also, there are constraints imposed by bureaucratic procedures, such as the endless arguments between regional and home offices or between divisions of the same organization. There are also constraints on decisions that are imposed by the demands of the executive role. A decisionmaker may feel that she cannot show friendliness to subordinates as it might be construed as a sign of weakness and would hamper negotiations with a lobbyist or other interest groups.

Perhaps one of the most important constraints is the lack of objective standards for assessing alternative outcomes, which can force the decisionmaker to be sympathetic to social and political pressures and special interests. Decisionmakers often rely on stereotypes, such as believing that the information of uneducated people is always unreliable, which results in biased decisions. Bias can be introduced by an individual decisionmaker's cognition of his or her role and intuitive assessment of the likelihood of the success or failure of the chosen course of action. And of course decisions are often made with insufficient or imperfect information, particularly in the case of environmental management.

Strategies

Given that we live in an imperfect world with many complexities, it is surprising that we have been able to make sound environmental decisions at all. Decisionmaking in natural resources management is divided into three general categories: satisficing, incrementalism, and stress management. *Satisficing* is the consideration of two policy alternatives at a time, which are examined sequentially and compared to one another. The best choice is then selected from these two. The goal of the satisficing approach is to look for the course of action or alternative that is just good enough and that meets a minimal set of requirements. This type of approach is cost-effective because the full range of alternatives is not researched, which would be too costly in time and money, and thus the collective resources of the decisionmaker or agency are used more efficiently. A negative aspect of this strategy is the limited range of alternatives from which to select the best choice. Satisficing is an appealing approach to managers because it is simple, and it is used in many other areas besides resource use decisionmaking.

Incrementalism is used when the problem or resource issue is not clearly defined or when there are conflicting goals, values, or objectives (Mitchell, 1979). Incremental decisions are made by "muddling through" as they come across an administrator's desk. He or she may not know what is wanted but they do know what should be avoided. As a result, incrementalism is not used to set broad policy guidelines as is the satisficing strategy, but rather to alleviate the shortcomings in the present policy in its day-to-day administration. This approach is regularly used to cope with the bureaucratic politics that many times result in compromising and shifting coalitions. Incrementally made decisions are often disjointed and seemingly contradictory, and reflect minute changes in policy.

The third strategy, *stress management,* is the approach most commonly used in government. Stress management is the response to an issue once it becomes a critical problem. It begins with a seat-of-the-pants planning effort to come to grips with the looming impact of the problem, and policy is then determined on a piecemeal basis to deal with the immediate problem at hand. There may be little consideration of long-term effects in the rush to get something done quickly. For example, when it was realized that certain industries contributed to local air pollution, regulations were put into effect in the 1970s that required higher smokestacks so that the pollutants would not afflict nearby communities. In the long run, however, this stress management decision may have a larger negative impact, as these airborne pollutants are contributing to the acid rain problem that may lead to major deforestation and water pollution problems hundreds of miles from the smokestacks. Thus with stress management choices, there is no time for a discussion of larger policy questions. All decisions must be made immediately and implemented as quickly as possible (Kasperson, 1969), and there is very little time to discuss all the alternatives or the implications of new rules and regulations. Stress management has often been referred to as "crisis management" for good reason. Unfortunately, many of our environmental regulatory agencies routinely operate in this fashion.

You might think that the cumulative effect of all of these imperfections in the decisionmaking process would prevent good decisions from ever being made. Some might agree. But in fact with most decisions of this nature there is a wide range of opinion on how problems should be approached, and in most cases only a portion of the population could be completely satisfied with the result. That is of course the nature of the political process. But the important thing to recognize is that the push and pull of politics goes on at many levels of decisionmaking—not just at election time. The administrator and enforcer are just as susceptible to the forces that sway decisions as is the legislator.

The Role of Public Interest

Public interest can be defined in many ways, as there are many different "publics." At the international level, for example, who constitutes "the public" and what is the public interest? At the national level, perhaps these are easier questions to address, largely because of our penchant for opinion polls.

Public opinion regarding environmental issues has always been strong, yet this support has not been translated into electoral power. In the last decade, in particular, the public has endorsed stronger environmental laws even if improved environmental quality means higher prices and costs (Dunlap, 1987). In fact, a poll in July 1989 found that about 80 percent of the respondents agreed that protecting the environment was so important that requirements and standards could not be too high, and that continued improvements in environmental quality had to be made regardless of cost (Suro, 1989).

Despite this overwhelming support, environmental issues still do not decide national elections. At the national level, this concern is often tapped by environmental activist groups that are able to mobilize public support and increase their membership and ultimate lobbying positions. There was a marked rise in membership in many environmental organizations during the early Reagan years, largely in response to his policies as implemented by James Watt at the Interior Department and Anne Gorsuch Burford at the Environmental Protection Agency. In the ensuing national furor over the management abilities of these two individuals, culminating in their resignations, Reagan's popularity never waned. Environmental groups, on the other hand, saw a sudden and strong upsurge in members.

There are many types of public interest groups, each with a particular cause and management style. Some groups are conservative and work with lobbyists. Other groups are more radical and often take their message to the forest, oceans, or streets, wherever they can command media attention. Table 3.2 lists some of the different types of public interest environmental groups that are active today. This is not an exhaustive list, but is provided as an illustration of the diversity and abundance of different "public interests." It is important to understand that environmental groups make decisions just like any other organization and are subject to the same pressures and stresses. Just because it is the Sierra Club or the Natural Resources Defense Council does not mean that their decisions are perfect and unbiased.

TABLE 3.2   Public Interest and Environmental Groups

Advocacy
  Clean Water Action Project
  Common Cause
  Cousteau Society
  Defenders of Wildlife
  Ducks Unlimited
  Earth First!
  Environmental Action Foundation
  Friends of the Earth
  Fund for Animals
  Fund for Renewable Energy and the
    Environment
  Greenpeace
  Izaak Walton League
  League of Conservation Voters
  National Audubon Society
  National Wildlife Federation
  The Nature Conservancy
  Physicians for Social Responsibility
  Planned Parenthood
  Rain Forest Action Network
  Sierra Club
  Trout Unlimited
  Union of Concerned Scientists
  The Wilderness Society
  World Wildlife Fund
  Zero Population Growth

Litigation
  Environmental Defense Fund
  Natural Resources Defense Council
  The Public Citizen
  Public Interest Research Group

Research/Education
  Center for Marine Conservation
  Center for Science in the Public Interest
  Center for the Study of Responsive Law
  Citizen's Clearinghouse of Hazardous Waste
  Conservation Foundation
  Environmental Law Institute
  Institute for Local Self Reliance
  Population Reference Bureau
  Resources for the Future
  World Resources Institute
  World Watch

Industry
  American Petroleum Institute
  American Water Well Association
  Atomic Industrial Forum
  Chemical Manufacturers Association
  Edison Electric Institute
  Keep America Beautiful
  National Solid Waste Management Association

THE "NEW" ENVIRONMENTAL POLITICS

There are two additional factors that currently influence environmental decisionmaking. The first is the increased use of the referendum process, whereby voters are asked to decide on complex environmental issues. One of the best examples of this new approach to environmental legislation is California's new Toxics Law, otherwise known as Proposition 65 (see Issue 3–3).

The other factor is a shift from the top-

ISSUE 3–3 California's Toxic Law (Proposition 65): Public Involvement at the Extreme or the Wave of the Future?

In November 1986, Californians overwhelmingly (63 percent to 37 percent) passed Proposition 65, the Safe Drinking Water and Toxic Enforcement Act. This law is the first of its kind and requires that warnings be posted wherever people are placed at "significant risk" of exposure to toxic chemicals. Significant risk is defined as one excess cancer case per 100,000 people exposed over a lifetime. The exposure applies to the workplace, in consumer products, or in the environment. At first, there were only 29 chemicals listed, but this has been increased to 300 or so by the courts and the Republican governor. About 260 of the chemicals are described as probable carcinogens based on animal testing, while another 35 are listed as reproductive toxins. The uniqueness of this legislation is that it does not seek to ban toxics outright, but merely requires that industry not put any of these chemicals into drinking water and not expose anyone to them without first providing a clear warning as to the nature of toxicity. Market incentives are used to reduce the consumer's exposure to toxic chemicals.

As signs appeared in supermarkets, restaurants, gasoline stations, and hospitals, the public debate on whether or not the law is working began in earnest. Gasoline, alcoholic beverages, and tobacco products all have warning labels. In addition to many scientific questions (e.g., what is no significant risk?), the mechanisms for alerting the public to the dangers of toxic chemicals are becoming quite controversial. The grocery, cosmetics, and drug industries want their products regulated under the purview of the Food and Drug Administration. Supermarkets, in particular, did not want the responsibility for posting individual warnings on shelves and demanded that producers and manufacturers provide them on products, which of course they were unwilling to do. In a test case involving tobacco companies, the California attorney general sued eight retailers and twenty-five tobacco companies for failure to comply with warning requirements under the law. Vons, the largest supermarket chain in the state, also refused to carry tobacco products until warnings were placed on labels. In March 1989 the suit was settled out of court, with the tobacco companies capitulating. All manufacturers were thus placed on notice and were forced to comply with labeling requirements. The national significance of this test case is enormous. If manufacturers are forced to provide warning labels on products they sell in California, then they are also more likely because of cost, legal liability, and convenience to do so elsewhere.

Whether or not the legislation is affecting consumer behavior and choice is unknown at the moment. What is clear, however, is Proposition 65's impact on manufacturers who must label their products as containing hazardous substances. This may act as a deterrent and force industry to assess exactly how much of those hazardous ingredients are really necessary in the product's formulation.

Other states are beginning to follow suit. Proposition 65-type legislation is pending in many states. Not to be outdone in November 1990, California voted on the "Big Green" initiative, the most sweeping and far-reaching legislative proposal in the state's history. The bill would ban 19 cancer-causing pesticides still in widespread use; it would limit emissions of greenhouse gases and clear-cutting in the state's forests; it would permit offshore oil drilling only in the case of national emergencies; and finally, it would create an elected position for an environmental advocate who would enforce the law. Unfortunately the measure lost (67% voted no) in a wave of anti-environmental losses not only in California, but nationwide (Mackerron, 1989; Reinhold, 1989, 1990; Russell, 1989).

down legislative approach in which Congress passes national laws and states adhere to them to a more bottom-up one in which individual states set policy that is ultimately nationalized. One of the most significant legacies of the Reagan administration was to shift environmental responsibility from the federal government to state and local governments (see Issue 3–1). The result was a fundamental transformation in how laws are made in this country. Beset by inactivity at the national level, state legislators devised their own laws to tackle pollution issues within their state but not exclusive to them. For example, in 1987, legislators in Sacramento, California, insisted that refiners change the mix of ingredients in gasoline to inhibit evaporation since these vapor fumes were a major source of hydrocarbons in Southern California. New York, New Jersey, and the six states in New England followed suit a year later. By 1989, the U.S. EPA announced a major national program for controlling evaporation of unburned fuel. "As California breathes, it seems, so breathes the nation," wrote one reporter in *The New York Times* (Wald, 1989, p. A23). California is clearly the policy innovator for clean air legislation as it has the worst air quality in the nation and hence the greatest necessity to clean it up. Another innovative state is New Jersey, which experienced the garbage crisis before anyone else. In response to the mounds of solid waste generated daily by its residents, the state developed a comprehensive recycling master plan that mandates the recycling of 25 percent of the municipal solid waste stream. Passed as legislation in 1980, this program has become a model for the rest of the nation.

Why are these interstate problems being solved at the state rather than national level? Some point to the fact that many states have such severe pollution problems (e.g., Los Angeles smog) that they cannot wait for Washington to act. As a consequence, if California acts, and doesn't fall flat on its face, other states may adopt their programs. In addition, aggressive national lobbyists don't often frequent state houses, which means that the likelihood of passing a controversial piece of legislation (meaning one that industry does not favor) is greater at the state rather than na-

tional level. Finally, some argue that state legislators are more in tune with political change and thus more responsive to local environmental concerns. This immediately transfers voter support for environmental concerns into political action. The trend at the national level is less clear.

REFERENCES AND ADDITIONAL READING

Carson, R.L. 1962. *The Silent Spring*. Boston: Houghton Mifflin.

Council on Environmental Quality. 1980. *Environmental Quality: The Eleventh Annual Report*. Washington, DC: U.S. Government Printing Office.

———. 1986. *Environmental Quality: The Seventeenth Annual Report*. Washington, DC: U.S. Government Printing Office.

Dunlap, R. 1987. Polls, pollution, and politics revisited: Public opinion on the environment in the Reagan era. *Environment* 29(6): 6–11, 32–37.

Hardin, G. 1985. *Filters against Folly*. New York: Penguin Books.

Huth, H. 1957. *Nature and the American: Three Centuries of Changing Attitudes*. Berkeley: University of California Press.

Janis, I.L., and L. Mann. 1977. *Decision Making: A Psychological Analysis of Conflict, Choice, and Commitment*. New York: Free Press.

Kasperson, R.E. 1969. Political behavior and the decision making process in the allocation of water resources between recreational and municipal uses. *Natural Resources J.* 9: 176–211.

Lamm, R.D., and T.A. Barron. 1988. The environmental agenda for the next administration. *Environment* 30(4): 16–20, 28–29.

Leopold, A. 1949. *A Sand County Almanac and Sketches Here and There*. New York: Oxford University Press.

Mackerron, C.B. 1989. Industry is learning to live with Proposition 65. *Chemical Week*, July 12, pp. 18–20.

Malone, T.F., and R. Corell. 1989. Mission to planet Earth revisited. *Environment* 31(3): 6–11, 31–35.

Marsh, G.P. 1864. *Man and Nature, or Physical Geography as Modified by Human Action*. New York: Scribner.

Mitchell, B. 1979. *Geography and Resource Analysis*. London: Longman.

Nash, R. 1982. *Wilderness and the American Mind*, rev. ed. New Haven, CT: Yale University Press.

Nicholson, M. 1970. *The Environmental Revolution: A Guide for the New Masters of the World.* New York: McGraw–Hill.

O'Riordan, T. 1976. *Environmentalism.* London: Pion.

O'Riordan, T., and R.K. Turner. 1983. *An Annotated Reader in Environmental Planning and Management.* Oxford: Pergamon Press.

Pepper, D. 1986. *The Roots of Modern Environmentalism.* London: Croom Helm.

Reinhold, R. 1989. California alliance proposes vote on broad environmental measure. *The New York Times*, October 11, p. A1.

———. 1990. Politics of the environment: California will test waters. *The New York Times*, April 27, p. A1.

Russell, C. 1989. Forewarned is fairly warned. *Sierra* 76(6): 36–44.

Sandbach, F. 1980. *Environment, Ideology, and Policy.* Montclair, NJ: Allanheld, Osmun.

Suro, R. 1989. Grass-roots groups show power battling pollution close to home. *The New York Times*, July 2, p. A1.

Swem, T., and R. Cahn. 1983. The politics of parks in Alaska. *Ambio* 12: 14–19.

Udall, S. 1963. *The Quiet Crisis.* New York: Holt, Rinehart.

Vale, T.R. (Ed.). 1986. *Progress against Growth: Daniel B. Luten on the American Landscape.* New York: Guilford Press.

Wald, M. 1989. Recharting war on smog. *The New York Times*, October 10, p. A1.

Wood, W.B., G.J. Demko, and P. Motson. 1989. Eco-politics in the global greenhouse. *Environment* 31(7): 12–17, 32–34.

TERMS TO KNOW

Carrying Capacity
Hetch-Hetchy
Homestead Act
Incrementalism
Mining Act
Multiple Use
NEPA
Satisficing
Stress Management
Sustained Yield
Taylor Grazing Act
Timber Culture Act

STUDY QUESTIONS

1. What is the significance of Hetch-Hetchy in the preservation versus conservation debate?

2. How would you characterize each of the phases in the development of natural resources policies in the United States?

3. How have the following pieces of legislation shaped the natural resource and environmental policies in the United States over the last century?
   (a) NEPA
   (b) Homestead Act
   (c) Taylor Grazing Act
   (d) Superfund

4. What are the primary differences among the three strategies of decisionmaking and under what circumstances is each most applicable?

5. How does the Alaska Lands Bill demonstrate the politics of environmental legislation and the role of special interests in the process?

6. Explain the difference between top-down legislation and grass-roots initiatives in environmental decisionmaking.

4

The Ecological Bases of Natural Resources

INTRODUCTION TO THE STUDY OF ECOSYSTEMS

Ecology and *ecosystem* are terms that were popularized almost to the point of meaninglessness in the 1970s, but they are no less important and are at the center of environmental management. We see signs that read, "Don't litter—save the ecology," and we may have a feeling that the word means natural beauty, or baby seals, or clean air and water. In fact, ecology did not suddenly spring into existence on the first Earth Day created to raise conservationist consciousness back in 1970. Ecology has been around for over one hundred years and describes a complex field of study.

It is probably no coincidence that we find the first uses of the word ecology in the second half of the nineteenth century, at about the same time that naturalists were first beginning to worry about large scale natural resources depletion. Although the term was probably in use earlier, in 1870 the German biologist Ernst Haeckel defined it as "the study of all the complex interrelations referred to by Darwin as the conditions of the struggle for existence" (Haeckel, 1870, cited in Kormondy, 1969).

More recently, Kormondy has referred to ecology as "multidisciplinary and almost boundless in its concern" (Kormondy, 1969, p. ix) and suggests that we in effect move into other fields of study when we cease to be interested in the interrelationships between processes but focus instead on any one process. That is, when we look at the interactions between the squirrel and its food supply, we are ecologists. When we turn to the physiology of the squirrel, we have become zoologists.

Thus the heart of the study of ecology is the interrelationships between animals and plants and the living and nonliving components and processes that make up their environment. This is why the study of ecological systems is so basic to the conservation of natural resources. Without an understanding of how natural systems work, we cannot begin to conserve, manage, and protect them.

ECOSYSTEMS AS FUNCTIONAL UNITS

An ecosystem can encompass a large or small geographic area and usually consists of several organisms whose needs and requirements are complementary, so that the available resources are used in a stable and nondepleting fashion. It can be difficult to define the precise boundaries of an ecosystem, as organisms are often participants in more than one. *Ecotones* or transitional zones are the more flexible alternative to outlining a sharp boundary (Fig. 4.1, Fig. 4.2). Within a single ecosystem, researchers tend to separate the stable plants and animals into *communities*. These are further subdivided into local societies or colonies, each containing a population of one or more species. Finally, the ecologist can examine the individual organism's function in this larger system.

An ecosystem is a system in which matter and energy are exchanged between ecosystems and with the larger environment. The ecosystem receives *inputs* of energy and

Figure 4.1　A coastal wetlands ecosystem. The shallow bay and its estuarine ecosystem are clearly visible in this view of Cape Canaveral National Seashore.

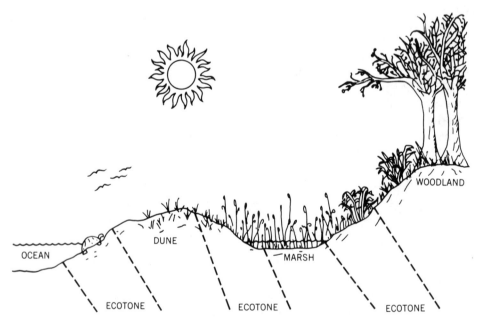

Figure 4.2　Natural ecosystems. The boundaries between different ecosystems are often difficult to define. *Ecotones* are transitional areas between two ecosystems, with plants and animals from both, and are a more accurate reflection of reality. An ecotone is more diversified and usually more productive than a simple ecosystem.

material, which are stored, utilized, or flow through the ecosystem and leave as *outputs*. Interaction between the physical environment of the Los Angeles basin and the human patterns imposed on it produces a complex picture of inputs and outputs (Fig. 4.3). In this urban ecosystem, inputs include raw materials and other imports, immigration of new residents, relatively clean Pacific air, water supplies, and electric power. Within greater Los Angeles, products are created for export, such as air pollution, and emigrants move on in search of other opportunities. This diagram is of course a simplification and presents only a few of the major elements that make up the input–output model of an urban ecosystem (see Detwyler and Marcus, 1972).

THE GLOBAL ENVIRONMENTAL SYSTEM

Although much of the research on ecosystems has focused at small scales such as individual communities or relatively homogeneous ecological regions, there is growing recognition that the entire earth may be viewed as a single environmental system. We now recognize that events occurring in one area may have such far-reaching impacts as to be essentially global in nature. For example, deforestation in the Amazon basin and other tropical areas is a significant contributor to the worldwide increase in atmospheric carbon dioxide content, which could lead to global climatic changes. Fluctuations in ocean circulation in the east-

ern Pacific were recognized as a factor in the decline of the Peruvian anchovy fishery in the 1960s, but now we also realize that these events play a major role in weather patterns throughout the Western Hemisphere and probably the entire globe. The explosion at a nuclear reactor at Chernobyl in the Soviet Union spewed a plume of radioactive pollutants that spread across most of Europe and was detected at monitoring stations around the world.

The integrated nature of the world environmental system is the basis of the Gaia hypothesis, a controversial but stimulating view of the earth (Lovelock, 1979). The Gaia hypothesis suggests that the earth functions as a unified, self-regulating ecological system that has internal feedback mechanisms not unlike those of a single organism. For example, changes in carbon dioxide content may cause changes in rates of plant photosynthesis, which in turn remove carbon dioxide from the atmosphere. Although the Gaia hypothesis has been much criticized (Kirchner, 1989), in recent years it has served as a stimulant to interest in the connections between the global biological and physical systems.

ENERGY AND MATERIAL CYCLES IN ECOSYSTEMS

Natural resources come from the earth's physical environment, and to manage a natural

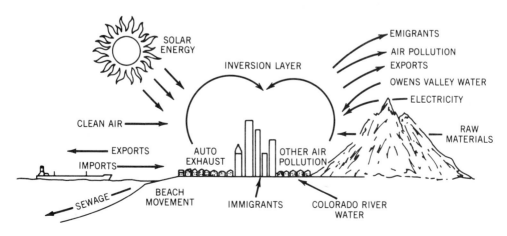

Figure 4.3 An urban ecosystem. This simplified and idealized model of the Los Angeles urban ecosystem shows some of the physical, social, and economic inputs and outputs.

resource for sustained use we need to understand the workings of the environment. Without this knowledge, it is possible to permanently damage or destroy a valuable resource. In such situations, where a resource is utilized in ignorance of the workings of the environment, damage can spread to other portions of the natural or built world. For example, in the nineteenth century, farmers moved into the dry lands of Oklahoma and West Texas, with little concern for the fact that they were growing crops in a much drier region than the one they had moved from. Thus their cropping, tilling, and soil conservation methods were based on the workings of a more humid environment. When low farm prices and a series of dry years struck these semiarid lands in the 1930s, environmental disaster followed. Topsoil was blown to distant regions, and thousands of people were forced to migrate in search of new livelihoods. The soil and water resources were depleted, and interrelated natural systems were adversely affected. Only since the introduction of agricultural practices that recognize the limitations and requirements of semiarid lands have we seen some recovery in this region (see Chapter 7).

Numerous other examples attest to the damage to resources when they are utilized in ignorance of environmental systems. These include the accelerating contamination of water supplies caused by mismanaged waste disposal and the increasing acidification of rainfall resulting in damage to trees and fish. These problems have global implications for the future availability and quality of our most basic resources.

Good resource management depends on understanding the natural processes controlling the availability of natural resources. In any specific case, quite sophisticated scientific knowledge is needed. This is why detailed environmental impact assessments and similar studies are routinely conducted by resource managers. But at a more general level, it is important to understand some of the basic characteristics of natural systems before analyzing specific resources in more detail. This section deals with the general characteristics of energy and material cycles in the environment and their relation to ecological systems and natural resources.

ENERGY TRANSFERS

Energy in ecosystems (and human systems) is ultimately derived from the sun. This energy passes through a series of storages via many paths, before finally being returned to space as radiant energy. There are two fundamental laws governing all energy transfers, called the first and second laws of thermodynamics.

The *first law of thermodynamics* is the law of conservation of energy, but it also governs conversion of matter into energy. It simply states that in any energy transfer, the total amount of energy is unchanged; energy is neither created nor destroyed. Another way of saying this is "you can't get more out than you put in." The second law is called the *law of entropy*, and it is a little less obvious than the first. It says that any time energy is converted from one form to another, the conversion is inefficient. Energy is always converted to a less concentrated form or dissipated as heat. Another way of saying this is "not only is it impossible to get more out than you put in, but you can't even break even." Entropy is a measure of the degree of organization present. Greater entropy means greater disorganization or randomness. The following two examples may help to illustrate these concepts.

The first example is the conversion of solar energy to food energy by *photosynthesis*. A leaf on a plant is exposed to sunlight, and this stimulates a chemical reaction in which carbon dioxide and water are converted to carbohydrates, with oxygen given off as a by-product. In the process, however, the leaf must be heated, and this causes a loss of energy by radiation or convection from the leaf surface. In addition, water must be moved through the leaf stem to deliver nutrients to the leaf and is also evaporated by the leaf as a cooling mechanism. This water loss involves a conversion of water from liquid to vapor form, which requires energy. Finally, plants must also respire. Respiration is a process in which food energy is converted to heat energy, which is then dissipated. When all these things are considered together in an *energy budget* for a single plant or for an entire plant community, only a very small fraction of the incoming solar energy is converted to food energy or *biomass*, generally about 1 percent or less. The rest of the energy is reflected, reradiated, or used in the conversion of liquid water to water vapor.

A coal-fired electric generating plant provides a second example. Coal, of course, is formed by the chemical modification of formerly living matter, mostly plants. The energy released was first stored by plant photosynthesis at some time in the geologic past. When the coal is burned, some heat is lost up the smokestack, but most of the heat is used to convert water to steam. The steam then drives turbines, which drive generators, which in turn produce electricity. The steam is cooled in the process, but not enough to condense it, although it must be returned to the boiler as water. To do this it must be cooled, usually by dissipating the heat in the nearest river or other body of water. Heat is also produced by the generator and by friction in moving parts, and this must be dissipated as well. In the end, only about 35 percent of all the heat stored in the coal is finally converted to electric energy. The rest is dissipated as heat, either in the stack gases or in the steam condensing system. This dissipation of energy is an example of entropy.

Ecosystems consist of all the living organisms in a defined geographic area, together with all the physical entities (soil, water, dead organic matter, and so on) with which they interact. As such they are exceedingly complex, and the energy and material transfers within them are difficult to quantify. Several important studies of energy transfers within ecosystems have been done, however, and from these some generalizations are possible. As one type of organism in an ecosystem consumes another, a pattern of energy flow through the ecosystem is set up, called a *food chain* (Fig. 4.4). Some food chains are simple, for example, when a plant is consumed by a rabbit, which is consumed by a fox. Such a simple chain is usually part of a more complex *food web* in which several animals and plants may be dependent on one another. Many organisms eat more than one kind of food and may in turn themselves be appealing to several other species.

Energy is transferred from one *trophic level* to another within the chain or web. Terrestrial green plants are producers, as they convert solar energy to food energy at the first trophic level. Consumers can in turn be classified as primary consumers, which feed on producers at the second trophic level, secondary consumers, which feed on primary consumers at the third trophic level, and so forth. In addition there are decomposers, which feed on dead organic matter and return nutrients to the soil or water where they become available to producers. There may be fourth- or fifth-level consumers, but rarely do we find more than five in an ecosystem, as the energy produced at the first level has been mostly consumed at intermediate levels. Human beings are able to take advantage of the food energy at different levels because we can consume energy in the form of both plants and animals. There is some debate over whether or not we are wasteful of the world's food energy because our diets are high in animal products. It is generally more efficient in terms of energy production and consumption to obtain our food directly at the first trophic level.

Figure 4.4 illustrates a relatively simple food chain. Notice that at each step in the system, energy is either stored as biomass (the living and dead organic matter in an ecosystem) or used in respiration. Most of the energy consumed at any given level is used in organism metabolism, with only a small percentage being stored, as biomass, and available for the next higher level to consume.

BIOGEOCHEMICAL CYCLES

Just as energy flows through an ecosystem in a cyclic manner, so do materials necessary for life—carbon, oxygen, nitrogen, potassium, water, and many others. The paths these substances take in the environment are called *biogeochemical cycles*. Some biogeochemical cycles are regulated by large storages in the atmosphere; the nitrogen cycle is a good example of this type. Others are dominated by terrestrial storages, usually in rocks and sediments. The phosphorus, potassium, sulfur, and calcium cycles are examples of this latter type. Although the cycles differ because of the different chemical and biological processes regulating them, the patterns are generally similar and we will only discuss four of the important biogeochemical cycles: the nitrogen, phosphorus, carbon, and hydrologic cycles.

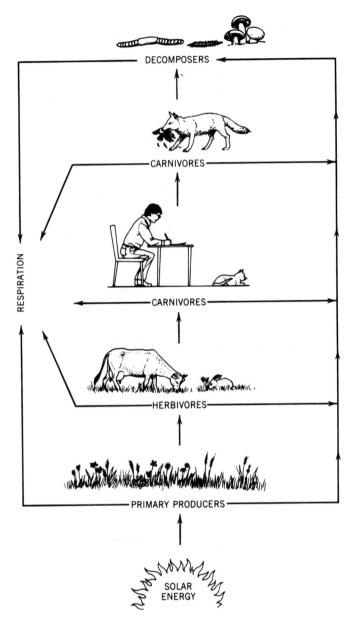

Figure 4.4 Food chain. Herbivores, or primary consumers, eat producers and are then consumed by carnivores. Sometimes a food chain can support additional trophic levels of consumers, before decomposers take their turn.

Nitrogen comprises about 80 percent of the earth's atmosphere, and most of the earth's nitrogen is in the atmosphere at any given time (Fig. 4.5). Nitrogen is also an essential nutrient and a fundamental component of many proteins. Nitrogen cannot be directly used by most organisms in its gaseous form, and for it to be available to living matter it must be fixed or incorporated in chemical substances such as ammonia, nitrates, or organic compounds that plants are able to use. Some nitrogen is added directly to the soil as impurities in rainfall, primarily nitric acid, but the much more important mechanism is the action of nitrogen-fixing bacteria, some of which live in association with plant roots. These bacteria are able to extract nitrogen directly from the air. Some plants, such as legumes, have sym-

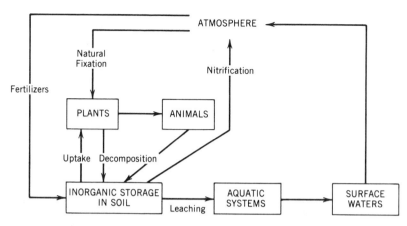

Figure 4.5   The nitrogen cycle. The atmosphere provides the primary storage of nitrogen, which is unusable by plants in its gaseous state and must first be converted by nitrogen-fixing bacteria before it can be used by plants.

biotic or mutually beneficial relationships with particular nitrogen-fixing bacteria, but many other plants also accommodate nitrogen-fixing bacteria, and some nitrogen fixers are not dependent on the environment of plant roots at all. Once nitrogen is incorporated in organic matter, it follows much the same route as energy in the food chain, passing from producer to consumer and ultimately to decomposer. Decomposers return nitrogen to the soil in mineral forms such as ammonia that are again available to plants. In addition, nitrifying bacteria convert nitrogen from ammonia to nitrates and eventually to the gaseous forms N_2O, NO, and N_2, which are returned to the atmosphere. Finally, some nitrogen is leached from the soil or incorporated in runoff and makes its way into groundwater, rivers, lakes, and the sea, from which it can be returned to the atmosphere.

The phosphorus cycle (Fig. 4.6) is a good example of a biogeochemical cycle that is dominated by terrestrial rather than atmospheric storage. Phosphorus, an essential nutrient, is found primarily in rocks and enters the soil by weathering of those rocks. But many rocks contain little phosphorus, and areas underlain by nonphosphate rocks must derive their phosphorus from trace amounts contained in rainfall. Once in the soil, phosphorus travels through the food chain, ultimately being returned to the soil by decomposers. Considerable amounts of phosphorus are leached or eroded from the soil, however,

and this phosphorus eventually accumulates in the sea, where it is concentrated in the bones of fish. As the fish die and their bodies decay, phosphorus is deposited on the ocean floor, and eventually it is incorporated in sedimentary rocks. Fish-eating birds excrete large amounts of phosphorus, and their dung, or guano, which accumulates on rocks or offshore islands where seabirds roost, is an important source of phosphate fertilizer. Fish bones from processing plants are also used as fertilizer in some parts of the world. In the United States, most of our phosphate fertilizer is derived from mining of phosphate-rich rocks.

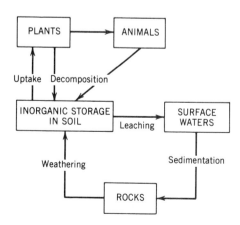

Figure 4.6   The phosphorus cycle. Phosphorus naturally enters the environment through the weathering of rocks. Human uses of phosphorus include phosphate fertilizers and detergents.

One of the most important biogeochemical cycles is the carbon cycle (Fig. 4.7), which utilizes large storages in the atmosphere, in living organisms, and in rocks. Carbon dioxide in the atmosphere enters plant leaves, and through photosynthesis is incorporated in living matter to form a basic part of starches, sugars, and other foods. As it passes through the food chain, carbon dioxide is returned to the atmosphere by respiration of consumers and decomposers. But significant amounts of organic matter accumulate in soils, marshes, and lake bottoms and this organic matter is largely carbon. Some of it may be oxidized from time to time, but most is semipermanently stored in sediments. In addition, large amounts of carbon exist in the oceans, both in living organisms and as dissolved carbon dioxide. Carbon is continually deposited on the ocean floor in sediments, which over time become sedimentary rocks. Limestone, which is primarily calcium carbonate ($CaCO_3$), is formed in this way as are fossil fuels. Carbon in rocks reenters the atmosphere through weathering and erosion of rocks and by combustion of fossil fuels. In the last few hundred years humans have removed and burned much more

carbon from terrestrial storages of coal, oil, and natural gas than has been returned in that time, and the atmospheric concentration of carbon dioxide has increased accordingly. In addition, clearing of forests and depletion of soil organic matter by poor land management practices have reduced these storages of carbon and contributed to the increase of atmospheric carbon dioxide.

Another example of an important environmental cycle is the hydrologic cycle (Fig. 4.8), which is not a biogeochemical cycle in the same way as the others just discussed, but is more of a regulator of flows of nutrients and energy. The hydrologic cycle is the set of pathways that water takes as it passes from atmosphere to earth and back (Fig. 4.9). It is primarily regulated by climate, but the terrestrial components of the cycle—rivers, lakes, soil, and groundwater—are also regulated by the characteristics of surficial materials and by topography. Analysis of water budgets, which quantify various components of the hydrologic cycle, is essential for water management.

Beginning with the atmosphere, water is delivered to the earth surface by precipitation. Rain strikes the leaves of plants, and some

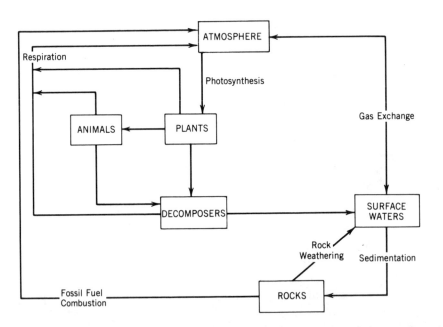

Figure 4.7 The carbon cycle. Carbon is stored in the form of carbon dioxide in the atmosphere, in plants, and in the decayed remains of organic organisms found in rocks and oceans. Fossil fuel combustion has altered the normal carbon cycle by removing carbon from terrestrial storage, burning it, and returning it to the atmosphere faster than it can be placed into storage.

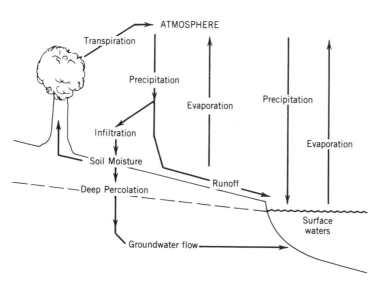

Figure 4.8 The hydrologic cycle. Water flows in the environment play a major role in regulating material and energy cycles.

remains there and is evaporated, but most reaches the soil surface. Once on the soil, the water may either evaporate, soak into the soil, or run off. Several factors determine how much water soaks in and how much runs off, but the primary controls are the rate at which rain falls, or precipitation intensity, and the ability of the soil to soak up water, or its *infiltration capacity*. These factors are of critical importance in controlling soil erosion, and

they will be discussed later in that context. Water that runs off the soil surface or through the regolith enters stream channels and becomes surface water. Surface waters flow by gravity to the ocean via rivers, lakes, swamps, and so on. Depending on climatic factors such as atmospheric humidity and temperature, varying amounts of surface water are lost by evaporation.

Precipitation may add directly to surface

Figure 4.9 Precipitation. Moisture held in storage in the atmosphere precipitates out as rain, illustrated by this thunderstorm. The water is used by plants, runs off into surface waters, or percolates through the soil for storage as groundwater.

water, but it is also temporarily stored in the soil, where it is available to plants. As plants use water it is returned to the atmosphere by evapotranspiration from their leaves. Water that is not used by plants percolates into the ground, where it eventually reaches a level below which the pores in the rocks are saturated, known as the *water table*. Water in this saturated zone is called *groundwater* and flows by gravity, and over long periods of time it may return to the surface in valleys and become surface water. The rate of flow of groundwater is considerably less than that for surface water, and depending on subsurface characteristics very large amounts of water may be stored there. Groundwater flow is primarily responsible for maintaining river flow during periods between rains. Eventually, most water is returned to the atmosphere, either by evapotranspiration by plants or by evaporation from surface waters, particularly the oceans. Some water may be stored for such long periods of time, such as in groundwater, ice caps, and isolated deep water bodies, that it is essentially removed from the cycle.

These environmental cycles are of enormous importance in regulating natural processes and the viability of natural resources is strongly affected by them. They provide the major means by which resources are renewed following harvesting. For example, when a forest is logged, the environmental system of the forest is drastically altered. Removal of trees causes a reduction in evapotranspiration, with a corresponding increase in water moving both through and over the soil. This increased water movement, together with the decay of plant matter left behind (stumps and smaller branches and leaves), contributes to a greatly increased removal of nutrients from the area, both dissolved and as part of soil particles. Were it not for weathering, nitrogen fixation, and other additions of nutrients over time to replace these losses, the soil would be less able to support the regrowth of the forest for future harvest. Similarly, grazing, cultivation, and water resource development depend on replacement of substances by these natural cycles. Additionally, the timing of these cycles may place significant constraints on human use in the same way that finite, or stock, resources impose constraints. Clearly "renew-

able" resources also have an element of finiteness.

The operation of biogeochemical cycles also has implications for activities that disturb some portion of the cycle, by either removing or introducing substances. The use of nitrogen fertilizers in agriculture causes a substantial increase in the inorganic nitrogen content of the soil. This increase of course benefits crop plants, but it also leads to greater leaching of nitrogen by water and hence greater nitrogen concentrations in rivers and lakes draining agricultural areas. This added nitrogen causes serious pollution problems in some areas, as it not only modifies aquatic ecosystems to trigger algal blooms but is also potentially dangerous to humans if consumed in drinking water. By modifying the nitrogen inputs to the soil we also change conditions farther downstream, often with undesirable consequences. A second example relates to the use of pesticides in the environment. An insecticide may be intended to act on only one small component of an ecosystem—the population of some particular insect species—but the food chain can carry both food and unwanted substances to other organisms, with unforeseen and damaging effects.

Thus biogeochemical cycles serve as conduits for substances from one part of the environment to another. They also cause the effects of human activities to extend beyond the immediate area of impact. For these reasons, we have become increasingly aware of the interrelatedness of natural resources, particularly renewable resources, and of the need to understand these phenomena completely in order to manage these resources properly.

ECOSYSTEM CARRYING CAPACITY AND POPULATION GROWTH

No matter how complex or simple the ecosystem, its component organisms are always working to reproduce themselves and to find adequate food. Obviously, the number of organisms cannot exceed the amount of food available to them for very long, or the equilibrium of the ecosystem will be threatened. For an ecosystem to maintain equilibrium, population size and food supply must be stable over the long run, though there can be short-term fluctuations. As a result, we find an intricate relationship between the size of populations of the different species in an ecosystem and between their competitive or complementary food needs relative to other populations in that ecosystem. These relationships can change over time, as the ecosystem's population dynamics shift in response to internal and external changes (see Issue 4–1).

With ample food, living space, good health, and no predators, a species population could grow at its *biotic potential*. This is the maximum rate of population growth resulting if all females breed as often as possible, with all individuals surviving past their reproductive period. Obviously, a species breeding at an exponential rate of increase would soon outstrip the available food supply for it and other species in its ecosystem. Just as obvious, various types of *environmental resistance,* such as exhaustion of the food supply, adverse weather, and disease, would ensure that the population is kept at a level far below its biotic potential. In systems terms, environmental resistance is a good example of negative feedback. For example, as a population grows, its food consumption increases and food becomes harder to find. As food becomes scarce, competition for food intensifies and survival of organisms to reproductive age is less likely, and thus population growth is reduced.

Although these inhibitions on population growth prevent exponential rates of increase, there are several fairly predictable growth patterns for populations within ecosystems (Fig. 4.10). A *sigmoidal growth curve* describes a population with only a small difference between the rates of growth (birth and immigration) and decline, as a result of disease, predation, uncertain food supply, and other forms of resistance. Over time, however, the population may increase more rapidly as long as there is enough food and other necessities. Eventually, the resources that a population demands may exceed those available for its use, and environmental resistances such as disease and malnutrition will put a damper on the rate of increase.

The near-level portion of the sigmoidal curve suggests a zero growth rate in which births plus immigrations equal deaths plus emigrations. In fact, this is an equilibrium situation in which biotic potential equals environmental resistance. The *carrying capacity* for this species in this ecosystem has been reached, which is the maximum number of organisms of one species that can be supported in the given environmental setting. Extinction of a species can occur when a population fluctuates dramatically, dropping so low that the species cannot reproduce quickly enough to remain in competition with others for available resources. These factors provide the biological basis for renewal resources management (see Issue 4–2).

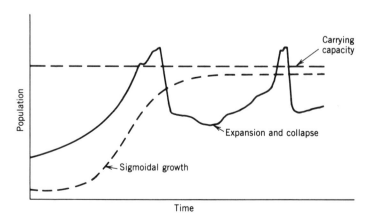

Figure 4.10 Population patterns in ecosystems. Populations can stabilize below carrying capacity. If the carrying capacity is exceeded, however, populations collapse and dieback can occur.

THE PRINCIPLE OF LIMITING FACTORS

One of the most important principles relating populations to ecosystem characteristics is the *principle of limiting factors*. There are usually many factors (nutrients, physical site characteristics, and so on) that are necessary for an organism to exist, and the availability of these factors varies from site to site, with some factors plentiful while others are rare. An organism requires different environmental conditions in varying degrees or in different amounts, and there is no reason to assume that every condition is available in exactly the amount required. Small changes in limiting factors may have profound effects. Similar changes in nonlimiting factors may have little or no effect.

Plant nutrients provide a simple example. A particular plant may require sunlight, water, a stable substrate, and a variety of nutrients from the soil. These nutrients may include nitrogen, phosphorus, potassium, magnesium, copper, zinc, and many other elements. They may all be available in plentiful supply except one, say, phosphorus. The rate of growth of the plant will be restricted by the lack of phosphorus, even though there is more than enough of the other nutrients. In this situation, nitrogen fertilizer applied to the soil will do nothing to help the plant, but phosphorus fertilizer will be very effective. Phosphorus is thus said to be the limiting factor in this case.

Nutrients are not the only factor that can be limiting. Sunlight, carbon dioxide, frost, or any other environmental characteristic that an organism requires may be limiting. If substances are present in excessive quantities that may poison an organism, they can also be considered limiting. Predators are often limiting factors for animal populations. It is usually difficult to determine just what factor or factors are limiting in any given situation, but clearly this information is essential to predicting the effects of environmental changes on ecosystem development, and illustrates the critical importance of sound environmental knowledge for informed resource management.

TOXIC SUBSTANCES IN ECOSYSTEMS

One of the most significant impacts humans have had on the environment in recent decades is the creation and release of a wide variety of chemical substances into the environment, some of which have significant adverse effects on natural organisms and/or on humans. Ecological processes are very important in the study of toxic substances, both because ecosystems are affected by toxic substances and because ecological processes, like the biogeochemical cycles discussed earlier, are important in distributing toxic substances through the environment. Problems associated with toxic substances are discussed throughout this book in relation to various resource issues. The following sections provide an introduction to some of the general problems and characteristics of toxic substances.

DEFINITIONS AND SOURCES

Different definitions of toxic substances are used in different circumstances; here we will consider a *toxic substance* to be any substance in the environment that is harmful to humans, plants, or animals at very low concentrations. In practice, most of the toxic substances we examine are hazardous to humans and other animals, and by low concentrations we usually mean parts per million or less. There are thousands of toxic substances that are of environmental concern, and lists of known toxic substances change frequently as new information on toxicity and/or environmental concentrations becomes available. Toxic substances are derived from a multitude of human and natural sources and move along many different environmental pathways. In the following sections we provide a glimpse of the diversity of toxic substances and their sources.

Industrial Releases

Manufacturing activities are an important source of toxic substances in the environment, and recently the Environmental Protection Agency completed a comprehensive inventory of industrial toxic substances releases. The inventory was required by the 1986 Superfund

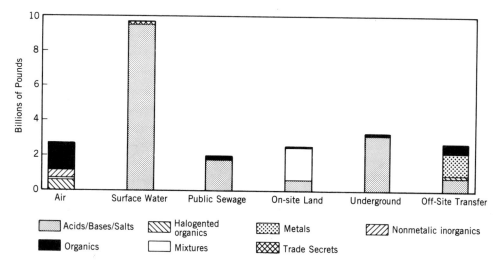

Figure 4.11 Toxic Release Inventory releases and transfers by chemical class, 1987.

Amendments Reauthorization Act's (SARA) Title III, called the Emergency Planning and Community Right-to-Know Act. In the 1987 Toxic Release Inventory (TRI), data on 309 different substances were collected for the first time. Table 4.1 is a list of the top 10 chemicals released in the greatest quantities, and Fig. 4.11 illustrates the types of releases for various classes of substances. The total reported releases amounted to about 22 billion pounds (10 billion kg) of toxic substances in 1987, or an average of about 10 pounds (4.5 kg) per acre of land per year (U.S. Environmental Protection Agency, 1989). Obviously not all releases are ultimately deposited on land and this average is not particularly

TABLE 4.1 Top 25 Toxic Release Inventory Chemicals and Their Release, 1987

Rank	Chemical	Total Released (Million Ponds)	Air	Surface water	Public Sewerage	Land	Underground Injection	Off-Site Transfers
1	Sodium sulfate	12,079.6	0	75.0	8.7	0.8	14.4	1.1
2	Aluminum oxide	2,435.0	3.4	1.5	0.1	57.2	2.3	35.4
3	Ammonium sulfate	917.8	0.7	9.8	20.6	0.8	66.6	1.5
4	Hydrochloric acid	656.7	8.0	2.1	8.8	1.8	63.0	16.3
5	Sulfuric acid	642.8	3.0	12.1	15.6	12.3	21.2	35.9
6	Sodium hydroxide	626.8	1.3	12.6	38.2	21.0	5.5	21.6
7	Ammonia	444.5	71.5	7.1	8.3	1.1	10.8	1.2
8	Methanol	419.5	46.7	5.9	22.0	3.5	4.7	17.1
9	Toluene	344.6	75.0	0.1	1.0	0.5	0.4	23.0
10	Phosphoric acid	343.9	0.5	37.5	4.5	54.4	0	3.1

Source: U.S. Environmental Protection Agency (1989), p. 18.

meaningful for any one place, but it gives an indication of the magnitude of the situation. The majority of TRI releases are actually discharged into surface waters, followed by underground injection and then air emissions.

End-Use Releases

Many toxic substances are released to the environment deliberately and for beneficial purposes. Pesticides are an obvious example of this. In 1986 over 1 billion pounds (455 million kg) of pesticides were produced in the United States (U.S. Bureau of the Census, 1989), and most of this was released to the environment in applications ranging from large-scale agricultural uses to individual use of insect repellents. Another example is the use of tributyl tin as an antifouling agent in marine paints.

Lead is an important toxic substance that has received much attention in recent years. Lead is toxic to humans and has been used as an additive in motor fuels for decades. In the early 1970s, increasing concern over air pollution led to the requirement that cars be equipped with catalytic converters to reduce hydrocarbon emissions. Lead in fuel damages these converters, and so lead-free gasoline was introduced, with the added benefit of reduced lead emissions. Today virtually all gasoline sold in the United States is lead-free, and cars with or without catalytic converters are using lead-free gasoline. The result has been that lead concentrations in the air and water decreased markedly in the 1980s (see Chapter 13).

Natural Toxins and Pollutants

Many toxins have natural origins besides their human-caused presence in the environment. For example, most toxic metals are present in rocks and soils and are naturally released to water and biota by processes of rock weathering and water flow in soils. Many plants produce toxic organic chemicals, some of which are released directly by plants and others of which are produced by processes of biochemical decay.

Under most circumstances these natural sources of toxic substances do not present major problems, either because the concentrations involved are low or because ecosystems are adapted to them. However, there are circumstances in which human activities aggravate, or are aggravated by, these natural sources. One example is when toxic substances have both human and natural sources. Metals are a good example. Several metals are natural constituents of water, but usually in relatively low concentrations. In some cases, however, human sources of these metals may cause the total concentrations to rise to toxic

---

ISSUE 4–1   Tamarisk: Unchecked Growth

Species that are introduced to a new environmental setting often experience a population boom period because they occupy underutilized portions of one or more ecosystems or else are more aggressive than the native species. Examples abound, such as the kudzu vine that was introduced as a ground cover in Florida and has spread throughout the South, or the rabbit, which when introduced to Australia caused great environmental damage through competing with sheep, another introduced species.

The tamarisk, or salt cedar (*Tamarix pentandra*), was introduced to the American Southwest in the nineteenth or twentieth century as a rapid-growing and drought-resistant tree that was suitable for windbreaks and shade.

It soon escaped from cultivation, taking over riverbanks and moist areas and crowding out native species.

Only since the 1930s has tamarisk come to be seen as a problem. In the mid-1930s, it was still being planted along eroding streambanks in New Mexico and along the property lines of many farms. To emphasize how rapidly it spread and became a problem, in 1936 the mapped vegetation of the Rio Grande River Valley (of Colorado, New Mexico, and Mexico) revealed that tamarisk was present, though not over large areas. In 1947, eleven years later, 60,640 acres (24,500 ha) were covered (Hay, 1972).

The tamarisk was able to invade because the Rio Grande's farming and natural ecosystems had been weakened by sedimentation and salini-

levels, creating or increasing hazards to humans and other organisms. Another possibility is that toxins are present naturally in relatively harmless forms, but human actions release these toxins to the environment. An example would be acid precipitation, which may result in a decrease in soil pH and thus cause metals that were in insoluble forms to be released and taken up by plants or enter surface water. This may be one of the mechanisms by which acid precipitation damages trees. Natural substances may also combine with pollutants of human origin to produce new toxic substance problems. An example of this is the production of a group of substances called trihalomethanes in drinking water, which arises from the combination of natural organic substances (such as the products of plant decay in streams) with chlorine added to water to reduce bacterial concentrations.

The fact that some toxic substances have both natural and human origins makes management and control efforts particularly difficult. It may be possible to control some human sources, but not all, and sometimes we eliminate human sources but still find the pollutant present because of natural sources. If a pollutant is found in the environment, it is often difficult to determine how much of it is natural and how much human in origin. These uncertainties are often used to political advantage by those attempting to point a finger at polluting industries, for example, or by those trying to avoid pollution control efforts.

PROCESSES OF POLLUTANT DISTRIBUTION AND DECAY

Once pollutants are introduced to the environment, they migrate within it and their concentrations change as a result. The processes of pollutant movement in the environment are obviously critical to understanding and evaluating their impacts on resources. In the following sections we will examine three different mechanisms by which the concentrations of pollutants change through time: pollutant decay, bioconcentration, and physical transport from one place to another.

Pollutant Decay

Some pollutants gradually decay in the environment and become less toxic over time. This is true for compounds such as pesticides, but not for elements, such as metals. *Biochemical decay* may be accomplished in organisms that ingest pollutants, or it may take place as a result of exposure to water, sunlight, and other substances in the environment. Some pollutants are very stable in the environment, and it

---

zation. The moist, silty banks along the Rio Grande were the perfect environment for the tamarisk. In addition, dam building resulted in more sedimentation that created shallow deltas that the tamarisk was better prepared to utilize than were any native species.

Why is the tamarisk a problem? Its dense growth along the banks further restricts water flow, which leads to more sediment deposition, waterlogging of soils, and more and better tamarisk habitat. Because the tamarisk exudes salt from glands, it can tolerate saline water but pollutes the soil surface, making agriculture impossible. In addition, the tamarisk consumes a great amount of water. In 1947 tamarisk was estimated to be responsible for 45 percent of the total water consumption in the Rio Grande Valley. On an annual basis, 2.5 acres (1 ha) of tamarisk consume about 430,000 cubic feet (12,200 m^3) of water, or a depth of 4 feet (1.22 m) (Hay, 1972).

Chemicals, burning, mowing, plowing the roots, and bulldozing have been used to try to control the tamarisk. Some of these solutions have caused more environmental problems, including chemical contamination of soil and water and increased erosion.

Overall, tamarisk is a species that has been able to take advantage of a weakened ecosystem or systems, and its population size and areal extent have spread beyond all the expectations of those who introduced it. At present, the tamarisk remains prosperous and largely unchecked in the arid West.

is this stability that may cause them to become a problem. Persistent pesticides, so named because they are relatively stable in the environment, are an example. Many compounds of carbon, hydrogen, and chlorine (chlorinated hydrocarbons) are resistant to decay. Persistent pesticides such as DDT and chlordane are examples of chlorinated hydrocarbons that have been restricted from use in the United States because of their danger to organisms and the environment.

Other pollutants decay quite rapidly, and their concentrations decrease through time. Most of the pesticides in use today do decay in the environment and so have relatively short-term impacts. As a rule this decay is advantageous, although it sometimes requires that pesticides be applied in higher concentrations to overcome the effects of rapid decay.

Bioaccumulation and Biomagnification

Some pollutants are selectively accumulated by organisms that consume or are exposed to them in the environment, and in many cases this is an important mechanism of toxicity. This is called *bioaccumulation* and is particularly important for metals and some organic compounds. Plants and animals absorb pollutants through their food, through skin contact, or through the air. If the pollutant has a tendency to bind with other substances in the organism, then it may accumulate over time. Usually the pollutant will accumulate in a particular part of the organism, for example, iodine tends to accumulate in the thyroid gland. As this accumulation continues, the concentration of the pollutant in an individual organism rises, sometimes to toxic levels.

Biomagnification is a process whereby the concentration of a substance in animal tis-

---

ISSUE 4–2   Getting a Handle on Cod

A wooden model of a codfish hangs in the Massachusetts statehouse in Boston. It was placed there in recognition of the role this species played in the colonization of New England. Although codfish is a part of history, it is also a modern-day headache for New England's fishermen, biologists, and politicians.

In 1976 the U.S. Congress unilaterally declared a 200-mile-wide (325 km) exclusive fishing zone, over the objections of then-President Ford and the State Department. The key sponsor of the legislation was Congressman Gerry Studds, representing Cape Cod and the fishing port of New Bedford. He pleaded for the immediate protection of cod, haddock, and yellowtail flounder stocks from overfishing by the fleets of huge Soviet and Japanese fishing vessels on Georges Bank, 50 miles (80 km) off the cape. Thus, the Fishery Conservation and Management Act was passed, halting virtually all foreign fishing off New England. Fearful of further overfishing, the federal government also imposed catch limits on domestic fishermen, based on complex biological assessments of cod, haddock, and yellowtail flounder populations. Eleven weeks after the quotas were established, fishermen exceeded the entire 1977 groundfish quo-

tas. Chaos followed, with management regulations changing thirty times and quotas increasing five times within a two-and-one-half-year period. Fishermen claimed that there were more cod on Georges Bank than ever before and biologists admitted that the margin of error in their population estimates was at least as large as the quotas they had proposed.

How did this situation arise? Management of renewable resources has two often conflicting objectives: (1) maximizing economic return and (2) preserving the sustainable nature of the resource. To meet these objectives, biologists calculated the surplus production of a species beyond that required to renew itself. This surplus is defined as the *maximum sustainable yield* (MSY). The MSY is the largest average catch that can be harvested indefinitely under existing environmental conditions. It is calculated using various population models, that combine such variables as the recruitment of young fish into the harvestable population, reproductive rates, and natural mortality. The concept of MSY assumes that a wildlife population produces a harvestable surplus when the size of the population is kept at an intermediate level. Growth rates,

sues is increased step by step through a food chain. As a rule of thumb, it takes about 22 pounds (10 kg) of food to make 2 pounds (1 kg) of tissue in the consumer. If a substance has a tendency to be retained in animal tissues rather than metabolized or excreted, then its concentration in those tissues could be increased by as much as 10 times for every step in the food chain. When a food chain has many steps, the ultimate concentration in the top predator may be quite high.

Many of the persistent pesticides accumulate in fatty tissues of animals and tend to be concentrated in the food chain. Although concentrations in most waterways now generally range from not detectable to parts per billion, fish and bird tissues frequently contain DDT and other pesticides at the parts per million level. Average concentrations of DDT and its metabolites in human tissues in the United States were about 8 ppm in 1970, but declined to 5 ppm by 1976, with further gradual declines in the 1980s (Council on Environmental Quality, 1989). Other hazardous substances that have become bioconcentrated include polychlorinated biphenyls (PCB's) and strontium-90, which tends to concentrate in bone tissues. Persistent pesticides are generally found in higher concentrations in aquatic sediments than in the water, and it is likely that they will be found in animal and human tissues for a long time.

Distribution in the Environment

Because toxic substances are dangerous at relatively low concentrations, transfers of small amounts from one place to another may be of significance. Many processes are involved, including transport in surface and groundwater, in air, dust, and sediments, and through organ-

reproduction, and recruitment are theoretically higher when older, slow-growing members are removed and competition for food, space, and other factors is reduced.

The principle of MSY is used in the management of timber, game species such as deer, and most marine fisheries. However, the concept of MSY has been less than successful in the real world of fisheries management. First, traditional MSY calculations require a species-by-species approach. A "desirable" species is identified and the surplus production is calculated, keeping all other variables constant. Thus, predator–prey relationships are ignored, and a value judgment is made about the importance of a particular species. People interested in the preservation or enhancement of an entire ecosystem, as opposed to a specific species, therefore consider the MSY approach dangerously exploitative. Conversely, hunters and fishermen distrust the MSY concept because catch is dictated strictly on biological grounds, ignoring economic considerations.

Second, a MSY calculation assumes that other variables affecting the population remain constant. In the case of New England's cod, haddock, and yellowtail flounder, it was this limitation in the MSY calculation that created chaos in the fishing industry between 1977 and 1980. For example, a comparison between the yearly expected surplus of flounder and water temperature indicates that temperature has more impact on population size than does predicted fishing mortality. In another example, scientists have discovered that it is the flow of the Mississippi River, not the size of the catch, that is most important in determining the number of shrimp available for harvest each year in the Gulf of Mexico.

Scientists and politicians now realize that MSY is an overly simplistic approach to managing renewable resources. Federal laws on fisheries, marine mammals, and timber therefore now require managers to determine the optimum yield of a species, taking into account environmental variables, economic interests, and the biological uncertainties of managing entire ecosystems. Although it is a more realistic approach to management, the calculation of optimum yield is a delicate balancing act between competing interests. In the future, fishery biologists may have to be equally adept at political mediation as well as population biology (Warner 1982; Warner, et al., 1981).

isms. Often a pollutant deposited in one medium turns up in another. For example, organic compounds in wastes disposed of in a landfill may enter groundwater, flow into surface water, be taken up by fish, and be passed through the food chain. Or soil in a mine tailings pile containing high concentrations of metals may be eroded by wind and transported considerable distances before being deposited.

Management problems become more complex as a result of the low concentrations that must be examined and the mobility of toxic substances from one medium to another. Not the least of these problems is the expense of sampling and analyzing environmental materials for concentrations of a wide range of substances at the parts per million (ppm) or parts per billion (ppb) level. Laboratory analyses for some substances cost in excess of $1000 each, in addition to sampling costs. But more troublesome is the development of regulatory mechanisms that deal with several different media simultaneously. For example, a substance may be relatively benign when found in soil but be very hazardous in water. Regulations governing disposal of wastes on land must include some means to evaluate the likelihood that pollutants will enter water and the concentrations in which they may occur. Such regulations become extremely complex, and are both difficult and costly to enforce.

Uncertainty in Toxic Substances Management

The problems of managing toxic substance pollution are many, but perhaps the most difficult problem is that decisions must be made with less than adequate information. In the first place, there are a great number of substances (at least several hundred) that may be toxic to humans or other organisms. For many of these we have very little information on the exact concentrations at which toxicity occurs, and even less information on their concentrations in the environment. Assessment of the risk to humans associated with exposure to a substance becomes one of extrapolation from very limited information, and the conclusions we draw are necessarily shaky (National Research Council, 1983). On the one hand we seek to eliminate any chance of adverse health impacts associated with a pollutant, and on the

other we cannot do this with any certainty unless we reduce exposures to very low levels, often at very high (and weakly justified) costs.

ECOLOGY, NATURAL RESOURCE USE, AND CONSERVATION

Careful and painstaking research by ecologists provides a strong argument for thoughtful management of resources. The complexity of ecosystems is such that one can never assume that an action will only affect the immediate location. The vast body of ecological research that has accumulated in the last few decades has shown that the interconnectedness of ecosystems almost always leads to more far-reaching and often unexpected effects. Without a recognition of this fact, disruption in natural systems is likely to occur and lead to further disruption of connected systems or possibly to a domino effect in which distantly related systems and organisms may suffer.

We must always keep in mind that the ecological viewpoint is open to political uses, as are all scientific approaches. Ecosystems are both real and abstract (Kormondy, 1969). It is the abstract idea of interrelatedness that can be used by individuals or organizations eager to protect some special interest from change or development. They may argue that because everything is interrelated, then if a certain stream is dammed, this act will eventually lead to the collapse of civilization, or life on earth. Ecology as a serious field of study makes no such sweeping guarantees or generalities. In the context of resource management it needs to be used in a sober and factually based manner.

REFERENCES AND ADDITIONAL READING

Council on Environmental Quality. 1989. *Environmental Trends*. Washington, DC: U.S. Government Printing Office.

Detwyler, T.R., and M.G. Marcus (Eds.). 1972. *Urbanization and Environment*. Belmont, CA: Duxbury Press.

DeYoung, R., and S. Kaplan. 1988. On averting the tragedy of the commons. *Environ. Management* 12: 273–283.

Hay, J. 1972. Salt cedar and salinity on the upper Rio Grande. In M.T. Farvar, and J.P. Milton (Eds.), *The Careless Technology: Ecology and International Development*. Garden City, NY: Natural History Press.

Kirchner, J.W. 1989. The Gaia hypothesis: Can it be tested? *Rev. Geophys.* 27(2): 223–235.

Kormondy, E.J. 1969. *Concepts of Ecology*. Englewood Cliffs, NJ: Prentice–Hall.

Lovelock, J.E. 1979. *Gaia, a New Look at Life on Earth*. Oxford: Oxford University Press.

Myers, N. (Ed.). 1989. *The Gaia Atlas of Planet Management*. London: Pan Books.

National Research Council. 1983. *Risk Assessment in the Federal Government: Managing the Process*. Washington, DC: National Academy Press.

Robertson, G.P. 1986. Nitrogen: Regional contributions to the global cycle. *Environment* 28(10): 16–20, 29.

Simmons, I.G. 1981. *Ecology of Natural Resources*, 2nd ed. London: Halstead Press.

Turk, J., *et al.* 1975. *Ecosystems, Energy, Population*. Philadelphia: W.B. Saunders.

U.S. Bureau of the Census. 1989. *Statistical Abstract of the United States*. Washington, DC: U.S. Government Printing Office.

U.S. Environmental Protection Agency. 1989. *The Toxic Release Inventory: A National Perspective*. EPA 560/4-89-005. Washington, DC: U.S. Government Printing Office.

Warner, L.W. 1982. The conservation aspects of the Fishery Conservation and Management Act and the protection of critical marine habitat. *Natural Resources J.* 23: 97–130.

Warner, L.W., *et al.* 1981. Practical application of the conservation aspects of the Fishery Conservation and Management Act. *Harvard Environ. Law Rev.* 5(1): 30–70.

Watts, D. 1971. *Principles of Biogeography*. New York: McGraw–Hill.

TERMS TO KNOW

Bioaccumulation
Biochemical Decay
Biogeochemical Cycles
Biomagnification
Biomass
Biotic Potential
Carrying Capacity
Communities
Ecology
Ecosystem
Ecotone
Energy Budget
Environmental Resistance
First Law of Thermodynamics
Food Chain
Food Web
Groundwater
Infiltration Capacity
Input
Law of Entropy
Maximum Sustainable Yield
Output
Photosynthesis
Principle of Limiting Factors
Respiration
Sigmoidal Growth Curve
Toxic Substances
Trophic Level
Water Table

STUDY QUESTIONS

1. What are the differences among ecosystems, ecotones, and communities?

2. What are some of the adverse effects of disrupting the carbon, nitrogen, and phosphorus cycles?

3. How does environmental resistance provide negative feedback within an ecosystem?

4. Describe the principle of limiting factors and explain the role of this principle in the functioning of ecosystems.

5. How do pollutants change their concentrations over time in ecosystems?

6. What is the Gaia hypothesis and how does it help us to understand global environmental systems?

Population: The Human System and the Human Condition

INTRODUCTION

The world's population is increasing rapidly. In 1980, global population was estimated at 4.5 billion, and by 1990 it had reached 5.3 billion (Population Reference Bureau, 1990). One-fifth of this total or 1.1 billion lived in China, the world's most populous country, with another 853 million living in India. The United States had 251 million people.

As the world's population increases so does its use of resources. Environmentalists and population theorists such as Paul Ehrlich and Lester Brown and economists such as H.E. Daly and N. Georgescu-Roegen continue to warn of increased population pressures on natural resource consumption. People must be fed, housed, and clothed, and the more people there are, the more food resources, housing materials, and fibers must be produced. Other theorists, such as economist Julian Simon and writer Ben Wattenberg, are confident that population growth does not mean a drop in standards of living.

POPULATION GROWTH: GOOD OR BAD?

The population problem, or crisis to some, is not a recent phenomenon. In 1798, the British economist *Thomas Malthus* foresaw some of the world's current population problems. Malthus wrote that populations increase in size geometrically, that is, they double in size in a fixed time period. Geometric growth is shown by the J-shaped curve in Fig. 5.1. Malthus also wrote that food supplies increase arithmetically, that is, they increase by addition of a fixed amount in a given time period. Arithmetic growth is shown as a straight line in Fig. 5.1. Eventually, he said, population growth would outstrip the food resources (assuming, of course, no new resources are developed) with catastrophic consequences—mass starvation, poverty, and collapse of economic and social systems.

Debates continue today over the relationship between population growth and resource scarcity. *Neo-Malthusians* take the same perspective as Malthus yet argue for strong birth control measures to postpone or delay population growth to below the limit of resource availability. Advocacy of birth control to stabilize population growth, instead of expecting nature to do the job through famine and war, differentiates neo-Malthusianism from the original form.

A nineteenth-century critic of Malthus, Karl Marx, stressed that there was no single theory of population growth and resource use. Increased population growth did not by itself, as Malthus suggested, result in excessive resource use and a lowering of the standard of living of individuals. Marx felt that poverty was caused by the economic system, which exploited labor for the benefit of the elite. He believed the cause of poverty was economic, not solely an increase in numbers of people.

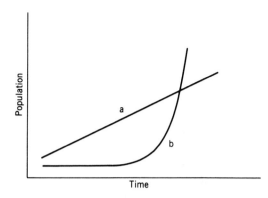

Figure 5.1 Arithmetic versus geometric growth. Arithmetic growth (*a*) follows a straight line, increasing by addition. Geometric growth (*b*) follows a curve, increasing by multiplication.

In the twentieth century Esther Boserup (1965, 1981) has suggested that population growth may be beneficial in providing a stimulus for the improvement of the human condition. She suggests that population growth intensifies land use, resulting in increased agricultural production. The end result will be that all individuals benefit from the increased production and thus achieve a higher standard of living. She suggests that Malthus was incorrect in his assumption that increased population led to increased poverty, starvation, and war.

Today some population experts anticipate some form of population catastrophe in the near future. Others, however, are confident that human needs can be met no matter how large the world's population becomes. The following historical perspective and some of today's population numbers may help you decide where you stand on this issue.

A SHORT HISTORY OF WORLD POPULATION GROWTH

Although it is impossible to accurately measure the world's human population in the distant past, demographers and archaeologists, among others, have developed low to high ranges for population size and growth over thousands of years. These estimates change, of course, with new evidence such as the unearthing of ancient communities, new dating methods, and new theories. The world human population at the end of the most recent ice age, about 10,000 years ago, was somewhere between 2 and 10 million people. It had taken perhaps 1 to 2 million years for the population to grow to this size. When we consider that population has burgeoned to 5.3 billion in the past 10,000 years—and most of that in the last 300 years—it is clear that extraordinary changes have taken place in all aspects of human life to adjust to this astonishing growth (Fig. 5.2).

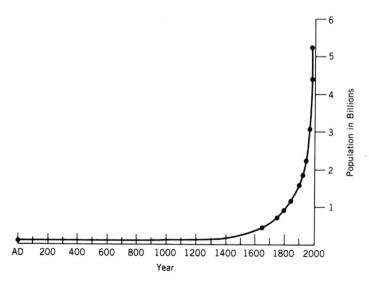

Figure 5.2 World population growth. World population growth was slow and steady until about A.D. 1700 to 1750. Since then, population has expanded rapidly.

From 8000 B.C. to A.D. 1 the population doubled almost six times, to between 200 and 400 million. The doubling time was more than 1000 years. One should realize, of course, that this growth was not steady and smooth. A close look would reveal sudden rises and drops due to the vagaries of famine, war, and disease over small and large regions. The tendency, however, was toward growth. Between A.D. 1 and 1750, growth continued at about the same rate, ultimately reaching 750 million by 1750. Though scholars differ, there is no doubt that the technological developments of agriculture and irrigation, in the first few thousand years after the ice retreat, had much to do with this population increase, as did warmer weather worldwide.

Since 1750 the world's population has begun its modern climb, beginning in Europe. It took only 150 years, from 1750 to 1900, for the population to double from 750 million to 1.5 billion. The population doubled once again between 1900 and 1965, a doubling time of 65 years. *Doubling time* is the number of years it takes a population to double in size assuming a constant rate of natural increase. The lower the number of years to double in size, the faster the growth rate. However, just because a nation's doubling time is 32 years in 1990 does not mean that it will have double the population 32 years from now. Many factors, such as war, disease, social pressure, government programs, immigration and emigration, may affect the doubling time on a year-to-year basis. In 1990 the worldwide doubling time was 39 years. This means that, theoretically, in the year 2029, 39 years from 1990, the world's population would be about 10.4 billion, and a hundred years from 1990, in 2090, the global total would be 32 billion. But experts do not expect this to happen. Recent projections made by the World Bank, taking into account all the above-mentioned factors (and one not included: space-travel!), suggest that population growth rates over the next decade will slowly decline and that it will take 100 years to reach 10.4 billion people (Population Reference Bureau, 1990). Population projections to the year 2000 place the world's population at about 6.5 billion, reaching 7 to 8 billion in 2020.

Where was the growth and where is the growth likely to occur in the future? After 1750, Europe's population mushroomed, and the resulting crowding and poor conditions had a great impact on the settlement of the Americas, Australia, and New Zealand and on European imperialism worldwide. Europe needed raw materials to support its astonishing human and economic growth, and those resources were available in Africa, Asia, the Americas, and the Indian subcontinent. During the twentieth century, the benefits of the Scientific Revolution that led to Europe's boom—the germ theory of disease, ideas about cleanliness, vaccinations, agricultural improvements—were introduced to the rest of the world, and population growth shifted to Europe's former colonies.

Estimates of future population growth, called population projections, are shown for selected countries in Table 5.1. In 1990 the fastest-growing areas were Kenya, with a doubling time of 18 years, and the Gaza Strip at 16 years. The U.S. population doubling time, at 92 years, is intermediate. At the low end are Hungary and West Germany, two countries where population growth is negative: more people are dying than are being born. Europe as a whole is going through a period of low natural population growth. However, these numbers do not include the effects of high immigration to these countries from their former colonies, nor an equally high emigration from eastern and central European countries to western European ones. These issues will be discussed later.

WHY HAS THE HUMAN POPULATION RISEN SO DRAMATICALLY?

There are many explanations for this extraordinary population increase over such a short period of humanity's life span on earth. One idea is that a broader worldwide food base developed because of increased trade; another is that humanity developed an eventual (after a two-century-long period of fluctuation) rise in overall disease resistance, also a result of increased trade and travel. It has been suggested that numbers began to rise in the wake of better medical technology and theory, leading to a drop in infant and child mortality rates, and an increased life span for large segments of the world's population. Let us discuss the

TABLE 5.1   Population Projections

	Population Estimates (Millions)		Annual Increase (%)	Doubling Time (Years)
	1990	2000		
World	5321	6292	1.8	39
Industrialized countries	1214	1274	0.5	128
Less industrialized countries	4107	5018	2.1	33
Regions				
Africa	661	884	2.9	24
Asia	3116	3718	1.9	37
North America	278	298	0.7	93
Latin America	447	535	2.1	33
Europe	501	515	0.3	266
USSR	291	312	0.9	80
Oceania	27	31	1.2	57
Selected countries				
People's Republic of China	1120	1280	1.4	49
India	853	1043	2.1	33
Indonesia	189	224	1.8	38
Bangladesh	115	147	2.5	28
Pakistan	114	149	3.0	23
Philippines	66	83	2.6	27
Thailand	56	64	1.5	45
South Korea	43	46	1.0	72
Nigeria	119	161	2.9	24
Burkina Faso	9	12	3.2	21
Kenya	25	35	3.8	18
Zimbabwe	10	13	3.2	22
Namibia	1.5	2	3.2	22
Nicaragua	4	5	3.3	21
Brazil	151	180	1.9	36
Colombia	32	38	2.0	34
Canada	27	29	0.7	96
United Kingdom	57	59	0.2	301
Ireland	3.5	3.5	0.6	108
East Germany	16	15.5	0.0	6930
Italy	58	59	0.1	1155
Australia	17	19	0.8	90
Vanuatu	0.2	0.2	3.2	22

Source: Population Reference Bureau (1990).

possibilities and implications of present and future growth rates.

POPULATION DYNAMICS

There are two helpful tools for examining the human population system. The first includes the rate and causes of population growth and is called *population dynamics*. The second is the location of growth, that is, its spatial distribution around the world. Both are essential to our understanding of current and future population trends. In examining population dynamics, a first question is: How and why do populations grow? There are three factors that contribute to population growth. These are rates of natural growth/decline, the age structure of a population, and immigration/emigration.

NATURAL GROWTH

Natural growth (sometimes called natural increase or decrease) is a simple measure of population growth, that examines the differences between births (fertility) and deaths (mortality) in a given group. *Birth* and *death rates* are normally expressed as rate of occurrence per 1000 people. For example, if 3000 babies were born in a population of 150,000, then the birth rate would be 20 per 1000.

Rates of Natural Increase

Natural increase is the difference between birth and death rates and is expressed as a percentage figure. An annual natural growth rate of 0.8 percent, roughly that of the United States, means that a country is increasing in population by 0.8 percent each year. At present, this translates to about 2.0 million people annually.

Annual growth rates and natural increase must be considered in combination with the actual population figure. A small annual growth rate of a small population is significantly different from a comparable annual figure for a much larger population. India and Lebanon, for example, had identical annual growth rates of 2.1 percent in 1990. India, with a base population of 853 million will increase by 17.9 million annually. Lebanon, on the other hand, has a much smaller population base, 3.3 million people. With an annual growth rate of 2.1 percent, the country will add only 69,300 people annually (Table 5.1).

Fertility Rates

The simplest measure of fertility is the birth rate. Another measure that is often used is the total *fertility rate*, a measure of the average number of children a woman has in her reproductive years (ages 15 to 49). One of the most important reasons for a decline in the rate of natural growth in the United States has been a steady decline in the number of children born per family. In 1990, for example, the total fertility rate among American women was 2.0. This means that, on the average, every American woman has 2.0 live births during her lifetime. The total fertility rate in the United States has steadily declined since the 1950s (Table 5.2), although from 1985 to 1990 a small increase was apparent.

TABLE 5.2   U.S. Fertility Rates

Year	Rate
1950	3.3
1960	3.4
1970	2.5
1980	1.8
1983	1.8
1985	1.8
1989	1.9
1990	2.0

Source: Council on Environmental Quality (1988); Population Reference Bureau (1990).

On a global scale, the total fertility rate was 3.5 in 1990. The rate is significantly higher in the less industrialized nations (4.0) than in the more industrialized nations (2.0). If one excludes China from the less industrialized nations, the total fertility rate increases to 4.6. There are some very distinct regional differences. For example, Africa has a total fertility rate of 6.2, versus 3.6 in Southeast Asia and 3.1 in the Caribbean. Although total fertility rates are high in some regions of the world, this is partly offset by high mortality rates in some of these areas (most notably Africa). Rwanda had the world's highest total fertility rate (8.3) in 1990, but also has a high mortality rate (17 per 1000). High fertility rates, then, do not necessarily imply high annual growth rates.

For decades, debate has continued over whether or not high-growth nations should work to decrease their fertility rates. As an example, the People's Republic of China (total fertility rate 2.2) instituted a one-child limit for all families (Fig. 5.3) during the 1970s. Although the policies varied from province to province, in some the birth of a second child resulted in the loss of state medical and school aid, ostracism, and official criticism. A third pregnancy brought strong pressure from the community for an abortion (Greenhalgh and Bongaarts, 1987).

Accustomed to large families and desirous of having boys, many Chinese found the policy very difficult to live with. Reports of female infanticide, while true, remain very controversial, because those in favor of population control do not like to admit to such abuses, which often provide ammunition to those who would

Figure 5.3 One-child family policy in China. The Chinese government has encouraged late marriage and has imposed economic penalties on families with more than one child. This has resulted in a significant lowering of the country's fertility rate. The wall poster in Chengdu, Sichuan Province, praises the merits of one-child families.

abolish all limits to growth. In recent years Chinese policies have eased somewhat as urban–rural and ethnic differences have begun to play a role in family planning.

India has struggled for 25 years to reduce birth rates with various economic and social incentives, as well as involuntary measures. Its most recent census revealed, however, that growth rates did not decline significantly between 1970 and 1990. There has been a decline in fertility in some countries primarily as a result of government-sponsored family planning programs. Not all family planning programs have been successful and there are many countries with continued high fertility rates.

Zero population growth (ZPG) is a term for the number of births that will simply replace a population, without further growth. It takes a total fertility rate of about 2.1 in developed nations or 2.7 in developing nations to maintain a population at a constant size, assuming a stable age structure and no net migration. The difference is explained by higher mortality rates in the developing nations, which require a higher birth rate to offset losses. A total fertility rate of less than 2.1 would eventually lead to population decline, assuming no net immigration. To achieve ZPG

globally, a total fertility rate of about 2.5 is needed, but a much lower rate (below *replacement levels*) would be needed in some regions to stabilize population. Even if a ZPG fertility rate were reached, which is highly unlikely in this century, the population would continue to expand simply because of its age structure.

AGE STRUCTURE

The second factor that contributes to overall population change is the *age structure* of a population. A short discussion of the profiles of populations by age and sex will give us the key to understanding whether a country has an expanding, declining, or stable population.

How is a population's profile drawn? The *population pyramid* is a visually striking representation of the age and sex structure of a population (Fig. 5.4). To make up a pyramid, a population is classified in age groups or *cohorts* by 5-year intervals (0–4, 5–9, 10–14, etc.) and by sex. The actual number of people or the percentage of a population that falls into each of these age categories is then graphed. The percentage of males in specific age groups is shown on the left and the percentage of females on the right. The general shape of the

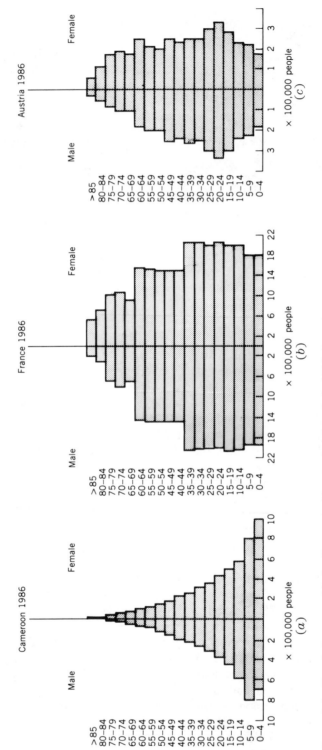

Figure 5.4 Population pyramids for Cameroon, France, and Austria in 1986. Cameroon has a broad-based pyramid, indicating large numbers of young people whose childbearing years are in the future. France and Austria have narrow-based pyramids, typical of more stable populations. (*Source:* Data from United Nations, 1988.)

pyramid indicates the relative growth of the population.

For example, a rapidly expanding population such as Cameroon's (Fig. 5.4a) has a very broad base because a large percentage of the population is less than 14 years of age, that is, many children are being born to each mother. The fertility rate for Cameroon women is 5.8. Many of the developing nations have population pyramids of this shape. One hundred years ago, the U.S. population had a similar shape, as did the countries of Europe.

Stable populations such as France (Fig. 5.4b) have population pyramids with narrower bases; children are being born, but at a lower rate. As the population ages, the actual number or percentage in each cohort declines due to mortality. In stable populations such as those of France, the United States, Canada, and the Scandinavian countries, the pyramid maintains a stable shape over the years.

A declining population, such as Austria's (Fig. 5.4c), is one in which the base of the pyramid is small, because few children are being born; there is a bulge in the reproductive and/or postreproductive age categories. Germany (East and West) is another good example of a declining population. Even as some countries are worried about having too many people, the European countries that were centers of population growth a century ago now worry about the political and economic effects of a shrinking population. During the 1980s, a declining population in Romania resulted in strict prohibitions on birth control. Women were simply not allowed to practice family planning and were forced to have children they did not want or could not afford or face social and economic sanctions. Abortions were illegal and performed in back alleys, resulting in many unnecessary maternal deaths. Only after the death of the Romanian dictator, Nicolae Ceaușescu, did the rest of the world hear about these propopulation policies and see how crowded Romanian orphanages were as a result.

Right after World War II and into the 1960s, the U.S. fertility rate was at a modern-day high, with an average of slightly more than three children being born to each mother. These baby boomers have not been reproducing at the high rate of their parents, and even with their huge numbers, since 1970 there has been a decrease in the number of people under age 14. As the baby boom cohort ages, so does the overall age of the U.S. population. The median age in 1970 was 28, in 1980 it was 30, by 1990 it was 32.1, and it is projected to rise to 36.3 by 2000 and to 40.8 in 2030 (Barringer, 1989). Declining birth rates and the general aging of the *baby boom* cohort of the 1950s, coupled with a long life expectancy, account for this trend.

The economic effects of this drop are being felt: employers are having a hard time filling jobs with teenage and young adult labor. These young people (that is you, the reader) are able to pick and choose among careers and job openings. This "baby bust" labor will be in demand to fill the huge number of entry-level positions created by the baby boomers. Debate has begun over how this smaller group of employees will be able to support the boomers with Social Security taxes when that notorious generation (that is us, the authors) reaches retirement.

Some experts believe that from the early 1980s to the present, the United States has been undergoing a baby "boomlet" as women born in the post-World War II boom are having babies somewhat later in life than did earlier generations. Because they are having smaller families than did their mothers, however, the overall effect is still one of a decline in growth.

Population pyramids similar to those of the United States can be found throughout the industrialized world. Nearly 66 percent of the population in these countries is in the work force age groups, ages 15 to 64. The young comprise about 22 percent of the total population, and the old around 12 percent. In contrast, 36 percent of the population in developing nations is under 15 years of age, and another 60 percent of the population is of working age. In these less industrialized nations, only 4 percent of the population, on average, is 65 and older.

Demands for food and education will be difficult to provide for these youthful populations under current political and economic conditions. Out of a worldwide population of 5.3 billion, there are 1.8 billion people worldwide aged 15 years or younger; many of these live in Africa, where fertility rates are high. Poverty is clearly a problem related to population growth. In 1989, for example, 1.2 billion people lived in absolute poverty—mostly in sub-Saharan Africa (62 percent), Latin America (35 percent), Asia (25 percent), and North Africa and the Middle East (28 percent). Numerically, children are plagued the most by poverty. In many areas, as poverty increases, so does population, since many poor people feel that more children can help produce income. In other words, the gap between the rich and the poor widens with increased population. In addition to population growth, poverty is also related to global economic cycles, land degradation, and migration. Millions of people migrate from relatively self-sufficient farming livelihoods in rural areas to cities in search of paid wage employment, thus placing enormous stress on the world's cities. Some of the possible reasons for this pattern are discussed in the following section.

MIGRATION

Migration, which includes immigration and emigration, is the movement of individuals from one location to another. It has no influence on global population projections but does have a significant impact at national, regional, and local population levels. Migration flows are caused by lack of economic opportunities, group conflicts between and within nations, and environmental disruption (see Issue 5–1). These flows can be permanent or temporary (Fig. 5.5).

Causes and Effects

Early migration to North America was of two basic types. Free immigrants came in search of a better life, and forced immigrants, or slaves, helped make life easier for others. By the late nineteenth century, mass migration increased the flow greatly as entire ethnic or regional groups decided collectively to move to the

---

ISSUE 5–1 Environmental Refugees

John Steinbeck's novel *The Grapes of Wrath* tells the story of the economic and environmental degradation of the Great Plains during the 1930s. It chronicles the migration of Okies from their home state of Oklahoma to California in search of a better life after being forced off the land by drought and economic hardship. This fictionalized version of historical events is a good example of *environmental refugees*, people who are forced to relocate because some environmental event makes their current residence uninhabitable.

There are many events that can cause environmental disruption and these are generally referred to as environmental hazards. They can be either short term or long term, cover small areas or large, and originate from either natural or technological events. The results, however, are similar: often, the only response people have is to flee their homes either temporarily or permanently.

Natural disasters cause widespread damage and the world's vulnerability to natural disasters is increasing as people are moving into more

marginal lands because of population pressures. Droughts in the Sahel region of Africa over the last two decades have forced the migration of 2 million people from Burkina Faso, Chad, Mali, Mauritania, and Niger. The widespread desertification and land degradation, initiated by a natural event and exacerbated by human activity, have rendered parts of the region largely uninhabitable. Floods, another type of natural hazard, constantly plague large parts of the world from Bangladesh to Texas. In 1974, for example, the monsoon rains resulted in catastrophic floods that killed 3000 in Bangladesh and displaced thousands more. In the spring of 1990, parts of southeast Texas along the Trinity River were under water for weeks and months. Those residents became temporary environmental refugees. Again, although the event was natural, people became vulnerable because of their location. They built their homes in a very marginal area, a floodplain, which by its very definition means that it floods on a recurrent basis.

Technological hazards are also increasing

Figure 5.5 Refugees in Kobo, Ethiopia, 1984. The Sahelian drought and political instability forced the migration of millions of Africans in search of emergency food and water supplies.

the number of environmental refugees. In 1986, the nuclear power plant accident in Chernobyl, USSR, forced the evacuation of 100,000 people. Years later, nearly 2600 square kilometers are deemed uninhabitable because of continued high levels of radioactivity. Chemical disasters are also taking their toll in both industrialized and nonindustrialized countries. Between 1962 and 1971 nearly 19 million gallons of the herbicide 2,4,5-T, called Agent Orange, was sprayed on the Vietnamese land by the U.S. government during the Vietnam War. Nearly 10 percent of the country was affected, much of it arable land: 10 percent of the inland forests, 36 percent of the mangrove, 3 percent of cultivated land, and 5 percent of floodplains and small settlements (Hay, 1982). Thousands of Vietnamese were forced off the land into cities since the dioxin-contaminated land had now become marginally productive. Dioxin-contaminated soil has also forced the permanent evacuation of entire neighborhoods in the United States: Love Canal, New York, and Times Beach, Missouri. A dioxin explosion at a Seveso, Italy, plant in 1976 resulted in the evacuation of 800 people from their homes for over a year.

It is clear that the number of environmental refugees will increase during the 1990s. Sea level rise may affect millions living in low-lying coastal areas. Chemical contamination will increase from the manufacture, use, and disposal of hazardous waste. Industrial pollution, already a severe problem in parts of eastern and central Europe, may ultimately force people out of the most polluted regions for health reasons. Already in many of these places, children are routinely sent out of the area for the summer months in order to breathe clean air. It is hard to predict the extent and timing of environmental refugees. What we do know is that exposure of human population to environmental hazards is increasing and as we contaminate habitable land and move into less marginal areas, we place increased population pressures on the existing land, thereby reducing its carrying capacity. Perhaps the Malthusianists were right (Jacobson, 1988)!

United States and Canada, largely in search of better economic opportunities, as conditions became too crowded in "the old country."

Since World War II, the international migration flow has to a large extent reversed, with the largest percentage of migrants moving from less industrialized nations to European and North American urban areas. The principal destinations of transnational migrants from 1950 onward have been the United States, Canada, Australia, and New Zealand, with large numbers moving to Europe and Great Britain as well. All of these countries currently have low birth rates and the native population is stabilizing or shrinking. These new immigrants account for much of the increase in population in these countries. This trend is accelerated by war and genocide, for example, the expansion of the Vietnamese population in the United States since the end of the Vietnam War. It also contributes to racial tension: the 3 million residents of Hong Kong with British passports have been told by the British government that they are not welcome in Great Britain when the People's Republic of China reclaims Hong Kong in 1997.

As a result of increasing numbers of migrants to the industrialized world, some countries have devised restrictive policies for immigration, maintaining that the immigrants are stealing wages from native-born citizens. Of course there is usually a large component of fear and dislike—racism—on the part of natives regarding these new residents. Though disliked, the peoples of the Middle East, Asia, and Africa are allowed to enter on a temporary basis to work the jobs that declining populations cannot or will not fill. In Europe these temporary residents are called "*guest workers*"; in South Africa, black labor is the backbone of the economy but blacks are excluded from government or citizenship. In the 1980s, fears of an unending flood of illegal immigrants from Mexico into the United States led to legislation forcing immigrants to register and be monitored more closely, so that they cannot disappear into the U.S. economy.

This situation is only a symptom of a larger problem, that is, population pressure and perceived lack of opportunity in many less industrialized nations. People were once pulled off the land into the cities by the attractive opportunities available there. Now they are pushed off the land because their parents cannot subdivide the small farm between siblings any further, and no new land is available. A move to the regional or capital city brings no satisfaction since these areas are overcrowded and unable to provide basic services (sanitation, electricity, and housing) for the new immigrants.

Clearly, this situation will worsen as populations continue to grow and economic opportunity does not increase in rural areas. When the population boom hit Europe in the eighteenth century, the overcrowded countries had empty lands to spread into, and where the land was not empty, as with the native populations of the Americas, the Europeans simply conquered by force. Today there are no empty lands for the peoples of Asia and Africa to spread into. The situation is somewhat better in Central and South America, although even there settlers are chastised by the industrialized, environmentally sensitive countries for their environmentally destructive methods of settlement. Many peasants still remain landless, thus increasing the likelihood of poor stewardship of the land.

Immigration to the United States

The United States has long been a symbol of freedom for those seeking a better life; this was very poignantly brought home in June of 1989, when protesting students in Beijing, China, constructed a Statue of Democracy modeled after the U.S. Statue of Liberty. As a result of this country's popularity, however, the United States must deal constantly with an unending flow of people who want to settle here. Over the past centuries, immigration regulations have waxed and waned in their strictness (see Table 5.3).

A quota system was enacted by the U.S. Congress in 1921, strictly limiting the number of immigrants from "undesirable" countries, which in those days meant southern Europe. Although quotas on the basis of national origin were abolished in 1965, Congress still determines annually what total number of immigrants will be allowed, and this total is divided among all countries. For example, in 1988, 20,000 was the cap for each country.

TABLE 5.3 Immigrants Admitted to the United States from All Countries

Selected Years	Number
1820–1830	152,000
1841–1850	1,713,000
1861–1870	2,315,000
1881–1890	5,247,000
1901–1910	8,795,000
1921–1930	4,107,000
1941–1950	1,035,000
1961–1970	3,322,000
1981–1988	4,711,000

Source: U.S. Bureau of the Census, 1990.

Major changes have taken place in the U.S. immigration laws during the 1980s. The Refugee Act of 1980 was established to admit refugees of humanitarian concern to the United States; this allows the President some direct power in determining which of our overseas allies are in most need of rescue and resettlement in reward for services rendered to U.S. interests.

In 1986, the Immigration Reform and Control Act became law after much debate and soul-searching on the part of Congress. This 1986 Act is an attempt to bring under control the enormous numbers of people who have immigrated to the United States illegally, mostly from Mexico and Central America. Aliens who had been in the United States since before January 1, 1982, were offered a form of amnesty. They were required to come forward and register, first for temporary residence and after 18 months for permanent residence. Employers who knowingly hire *illegal immigrants* can now be fined. Those persons who enter the country as seasonal farm workers are now in a special temporary category that keeps strict tabs on their whereabouts and provides them with little chance of moving up the employment ladder. About three million aliens have applied for amnesty, either as future citizens or as temporary farm workers.

What effects, if any, has the 1986 Act had on the flow of illegal immigrants from south of the border? It is estimated that anywhere between several and perhaps 12 million people have entered the United States via Mexico in recent decades; clearly, the 1986 Act missed a few! Half of the applications under the 1986 program were from California, and over 70 percent of all applicants nationwide said they came from Mexico. A 1989 study by the Urban Institute indicates that the flow of illegal immigrants is down substantially, but is far from negligible: nearly 1.3 million Mexicans have entered illegally since the Act was made law in 1986, but this number would have been as high as 2 million if not for the new laws and amnesty program. The report suggests that of the 700,000 who might have come but did not, 12 percent were thwarted by border patrols, 17 percent were channeled into the temporary farm workers program, and 71 percent did not come for fear of the new law's impact on their chances for success in the United States. Overall, however, it is too soon to draw conclusions on the long-term impact.

In 1989, the two Houses of Congress debated the possibility of setting aside some immigration numbers for immigrants whose skills were needed in the United States. Skilled workers are in short supply because of the "baby bust" of the 1960s and 1970s. However, total allowable immigrants to the United States from abroad are at present about 600,000 a year, including refugees, country quotas, relatives, and several other exceptions to the rules and quotas (Suro, 1989; Rasky 1989).

Behind these laws lie a number of debates, assumptions, and questions of racism. Why are Americans afraid of the influx of people from south of the border? Why are we trying so hard to control their entry? In past years the cry has been that these aliens will take jobs away from "real" Americans. In the present economic climate, this is untrue: entry-level jobs are going begging across the nation. Some environmentalists attest that the United States is already too crowded and that allowing in "all of Mexico" will put terrible strains on our resources. Others suggest that racism is really at the heart of the matter. An interesting study by economist Julian Simon suggests that immigrants may put strains on a country in the short term, but over the long term new residents will provide a boost for the country as a whole (Simon, 1986). However, Simon minimizes environmental issues in making his pro-immigration arguments.

PATTERNS OF POPULATION GROWTH OVER TIME

The general pattern of rapid population growth in recent centuries can be explained by a combination of the changes in fertility and mortality rates (Fig. 5.6). Prior to the Industrial Revolution with its attendant social changes and medical advances, most human populations had both high fertility rates and high mortality rates and relatively stable populations. In recent centuries in the industrialized nations, mortality rates began to decline as a result of increased standards of living and medical care. This decline preceded the decline in fertility. The result was a period of time in which fertility rates were substantially greater than mortality rates, and population increased accordingly.

This period of increase was characterized by a particularly broad-based population pyramid. It was also during this era, the eighteenth and nineteenth centuries, that the large populations of Europe found an outlet by settling in North America, Australia, and other frontier areas. Later, social changes brought about in part by the Industrial Revolution led to a decline in fertility in the industrialized nations, so that the base of the population pyramids narrowed and populations stabilized. Thus Europe and the Americas have passed through their own period of intense population growth.

In the less industrialized nations, however, mortality rates have declined substantially, but a decline in fertility is not yet clearly in sight. This is the fundamental reason for the high rates of population growth in the world as a whole, and in the less industrialized nations in particular.

SPATIAL DISTRIBUTION OF POPULATION

Currently, the most rapid population growth is taking place in the less industrialized countries. Recent United Nations projections suggest a rise in population worldwide to 8.5 billion by 2035. Only 200 million people, during the next 35 years of growth, will be born in the industrialized countries; the other 3 billion new human beings, making up 95 percent of the projected growth, will greet life in the less industrialized countries (Keyfitz, 1989). This rapid population growth in the developing world will increase the pressure on an already stressed economic and environmental system.

Much of the growth has occurred in urban places in both the industrialized and less industrialized nations (Fig. 5.7). Movement away from rural areas, where in most cases the population was largely food self-sufficient, has complicated the population pressures in the

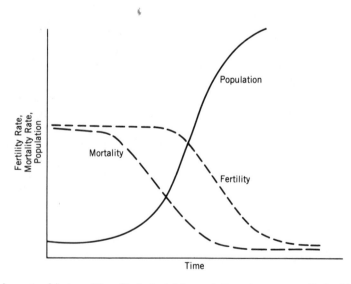

Figure 5.6   The demographic transition. Preindustrial populations have generally had high birth rates and death rates. When death rates fall before birth rates, population rises rapidly.

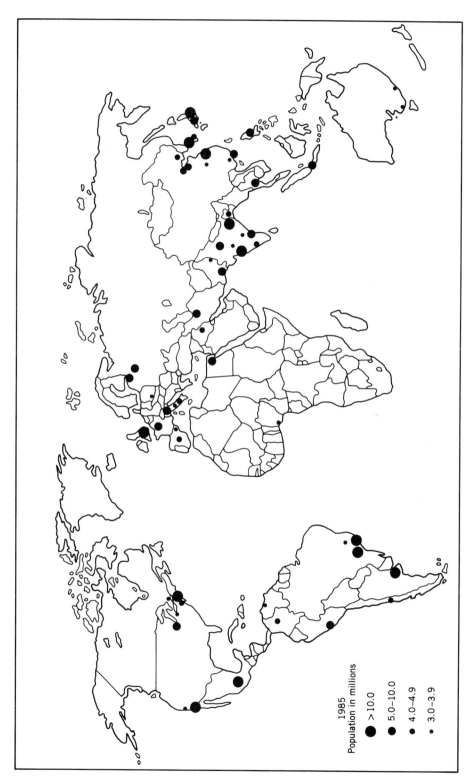

1985
Population in millions

● >10.0

● 5.0–10.0

• 4.0–4.9

· 3.0–3.9

Figure 5.7 Major metropolitan areas of the world, 1985. In most of the world, cities are growing much faster than rural areas.

less industrialized nations. It certainly has intensified the pressures on usable resources, including space, water, and food, and it taxes national abilities to promote social and economic welfare. This trend toward increasing urbanization is a major problem facing the less industrialized nations in the future.

Even if one assumes moderate growth rates, urban places such as Mexico City will rise from a 1985 population of 16,901,000 to 27,872,000 by 2000 (Table 5.4). It is estimated that the urban areas of the less industrialized nations are growing at a rate 2 1/2 times that of the industrialized nations. In 1950, there were 70 cities worldwide with 1 million or more inhabitants. By the year 2000, one estimate gives 276 million-plus cities, the majority of these in the less industrialized nations. In A.D. 1900, 5 percent of the world's population lived in large cities. By 2000, between 40 and 70 percent of the world's population will live in urban areas of 20,000 or more people (Newland, 1980). Within our lifetimes, then, more than half of the world's population may find itself living in cities.

Internal migrations are a cause for concern in both the industrialized and less industrialized nations. In the latter, internal migrations feed urban growth, and this movement from rural areas to urban centers is placing severe demands on governments in terms of provision of food, sanitary facilities, jobs, housing, and other necessities. Similar shifts within the U.S. in recent years (Table 5.5) have caused local strains on resources in many high-growth areas.

POPULATION GROWTH: RESOURCES AND PEOPLE

There is a finite amount of arable land in the world. Many experts suggest that at some future date the carrying capacity of available resources may be reached, and the human population will be plunged into a series of famines and resource wars until the population is reduced to a level that is within the boundaries of available resources. One alternative to this scenario is to control or limit population growth. Although reproduction is a private act between individuals, it does have profound social and economic consequences and as such is a social issue. Many planners and resource experts believe that limiting the world's population growth is the only way to ensure a stable and prosperous future.

TABLE 5.4   Population Projections for Major World Cities

City	1985	2000
The top four		
Tokyo–Yokohama, Japan	25,434,000	29,971,000
Mexico City, Mexico	16,901,000	27,872,000
Sao Paulo, Brazil	14,911,000	25,354,000
New York, U.S.A.	14,598,000	14,648,000
Selected others		
Moscow, U.S.S.R.	9,873,000	11,121,000
Los Angeles, U.S.A.	9,638,000	10,714,000
London, U.K.	9,442,000	8,574,000
Essen, West Germany	7,604,000	7,239,000
Lagos, Nigeria	6,054,000	12,528,000
Beijing, China	5,608,000	5,993,000
Bogota, Colombia	4,711,000	7,935,000
Dhaka, Bangladesh	3,283,000	6,492,000
Toronto, Canada	2,972,000	3,296,000
Budapest, Hungary	2,297,000	2,335,000
Birmingham, U.K.	2,211,000	2,078,000

Source: U.S. Bureau of the Census 1990.

TABLE 5.5 U.S. Population Growth

Components of Change (Millions):

Year	Births	Deaths	Immigration	Net Change
1970	3.74	1.93	0.44	2.25
1980	3.61	1.99	0.84	2.47
1987	3.81	2.12	0.60	2.29

Metropolitan Growth:

Years	Population (Millions)	Growth (%)	Nonmetropolitan (%)	Metropolitan (%)
1960–1970	204.4	13	4.4	17.0
1970–1980	226.5	11.4	13.9	9.1
1980–1987	243.4	7.5	4.1	8.7

Regional Population Growth:

Region	% Change 1970–1980	% Change 1980–1987	1987 Population (Millions)
West	24.1	15.0	49.7
South	20.1	11.3	83.9
Middle West	4.1	1.0	59.5
Northeast	0	2.4	50.3

Source: U.S. Bureau of the Census (1989); Council on Environmental Quality (1988).

On the other hand, there are many who resist the concept of control of reproduction. Julian Simon, an American economist, maintains that there is no population problem. He states that every new human being is a new source of mental creativity to help solve humanity's problems, to invent new resources, and to increase the productivity of existing resources so that the earth can support an infinite number of people (Simon, 1981, 1986; Wattenberg and Zinsmeister, 1985). Unfortunately, many of these population optimists fail to take into account the wear and tear on the environment of so many additional persons: by the year 2025 there will be four times the number of cars on the planet as there are today (Keyfitz, 1989)!

For religious and moral reasons, formed in an era when there was no fear of a limit to resources, millions of Americans and probably billions worldwide resist the idea of birth control. This viewpoint at home has had international repercussions for the world's population control programs. During the 1980s, the Reagan administration refused to contribute the United States' portion of the budget to United Nations programs that had anything to do with population control. Spokesmen (and we deliberately use "men" here) maintained that no U.S. dollars would be used to pay for abortions. As a result, many countries have been forced to curtail their population control programs. The bulk of the United Nations' efforts are, of course, aimed at education and contraception, not abortion. However, by using the highly emotional issue of abortion as a cover, progrowth activists in the United States have contributed, indirectly, to a rising world population.

For most people in the less industrialized countries, where farming has been the key to prosperity, another child has always meant another pair of hands to help out. Until very recently, parents might produce ten offspring, only to have over half of them die before adulthood. Now, better infant health care and, to some extent, improved nutrition enable more children to make it to adulthood. The economic need for having many children is now less pressing, and in its place are new reasons for limiting family size. However, ideas are slow to change, often for good reason. There is no guarantee that good times will last, and children are for many the greatest and perhaps only pleasure in a hard life.

Politically, population control is a complex issue at home and abroad. As mentioned earlier, the industrialized nations went through a period of rapid population growth from the middle of the eighteenth to the early nineteenth century. This was also the period of colonization and settlement by those countries. Many people in the less industrialized nations say it is now their turn to do the same, and they argue that they have the same rights to reproduction and resource use as have the industrialized nations. Any attempt to control their growth is seen as racism on the part of the older powers, out of fear that these new centers of population growth will also become new power centers. Whatever the arguments, it is undeniable that there is a strong tendency worldwide toward at least considering population control, and this consideration is directly tied to fears over resource depletion. Notable successes are the family planning efforts in Indonesia, Thailand, and South Korea (Keyfitz, 1989).

FERTILITY CONTROL AND FAMILY PLANNING

Family planning programs in the United States were first institutionalized in the form of birth control clinics in the 1920s. The first birth control clinics were established in New York City by Margaret Sanger, a leader in the women's rights movement. Sanger was concerned with the suffering of women who had too many children, too close together, with no options for fertility control other than illegal abortions. The first birth control clinics were designed to liberate women from the traditional roles of wife and brood mare and to allow women to exercise active control over the number and spacing of births of their children. These early clinics met with strong resistance, in much the same way that the equal rights movement met resistance over half a century later. For a time in this country, diaphragms were illegal and had to be smuggled in from Europe by birth-control advocates.

The link, however, between a woman's role in her society and her desire to increase or decrease the size of her family is a strong one. An understanding of women's roles in society is a prerequisite for any successful family planning effort.

Family planning programs are generally voluntary in nature. In the less industrialized nations, however, many countries have found it necessary to implement compulsory programs or incentives to encourage family planning. Prior to 1965, only a handful of less industrialized nations had officially supported family planning programs. The international spread of family planning began after 1965 and quickly gained momentum in the next ten years (Fig. 5.8). By 1975, only 3 of the 38 less industrialized nations with populations greater than 10 million had no officially adopted family planning programs. These were Burma, Peru, and North Korea. Five years later, all but a few Third World countries had family planning policies, although some were only on paper (Brown *et al.*, 1979).

Indonesia's example illustrates the use of modernism mixed with tradition. In 1980, after ten years of work, 40,000 information and distribution centers had been set up in the country's villages. Free contraceptives have been accompanied by a relentless public relations campaign: the ideal family is "small, happy, and prosperous." Imagine having to listen to the national family planning jingle every time a train passes a railroad crossing! These and related efforts have been successful. Although abortion is illegal in Indonesia, the fertility rate has dropped from 5.6 to 3.4 children per woman since the early 1970s. Since that time, the number of couples using contraceptives has risen from 400,000 to 18.6 million (Keyfitz, 1989).

Experts suggest that those programs receiving good governmental support and economic assistance will be the most successful in

Figure 5.8 Family planning in Jendouba, Tunisia. Education is the key to success for family planning efforts. In Tunisia, the emphasis is on integrating health care (maternal and child), nutrition, and family planning. Notice the absence of the fathers in this family planning class.

bringing down the fertility rate. A well-planned program must include not only the distribution of contraceptives but also increased education about their use. The bitter reaction by many to India's IUD (intrauterine device) program is a case in point. The IUD was being adopted by many Indian women as a method of contraception. Family planning personnel would visit rural villages and, after medical examinations, insert the IUDs. The doctors failed to warn the women, however, of potential side effects. When these became apparent, rumors spread and the program virtually collapsed overnight. Similar reactions to the IUD have followed in the United States.

NON-FAMILY PLANNING

In those nations where standards of living and increased literacy have helped to improve women's status, fertility has declined (see Issue 5–2). There are a number of specific factors that have influenced the decline in fertility, including increased educational levels of women, increased female employment outside the home, and marriage at a later age. All of

these create conditions that motivate women to limit the size of their families (Newland, 1977). However, family planning programs in countries with strong pro-natalist cultures, especially in Africa and Asia, have met with little success. In most less industrialized countries, however, the signs are clear that this generation wants smaller families than did its predecessors (Keyfitz, 1989).

Increased educational levels have opened opportunities other than motherhood to many women. The acquisition of more knowledge has not only made these women more aware of family planning and contraceptive information but has also increased their knowledge of the need for family planning. Also, increased education influences one's goals and aspirations and as a woman receives more education she may seek new alternatives or life-styles and perhaps a career. Lastly, educated women realize the value of education and want to have their own children educated as well. To do so effectively and in some cases economically, these women feel the need to limit the size of their families.

Increased female employment outside the home is another factor that has contributed to declining fertility rates. The need for two income earners in North American households is a response to increasing economic pressures. With a large percentage of women now in the labor force, large families are not as easily sustained as when women were mainly homemakers. According to the U.S. Census, over half of the nation's married women work outside the home.

Delaying the age of marriage has also contributed to declining fertility. If a woman is marrying later in her life, in the late 20s or early 30s, the number of children she can bear will be lower. This practice has been used for years in the People's Republic of China as a method of family planning and has shown mixed results.

In opposition to these trends, however, are the pro-growth advocates, who are also largely in favor of women returning to their traditional roles as moms and homemakers only. To choose to be a homemaker is fine, but women should be able to have other choices as well.

The 1989 decision by the U.S. Supreme Court limiting access to abortion is seen by many as the first step by traditionalists who want to push women back into the home, tied to the raising of large families. It is probable that many contraceptive methods, taken for granted by women for decades, may soon be under attack.

This would be a great blow to the birth control programs and clinics run by Planned Parenthood and other groups who are struggling to introduce family planning to teenagers, the females at most risk for early, unwanted, and multiple pregnancies. Many young girls and women are struggling in great poverty to raise large families, with no hope of school or jobs for themselves or their children. As with their more fortunate sisters who have jobs and choices and small families, contraception and education are the key to survival; but political trends at the top in this country suggest that assistance will be increasingly hard to find.

ISSUE 5–2   Brazil's Fertility Rate Drops Nearly 50 Percent: Why?

Something unanticipated has happened in Brazil. Since 1970, the fertility rate in this huge South American country has declined by almost one-half, from 5.75 children per woman to about 3.2 today.

Of course, there are other countries with rapid, precipitous drops, but these examples are either in the developed world or are the result of strong government policies, such as China's stringent one-child policy and government-led programs in Colombia and Mexico. There are also the conspicuous policy failures, such as in India, where all the family planning campaigning in the world cannot seem to make a dent in the birth rate. To make Brazil's situation all the more puzzling, its present population of 145 million is overwhelmingly Roman Catholic, a religion that discourages birth control, and Brazil's government has no government birth control policy.

So why is Liliana Duque's experience now regarded as typical in Brazil? She comes from a family of twelve children, she herself had three, and her daughter plans to have two. This represents a *demographic transition,* compressed

into a little over a generation and not accompanied by many of its usual characteristics. According to demographer George Martine, Brazil's sudden self-induced fertility decline is unprecedented in human history (Brooke, 1989).

There are several known causes for this fertility drop. The first is the government's withdrawal from the fertility issue. In the 1960s, Brazil's military government encouraged big families, and both government and church were hostile to family planning. What has changed is that both authorities are now silent on the subject and allow couples to decide for themselves. Universal access to contraception has also helped. In the 1960s, only 5 percent of fertile married women used contraceptives, and today that figure is 66 percent. In a Roman Catholic country, it is not surprising that abortions are illegal, nor is it surprising that so many are carried out nevertheless: 3 million illegal abortions take place annually in Brazil.

The improved status of women has also contributed to Brazil's fertility decline. Brazil's two most popular forms of birth control are the pill

FUTURE POPULATION ESTIMATES AND CONCLUSIONS

Population control programs are having an effect on worldwide population growth, according to the United Nations Population Division. Although the world's population is growing rapidly and in some places is totally out of control, indicators are clear that the rate of growth is slowing. The world's annual population growth rate dropped from 2.4 percent in 1965–1970, to 2 percent in 1980–1985, to 1.8 percent in 1990. This slow, downward trend means that between 1980 and 1985, the world's population increased by 9 percent, but that it will increase by only 4 percent in a five-year period early in the next century.

However, don't expect world depopulation in your lifetime. There are so many babies being born today that it will be a century and longer, even by the best estimates, before the engine of growth begins to slow. By 2020, a middle-of-the-road estimate indicates a rise from 5.3 to 8.2 billion people (Keyfitz, 1989; Population Reference Bureau, 1990).

Population growth and resource use are intertwined and interdependent. The world is still undergoing a massive population boom that began several hundred years ago, and it is far too soon to know what the end results will be for the human race. In future decades we may see deprivation and suffering due to worldwide resource shortages or inequities in resource distribution. Perhaps there will be a cataclysmic collapse of the human population, with effects akin to those wrought by the European plagues of the late Middle Ages. Some argue that the modern plague is already here: AIDS. Certainly the social and economic effects of AIDS will be profound in the areas of Africa where it is rampant, and may lead to great changes in our country as well.

On the other hand, we all may get used to living close together and may adapt creatively to the conditions and new resources as the world becomes an urban and crowded place.

---

and female sterilization, which require Brazil's women to take an active role in determining their own fertility. Birth control pills can be purchased without a prescription, and the largely irreversible tube-tying choice has been made by 27 percent of married Brazilian women (the U.S. level is 17 percent); only 0.8 percent of Brazil's married men have opted for sterilization. There is also a new constitutional clause for a 4-month maternity leave. This 1988 law was intended to encourage women to both work and have babies: however, in actuality women workers find they are penalized for remaining fertile. Many employers now demand sterility certificates as a precondition for hiring or conduct regular urine-pregnancy tests of their women workers. This punitive response certainly suppresses childbearing among Brazil's working women.

Economic changes within the family and Brazilian society are also important. In the classic tradition of the demographic transition, family size declines as real income rises—this was the experience in Europe and North America. In Brazil, however, real income has declined in a stagnant 1980s economy, but the poor maintain that they cannot afford more children, even though many babies die before their first birthdays, victims of unsanitary conditions and malnourishment. Last, but not least, the role of television has been extremely influential. Researchers suggest that in the absence of real prosperity, Brazilians are absorbing the values of the good life by watching television. Demographer Martine maintains that the image of urban life communicated by television is a middle-class, prosperous existence (Brooke, 1989).

For fertility levels to drop, say proponents of the demographic transition, a population must become urban and industrialized and experience a rise in quality of life. Apparently, these can be acquired via television fantasy alone. Brazil's evening soap operas emphasize that sexuality and procreation can be separated, that large families are poor and miserable, and that small families are affluent. In the absence of real prosperity, Brazil's population—especially its women—has made the move to low birth rates on the basis of expectations alone.

Certainly, however, the time is past when one group of people can utilize a resource without concern for the effects of that use on others. We are already a bit too crowded for that kind of behavior, and resource management is a real worldwide necessity that at present is in short supply.

REFERENCES AND ADDITIONAL READING

Barringer, F. 1989. Waiting is over: Births near 50s level. *The New York Times*, October 31, p. A13.

Boserup, E. 1965. *The Conditions of Agricultural Growth*. Chicago: Aldine.

———. 1981. *Population and Technological Change*. Chicago: University of Chicago Press.

Brooke, J. 1989. Decline in births in Brazil lessens population fears. *The New York Times*, August 8, p. A1.

Brown, L.R., *et al*. 1989. *State of the World, 1989*. Washington, DC: Worldwatch Institute.

Conservation Foundation. 1982. *State of the Environment, 1982*. Washington, DC: Conservation Foundation.

Council on Environmental Quality. 1988. *18th and 19th Environmental Quality Annual Reports*. Washington, DC: U.S. Government Printing Office.

Daly, H.E. 1977. *Steady-State Economics*. San Francisco: W.H. Freeman.

Durning, A.B. 1989. *Poverty and the Environment: Reversing the Downward Spiral*. Worldwatch Paper #92. Washington, DC: Worldwatch Institute.

Erlich, P. 1968. *The Population Bomb*. New York: Ballantine Books.

Georgesu-Roegen, N. 1979. Comments on papers by Daly and Stiglitz. In V. K. Smith (Ed.) *Scarcity and Growth Reconsidered*. Baltimore: Johns Hopkins University Press.

Greenhalgh, S., and J. Bongaarts. 1987. Fertility policy in China: Future options. *Science* 235: 1167–1172.

Gruson, L. 1989. Emigrants feathering their old nest. *The New York Times*, July 18, p. A4.

Harvey, D. 1974. Population, resources, and the ideology of science. *Econ. Geography* 50: 256–277.

Hay, A. 1982. *The Chemical Scythe: Lessons of 2,4,5-T and Dioxin*. New York: Plenum.

Holdgate, M.W., Kassas, M., and White, G.F. 1982. World environmental trends between 1972 and 1982. *Environ. Conservation* 9: 11–29.

Jacobson, J.L. 1988. *Environmental Refugees: A Yardstick of Habitability*. Worldwatch Paper #86. Washington, DC: Worldwatch Institute.

Keeley, C.B. 1982. Illegal migration. *Sci. Amer.* 246(3): 41–77.

Keyfitz, N. 1989. The growing human population. *Sci. Amer.* 261(3): 118–127.

Malthus, T.R. 1976. An essay on the principle of population. In Appleman, P. (Ed). *An Essay on the Principles of Population: Text, Sources and Background, Criticism*. New York: Norton.

National Research Council. 1989. *A Common Destiny: Blacks and American Society*. Washington, DC: National Academy Press.

Newland, K. 1977. *Women and Population Growth: Choice beyond Childbearing*. Worldwatch Paper #16. Washington, DC: Worldwatch Institute.

———. 1980. *City Limits: Emerging Constraints on Urban Growth*. Worldwatch Paper #38. Washington, DC: Worldwatch Institute.

Population Reference Bureau. 1990. *1990 World Population Data Sheet*. Washington, DC: Population Reference Bureau.

Preston, S.H. 1986. Population growth and economic development. *Environment* 28(2): 6–9, 32–33.

Rasky, S. F. 1989. Senate votes to ease immigration for professionals and Europeans. *The New York Times*, July 14, p. A1.

Simon, J. 1981. *The Ultimate Resource*. Princeton, NJ: Princeton University Press.

———. 1986. *Theory of Population and Economic Growth*. Oxford/New York: Basil Blackwell.

Stokes, B. 1980. *Men and Family Planning*. Worldwatch Paper #41. Washington, DC: Worldwatch Institute.

Suro, R. 1989. Employers are looking abroad for the skilled and the energetic. *The New York Times*, July 16, p. D4.

United Nations. 1988. *Demographic Yearbook, 1986*. New York: United Nations.

U.S. Bureau of the Census. 1981. *Population Characteristics*. Series p-20, #374. Washington, DC: U.S. Government Printing Office.

U.S. Bureau of the Census. 1989. *USA Statistics in Brief*. Washington, DC: U.S. Government Printing Office.

U.S. Bureau of the Census, 1990. *Statistical Abstract of the U.S.* Washington, DC: U.S. Government Printing Office.

Urban Institute. 1989. *U.S. Immigration Reform and Control Act and Undocumented Immigra-*

tion to the United States. In co-operation with the Rand Program for Research and Immigration Policy. Washington, DC. Urban Institute.

Wattenberg, B. and K. Zinsmeister (Eds.). 1985. *Are World Population Trends a Problem?* Washington, DC: American Enterprise Institute for Public Policy Research.

TERMS TO KNOW

Age Structure
Baby Boom
Birth Rate
Cohort
Death Rate
Demographic Transition
Doubling Time
Environmental Refugees
Fertility Rate
Guest Workers
Illegal Immigrants
Thomas Malthus
Natural Increase
neo-Malthusianism
Population Dynamics
Population Pyramid
Replacement Level
Zero Population Growth

STUDY QUESTIONS

1. What is the significance of geometric versus arithmetic growth?
2. Why is the spatial distribution of population growth so important?
3. What are the major demographic differences between less developed and more developed nations?
4. Why do people resist birth control measures? What incentives to use them do some nations provide?
5. At what time did the U.S. population pyramid resemble that of a developing nation?
6. What were the three major migration patterns of people who came to the U.S?
7. What will world population patterns be like in 2000, according to recent projections?

Land Resources

INTRODUCTION

In the preceding chapter, we examined the distribution of people around the world and the variation in population densities from place to place. Population density is an important measure—it represents the number of people in relation to the fundamental resource that sustains them: the land. In this chapter we will examine the characteristics, distribution, and use of the world's land resources.

Land is the most fundamental natural resource because it provides nearly all the food we use today, from the world's agricultural and grazing lands. There is some possibility of increasing the amount of food we obtain from the oceans, as will be discussed in Chapter 12. Also, innovative forms of agriculture may not depend on soil but may be carried out in built environments either in rural areas or on the tops of buildings. But these alternatives to conventional agriculture have little promise of feeding large numbers of people in the near future, and land will continue to be the ultimate source of most food.

Land is also necessary simply to provide space on which to live. We are certainly capable of living in much less space than is currently available, if we can learn to live at the high population densities that characterize most cities. In many areas of the world, particularly the United States, growth in urban populations has taken place at the same time as the number of people living in rural areas has declined. But population growth, even at high densities, inevitably means that more land must be used to accommodate those people, either for residential uses or for the variety of other demands an urban population makes:

roads, airports, reservoirs, commercial districts, and so on.

Finally, even land that is not intensively used as agricultural or urban land satisfies important human needs. Recreation, water supply, and wildlife habitat are common uses of nonagricultural rural land. These uses are valued highly enough that in much of the world such lands are dedicated to these purposes, and competing uses are restricted.

As the world's population grows, more and more demands are placed on a finite land base. Increased intensity of land use will meet some of these demands, but in many cases land use demands are mutually incompatible. Land use decisions must then be made—decisions that necessarily limit the amount of land available for various purposes. Land use allocation has become the focus of many debates in environmental management and will increasingly govern many natural resource decisions.

GLOBAL LAND RESOURCES

BIOREGIONS

One way to look at the world's land resources is in terms of their general ecological characteristics. A region's resources and environmental capabilities are closely tied to the basic characteristics of its ecosystems, which are themselves related to the prevailing geologic, topographic, soil, and climatic environment. Ecological regions, or *bioregions*, can serve as a valuable framework for environmental management decisions—a framework that is primarily based on natural resources rather than their use by humans, although human factors can be combined with natural ones in classifying resource areas. The rationale for delimiting bioregions is that they form a rational basis for resource assessment and management decisions. Such regions have a certain amount of internal homogeneity and presumably similar policies should be applied within them, whereas different ecological areas may demand different policies. Unfortunately political boundaries usually have very little correspondence to natural ones, and it is often more expedient to base resource management strategies on the political map than on the ecological map. But at somewhat smaller scales, within nations or cooperating groups of nations, bioregions offer considerable potential for guiding the management process.

Ecosystems are also useful to the researcher because they are large enough to be a reasonably representative slice of the environment, yet not so large as to be unmanageable. Ecosystems are themselves ultimately part of larger systems. At the broadest level is the *biosphere*, the worldwide envelope of organic and inorganic substances within which all life functions. Envision the millions of tiny and large ecosystems that make up the biosphere, and try to comprehend the awesome complexity of the interactions and "meshing of gears" that have developed over billions of years so that this global system can function smoothly.

The concept of *biome* helps us make sense of the patterns of interaction between plants, animals, and the physical environment. A biome is a major ecological region within which plant and animal communities are broadly similar, both in their general characteristics and in their relations to each other and to the physical environment. Because biomes are defined on the basis of organism–environment interactions, it is within each of the world's major biomes that the researcher can make sense of individual ecosystems.

THE WORLD'S MAJOR BIOMES: A BRIEF SUMMARY

Figure 6.1 is a map of the major world biomes. Looking first at the equator, the equatorial or *tropical rainforest* is an exuberant response to a rainfall schedule that is year-round and frequent, with little variation in day-length or seasonal change. The resulting vegetation cover is a complex array of broad-leaved evergreens, trees that constantly shed some leaves but are never bare. There is a larger diversity of species in the rainforest than elsewhere. For example, an acre of forest in the northeastern United States might sustain five to ten tree species, whereas an acre of tropical rainforest might yield several times that many. In addition, tropical species are often unique to only a very small area of rainforest, unlike their northern counterparts which are found over a very wide geographic area. Tropical rainforests straddle the equator, with the largest areas found in the Amazon basin (Brazil), in Indonesia and the Southeast Asian peninsula, and in Africa's Zaire basin.

Moving south and north from the equator, one finds a seasonally drier climate and a correspondingly less heavily vegetated biome called *savanna*, which occurs near latitude 25 degrees north and south, notably in Africa, South America, and Southeast Asia. Most savanna is located in the tropical wet and dry climate zone and is characterized by heavy summer rainfall and an almost completly dry winter season. The characteristic vegetation varies from open woodland with grass cover to open grassland with scattered deciduous trees. Researchers generally agree that much of Africa's savanna is derived not from natural processes but from the human use of fire. If this is true, savanna is perhaps the oldest of human-shaped landscapes.

The dry climates that produce the *desert* biome are found in two locations worldwide: in the subtropical latitudes as the result of high pressure zones and in the mid-latitudes in continental interiors far from ocean moisture. Deserts vary from the cartoon image of bare rock and blowing sand dunes where no rainfall is recorded year after year to areas with shrubs and 4 to 12 inches (100 to 300 mm) of rain a year. *Potential evapotranspiration,* or the amount of water that would be evaporated or transpired if it were available, is much higher, leading to a water deficit. Desert vegetation consists of plants with special structural adaptations that enable them to store moisture, to retain it under waxy leaves, and to search for it via long root systems. These species complete

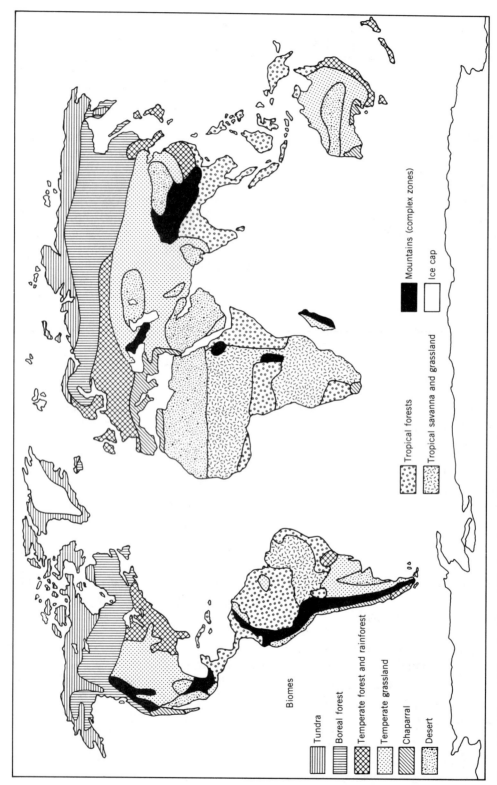

Figure 6.1 The world's major biomes. The broad geographical distribution illustrates the diversity of ecosystems found throughout the world. (*Source:* Council on Environmental Quality, 1989.)

Biomes

Tundra

Boreal forest

Temperate forest and rainforest

Temperate grassland

Chaparral

Desert

Tropical forests

Tropical savanna and grassland

Mountains (complex zones)

Ice cap

their brief life cycles during the short rainy season.

The subtropical deserts are the largest on earth and include the Sahara Desert, which stretches across Africa eastward to join the Arabian, Iranian, Afghani, and Pakistani deserts. Other subtropical deserts are found in the southwestern United States, northern Mexico, Australia, Chile, Peru, and southern Africa (Fig. 6.2). Continental deserts are found in the interiors of Northern Hemisphere continents: between the Caspian and Aral seas in the Soviet Union, the Gobi Desert in Mongolia,and between the Rocky Mountains and the Sierra–Cascade ranges in the United States.

The Mediterranean biome is named after the region that stretches around the Mediterranean Sea, characterized by a cool, moist winter and a hot, dry summer. Typical vegetation consists of a thorny, glossy, and sometimes impenetrable mass of fire-prone species called *chaparral*. Mediterranean climate and chaparral are found in other coastal locations between 30 and 45 degrees latitude north and south of the equator, including coastal southern California, Chile, South Africa, and parts of southern Australia.

The mid-latitude *grasslands* are found at 30 degrees north and south latitude in semiarid interior areas. With not quite enough moisture to support trees and shrubs, these fire-prone grasslands once stretched from Texas to Alberta and Saskatchewan in North America, before being put to the plow in the nineteenth and twentieth centuries. The grasslands of South America in Argentina and Uruguay have also been converted to agricultural development. The grassland steppes of the Ukraine in the USSR continue east as far as Manchuria in China.

The vast mid-latitude or *temperate forests* (Fig. 6.3) once stretched from 30 to 50 degrees north and south latitude across the eastern United States, much of northwestern Europe, eastern China, Japan, and small areas of South America, Australia, and New Zealand. With the colonization and population growth of the last several centuries, much of this deciduous (in the United States) and mixed deciduous/evergreen (in Europe) woodland cover has been removed. The characteristic climate of this region is cold winters and warm summers, with average annual precipitation generally equal to or greater than potential evapotranspiration.

The *boreal*, or northern coniferous, biome is located between 50 and 60 degrees north latitude (there being no significant land mass at this latitude south of the equator). In contrast to the diversity of the tropical rainforest, the number of species in this biome is extremely limited. These woodlands stretch in a belt across Alaska, Canada, and as far south as the northern portions of Michigan, New York, and New England in North America. In Europe this belt continues across Scandinavia and the

Figure 6.2   Desert biome. The organ pipe cactus (*Lemaireocereus Thurberi*) preserved in the Organ Pipe National Monument, Arizona, is one type of xerophytic plant that characterized the deserts in the Southwest.

Figure 6.3   Temperate forest biome in Nicolet National Forest, Wisconsin. This biome is characterized by mixed hardwood species, such as maple, elm, black ash, and ash.

Soviet Union. Mean monthly temperatures range from -20° F (-29° C) in the winter to 75° F (24° C) in the brief summer. Precipitation is moderate, but because of the relatively cool temperatures there is usually a moisture surplus for the entire year. The vegetation cover is dominated by fir, spruce, and pine, which have thick needles and bark to withstand the cold. In the far north, trees only one meter high may be one hundred or more years old.

At this tree line boundary the *tundra* biome begins, generally poleward of 60 degrees north and south latitude. The average temperature of the growing season does not exceed 50° F (10° C) for more than a few weeks, which prohibits tree growth. Much of this area is underlain by *permafrost*, or permanently frozen ground. With low precipitation, the tundra is often called a frozen desert; in its brief thaw, like the warm deserts, a low and

colorful mat of shrubs, mosses, lichens, and grasses temporarily springs up.

The preceding descriptions present a highly simplified picture of a complex patterning of biomes. There are numerous exceptions to the commonly occurring biomes, caused by microclimate, soil variability, and human impact. The main point to note is that vegetation and climate have interacted over millions of years, resulting in adaptive vegetative patterns. We should remember that portions of these biomes have been altered by the work of humanity, and this is the cause of much discussion and dissent among those who would conserve and those who would develop and further alter these biomes.

WORLD LAND USE PATTERNS

The total land area of the world (excluding Antarctica) about 32 billion acres (13 billion ha) (Fig. 6.4). The best data on world land use are provided by the Food and Agricultural Organization of the United Nations. The FAO classifies land as *arable* (capable of producing crops through cultivated agriculture), permanent pasture (land that is suitable and available for grazing animals, regardless of the dominant vegetation type), forest and woodland, and other (including parks, urban areas, roads, deserts, and other nonagricultural areas). Using this classification, about 10 percent of the world's land is used for arable agriculture, and another 25 percent for permanent pasture. Thirty-one percent of the world is in forest and woodland, while 33 percent is in other uses. The continents vary considerably in the proportions of land in these uses. For example, Europe (excluding the USSR) is 30 percent arable, and Oceania, Africa, and South America are only 5 to 7 percent arable. There are similar variations in the proportions of land in other uses (see Table 6.1).

There are some notable trends in world land use as seen in Table 6.1. In the period 1970 to 1987, there were minor but significant increases in the amount of arable land, most importantly in Third World areas of Africa, South America, and Asia. In the wealthier parts of the world (North America, Europe, Oceania, and the USSR) there was very little change in

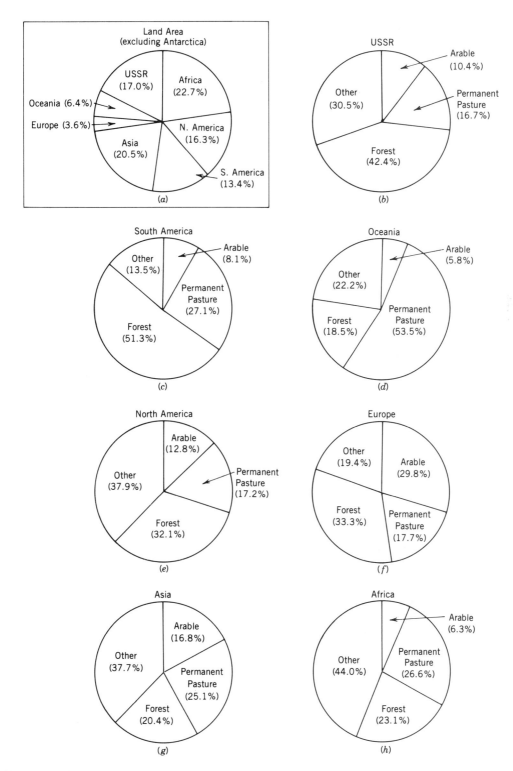

Figure 6.4 World land use, 1987. (a) Areas of world regions (b) through (h): Percent of land area in arable agriculture, permanent pasture, forest, or other uses. (Source: FAO, 1989).

TABLE 6.1 World Land Use, 1970–1987 (in millions of hectares)

	Africa	North America	South America	Asia	Europe	Oceania	USSR	Total
Land area	2966	2136	1753	2677	473	843	2227	13,075
(% of world)	23	16	13	20	4	6	17	100
Arable land 1987	188	274	142	451	140	49	233	1476
(% of region)	6	13	8	17	30	6	10	11
Arable land 1981	181	265	126	455	141	46	232	1452
(% of region)	6	12	7	17	30	5	10	11
Arable land 1970	169	267	112	444	145	43	233	1413
(% of region)	6	13	6	17	31	5	10	11
Permanent pasture 1987	788	368	475	679	84	450	372	3214
(% of region)	27	17	27	25	18	53	17	25
Permanent pasture 1981	784	352	450	604	87	466	374	3117
(% of region)	26	16	26	23	18	55	17	24
Permanent pasture 1970	786	357	433	622	89	466	375	3127
(% of region)	27	17	25	23	19	55	17	24
Forest/woodland 1987	686	686	900	539	157	156	944	4068
(% of region)	23	32	51	20	33	19	42	31
Forest/woodland 1981	696	683	942	546	155	151	920	4094
(% of region)	23	32	54	20	33	18	41	31
Forest/woodland 1970	728	697	981	551	150	182	920	4210
(% of region)	25	33	56	21	32	22	41	32
Other land 1987	1304	810	237	1010	92	187	679	4319
(% of region)	44	38	14	38	19	22	30	33
Other land 1981	1305	829	235	1072	90	179	702	4413
(% of region)	44	39	13	40	19	21	32	34
Other land 1970	1283	814	228	1060	88	152	700	4325
(% of region)	43	38	13	40	19	18	31	33

Source: Food and Agricultural Organization (1989).

the area cultivated. The increases in arable land were caused by expansion of cultivation into areas that were previously forested to meet the food demands of a rising population. The fact that woodlands are being cleared to make way for cultivation indicates that agriculture is being forced onto poorer and poorer land, with concomitant increases in problems of erosion, unfavorable moisture conditions, poor fertility, and so on. The impact of this land clearing is seen in the decrease in forest and woodland; in this 17-year period, the amount of forest and woodland worldwide decreased by 35 million acres (142 million ha), or by over 3 percent. About two-thirds of this deforestation was in South America, primarily in the Amazon basin.

In this same period there were only minor changes in the amount of land in permanent pasture. The most notable increases are in South America and Asia. Increases in permanent pasture result from forest clearing in South America, whereas in Asia they primarily represent expansion of pasture into areas previously classified as other land. The amount of land in "other" uses changed little overall, though there were substantial decreases in Asia and small increases in several other areas. The major factors in these changes were expansion of pasture areas, urban development, and the establishment of large areas for parks and wildlife reserves.

U.S. LAND RESOURCES

The total land area of the United States is 2.265 billion acres (917 million ha) (Fig. 6.5). U.S. land is usually classified under a different system than that used by the Food and Agricultural Organization discussed in the preceding section. Arable land is defined as farmland or cropland. *Farmland* is land in farm units and includes both cultivated land and land in woodlots, pasture, feedlots, and similar uses that are part of the farm but not cultivated. *Cropland* consists of land that is actually cultivated and planted on a regular basis and includes cultivated fallow and temporary pasture that is part of a crop rotation system. *Rangeland* is land on which the native vegetation consists of grasses and similar plants suit-

able for grazing animals. *Pasture* is land on which these plants are not native, but they are cultivated for use by grazing animals. Most of the rangeland in the United States is in the semiarid western states, whereas most pastureland is in areas where the natural vegetation is woodland.

Using these terms, the Council on Environmental Quality (1989) reported that U.S. land consists of about 18 percent cropland, 26 percent pasture and range, 29 percent forest, 12 percent in special uses (including transportation, parks and wildlife areas, farmsteads, and military uses), and 12 percent unclassified. About half of the unclassified land is in Alaska, and another 47 million acres (19 million ha) of unclassified land is in urban or built-up areas. This urban land amounts to about 2 percent of the area of the United States. Also included in unclassified areas are some desert lands and rock or ice areas of mountains.

This land use pattern has undergone many changes since Europeans arrived in North America. Obviously there was very little cropland prior to European settlement and substantially more forest. Most of the forest clearance took place during the eighteenth and nineteenth centuries, and forest area reached a minimum in the late 1800s or early 1900s—earlier along the eastern seaboard and later in the central and southern states. As settlement and agriculture spread westward from the early 1600s to the 1920s, forestlands in the east were cleared and tallgrass prairie was plowed under. Land that wasn't cleared for farming or pasture was cleared for other purposes, usually to provide fuel and building materials. But as the productivity of agriculture grew in the nineteenth century, eastern lands less suitable for farming were abandoned and gradually reverted to woodland, so that much of the eastern United States today is reforested. But the tallgrass prairie of the eastern plains and most of the forest of the central states have been replaced by farms, and so what was once oak forest or grassland is now fields of corn, soybeans, and wheat.

In addition to this dramatic land use change, there have been equally drastic changes covering smaller areas as cities and other developed areas have expanded. Urban lands now occupy about 2 percent of the coun-

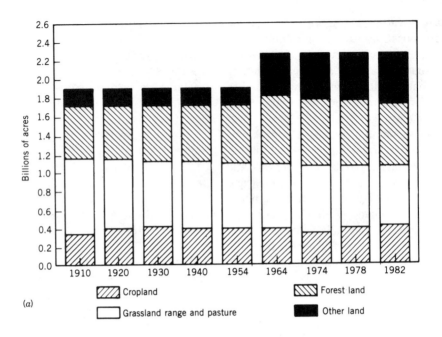

(a)

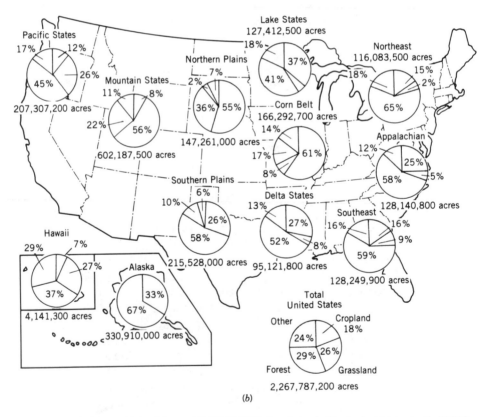

(b)

Figure 6.5   Land use in the United States (1910–1982). Land use is illustrated historically (1910–1982) (*a*) and regionally (*b*) for 1982. (*Source:* Council on Environmental Quality, 1989.)

try, and transportation uses occupy another 1 percent. Reservoirs also have taken substantial areas. The amount of land in urban uses continues to increase at about 1.3 percent per year (CEQ, 1989). Rural areas are also being committed to new uses, most importantly as parks and wildlife areas. National parks occupy over 3 percent of the land area of the United States, and national wildlife refuges and designated wilderness areas each cover an additional 4 percent of the nation's land (CEQ, 1989).

About a third of the U.S. land is in public ownership. In areas of the eastern United States that were territories of the original British colonies, land was granted by the British government to various companies and private individuals, or was granted by the states as payment for military service, and almost all land has been in private hands since the late eighteenth century. But most of the land west of the Mississippi River (excluding Texas) was acquired by the U.S. government by treaty or purchase. Through homesteading, grants to railroads, and other means, most of the more productive land came under private ownership, mostly in the second half of the nineteenth century. But semiarid and arid areas and high mountain areas that were not desirable for agriculture remained unclaimed into the early twentieth century. Many of the mountainous areas were reserved as National Forests, and so most federally owned land consists of these arid and/or mountainous areas in the western United States. Thirty-two percent of U.S. land is in federal ownership, 7 percent is state owned, 2 percent is owned by American Indians, and the remaining 59 percent is in private hands (CEQ, 1989).

LAND USE PROBLEMS

Land use decisions are probably the most important single issue in environmental management, for land use essentially defines what kinds of resources we exploit and the extent of environmental impact associated with our activities. If a parcel of land is used for agriculture, then not only does this contribute to our total food production but it also means that runoff from that land will contain certain byproducts of agriculture (sediment, nutrients, and pesticides) in nonpoint water pollution. The use of a parcel of land for one purpose has implications for other parcels: urban growth may mean a demand for recreational lands nearby, or the need for watershed protection in other areas to supply a growing population with drinking water.

In most of the world, land use decisions are made through some process of balancing competing interests. In market economies, allocation of land among various uses is generally determined by the relative income that can be generated at any given time. Agricultural land near cities is sold for urban development because those uses generate greater profits for the landowner than agriculture (Fig. 6.6). Similarly, farmers shift land among crops, pasture, and other uses depending on production costs and the return on investment for various commodities.

Governments play a role in this process in market economies as well as in centrally planned economies. Public interests are served by allocation of land to transportation, parks, water resources, defense, and similar

Figure 6.6 Suburban encroachment into prime agricultural lands. Suburbanization is one of the main factors contributing to the loss of agricultural land in places like California, where the high cost of housing has forced residents to locate in previously agricultural areas in the Central Valley.

common needs. In most countries there is also regulation of the patterns as well as types of land uses. In the United States this is accomplished by zoning laws, usually at the local level, which are generally designed to separate incompatible uses, such as industry and residences. Land use regulations are also used to ensure adequate open space, such as through the designation of greenbelt areas around cities, and for environmental protection as in restrictions on development in wetland areas (see Issue 6–1) and prohibition of waste disposal on floodplains.

As populations grow and land becomes scarcer, competition for land resources and the intensity of debate over land use decisions inevitably increase. There are many examples of such problems, ranging from the restriction of oil exploration or timber harvesting from wildlife refuges to local debates over where to locate a sewage treatment plant. The following sections provide examples of two important land-related issues: solid waste disposal and mined-land reclamation.

SOLID WASTE DISPOSAL

In preindustrial times, when populations were lower and more dispersed and rates of production and consumption of goods were much lower, waste disposal was a much smaller problem than it is today. Of course there have been waste dumps for millennia, and ancient ones are invaluable to modern archaeologists. But in modern urban-industrial societies, with populations exceeding 1000 per square kilometer in extensive megalopolitan regions, the problem is on a different scale. In the 1980s it reached crisis proportions in much of the United States.

Solid waste generation in the United States has steadily increased in recent decades as the nation has become wealthier and consumed more goods (Fig. 6.7) (see Issue 6–2). Per capita solid waste generation is currently about 3.4 pounds per person per day, or about 160 million tons per year nationwide (Office of Technology Assessment, 1989). Figure 6.8 illustrates the content of municipal solid waste. About 11 percent of this waste is recovered (primarily paper and paperboard) and 6 percent is processed for energy recovery by combustion or pyrolysis. About 92 percent of the remaining 3 pounds per person per day is disposed of in *landfills*; most of the rest is burned (Forester, 1988).

There are thousands of operating landfills in the United States today, but the number is declining rapidly. In 1976 the number of operating landfills was about 30,000 nationwide; by

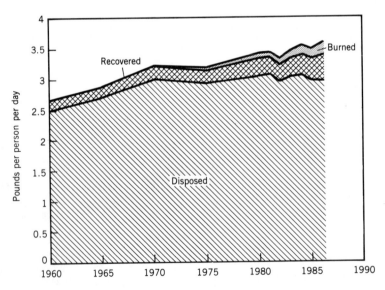

Figure 6.7   Disposition of solid waste in the United States, 1960–1986. Most solid waste is disposed of in landfills, but the portions recovered and burned are slowly increasing. (*Source:* U.S. Bureau of the Census, 1989.)

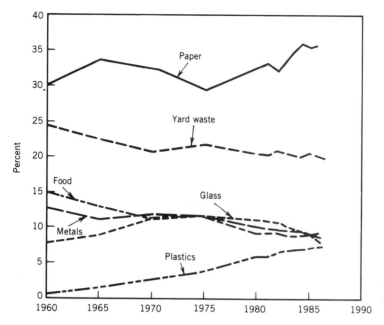

Figure 6.8   Composition of municipal solid waste in the United States, 1960–1986. Paper and yard waste have consistently accounted for more than half of the waste stream, with smaller portions of metal, food, glass, and plastic. The plastic content of solid waste has steadily increased. (*Source:* U.S. Bureau of the Census, 1989.)

1984 this decreased to slightly over 9000, and a 1987 survey put the number at 6584 (Forester, 1988). This decline is the result of an increased awareness of the environmental impacts of landfills, particularly the potential for groundwater pollution. Until recently most landfills were sited on whatever low-value land was available, without regard for environmental impacts other than unpleasant odors experienced nearby. But with the great increase in awareness of groundwater pollution problems in the 1970s and 1980s, many new restrictions on landfill siting and operation have been imposed. Many operating landfills were closed, and the number of potential sites for new ones was greatly reduced (Fig. 6.9).

Figure 6.9   Landfills. The number of operating landfills is rapidly declining, forcing to reevaluation of our consumptive habits and how we manage our solid waste.

(a)

(b)

Figure 6.10   Surface mining and land use changes. Surface mining causes great scarring on the land (a). Eleven years after reclamations (b), the land here in Wise County, Virginia, is shown restored to its approximate original topography.

The landfill crisis is one of many examples of the need for sites for special land uses that are not easily compatible with other uses. Other examples include nuclear power plants, mineral extraction facilities, chemical waste processing facilities, and similar potentially hazardous or noxious land uses to which many people say "not in my backyard." The not-in-my-backyard dilemma is a result of the growing awareness of environmental (and especially toxic substance) problems associated with modern industrial society, in an era of intense competition over land use. This competition can only intensify as world population increases and more people demand more things from a finite land base.

MINED-LAND RECLAMATION

Incompatibility is one important land use problem; another is the irreversibility of many land use decisions. Once a city or a reservoir is built, and land is converted to a new use, it is virtually impossible to reverse this action. Construction of houses and roads destroys the underlying soil, eliminating the possibility of agricultural use. Reservoirs fill with sediment, obliterating the previous soil surface and al-

tering the shape of the land. The Reagan administration proposed draining the controversial Hetch-Hetchy reservoir in California and allowing it to revert to parkland, but this proposal was more a political gesture than a realistic plan.

An example of a partially irreversible land use change is that caused by surface mining (Fig. 6.10). This is particularly sensitive on prime agricultural land—land on which crops can be produced for the least cost and with the least damage to the resource base. In surface mining for coal, for example, usually the soil and some overburden beneath it are first re-

---

ISSUE 6–1 "No Net Loss": For Whom?

What is a wetland? We have many names for it: swamp, marsh, bog, fen, peatland, bottomland, wet meadow, slough, and pothole are just a few. Some of the names have negative connotations, because until recently wetlands, whatever their name, were synonymous with wastelands. Ever since human beings began to manipulate the environment for their own uses, wetlands, both marine and freshwater, have been targets for "reclamation": the only good wetland, people believed, was a drained, filled-in, or paved-over one. Boston's Back Bay, Chicago's Loop, and most of New Orleans, now covered with skyscrapers, were once soggy wetlands and considered to be an unproductive nuisance: a source of disease, a breeding ground for harmful insects, a place of decay.

In the United States it is estimated that over half of the country's wetlands are gone: of the 200 million acres (81 million ha) of wetlands present in the contiguous 48 states at the time of European settlement, only 95 million acres (38 million ha) remain. From the mid-1950s to the mid-1970s, 11 million wetland acres (4.5 million ha) were converted (550,000 acres or 223,000 ha annually), mostly to farmland but also to land for suburban housing, mining, and landfills. About 5 percent of the total loss was due to natural causes, such as erosion, subsidence, and storms. Since the early 1980s, environmental record-keeping has been much reduced, but estimates of continued wetland loss range from 240,000–360,000 acres (97,000–146,000 ha) per year.

Since 1975 there has been limited federal protection of wetlands, but nonetheless wetland loss has continued. Beginning in 1985, the U.S. Congress prohibited subsidies and other federal support for farmers growing crops on newly converted farmlands, and debate is intense over whether or not the "no-net-loss" principle introduced by the National Wetlands Policy Foundation in 1988 should become law. Property owners and real estate developers are adamantly opposed to the concept, which proposes that there be no more wetlands lost: if farmers or developers want to fill in wetlands then they must simultaneously create wetlands elsewhere or reconvert former wetlands to their natural state, resulting in no net loss of wetlands.

Why all this debate over land that was until recently regarded as less than worthless, land that was being "improved" by filling it in? First, in an increasingly crowded world, any open land is seen as more valuable, either for use or for conservation, and second, careful scientific study has revealed that wetlands are not simply the dumps of the natural world. They are complex, thriving, and biologically healthy and provide "services" to a broad range of species—including human beings—that are essential to their survival.

- They absorb floodwaters by holding a river's excess flow until a flood peak has passed and the river can handle the drainage. When riverside wetlands are

moved. The coal is then extracted, and the overburden and soil are replaced. In the past the replacement of overburden was minimal; generally overburden was simply dumped on areas that had already been mined with no further surface improvements. In 1977 the Surface Mining Control and Reclamation Act was passed, which requires *mined-land reclamation*, in which the land is restored to its approximate original topography and capabilities.

As will be discussed in the next chapter, soil has distinct layers that vary in thickness from a few inches to a few feet and develop over periods of hundreds to thousands of years. To remove soil from a large area, store it for a few months or years, and then replace it

and restore its original productivity is not a simple matter. Generally, the federal Office of Surface Mining, requires that mine operators remove and replace individual soil horizons separately so as to leave a soil that is as close to the premining condition as possible.

This problem is a minor one nationwide, because only about 10,000 acres (4050 ha) of prime farmland, or about 0.003 percent of the nation's prime farmland base, are disturbed by surface mining annually (Plotkin, 1986). But locally the agricultural impacts can be significant, particularly in Illinois. Mining companies have made major efforts to develop techniques for restoring soil productivity in these areas, and considerable progress has been made. Although enforcement of surface mining laws

---

paved over, the effects can be disastrous in urban areas.

- They are our nation's fish nurseries. Wetlands have high rates of plant growth and rich fauna and flora, creating ideal spawning and feeding conditions. When wetlands are polluted or converted to other uses, fish populations decline.

- Wetlands purify groundwater. If kept at manageable levels, pollutants are absorbed from water by wetland shrubs and trees, thus cleaning the water that flows through. Much of this water seeps underground to be reabsorbed into the groundwater supplies that humans rely on. When wetlands are converted to development or used as pollution sinks, this filtration and cleansing process comes to an abrupt halt, and our water supplies can become undrinkable.

- Wetlands are critically important to birds and waterfowl as protected places to breed, nest, and rest on long migratory flights. The wetland areas most threatened by farmland conversion are the prairie potholes of the upper Midwest, where glaciers left ice chunks that melted, resulting in hundreds of thousands of small ponds and lakes. Farmers object that you cannot grow wheat in these areas and so have brought in bulldozers and backhoes to build miles of drainage ditches. But you

cannot grow ducks on stubble, and the estimated 80 percent of the U.S. ducks that use this region have been severely affected by this massive habitat loss.

The recent turnabout in the valuation of wetlands has left many farmers and property owners profoundly confused. According to the environmental values prevalent until the 1970s, humankind benefited from the extermination of that pestilent landform, the wetland. Wetlands had little economic value and were regarded as a nuisance until they were converted to other uses. Wetlands adjacent to prime commercial lands were the ideal targets for development: buy them for next to nothing, put up a sign reading "clean fill wanted," and you've got a pad for a gas station in no time. So the sudden reversal of wetland values has left property owners angry and disappointed.

Economic incentives may be necessary to encourage the "no-net-loss" principle and to ease its transition into law. Tax breaks for land donations to reserves, subsidies to farmers who retain wetlands instead of converting them, and outright purchase of wetlands by private organizations and public governments are the main strategies at present, and are being used to save Georgia's Okefenokee Swamp, Florida's Everglades, the Mississippi River delta, and thousands of other locations in the Southeast, upper Midwest, and the northeastern coastal states (Stevens, 1990).

has been lax at times, there is evidence that restoring productivity is technically feasible, and questions of cost are probably more important than technological problems in restoration of mined lands.

LAND USE POLICY IN THE UNITED STATES

Under the U.S. Constitution, the power to regulate land use is in the hands of the states, but in most states land use policy is made at the local (municipal and/or county) level. Where land use is regulated, regulations take the form of *zoning* laws, in which a government agency prepares a map of acceptable uses for the land within its jurisdiction. These maps are based primarily on existing uses, with desired future uses designated for undeveloped areas. A property owner is obliged to use the land according to these zoning regulations, unless specific permission for a variance to the stated plan is granted. In most of the United States, zoning is only enforced in relatively densely populated areas. Virtually all cities are zoned,

as are most counties in areas of rapid urban development. In recent years, as development pressure has grown along with the desire to preserve land in rural areas, conflicts over land use have prompted state governments to expand land use controls (see Issue 6–3). Several states now have statewide land use regulations, and this trend can be expected to continue.

Although land use control is a power of state government, the federal government also exerts its influence. In the eighteenth and nineteenth centuries the prevailing policy was to encourage as much development as possible, and this was accomplished through programs for transfer of federal land to private hands. But beginning in the late nineteenth century, there has been increasing planning and management of federally owned lands, particularly by the Forest Service and the Bureau of Land Management, which together control the bulk of federal lands. More recently, there have been measures to influence, if not control, land use on some sensitive lands. Most notable are measures to preserve wetlands, establish wildlife reserves and protect

---

ISSUE 6–2   Pampers, Huggies, and Luvs in the Environment

Eighty-five percent of moms and dads in this country use disposable diapers on their infants. Considering that an average baby uses 10,000 diapers before she or he is toilet-trained, this adds up to a phenomenal number of diapers. In 1988, 18 billion single-use diapers (the euphemism for disposable diapers) were sold in the United States, netting $3.5 billion in sales. This means that 18 billion diapers must also be disposed per year, a staggering 12,300 tons of waste per day. Recent estimates suggest that disposable diapers constitute between 2 and 4 percent of all municipal solid waste. Since many parents do not remove fecal material from the diapers, nearly 3 tons of baby poop are landfilled each year. Fecal contamination of groundwater is a worrisome health issue.

Disposable diapers were first developed in the 1950s. The largest manufacturers are Procter and Gamble (Pampers and Luvs) and Kimberly Clark (Huggies). Procter and Gamble

patented a remarkable way to make parents' life easier, but the convenience took a while for the American public to embrace. In 1961, Pampers had less than 1 percent of all diaper sales since most parents were still using cloth diapers. By 1990, Pampers cornered the market with 85 percent of all sales. As newborn babies left the hospitals, new mothers and fathers were treated to care packages provided by the baby industry—lotion, powder, and of course, disposable diapers. Parents are programmed early on that disposable diapers make sense: easy to use with no pins, just resealable flaps, super absorbency so baby has less diaper rash, and of course very little mess, just wrap up and throw away.

Most disposable diapers are two-thirds cellulose and thus potentially biodegradable, but the remaining one-third is plastic. It takes over one billion tons of wood pulp and 75,000 metric tons of plastic to produce the 1.8 billion diapers sold in 1988. So-called degradable diapers take

wildlife habitat, and restrict agricultural use of erodible lands.

Clearly, issues of land use are intimately involved with virtually every environmental or natural resource question. Every piece of land has several potential uses, and usually these uses are incompatible. Land cannot be used as a strip mine and a farm at the same time; logging and wilderness are by definition mutually exclusive. At the same time, many uses are mutually compatible: moderate-intensity recreation is compatible with water resource development, and agriculture is compatible with open space preservation. Even if these compatibility questions can be worked out, other difficult issues remain. A decision to convert a forested area to agriculture, or to reduce loss of agricultural land through a preferential property tax system, or to open an agricultural area to urban uses, implies a wide range of physical and economic impacts. These are the clear and visible aspects of environmental policy and are the frequent battleground in the natural resources debate.

REFERENCES AND ADDITIONAL READING

Caves, R.W. 1990. Determining land use policy via the ballot box: The growth initiative blitz in California. *Land Use Policy* 7: 70–79.

Council on Environmental Quality. 1989. *Environmental Trends*. Washington, DC: U.S. Government Printing Office.

Feder, B.J. 1989. What's new in diapers. *The New York Times*, March 12, pp. C3–15.

Food and Agricultural Organization. 1989. *1988 FAO Production Yearbook*. Rome: United Nations, Food and Agricultural Organization.

Forester, W.S. 1988. Solid waste: There's a lot more coming. *EPA J.* 14(4): 11–12.

Lewis, J. 1989. What's in the solid waste stream? *EPA J.* 15(2): 15–17.

Lyman, F. 1990. Diaper hype. *Garbage* 2(1): 36–40.

Morgenson, G., and B. Eisenstodt. 1990. Profits are for rape and pillage. *Forbes*, March 15, pp. 94–100.

Office of Technology Assessment. 1989. *Facing America's Trash: What Next for Municipal*

500 years or so to break down because they need water and oxygen to do so, which are noticeably absent in modern airtight and watertight landfills. In addition, the "degradable disposable" diaper with the cornstarch-based plastic backing uses just as much wood pulp and plastic as the conventional disposable one.

Until very recently, it was virtually impossible to find cloth diapers or a diaper service in many parts of the country even if you were willing to pay more. Things have finally changed. Cloth diapers are making a comeback and so are diaper services. Cotton diapers can be reused up to 150 times before they finally give out, and it takes only six months for them to degrade in landfills. Because of a large influx of cloth diapers from China in the mid-1980s, U.S. manufacturers cut production by 45 percent. In 1987, the United States placed import restrictions on Chinese cloth diapers to 1.34 million pounds to enable U.S. manufacturers (Gerber Products and

Dundee Mills) to compete in this growing market. Rather than entering the diaper vendor market (the diaper services), however, the American manufacturers are concentrating on retail sales (estimated worth $35 million) for the 48 million cloth diapers sold each year.

The economics of disposable versus cloth diapers are interesting as well. Disposables were always marketed as costing more (up to 50 percent more), but the convenience was supposedly worth it. A single-use diaper costs about 22 cents, whereas a so-called biodegradable diaper costs between 26 and 39 cents. If one includes washing, labor, electricity, fuel, and so forth, cloth diapers cost 13 cents each, whereas a diaper service charges about 15 cents. So why aren't more parents using cloth since it makes both environmental and economic sense? Perhaps you can reverse the diaper trend by demanding that your children be swathed in cloth rather than plastic (Feder, 1989; Morgenson and Eisenstodt, 1990, Lyman, 1990).

Solid Waste. OTA-0-424. Washington, DC: U.S. Government Printing Office.

Plotkin, S.E. 1986. From surface mine to cropland. *Environment* 28(1): 17–20,40–44.

Schumacher, E.F. 1973. *Small is Beautiful.* New York: Harper & Row.

Soil Conservation Service. 1987. *Basic Statistics, 1982 National Resources Inventory.* Iowa State University, Statistical Laboratory, Statistical Bulletin 756. Ames: Iowa State Univ. Statistical Laboratory.

Stevens, W.K. 1990. Efforts to halt wetland loss turn their attention inland. *The New York Times,* March 13, pp. C1, C12.

U.S. Bureau of the Census. 1989. *Statistical Abstract of the United States.* Washington, DC: U.S. Government Printing Office.

U.S. Department of Agriculture. 1989. *The Second RCA Appraisal.* Washington, DC: U.S. Department of Agriculture.

TERMS TO KNOW

Arable Land
Biome
Bioregion

ISSUE 6–3   Citizens in Control: Planning Via the Ballot Box

Who is best able to make decisions—our elected leaders or we ourselves? This question is becoming increasingly important for environmental policy matters. Citizens in California, dissatisfied with inaction by local and state governments, are taking matters into their own hands directly via the ballot box.

The California Supreme Court describes voter initiatives as "in essence a legislative battering ram which may be used to tear through the exasperating tangle of the traditional legislative procedure and strike directly toward the desired end" (quoted in Caves, 1990). Today, officials receive conflicting messages from their electorate, as some citizens continue to root for growth at any cost, while others demand immediate action on new quality-of-life issues.

Along with the development of an environmental awareness among the general public has come a desire for action. A generation or more ago, people accepted their fates as shopping centers sprang up in quiet neighborhoods, super-highways were built through parklands, and factories dumped wastes into local streams. These indicators of growth were regarded as the necessary price of prosperity, but not anymore. Quiet, everyday citizens are no longer willing to pay this price, and they feel that something is wrong with growth if it requires such sacrifices. For many Americans—and people elsewhere—the quality of life is now as important, if not more so, than the growth that accompanies prosperity.

This new attitude strikes a blow at the core of the American way of life, which was built on the basic beliefs that growth is good and bigger is better. When E.F. Schumacher introduced the pro-environment motto "small is beautiful" in 1973, his views were embraced by a small minority of Americans. After all, the United States' greatness stems in part from its having the most, of being able to construct the biggest, and its citizens being willing to forsake other amenities in order to get ahead and be first. America's cities have traditionally vied for titles of "largest population," "largest area," "the most industry," and so on. But growth is no longer synonymous with good in the minds of many Americans.

Most American communities were established according to the old growth-oriented rules, and city governments are set up to continue this trend. Land acquisition and use, zoning, tax incentives to business, suburbanization, highway construction, all are oriented toward growth-based industries such as real estate and construction, as well as the general desire to expand business activity. These giant urban engines are now ever-so-slowly turning in a new direction, toward land use controls, population caps, pollution control, and moratoria on industrialization.

California is a hotbed of this ballot box land use planning, as citizens have had the right since 1911 to vote directly on municipal (city-level) ordinances and to reject or approve ordinances

Biosphere
Boreal Forest
Chaparral
Cropland
Desert
Farmland
Grassland
Landfill
Mined-Land Reclamation
Pasture
Permafrost
Potential Evapotranspiration
Rangeland
Savanna
Solid Waste
Temperate Forest
Tropical Rainforest
Tundra
Zoning

STUDY QUESTIONS

1. What are some of the major biomes of the world? What are their characteristics?

2. Why is the concept of bioregions useful in environmental management?

3. Consider a land use issue facing your local area. What are the alternatives being considered? Which land uses are compatible, and which are incompatible? What are the environmental implications of the decision?

4. How have the relative amounts of land in forest, cropland, rangeland, and other uses in the United States varied in the past 100 years?

5. What are the major land use trends taking place in the world today? How are land uses changing in poor as opposed to wealthy countries?

---

passed by their city councils. Other western states and Ohio, Massachusetts, Maine, and Maryland allow citizen initiatives at the municipal levels, as do a number of other countries (Caves, 1990). Some recent examples of land use planning via direct democracy include:

- Portland, Maine: Voters approved a restriction on a portion of the city's waterfront to limit buildings solely to marine uses.

- Ocean City, Maryland: Troubled at the number of high-rise buildings for vacationers, voters approved a stop to any construction high enough to cast a shadow on another person's property.

- Cape Cod, Massachusetts: In the face of galloping recreation and retirement-related growth, voters approved two nonbinding referenda to stop development and create a regional planning authority.

- Seattle, Washington: A voter-controlled downtown development plan restricts the amount of new office space and limits building height.

In California, where the tradition of citizen-initiative legislation is strongest, voters have had state-level opportunities to control property taxes and restrict coastal development, and at the municipal level to decide on issues relating to the environment, political reform, rent control, property tax relief, the death penalty, nuclear power and weaponry, and public disclosure of toxic and hazardous materials use. Between 1971 and 1986, over 150 local land use issues were on the ballot in California elections.

The San Diego region of southern California is projected to grow by over 26 percent between 1986 and 2000, a rate higher than the California average and twice the national average. Citizens who were concerned about the environmental and quality-of-life consequences of recent defense industry growth introduced 18 growth-control ballot measures between 1985 and 1988. Ten were voted into law. These initiatives relate to control over the number of dwelling units, availability of public facilities in new neighborhoods, citizen control over zoning, and open space preservation, among many other issues.

Is ballot box planning good or bad? Those who dislike it ask: Are average citizens capable of comprehending complex socioeconomic issues? Are small groups manipulating the larger citizenry into supporting elitist growth-control measures? Is planning possible when citizens can continually interfere with it? Those who support it respond that the more citizens participate, the better our government is, and that ballot initiatives educate the public and serve as signals to government that its populace is unhappy and wants changes. In any case, citizen-based voter initiatives are on the rise as everyday people struggle to protect and enhance what they see as the good life (Caves, 1990).

7

Agricultural Resources

INTRODUCTION

To Thomas Jefferson, the future of American agriculture was based on the family farm, providing subsistence to the family that owned and ran it, with any surplus sold to supply nonfarm families with food and bring cash income to the farmer. This vision was realized for the first 150 years of U.S. history, when westward expansion of settlement, aided by government land grants to soldiers and homesteaders, facilitated the establishment of family farms in the fertile Midwest. But over the last century the introduction of hybrid corn and heavy machinery changed the economics of the farm. No longer was 160 acres a reasonable size farm for a family to operate. Instead, it was possible to cultivate much larger areas with only a few workers. Changing agricultural technology increased the capital requirements of farming so that land itself was no longer the major requirement for farming; access to large amounts of capital was also necessary. The mid-twentieth century, then, has seen a shift away from the small family farm toward large farms run as businesses, many still family owned but more and more owned by corporations. This change in the needs and aspirations of farmers has changed the way farmland is managed.

The world agricultural situation has also changed. Increased trade, famine, and poverty in much of the world have heightened awareness of agricultural production as a global resource. American farmers today serve markets around the world, and production is thus affected by world market and trade factors. Although American agriculture is immensely productive and the United States is a major food exporter, it has yet to make a significant contribution to alleviating food shortages in the Third World.

THE WORLD AGRICULTURAL RESOURCE BASE

The total land area of the world is about 32 billion acres (13 billion ha). Of this, only about 12 percent is presently *arable*, or suitable for cultivated agriculture (Alexandratos, 1988). Figure 7.1 is a map showing the distribution of arable land in the world. One Food and Agricultural Organization (FAO) estimate suggests that between 1983 and 2000, 405 million acres (164 million ha) must be brought into use just to keep pace with population increases (Alexandratos, 1988). The potential for increased arable land worldwide is more than double that presently cultivated, but it is unlikely that this land area will ever be placed in production. Rather, more realistic estimates of the potential increase in arable land over the next few decades are on the order of 10 percent. Much of the potentially arable land is semiarid or arid and would require irrigation or has other limitations such as forest cover, poor drainage, or steep slopes. Large increases in agricultural land would require major technological advances in water supply, plant breeding, and cultivation techniques, as well as displacing other land uses such as forestry and grazing. Technological advances and replacement of these other resources require large amounts of capital, which is not likely to be available in the areas where it is needed most.

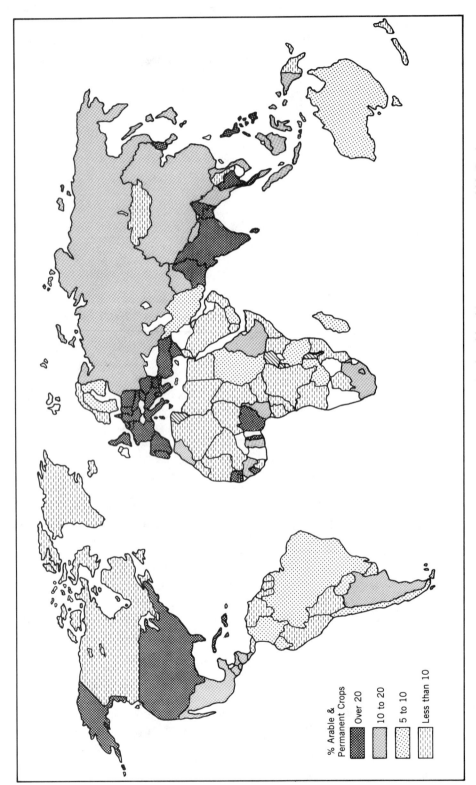

Figure 7.1 World agricultural land. Percent arable land and land in permanent crops, 1988 (FAO, 1989).

Arable land is not uniformly distributed in relation to population. Although Asia has the most arable land, it also has an immense population to feed. On the other hand, North America has much arable land and a relatively small population. When we consider that American agriculture generally produces higher yields per acre than systems where fertilizers and pesticides are less available, the disparities from one area to another are even greater.

The world's food supply is based on about 30 major crops. The top 7 (wheat, rice, maize, potatoes, barley, sweet potatoes, and cassava) have annual harvests of 100 million metric tons or more, and these 7 account for more than half the harvest of the top 30 crops. In terms of global meat supply, 7 species provide more than 95 percent of all meat production. Pigs and cattle are first and second, poultry is third, followed by much smaller contributions from lamb, goat, buffalo, and horse (Crabbe and Lawson, 1981; Harlan, 1976). Meat supplies about 17 percent of the calories and 35 percent of the protein that humans consume.

There are great disparities in the amounts and kinds of food consumed in rich and poor nations, with rich nations not only eating more, but also better. Increasingly around the world, locally domesticated and harvested plants and animals are being replaced by these relatively few global food sources, either grown locally or imported. This replacement is the result of many complex factors, including increased trade, mechanization, the spread of high-yielding varieties, and cultural change. Some experts decry this loss of food source flexibility, in the belief that a broader base of food crops is safer in case of widespread plant diseases. A broad crop base can also reduce susceptibility to weather fluctuations and climatic change.

Agricultural production has been increasing in the Third World as a result of cultivation of new land and improved production on a per hectare basis, but population is also rising. Over a 15-year period to the mid-1970s, 92 nations with developing market economies expanded their food production at a rate of 2.6 percent per year, just barely keeping even with population growth (Fig. 7.2).

One success story is found in India, where even after severe droughts the agricultural improvements of the last 15 years have made it possible to produce enough food for self-sufficiency. This has been achieved through planning by the Indian government and development experts, and with the expanded use of fertilizers, irrigation, and high-yielding crop varieties. However, uneven food distribution remains a problem, as it is estimated that nearly half of India's population eats less than two meals a day (Kaufman, 1980).

In other parts of the world the situation remains critical. In 1982, a drought in southern Africa destroyed hopes for increased self-sufficiency in that region. Botswana, Namibia, Mozambique, Zimbabwe, and South Africa were reduced once again to importing grain. A 1982 FAO survey listed 24 countries with "serious food shortages," 19 of these in Africa. Faced with rising costs of fuel oil, conversion to cash crops for sale or export, rising populations, warfare, and uncertain weather, it is a continuing struggle for these and other countries to attain food self-sufficiency.

THE U.S. AGRICULTURAL RESOURCE BASE

About 70 percent of U.S. land is classified as agricultural land. "Agricultural land" is a broad term, however, and includes cropland, rangeland, forestland, and pastureland. Cropland, or land on which crops are presently grown, comprises only about 25 percent of agricultural land. The cropland area of the United States amounts to about 1.5 acres (0.6 ha) per person, as compared with the global average of 0.8 acres (0.32 ha) per person.

America has always been a land of agricultural abundance, with a large area of arable land and a relatively small population. Through the first two centuries of European settlement in North America, agriculture was based largely on a fertile soil resource, supplemented in some sectors by cheap slave and indentured labor. In the mid-nineteenth century, the opening of the Great Plains was facilitated in part by the development of the steel plow, one of many major innovations contributing to the

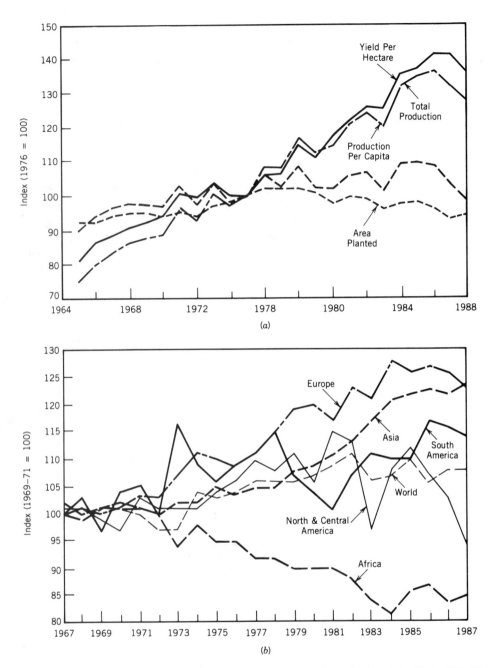

Figure 7.2(a)   World food production. World cereals production indices, 1964–1988 (1975-100). Yield per acre has steadily increased, causing an increase in total production without a substantial increase in area planted. Per capita production increased substantially in the 1970s and early 1980s, but declined in the late 1980s. (*Source:* FAO, 1989; previous editions of the same volume back to 1968.) (*b*) Per capita food production indices (1969–1971–100) for selected regions.

growth of U.S. agricultural production. Today the U.S. agricultural system is among the most technologically advanced in the world.

American agriculture is based on high and continual inputs of capital and replacement of animal power and human labor by machines, which has resulted in drastic reductions in the number of farms and farm workers. This has culminated in an agricultural system that, unlike those in traditional societies, is operated as a complex of small and large businesses whose primary goal is earning money rather than producing food for subsistence. This system has come to be known as *agribusiness.*

THE UNITED STATES AND THE WORLD FOOD SITUATION

U.S. agriculture dominates food exports in the world economy, with American grain exports accounting for over half of the world total. American agriculture feeds many more people than live in the United States, and there is potential for even greater food exports. In addition, the average American consumer pays a much smaller portion of disposable income for food than those in most of the rest of the world.

Farming in the United States has been profitable at times and unprofitable at others. This is illustrated by recent trends in area harvested, yields, and total production of corn (Fig. 7.3). In the early 1970s, increasing world demand for grain and government policies favoring exports stimulated farmers to increase production. Area planted expanded, and with relatively favorable weather, yields and total production rose substantially. This period was also one of considerable investment in agricul-

tural land and machinery. But bumper harvests in the late 1970s kept prices down, while inflation continued to force costs and interest rates up. In 1981, farm debts stood at $194.5 billion, double the 1975 figure, and by 1983 they were $216 billion. Over the same period, farm expenses rose from $75.9 billion to $141.5 billion annually, with a 1981 net farm income of $22.9 billion as compared to $24.5 billion in 1975. Prices paid for crops rose 34 percent from 1977 to 1981, while fuel prices went up 113 percent. In the mid-1980s this decline in profitability, coupled with government policies aimed at reducing production, led to a substantial decline in area harvested, with associated production declines. In the late 1980s the situation improved as a result of a combination of lower interest rates, lower acreages planted, and stable prices for inputs such as fuel and chemicals, and by 1990 farming was again becoming profitable.

Because the United States exports so much food, American agricultural prosperity is closely linked to world agricultural markets. These markets exert an important influence on agriculture in both the rich and the poor nations. In recent decades the general pattern has been one of government policies that encourage production by keeping domestic

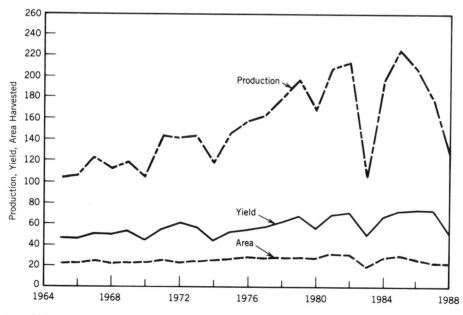

Figure 7.3 U.S. corn production, 1965–1988. (*Source:* FAO, 1989.) Production is shown in millions of metric tons. Yield is shown in hundreds of kilograms per hectare. Area harvested is shown in millions of hectares.

prices high and that encourage exports by subsidizing such sales. This has the effect of keeping world market prices low, and thus making it difficult for poorer nations to export agricultural products. At the same time, many Third World nations have followed policies that keep their domestic prices low in order to keep food within reach of their poorer citizens. These low domestic prices in Third World countries discourage production there, and most Third World nations lack the foreign currency needed to import enough food to meet their needs. The situation is therefore one of considerable imbalance: the United States and other wealthy nations overproduce and the Third World underproduces, in a world market that makes it difficult for rich nations to sell to poor ones.

THE IMPORTANCE OF GOVERNMENTAL AGRICULTURAL POLICIES

Throughout the world, in capitalist and socialist economies alike, agriculture is considered to be of fundamental importance to national welfare—including social and cultural issues as well as economic prosperity and food supply. Because of this, virtually every government in the world intervenes in the agricultural system in a variety of ways. Most important among these policies are those intended to affect the quantity of production and the prices of agricultural commodities.

In most capitalist countries, these policies take the form of economic incentives or disincentives for production. In the United States, for example, the Department of Agriculture has programs that provide a form of insurance to farmers against crop failure. If a harvest is low because of bad weather or disease, or if prices are too low at harvest time for the farmer to sell the crops for a good return on investment, the government in effect buys the crop at a guaranteed price. There are also programs to limit production and thus keep prices high. In many cases farmers are only allowed to receive government subsidies or price guarantees if they agree to limit the amount of land they cultivate.

Since the depression of the 1930s, the thrust of most U.S. agricultural policies has been to subsidize agricultural income and maintain higher prices than would occur in a free market, while restraining production and pursuing conservation goals. These policies have had the effect of generating more production than the market can absorb, and the government has accumulated surpluses of agricultural commodities. Some of these surpluses have been sold on the world market, usually at prices below domestic levels, while others have been given to famine relief and welfare programs. In Western Europe similar policies have been pursued, with the result that enormous surpluses of many commodities have accumulated.

In many Third World countries, a very different approach has been taken. There, where poverty and malnourishment are continual problems, it has been common to keep food prices artificially low in order to make food more available to the poor. But unless the government buys food at a high price from the farmer and then sells it at a low price, these price controls have the effect of reducing incentives for farmers to produce. Thus farmers have not been willing or able to make the investments necessary to increase agricultural production to meet the needs of growing populations.

Recently the nature of these policy effects has been more widely recognized, and many governments are beginning to reorient their agricultural policies. The Food Security Act of 1985 in the United States represents a significant step in that direction. Although reductions in price supports had been occurring for years, such reductions were made a more central part of the farm policy program. The 1985 Act also contained important environmental provisions, most important of which are incentives designed to reduce the cultivated acreage of erodible land and wetlands. Elsewhere in the world there is similar pressure to reduce governmental intervention in agricultural markets, and thereby address the tremendous imbalance between overproduction in wealthy countries and underproduction in poor countries. But changes in agricultural policies inevitably have wide-ranging social and political consequences, and affected interest groups often resist and slow this trend.

MODERN AMERICAN AGRICULTURAL SYSTEMS

American agriculture today includes both mixed and monocultural cropping systems. *Mixed cropping* systems are agricultural systems that combine several different crops in a single farm unit. They usually include crops both for human consumption and for fodder (animal feed). Mixed cropping is used in areas where several different crops can be grown with roughly the same profit per acre and in dairy farming areas. A typical dairy farm in the northeastern United States might include corn and alfalfa grown for fodder for dairy cattle, with milk marketed for cash income. By producing several different animal and vegetable products simultaneously, mixed farming systems make efficient use of the land resource while minimizing susceptibility to unfavorable weather or market conditions for any one commodity. Mixed systems benefit from crop rotation, in which the crops grown on a given parcel of land are changed from year to year or season to season, thus reducing depletion of particular nutrients. These farmers also may make greater use of plants by feeding otherwise unused parts of plants to animals and by returning some organic matter to the fields in the form of manure.

Monoculture is an agricultural system in which just one crop is cultivated repeatedly over a large area. Other, much more distinctive characteristics of modern monocultural systems include a reliance on technology (in the form of machines), specialized plant varieties, fertilizers, and pesticides. This technological agriculture is most developed in the United States, but is found in most of the wealthy nations of the world. Monoculture is necessary to take advantage of the labor-saving benefits of machines. Additional benefits include economies of scale and more efficient marketing. Plant varieties are bred that not only produce high yields but that also have a high degree of uniformity of plant dimensions and ripening time. If an entire 160-acre field is to be harvested at one time by machines that harvest 12 rows at a pass, then clearly all the plants must mature at the same time. A food production system that is primarily monocultural is a highly specialized one. It must have the capac-

ity to store produce over long time periods and transport it efficiently from one area to another.

One consequence of the uniformity of plants in monocultural systems is their susceptibility to disease and pest infestation. If an insect that can successfully attack a particular variety takes hold, large fields can be devastated quickly. For this reason, substantial inputs of pesticides are normally required. Many of these specialized plant varieties also require large inputs of fertilizer or irrigation water to realize maximum yields. In addition, the machines, fertilizers, and chemicals require large amounts of energy, in the form of fossil fuels and electricity, to operate or produce.

Monoculture under these conditions produces very high yields of uniformly high quality. As a result, the value of crops on a per acre basis is very high. But to achieve this high-value harvest, much capital is needed to purchase the inputs of production—land, machines, seed, fertilizer, and so on. It is a capital- and energy-intensive system rather than a labor-intensive one. In recent years, capital has become an increasingly costly input for American farmers, and at the same time there is growing concern about the negative aspects of agricultural chemicals. There are indications that American agriculture may be turning away from intensive use of chemicals, although it is not clear whether other factors of production (such as labor) would be substituted or yields per acre would be allowed to decline. These trends will be discussed further later in this chapter.

COMPONENTS OF AGRICULTURE

SOIL

Soil is the uppermost part of the earth's surface, which has been modified by physical, chemical, and biological processes over time. It is the essential medium for plant growth, and is a complex and dynamic mixture of solid and dissolved mineral matter, living and dead organic matter, water, and air. Soil is formed over long periods of time, usually thousands of years.

Many factors affect soil formation, including climate, parent material, topography, erosion, and biological activity. Climate affects soil by determining the amount of water that may enter the soil from rainfall, and the amount that can be drawn from the surface by evaporation. Climate also determines soil temperatures, which are important in regulating chemical reactions in the soil as well as influencing plant growth. *Parent material* is the mineral matter on which soil is formed. It affects the soil by supplying the mineral matter that forms the bulk of the soil. Parent material has a fundamental influence on *soil texture,* which is the mix of different sizes of particles, and on the chemical characteristics of the soil.

Topography influences soil primarily by regulating water movement within and over the soil. On slopes, water moves down and laterally through the soil, providing drainage. In low-lying areas water accumulates, and soils may become waterlogged. Along stream courses sediment may accumulate, producing fertile alluvial soils. Topography also affects the rate of erosion. *Erosion* is the removal of soil by running water or wind. It is a natural process that can be greatly accelerated by human influences such as vegetation removal. The rate of erosion relative to the rate of new soil formation is an important determinant of soil characteristics.

Finally, biological activity is what makes soil the distinctive, living, dynamic substance it is, rather than just an accumulation of sterile rock particles. Biological activity includes the growth and decay of plants and animals in and above the soil. It contributes organic matter to the soil, which constitutes the basic storage of nutrients for most ecosystems. Biological activity also aids in the physical modification of the mineral soil by contributing organic acids that break down rocks, by exerting physical forces that fracture rocks, and by stirring and aerating the soil so that water and air may penetrate below the surface. Vegetation cover regulates water losses by evapotranspiration and protects the soil from excessive erosion. The type of vegetation is also important in determining soil characteristics. For example, the thick grass cover of a prairie leads to the development of an organic-rich and uncompacted topsoil that is not usually found in forest soils. In short, biological activity plays a

fundamental role in soil formation and helps maintain the ability of soils to support life.

Soil is a four-dimensional medium: it varies vertically, in the two horizontal dimensions, and through time. In the vertical dimension, most soils exhibit several layers, or *horizons,* with different characteristics. Figure 7.4 shows a generalized soil profile for humid midlatitude regions. The uppermost horizon is called the A horizon. This layer contains the most organic matter, and it is usually a zone from which dissolved materials are removed by downward percolation of water. It includes

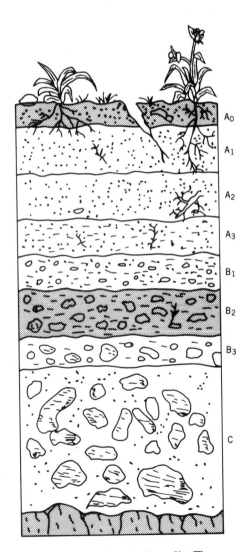

Figure 7.4   A generalized soil profile. The characteristics of the individual soil horizon vary between different soil types (see text for explanation of types).

an upper litter layer (the A_0 horizon), a zone of moderately high organic content (A_1), a zone of maximum downward movement of clays and dissolved materials (A_2), and a zone (A_3) that is transitional to the next lower horizon. The B horizon is a layer of accumulation of materials removed from the A horizon. It is usually lower in organic content than the A horizon and is often rich in clay. The C horizon consists of partially weathered parent material. It is much less altered than the upper layers, and some dissolved materials removed from the A and B horizons may accumulate in the C horizon. Below the C horizon is unweathered parent material.

These layers are found in most well-developed soils in humid mid-latitude environments, but their characteristics vary from place to place depending on variations in the soil-forming factors of climate, topography, and so on. In semiarid and arid areas, upward water movement caused by high evaporation rates at the surface may result in the accumulation of dissolved minerals in the A horizon. On hilltops, rapid drainage may cause considerable removal of minerals, whereas in poorly drained lowlands, saturated conditions can lead to the accumulation of organic matter that is not broken down because of the lack of oxygen.

The way in which individual soil particles group together in aggregates is called *soil structure*. Some common soil structures include platy, prismatic, blocky, and spheroidal. Soil structure is important in determining the water holding capacity of soil and the speed with which water soaks into and through the soil. Plowing, compaction, oxidation of organic matter, extraction of nutrients by plants, or desiccation can sometimes destroy soil structure to the detriment of its water holding properties.

Soils develop slowly from unweathered bedrock to a complete soil profile. The rate of new soil formation varies from place to place, but as a rule it is very slow in human terms, requiring hundreds to tens of thousands of years. Eventually, soils reach an equilibrium with the prevailing climatic, topographic, and biological conditions, and they then retain fairly constant properties. But even in this equilibrium condition, new soil is being

formed. Erosion is part of the natural soil system, and soil eroded from the surface must be replaced by formation of new soil from parent material. If the soil erosion rate is high, then the soil may not develop as thickly or as completely as in areas of low erosion rates. Alluvial soils that continually receive inputs of new material at the top of the profile also show incomplete development.

Soils vary greatly in their ability to support agricultural production, depending on their fertility, water holding characteristics, temperature, and other factors. *Soil fertility* is defined as the ability of a soil to supply essential nutrients to plants, which is dependent on both the chemical and textural properties of the soil. Generally soils that have a high proportion of clay and organic matter also have high fertility, as these substances have the ability to store and release nutrients. Sandy soils, on the other hand, generally have lower amounts of nutrients available to plants, although as little as 10 to 15 percent fine particles may be sufficient to supply the needed nutrients. The abundance of various elements in the soil, such as phosphorus and calcium, is also important. This is often controlled by the chemical composition of the bedrock and the degree of leaching of these nutrients by water percolating through the soil.

The *water holding capacity* of a soil is primarily determined by its texture. As a rule, coarse-textured soils have low capacities to store water, whereas clayey soils can hold large volumes of water in the upper parts of the profile. At the same time, however, clay soils may be poorly drained, with the tendency to become waterlogged, which prevents air from reaching plant roots. Waterlogging is particularly common in humid areas, on floodplains, or on other flat land. In addition, irrigated areas often experience waterlogging if irrigation causes a rise in the local groundwater table.

The productive capabilities of soils are thus of fundamental importance in determining what plants can be grown, what particular management techniques should be used, and what typical yields will be. The U.S. Soil Conservation Service has developed a system, called the *Land Capability Classification System*, for assessing and classifying this productive capacity (Table 7.1). There are eight major capability classes, designated I through VIII, with classes I through IV indicating arable land and classes V through VIII indicating land useful for grazing or forestry. For both agriculture and other uses, the first category includes land that is nearly ideal for production, with little or no limitations of fertility, drainage, and so on. The next two classes include land with increasing degrees of limitations, including such problems as poor drainage, excessive erosion hazard, poor water holding capacity, and the like. The fourth class is land that is generally not usable. Note that the land in the United States is about equally divided between suitability for agriculture and suitability for forestry or grazing, and that in each of these groups about 80 percent of the land has some limitations for use. This further indicates the great importance of proper land management techniques that are adapted to the inherent capabilities and limitations of each land unit.

Such capability classifications are just part of the work of the U.S. Department of Agriculture's Soil Survey, which includes nationwide mapping of soil types, their physical characteristics, and their productive capabilities. These maps are of great use to farmers and land use planners in their attempts to make the best possible use of the soil resource (Fig. 7.5).

WATER

Water is of course essential to plant growth and is supplied to crops naturally by rainfall and artificially by irrigation. Rainfall farming is entirely dependent on the weather to provide a sufficient, but not excessive, supply of moisture to plants. If there is not enough, plants wither and die; if there is too much, the soil cannot be worked, crops rot in the field, or roots suffocate from lack of air. The amount and timing of rainfall are major determinants of what can be grown, where, and when. In areas without irrigation, rainfall variability is a major cause of year-to-year variations in yields. Droughts, early rains, and late rains take their tolls in crop failures or low yields in many regions of the world each year. Some climatologists feel that in the future climates will change or become more variable (Issue 7.1), and if this is the case such yield fluctuations will become an even more severe problem than they are today.

In those parts of the world with sufficient and reasonably dependable rainfall, crops can be grown without irrigation. But about 13 percent of the world's arable lands are arable because water has artificially been made available to plants. Also, much of the land deemed potentially arable will become so only through irrigation. The distribution of irrigated lands in the United States is illustrated in Fig. 7.6.

There are four major types of *irrigation* used in the world today: flood, furrow, sprinkler, and drip. *Flood irrigation* involves inundating entire fields with water, or allowing water to flow across entire fields. The most widespread use of flood irrigation is in growing paddy rice, primarily in southern and eastern Asia. Rice fields are quite flat and bounded by dikes. During the wet season the fields are

---

TABLE 7.1   Land Capability in the United States

Capability Class		Percentage of U.S. Nonfederal Land
I	Few limitations on use	3
II	Moderate limitations for agricultural uses	20
III	Severe limitations that reduce the choice of plants or require special conservation practices	20
IV	Very severe limitations for cropping	13
V	Few limitations for pasture or woodland uses	2
VI	Moderate limitations for pasture or woodland uses	19
VII	Very severe limitations for pasture or woodland uses	20
VIII	Generally suitable only for wildlife, recreation, or aesthetic purposes	3

Source: Soil Conservation Service (1980).

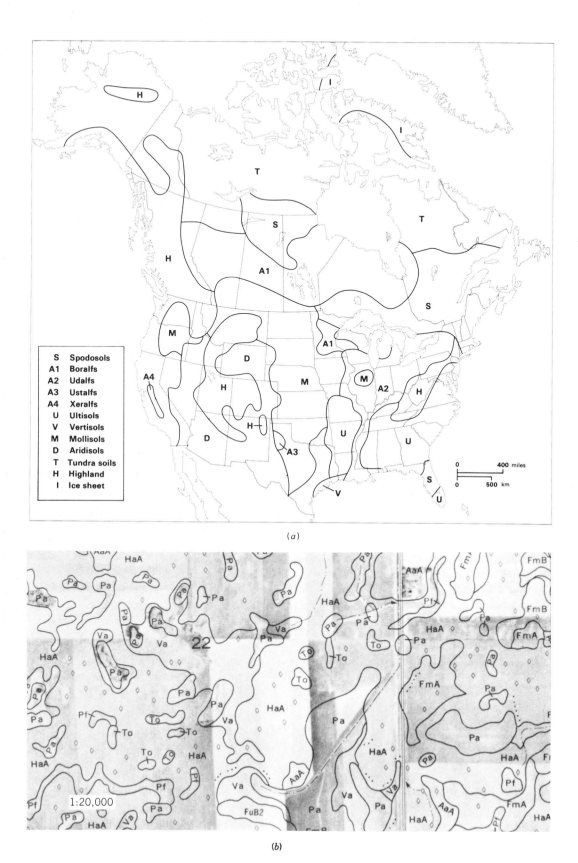

Figure 7.5 Soil maps. a) Generalized map of soils of North America. b) Detail of a U.S. Soil Conservation Service soil map of an area in Southern Minnesota, illustrating local variability in soil types.

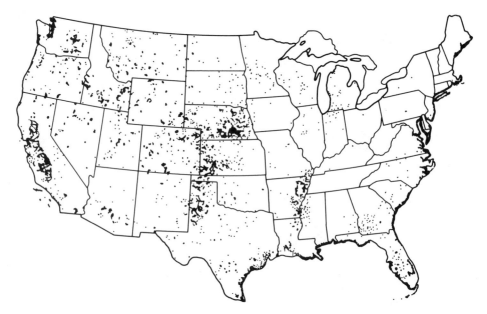

Figure 7.6   Irrigated land in U.S. farms, 1982. (Source: Bajwa, et al. 1987.)

ISSUE 7–1   Agriculture, CO$_2$, and Climate: The Only Certainty Is Change

When extreme weather occurs, one of the most obvious and immediate effects is on agriculture. Farming is vulnerable to a wide variety of bad weather: cool spring weather delays growth, wet spring weather delays planting, autumn rains prevent harvesting, and drought and early frost damage crops. All of these take their toll on crop yields. At the same time there can be especially good weather: summer rain, dry weather to help crop ripening, and warm spring weather often contribute to bumper crops in the United States. Weather variability has obvious impacts on U.S agricultural production, although the American consumer rarely notices these effects directly. In poorer countries vulnerable to food shortages, a drop in production has an immediate impact on diet and health.

Climatologists are predicting changes in global weather, largely as a result of increasing atmospheric CO$_2$ concentrations. What does this mean for agriculture? Will the changes be good or bad? Will higher atmospheric CO$_2$ levels mean more plant growth? The effects of CO$_2$-induced climatic change on agriculture are difficult to predict, but it seems certain that they will be significant.

It is generally recognized that the anticipated global warming associated with the greenhouse effect will include a wide variety of cli-

matic shifts and not simply a rise in temperature. The temperature rise will be significant—probably greatest at high latitudes and modest in the tropics. But there will also be shifts in storm tracks and in the prevailing wind and pressure patterns. In some locations this may mean warmer or wetter weather, and in other places cooler or drier weather. Many forecasters anticipate hot and dry conditions in the central United States, which would probably be damaging to corn production. But a warming trend would also make many northern areas that now have summers that are too short and cool for crops more favorable for agriculture.

Although climatologists working with global climate models may make predictions of how the climate in a given place may change, there is a great degree of uncertainty surrounding such specific predictions. Only recently has a consensus emerged that there will be an increase of average temperature worldwide, and as yet there is little agreement on conditions in specific agricultural areas. It is reasonable to assume, however, that within the next decade or two we will have a clearer idea of how regional-scale climatic patterns will change (or are changing right now). When this knowledge is available, we will be in a better position to analyze likely shifts in growing regions for various crops. But these

flooded, and rice seedlings are planted in standing water. Later the fields are drained, and the rice ripens in a relatively dry field. Flood irrigation is also used to irrigate pastures in some areas. *Furrow irrigation* (Fig. 7.7*a*) also requires very flat land, but in this case the water flows between rows of plants, which are grown on low ridges. Water is delivered to the furrows by small ditches or in pipes and applied as needed throughout the growing season.

Sprinkler irrigation (Fig. 7.7*b*) requires substantially more equipment than flood or furrow irrigation. In sprinkler irrigation, water is pumped under pressure to nozzles and sprayed over the land. Nozzles may be fixed or moved across a field manually or automatically. Sprinkler irrigation usually results in much higher evaporative losses than other methods, but in areas of very permeable soils seepage losses are important, so that sprinklers are preferred to furrow irrigation. *Drip irrigation* is a relatively recent development and is used primarily in orchards and vineyards. Each plant has a small pipe that delivers water at a controlled rate directly to the base of the plant. The water drips out very slowly so that little is lost to evaporation or to seepage. It is an expensive system to install, but it is cost-effective in areas where water is scarce.

Irrigated agriculture generally produces high yields as long as water is available. This is because the other environmental characteristics of dry lands, plentiful sunshine and warm temperatures, are conducive to crop growth. This high productivity is not without its costs, however, and in many areas of the world waterlogging, salt accumulation, groundwater de-

changes will probably take place over decades, and our past experience of world agricultural patterns makes it clear that climate is only one of several factors affecting agricultural production. Unforeseen changes in other factors, such as mechanization, development of new crop varieties, or economic factors, may contribute at least equally with climate in determining the future geography of crop production. In addition, the complex biochemical interactions between increased atmospheric CO_2 and plant growth adds another layer of unpredictability.

Carbon dioxide not only plays a central role in the earth's atmospheric circulation but is also an essential input to photosynthesis. The concentration of carbon dioxide in the atmosphere affects the rate at which plants remove that gas from the air and store it as biomass: the more CO_2 in the air, the faster plants photosynthesize. If plants grow faster, then crop yields may also increase.

To understand the importance of this effect, we must recognize that different plants use different biochemical processes in photosynthesis. Two of these are the C_3 and C_4 processes. C_3 plants, including wheat, barley, rice, and potatoes, respond well to increases in atmospheric CO_2, whereas C_4 plants such as corn, sorghum, and sugarcane do not (Parry, 1990). Increases in CO_2 concentration also affect the efficiency of water use by plants: the more CO_2 present, the less water is used per unit of plant growth. This means that in areas of water shortage, higher CO_2 concentrations are likely to have beneficial effects on production.

Predicting the effects of all of these changes on world agricultural production is clearly impossible at this time. The effects at any given place depend on what varieties of crops are grown, whether water availability is an important limiting factor, and how other factors of production (fertilizer, seed, energy, machinery, and so on) change—too many unknowns even for the most careful analyses. But we can make three simple generalizations. First, farmers need to be prepared for change. They should avoid growing crops that are easily damaged by unusual weather and should concentrate on varieties that are relatively robust. Second, we should expect the geography of crop production to change: areas that are important for one crop today may be growing something different in the future, areas that have no crops today may become productive, and currently viable regions may cease to produce. And third, agricultural research needs to be directed toward developing new crops and adapting old ones to a wide array of possible future climatic conditions.

(a)

(b)

Figure 7.7   Irrigation methods. (a) Furrow irrigation in Texas, (b) Center pivot sprinkler irrigation in Nebraska.

pletion, and disease are serious side effects of irrigation. In some areas, salinization is severe enough that it is forcing abandonment of formerly productive land. In parts of the arid western United States, much of the environmental damage associated with irrigation can be attributed to government policies that provided water at artificially low prices. These subsidies encourage inefficient use of water, such as for production of hay. This excessive use has contributed greatly to the salinity problems in the lower Colorado River.

Although in most of the world's farming regions water is already being used intensely, there are significant opportunities to increase irrigation. One estimate is that there is a potential for irrigating an additional 248 million acres (100 million ha) between 1983 and 2000, accounting for about two-thirds of the projected increase in arable land in that time period (Alexandratos, 1988). If this occurs, increased irrigation can make a significant contribution to increased food production in many areas, particularly Asia.

FERTILIZERS AND PESTICIDES

Average yields of grains worldwide have increased over 50 percent in the last 20 years, and most of this increase has been due to increases in the use of *fertilizers.* Fertilizer use has increased over four times in that same 20-year period (Fig. 7.8). It is generally agreed that fertilizers will continue to play the dominant role in increasing grain yields for some time to come (Scrimshaw and Taylor, 1980). One of the main reasons for this is the development of high-yielding plant varieties that require large inputs of fertilizer to realize their potential. In addition, fertilizers may make production possible on otherwise marginal land.

The three most important nutrients required by plants are nitrogen, phosphorus, and potassium. Nitrogen is ultimately derived from the atmosphere, but it is made available to plants by nitrogen-fixing bacteria. It is the nutrient that is most often deficient and that is most widely applied to crops. Additions in amounts of 45 to 90 pounds/acre (50 to 100 kg/ha) may increase yields from 1.5 to 3 times, depending on plant variety and inherent soil fertility. Nitrogen fertilizers are manufactured from natural gas, and the most commonly used forms are ammonia (NH_4) and urea ($CO(NH_2)_2$). Phosphorus is usually present in small quantities in soils, but it is often found in relatively unusable forms. It is usually applied as superphosphate or as phosphoric acid, which are manufactured from phosphate rock or from guano (bird dung) deposits found in some coastal areas. In soils, potassium is usually found in larger quantities than phosphorus because it is a more abundant constituent of most rocks. It is also demanded by plants in large quantities, and in many areas potassium fertilization is important. In some areas local soil conditions or the

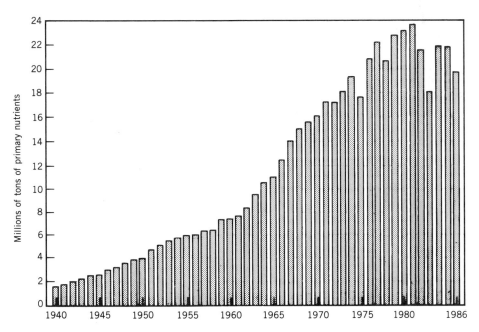

Figure 7.8 Farm fertilizer use, 1940–1986. Fertilizer use has rapidly increased since World War II, and peaked in the early 1980s. Since then, there has been a slight decline. (*Source:* Council on Environmental Quality, 1989.)

particular needs of plants require that other fertilizers be added, with lime (a source of calcium and magnesium as well as a regulator of soil pH) being the most common.

Organic fertilizers (primarily manure) have historically been the most important source of nutrients, especially nitrogen. Organic fertilizers also aid in maintaining good soil structure and water holding capacity by keeping soil organic matter content high. In the wealthy nations inorganic fertilizers are today more important, but in the developing nations manure is still the most common fertilizer. In most areas manure supplies are quite limited, and manure is more difficult to apply than other forms of fertilizer. Manure is low in nutrient content relative to synthetic fertilizer and is not capable of providing the large inputs of nutrients demanded by high-yielding crop varieties. Increasingly, therefore, inorganic sources of nutrients have been replacing organic sources and this trend can be expected to continue.

Pesticide is a general term used to refer to any of a number of chemical agents used to control organisms harmful to plants, including insects, fungi, and some types of worms. Pesticides include insecticides, rodenticides, fungicides, and others. Herbicides are used to control weeds. The use of pesticides and herbicides has accounted for a large part of recent increases in crop yields, particularly in the wealthier nations. There are thousands of different kinds of pesticides and herbicides, and the vast majority are complex organic compounds manufactured using petroleum as an important raw material. Among insecticides, organochlorines, organophosphates, and carbamates are important types.

The large-scale use of pesticides in agriculture began in the 1950s. Among the first widely used insecticides were organochlorines such as DDT, aldrin, dieldrin, and chlordane. In the 1960s and 1970s these were largely replaced by organophosphates for most uses, in part because insects began to develop resistance to the effects of organochlorines and in part because organophosphates break down more rapidly and therefore are less likely to accumulate in the environment. Today many different types of chemicals are used (Fig. 7.9). Among the small-grain crops, pesticides and herbicides are used most intensively on corn, soybeans, and sorghum. Most fruits and vegetables are susceptible to damage by insects, fungi, and other pests, and various pesticides are used depending on specific circumstances.

The dangers of pesticide use have been widely discussed since the early 1960s, and the use of pesticides has been regulated in many ways. But in general their use has increased continuously since their introduction. As will be discussed in a later section, there are now signs that this trend may be reversed.

Figure 7.9   Aerial application of insecticide to lettuce field in California.

SEED

Ever since the development of agriculture farmers have practiced crop improvement through seed selection. Observant of the variations in a single crop, farmers saved seed from those plants that possessed the characteristics they preferred, and planted these seeds the following year. Over a period of thousands of years, this process led to the development of the world's major modern crops. One of the most spectacular examples of this long-term process is maize, or corn. Since 6000 B.C., corn has been altered from a small grain head to its present size and productivity. The success of hybrid corn varieties was a major factor contributing to a large increase in acreages of corn planted in the United States over the past few decades. Another example is the kale species *Brassica oleracea*, which has been altered into several distinct vegetables by selection for different characteristics. These include broccoli, brussels sprouts, and cauliflower, among others.

Since the early twentieth century, the application of Mendel's laws of genetics has sped the process of selection (Issue 7-2). Not only does this allow the creation of new plant varieties, but hybrid seeds tend to produce more vigorous plants than nonhybrid varieties, and thus substantial increases in yield have been achieved. More recently, advances in bioengineering are making it possible to manipulate the genetic material directly, so that alterations can be made in a single generation of a plant species. Thus those farmers who can afford to pay for these sophisticated seeds can choose among a wide array of disease, insect, and drought resistance, and for specific fruit or grain size, flavor, ripening time, packing and processing qualities, and so on.

As a result of selection experiments pioneered by N.E. Borlaug in the 1940s, advanced varieties of wheat, rice, and other staples were first made available to Third World farmers in the early 1960s, an era that is now called the *Green Revolution*. These seeds guaranteed much greater productivity as long as the farmer also applied increased amounts of fertilizer, pesticides, and/or water. Of course, these things cost money, and so some farmers have profited from the new seeds while oth-

ers have not. There is no disputing, however, the effects the seeds have had on worldwide crop production. Between 1950 and 1970 per capita grain production increased 30 percent (Brown, 1980).

One example of the great benefits of seed and fertilizer combinations is found in Mexico, in the decades from 1950 to 1970. Wheat production during this period increased from 330,600 tons (300,000 tonnes or metric tons) per year to 2.9 million tons (2.6 million tonnes), an eightfold increase. Over the same period, corn output increased 250 percent, the bean crop doubled, and the sorghum crop increased 14-fold. By the 1970s a leveling trend was seen, and population began to catch up with this vastly increased output. Seeds cannot do the job alone, especially when there is not enough water for irrigation. Much of Mexico's remaining cropland is marginal for agriculture, and inequities in land ownership prevent small holders from earning enough to pay for Green Revolution materials (Wellhausen, 1976). Ten agricultural research and training centers in Africa, Asia, and Latin America are financed by a variety of governmental, public, and private concerns and are presently designing seeds to fit local conditions.

There is some evidence that, at least in the United States and other countries with technologically advanced agriculture, the "miracle seed" productivity is leveling off. It is suggested that this is in large part due to diminishing returns from the addition of more fertilizer. Experts argue, however, that there is still room for greatly increased productivity in the Third World, where chemical fertilizers are as yet underutilized (Wortman, 1976).

In recent years, controversy in the seed development industry has focused on the granting of seed patents to large agribusiness concerns. Such patents allow seed developers to collect royalties for use of seeds, and thus provide a greater economic incentive for research and development into new crop varieties. But some see this as yet another cost for farmers and consumers and another potential barrier to increasing production. In addition, the abandonment of older low-yielding varieties is threatening some of these varieties with extinction, though efforts are being made to preserve seeds in gene banks (see Chapter 16) (National Academy of Sciences, 1972).

LABOR, MACHINES, AND ENERGY

To grow crops, soil must be tilled, weeds removed, and plants harvested. Until the nineteenth century in North America, most of this work was done by human and animal labor, using simple tools such as plows and hoes. Today, heavy machinery driven by fossil fuels predominates (Fig. 7.10). In the nonindustrialized countries, an impetus toward mechanization was introduced as part of the Green Revolution "package."

In the United States, Canada, and other countries dependent on mechanized production, the percentage of the labor force employed as farmers has dropped steadily. In 1850, 64 percent of the U.S. labor force was made up of farmers; this had dropped to 3.1 percent by 1982. In the early days of mechanization, these millions of workers were absorbed by the availability of industrial jobs in cities. From 1950 to 1980, the number of people on farms and the number of farm workers have dropped, respectively, from 23 and 9.9 million to 6 and 3.7 million (Rasmussen, 1982). In this period the demand for underskilled labor in industry also dropped, aggravating problems of unemployment. In addition, much of the remaining nonmechanized farm work is performed by seasonal and permanent legal and illegal immigrants to the United States who have become an essential cog in the nation's economic machinery.

The technological developments in agriculture involving farm machinery have had

---

ISSUE 7–2   Genetic Manipulation and New Supercrops

The words "genetic manipulation" and "gene transfer" are easily pronounced, but what exactly do they mean? How does a scientist actually move one particular gene from one species into another to create a new and improved crop? Strangely enough, a tumor-causing bacterium was the pioneer vehicle for gene transfer. In the late 1970s, the plant pathogen *Agrobacterium tumefaciens* was found to actually transfer and integrate its genes into the plants it infected to create the characteristic tumorous growths of crown gall disease. Further research revealed that, if additional genetic material was inserted into the *Agrobacterium*, this new DNA would accompany the infectious gene transferral. So, the question arose: Can we separate this gene-transferral ability of *Agrobacterium* from its disease-causing ability? This was achieved by the mid-1980s, and by 1989 gene transfers had been used toward improvement of thirty economically important species, including tomato, potato, cotton, apple, rice, and corn.

Other methods of introducing DNA into another species are becoming increasingly varied and flexible. A "particle gun" pushes DNA through a cell wall on the surface of minuscule (0.5 to 5 microns) metal particles traveling at speeds of one to hundreds of meters per second. Corn, tobacco, and soybean cells and plants have been altered in this fashion; the particle gun can move commercially valuable genes directly into plants, thus speeding up the transformation process. Researchers are also experimenting with gene transfer via pollen, injection of DNA into a plant's reproductive parts, and microinjection into embryo plants.

The squeamish among us may wince at these techniques, even while realizing that they are just the latest methods in the age-old art and science of plant improvement. Humans have been selecting and interbreeding plants for thousands of years. These new techniques speed up the process of selecting for specific desired plant characteristics, and by the beginning of the next century the marketplace will be seeing the introduction of genetically engineered soybean, cotton, rice, corn, oilseed, rape, sugar beet, tomato, and alfalfa crops.

What improvements do farmers and lab researchers dream of?

- Farmers use herbicides to kill weeds; sometimes these chemicals also harm the field crop as well, or are absorbed in quantities that may be toxic to the consumer. New plant varieties may contain a genetically coded tolerance for such popular herbicides as Roundup, Glean, and

Figure 7.10   Combine-harvesting of wheat in Washington.

Oust. In addition, an introduced gene in such crops as corn and soybean will detoxify the herbicide once it enters the plant.

- Certain bacteria are lethal to insect pests; tomato, tobacco, and cotton plants containing killer genes from these bacteria are proving to be much more resistant to insect damage.
- Plant diseases such as alfalfa mosaic virus, cucumber mosaic virus, and potato virus X can be devastating once they infect a field or farming region. Tomatoes and other crops are among the species being made resistant to viral infection.

In the near future, genetic engineers will be able to control the speed at which leaves, flowering parts, seeds, and other organs develop, as well as the plant location of these parts. They will be able to protect a plant against heat shock, wounding, or a deficiency of soil nutrients, and will be able to eliminate undesirable plant characteristics. This fine-tuning will be possible as genetic "maps" are developed, in which the thousands of genes possessed by a species are each individually pinpointed, so that extremely precise, gene-by-gene manipulations can be carried out.

As in so many areas of modern life, plant genetic technology is progressing faster than our culture's ability to deal with it. Gasser and Fraley (1989) suggest that before any of these new superplants can enter the marketplace, a series of societal hurdles must be scrambled over.

The U.S. government regulates the safety of genetic engineering research; so far, research on plants has not received the adverse publicity that focused on research on other life-forms, and by the end of 1989 an estimated thirty field tests had been carried out. The U.S. Department of Agriculture and other agencies are responsible for ensuring the safety of these experiments and of any new crops, and to date they have found no cause for concern, although innovations such as this may have very different effects when applied on a large scale than when observed in small tests. Following these small-scale tests are the large, multifield studies, and scientists are working with food, chemical, biotechnology, and seed companies to develop guidelines for the next step to commercialization.

Patent protection for these new species is also an issue. Companies want assurances that they will receive all the profits from these expensive research programs. Most recent patent legislation and court decisions have ruled in favor of company ownership of plant materials, but

their greatest effects in the industrialized, wealthier nations. It is estimated that agricultural production per farm worker increased sevenfold between 1850 and 1980 (Rasmussen, 1982).

For example, grain production was revolutionized through a series of inventions. The plow evolved from a wooden horse- or ox-drawn implement to today's gang plow with up to 16 blades and capable of plowing 10 acres (4 ha) per hour. Reaping and threshing of grain were once done with sickles, scythes, and human muscle power. Today the diesel-powered combine both harvests and threshes grain at a rate of up to 12 acres (5 ha) an hour. These machines need a single human operator who rides in an air-conditioned cab. Labor shortages during World War II forced farmers to increase their use of machinery, further eliminating the need for large farm crews.

The amount of petroleum products required to fuel this mechanical transformation is enormous. Recent studies estimate that 1974 energy use in American agriculture was 2000 trillion BTU (British Thermal Units), or about 2150 BTU/acre (5300 BTU/ha) (Council on Environmental Quality, 1981b). Comparable figures for systems using animal power vary depending on how energy is accounted for, but fossil fuel use per hectare is commonly 10 percent or less of that in wealthy nations. In comparing total energy inputs with total energy outputs per hectare of land, the energy efficiency of modern, machine-powered, and chemical-intensive agriculture is substantially lower than that of traditional animal-powered methods (Sinha, 1986; Slesser, 1986), but of course yields per acre are higher under energy-intensive techniques. The largest uses in mechanized agriculture are fuels for tilling, planting, harvesting, transport, and water pumping for irrigation. In addition, heat and light are needed for livestock and poultry production, crop drying, and frost protection. Energy is also utilized in the form of agricultural chemicals, and this amounts to more than a third of the total energy used in U.S. agriculture. The Global 2000 report summarizes recent estimates of potential energy savings and concludes that more efficient practices in operations such as cultivation, crop drying, and transportation could bring savings of 50 percent of the energy used in cultivation and 10–20 percent in irrigation (CEQ, 1981a). Substantial savings are also possible through more careful selection and use of fertilizers.

SOIL EROSION: A PROBLEM MANY ARE UNWILLING TO FACE

PHYSICAL PROCESSES

Soil erosion on agricultural lands takes place by three major processes: overland flow (or runoff), wind, and streambank erosion. Of these, overland flow erosion is the most widespread, and in most agricultural areas it is quantitatively the most important. Wind erosion occurs primarily in arid and semiarid areas, where the soil can become dry enough for wind to pick up particles. Streambank erosion is limited to fields that border streams, and though locally significant it is not a major factor in soil erosion worldwide.

Accelerated *overland flow* erosion is primarily the result of intense rainfall on bare

---

enough doubt exists both in the United States and abroad to make companies wary of investing too heavily in this new research. Patenting certainly means that new varieties will be expensive to use, and only farmers with ready access to capital will be able to take advantage of the new super plants.

Questions also arise regarding public unease about the moral and safety-related aspects of genetic engineering. Strangely, though people are extremely worried in general about genetic alterations to many bacterial and animal species, the same fears are not stirred up about plant species and their diseases. Perhaps this is because people have been altering plants for so long, with largely beneficial results, or perhaps it is because people cannot realistically envision a plant disease or species running amok in the same destructive fashion as a mutated form of smallpox or AIDS, even though the potential exists among plants as with any other organism.

ground. Raindrops striking a bare soil surface break up clumps of soil into individual particles. These are moved by the splash made on raindrop impact, and compact the soil surface so that water is less able to soak in, thus reducing the *infiltration capacity*, or the maximum rate at which soil will absorb water. When the precipitation intensity exceeds infiltration capacity, water flows across the surface as *overland flow* rather than soaking in. When overland flow rates are particularly high, small stream channels called rills (Fig. 7.11) may be formed to carry the water away.

Soil erosion due to overland flow varies considerably from place to place. Some areas are extremely susceptible to erosion, whereas in other areas it is a minor problem. Some of the major factors influencing the severity of erosion are topographic factors such as slope steepness, the inherent susceptibility of the soil to erosion, the intensity and frequency of rainfall, and the cropping and management practices of the farmers.

The characteristics of the soil itself that influence erosion, or the *soil erodibility*, include infiltration capacity and cohesiveness. Soils with a high infiltration capacity will generate less overland flow, and so less erosion will occur. The ability of overland flow to detach and transport particles is affected by the cohesiveness of the soil, or the tendency of particles to stick together. Cohesiveness is determined by many factors, but an important one is the organic matter content of the soil. Organic matter adds cohesiveness, as well as water and nutrient storage capacity, to the soil.

Rainfall intensity is a major factor in soil erosion rates, with intense storms causing the most erosion and gentle rains causing very little. The ability of a given storm to cause erosion can be measured, and Fig. 7.12 is a map of the average annual *erosivity* of rains in the United States. The Southeast has the most erosive rain, with somewhat lower values in the North and Midwest. In some areas of the country, particularly the Pacific Northwest, snowmelt is also important in causing erosion.

Finally, and most importantly, cropping and management practices are very significant to overland flow erosion. Cropping practices include what kinds of crops are grown and when they are planted. Row crops, such as corn and soybeans, tend to allow more erosion than do continuous cover crops such as wheat or hay. If the field is bare during part of the year, then that will be the time when there is the greatest susceptibility to erosion. As the plants grow and mature, they cover a greater amount of the ground and erosion susceptibility decreases. In most cases the time of planting is dictated by plant characteristics and weather, but there are situations when particular crops that provide greater cover at times of more erosive rainfall may be chosen. In addition, the decision of whether or when to plow stubble under has effects on erosion susceptibility. This is an example of a management practice. Others include the choice of various conservation techniques such as contour plowing, terracing, or minimum tillage, practices that are discussed in following sections.

The role of weather, soil characteristics, topography, and land management techniques in controlling soil erosion is illustrated by the *Universal Soil Loss Equation* (Wischmeier and Smith, 1978). This equation is a statistical technique for predicting average erosion by rainfall under a variety of climatic, soil, topographic, and management conditions. It is based on many years of U.S. Department of Agriculture research on experimental farms in

Figure 7.11 Rill erosion on sloping cropland in western Iowa.

Figure 7.12   Average annual rainfall erosivity for the United States. High rates of rainfall erosion are found in the humid East, particularly the Southeast. (*Source:* Soil Conservation Service, 1975.)

which field characteristics could be controlled and erosion rates measured. It takes the form

$$A = R \times K \times LS \times C \times P$$

where A is the average soil loss in tons per acre per year, R is the rainfall factor, K is soil erodibility, LS is the slope length and steepness factor, C is a crop factor that measures the effect of vegetation cover in reducing erosion, and P is a management practice factor that measures the effects of practices such as contour plowing. The use of the equation is illustrated in Table 7.2. The R factor is based on the intensity and kinetic energy of rainfall at the location considered. The K factor is a number such that when multiplied by R the average erosion rate for a standard plot is obtained. The standard plot is one that is 72 feet long, with a 9 percent slope, kept in continuous bare fallow and plowed upslope and downslope. The LS, C, and P factors are the ratios of erosion rates for particular conditions to erosion rates on a standard plot. In the example in Table 7.2, the C factor for continuously planted corn in central Indiana is .275, indicating that the vegetation cover provided by the corn reduces erosion to about 28 percent of that on bare ground. The Universal Soil Loss Equation (USLE) has undergone significant refinement

over the years, and a revised USLE was released in 1989. The USLE is useful in estimating average erosion rates under a wide range of

---

TABLE 7.2   Examples of a Calculation Using the Universal Soil Loss Equation

A 4-year rotation of wheat-with-meadow-seeding, meadow, corn, corn in central Indiana, on 4 percent slopes 220 feet long, contour plowed.

R factor: 175
K factor for silt loam soil with fine granular structure and moderate permeability: 0.48
LS factor for 4 percent slopes 220 feet long: 0.6
C factor for wheat-with-meadow-seeding, meadow, corn, corn: 0.119
P factor for contour plowing on 4 percent slope: 0.52
Soil
  loss = A = 175 × 0.48 × 0.6 × 0.119 × 0.52 = 3.1 tons/acre/year
Soil loss, with conditions the same as above but plowing upslope and downslope instead of on contour: 6.0 tons/acre/year
Soil loss, with conditions the same as above but with contour cultivation of corn continuously instead of rotation: 7.2 tons/acre/year

Based on Wischmeier and Smith (1965) and Wischmeier (1974).

conditions, and thus is a valuable tool in selecting appropriate conservation techniques. Its use as a soil conservation tool is discussed later in this chapter.

Wind erosion occurs when there is a combination of high wind velocities and a soil surface that is easily eroded. High wind velocities are obviously dependent on weather conditions, and some areas are windier than others. Vegetation cover is more important as it controls wind speed at the soil surface. Plants are very effective at reducing surface wind velocities, and wind erosion is essentially negligible under continuous vegetation cover.

The shape of the soil surface is also important in slowing wind velocities and soil erosion. If the ridges and furrows of a plowed field are perpendicular to the wind, the rate of erosion will be much less than if the field is plowed parallel to the prevailing wind direction. Soil texture is also important. Soils that have a high clay content and/or high organic content are generally less susceptible to wind erosion than sandy soils, although there are many exceptions to this generalization. Soil moisture is also significant to wind erosion. Moderate levels of soil moisture tend to hold soil particles together, and as long as the soil surface is moist very little wind erosion will occur. Dry weather can dry out the top few millimeters of a soil even though deeper layers are moist, and thus a bare soil may be susceptible to wind erosion at any time of the year.

Vegetation acts to reduce the rate of erosion in nearly every aspect of both water and wind erosion processes. The leaves of plants intercept raindrops, slowing them down and allowing the water to reach the soil slowly instead of with a strong impact. In addition, the stems of plants and the litter of dead leaves on the soil surface slow down overland flow, reducing its ability to transport soil particles. Finally, a good vegetation cover helps to stir the upper parts of the soil profile, keeping it rich in organic matter and permeable so that a high infiltration capacity is maintained. When vegetation is removed, such as by plowing to prepare the soil for crops, the soil is left bare, and the increases in raindrop impact, overland flow volumes, and flow velocity that result cause accelerated erosion. Similarly, vegetation slows down wind at the soil surface and

protects it from intense sunlight or drying winds that could make it more susceptible to wind erosion.

Accelerated erosion has physical effects on the soil that not only reduce its fertility but may also make it more susceptible to further erosion. Erosion removes the upper portions of the soil profile, which are usually the portions that contain the most stored nutrients and organic matter and that are therefore most important for soil fertility. These upper layers are often very important in maintaining a high infiltration capacity and in storing soil moisture. Thus when the surface horizons are removed, the lower layers are exposed and the soil may be less able to absorb and store moisture, less fertile, and even more susceptible to erosion.

EXTENT OF THE PROBLEM

Accelerated soil erosion is found on virtually all cultivated lands, but the extent of the problem varies greatly from place to place. The results of a U.S. Department of Agriculture survey of sheet and rill erosion on U.S. lands (U.S. Department of Agriculture, 1989) are summarized in Fig. 7.13. The greatest rates of soil erosion are found in the Southeast and in the Corn Belt states, with average rates ranging from 4 to 6 tons per acre (8 to over 12 tonnes/ha) per year. Wind erosion is mapped in Fig. 7.11*b*. It is most severe in the western Great Plains states, at rates similar to those of rill erosion in the East. The sum of wind and water erosion is mapped in Fig. 7.14. Rates of 4 to 6 tons/acre (8 to over 12 tonnes/ha) per year correspond to a loss of about 0.2 to 0.4 inch (0.5 to 1 cm) from the soil surface in 10 years. If we recognize that the top 4 to 12 inches (10 to 30 cm) of most soils hold the greatest proportion of the nutrients and organic matter, then these rates may lead to removal of much of this very fertile layer in just a few decades.

The effect of this erosion on crop production is difficult to assess, primarily because there are relatively few opportunities to quantitatively measure these effects directly today or to predict future consequences of erosion. There are so many factors that affect crop yields that it is nearly impossible to determine

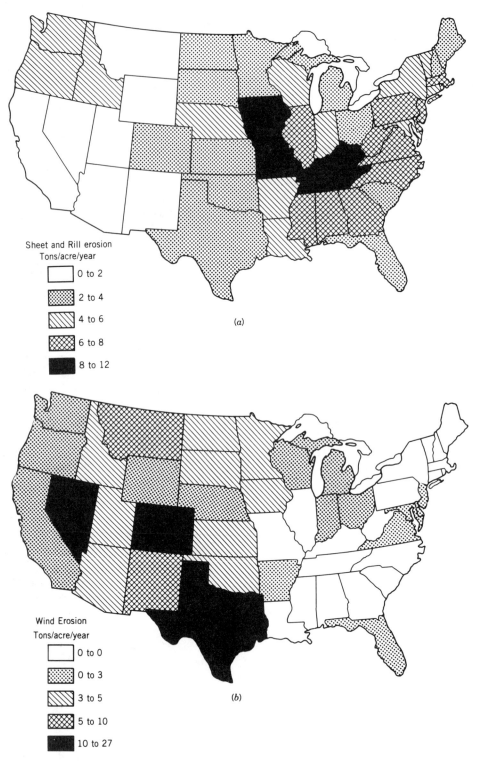

Figure 7.13   Soil erosion on U.S. cropland. (*a*) Rates of sheet and rill erosion on cropland, 1982. (*b*) Rates of wind erosion on cropland, 1982 (*Source:* USDA, 1989.)

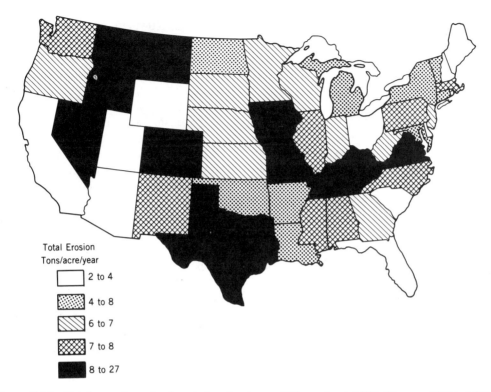

Figure 7.14   Total rate of erosion by wind and water on U.S. cropland, 1982. (*Source:* USDA, 1989.)

the effects of changes in single factors such as inherent soil fertility. This is particularly true when the adverse effects of excessive soil erosion accumulate very slowly and are masked by changes in farming techniques, weather, or farm economics.

One criterion commonly used to determine how much erosion is tolerable is the rate of new soil formation. Soil is continually being formed, and if the rate of erosion can be kept equal to or less than this rate, then the long-term viability of the resource is not jeopardized. The rate of new soil formation is itself difficult to determine, but working estimates have been made for most of the major agricultural soils in the United States. For the most part these estimates range from about 0.5 to 5 tons/acre (1 to 10 tonnes/ha) per year. In 1982, the most recent year for which data are available, the rainfall erosion rate exceeded the tolerable rate on 106.3 million acres (43 million ha) of cropland, or 21 percent of the total cropland in the nation. This does not in-

clude wind erosion, which exceeds rainfall erosion in some of the Great Plains states.

A few studies have been conducted on the reductions in crop yields that occur as a result of erosion, with other factors being held constant. These show that losses can be significant, particularly if erosion over periods of several decades is considered. Larson *et al.* (1983), for example, conclude that for some soils in the upper Midwest, as much as 15 to 20 percent of the productive capability of the soils may be lost in 50 years of erosion, although in most cases projected losses were less. Nationwide, water erosion at current rates is estimated to result in the loss of 1.8 percent of the soil productivity over a 100-year period. The figures are much higher in the Northeast (7.1 percent), Appalachia (4.7 percent), and the Corn Belt (3.5 percent) (USDA, 1989). In the long term this loss of soil productivity is significant, particularly when we consider a growing population and likely world food demands. But on a per year basis, the losses are very small, only a fraction of a percent.

CONSERVATION TECHNIQUES

Over the years many techniques have been developed to control erosion while still allowing efficient agricultural production. Some of these, such as crop rotation, have been known for centuries, whereas others have been developed fairly recently. Some of the important techniques are discussed in this section.

Crop rotation is a farming method that is primarily aimed at maintaining soil fertility, but by so doing plant growth is enhanced and erosion reduced. Crop rotation simply means that over a period of several years the crops grown on a field will change in a systematic pattern. Some crops demand more of some nutrients than others, and by changing crops from year to year excessive depletion of nutrients can be prevented. Typical rotation patterns may include fallow periods or plantings of crops like alfalfa that restore some nutrients to the soil. Often such crops are plowed under rather than harvested, a technique called green manuring. Crop rotation may also allow the ground to be covered a greater percentage of the time, thus reducing erosion. Some rotation patterns may repeat one or more crops, such as a rotation of corn, corn, oats, and hay. In the short run this may require planting less profitable crops in some years, which may reduce the ability and willingness of farmers to use this technique.

Contour plowing is another important soil conservation method. It involves plowing across a slope, or on the contour, rather than up and down a slope. Contour plowing reduces erosion by causing water to be trapped in the furrows where it can soak in, rather than running down the furrows and causing erosion. It is thus also a water conservation technique. On hilly land, contours are rarely straight, and so contour plowing requires plowing in curvy lines across a field. Field boundaries rarely follow the contours, and so this usually results in irregular-shaped patches and some unused land, making it more time-consuming and perhaps less profitable for the farmer than plowing in straight rows parallel to the borders of a rectangular field.

Contour plowing is often used in conjunction with *terracing.* Terracing involves constructing ridges or ditches parallel to the contours, which trap overland flow and divert it into drainage channels, thus preventing it from continuing downslope and causing erosion. In some parts of the world, notably Southeast Asia, terraces are constructed with flat surfaces for ponding of water and rice production. In the United States most terraces are subtle ridges on sloping fields, and in many cases the farmer plows and plants on them as if they were not there. Contour plowing, terracing, or crop rotation may be combined with *strip cropping,* in which crops are planted in parallel strips along the contour or perpendicular to prevailing winds. One strip may be planted with a less protective crop or left fallow, while the adjacent strip has a protective cover. Soil eroded in one area is deposited nearby, and little of the soil is lost.

With regard to wind erosion, the most useful prevention methods are *stubble mulching* and *windbreaks.* Stubble mulching simply means leaving plant residue on the ground between growing seasons rather than plowing it under immediately after harvest. Windbreaks are lines of trees planted perpendicular to the most erosive winds. Both of these techniques act to reduce wind velocity at the soil surface and thus reduce erosion. Some of these methods are illustrated in Fig. 7.15.

Another conservation technique that is rapidly gaining acceptance is *minimum tillage,* or *conservation tillage.* This is a technique that reduces erosion by minimizing the number of times a plow or other implement is passed through the soil. It reduces erosion because the crop residue is usually left on the surface through the winter rather than plowing it under in the fall. In addition, undisturbed soils will maintain a thin crust that is more resistant to erosion than a disturbed soil. Minimum tillage also greatly reduces the fuel costs of operating a tractor, a factor that has become increasingly important in recent years. One of the major drawbacks of minimum tillage is that instead of physically removing weeds by plowing, herbicides are used to a greater extent, which increases the risk of the harmful side effects of these chemicals.

One of the greatest advances in soil conservation was the development of the Universal Soil Loss Equation, which has been refined so that an extension agent can easily estimate the amount of erosion that will be expected to occur on a specific field, assuming particular practices by the farmer. It is then possible to choose the mix of cropping and management practices that best suits the needs of the farmer and minimizes erosion. The range of alternatives to control erosion is usually large, so that in theory most farmers should be able to find a combination of crop types, planting times, and conservation practices that still allows a profitable farm operation. In practice, however, the equation has enjoyed only limited success, largely because of economic constraints on farmers.

THE ECONOMICS OF EROSION

Decisions on how to manage agricultural land are made by individual farmers, who, like any individuals operating businesses in the short run, are primarily concerned with maximizing their incomes. Farmers are aware of the threat of erosion to the productivity of their lands (which in the long run is destruction of their capital base), and most feel that more should be done to prevent it. The problem is that their management decisions must consider the costs of inputs of seed, fertilizer, irrigation water, fuel, pesticides, and so on, relative to the value of the crops that will be produced. Inputs of fertilizers and pesticides will generally result in substantial increases in crop yields, and so variations in these inputs are much more significant to short-term returns than long-term reductions in inherent soil fertility caused by erosion. Most farmers in the United States today are struggling under enormous debts, and farm prices have not been high enough to pay off loans and provide a comfortable profit. This profit is necessary if farmers are to restrict planting, invest in erosion control structures, or otherwise constrain their activities.

Government officials concerned with soil conservation have recognized this problem and since the 1930s have implemented programs to ease the economic burden of soil conservation. One important method is payments to the farmer in exchange for planting soil-conserving cover crops such as alfalfa instead of more profitable, but nonprotective, crops. Such payments serve a second purpose, that of reducing farm production so as to increase prices. In addition to these payments, subsidies are made available from time to time to pay for capital improvements such as construction of terraces or gully control. Finally, Soil Conservation Service extension agents provide technical assistance to farmers by making available information on different erosion control methods and how they can be incorporated into a profitable farm management plan.

In spite of these measures, the erosion problem persists. In the late 1970s and early 1980s, economic difficulties led farmers to plant on more and more land, rejecting cover crops in favor of more profitable row crops. The large machinery in use today is not well suited to terraced fields, and in many areas terraces have been destroyed. These trends have prompted new warnings on the severity of the erosion problem, but no new government programs have emerged to deal with it. Many experts feel that as long as new agricultural technologies can increase yields at the same time as erosion control reduces either yields or profits, few farmers will do much to control erosion. Although farmers might be willing to accept mandatory programs to control erosion, they would only be willing to do so if society as a whole, through the government, compensated farmers for reduced incomes (Seitz and Swanson, 1980).

AGRICULTURAL LAND CONVERSION

As discussed earlier, the amount of land on which crops are planted in any given year is only a portion of the available agricultural land. The amount of cropland changes through time, increasing as new land is cleared or irrigation water is made available, and decreasing as land is converted to other uses or lost from agricultural uses as a result of erosion, salinization, or other degradation processes. The actual amount of land that is in crops at any time is a function of farm economics, available technology, and demand for land for other uses. In any event, the

(a)

(b)

Figure 7.15   Soil conservation methods. (a) Windbreaks in Wisconsin. (b) Contour plowing and terraces in Iowa. (c) Contour strip cropping in Maryland. (d) Chiseling to till soil while leaving mulch on the surface in South Dakota.

total amount of potentially arable land is finite.

Worldwide there are tremendous pressures on the available land base, as growing populations seek living space and resources. These pressures cause land to be more or less permanently allocated to nonagricultural uses, irreversibly limiting potential arable land area. In a world already experiencing problems of food supply, this indicates even greater problems in the future.

(c)

(d)

CAUSES

There are many reasons why agricultural land is lost to other uses, and often it is difficult to separate them. Some of the major factors are urban growth, water resource development, changing farm economics, and land degradation. Conversion of cropland to residential, commercial, industrial, and transportation uses is an irreversible change that accompanies urban growth. In the United States this process consumes about 1 million acres (400,000 ha) annually. Most of this occurs at the urban fringe, where new shopping centers, housing developments, and highways are being constructed. The principal reason for the change in land use is simply that the land can return a greater profit to its owner from nonagricultural than agricultural use. Through the open market system, society is demanding more urban and residential land and less agricultural land. In this case, however, the change at any given location is irreversible. Houses can be torn down to build highways, and factories can be converted into apartment houses, but once land is paved, sewers installed, and buildings erected, it cannot be returned to agricultural use except at prohibitive cost. What can be done, of course, is to convert other agricultural land into cropland to replace what has been lost.

If we accept that there is a genuine need for urban land, then some cropland must be sacrificed for these uses. An important question is whether the conversion is made efficiently, that is, to minimize the land loss and to convert poor-quality land rather than the best cropland to urban uses. There is a tendency for development to take the best cropland rather than less productive land. This is because the best land for agriculture is usually the more level land, often in accessible areas such as river valleys, which are also the best sites for shopping centers, highways, and so on. It seems that in the United States today, the conversion is not being made as efficiently as it might, largely because simple proximity to cities often makes agriculture difficult.

Near an expanding urban area, several processes contribute to loss of agricultural land. First, demand for land causes land values to rise. If property taxes are based on land value, then the farmers' taxes rise, making farming less profitable. As farmers see land around them being sold to developers, they recognize that they too are likely to sell out in the near future. They are then reluctant to make major investments in farm equipment or improvements that will keep the farms competitive in the long run and that will take longer to pay for themselves than the expected life of the farm. In addition, the rural economic system begins to be replaced with urban-oriented businesses, and farm supplies and occasional labor become more difficult to obtain. In many areas farm vandalism and theft perpetrated by urban residents further hinders farming operations. Urban residents also complain about nuisances such as odors, dust, and pesticides. All of these factors together tend to encourage farmers to abandon agriculture and sell out to land speculators, often much sooner than would be the case if these additional pressures were not acting.

Urban demands for land extend well beyond the suburban fringe. Cities need water, and dams that impound water also inundate substantial acreages. In the United States, about 29 percent of the land lost annually is lost to water uses, mostly reservoirs and catchment areas, and 71 percent of the loss is to urban uses (Schmude, 1977). In many cases, inundated bottomlands were the most fertile lands. In areas where water is in short supply, allocating water for urban uses often precludes other uses such as agricultural irrigation. In Arizona, for example, accumulation of salts in soils and depletion of groundwater have limited productivity to the point where farms are being abandoned. If more water were available, these farms could remain productive, but rapid population growth is causing available water to be diverted to cities. Electric power transmission lines and petroleum pipelines also take rural land, in the process sometimes breaking up fields and making farming more difficult.

EXTENT AND SEVERITY

Few reliable data are available on a global level that would indicate how much agricultural land is lost to other uses. Urbanization is a worldwide phenomenon, but losses are presently masked by opening of new lands, so that on a global level arable land is increasing slightly. At the national level, the rate of agricultural land conversion to other uses has varied between about 1–2 million acres (405,000–810,000 ha) per year. The highest rates of conversion in recent years occurred in the late 1960s and 1970s, when up to 2.1 million acres (850,000 ha) per year were lost to urban uses. Since 1977 the rate has declined, and between 1977 and 1982 it was about 1 million acres (405,000 ha) per year. This annual loss represents about 0.1 percent of our cropland base. A substantial amount of the land lost was prime farmland—the very best land for farming. Between 1967 and 1975, about 1 million acres (0.4 million ha) per year of prime farmland were lost. Not all prime farmland is presently cropped, and much of what was lost was not in production at the time.

The question of whether these losses constitute a serious problem is open to debate. The primary considerations in such a debate are (1) what are the expected and future demands for farmland and (2) can these demands be met by the available land plus new land that may be brought into production? It is clear that future demands for farmland, on a worldwide basis, will be tremendous. World population is expected to reach 6.3 billion by the year 2000, and even though there is substantial uncultivated land in the world, relatively little of it is likely to be brought into production (Paulino, 1986; Swaminathan, 1988). This is because much of the reserve land is in parts of the world where it is not needed (such as the United States, Brazil, and Zaire), and most of the available land is of relatively poor quality for agriculture. The result will be a decline in arable land per capita. This will require substantial increases in yield per hectare, which can only occur with increases in cropping intensity and the use of fertilizers, pesticides, irrigation water, and high-yielding varieties. Such increases will probably occur only with substantial increases in the cost of food, and will in turn lead to accelerated erosion. If more land were available, more food could be produced at relatively low cost, with an associated improvement in diet for the poorer nations of the world.

In the United States, population is not rising rapidly and there is no reason to believe that improvements in agricultural technology will not be able to keep pace with domestic demands. However, the United States is a major food exporter, and if it is to maintain and expand that role in the future it must have as much good-quality land as possible. Furthermore, preservation of the most productive land for agriculture allows us to produce food on fewer acres with lower inputs of fertilizer and less erosion, with associated water quality benefits.

PRESERVING AGRICULTURAL LAND

Several institutional measures have been devised to limit the conversion of agricultural land to other uses. The most common of these is property taxes that are based on the use value of land rather than on the market value. Thus if a parcel of land is in agricultural use it is taxed at a rate that reflects the relatively low profits that can be made by that use, rather than the higher value of the land if it were sold for development. This eliminates the effect of excessive taxes on farmers in urbanizing areas. A second method that has been used in several areas has been the establishment of agricultural districts. These are productive areas that are designated as areas that should remain agricultural, while other areas around them are allowed to be developed. Landowners within agricultural districts receive tax advantages for maintaining agricultural land use, and various measures are used to restrict or prevent conversion of farmland to other uses. In New Jersey, this concept includes the sale of development rights by farmers in agricultural districts. Development rights are purchased by land developers, who may then build at higher than normal densities in planned growth areas. The farmers who sell these rights then gain the profits associated with increased land values without having to give up farming. In other areas, development rights have been acquired directly by local or state governments.

These measures have met with limited success. In some areas, such as New Jersey and Long Island, New York, farmland preservation has strong public support, and innovative laws have been passed to preserve the remaining agricultural areas. Yet conversion continues. To some extent the causes are national in scope, with competition from farmers in one part of the country constraining preservation actions in another part. Under these circumstances it is difficult to prevent farm abandonment, and once land is no longer farmed it is difficult to prevent a farmer from selling to developers. Unless there is a considerable growth in strong land use planning efforts at a regional as well as local scale, it appears that the only thing that will stop conversion of farmland to other uses will be large increases in food prices.

TOXIC SUBSTANCES IN AGRICULTURE

Pesticides have been a boon to modern technological agriculture, but they also have harmful side effects. The primary side effects of concern are health hazards to agricultural workers using the pesticides, health effects on the general population through contamination of food, water, and air, and adverse ecological effects.

The most severe human health hazards associated with pesticides are those associated with occupational exposure of farm workers handling the substances. Workers in the field at the time of application are exposed, as are those handling crops at harvest time. Accidental exposure is also a major concern. Although there has been regulation of pesticides to limit effects beyond the farm as well as on it, major problems remain. For example, the nonpersistent pesticides that are generally used today do not accumulate in high concentrations in the environment. However, they are highly toxic at the time they are applied, hence those in contact with pesticides at that time are most at risk (Johnson, 1982).

The general population is also exposed to agricultural chemicals, primarily through consumption of foods containing these chemicals but also through transport of pollutants in water and air. Although these exposures are less acute than those faced by agricultural workers, the number of people affected is much greater.

The combined hazards of pesticide use are great, but so also are the benefits in terms of increased yields. Concern for the problems associated with massive pesticide use has prompted research on alternative methods of pest control, most importantly *integrated pest management*. This approach recognizes that there are several different means to control pests, including pesticides, crop rotation and other habitat controls, biological controls such as predator introduction, and other techniques. No single technique is likely to be completely successful in any given place, but for each particular set of agricultural needs and pest problems it should be possible to use a mix of different control techniques tailored to the situation. This approach will require considerable research and development before it can be widely used, but it offers the greatest promise in solving pest problems without poisoning humans or the environment.

Many scientists and others concerned with the use of agricultural chemicals have long warned of dangers and advocated alternative approaches. But for the most part the governmental and university researchers and advisors who guide most U.S. agricultural technology have maintained that productive agriculture depends on substantial chemical inputs.

There are recent indications of a major change in the direction of policy in this area. In 1989 the National Academy of Sciences released a report describing a 5-year study of practices and yields on farms that successfully use few or no chemical inputs (Schneider, 1989). The study examined farms that have successfully eliminated or dramatically reduced use of chemical fertilizers and pesticides. The farms in the study were from a wide range of environments and produced crops such as corn, soybeans, wheat, and garden vegetables. Using innovative methods, they were able to produce these crops with yields per acre and profits that rivaled those of conventional farms. Most of the farms studied relied on intensive management, including techniques such as crop rotation, biological pest control, special cultivation techniques, and highly selective use of pesticides. What is most intriguing about the study is the reaction it received in Washington, DC: officials of the U.S. Department of Agriculture, which is usually strongly supportive of conventional techniques, were pleased with the report and welcomed the changes in agricultural practices recommended by it.

This development came at a time when there is increasing evidence that farmers are working to reduce pesticide use, and the trend is likely to take hold in the 1990s. Examination of recent trends in pesticide use, for example, suggests that insecticide use is on the decline (Fig. 7.16). Herbicides, which are used intensively in modern minimum-till and no-till methods, are still used intensively, but their use does not appear to be growing even though more and more farmers are adopting reduced tillage techniques. A reduction in agricultural use of these chemicals is likely to bring about improvements in many aspects of the food system, from the health of farm laborers to reduction of pesticide residues in processed foods, as well as reductions in groundwater pollution (see Issue 7–3). Development of government policy with regard to use of chemicals in agriculture is likely to be an important area of debate in the 1990s (Lighthall and Roberts, 1988).

THE "SUSTAINABLE AGRICULTURE" MOVEMENT

Another recent development in U.S. agriculture has been the widespread recognition that the practices that prevailed in the 1960s and 1970s cannot be carried on indefinitely without significant adverse effects. Although environmentalists have been warning of problems in agriculture for years, two key research efforts have contributed to this new trend. These developments have given rise to the promotion of agricultural practices that can be continued indefinitely without long-term damage to the productivity of the land, otherwise known as *sustainable agriculture.*

The first breakthrough was an effort by the U.S. Department of Agriculture to document the long-term effects of erosion on soil productivity. By the early 1980s, sufficient evidence on these effects was amassed to allow routine estimation of such productivity declines, and such estimates are a part of the Second Resource Conservation Act Appraisal, released in 1989 (USDA, 1989).

The second important research effort was an examination of groundwater contamination by agricultural chemicals. This included several federal studies, but probably the most significant was a statewide study of agricultural contamination of groundwater in Iowa (Hallberg, 1985). This study demonstrated that the problem is significant and widespread, and that continued use of pesticides at increasing rates would almost certainly result in severe degradation of groundwater quality in many agricultural areas.

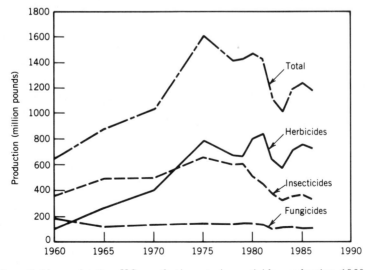

Figure 7.16 U.S. pesticide production. U.S. synthetic organic pesticide production, 1960–1986, in millions of pounds per year. (*Source:* U.S. Bureau of the Census, 1989.)

The sustainable agriculture movement is a renewal of efforts that have been under way for decades to convert American agriculture to methods that do not degrade the environment or the ability of the agricultural system to produce future yields at least as high as those at the present. It is a grass-roots movement attempting to convince farmers to reduce pesticide use and adopt soil conservation techniques that will make agricultural land a truly renewable resource rather than a stock resource that is used for a period of time and then abandoned. Although it is difficult to define precisely what farming techniques constitute "sustainable agriculture," they generally involve intensive soil conservation measures and minimal use of pesticides and inorganic fertilizers. At the present time the number of farmers using these methods is relatively small, mostly in specialized crops such as fruits

---

ISSUE 7–3 Back to the Organic Garden

Prior to World War II, most farms and home gardeners practiced organic farming methods. Organic methods do not rely on synthetic chemical inputs (fertilizers or pesticides) and instead use crop rotation and manure to maintain soil fertility, and biological and mechanical methods to control pests. This is a stricter form of sustainable agriculture.

Consumer concern over pesticide residues in food has prompted a demand for organic produce. A 1989 Natural Resources Defense Council report created a public outcry when it claimed that children have a greater risk of cancer than adults from pesticide residues on food because of their lower body weight and increased consumption of fruit, particularly apples and bananas. In response, Alar, a chemical that is applied to apples and peanuts, was removed from the market, which cost apple growers millions of dollars. EBDC, a fungicide used on many fruits and vegetables, also was banned. Aldicarb (Temik), used on potatoes and imported bananas, was restricted as well. As the public concern continued, more and more people wanted to purchase "pesticide-free" produce.

Organic gardening is a perfectly reasonable alternative for chemically dependent agriculture on a small scale. The backyard garden is ideal. On larger scales, however, organic gardening is more difficult, and thus the produce is more costly. Consumers, however, are willing to pay more for organically grown fruits and vegetables. Unfortunately, farmers have been slow to capitalize on this trend. Today organic produce makes up less than 1 percent of the U.S. market, and most experts think that this may climb, but probably not exceed 10 percent.

How can you tell whether produce is organically grown? Certification of organic produce has always been a problem, especially in the large supermarket chains. In 1980, for example, only two or three states had organic produce laws. By 1990, 15 had passed such legislation, including Washington, Oregon, California, Montana, Nebraska, North Dakota, South Dakota, Minnesota, Wisconsin, Iowa, Maine, Vermont, New Hampshire, Massachusetts, and Texas. Since the Alar scare, organic farmers cannot keep up with the demand. There is hope on the horizon for larger-scale organic farming.

In 1990, the Organic Foods and Production Act was introduced in the U.S. Congress. The act promotes organically grown foods through national standards of production and certification requirements for interstate commerce. In order to be labeled "organic," products must be grown without the use of synthetic chemicals and on land that has not had synthetic chemicals applied within the last three years. Also, the products must come from a farm that has been certified as organic by a qualified inspector. Soil amendments must adhere to the National List of approved and not-approved items. The Organic Foods Bill also has provisions for organically grown animal products. Finally, violators of the organic labeling laws are subject to civil penalties (imprisonment up to five years) and fines not to exceed $100,000.

As a consumer, you can now rest a little easier. If you want to buy organic produce, it should be available at your local A&P, Pathmark, Ralphs, Safeway, Grand Union, Piggly Wiggly, or Krogers supermarket in addition to the local health foods store. On the other hand, if you really want to be sure that you are eating organic foods, start your own organic garden (Burros, 1989).

and vegetables. But the number of farmers producing grain, meat, and dairy products using sustainable methods is increasing, and this trend is likely to continue as long as the costs of chemical inputs remain high and the need to maximize yield per acre is low (Madden, 1987).

CONCLUSIONS

Debate continues regarding the future of world agriculture. There are millions of hungry people in the world today, yet crop production increases are leveling off in the "breadbasket" nations of the world. Self-sufficiency in food production is far from a reality in many nations.

Some ecologists accept the inevitability of large-scale epidemics and die-offs of the human population to return it to a stable size. On the other hand, many food production experts in the wealthier nations encourage further transferral of mechanized agriculture to the less affluent, with the implication that the American system should be adopted worldwide. This would have to be accompanied by a massive industrialization program to employ the billions of farmers and families pushed off their land by mechanization and other economies of scale. There are immense social, environmental, and economic implications of such a transformation.

Many countries are attempting to stimulate a return to small-scale, subsistence-oriented farming for their rural residents, but are fighting a massive flow of people to the cities. It is unlikely that these plans can be effective without a strong guarantee to farmers that they can turn a profit growing food for themselves and others. This is impossible under most present-day land ownership and cash-crop-oriented systems.

In the United States, technological improvements will probably continue to produce increases in crop yields, and America will continue to be a major food exporter. Concerns for the future of agricultural resource development revolve mainly around the problems of energy efficiency, pesticide use, and soil erosion. Energy prices are particularly important to farm income. Although energy prices fluctuate, it seems clear that in the long run they must increase. There is growing concern over the ecological and health effects of pesticide use, as pests become resistant to them and as farmers turn more to chemical, rather than mechanical, means for controlling weeds. At the same time, there are indications that in the United States, at least, pesticide use may have peaked, and farmers may be embarking on a new technological revolution that will both reduce pollution and conserve soil. Nonetheless, soil erosion continues at unacceptable rates in many areas of the United States. Although it will probably not be an acute problem causing abandonment of land, it will be a chronic problem that will ultimately force farmers to increase inputs of fertilizer and possibly organic matter to replace lost nutrients and to improve deteriorating soil structure. All of these factors will further increase the cost of producing food and fiber. Thus it seems that the United States will continue to be an important food provider, but that food prices will probably have to rise substantially in the next few decades to allow this production to take place.

REFERENCES AND ADDITIONAL READING

Alexandratos, N., 1988, *Agriculture toward 2000.* Rome: Food and Agriculture Organization.

Bajwa, R.S., W.M. Crosswhite, and J.E. Hostetler. 1987. *Agricultural Irrigation and Water Supply.* USDA Agricultural Information Bulletin 532. Washington, DC: U.S. Department of Agriculture.

Brewer, M.F., and R.F. Boxley. 1981. Agricultural land: Adequacy of acres, concepts, and information. *Amer. J. Agric. Econ.* 63: 879–887.

Brown, L. 1980. *Food or Fuel: New Competition for the World's Cropland.* Worldwatch Paper #35. Washington, DC: Worldwatch Institute.

Buckman, H.O., and N.C. Brady. 1969. *The Nature and Properties of Soils,* 7th ed. New York: Macmillan.

Burros, M. 1989. A growing harvest of organic produce. *The New York Times,* March 29, p. C1.

Council on Environmental Quality. 1981a. *Global 2000 Report to the President.* Washington, DC: U.S. Government Printing Office.

———. 1981b. *Environmental Trends.* Washington, DC: U.S. Government Printing Office.

————. 1989. *Environmental Trends*. Washington, DC: U.S. Government Printing Office.

Crabbe, D., and S. Lawson. 1981. *The World Food Book*. London: Kogan Page.

Duffy, M., and S.R. Johnson. 1988. Agriculture and ground-water pollution in Iowa. *EPA J.* 14(3): 19–21.

Food and Agriculture Organization. 1989. *1988 FAO Production Yearbook*. Rome: United Nations, Food and Agriculture Organization.

Gasser, C.S., and R.T. Fraley. 1989. Genetically engineering plants for crop improvement. *Science* 244: 1293–1299.

Hallberg, G.R. 1985. *Agricultural Chemicals and Groundwater Quality in Iowa: Status Report 1985*. Ames: Iowa State University Cooperative Extension Service.

Harlan, J.R. 1976. The plants and animals that nourish man. *Sci. Amer.* 235(3): 88–98.

Heady, E.O. 1976. The agriculture of the U.S. *Sci. Amer.* 235(3): 107–127.

Hulse, J.H. 1982. Food science and nutrition: The gulf between rich and poor. *Science* 216: 1291–1294.

Johnson, K. 1982. Equity in hazard management. *Environment* 24(9): 28–38.

Kaufman, M.T. 1980. No longer a charity case, India fills its own granaries. *The New York Times*, August 10. p. D22.

Larson, W.E., *et al.* 1983. The threat of soil erosion to long term crop production. *Science* 219: 458–465.

Lighthall, D.R., and R.S. Roberts. 1988. Agricultural chemicals and groundwater quality: The political economy of policy responses. *Environ. Professional* 10: 211–222.

Madden, P. 1987. Can sustainable agriculture be profitable? *Environment* 29(4): 19–20, 28–34.

National Academy of Sciences. 1972. *The Genetic Variability of Major Crops*. Washington, DC: National Academy of Sciences.

Parry, M. 1990. The potential impact on agriculture of the greenhouse effect. *Land Use Policy* 7: 109–123.

Paulino, L.A. 1986. *Food in the Third World: Past Trends and Projections to 2000*. Research Report 52. Washington, DC: International Food Policy Research Institute.

Rasmussen, W.D. 1982. The mechanization of agriculture. *Sci. Amer.* 247(3): 77–89.

Schmude, K.O. 1977. A perspective on prime farmland. *J. Soil and Water Conservation*. 35: 240–242.

Schneider, K. 1989. Science Academy says chemicals do not necessarily increase crops. *The New York Times*, September 8. p. A1.

Scrimshaw, N.S., and L. Taylor. 1980. Food. *Sci. Amer.* 239: 79–88.

Seitz, W.D., and E.R. Swanson. 1980. Economics of soil conservation from the farmer's perspective. *Amer. J. Agric. Econ.* 62: 1084–1088.

Sinha, S.K. 1986. Energy balance in agriculture: The developing world. In M.S. Swaminathan and S.K. Sinha (Eds.), *Global Aspects of Food Production*, pp. 57–84. Oxford: Tycooly International.

Slesser, M. 1986. Energy balance in agriculture: The developed world. In M.S. Swaminathan and S.K. Sinha (Eds.), *Global Aspects of Food Production*, pp. 47–56. Oxford: Tycooly International.

Soil Conservation Service. 1975. Procedure for computing sheet and rill erosion on project areas. *Technical Release 51*. Washington, DC: U.S. Government Printing Office.

————. 1980. *America's Soil and Water: Condition and Trends*. Washington, DC: U.S. Government Printing Office.

————. 1987. *Basic Statistics, 1982 National Resources Inventory*. Iowa State University, Statistical Laboratory, Statistical Bulletin 756. Ames: Iowa State Univ., Statistical Laboratory.

Swaminathan, M.S. 1988. Global agriculture at the crossroads. In H. DeBlij (Ed.), *Earth '88: Changing Geographic Perspectives*, pp. 316–329. Washington, DC: National Geographic Society.

U.S. Department of Agriculture. 1981. *RCA Appraisal, Parts 1 and 2*. Washington, DC: U.S. Government Printing Office.

————. 1989. *The Second RCA Appraisal*. Washington, DC: U.S. Government Printing Office.

U.S. Department of Agriculture and Council on Environmental Quality. 1981. *National Agricultural Lands Study, Final Report*. Washington, DC: U.S. Government Printing Office.

Water Resources Council. 1978. *The Nation's Water Resources, 1975–2000*. Washington, DC: U.S. Government Printing Office.

Wellhausen, E.J. 1976. The agriculture of Mexico. *Sci. Amer.* 235(3): 128–153.

Wischmeier, W.H. 1974. New developments in estimating water erosion. *Proc. 29th Annual Meeting, Soil Conservation Soc. Amer.*, pp. 179–186.

Wischmeier, W.H., and D.D. Smith. 1965. Predicting rainfall erosion losses from cropland east of the Rocky Mountains. *USDA Agricultural Handbook 282*. Washington, DC: U.S. Government Printing Office.

———. 1978. Predicting rainfall erosion losses–A guide to conservation planning. *USDA Agricultural Handbook 537.* Washington, DC: U.S. Government Printing Office.

Wortman, S. 1976. Food and agriculture. *Sci. Amer.* 235(3): 30–39.

TERMS TO KNOW

Arable Land
Conservation Tillage
Contour Plowing
Crop Rotation
Drip Irrigation
Erosion
Erosivity
Fertilizer
Flood Irrigation
Furrow Irrigation
Green Revolution
Gully
Horizons
Infiltration Capacity
Integrated Pest Management
Irrigation
Land Capability Classification
Minimum Tillage
Mixed Cropping
Monoculture
Overland Flow
Parent Material
Pesticide
Rill
Soil

Soil Erodibility
Soil Fertility
Soil Structure
Soil Texture
Sprinkler Irrigation
Strip Cropping
Stubble Mulch
Sustainable Agriculture
Terracing
Universal Soil Loss Equation
Water Holding Capacity
Windbreaks

STUDY QUESTIONS

1. What is meant by "sustainable agriculture"?
2. What are some of the causes of loss of agricultural land to other uses?
3. What are some of the important environmental hazards associated with the use of pesticides in agriculture?
4. How do flood, furrow, sprinkler, and drip irrigation vary in costs and efficiency?
5. What are some of the most important soil conservation techniques?
6. What are the world's major food crops?
7. What is the Green Revolution?
8. How do energy inputs and efficiency differ between mechanized agriculture and traditional animal-powered agriculture?
9. How do low food prices affect food availability in the Third World?

8

Rangelands: Food Resources for Animals

INTRODUCTION

Several resource issues are of particular importance in predicting and planning for future world supplies of meat, milk, and hides. These issues include the variability of rainfall patterns in lands already marginal for grazing, overgrazing, competing land uses, ancient cultural traditions, and the efficiency of using meat for food. In this chapter we will look at the quantity and quality of grazing lands, both globally and within the United States. As defined by the U.S. Forest Service, *range* is land that provides or is capable of providing forage for grazing or browsing animals. This includes grass, shrub, and forest lands that can support nutritive plant species, both native and introduced, natural and managed (U.S. Forest Service, 1981).

Human beings and domestic animals have depended on one another for thousands of years. In fact, one way of defining a *domesticate* is its inability to survive without human assistance. As with the plants that are now our major crops, so have our major food animals been carefully chosen generation by generation and bred for those characteristics that we find valuable, such as thick wool, milk and meat, and resistance to disease. As a result, characteristics that enable an animal to survive in the wild, such as intelligence or agility, are often not found in our domesticated animals. Thus they and we are mutually dependent for survival. For optimal production, herders and ranchers must provide livestock with high-quality food and ensure that the land grazed is not overused.

Most of the world's grazing lands are in semiarid climates, for in these low-rainfall areas the land generally cannot support arable agriculture without irrigation. Palatable grasses and low shrubs, however, are available to livestock (Fig. 8.1). Animals are grazed on other lands, too, usually mountainous areas and forests, both of which are unsuited for agriculture. Through the ages, livestock have been able to make use of land that was otherwise useless for human occupancy. In the United States, cattle grazing was the early backbone of the western states' economy, and in fact contributes to much of the region's folklore. Today raising and selling cattle is part of the nation's agribusiness industry. There are often conflicting demands on the land available for grazing, and a debate ebbs and flows over the comparative value of meat versus grain production for national and global food supplies.

USE AND ABUSE OF RANGELANDS: A GLOBAL VIEW

Range, or grazing land, provides forage for limited numbers of domestic animals. *Overgrazing* occurs when the numbers of animals on these lands exceed carrying capacities. Several areas of the world, notably the dry lands around the Mediterranean Sea, have been long overgrazed, with resulting problems of devegetation, erosion, and ultimately the threat of desertification. *Desertification* is the process of land becoming more desertlike as a result of devegetation and related soil deterioration, aggravated by drought. It occurs in parts of all

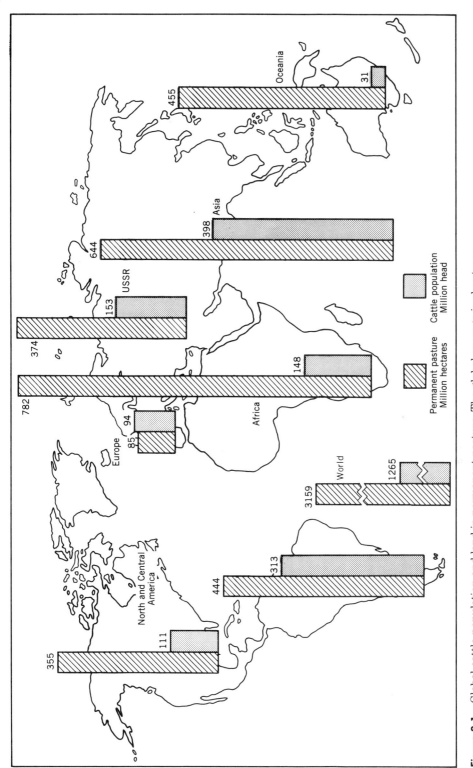

Figure 8.1 Global cattle population and land in permanent pasture. The global average is about one animal for every three hectares. Europe and Asia have large numbers of cattle relative to pasture area, while Africa and Oceania have smaller cattle populations per hectare. Africa has more pastureland than any other continent. (Source: Data from Crabbe and Lawson, 1981) World Resources, 1988.

the major semiarid regions of the world. There are several misconceptions about the causes of desertification. One is that global rainfall is decreasing. There is no evidence that modern desertification is the result of climate change, although droughts play a major role in the process. Also, we often hear statements about "advancing deserts"; this is also inaccurate. Deserts do not move—they are created in place by overuse of a sensitive resource.

LIVESTOCK USE PATTERNS

The herding of animals is an ancient system of arid lands resource use. Patterns of life dependent on livestock developed thousands of years ago in Asia and Africa and are still important to a remnant population of between 30 and 40 million people worldwide (World Resources Institute, 1988). Most of the world's *pastoralists* are located in Africa (55 percent), Asia (29 percent), and parts of Central and South America (15 percent). The traditional *pastoral nomad* is not oriented toward the production of large quantities of meat and dairy products for market. Instead, products of the sheep and goat herds of Asia and cattle herds of Africa are used locally or traded on a small scale. The past 100 years have seen a decline in the numbers of these pastoral nomads as a result of settlement in permanent locations. The process of *sedentarization* has been enforced by governments that encourage herding groups to settle in villages and that control the crossing of national borders. Additionally, many nomads have left their herds and families for work in urban areas.

In other agricultural systems, livestock are of varying importance. For example, in the wet rice cultivation regions that provide food for the populations of the Far East, there is little room on cultivated acreage for growing animal feed. Thus meat and dairy products play only a small role in the diet of southern and eastern Asia. This is changing, however, as American-style fast-food chains and the high-status appeal of beef make inroads into the traditional eating habits of the region.

With the nineteenth-century settlement of drier areas in the Americas and Australia, it became environmentally and financially feasible to raise and transport large numbers of livestock for transport to distant markets. The vast open stretches of shrub and grassland were well-suited for grazing, as there was not and still is not today enough rainfall for any other agricultural system except for risky *dry farming*. There are important differences between the traditional Asian and African pastoralism and cattle raising in the more recently settled drylands. One is that livestock raising in the Americas and Australia is oriented toward meat instead of milk consumption. The newer system is also more highly dependent on a technologically complex set of elements, including truck transport, antibiotics, and other food supplements.

Another element of these newer livestock raising patterns is the grazing land itself, which can be brought more fully under the control of human managers than was technologically possible for Old World nomads. The main tool available to the nomad for range improvement or alteration was fire. The American farmer can alter vast stretches of land with defoliants, irrigation systems, and introduced seeds and can use helicopters, trucks, and bulldozers as tools. Even with these new developments, however, the problems of overuse, degradation, and erosion loom as large in these modern systems as they have for millennia in the drylands of Asia and Africa.

LAND DEGRADATION

A number of factors contribute to the degradation of the world's rangelands. Overgrazing, the expansion of cultivation, the conversion of rangeland to cropland, and increased human population pressures are all taking their toll on the rangeland conditions worldwide. The degradation on drylands (arid and semiarid lands) is particularly acute. Desertification now threatens about one-third of the world's land area (18.5 million square miles or 48 million km^2) (World Resources Institute, 1987). Figure 8.2 is a world map of the main areas affected by desertification. Many of these areas are in the semiarid regions of western and eastern Africa, northern China, and Southwest Asia.

The sharp rise in population in these areas has led to an ever-increasing demand for food. In addition, improvements in the overall stan-

Figure 8.2 World areas affected by desertification. Regions with a high risk of desertification are in the semiarid regions of Africa, northern China, and southwest Asia. A primary area of concern is the Sahel region of Africa, located along the southern margin of the Sahara Desert. (*Source:* World Resources Institute, 1987.)

dard of living and increased use of animal protein in fulfilling dietary needs have resulted in a subsequent increase in *ruminant* resources (cattle, sheep, and goats). For example, cattle populations increased 41 percent between 1950 and 1984, while sheep and goat populations increased by 38 percent during the same time period (Wolf, 1986). This rate of growth slowed during the 1980s, which saw only a 4 percent increase in cattle and an 8 percent increase in sheep and goats (Table 8.1). Regionally, however, substantial increases in ruminants occurred in Asia (cattle and buffalo), the Far East (sheep and goats), and Latin America (buffalo). Decreases in ruminant populations were found in North America, Oceania, and Western Europe (cattle).

This increase in animal populations means a rise in the use of grazing lands and is thus a major cause of recent desertification in places like Africa. For example, in the Republic of the Sudan, located on the southern margins of the Sahara Desert, there is evidence that the line separating scrub from barren lands shifted 56 to 62 miles (90 to 100 km) between 1958 and 1974 (Eckholm and Brown, 1977). Desertification in the *Sahel* was particularly severe during the 1968–1973 drought.

However, about three-fourths of the world's ruminants are no longer totally raised on range resources as countries increasingly move toward intensive livestock production. Farming and the use of forage crops such as alfalfa now contribute to the animals' feed. This pattern is true not only in the developed world but more so in the developing countries. For example, in India, 91 percent of ruminant feed is derived from forage crops, whereas 4 percent comes from rangelands. In the United States, 84 percent of the feed is from forage crops (Wolf, 1986).

THE HUMAN CONTEXT

According to a study done for the U.N. Conference on Desertification (Kates *et al.*, 1976), an estimated 50 million people worldwide are directly affected by desertification. The 3 million residents of the world's drylands who are dependent on traditional and modern animal-based livelihood systems are disproportionately affected by desertification.

The origins of desertification are complex. The condition develops from the interaction between agriculture-based, animal-based, and urban-based livelihood systems in semiarid areas, fluctuations in the natural environment, and changes in human social systems. These changes include the growth and decline of human populations, alterations in and losses of traditional life-styles, and changing governmental directions (Kates *et al.*, 1976). All of these societal and institutional factors work with natural factors to bring about desertification. For example, changes in carrying capacity are brought about by rainfall variations. Pastoralists want to keep as many cattle as their land can tolerate; to keep fewer would mean less income and decreased economic stability.

It takes years to build up a herd if it is accomplished by reproduction alone. The herd represents savings, which should be depleted as slowly as possible if the length of drought is uncertain (Fig. 8.3). In times of plentiful rain and good forage, pastoralists increase herd sizes to make use of the expanded resource. During droughts, forage production and carrying capacity are reduced, and overgrazing results. Animals are slaughtered to provide food and income, which reduces grazing pressure, though not before considerable damage is done to vegetation and soil. This pattern is a common one and is a result of the lag time between changes in the forage supply and changes in the affected animal population. Thus in times of increasing carrying capacity the range is understocked, and it is overstocked when carrying capacity is decreasing. The only ways to avoid this problem are either to continually ship animals long distances from areas short in forage to areas with surplus or to keep herd sizes at a constant low level well below carrying capacity for all but the worst years. For many of the poorer countries of the world, these changes would require expensive government regulation and a further reduction in the freedom of the traditional pastoral nomad. It should be noted that especially in Africa, national boundaries add another constraint in that they interfere with the traditional migration routes of pastoral nomads.

TABLE 8.1 World Ruminant Resources, 1988 (Millions)

Region Total	Sheep and Goats	% Change 1979–1988	Buffalo	% Change 1979–1988	Cattle	% Change 1979–1988	Total
North and Central America	12	−1.3	—	—	111	−13.0	123
Western Europe	111	14.4	0	−24.2	94	−6.2	205
Oceania	231	12.1	—	—	31	−8.6	262
Other developed countries	36	−4.7	—	—	17	−8.3	53
Africa	287	10.4	—	—	148	7.2	435
Latin America	152	5.3	10	49.2	313	8.2	475
Near East	208	−1.0	3	−7.2	53	2.4	264
Far East	267	20.9	111	11.8	262	2.2	640
Asia	200	−0.3	24	13.5	83	29.0	307
Eastern Europe and USSR	188	1.0	0	13.5	153	2.9	342
Total	1692	7.8	141	−11.8	1265	3.8	3106

Source: Food and Agriculture Organization (1988).

Figure 8.3   Sheep herding in Iraq. The herd is usually the pastoralist's most valuable asset.

The number of people at risk from land degradation will only increase as human population levels rise, particularly in developing countries. In many countries, population pressures have already stretched the land's productive capability, and to ensure human survivability, restoration of degraded lands will be necessary. The process, however, is slow and costly. The costs of such efforts not only reflect remediation of the biological and geophysical systems, but they must include the social systems as well, including labor. As an example, the FAO spent $289 million between 1985 and 1987 to improve African agricultural lands and estimates that another $1 billion is needed for rehabilitation in selected countries like India, Ethiopia, Indonesia, Pakistan, and Kenya (World Resources Institute, 1988). Recent estimates suggest that $70 billion is needed to fight desertification on grazing lands worldwide (World Resources Institute, 1988).

GRASS FOR ANIMALS, MEAT FOR PEOPLE

RANGELAND ECOLOGY

Most of the world's prime grazing lands are natural grasslands found in semiarid and subhumid areas. Grasses do well in a semiarid climate for several reasons. When water is in short supply, it takes precedence over sunshine as a limiting factor (see Chapter 4). Trees, which require relatively large amounts of water, do not compete well. Grasses and other plants that can grow and reproduce in a short wet season are better equipped to survive. In addition, aridity increases the likelihood of fire, and this also favors grasses. Trees take longer to regenerate after fire than do grasses, and frequent fires may prevent trees from taking hold. Many of the world's grassland areas exist because of frequent fires, either of natural or human origin.

The ability of grasses to grow rapidly when conditions are favorable, combined with the variability of precipitation in semiarid areas, leads to seasonal and annual variations in the amount of grass that grows in grassland areas. This means that the number of herbivores that can be supported by the land also varies. Under natural conditions, populations of these grazing animals such as rodents and deer are kept in check by competition for available food. But the population levels of domestic animals are controlled by humans, not by natural conditions. To maximize animal production in the short run, herders often exceed the carrying capacity of the land, which results in damage to the vegetation.

Grazing affects plants in several ways. Plants are reduced in size by grazing, which usually inhibits their ability to photosynthesize and grow. Animals damage plants by trampling, which is particularly detrimental to young plants. The reduction in plant cover caused by grazing leads to a deterioration in soil conditions that also inhibits plant growth. On the positive side, the seeds of some plant species are spread by grazing animals, either by being eaten and excreted or by being attached to fur. Other plant species may be inhibited from reproducing under grazing pressure, for example, if their seeds are digested. Finally, grazing may stimulate plant growth by reducing competition among plants for moisture or nutrients, and thus the plants may be able to replace some of the biomass taken by animals.

Range plant species vary in their ability to survive and reproduce under grazing pressure. Some species may be able to quickly regenerate leaves lost to animals, whereas others cannot. Some are relatively unaffected by trampling, and for others this is fatal. Most importantly, some species are more palatable to grazing animals and thus are eaten first, and some are less palatable and are eaten only after the desirable forage is consumed. These differences in susceptibility of plants to grazing impact are the basis of the ecological changes that result from grazing.

Range ecologists classify plant species in a particular area as decreasers, increasers, or invaders. *Decreasers* are plant species that are present in a plant community but decrease in importance (as measured by numbers of plants or percentage of ground covered) as a result of grazing. They are generally the most palatable plants, but they may also include species that are negatively affected by animals in other ways, such as by trampling. *Increasers* are species that were present prior to grazing and that increase in importance as a result of grazing. They may be less palatable species, or they may increase simply because there is less competition from the decreasers for water or nutrients. *Invaders* are species that were not present prior to grazing but that are able to colonize the area as a result of the change in conditions.

No species can be classified as decreaser,

increaser, or invader without reference to a particular site. A species may be an increaser in one area and an invader in another, or it may be a decreaser in one area and an increaser in another. For example, big sagebrush (*Artemisia tridentata*) is present on much of the rangelands of the United States, and over most of this area it is an increaser (Fig. 8.4). Although it is high in nutrients, it is unpalatable to cattle and sheep except when other forage is unavailable. Big sagebrush is also unaffected by trampling. In some areas of the American West, it was insignificant or not present prior to the onset of grazing in the nineteenth century, but today it is a dominant species. In these areas it is an invader.

Mesquite (*Prosopis juliflora*) is another example of an increaser or invader that is today perceived as inferior to grass cover as a food source for livestock, even though its fleshy pods were a major food source for the southwestern American Indians and their livestock (see Chapter 1). Mesquite has taken over large areas of grassland, affecting an estimated 70 million acres (28 million ha) of range in the American Southwest over the past century. Its spread is directly attributable to overgrazing. In search of food on land with little grass cover, cattle eat mesquite pods and deposit them in their dung on grasslands that have been overgrazed. Subsequently, grasses are unable to compete with the better-adapted mesquite (Harris, 1971; Vale, 1978).

As a final example, some grasslands that supported perennial grasses before grazing began are now covered mainly by annual grasses (Fig. 8.5). The annual grasses, by spreading large numbers of seeds each year, can replace themselves even though the plants are eaten or trampled. The perennial grasses, on the other hand, produce fewer seeds, and thus once trampled or eaten are less able to reproduce.

Overgrazing not only causes changes in plant communities, but it also affects the soil resource. Removal of plant cover and compaction of the soil by trampling reduce infiltration capacities, resulting in greater erosion and reduced soil moisture. Thus it becomes more difficult for remaining plants to survive, or for new seedlings to take hold. The process is reversible, but this requires significant reduction

Figure 8.4   Sagebrush rangelands in New Mexico.

in grazing pressure and in many cases active range improvement measures.

Accelerated erosion caused by grazing has plagued most of the world's semiarid lands. In the southwestern United States, for example, vegetation removal has caused significant increases in soil erosion rates over wide areas. This erosion is caused by both wind and water, but water erosion is particularly dramatic. Large gullies called *arroyos* have been cut in valley floors over much of the West. The period 1880 to 1930 was one of particularly intense arroyo formation, and some attribute this to the effects of cattle, although other factors may also be responsible (Cooke and Reeves, 1976).

Figure 8.5   Grasslands in California.

THE ENERGY EFFICIENCY OF MEAT PRODUCTION

Beef production in the United States involves raising cattle on rangelands or farms and transporting them to feedlots, where they are fattened with grain so that their meat will be well-marbled. Consumer preferences and grain prices influence forage versus grain consumption by cattle. In the 1950s the price of grain was low, enabling U.S. feedlot operations to accept younger cattle. Grain contributed a higher percentage of an animal's finished weight in the 1950s than 20 years later, when high grain prices led meat producers to rely more heavily on grazing.

In the mid-1970s, the high cost of grain led to an alteration in USDA grazing standards for beef. In 1975, the standards were changed so that a smaller percentage of grain in the diet could still result in the meat being labeled "USDA Choice." In addition to the cost factor, other reasons have emerged for reducing the amount of marbling in beef. Consumer groups have advocated fat reduction in beef by reducing the grain consumed. Their principal reasons include the health benefits of a lowered consumption of cholesterol found in animal fat and the freeing of grains and croplands to feed hungry people instead of cattle (USFS, 1981).

Humans are omnivores, in that they consume both plant and animal foods. Meat is a high-quality food because it contains a high proportion of protein and other important nutrients. The efficiency of converting vegetable food energy to animal food energy in the United States is about 5 percent (Cook, 1976). That is, 20 calories of food energy as feed (range grasses and grains in the feedlot) are needed to produce one calorie of food energy as meat on the table. A balanced vegetable diet can also provide these same nutrients found in meat.

If the food used to produce meat is grown on land that could be used to grow grain for human consumption, then we are in effect substituting a substantial amount of vegetable food for a small amount of meat, which would seem to be unwise in a world short of food. On the other hand, meat produced by grazing animals on land that is not otherwise usable for food production represents an important increase in available food supplies. Thus range animals can be a means of converting otherwise unusable vegetable matter to valuable food, even if the efficiency of conversion is relatively low. It is when livestock are fed high-quality corn and other grains that the questions of efficiency and equity arise. These issues are particularly important in Central and South America, where forest conversion to grasslands for cattle production has been largely stimulated by North American tastes for hamburger (see Issue 8–1).

U.S. RANGELAND RESOURCES

HISTORICAL DEVELOPMENT OF RANGELAND USE

Prior to European colonization, North America's wide open spaces were home to huge herds of elk, buffalo, and pronghorn antelope, with an estimated 23–34 million head (Wagner, 1978). Cattle domestication was unknown until Spanish settlers brought livestock to their New World settlements in the early sixteenth century. The American Indians had not found any need to harness animal power, as their agriculture was performed with hand tools and loads were carried manually or dragged. Wild animals for meat and hides were plentiful and widely available, so there was little need to bring them under human control.

The Spaniards and later colonists brought with them a cattle-based livelihood system adapted to European culture and resource availability. These settlers were accustomed to the crowded conditions and overgrazed lands of Europe. In contrast, the apparently limitless grazing opportunities available in North America helped build a cattle-raising industry that today covers immense tracts of open range and is capital-intensive in feedlots. This has enabled Americans to have one of the highest per capita rates of meat consumption in the world.

The range resource was first utilized in the eastern parts of the continent and then moved westward with human settlement. The colonial settlers sent frontier-fattened cattle to city markets and were the precursors of large-scale stock raising that developed in Texas and other western states. By the 1840s, Texas cattle drives were delivering cattle to markets in Ohio, Louisiana, and California.

The boom period in both cattle and sheep raising came in the decades between the Civil War and the early twentieth century, by which time the once-wild frontier areas were being transformed for farming and urban uses. During the 1870s, expansion accelerated as the Great Plains Indian tribes were subdued and the vast buffalo herds decimated. Between 1870 and 1890 the cattle population in the West rose from between 4 and 5 million to over 26.5 million. Sheep raising was introduced in several locations, notably along the eastern seaboard and, during the eighteenth and nineteenth centuries, in New Mexico, Arizona, Texas, and California. Between 1850 and 1890 the estimated sheep population in the West rose from 514,000 to over 20 million (Dale, 1930).

The availability of free or low-cost forage on federally owned lands was essential to the profitability of the developing cattle industry. In addition to leasing the water and forage rights on government property, many ranchers obtained title to vast areas of federal land by evading the acreage limitations imposed by the 1862 Homestead Act (see Chapter 3). By the early twentieth century, the use of barbed wire had created boundaries to the great American pasture, and the days of open-range cattle and sheep drives wound down. These were replaced by truck and train transport to regional markets, notably Chicago, Minneapolis, Omaha, Dallas, and Denver.

The federal government has imposed several constraints on the traditional independence of the western rancher beginning with the establishment of the National Forest System (1905), passage of the Taylor Grazing Act (1934), and the establishment of the *Bureau of Land Management* (BLM) in 1946. Initially, ranchers were not permitted to let animals graze in the National Forest reserves, but a nominal fee system later permitted the land to be opened for use. Battles have raged ever since over the government's right to control numbers of cattle and the seasonality of grazing. The Taylor Grazing Act organized federal lands into a system of 144 grazing districts for joint management by the federal government and local stock raisers. Some cattlemen resisted this scheme and attempted to turn management of these lands over to the state governments. However, the effects of overgrazing were evident, and the Taylor Grazing Act's range rehabilitation plans received Congressional support. The Act was passed, but it remained underfunded and subject to constant disagreement between federal and local interests (Stegner, 1981a).

Today, 22,000 ranchers lease grazing rights from the BLM to graze 4 percent of the nation's beef cattle. A recent estimate suggests that ranchers lease lands at bargain prices. In 1982, for example, the BLM collected $20.9 million in grazing fees. The fair market value of these grazing rights indicates that $104 million should have been collected (Baker, 1983). More recently, monthly grazing fees on public lands cost $1.40 per animal, whereas grazing on private land costs an estimated $8.85 per animal. The government subsidy ($7.45) provides a strong incentive for ranchers to graze on government lands regardless of the quality of the forage. By 1990, grazing fees had increased to $1.81 per animal unit.

The BLM took over the administration of these and other public lands from the General Land Office and administered them in a similar manner until 1976. In that year Congress passed the *Federal Land Policy and Management Act* (*FLPMA*), which brought together thousands of pieces of legislation related to public land management. It also increased the power of the BLM to manage its 170 million acres (69 million ha) for the public good, with *multiple use* and *sustained yield* as guiding principles. Through the use of inventories, comprehensive plans, and public participation, the control of America's public lands began to slip away from the ranching, timber, and energy interests that had been influential at the state level (Stegner, 1981b; Nothdurft, 1981).

CURRENT RANGELAND STATUS IN THE UNITED STATES

In 1982, there were 735 million acres (297 million ha) of rangeland in the United States, and Alaska contains 232 million acres (94 million ha) of this total. In addition to this rangeland, there are about 320 million acres (130 million ha) of woodland that can be grazed. In the lower 48 states, 99 percent of the 503 million acres (203 million ha) of rangeland is found in 17 western states (Fig. 8.6). Only 1 percent is in the 31 eastern states, mostly in the South. Any potential for increased grazing in the East depends on more intensive grazing of forests or the removal of forest cover.

Most of the rangelands in the United States are on private lands. For example, in the six Great Plains states, 98 percent of the range is privately owned, and this area accounts for 25 percent of the range grazed in the lower 48 states. Only in the Pacific Northwest does federal land supply more than half of the grazed range (USFS, 1981).

There are serious problems of degradation on much of the nation's range, especially in the Southwest. The Forest Service defines *range condition* as "an estimate of the degree to which the present vegetation and ground cover depart from that which is presumed to be the natural potential (or climax) for the site" (USFS, 1981, p. 158). They use a four-class scale to judge range quality: excellent, good, fair, and poor (Table 8.2). This rating scheme is then applied to parcels of land and is used to measure the amount of forage produc-

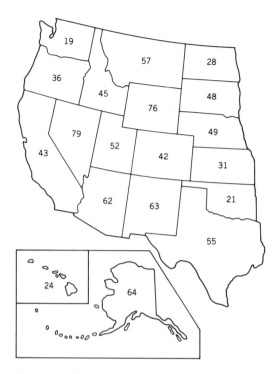

Figure 8.6 Rangeland as a percentage of total land area in the western United States. More than 75 percent of the land area of Nevada and Wyoming is currently classified as range. (*Source:* U.S. Forest Service, 1981.)

tion on that land. In 1982, the most recent assessment of range conditions showed that 59 percent of the nation's nonfederally owned range was in fair to poor condition (Soil Conservation Service, 1987). (Fig. 8.7) For federally owned lands, 46 percent of the rangelands was in fair to good condition (USFS, 1981). By 1986, 71 percent of BLM lands was labeled fair to good while 80 percent of USFS lands was in

TABLE 8.2   Range Condition Classification

Category	Definition
Excellent	More than 75 percent resemblance to the climax community
Good	51–75 percent
Fair	26–50 percent
Poor	0–25 percent

Source: USDA (1989).

satisfactory condition (CEQ, 1988). There is a gradient in quality running from north to south in the 17 western states, with the highest-quality range in the wetter north and poorer range conditions in the drier south. In the arid and semiarid intermontane states, including California, Arizona, New Mexico, Oregon, Idaho, and Texas, less than 40 percent of the range is in good to excellent condition. Most of the remaining western states have between 40 to 60 percent of their range in good to excellent condition (USDA, 1989). It is calculated that 37 percent of North America's arid lands is in a state of "severe" desertification. Within the United States, perhaps 225 million acres (91 million ha) (about 25 percent of the rangeland total) are in a state of "severe" or "very severe" desertification (Dregne, 1977; Sheridan, 1981a).

Nationally, only 33 percent of the range is adequately protected from deterioration. Sixty-two percent of the rangelands requires some form of conservation treatment to enhance the resource. Around 5 percent is so permanently damaged that conservation efforts are not suitable. Regionally, more than two-thirds of the range in the arid and semiarid states requires extensive treatment, ranging from livestock management and distribution of livestock (reductions in animals per hectare) to protect the vegetation from overgrazing to more expensive brush management techniques such as the destruction of weedy species, replanting, and so forth. Overgrazing protection is needed to conserve the majority of rangelands in California, Minnesota, North Dakota, and South Dakota. Brush management and brush improvement are needed in the remaining states (Table 8.3).

Taking a broader view beyond the health of the region's ecosystems, the grasslands are in slightly better condition than the shrublands. The mountain meadows, grasslands, and the Great Plains ecosystems are generally in better condition than the semiarid and arid range of the West and Southwest. This is a function of many factors, including a shorter grazing history, different management practices, and greater moisture availability. All of these enable an area to recover more rapidly when grazing pressures are removed (USFS, 1981).

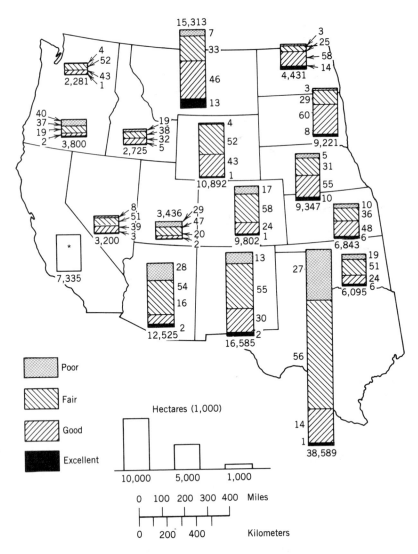

*unable to assess as mostly annual grasses

Figure 8.7 Condition of rangeland in the United States in 1982. In the continental United States, only 46 percent of the nation's rangeland is classified as either in fair or good condition. (*Source:* U.S. Department of Agriculture, 1989.)

RANGELAND DEGRADATION

Rangeland degradation in the United States has many causes, and two case studies help illustrate that poverty, carelessness, and fluctuating climatic conditions can contribute to the spread of desertlike conditions. In the case of the Navajo Indians of Arizona and New Mexico, very severe rangeland degradation is caused by too many people, with few economic alternatives, being crowded onto too little land. During the past century, the Navajo population has multiplied by a factor of ten, while the land available has only tripled. From the late 1930s, when overgrazing was first tackled by the U.S. government, the Navajo's sheep population has grown from an estimated 1.3 million to 2.17 million in the early 1980s (Sheridan, 1981b). When one considers that the U.S. government believes that the 15-million-acre (6-million-

TABLE 8.3   Percentage of Acreages Needing Conservation Treatments in the United States

State	Area Needing Treatment	Treatment type		
		Erosion Control	Overgrazing Protection	Brush Management
Arizona	74	6.0	35.9	58.1
Arkansas	67	6.0	6.0	88.0
California	43	29.0	42.0	29.0
Colorado	69	17.8	34.6	47.6
Florida	78	0.5	5.4	94.1
Idaho	72	4.7	24.2	71.1
Kansas	53	5.6	35.0	59.4
Louisiana	80	0	50.4	49.6
Minnesota	37	1.3	51.2	47.5
Missouri	79	7.4	14.7	77.9
Nebraska	31	4.9	45.5	49.6
Nevada	54	6.0	17.4	76.6
New Mexico	69	28.7	24.6	46.7
North Dakota	29	9.1	65.3	25.6
Oklahoma	61	8.0	20.0	72.0
Oregon	80	11.9	10.4	77.7
South Dakota	40	5.4	65.6	29.0
Texas	74	1.9	10.5	87.6
Utah	83	27.1	37.1	35.8
Washington	67	8.0	21.8	70.2
Wyoming	61	15.5	31.1	53.4

Source: USDA (1989).

ha) Navajo reservation has a carrying capacity of 600,000 sheep, the problem of overgrazing becomes quite clear.

What are the environmental effects of this overgrazing, and why do the Navajo continue it? Most of the land surface of the reservation is badly eroded, and the plant cover the animals rely on for food is not being maintained. Until recently the Navajo have had few alternatives, and conflicts between traditional livelihood patterns and high unemployment rates (over 60 percent) forced the Navajo to continue their overgrazing practices. Since sheep and cattle herding remain the major source of income for many Navajo, they are naturally unwilling to reduce animal population levels to reach what they see as a U.S. government-generated ideal called carrying capacity that could threaten their own security.

In the Rio Puerco basin of New Mexico, the BLM finds itself in a losing battle to reduce overgrazing in what is perhaps the most environmentally degraded western river basin

(Sheridan, 1981b). First settled by poor Spanish families in the late eighteenth century, the Rio Puerco basin was called the "bread basket of New Mexico" by the late nineteenth century. During this period there were about 240,000 sheep and 9000 cattle on the 3.7-million-acre (1.5-million-ha) range. Villages and farms prospered along the river.

During the 1880s, a period of adverse weather conditions developed from which the Rio Puerco basin and other parts of the dry West have yet to recover. Water tables fell, arroyos grew, and eroded sediment flowed out of the Rio Puerco and into the Rio Grande. It is estimated that between 1885 and 1962, 1.1 to 1.5 billion tons (1 to 1.4 billion tonnes) of sediment were eroded. Today it is estimated that 3.6 billion tons (3.3 billion tonnes) are eroded annually (USDA, 1989).

How did this situation develop and what are some of its effects? There is some question as to whether overgrazing or climatic changes were the major cause of the initial arroyo cutting. Perhaps a minor change in precipitation patterns was sufficient to initiate arroyo cutting, with continued erosion aggravated by overgrazing. At any rate, arroyos, once a minor landscape feature, now dominate the basin. In the 1930s typical arroyos were a little over 100 feet (30 m) wide. On either side of these arroyos were lands still suitable for grazing and irrigated farming. Today, however, that land is being eaten away, and the average arroyo width is now 300 feet (91 m). Socially, the effects have been severe, and many former riverside villages are just ghost towns today.

Grazing continues in the basin, though at reduced levels. The BLM, which manages a quarter of the basin's land, estimated in 1975 that 55 percent of the area's public land was undergoing "moderate to severe" erosion (U.S. Bureau of Land Management, 1978). This will increase, BLM predicts, to 73 percent by the year 2000 if current grazing practices continue. The ranchers who hold grazing permits are being restricted in the number of animals they can graze on public land, and BLM's plans

include a schedule of a fallow year for about a third of the land at any given time. Fences, wells, rainwater catchments, water tanks, and reseeding are also options; however, with three-fourths of the basin's land in private hands, the BLM can only restore a small portion of the degraded range. In addition, critics doubt that the most delicate soils can recover in a year's time, and the lack of any plant litter over large areas makes seed germination difficult (Sheridan, 1981b).

RANGE MANAGEMENT AND IMPROVEMENT TECHNIQUES

The BLM and predecessor agencies have struggled from their inception to reduce overgrazing. Today's grazing allotments (numbers of animals permitted per acre) were established according to 1930s estimates of historical rangeland use. It is suggested that the 1930s cattlemen provided the government with inflated figures of past cattle populations.

ISSUE 8–1   Billions of Burgers

North Americans consume billions of hamburgers each year as we are endlessly told in fast-food advertising ("over 70 billion burgers sold"). Americans eat more than 70 pounds (32 kg) of beef per person each year. An ordinary house cat in this country eats more beef than the average Central American. To meet this demand, the United States must import beef from other nations. In 1986, for example, 1 million tonnes of beef and veal were imported to the United States (USDA, 1986), about a third of this from Central America. Other supplying countries include Australia, New Zealand, Brazil, Argentina, Dominican Republic, and Haiti. To accommodate this enormous demand, some beef-producing countries are rapidly converting forests into grazing lands. Nowhere is this more serious than in Central America.

Currently, about two-thirds of the arable land in Central America is in cattle production. In the 1970s there was a rapid expansion of the Central American cattle industry in response to the U.S. demand for inferior cuts of beef that

were primarily used in the fast-food industry. Prior to this time, the Central American cattle industry was concentrated along the Pacific Ocean in the coastal regions. As the number of cattle increased on the grazing acreage, more overgrazing occurred in the Pacific lowland region. As a result, cattle production slowly encroached into the Caribbean lowlands region by the cutting down of tropical rainforests to create new grasslands. The increased pressure for land conversion was directly related to the North American appetite for hamburgers. The expansion of the cattle industry, including meat packing and processing, was assisted by loans to the host countries from the World Bank, in the form of development assistance.

Why is Central American beef so important to the United States? Why can't the demand be met with less destruction of the tropical rainforests in the region? Central American cattle rely on forage, whereas North American cattle are fed grains, and the meat of forage-fed cattle has less fat. In a diet conscious society, lean meat

Thus in agreeing to reduce their allotments, many ranchers may in fact do very little (Sheridan, 1981a).

The best way to manage rangelands is to maintain animal populations at or below carrying capacity. Carrying capacity varies from location to location and from year to year. Range ecologists have developed techniques for estimating carrying capacity based on vegetation type, average precipitation, soil characteristics, and other data. It remains difficult, however, to predict rainfall months in advance, so planning herd sizes to suit range conditions is sometimes a problem. Over the long run, though, it is possible to determine fairly closely just how many animals should be allowed to occupy a given piece of land, and under what conditions. For most of the federally owned lands this long-term planning is done by the BLM; for privately owned lands it is the responsibility of the landowner.

Rangeland that is damaged by overgrazing is not lost forever; it will recover if grazing pressure is reduced. In contrast to this passive method, there are several active techniques that are used to improve range quality. These include mechanical, chemical, and biological control of undesirable plants, and burning, seeding, fertilization, and irrigation (Vallentine, 1989). Mechanical brush control by plowing, bulldozing, or dragging heavy chains across the land is widely used to control sagebrush, mesquite, juniper, and other undesirable species. In some cases the slash from such operations is burned, and in others it is left as an erosion control measure. In some areas goats are used to control woody species, as they will strip plants of leaves and eat entire seedlings while cattle will not. Care must be taken that the goats do not overgraze the range, however, or desirable species will also be lost.

Herbicides are widely used, through aerial and ground applications, sometimes in combination with other control methods. Seeding and fertilization are usually used to stimulate

---

is in. In addition, Central American beef is inexpensive and the shipping costs are lower because of its proximity to the United States. Finally, U.S. health codes prohibit beef imports from countries with hoof and mouth disease. Countries like Brazil (where this disease is prevalent) must first process the beef by cooking, so that the finished product, such as pastrami, is allowable for import. For the primary producing nations in Central America (Costa Rica, Honduras, Nicaragua, and Guatemala), the beef is either frozen or refrigerated and shipped to points of entry into the United States. Once it passes inspection and is given the USDA grade stamp, the beef makes its way to you. The beef is widely used by fast-food chains and in fast-food processing. Many of our processed foods (lunch meat, chili, soups, beef stews, hash, TV dinners, baby food, and pet foods) are made from Central American beef. Unfortunately, the beef is hard to trace once it arrives in the United States as the commodity is bought and sold many times. Some fast-food chains readily admit to using such beef (Jack-in-the-Box, Burger King, and Roy Rogers), whereas others claim to use only 100 percent pure U.S. beef. McDonald's, for example, is adamant about the origin of its beef. A flyer titled "McDonald's and the Environment" states: "Nowhere in the world does McDonald's purchase beef from rain forest land. We do not, have not and will not purchase beef from rain forest (or recently deforested rain forest) land."

As we continue to enjoy hamburgers, current estimates place the rate of tropical rainforest loss in Central America at more than 1550 square miles (4000 km^2) per year. This equals a stunning 4 square miles (11 square kilometers) every day. Beef production will continue as long as demand remains high. The fast-food industry may not be the sole culprit since it is really you and I who demand a quarter-pounder with cheese, or a Whopper. Until our consumption of beef is reduced and we are no longer a hamburger society, the problems of overgrazing and deforestation will continue in Central America.

growth of forage plants after removal of brush. Irrigation is a very costly method of range improvement and is only used in special circumstances. These range improvement measures, though expensive, can be very effective in increasing the available forage, sometimes by as much as 5 to 10 times. In some areas, notably Arizona, conversion of shrubs to grassland is justified as a method of increasing water runoff for agricultural and urban uses as well as providing forage for cattle.

Rangeland improvement measures are used on both private and public lands. The federal government, particularly the BLM, plays a major role in attempting to repair some of the damage done by overgrazing in the past. In 1979, BLM began a 20-year program to improve the rangeland it administers, including range improvement on 139 million acres (55 million ha) and erosion control on 148 million acres (60 million ha). The goal of the program is to double annual forage production on BLM lands from 5.6 million to 11.2 million tons (5.1 to 10.2 million tonnes) annually.

An experimental stewardship system has been devised that provides for collective management by ranchers and government agencies of five range areas. A BLM proposal would permit certain ranchers to carry out the range improvements at their own expense in return for lengthened grazing leases (Baker, 1983).

RANGELAND RESOURCE ISSUES

There are many controversial issues regarding rangeland management. One issue is predator control, particularly the coyote, which is seen as a menace to sheep ranching (see Issue 8–2). Another issue is the notion of the privatization of land and grazing on those public lands for profit. Western ranchers claim their right to graze cattle and sheep on federal lands and maintain that a small fee is appropriate. Others contend that grazing fees on public lands should be competitive with grazing fees on private land so as to discourage further deterioration of the rangeland resources. Grazing fees are based on the amount of forage on an

---

ISSUE 8–2 Coping with Coyotes

One of the more controversial issues surrounding grazing in the western United States is the effect of coyotes on grazing animals, particularly sheep. Sheep ranchers claim that coyotes kill substantial numbers of sheep on the open range, and accordingly most ranchers support measures to reduce coyote populations. On the other hand, many wildlife experts maintain that although coyotes do kill sheep, their overall effects on ranching activities may be positive rather than negative. In any case killing coyotes does not solve the problem.

Coyotes (*Canis latrans*) are smaller relatives of wolves, being about a foot and a half high and weighing 20 to 35 pounds (Pringle, 1977). They are omnivores and live on a diet of small rodents (such as mice and rabbits), carrion, and plant materials. They live in small packs, but unlike wolves they do not hunt in packs, preferring to hunt alone or in pairs. Wolves are their natural enemies, and as the wolf population expanded through the West, ranchers killed off most of the wolves that lived there. Removal of

the wolves allowed the coyote to significantly expand its range, and this expansion continues today.

In a landscape composed of ranches, farms, and undeveloped land, coyotes are able to find plenty to eat. In addition to their primary staples of mice, insects, and other small prey, they are able to kill lambs and chickens and occasionally raid a vegetable garden or farm. Coyotes are not as wary of humans as are wolves, and they even live in suburban areas of Los Angeles, Denver, and other cities, where they can find garbage and other food not found in wilder areas. They are generally regarded as pests, and most states allow unlimited year-round hunting of coyotes.

Over the years ranchers and government agencies (particularly the BLM) have tried many techniques to reduce coyote populations, but with little success. Coyotes are too numerous and too cautious to be hunted effectively, and so traps of various kinds are frequently used. These have included poisoned bait, traps set with explosive charges, and toxic collars on sheep.

allotment (a federal grazing area). The forage is defined in *animal unit months* (AUM) and is the amount of forage needed to support a cow and her calf, or an adult bull, steer, or mule, or five sheep or goats. In recent years, the federal government has not generated enough money from grazing fees to pay for the labor to manage the grazing fees program.

A related issue is the changing dietary habits of Americans in particular and Europeans more generally. There has been a 20 percent decline in red meat consumption since 1975. Although Americans still consume 28 percent of the world's beef, they are demanding less of it, and in leaner cuts. As a result, American beef is raised for a longer period on forage, thus placing even more stress on the rangeland resources. In Europe, American beef is now banned if it contains growth hormones (which are used to reduce the amount of time needed to fatten an animal). In addition, the livestock industry is experimenting with other types of meat (e.g., water buffalo) in an attempt to satisfy the desire for leaner cuts

of beef. Finally, at the international level, one of the most controversial issues concerns the conversion of forests into grasslands for the purposes of grazing cattle. This has widespread ecological effects, which are discussed in Issue 8–1.

THE FUTURE OF RANGELAND RESOURCES

At present, the world's rangelands are overgrazed. In drier areas this overuse has led to soil and vegetation loss associated with the spread of desertlike conditions. There is potential for expansion of both the world's rangelands and its deserts. If the best management techniques are brought into use, as developed in both traditional and modern animal-based economies, the world's rangelands can be strengthened and in fact expanded, while the extent of desertification can be reduced.

In the United States, for example, the U.S.

These methods have stirred the ire of wildlife groups for several reasons. Among these are that traps and poisons also kill other predators that may be rare or endangered (such as eagles, bobcats, or badgers), as well as nontarget animals, such as dogs. Some range ecologists also argue that the coyote may benefit grazing animals by helping to control populations of smaller herbivores (especially rabbits) that compete with large herbivores such as cattle or deer for forage. Sheep, however, and particularly lambs, are small enough to be killed by coyotes, and they probably do not enjoy this beneficial effect.

Compound 1080 (sodium fluoroacetate), a poison used in coyote control, was banned in 1972 after environmentalists sought legal action claiming that the practice of baiting carcasses led to indiscriminate deaths of nontargeted species like the bald eagle. Nearly a decade later, ranchers found a sympathetic ear in the Reagan administration, which pressured the EPA to permit the use of Compound 1080 in closed collars. Baited collars were placed on the sheep, so that

when a coyote seized the sheep by the neck, it would puncture the collar as well and ingest a lethal amount of the poison. The practice was short-lived, however, as the EPA finally banned all use of Compound 1080 in 1988, including its use in closed sheep collars.

In spite of efforts to reduce or control coyote populations, they continue to expand their range and are now appearing in the eastern United States. Coyotes are very adaptable animals and are able to prosper in a wide range of environments. Their populations grow rapidly when food is plentiful, and litters tend to be larger when population densities are low. This adaptability is probably the primary cause for the lack of success of coyote control programs. Many range managers are now recommending that coyotes be controlled selectively, such as by limiting control to areas where lambs are unprotected. In addition, the most effective way to reduce losses of sheep to coyotes may be by protecting the sheep with fences and guard dogs, rather than attempting to eradicate the coyotes.

Forest Service advocates increased but intelligent use of the nation's rangelands. They estimate that in 1976 only one-third of the biological potential for grazing was utilized. In other words, if these resources are managed for their highest productivity then they could withstand three times the amount of grazing without any detrimental effects. The USFS recommendations include shifting grazing to more efficiently productive ecosystems, intensifying the use of management techniques on both private and public rangelands, improving the amount and quality of forage produced, constructing livestock control and handling facilities, reducing loss of forage to fire, insects, and diseases, and reducing livestock losses to disease, parasites, and predators (USFS, 1981). However, these recommendations are frequently intrusive, as their implementation would mean changes in the livelihood patterns of the American rancher. If attempted in other areas of the world, the human impacts would be even more severe. In addition, many of the improvements suggested are extremely costly and might be difficult to justify in terms of the increased value of the animals produced.

At the same time, population pressures on rangelands continue, and there are few opportunities to do the one thing that is virtually guaranteed to improve range quality—reduce the number of animals using the land. In addition, it seems unlikely that rangeland conditions will improve worldwide under present climatic patterns and intensive use. Instead, we will probably see a continuing patchwork of range improvement in some areas, degradation in others, both shifting with the weather and with human fortunes.

REFERENCES AND ADDITIONAL READING

Baker, J. 1983. The frustration of FLPMA. *Wilderness* 47(163) (Winter): 12–24.

Cook, E. 1976. *Man, Energy, Society*. San Francisco: W.H. Freeman.

Cooke, R.U., and R. Reeves. 1976. *Arroyos and Environmental Change in the American Southwest*. New York: Oxford University Press.

Council on Environmental Quality. 1981. *Global 2000 Report to the President*. Washington, DC: U.S. Government Printing Office.

————. 1988. *Annual Report 1987–88*. Washington, DC: U.S. Government Printing Office.

Dale, E.E. 1930. *The Range Cattle Industry*. Norman: University of Oklahoma Press.

Dregne, H. 1977. Desertification of the world's arid lands. *Econ. Geography* 52: 332–346.

Eckholm, E., and L.R. Brown. 1977. *Spreading Deserts—The Hand of Man*. Worldwatch Paper #13. Washington, DC: Worldwatch Institute.

Food and Agriculture Organization. 1988. *Monthly Bulletin of Statistics, Volume 4*, pp. 34–35. Rome: United Nations, Food and Agricultural Organization.

Grigg, D.B. 1974. *The Agricultural Systems of the World, An Evolutionary Approach*. London: Cambridge University Press.

Harris, D.R. 1971. Recent plant invasions in the arid and semiarid southwest of the U.S. In T.R. Detwyler (Ed.), *Man's Impact on Environment*, pp. 459–475. New York: McGraw–Hill.

Kates, R.W., D.L. Johnson, and K. Johnson. 1976. *Population, Society, and Desertification*. Worcester, MA: Clark University.

Myer, N. 1981. The hamburger connection. *Ambio* 10(1): 3–8.

Nothdurft, W.E. 1981. The lands nobody wanted. *Living Wilderness* 45(153): 18–21.

Pringle, L. 1977. *The Controversial Coyote*. New York: Harcourt, Brace, Jovanovich.

Sheridan, D. 1981a. Can the public lands survive the pressures? *Living Wilderness* 45(153): 36–39.

————. 1981b. Western rangelands: Overgrazed and undermanaged. *Environment* 23(4): 14–20, 37–39.

Soil Conservation Service. 1987. *Basic Statistics, 1982 National Resources Inventory*. Iowa State University, Statistical Laboratory, Statistical Bulletin 756. Ames: Iowa State Univ., Statistical Laboratory.

Stegner, W. 1981a. Land: America's history teacher. *Living Wilderness* 45(153): 5–7.

————. 1981b. If the sagebrush rebels win, everybody loses. *Living Wilderness* 45(153): 30–35.

U.S. Bureau of Land Management. 1978. *Final Environmental Impact Statement—The Proposed Rio Puerco Livestock Grazing Management Program*. Washington, DC: U.S. Government Printing Office.

U.S. Department of Agriculture. 1986. *1986 Agricultural Chartbook*. Agricultural Handbook No.

663. Washington, DC: U.S. Government Printing Office.

———. 1989. *The Second RCA Appraisal, Soil, Water, and Related Resources on Nonfederal Land in the United States, An Analysis of Condition and Trends*. Washington, DC: U.S. Government Printing Office.

U.S. Forest Service. 1981. *An Assessment of the Forest and Rangeland Situation in the United States*. Forest Research Report No. 22. Washington, DC: U.S. Government Printing Office.

Vale, T.R. 1978. The sagebrush landscape. *Landscape* 22(2): 31–37.

———. 1983. *Plants and People: Vegetation Change in North America*. Washington, DC: Association of American Geographers.

Vallentine, J.F. 1989. *Range Development and Improvements*, 3rd ed. San Diego: Academic Press.

Wagner, F.H. 1978. Livestock grazing and the livestock industry. In H.P. Brokaw (Ed.), *Wildlife and America*, pp. 121–149. Washington, DC: Council on Environmental Quality.

Wolf, E.C. 1986. Managing rangelands. In L. Brown *et al.* (Eds.), *State of the World*, pp. 62–77. Washington, DC: Worldwatch Institute.

World Resources Institute. 1987. *World Resources 1987*. New York: Basic Books.

———. 1988. *World Resources 1988–89*. New York: Basic Books.

TERMS TO KNOW

Animal Unit Month
Arroyos
Decreasers
Desertification
Domesticate
Dry Farming
Federal Land Policy and Management Act (FLPMA)
Increasers
Invaders
Multiple Use
Overgrazing
Pastoral Nomads
Pastoralist
Range Condition
Rangeland
Ruminants
Sagebrush Rebels
Sahel
Sedentarization
Sustained Yield
U.S. Bureau of Land Management

STUDY QUESTIONS

1. What is the relationship between overgrazing and desertification?

2. What is the importance of the Taylor Grazing Act to the management of rangeland resources?

3. How has the Sagebrush Rebellion influenced the management of rangeland resources?

4. What are some of the ways in which plants are affected by grazing?

5. How can rangelands be improved?

6. Is it possible for a plant species to be both an increaser and an invader? Why or why not?

7. Some argue, from an energy efficiency standpoint, that humans should be herbivores rather than omnivores. Do you agree or disagree? Why?

9

Forests: A Multiple-Use Resource

INTRODUCTION

Forests are among the most widespread, versatile, and easily exploited of the world's natural resources. They are used for fuel, construction materials, paper, wildlife habitat, and erosion control. They are found in virtually all humid and subhumid regions of the world, from the tropics to the margins of the tundra. Forests are the natural vegetation in biomes with ample soil moisture and a sufficient growing season. They occupy areas of poor soil and steep slopes as well as high-quality lands. Trees can survive on marginal lands, so many forests remain intact even when there is great demand for agricultural land.

Forests are not inexhaustible and have been severely depleted in many areas of the world. In some cases, as in most of the wealthy nations, forests have recovered in recent decades and continue to be important renewable resources. But in many of the poorer countries, rapid population growth and rising fossil fuel prices have caused great increases in demand for wood, primarily for fuel. In these areas wood is in critically short supply, and *deforestation* is causing accelerated erosion and soil degradation.

In the United States and Canada, forests are both an economic and a recreational treasure. Often the debate over how to manage a U.S. forest comes down to one question: Which do we want to survive, hikers and owls or lumberjacks? Scientists are realizing, however, that we cannot think of the forest resource on a local, state-by-state, or even country-by-

country level. Forests, like air, tie the entire globe into a single interacting biological system. Trees are the earth's lungs: they absorb carbon dioxide, storing the carbon and releasing the remainder as oxygen. When trees die or are cut down, the earth's lung capacity is reduced; when trees are burned, the earth's lungs are clogged with massive releases of carbon dioxide, which may be contributing to the warming trend known as the greenhouse effect. Our global air quality and temperature are directly tied to the condition of the global forest resource.

In tropical areas, most notably the Amazon River Basin in South America, deforestation is proceeding rapidly to make way for other land uses (Fig. 9.1). The Amazon rainforest covers about 2.7 million square miles, (7 million km^2), or about 90 percent of the area of the contiguous United States, and extends into nine countries. In Brazil alone, 1.9 million square miles (4.9 million km^2)—the size of the United States west of the Mississippi River—is classified as Amazonian. Brazil is interested in developing its capability to produce fuel from biomass, as well as to increase agricultural output and meat production. It has constructed a highway into the Amazon rainforest to facilitate this development and is encouraging settlement there.

More than 45 percent of the world's tropical rainforests have been cleared, and the rate continues at about 1 percent annually (Brooke, 1989; Linden, 1989; Schneider, 1989; Wilson, 1989). Ecologists are concerned about the long-term effects of this clearing on soil

Figure 9.1 Clearing a tropical rainforest in the western Amazon, Brazil.

resources, species diversity, and the global "lung capacity," as well as the social impacts on native human populations. Rising demand for fuel and building materials, as well as a desire to open new lands for farming, suggests that the worldwide forest resource is in dire jeopardy. Associated with the depletion of the rainforests is a concern that the by-products of wood burning—for warmth, for cooking, for processing into other products, for land clearance—may be contributing to the development of the greenhouse effect.

Although the U.S. forest cover has shrunk dramatically in the centuries since the first European settlement, our forests are in good shape in comparison to many other nations. In fact, after 300 years of continual and often extravagant logging, the U.S. forest resource is today considered abundant and resilient, according to many measures. However, it often seems that there is not enough forest to go around, and the future stability of the resource is regarded by many to be in doubt.

How can a resource be abundant, yet scarce? It is possible because forests and their lands are used for an extraordinarily wide range of activities, and those who use and manage the forest resource disagree sharply over how much forest there is and how it should be used. For the decisionmaker in a paper products company, there is more forest than the nation could ever need, because forests are renewable when properly managed. But the wilderness preservationist feels that a second-growth forest is profoundly different from a forest that has never been cut and be-

lieves that forested wildlands should be protected from the ax forever. Prospectors and miners, another interest group, do not care about the trees so much as what lies underneath them. These several groups have *incompatible* management and use goals for forestlands. Most other users, such as the wide array of people who visit forests for leisure activity, are not at such extreme odds.

There is another, less tangible factor that influences American attitudes and policy toward forestlands. Fresh in the memory of many Americans is the forest cover of a century or more ago, so vast and unmeasurable that hundreds of thousands of settlers vanished into it, and did not emerge until they had cut much of it down. For those to whom the nation's forests retain this mythic appeal, any further loss of forest cover is seen as a tarnishing of American ideals and dreams. For these people, there is a sense of defeat attached to managing the forest resource, because in their minds the forests are still infinite, capable of absorbing all uses without overlap or conflict.

Concern for toxic waste production and the misuse of forestry chemicals adds another dimension to the traditional U.S. concern about resource abundance. Dangerous chemical by-products, such as dioxin, enter our rivers via pulpwood and paper products plants; the herbicides and pesticides used to enhance the growing environment for commercial trees can have lasting effects on other species as well.

This chapter provides a summary of both the natural and human aspects of the forest resource in the United States. The management of these forests, including the human actors involved, is also discussed.

FOREST ECOSYSTEMS

CHARACTERISTICS OF FOREST ECOSYSTEMS

Forests worldwide occupy 10.1 billion acres (4.1 billion ha), about 31 percent of the world's land area (World Resources Institute, 1988). Forests are found primarily in the more humid areas of the world because of greater moisture availability (Fig. 9.2). When moisture is not a

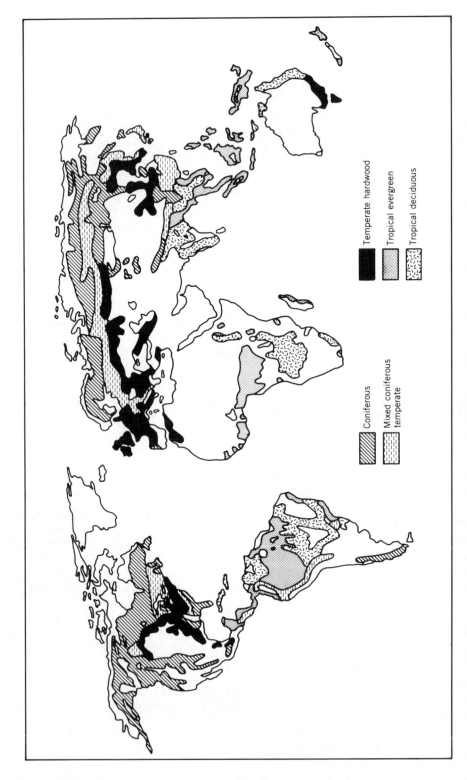

Figure 9.2 Major forest areas in the world. Forests occupy 2.66 billion acres (1.08 billion ha), 20 percent of the world's land area. (*Source:* Rand McNally, 1979.)

limiting factor, dominant tree species compete for sunlight by growing tall and producing broad canopies that shade out plants below.

Trees are more long-lived than most other plant types, and their growth rates are relatively low. Primarily because of their large size, trees contain large amounts of nutrients stored in living *biomass*. Forests are ecosystems in which most of the available nutrients accumulate in live trees over a long period of time. Relatively small amounts of nutrients are contained in herbs, shrubs, or the soil. In an experimental forest in New Hampshire, it was found that annual uptake rates of nutrients are a small fraction of the total amounts in storage. Restoration of ecosystem nutrients after forests are clear-cut may take several decades (Likens *et al.,* 1978). For most tree species the rate of growth (as measured by biomass) is relatively slow when the tree is young, primarily because it is small and does not have a large photosynthetic capacity. Growth rate increases as the tree gains a larger total leaf area and declines as it reaches maturity.

In many forests the amount of stored biomass reaches a steady state in which old trees die and their nutrients are taken up by younger ones. For a large portion of the world's forests, cyclic disturbances kill all or nearly all the trees at the same time, releasing nutrients and beginning a new cycle of forest growth. These disturbances can include fire, disease or insect infestation, windstorms, or other disturbances.

THE ROLE OF FIRE

In the past it was believed that fire was harmful to forests, but today it is recognized that forest fires are a natural and important part of most forest ecosystems (Mott, 1989; Romme and Despain, 1989). The 1988 fires in Yellowstone National Park (Fig. 9.3) focused attention on the fire controversy in newspapers and on television and radio news shows across North America.

Trees are susceptible to fire. Many species have adapted to this by developing mechanisms for rapid regeneration after fire, including sprouting from the root crown and seeds that are released or germinate only after being heated. Other species have characteristics that

Figure 9.3 Buffalo grazing on land burned in the 1988 Yellowstone fire.

protect against fire damage, such as low flammability or particularly thick bark.

Fires cause major, if temporary, disruption of the forest ecosystem. They consume dead and living biomass, and if severe enough kill most or all the trees. Water use and evapotranspiration are greatly decreased by the loss of live trees and shrubs, which results in increased runoff. In contrast, rainfall on a forested area is absorbed for use by the vegetation. When the surface conditions are changed by fire, less water is absorbed, and it runs in streams or sheets across the soil surface. This runoff causes accelerated erosion and also results in large losses of nutrients from the forest soil. Downstream, the eroded soil and nutrients contribute to sediment and dissolved solids loads in streams, and may contribute to eutrophication in lakes.

Fires also have beneficial effects. They allow the release of nutrients stored in dead biomass, which stimulates growth after the fire. They also remove old stands of timber that are particularly susceptible to insect or disease infestation, thus inhibiting the spread of pests. By removing the forest canopy, sunlight can reach ground level and rapid growth of early successional species is promoted, so beginning the process of reestablishment of the forest. Most importantly, though, frequent fires allow accumulated fuel to be burned off relatively harmlessly, preventing the severe fires that occur in areas of high fuel buildup. In many commercial forests, particularly the loblolly pine forests of the southeastern United States, ground fires are deliberately set from time to time to kill off plants that compete with the pines, so as to maintain an even-aged stand.

Forest ecosystems vary in their susceptibility to fire, and thus in how frequently fires occur. *Fire frequency* is the average number of years between successive forest fires at a given site. Some forests, like the chaparral woodlands of Southern California, are particularly susceptible to fire and have natural fire frequencies of 20 to 60 years. The pine forests that grow on areas of very sandy soils along the east coast of the United States also experience very frequent fires. Most forests, such as those in Yellowstone and the U.S. and Canadian north, have natural fire frequencies of 100 to 400 years. Fire frequency depends on many factors, including the rate of fuel accumulation, fuel moisture levels, and ignition sources.

There are three basic kinds of forest fires. *Ground fires* are fires that burn within the organic matter and litter of the soil. They smolder slowly and have little effect on trees. *Surface fires* burn on the ground surface, consuming litter but also the herbaceous and shrubby vegetation of the forest floor. They burn faster than ground fires, and may clear all the low vegetation of the forest, but have little effect on large trees. Finally, *crown fires* burn treetops as well as low vegetation, usually killing all or almost all aboveground vegetation. These fires are the most destructive to timber, wildlife, and the soil. Fires vary greatly in the temperatures that develop within the canopy and at ground level. Crown fires are much hotter than surface fires, but wind, fuel availability, and moisture levels are important influences on fire temperatures. Hotter fires are more destructive than cooler ones, particularly in that they consume greater amounts of organic matter. This results in greater postfire erosion and nutrient losses and retards the process of forest regeneration.

Prior to 1972, the long-standing policy of the U.S. Forest Service, U.S. National Park Service, and other forest management agencies was to fight all naturally started fires. This strategy, paradoxically, exacerbated the damage that fires cause. The easiest fires to extinguish are those that start during relatively wet and/or low wind conditions. These low-temperature fires cause only minor damage to the forest, while performing the valuable function of consuming available fuel.

The fires that are hardest to put out are those that occur during particularly dry, windy conditions, and/or that burn in areas where there is lots of fuel available. These fires tend to have relatively high temperatures and are more likely to be crown fires rather than surface or ground fires. By extinguishing the less harmful low-temperature fires, firefighters have permitted huge amounts of fuel to build up on the forest floor, which eventually will lead to the more severe crown fire.

Many Americans have grown up with the image of Smokey the Bear in his ranger hat warning us to "extinguish all fires, crush your smokes," and so on. With Smokey around to convince us that all fires are bad, it has been very difficult to change public and expert opinion toward the idea that several small fires are better than one big fire (Fig. 9.4).

Even without the public's general awareness, most U.S. agencies involved in forest

Figure 9.4   Smokey the bear. A long-time symbol of the Forest Service's policy of fire suppression, he is also used in anti-litter promotions (as pictured), and several other Forest Service campaigns.

management had adopted a "let-burn" policy by the middle of the 1970s. National parks have been conducting scientific studies to understand the fire history of their particular region, and many use deliberately set fires as a positive part of their management program (Romme and Despain, 1989). The National Park Service and the Forest Service formulated a common set of guidelines on the use of fire: one, the use of fire must be tailored to the environmental specifications and history of each site; two, naturally set fires are allowed to burn if the timing and location are right; three, unplanned human-caused fires are to be put out; and four, prescribed burns can be used only when conditions are right—cool and wet—so that the fire will not spread beyond the desired area (Matzke and Key, 1989).

Unfortunately, the conditions in Yellowstone in 1988 were not in the guidelines. The area was very dry; there were decades of fuel built up in the forests as a result of the previous policy of fire suppression; and dry, gusty winds were common. Both human-caused and natural fires took hold and went beyond the classification of crown fires, and were classified as firestorms. By the end of the brutal fire season of 1988, there had been 72,000 reported fires that burned over 4 million acres (1.6 million ha) in 23 states. Over one-fourth of this acreage was in the Greater Yellowstone Area Fire Command. About 45 percent of Yellowstone National Park's area was burned.

The reaction to this damage was very negative. Yellowstone is sacred in the minds of Americans, a symbol of endless wilderness, and to see it burned over, no matter how natural the process seemed to scientists, was terrible news. The fact that the fire's intensity was partly due to a long-standing policy of fire suppression was an irony that most Americans did not comprehend.

Today Yellowstone is a new park. It is open, with broad vistas, and brilliant, knee-deep greenery has taken over from the brooding darkness of the old forests. It is an excellent, even improved, wildlife habitat. In a century, perhaps, the park will resemble its pre-1988 appearance. In 1989, visitor numbers to Yellowstone were up substantially from previous years. And what of fire policy? Even before the fires were out in 1988, agency heads were meeting to evaluate and set future policy. The National Park Service reaffirmed its confidence in the positive role of fire, but strengthened and narrowed the guidelines so that if a "good" fire became "bad," action could be taken early enough to be effective. Unfortunately for the scientific view, American emotional opinion has the upper hand, and the Bush administration is requiring that *all* fires be fought until every park is in full compliance with the newer and stricter control guidelines (Christensen *et al.*, 1989; Elfring, 1989; Matzke and Key, 1989).

VARIABILITY IN TIMBER SUPPLY

TIMBER LOCATION AND TYPES

There are about 720 million acres (291 million ha) of forest land in the United States and 830 million acres (336 million ha) in Canada. To be classified as forest, 10 percent of a parcel of land must be forested and not developed for nonforest use. Most of the U.S. forest resources are concentrated in the Pacific Northwest, Alaska, and the East and Southeast regions (Fig. 9.5). In Canada, forests are located in the Pacific coast area—British Columbia—and in the central and eastern provinces.

Nearly two-thirds of the U.S. forestlands are rated as commercial forests. This means that the land is capable of growing at least 20 cubic feet of wood per acre ($1.4 \, m^3$ of wood per hectare) in a fully stocked stand on an annual basis (USFS, 1982). The timber produced is therefore commercially profitable. The remaining one-third of forestland is classified as noncommercial, and is categorized as parks, wildlife habitat, recreation, and wilderness.

Commercial forestland in North America is differentiated by the type of vegetation or tree species and is divided into *hardwoods* and *softwoods*. Hardwood forests generally consist of broadleaf and deciduous trees such as oak, maple, and hickory. In the United States, hardwood forests are primarily located in the northern and southern regions of the eastern half of the country (Fig. 9.6). Commercial hardwood stands are largely used for furniture making and flooring, although they are also important for heating. The total acreage of

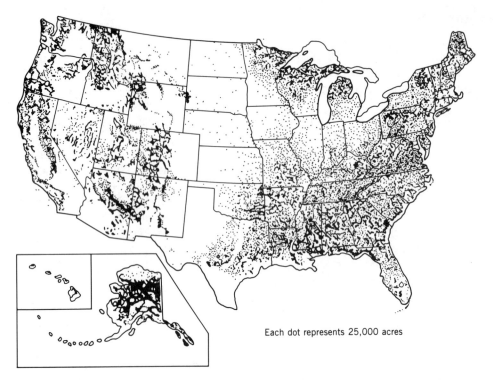

Figure 9.5 Forestlands in the United States. The nation's forests are concentrated in the Pacific Northwest, Alaska, the East, and the Southeast. (*Source:* Council on Environmental Quality, 1981.)

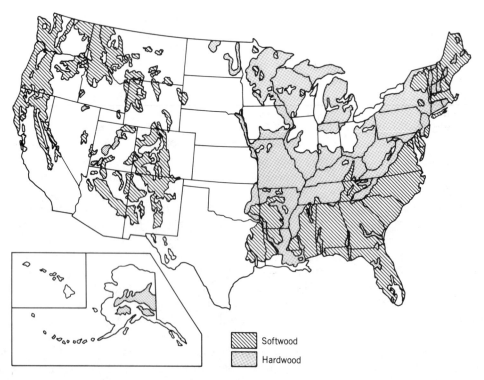

Each dot represents 25,000 acres

Softwood

Hardwood

Figure 9.6 Commercial forest by type and region. Hardwoods dominate in the South and East, and softwoods in the Southeast, Northeast, West, and Alaska. (*Source:* Haden-Guest *et al.,* 1956.)

hardwood stands in North America is greater than that of softwoods, but the timber is commercially less valuable because of the greater difficulty in harvesting.

Hardwood stands occur in mixed-species forests. Thus harvesting the valuable trees involves selective cutting as opposed to clear-cutting. This costs more because the hardwoods are not uniform in species, age, or height. As a result, the timber price is increased to cover the added costs of this custom harvesting, demand drops, and people settle for wall-to-wall carpeting in their homes instead of hardwood floors.

Softwoods are conifers, usually evergreens. The primary North American species are spruce, pine, and cedar, whose wood is softer and the grain is farther apart than in hardwoods. Softwoods are used primarily for paper products, lumber, and plywood. Softwood forests are located throughout North America but dominate in the Pacific Coast, Rocky Mountain, and Southern National Forest Service Regions (Fig. 9.7).

The economic value of softwoods is greater than hardwoods as a result of ease in harvesting and rapid growth of the trees. Softwoods grow in dense single-species stands at a relatively uniform rate and are easily harvested using clear-cutting techniques. Because of growth patterns and harvesting methods, the total volume of wood and the volume of wood per area are greater for softwoods than for hardwoods.

Most of our need for wood is for softwood, which comprised over 80 percent of total domestic production of lumber in 1987 (U.S. Department of Agriculture, 1988). Timber inventories rise when net annual growth (total growth less mortality) exceeds timber harvests, clearing, or removals (e.g., changes in land use) (Council on Environmental Quality, 1989). Net growth of softwood is presently highest in the South, with lower rates of growth in other regions. Hardwood is obtained from the North and the South, with the South having higher rates of net growth and harvesting. Net growth for the contiguous 48 states is

Figure 9.7 U.S. Forest Service regions. For management purposes, the United States is divided into four major forest regions: the Pacific Coast, Rocky Mountains, North, and South. These are further divided into 16 subregions. (*Source:* U.S. Forest Service, 1982.)

presently about 1.1 times the demand for softwoods and about 1.9 times the demand for hardwoods. There are significant variations in supply and demand from region to region. In the West, for example, harvesting of softwoods is slightly greater than net growth, resulting in depletion in that region. In the North and South, softwoods are still being grown at a rate higher than they are cut. In each of the major regions shown in Fig. 9.7, growth rates for hardwoods exceed current demands. Much of net growth is in smaller trees. Depletion of standing commercial timber may be greater.

FORESTLAND OWNERSHIP PATTERNS

In the United States, six different classes of forestland ownership are identified:

1. national forests owned and managed by the federal government, generally the U.S. Forest Service;

2. other forests owned by the federal government and managed by other agencies, such as the U.S. Bureau of Land Management and the National Park Service;

3. other publicly owned forests managed by state and county agencies;

4. private forests owned by forest or timber companies and managed by them, such as Boise Cascade, Weyerhauser, and Georgia Pacific;

5. private forests or woods that are part of farms or landholdings of individuals and managed by them; and

6. other lands that are private forests of mixed lots and ownership categories and cannot be placed in any of the other five groups.

Seventy-two percent of the commercial forestland in the United States is privately owned in small holdings and on farms (Table 9.1). Only about one-seventh of private, commercial forestland is owned by the giant forest industry companies. In the public sector, the federal government controls one-fifth of commercial forestland, and all but 2 percent of that is run by the U.S. Forest Service. Another 8 percent is publicly owned by states and other public agencies. About one-third of the country's forestland is noncommercial.

When ownership patterns are examined on a regional basis a number of interesting trends emerge (Fig. 9.8). Federal ownership dominates the western forests and is mostly managed by the Forest Service and the Bureau of Land Management. The timber industry dominates the ownership of forestland in Maine, South Carolina, and Florida. Private holdings by farmers and other individuals are the dominant type of ownership in the East. As a result of these patterns, public policies on forest issues also have a strong regional focus.

FOREST EXPLOITATION AND MANAGEMENT IN THE UNITED STATES

A BRIEF HISTORY

At the time of the European settlement of North America, forests covered about two-thirds of the United States. This forest was both a resource and an obstacle to the early settlers. It provided fuel and building materials but at the same time stood in the way of land clearance for agriculture. Timber was plentiful in most areas in the seventeenth and eighteenth centuries, and no one had to go far for wood. By the mid-nineteenth century, though, population and economic growth began to exert a great demand for wood, and supplies were diminishing. Local or regional shortages developed in the northeastern United States as the focus of timber harvesting moved west to the Great Lakes states. Writer and explorer Henry David Thoreau in his travels by canoe in the wilderness of central Maine found it notable to record the presence of towering white pines, as these were being harvested from remote areas even in the first half of the nineteenth century. Thoreau also complained of a chronic shortage of firewood in central Massachusetts.

Land area in forest cover continued to decline into the early twentieth century, largely due to clearing of land for agriculture (Clawson, 1979). By 1920, though, clearing of forestland had slowed. The increasingly productive agricultural lands of the Midwest had

TABLE 9.1 Ownership of U.S. Forestlands, 1988 (Thousands of Acres)

| Region | Federal | | State, County, and Municipal | Private | | Total Commercial | Non-commercial Forestlands |
	National Forest	Other		Forest Industry	Farmer, Other		
North	10,408	1,511	20,293	16,898	109,194	158,304	11,486
South	11,797	4,133	3,783	38,231	137,470	195,384	4,559
West	63,048	5,800	15,274	15,402	29,860	129,384	228,805
Total	85,223	11,444	39,350	70,531	276,524	483,072	244,849

Source: U.S. Department of Agriculture (1988).

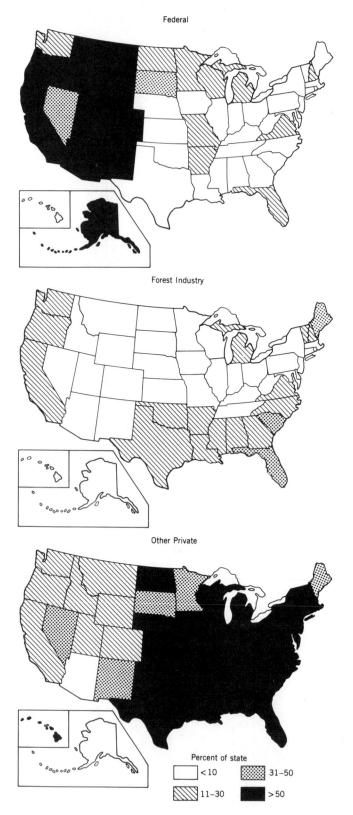

Figure 9.8 Ownership of commercial forestland. Federal ownership is dominant in the West and Alaska. Forest-industry ownership is most evident in the West, South, and Northeast. Other private holdings dominate in the East. "Percent of state" refers to the percentage of forestland in each state by ownership category. (*Source:* U.S. Forest Service, 1981.)

been competing with eastern agriculture for some time, and beginning in the nineteenth and continuing into the early twentieth century, farmland was rapidly being abandoned, primarily in areas within and east of the Appalachians. This farmland gradually reverted to forest, and as a result forest acreage in the lower 48 states has increased about 20 percent in the last 60 years.

Another important trend associated with timber harvesting and cropland abandonment has been a decrease in the average age of timber stands. This has had the effect of greatly increasing the net growth rate for timber, because young forests grow rapidly while an old forest has slower growth. Thus today we are growing slightly more timber than is being cut, and the standing volume of timber is steadily increasing, although problems of overcutting in some areas do exist.

Statistics show that supplies of wood for almost all purposes are available within the United States, and that we are presently harvesting below the sustained yield at the national level. At a regional level, however, the picture is somewhat different. In the North and South, the majority of forestlands are in small holdings such as farm woodlots, so that it is expensive for the large companies to arrange harvests on this piecemeal basis. In addition, many landowners do not find prices attractive enough. In the West, vast uninterrupted tracts of forestland make this region much more suitable for the large-scale harvesting methods of the large timber companies. Because of the size of tracts and the economics of harvesting, western timberlands are experiencing excess harvesting.

Timber companies are now running out of harvestable timber on their own lands and are demanding greater access to land owned by the federal government, mainly in the West (Fig. 9.9). Much of this land is also treasured as virgin forest and wildlife habitat; thus many conflicts are developing between preservationists and conservationists, not to mention loggers themselves (see Issue 9–1). To redress the balance between over-cutting in the west and undercutting in the east, the big companies must become willing to adjust their methods—and profit expectations—to fit the demands of harvesting on smaller parcels of land, in either federal or private ownership.

Figure 9.9 Earth First! protest. Earth First! activist chained to a tree to protest forest harvesting.

FOREST PRODUCT TECHNOLOGY

To better understand the changing supply and demand for timber, it is necessary to look at the uses to which wood is put. Until the twentieth century, wood was used almost exclusively for either fuel or lumber. Fuel was the major use until the mid-nineteenth century, when it was surpassed by growth in lumber use. Gradually fuelwood was replaced by other energy sources, and this use plummeted after the 1930s (Clawson, 1979). Beginning around 1900, wood began to be used to make plywood and pulp for paper, and these uses have increased steadily ever since. Demand for lumber also follows cycles in new housing construction. Today, for example, pulp production demands almost as much wood as lumber in the United States. In addition, wood chips and sawdust are now used to make boards rather than using whole pieces of wood. These fiber-based structural panels were produced at record levels in the early 1980s.

These varying uses require different kinds of wood. For example, just about any kind of wood can be burned, although hardwoods are better than softwoods for this purpose. Lumber, on the other hand, requires trees that are straight and as great in diameter as possible—in other words, old trees. Most lumbering requires softwoods, but specialized industries such as furniture construction use hardwoods. Plywood is made from large sheets of veneer only a few millimeters thick that are glued together. These sheets are not sawed from logs; they are peeled from a turning log with a large blade that can cut sheets that are hundreds of feet long. This means that plywood manufacture does not need logs of large diameter. Much younger trees can be used, provided they are softwoods, relatively straight, and free from knots. Similarly, pulp production

is not dependent on any particular size of log, and the tree species is more important than age. Particleboard and similar products are made using waste from other processes.

For the last several decades, demand for dimensional lumber has remained fairly constant, while most of the increased demand for building wood has been taken up by plywood. Thus while we still require many mature, large-diameter trees such as those from the Pacific Northwest, we are increasingly using smaller, younger trees such as those grown in the Southeast. Increases in energy prices have made fuelwood attractive for home heating, as well as for the generation of electricity in some areas. This has created a demand for the hardwoods that cover much of the abandoned farmland in the Northeast and may result in a reversal of the recent trend of increasing standing timber volume in much of the country.

ISSUE 9–1   Old Trees and Spotted Owls

As long as people can remember, logging and the timber industry have provided jobs and economic security for thousands of people living in the Pacific Northwest. As the fortunes of the timber industry rose and fell, so did the regional economies of Oregon and Washington. In Washington, for example, a portion of all timber revenues in the state are used to pay for state education and this is mandated by state law. When demand was high, and the resource was plentiful, few problems arose. But when demand slackened, the Pacific Northwest was plunged into an economic recession. During the feast years, logging companies cut many of the ancient trees and replanted very few. As the number of big trees dwindled, the timber companies set their sights on public land and argued successfully for increased access to the big trees on state and federal lands. All was going well for them until someone discovered the spotted owl, which lives in old-growth forests, and whose habitat is now severely threatened by the intense logging in the region.

Environmentalists have been concerned for years about the rampant logging of the virgin Pacific Northwest forest and the continued cutting of old-growth stands. Since many of these trees are centuries old, the logging companies would have completely depleted the resource unless some action was taken. Although many timber companies have extensive reforestation programs, the length of time for species maturation meant that the Northwest lumber companies would not see immediate returns on their reforestation efforts. Hence, the logging companies in Oregon and Washington were slow to shift to secondary growth stands and preferred to cut old-growth stands.

The opposition of environmentalists and other concerned citizens has been further galvanized because the timber market is now in a glut and because about 25 percent of the Pacific Northwest timber is exported to Japan and other Pacific Rim nations. The U.S. timber companies can afford to fell the trees and then wait for premium prices ($600 per thousand board feet) since only the United States and Chile export Douglas fir. So the timber companies keep logging and the environmentalists keep screaming.

The spotted owl controversy has made national news, and even before the species was officially listed as threatened the U.S. Forest Ser-

TOXIC SUBSTANCES INVOLVED IN WOOD PROCESSING

Anyone who has ever been downwind of a pulp plant knows how horrible it smells, although people can become accustomed to bad odors when the pay is good. To local workers, the sulfurous emanation from these factories is "the smell of money." However, we are beginning to realize that the processes involved in papermaking release tons of potentially dangerous substances into our air and water on an annual basis.

When logs are cut into chips for pulpmaking, the chips are soaked in bleaching agents that form toxic, chlorine-based compounds, including dioxin. More than 150 pulp mills in North America dump tons of chlorinated compounds, on average 35 to 50 tons (32 to 45 tonnes) per plant per day, into the air and water surrounding the plants. Dioxins and other related chemicals are showing up in the (unhatched) eggs of blue herons and in the fish downstream from pulp mills. What's worse is that all bleached paper products have the potential to be dioxin contaminated, and traces of this virulently poisonous substance have been found in disposable diapers, paper towels, paper plates, and coffee filters.

In the United States, there is clear evidence that the EPA worked in collusion with the paper products industry during the mid-1980s to suppress this information. In response to a 1988 lawsuit brought by the Environmental Defense Fund and the National Wildlife Federations, which the EPA lost, it issued new regulatory guidelines for the pulp and paper industry in 1990. The new regulations require that by 1993, pulp and paper mills must obtain permits for dumping waste into streams and those permits would be issued only if the mills reduce waste to levels con-

vice had declared 2.5 million acres (1 million ha) of national forest lands off-limits to logging in Washington, Oregon, and northern California. But the controversy continues and is most acute in the small lumber towns throughout the region. Washington's Olympic Peninsula is no exception. The Olympic Peninsula has some of the finest old-growth Douglas fir forests in the world. Olympic National Park encompasses 900,000 acres (364,000 ha), and another 650,000 acres (263,000 ha) are in a national forest. Washington state controls 365,000 acres (148,000 ha), while Native Americans control a similar size parcel. Lastly, private interests (the timber industry, families, private trusts, insurance firms, and other investors) control 1,750,000 acres (708,000 ha) in the area. In 1989, 5 million board feet of logs were exported to Pacific Rim countries (Japan in particular) from Washington's three ports: Seattle, Tacoma, and Everett. The livelihood of Forks, Washington (population 2600), is totally dependent on the logging companies and those citizens are some of the most vocal opponents of spotted owl and old-growth forest protection. About 10,000 jobs (a highly speculative number) may be lost throughout the Pacific Northwest to save the century-old western red cedar and Douglas fir tees and the spotted owls who live among them. The debate has been vociferous and violent. Environmentalists (most notably members of Earth First!) have chained themselves to trees to prevent cutting and have damaged logging trucks and equipment. Loggers have repeatedly threatened "environmentalist citizens" and USFS personnel.

The true culprit in this debate is not the spotted owl, but the inability of the majority of logging and timber companies in the Pacific Northwest to develop better management strategies based on sustainable yield. The forests of this area have been cut at rates far exceeding growth rates for several decades, and many feel that it is time for this resource depletion to stop. Sustainable yield practices would protect the habitat of the spotted owl by deferring harvest and maintaining old-growth stands while stabilizing the timber supply to ensure the regional livelihood of residents. This is not a clear case of environment versus economics, but a radically different and responsible approach to silviculture. Sustainable ecology supports sustainable economics (Mitchell, 1990).

sidered safe by the government. Furthermore, by 1995, the standards would be further tightened to require mills to install the best available technology to control dioxin levels to the lowest level feasible (Shabecoff 1990). Many European countries, most notably Sweden, are eliminating chlorine from the papermaking process, which will eliminate tons of chlorine from industrial wastes. Consumers may have to settle for speckled and brown paper products in place of the traditional whiter than white in exchange for a diminished threat from these toxics (Applebome, 1989; von Stackelberg, 1989).

CURRENT AND PROJECTED SUPPLY AND DEMAND

Current supplies and demand for timber in the United States are summarized in Tables 9.2 and 9.3. Annual net growth of timber and demand is shown for 1976, 1986, and projected to 2030. Net growth is the total increase by tree growth in volume of wood, less that lost to death, disease, storms, and rot. It is a measure of available new wood. The amount of standing lumber is much higher, but if more wood than net growth is cut, standing timber declines. Demand projections depend on certain assumptions about economic activity, most importantly the price of lumber. If the price is high, demand will be low, and vice versa. The projections shown are based on an assumption of equilibrium market conditions, where supply and demand are equal.

Looking more closely at Table 9.2, total U.S. demand for wood in 1986 was about 15.9 billion cubic feet (450 million m^3), an increase of 16 percent from 1976. Imports and exports are diverse, but the major ones include imports of lumber and pulpwood (primarily from Canada) and exports of lumber to Japan and other

Pacific Rim nations, and paper to Europe. Net imports supplied about 13 percent of U.S. demand in 1986, more than twice that of a decade earlier. By 2030, demand is expected to nearly double to 25.5 billion cubic feet (722 million m^3), with domestic sources meeting all of this increase. Much of the increase in demand is expected to be for hardwoods, partly because softwood supplies will become scarce and also because of the increased use of hardwood for fuel. Wood fuel demand is projected by the U.S. Forest Service to reach about 2 billion cubic feet (56.7 million m^3) per year by 2030, but these estimates may be reduced with the new emphasis on curbing carbon dioxide emissions.

By 2030, because of the increase in demand for both hardwood and softwood, it is expected that harvest will exceed net growth. In the critical western softwood areas (Table 9.3), net annual growth is expected to decline slightly, while it will increase in the South. In the North, a decline is predicted largely due to successional change in softwood to hardwood forests. Only in the North will net softwood growth exceed demand in 2030. In the North and South, it is estimated that hardwood demand will be nearly three times that of 1987. Hardwood supplies from the West will be low primarily because of the small amount of hardwood available there.

MANAGEMENT OF TIMBER RESOURCES

Prior to the turn of this century, forestry management in the United States consisted solely of cutting the timber and moving on. Great stands of mature forests were cut to make way for agriculture and progress. The public, the government, and the lumber companies be-

TABLE 9.2   U.S. Demand for Timber in 1976, 1986, and 2030 (Billion Cubic Feet)

	1976	1986	2030
Total domestic demand	13.4	15.9	25.5
Exports	1.8	2.3	1.3
Imports	2.8	4.4	3.8
Domestic supply	12.4	13.9	23.0

Source: U.S. Forest Service (1982, 1988).

TABLE 9.3   Projected Regional Net Growth and Harvest (Million Cubic Feet)

| | Softwoods | | | | | |
| | Net Growth | | | Harvest | | |
	1976	1987	2030	1976	1987	2030
North	1,600	1,336	1,374	705	751	1,088
South	6,158	5,849	6,488	4,471	5,741	6,303
West	4,461	5,550	5,189	4,762	5,372	4,988
Total	12,219	12,734	13,051	9,938	11,864	12,379
	Hardwoods					
	Net growth			Harvest		
	1976	1987	2030	1976	1987	2030
North	4,192	4,262	3,282	1,953	1,999	3,326
South	4,547	4,580	4,120	2,101	2,958	5,211
West	580	810	216	121	219	157
Total	9,319	9,653	7,618	4,175	5,176	8,694

Source: U.S. Forest Service (1982, 1988).

lieved that there was an abundance of trees and no real need to worry about the future supply of wood. In contrast to considerable achievements in forest management in Germany and other European countries, little attention was paid to maintaining this country's forests. Outcries from scientists and preservationists concerning forest deterioration finally reached the White House in the early 1900s and a new national forest policy was implemented. This involved the concept of sustained yield, which was advocated by *Gifford Pinchot*, the first Chief Forester of the United States under President Theodore Roosevelt. As we shall see later in this chapter, this concept became official policy in 1960.

THE CONCEPT OF SUSTAINED YIELD

The concept of *sustained yield* is an approach to the management of our biological resources. Sustained yield is the harvesting of a species at a rate equal to its rate of reproduction or maturation. The intent is that a resource is neither overharvested and depleted nor harvested before it is mature. The goal is preservation of both the quantity and quality of the resource.

As a philosophical concept, sustained yield is useful, but it has limitations as an everyday management tool, mostly in its application. For example, demand for wood fluctuates, particularly as building construction varies with the health of the national economy. This means that at some times it might be useful to cut in excess of the sustainable yield and at other times to cut much less. Also, in mixed-species forests, different trees mature at different rates. If the timber is harvested by clear-cutting, then for at least some trees the harvest will occur at the optimal time for maximizing sustained yield, yet sustained yield may not be practical for every parcel of land. On a regional or national basis, however, over a period of decades sustained yield may have some protective power for the forest resource.

HARVESTING TECHNIQUES

A variety of harvesting techniques is used in forestry management. Not all of these can be used interchangeably since they each have specific goals and impacts. The three most important are shelterwood cutting, selective cutting, and clear-cutting. A method for harvesting less valuable wood on small lots, called biomass harvesting, is also discussed.

Shelterwood cutting is a several-stage process requiring thinning and cutting. First, trees of poor quality are removed both from the forest floor and from the stand itself. This opens up the forest floor to more light, enhancing seedling growth and reducing competition. The remaining trees provide some shelter for the seedlings. When the seedlings take root and become established, some but not all of the remaining mature trees are harvested. Shelterwood cutting is an efficient technique in small plots with relatively homogeneous tree species. It is costly in terms of labor inputs in larger acreages and so is not widely practiced on large tracts of commercial forestlands.

Selective cutting is used only in forests of mixed age or in forests with trees of unequal economic value. The mature trees of the most desirable species are harvested while the others are left intact. In an oak–hickory forest, for example, the mature oaks might be selectively cut, leaving immature oaks, mature hickories and other species standing. Selective cutting is primarily used in hardwood forests. When used in mixed-species forests, selective cutting leads to a loss of diversity, which can have negative impacts on wildlife and other sectors of the forest environment. Selective cutting is costly and is appropriate only when the value of the harvested trees is high relative to those left uncut.

Clear-cutting is the most controversial harvesting technique of these three (Fig. 9.10). Currently, about two-thirds of U.S. annual timber production is harvested in this way. The technique involves cutting all the trees regardless of size or species and is appropriate when the trees are relatively uniform in species and age or when it would provide the most desirable form of regeneration. Clear-cutting, however, does remove the entire forest canopy and may cause soil erosion and wildlife habitat destruction. It also leaves a more scarred landscape than other harvesting techniques.

Loggers recently have developed a method for consuming whole trees of any size and shape, from any size tract. This *biomass harvesting* turns trees into wood chips, which are then sold to wood-fired power plants. Although demand fluctuates, many small- to medium-sized logging operations, especially in the Northeast, have found this harvesting technique to be quite profitable. Loggers may cut selectively or consume all standing timber, depending on the requirements of the job and stipulations of the landowner. This method has great economic appeal for harvesting the vast majority of U.S. forestlands—the small parcels in private hands. The jury is still out, however, on the possible environmental effects of bio-

(a)

(b)

Figure 9.10 Timber harvesting methods in Washington. (*a*) selective cutting; (*b*) block clear-cutting.

mass harvesting and its effect on nutrient recycling in the forest (Huyler, 1989).

ECOLOGICAL EFFECTS OF TIMBER HARVESTING

Timber harvesting affects forests in similar ways to fire. As trees are removed, sunlight reaches ground level and new growth is stimulated. The slash, or limbs and branches that are too small to use, is left on the ground and decays, contributing to nutrient release. On the other hand, increased runoff causes accelerated erosion and transport of nutrients out of the system, similar to the effect of fire.

There are, however, some important differences between timber harvesting and fire. Timber harvesting requires that heavy equipment be brought into the forest, including bulldozers, trucks, and yarding gear for moving the logs. Roads must be built to bring the equipment in and to carry the logs out. Driving vehicles over the forest soil, and dragging logs to truck loading areas, causes major damage to and compaction of the soil surface. This results in the acceleration of soil erosion at a much greater rate than would occur after most fires. This is particularly a problem in mountainous areas, such as along the Pacific coast of the United States and Canada. In these areas, the accelerated erosion includes both surface erosion and landsliding, and the resulting large amounts of sediment can move downstream and damage aquatic habitats and fish populations. This accelerated erosion has been the focus of much controversy in many areas, particularly the forests upstream from Redwood National Park in California. There the effects on streams in the park were so severe that the federal government was forced to curtail logging activities in upstream areas and to establish corridors where logging was prohibited along streams.

In addition to erosion, logging differs from fire in that fire-adapted species may not be stimulated to regenerate as quickly as they would after a fire. Many species require the heat of fire to stimulate germination or sprouting, and others require the massive input of nutrients that results from burning the forest. Slash left after the forest is cut may not release nutrients as rapidly as burned debris, and some nutrients are exported out of the area in the form of logs. In general, logging has impacts that are quite similar to fire. It is a catastrophic, but temporary, disruption of the ecosystem that removes large amounts of soil, nutrients, and biomass from the system, changes water yields, and increases stream temperatures as the process of reestablishing the forest cover begins.

METHODS OF REFORESTATION

Reforestation of cutover areas is carried out by natural regeneration, artificial seeding, and seedling planting. Natural regeneration simply means letting the forest regrow unaided by human activities, using seedlings that existed before harvest and natural seed sources re-

maining thereafter. Natural regeneration can be encouraged by using harvesting practices that leave seedlings in place or that leave some trees as seed sources.

Artificial seeding is usually done by broadcasting seed from aircraft where the forest terrain is rugged or isolated or where large acreages are involved. Seeding in this way accounts for only about 4 percent of the land artificially regenerated in the United States.

Seedling plantings are now used more commonly as a reforestation technique, primarily because the survival rates are higher and tree density can be more closely controlled. Planting is usually done by hand rather than by machine, particularly in rugged terrain.

Reforestation by planting and direct seeding has increased steadily since 1950. In 1986, for example, 1.8 billion tree seedlings were planted on 2.7 million acres (1.09 million ha) (Council on Environmental Quality, 1989). Much of this activity is occurring on industry-owned lands; only 11 percent of federally owned lands were reforested in 1986. Farmers participating in cropland diversion and soil conservation programs accounted for one-third of all tree plantings in 1986.

A basic tool of large-scale tree planting is the airplane, which is used to broadcast seed and to deliver follow-up loads of fertilizer, herbicides, and pesticides. However, concern is growing that what's good for the lumber industry may not be so good for the environment. Chemicals are sprayed aerially to clear a site for planting, to thin, to kill unwanted species, and to get rid of shrubs. Some of these chemicals are very long-lived in the environment and can harm wildlife and contaminate water supplies. Additionally, much of what is sprayed may drift away from the target and settle in adjacent areas— sensitive natural areas as well as in homes and yards.

A recent USDA leaflet reminds the sprayer that "You must also consider the environmental impact and potential effects on your neighbors' property. Then you must carefully apply the herbicide at the proper rate" (Miller and Bishop, 1989). However, there is little regulation beyond the availability of the leaflet. Throughout the 1970s and into the 1980s, defoliants similar to the notorious Agent Orange were sprayed in forested areas of Oregon's Coastal Range. Many people complained of health problems that they attributed to the spraying, including severe birth defects and high miscarriage rates. In recent years, the government has been unwilling to carry out the research necessary to determine the links between spraying and health problems (Boyd *et al.*, 1985; Ketchaw, 1978; von Stackelberg, 1989).

THREATS TO THE FOREST RESOURCE

There are a variety of natural and human-induced activities that threaten the world's and the nation's forests. Three of these are discussed: insects, disease, and acid precipitation.

INSECTS

Insects are a major cause of tree mortality, accounting for 26.3 million acres (10.6 million ha) in damage in 1987 (CEQ, 1989). The spruce budworm is a major pest in the eastern boreal forest, and major outbreaks peaked in 1978 when 12 million acres (4.8 million ha) were destroyed (Fig. 9.11). Its western counterpart, the western spruce budworm, attacked a record 10 million acres (4 million ha) of mixed coniferous forests between 1983 and 1986. Another major pest is the gypsy moth, which is not indigenous to the United States. It was brought from Europe in 1869, and the gypsy moth has caused extensive damage in the deciduous forests of New England, New York, New Jersey, and Pennsylvania. In 1981, the most serious outbreak of the gypsy moth defoliated 12.8 million acres (5.2 million ha). As its range extends, the gypsy moth will continue to damage the eastern forests; it has already been spotted in Delaware, Maryland, Virginia, and West Virginia.

Two lesser pests are also important regionally. The mountain pine beetle is a major pest in the lodgepole and ponderosa pine forests in the West. During the 1980s it caused extensive damage to more than 3 million acres (1.2 million ha) in the Pacific Northwest, Montana, and Idaho (CEQ, 1989). Finally, the southern pine beetle is a problem in the South,

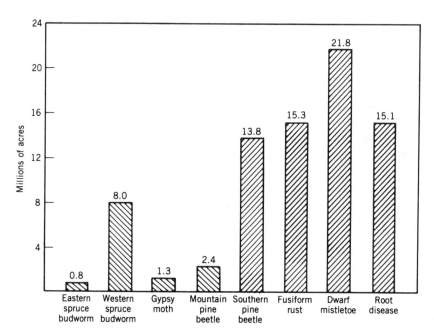

Figure 9.11   Acreages of forestland damaged by diseases and pests in 1987. (*Source:* Council on Environmental Quality, 1989.)

attacking southern yellow pine (particularly shortleaf and loblolly) stands. This pest is cyclic in its damage, with major infestations occurring every 7 to 10 years. The most recent outbreak began in 1986 when 26.4 million acres (10.7 million ha) were damaged.

DISEASE

Diseases also pose threats to the forest resource, and in 1987, 52 million acres (21 million ha) were damaged (Fig. 9.11). The most prevalent disease is fusiform rust, which primarily attacks slash and loblolly pines in the Southeast and accounts for 29 percent of the losses from all diseases. Root diseases account for another 29 percent and are more national in their occurrence. The dwarf mistletoe, a parasitic plant, is very widespread in North America. The plant survives by absorbing nutrients and water from its host. Conifers are particularly susceptible, especially western pines, firs, spruce, Douglas fir, larch, and hemlock. Southern pines, cedars, junipers, cypress, redwood, and sequoia species are relatively immune. In 1987, 42 percent of all disease losses were caused by dwarf mistletoe, affecting 21.8 million acres (8.8 million ha).

TREE BURNING AND ACID PRECIPITATION: GLOBAL IMPACTS

Although the scope of this book is concentrated on North America, especially the United States, there are some environmental issues that ignore national boundaries. Two of these are the effects of wood burning on both local and global air quality and the impact of acid precipitation on forest health.

In Brazil, the Amazon rainforest is being burned in small and large patches to make way for farms and cities. This burning releases large amounts of carbon dioxide into the atmosphere, where it joins the growing burden of CO_2 released by auto exhausts and fossil-fuel-burning factories and power plants. As will be discussed in greater detail in Chapter 14, this CO_2 load may be trapping heat in the earth's atmosphere and contributing to a global warming trend. Brazilians do not think it is fair that they should have to bring their development to

a halt because of the outcry of rich environmentalists from countries that are equally at fault in environmental matters. However, scientists are advocating the large-scale planting of trees worldwide to counteract the global warming effect.

How would tree planting work? Growing trees absorb CO_2, storing the carbon and releasing the oxygen. If burning trees makes the problem worse, goes the reasoning, why not plant trees to counteract Brazilian and other losses? One of the most startling aspects of this idea is that a tree planted in Indiana will help just as much, globally, as a tree saved in Brazil. We are all linked via the envelope of gases we call the atmosphere. The American Forestry Association wants to see 100 million trees planted in American cities and towns by 1992. Foresters are also developing new tree varieties that grow fast and absorb a greater load of CO_2, and one innovative environmental strategy has factories promising to plant trees to offset the deleterious effects of their fossil fuel use.

There are many drawbacks to these schemes, including the desperate need that growing populations have for fuel: newly planted trees would not survive very long in many countries. If one or two countries, such as the United States, were to undertake the growing of giant plantations as global "lungs," the plantations would have to be immense to have any effect on the global carbon budget. One estimate suggests that a forested area 1.5 times the size of the total U.S. forest cover, or more than 15 percent of the world's present closed-canopy forest cover, would be needed to absorb the excess carbon being produced annually. Clearly, the solution won't come soon or be cheap, but it is an exciting approach to work toward (Brooke, 1989; Sedjo, 1989; Stevens, 1989).

Another transboundary issue is that of acid precipitation. Factories and power plants produce a number of pollutants that are carried long distances before settling to earth. Sulfur dioxide (SO_2) and nitrogen oxide (NO_x) are two of these pollutants that have corrosive qualities. Acid rain is discussed in detail in Chapter 14, which also includes a discussion of the effects of acid precipitation on forests.

PRESENT-DAY U.S. FOREST POLICY

Forest policy in the United States is based on an attempt to balance many conflicting needs and desires. Foremost among these are the physical and biological constraints on forest productivity, the need for economic efficiency, the consideration of *amenity values,* and equity issues (Clawson, 1975). Until the early twentieth century, forest policy was dictated largely by considerations of economic efficiency—a sufficient supply of timber was available at a low price. Private timber interests played a dominant role in the formation of government policy, and U.S. Forest Service policies were those primarily developed in the Pinchot era. In the last half century, however, continued depletion of the country's forests and a growing public awareness of the need for conservation and preservation of wilderness areas have led to the incorporation of a broader range of goals into public forest policy.

LEGISLATIVE MANDATES FOR BALANCED USE

One of the first and most significant pieces of legislation passed regarding forest policy was the *Multiple Use Sustained Yield Act* of 1960 (MUSYA). Nontimbering interests had registered concern that the national forests were being cut down and that there were other values to a national forest than simply timber production. The passage of this act was significant in two respects. First, the U.S. Forest Service was made to recognize other uses of national forests. Second, the act established a balanced management approach recognizing four primary uses of national forests: timbering, watershed maintenance, wildlife habitat preservation, and recreation. Although these uses were conflicting, each was to be incorporated into specific management plans for each national forest in the country.

MUSYA was important because it acknowledged the balance between the economic, intangible, and ecological values of our national forestlands. The harvesting of timber, while still important, was to be done under the general principle of sustained yield advocated by Gifford Pinchot a half century earlier.

In 1974, the Forest and Rangeland Renew-able Resource Planning Act (FRRRPA) was passed. The purpose of this legislation was to clarify legally the management principles developed under the MUSYA. The FRRRPA required that the U.S. Department of Agriculture make an inventory and assess the quality of national forests every ten years and recommend a comprehensive management program. The program had to involve each of the four primary uses of forests as designated in the MUSYA. The Forest and Rangeland Renewable Resource Planning Act was designed to achieve a balance between economic efficiency, environmental quality, and social values in the management of national forests. It provided more practical guidance on how to do this than did the Multiple Use Sustained Yield Act.

Two years later in 1976, the FRRRPA was amended and became known as the *National Forest Management Act* (NFMA). This act provides operating policy for publicly owned forest resources in the United States and requires the development of integrated management plans for all 126 units of the national forest and national grasslands systems. The NFMA also established a number of specific policies involving clear-cutting, riparian protection, and the rate of timber harvesting on federal lands.

Under NFMA, the size of clear-cuts on federally owned lands is limited. In Douglas fir forests in the Pacific Northwest, for example, the maximum size of a clear-cut area is 60 acres (24 ha). In coastal Alaska, the size is 100 acres (40 ha) for hemlock and Sitka spruce forests. In the Southeast, clear-cuts of 80 acres (32 ha) are allowed on public lands with yellow pine forests, and 40 acres (16 ha) everywhere else.

The second provision involved protection of *riparian areas* or stream corridors. Management practices that seriously or adversely affect water quality, fish, or freshwater habitat are prohibited. This protection included a 100-foot (30.5-m) buffer strip between the body of water and any affected area.

The third specific policy developed under the NFMA was the regulation of the rate of harvest. Biological growth factors combined with physical factors (such as soil erosion, slope, and soil types) and economic factors were to be used in determining the rate of harvest. The primary concern was with harvesting immature trees, so the Act expressly prohibited commercial harvest until trees reach their peak of rapid growth and maturity.

One of the most significant outgrowths of recent forestry legislation was the establishment of wilderness reviews for all lands under the control of the U.S. Forest Service. Under federal mandate, those lands that qualified as wilderness were to be managed for both wilderness protection and use by the timber industry. Consequently the U.S. Forest Service had to develop a program to review lands for wilderness status, as required by the 1964 Wilderness Act (see Chapter 17). This internal procedure was called the Roadless Area Review and Evaluation Study (*RARE I* and *RARE II*). Major conflicts between the U.S. Forest Service and preservationists arose as a result

of this study, and neither side has been happy with the outcome.

Table 9.4 illustrates the nature of multiple use. In economic terms, national forests are most valued for timber production, which accounted for 90 percent of all receipts for 1987. The Forest Service costs in producing that timber (building roads and getting the product to market) greatly exceed the sales, resulting in below-cost timber sales. This difference between timber sale receipts and sales has been controversial. Grazing in the national forests, another type of multiple use, generated $8 million in revenues in 1987, while user recreation fees produced another $31 million. Mineral leases have been less important over the last decade and account for less than 5 percent of Forest Service revenue. There has been a significant rise in revenues from 1985 to 1987, mostly from increased timber sales (36 per-

TABLE 9.4   Multiple Use in the National Forests

Use	1985	1987
Timber cutting		
Volume (million board feet)	11,340	12,921
Value (million $)	724.5	1,019.0
Receipts (million $)	514.6	807.9
% of all receipts	81	90
Grazing		
Cattle, horses, burros (thousands)	1,565	1,410
Sheep and goats (thousands)	1,183	1,134
Use receipts (million $)	9.0	8.1
% of all receipts	1	1
Recreation		
Visitors (million visitor days)	225.4	238.5
User fees receipts (million $)	30.8	30.6
% of all receipts	5	3
Mineral leases/permits		
Fees (million $)	77.5	46.7
% of all receipts	12	5
Special land use		
Fees (million $)	4.0	5.1
% of all receipts	1	1
Total receipts	635.9	898.4

Source: U.S. Forest Service (1988).

cent), yet the timber is still being sold below what it costs to produce it.

To summarize the significance of this active period of forestry legislation, congressional intervention into management was the direct outgrowth of environmentalists' concern that the national forests were being harvested by private timber companies with U.S. Forest Service approval. There was also concern that the agency itself did not have the insight to develop a broader outlook in developing policy.

THE CONTINUING DEBATE

However, the more environmentally-oriented foresters within the Forest Service have recently begun to exert greater influence, and the agency is showing signs of becoming more conservation-minded (see Issue 9–2).

There are so many conflicting interests in forest management that debate will always be intense (Wondolleck, 1988). One of the issues that has loomed large since 1980 is privatization. *Privatization* involves the increased

---

ISSUE 9–2 Environmental Protection and the Will of the People

We expect people's political affiliations to reflect their feelings about natural resource use. In the 1970s, political liberals, a bipartisan mix of Republicans and Democrats, were responsible for the passage of much historic pro-environment legislation, and they were generally supported by Democrat Jimmy Carter in the late 1970s. In 1980 the Republicans, led by Ronald Reagan, moved into the White House and spent the next eight years dismantling all the environmental legislation they could get their hands on. The Republican trend in the White House has continued into the 1990s with George Bush. As an oil man and conservative capitalist, his instincts and preferences are anti-environment, but because of the massive resurgence of environmentalism in the United States he has been forced to promote his pro-development agenda in a subtle and quiet fashion.

The country's public agencies and departments tend to reflect the politics of the party in power. When a new president comes in, she or he chooses new cabinet members and appoints hundreds of people to government posts. Overnight a department can shift to a new policy direction. The policies of the U.S. Forest Service provide a vivid example of party politics, but suggest on a deeper level that changes at the top are not always reflected within an agency.

The U.S. Forest Service, as part of the U.S. Department of Agriculture, has always found itself with conflicting missions. On the one hand there is the conservation of the nation's vast public forestlands, and on the other hand is the desire to make money from those forests by cutting them down. Being in the Department of Agriculture instead of the Department of Inte-

rior doesn't help, as this implies that trees are regarded as basically just another crop. The Forest Service has its headquarters in Washington, DC, and the nation is divided into four forestry regions with a well-developed bureaucratic structure within each. At the bottom of this structure are the people who actually set foot in the forests, monitor their conditions, and make recommendations: the rangers in charge of particular forest districts. These are career civil servants, employees of the Forest Service, and most are trained in forestry and related fields at the university level. Generally their jobs are not jeopardized by political changes in Washington, but they are expected to obey any new policy directives. But do they?

In the northern half of Cherokee National Forest, in Tennessee near its borders with Virginia and North Carolina, are three national forest districts, each administered by a ranger. Near the end of the 1980s, geographer Bret Wallach visited the Cherokee to see what eight years of Reaganomics had done to the rangers and to the forest. At the time the forestry products industry was in effect running the Forest Service in Washington, and the head of the Forest Service had announced that he wanted national forest timber production to triple under his administration. How did this go over in the Cherokee?

Cherokee National Forest has had its ups and downs. The area had been in private hands earlier in the century, and there was *no* forest when the government took it over in 1940: uncontrolled logging had denuded the beautiful slopes and valleys that lie on the edge of the Great Smoky Mountains. The forest slowly returned, but only to a single generation's maturity, and by the 1960s the Forest Service's desire

purchase of federal timber by the timber industry. To meet expected demand, the industry must increase its supply of harvestable timber. Most of the private forestland is currently in use or in parcels that are too small to make cutting economical. Privately owned forests in the West are being harvested beyond a sustainable yield, and one of the few easy ways that the industry can increase the supply of timber is to purchase and harvest from publicly owned property (Table 9.5). The conflict arises when the timber companies want to in-

crease their purchases and thus increase the amount of timber harvested from these lands.

From a traditional economic perspective, privatization is the most advantageous to timber companies because the purchase of federal timber costs less and it is of higher quality than comparable timber on small private landholdings. Environmentalists are concerned about the already dwindling acreage set aside for recreation, wilderness, and ecosystem protection and thus oppose increased sales of federal timber. They feel that when the timber indus-

---

for production had opened the area to extensive logging roads and clear-cutting in the 20-year-old stands. In addition, instead of replanting the native hardwoods, the Forest Service was replanting faster-growing and more quickly harvestable pines.

During the heyday of the environmental movement in the 1970s, there was an overhaul of the Forest Service's trees-as-crops orientation. The 1976 National Forest Management Act redirected the Service's energies toward forest management for wildlife and recreation as much as for timber production. Public participation was provided for in the planning and review process that is now required, in place of the cozy timber deals with private loggers of earlier times.

Wallach's (1988) description of the Cherokee National Forest logging policies in the 1970s and 1980s reflects both a changing Forest Service and increasing resistance to commands from above. In 1981, when the Reagan administration took office, the Cherokee National Forest was running according to the dictates of a mid-1970s management plan that called for a 10 percent reduction in logging. This was a preliminary signal that a "crop" view was being overtaken by a "protect" view. In 1985, a plan based fully on the 1976 National Forest Management Act took over, and with it came a further 25 percent logging reduction. This was the result of hard work on the part of the Wilderness Society, and local chapters of the Sierra Club, Audubon Society, and other Tennessee pro-wildlife, anti-logging groups. By 1988, the Forest Service had approved a further cut in logging and had promised that one-third of the logging would be done with methods other than clear-cutting.

What a blow for local loggers! What a triumph for local environmentalists! But this was in 1988, at the height of the Reagan administration's attempt to triple logging in national forests. Why wasn't the Cherokee National Forest cooperating? What Wallach discovered was that no matter what is happening in Washington, for most rangers the forest comes first. He found that a landscape architecture-trained ranger was in charge of one Cherokee district, a new generation ranger with quiet dedication to conservation. In another district he spoke with the old-timer in charge and found that even though this man had made his career during the "trees as crops" decades, today he was a pro-conservation, pro-wildlife forest manager. To Wallach's amazement, he discovered that "thanks to Forest Service staff as well as environmentalist pressure, logging was going to become less and less important" in Cherokee National Forest, and "recreation and environmental quality were already dominant there" (Wallach, 1988). What is clear from this example is that the tide of environmentalism is running higher and stronger than any one party's politics:

> *People exaggerate the power of elected officials . . . [and] they confuse the will of those officials with what actually happens in the country. Here on the Cherokee the changes of the last eight years had run almost completely counter to what electioneering would lead one to expect. . . . This ought to make environmentalists realize that they have allies in unexpected places. It ought to make them take heart, regardless of election results.* (Wallach, 1988, p. 27)

TABLE 9.5   Net Growth of Timber in the United States by Species Group and Ownership Category, 1976–2030 (Million Cubic Feet)

Ownership	1976		1987		2030	
	Soft	Hard	Soft	Hard	Soft	Hard
National forest	2,442	651	2,680	617	3,374	397
Other public	1,076	879	1,370	963	1,218	413
Forest industry	2,866	1,207	3,216	1,151	2,328	1,174
Other private	5,877	6,643	5,457	6,861	4,890	5,597
Total	12,261	9,380	12,722	9,593	11,810	7,581

Source: U.S. Forest Service (1982), Ince *et al.* (1988).

try claims that it is running out of wood on private land, it is "crying wolf" in order to be able to cry "timber!" on federal property.

Among other issues that continue to be important are the allocation and protection of forestlands for water supply; forested areas are invaluable in collecting the rainwater runoff and snowmelt that are essential in refilling the reservoirs of the United States. Without this watershed protection, the quantity and quality of our country's water supply would be greatly diminished. Another issue is the methods used to harvest timber. Residents usually object to the results when clear-cutting is used nearby. Besides the degradation of area streams and rivers, the stark devastation can make the property line a little too neat. In the National Forests in northern California and Oregon, conflicts are also increasing between law enforcement officials and local marijuana growers who illegally use National Forest lands to cultivate their crop. The conflict has been so intense at times that growers set armed booby traps that injure law enforcement agents and unsuspecting hikers. Recreational use in many of these National Forests has been curtailed. The national forestlands are also under increasing pressure from business interests because of the vast mineral wealth found under them.

There is even division among those who call themselves environmentalists, with some opposing wood harvesting in general because of damage to wildlife and aesthetic values or because wood burning is an air pollutant and contributor to the greenhouse effect. On the other hand, many promote the use of wood as a renewable source of energy and raw materials. Once believed to be infinite, the U.S. forest resource is today a known quantity and its future is very much open to debate. The debate is taking place not only in the halls of Congress and in the public arena, but also among professionals within the Forest Service itself who are becoming increasingly vocal about abuses to our nation's forestry resources (see Issue 9–2).

REFERENCES AND ADDITIONAL READING

Applebome, P. 1989. Mill town agonizes over high dioxin readings. *The New York Times,* September 19, p. A10.

Boyd, R.J., *et al.* 1985. *Herbicides for Forest Weed Control in the Inland Northwest: A Summary of Effects on Weeds and Conifers.* General Technical Report INT-195. Ogden, UT: USDA Forest Service Intermountain Research Station.

Brooke, J. 1989. Rain and fines reduce fires in Brazil's Amazon. *The New York Times,* September 17, p. A22.

Christensen, N.L., *et al.* 1989. Interpreting the Yellowstone fires of 1988. *Bioscience* 39(10): 678–685.

Clawson, M. 1975. *Forests for Whom and for What?* Baltimore: Johns Hopkins University Press.

———. 1979. Forests in the long sweep of U.S. history. *Science* 204: 1168–1174.

———. 1982. Private forests. In P.R. Portney (Ed.), *Current Issues in Natural Resource Policy,* Chap. 9, pp. 283–292. Washington, DC: Resources for the Future.

Council on Environmental Quality. 1981. *Environmental Trends.* Washington, DC: U.S. Government Printing Office.

———. 1989. *Environmental Trends.* Washington, DC: U.S. Government Printing Office.

Elfring, C. 1989. Yellowstone: Fire storm over fire management. *Bioscience* 39(10): 667–672.

Gradwohl, J., and R. Greenberg. 1988. *Saving the Tropical Forests*. Covello, CA: Island Press.

Hapen-Guest, S., *et al*. 1956. *A world geography of Forest Resources*. New York: Ronald Press for the American Geographical Society.

Huyler, N.K. 1989. *Fuel Supply Structure of Wood Fired Power Plants in the Northeast: Loggers' Perspective*. Research Paper NE-624. Hubbard Brook, NH: USDA Forest Service Northeastern Forest Experiment Station.

Ince, P.J., J. Fedkiw, H.E. Dickerhoof, and H.F. Kaiser. 1988. *National Measures of Forest Productivity for Timber*. General Technical Report FPL-GTR-61. Washington, DC: U.S. Forest Service.

Ketchaw, D.E., coordinator. 1978. *Symposium on the Use of Herbicides in Forestry, February 21–28*. Washington, DC: U.S. Environmental Protection Agency.

Likens, G.E., *et al*. 1978. Recovery of a deforested ecosystem. *Science* 199: 492–496.

Linden, E. 1989. Playing with fire. *Time*, September 18, pp. 76–85.

Lugo, A.E. 1988. The future of the forest: Ecosystem rehabilitation in the tropics. *Environment* 30(7): 16–20, 41–45.

Matzke, G., and D. Key. 1989. Wildfire in the West's woods: Fire policy in the wake of the fires of 1988. *Focus*, Summer, pp. 1–2, 18.

Miller, J.H., and L.M. Bishop. 1989. *Optimum Timing for Ground-Applied Forestry Herbicides in the South*. Management Bulletin R8-MB 28. Atlanta: USDA Forest Service Southern Region.

Mitchell, J.G. 1990. War in the woods II: West Side Story. *Audubon* 92(1): 82–121.

Moran, E.G. 1981. *Developing the Amazon*. Bloomington: Indiana University Press.

Mott, W.P., Jr. 1989. Federal fire policy in national parks. *Renewable Resources J.* 7(1): 5–7.

Myers, N. 1984. *The Primary Source: Tropical Forests and Our Future*. New York: Norton.

Nations, J.D., and D.I. Komer. 1983. Rainforests and the hamburger society: Can the cycle be broken? *Environment* 25(3): 12–20.

Rand-McNally 1979. *Our Magnificent Earth*.

Romme, W.H., and D.G. Despain. 1989. The Yellowstone fires. *Sci. Amer.* 261(5): 37–46.

Schneider, S.H. 1989. The changing climate. *Sci. Amer.* 261(3): 70–79.

Sedjo, R.A. 1989. Forests a tool to moderate global warming? *Environment* 31(1): 14–20.

Shabecoff, P. 1990. Government says dioxin from paper mills poses no major danger. *The New York Times*, May 1, p. A17.

Shakow, D., *et al*. 1981. Energy and development: The case of Kenya. *Ambio* 10: 206–210.

Spurr, S.H., and B.V. Barnes. 1980. *Forest Ecology*, 3rd ed. New York: Wiley.

Stevens, W.K. 1989. To halt climate change, scientists try trees. *The New York Times*, July 18, p. A17.

U.S. Bureau of the Census. 1989. *Statistical Abstract of the United States*. Washington, DC: U.S. Government Printing Office.

U.S. Department of Agriculture. 1988. *Agricultural Statistics*. Washington, DC: U.S. Government Printing Office.

U.S. Forest Service. 1982. *An Analysis of the Timber Situation in the U.S. 1952–2030*. Forest Service Report No. 23. Washington, DC: U.S. Government Printing Office.

———. 1988. *U.S. Forest Facts*. Washington, DC: U.S. Government Printing Office.

von Stackelberg, P. 1989. White wash: The dioxin coverup. *Greenpeace* 14(2): 7–11.

Wallach, B. 1988. Taking heart from Upper East Tennessee: Politics in a National Forest. *Focus* 38(4):22–27.

Wilson, E.O. 1989. Threats to biodiversity. *Sci. Amer.* 261(3): 108–117.

Wondolleck, J.M. 1988. *Public Lands Conflict and Resolution—Managing National Forest Disputes*. New York: Plenum.

World Resources Institute. 1988. *World Resources 1988–89*. New York: Basic Books.

Wuerthner, G. 1989. The flames of '88. *Wilderness* 52(185): 41–54.

TERMS TO KNOW

Amenity Value
Biomass
Biomass Harvesting
Clear-cutting
Crown Fires
Deforestation
Fire Frequency
Gifford Pinchot
Ground Fires
Hardwoods
Multiple Use
Multiple Use Sustained Yield Act
National Forest Management Act
Privatization

RARE I and II
Riparian Areas
Selective Cutting
Shelterwood Cutting
Softwoods
Surface Fires
Sustained Yield

STUDY QUESTIONS

1. What is the cycle of forest growth?
2. Do forest fires ever benefit the environment? Why or why not?

3. What are the three basic kinds of forest fires, and what are the effects of each?
4. Describe each of the three most important wood-harvesting techniques. What are the pros and cons of each method?
5. Besides human activity, what are the major threats to forest resources?
6. What are three methods for reforestation of cutover areas? Which one is most appropriate for hardwood forests? For softwoods?
7. What are the four primary uses of the national forests, and how do these influence management decisions?

10

Water Resources: Supply and Demand

INTRODUCTION

The water system of the earth, the hydrologic cycle, involves huge quantities of water storage and transfer between the atmosphere, oceans, and the land (see Chapter 4). Most of the water in the hydrologic system, however, is unavailable for human use, because it is either saline (97 percent) or locked up in ice caps (2 percent) (Table 10.1). Although there is plenty of water on the earth, less than 1 percent of it is in a form that we can use.

The annual flow of fresh water over the land surface and through shallow groundwater systems amounts to about 9600 cubic miles (40,000 km^3) worldwide, or about .003 percent of the total amount of water in the world. This flow is precipitation less *evapotranspiration* (evaporation from the land surface plus transpiration from plants) on land surfaces and represents the amount that is theoretically available for human use. In practice, though, much less is available because water is not uniformly distributed on the earth's surface. Much of the runoff occurs in areas with low water needs, while many areas have large water demands but little available water. In addition, the flow is variable in time, with both regular seasonal variability and less predictable fluctuations such as droughts. As a result, much of the world is experiencing severe water shortages, which are made worse by the many demands we place on the hydrologic cycle and by deterioration in water quality. In the coming years these shortages can be expected to become more acute, with increasing popula-

tion and increasing water demand for irrigation, industrial, and household uses.

NATURAL WATER AVAILABILITY

Within the United States, there is considerable variation in water resources from place to place. Water availability also varies over time, with some years being wetter or drier than others. Because of this, it is often difficult to plan for future shortages or surpluses of water. To get around this problem, water resources are often described in terms of a water budget, which can be developed at the local, state, regional, or national levels. A water budget is an accounting of the major flows and storages in the hydrologic cycle. Table 10.2 illustrates

TABLE 10.1 World Quantities of Water in the Hydrologic Cycle

Location	Percentage of Total
Surface	0.0171
Freshwater lakes	0.009
Saline lakes and inland seas	0.008
Stream channels	0.0001
Subsurface	0.625
Soil moisture	0.005
Groundwater	0.62
Ice caps and glaciers	2.15
Atmosphere	0.001
Oceans	97.2

Source: Strahler (1975).

TABLE 10.2 Water Budget for the United States (Billions of Cubic Meters per Day)

Precipitation	15.9
Evaporation from wet surfaces	10.4
Reservoir net evaporation	0.06
Stream flow to oceans	4.62
Groundwater flow to oceans	0.38
Stream flow to Mexico and Canada	0.03
Consumptive use	0.40

Source: Water Resources Council (1978).

a generalized water budget for the United States.

SURFACE WATER AND GROUNDWATER

Water is found on the land in two basic forms: as surface water and as groundwater. Both of these function as important storages in the hydrologic cycle. *Surface water* is liquid water and floating ice above the ground surface, in rivers, swamps, lakes, or ponds. It is derived from direct precipitation or from subsurface sources.

Groundwater is water below the ground surface, in a saturated zone below the *water table* (Fig. 10.1). The water table is simply the top of the saturated zone, in which water fills pore spaces and cracks in rocks or sediments. Soil moisture above the water table is not considered part of groundwater. Groundwater is derived from downward percolation of rainfall through the soil, and in some areas from seep-

age of surface water. In addition, there are many areas of the world with substantial "fossil" groundwater storages that are derived from past humid conditions and are not being significantly replenished today. A porous body of material containing groundwater is called an *aquifer*. If the water table is free to rise with additional water, the aquifer is called unconfined. If there is an impermeable layer overlying the aquifer, it is called confined. Such impermeable layers are called *aquicludes*, and they are particularly important in segregating relatively clean groundwater from brackish or contaminated groundwater (Fig. 10.1).

Surface water and groundwater flow from high elevations to low ones. Surface water flows according to the shape of the land, following channels to the sea. But groundwater flows according to the slope of the water table and the permeability of the materials through which it moves. *Permeability* refers to the speed with which water will flow through a porous medium such as rock or sediments. The steeper the slope of the water table, or the greater the permeability of the ground, the faster water will flow. Usually the shape of the water table approximately parallels the shape of the land, so that groundwater flows from upland areas toward lowlands, but this is not always the case. For example, variations in the permeability of subsurface materials may affect flow rates and directions, sometimes causing drainage divides for groundwater to be different from those for surface water. Thus a

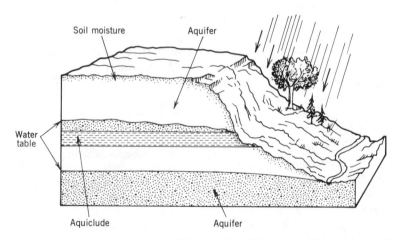

Figure 10.1 Groundwater. Water that is below the surface filling spaces in rocks or sediments is called groundwater. These storages can be used to meet water demand, but they are usually replenished slowly.

detailed knowledge of subsurface structures is necessary to understand how groundwater flows in any particular area. The locations of permeable and impermeable areas of rock or sediments are important not only for groundwater flow patterns but also for determining where water is stored and available.

SPATIAL VARIATION IN SURFACE WATER SUPPLY

Surface water supply is directly determined by precipitation and evapotranspiration rates, with runoff being the difference between the two. In the United States, average annual precipitation is relatively high in the southeastern states, the Appalachians, the Pacific Northwest, and in mountainous areas of the West, southern Alaska, and Hawaii (Fig. 10.2a). Water loss via evaporation and plant transpiration also affects water resource availability. Regionally, climate conditions influence evaporation and transpiration rates (Fig. 10.2b). For example, in semiarid areas, runoff is generally low because major evaporative losses occur shortly after the precipitation falls. Runoff, on a per area basis, is greatest in the Pacific Northwest, the Rocky Mountains, the Appalachians, and New England (Fig. 10.2c). Once this runoff is generated it flows into rivers and is transported to other areas.

Figure 10.3 is a map showing the average discharge for major American rivers. The Mississippi carries the most water, draining about 1.2 million square miles (3.2 million km^2) or 35 percent of the United States and carrying an average of about 620,000 cubic feet per second (cfs) (17,600 m^3/sec) to the ocean. The Columbia River is next, draining 258,300 square miles (669,000 km^2) and discharging an average of 235,000 cfs (6650 m^3/sec). The St. Lawrence River drains a larger area than the Columbia, but carries less water, and the Colorado River which drains 137,000 square miles (355,000 km^2) would discharge only about 17,000 cfs (480 m^3/sec) to the sea if it were not withdrawn for human uses. In addition to these, there are many smaller rivers, and immense amounts of water are also stored in freshwater lakes, especially the Great Lakes.

SPATIAL VARIATION IN GROUNDWATER SUPPLY

There are many different types of aquifers, depending on the nature of the materials and the source of water in them. Figure 10.4 shows the major aquifers of the United States. Although not every place has substantial groundwater available, these productive aquifers are widespread. The aquifer distribution pattern corresponds to geologic structures, including the extensive coastal plain deposits of the Southeast, sedimentary rocks, glacial deposits, and young sand and gravel deposits in the Midwest, and the accumulation of sediments in the West's intermontane valleys. In addition, most of the major river valleys (the Colorado and Columbia are notable exceptions) are underlain by relatively permeable channel deposits that are recharged by the stream flow of the rivers that formed them. Generally, areas without productive aquifers are mountain areas and much of the arid West, which have either too little or too brackish groundwater. In addition to the large aquifers shown, across the country there are smaller or less productive aquifers, many of which are important local water supplies.

TEMPORAL VARIABILITY IN WATER SUPPLY

There are two main ways of evaluating water availability: flow and storage. Flow is the rate at which water passes through a system; storage is the volume of water in the system at any given time. The ratio of flow to storage is especially important, as it determines the length of time required to replace stored water if it is depleted or contaminated. If the flow rate is high in relation to storage, then the water can be quickly replenished. However, such a system is susceptible to fluctuations in flow resulting from floods and droughts. On the other hand, if storage is high in relation to flow, then there is less short-term variability of flow, but it takes much longer to replenish stored water.

Rivers have very high ratios of flow to storage, and thus short-term fluctuations in discharge greatly limit the amount of water they can supply. Seasonal mean monthly discharges for rivers typically vary by one or even two

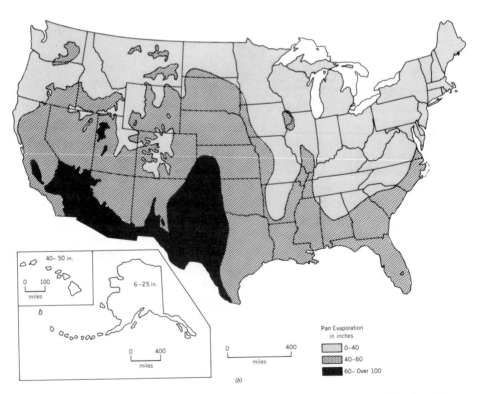

Figure 10.2   Surface water supply. The amount is determined by rates of precipitation (*a*), pan evaporation (*b*), and runoff (*c*). Notice the large amounts of runoff in the Pacific Northwest, where precipitation is also great. (*Source:* Council on Environmental Quality, 1989, p. 23.)

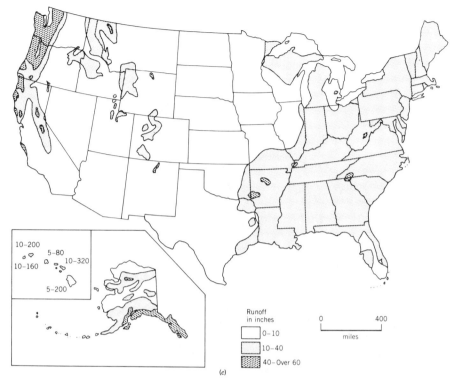

Figure 10.2 *(Continued)*

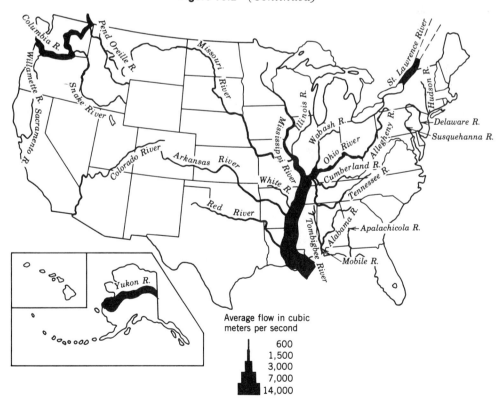

Figure 10.3 Average annual discharge of major U.S. rivers. The Mississippi dominates, with the Yukon, Columbia, and St. Lawrence also being major drainage systems. (*Source:* Council on Environmental Quality, 1989, p. 24.)

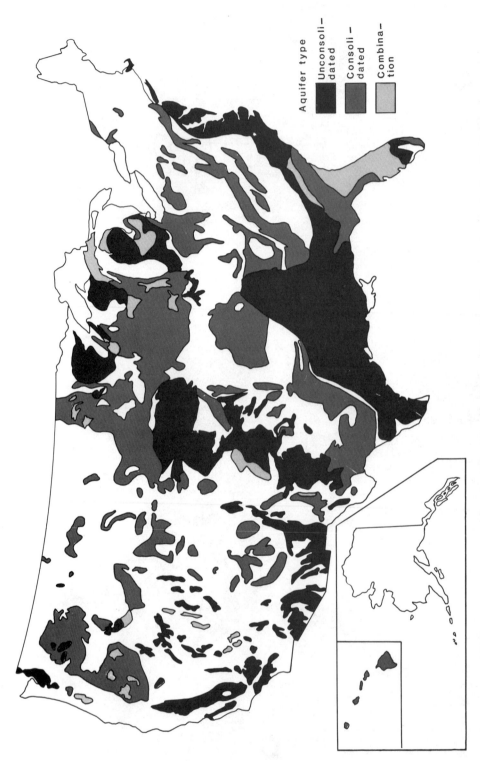

Figure 10.4 Major aquifers in the United States. Unconsolidated aquifers are composed primarily of recent deposits of sands and gravels. Consolidated aquifers consist of older permeable rocks. (*Source:* Adapted from Water Resources Council, 1978.)

Aquifer type

Unconsoli- dated

Consoli- dated

Combina- tion

orders of magnitude, depending on seasonal amounts of precipitation and evapotranspiration. This means that if the average flow in the driest month is 176 cfs (5 m³/sec), the flow in the wettest month may be 1765 or 17,650 cfs (50 or 500 m³/sec). In mid-latitude climates, the low-flow periods are usually in the summer because plants are using more water then. Summer is also the time when demand for water is higher, as people water lawns, wash cars, open fire hydrants, and fill swimming pools. As a result, the amount of water we can count on from a river is much less than the total amount that flows in it over the year. In addition, precipitation variations from one year to the next further reduce the amount of water we can depend on from rivers. The short- and medium-term variation in stream flow of U.S. streams is shown in Fig. 10.5. The drought years of the 1930s and the early 1960s stand out. These two decades serve as the baseline record of low flow, as there has not been a prolonged period of drought since. Water supply planners in New Jersey, for example, utilize these two decades for their worst-case scenarios.

Overall, water supplies must be planned for the years with flows well below the mean. If we want the supply to be adequate at least 95 percent of the time, for example, the discharge demanded must be equaled or exceeded in an average of 19 out of 20 years. For the Northeast, this demand value is generally about 60 percent of the mean discharge on an annual basis. In the Missouri River basin it is about 40 percent of the mean; for the Rio Grande, it is only 17 percent. This supply problem is compounded by the fact that *droughts* often last more than one year, so that there may be a succession of three or four dry years in a row, instead of a dry year always being followed by a wet one.

Groundwater supplies, on the other hand, usually represent very large storages of water in relation to flow. Aquifers are usually recharged very slowly, and large ones are not significantly affected by seasonal variations in precipitation or even year-to-year climatic fluctuations. However, smaller aquifers, especially shallower ones, are affected by short-term weather patterns, though less than rivers are.

USES OF WATER

Water is used for a wide variety of purposes, and these have very different quantity, quality, and timing characteristics. The type of use can be evaluated by whether it takes place in the stream or elsewhere, and by whether the water is returned to the stream after use. Before

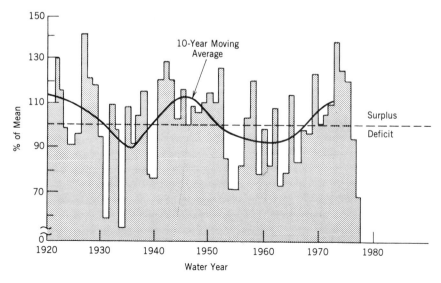

Figure 10.5 Variability of stream flow in the United States. Ideally, water supplies should be planned to anticipate the low-flow years. (*Source:* Water Resources Council, 1978.)

proceeding, then, let us define a few terms that describe these aspects of water use. *Withdrawal* is the removal of water from a surface or groundwater source for a variety of purposes such as municipal, industrial, or irrigation use. *Consumption* is the use of that water in such a way that it is not returned to the stream or aquifer; instead, it is returned to the atmosphere by evapotranspiration. *Instream uses* do not require removal of the water from a river or lake; these include navigation, wildlife habitat, waste disposal, and hydroelectric power generation.

Water demands fluctuate from year to year depending on weather patterns. In wet or cool years, demand is usually lower, whereas in dry years demand is greater. To evaluate long-term trends it is useful to average these short-term fluctuations. For example, both water withdrawals and consumption have risen steadily since the 1960s (Fig. 10.6). Since 1980, freshwater withdrawals and consumption have declined somewhat. Surface water remains the primary source of water withdrawals, a pattern evident from the 1950s.

Groundwater withdrawals have continued t increase since the 1950s as well (Fig. 10.7).

FUNCTIONAL USES

Withdrawal and consumptive uses of water are often defined by specific categories (or functions) of use. These include public supply, rural supply (domestic and livestock), industrial, irrigation, and hydroelectric power generation (an in-stream use).

Public and rural supplies include both domestic and commercial uses of water, including those that we are familiar with in our everyday lives at home or at work. They include washing, cooking, drinking, lawn watering, sanitation, and the like. About 86 percent of the U.S. population is served by municipal water supply systems, while the remaining 14 percent have individual domestic systems (usually wells). By the year 2000 it is expected that 90 percent will be served by centralized water supply systems (Water Resources Council, 1978). In centralized systems the average domestic water use is about 100 gallons (377

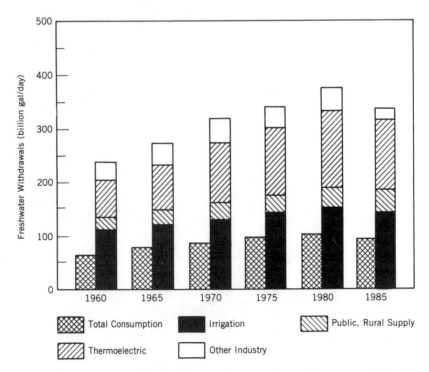

Figure 10.6   Trends in the U.S. freshwater withdrawls and consumption by use, 1960–1985. (*Source:* Council on Environmental Quality, 1988, p. 117.)

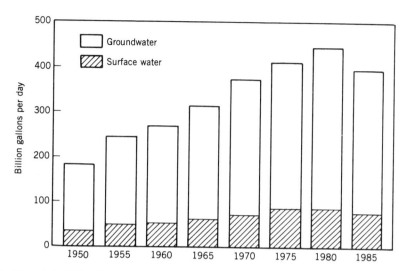

Figure 10.7 Trends in U.S. off-stream water use by source of withdrawal 1950–1985. (*Source:* Council on Environmental Quality, 1989, p. 30.)

liters) per person per day, and commercial uses add another 57 gallons (215 liters) per day. In individual systems, domestic use is less. The difference is that municipal use also includes delivery losses, fire protection, street washing, park maintenance, and similar community functions. This per capita use is not expected to change very much in the next few decades, although the total amount of water demanded for these uses will increase as population increases. Domestic and commercial uses are not highly consumptive, with most of the water being returned via individual or community sewage systems. On the average, about 26 percent of this use is consumed.

The use of fresh water in industry is much greater than domestic and commercial use, averaging about 611 gallons (2311 liters) per person per day in 1982 (Table 10.3). The largest industrial use is for the production of electric power, which accounts for almost two-thirds of all industrial withdrawals. Large amounts of water are withdrawn for coolant purposes, totaling 411 gallons (1557 liters) per person per day in 1982 (Table 10.3). Very little (around 26 percent) of this water is consumed, however. In the future, this use will also increase and more of the water will be consumed when evaporative cooling systems, rather than once-through convective systems, become

TABLE 10.3 Total U.S. Withdrawal and Consumption by Functional Use, 1982

	Withdrawals		Consumption	
	Total (Billion Liters/Day)	Per Capita (Liters/Day)	Total (Billion Liters/Day)	Per Capita (Liters/Day)
Domestic	79.86	338	21.95	93
Commercial	45.42	192	14.00	59
Industrial	545.42	2311	60.18	255
Thermoelectric	367.52	1557	15.52	66
Manufacturing/mining	177.90	754	44.66	189
Agriculture	498.11	2111	302.42	1281
Irrigation	489.78	2075	295.23	1251
Livestock	8.33	35	7.19	30
Total fresh	1168.81	4953	398.56	1689
Total saline	272.52	1155	8.33	35

Source: U.S. Department of Agriculture (1989).

more widespread. There have been some attempts, however, to use recycled wastewater for cooling in some of these facilities (see Issue 10–1). The manufacturing of paper, related products, and steel, the production of petroleum, coal, and chemicals, and food processing are also important industrial uses of water. Most of the water is used for cooling or washing purposes, and thus is not consumptive. In 1982, only 25 percent of manufacturing withdrawals was consumed. Some industries recirculate water through their plants, cooling it or cleaning it at the plant site. It is hoped that recirculation will become more widespread in the future, largely as a means to reduce water pollution. This will result in a decline in water withdrawals. Consumption, however, is still expected to increase.

By far the largest use of water in the United States, in terms of both withdrawal and consumption, is agriculture. Irrigation is the major component, and livestock watering accounts for only about 2 percent of agricultural use. Agricultural use amounted to about 560 gallons (2111 liters) per person per day in 1982, or about 43 percent of the total water withdrawals in the United States. Irrigation is also the most consumptive of all major uses, accounting for 80 percent of the total consumption and 34 percent of all water withdrawn in 1985 (Council on Environmental Quality, 1989).

The U.S. irrigation budget in (Fig. 10.8) illustrates the flows and losses of water in this system. To conserve more of the water, irrigation systems must become more efficient. Table 10.4 shows some of the major irrigation methods and their efficiency ratings. Irrigation efficiency is defined as the volume of applied water in the root zone that is used by the crop. It is expressed as a percentage of the volume of water diverted from surface sources or pumped from groundwater supplies (U.S. Department of Agriculture, 1989, p. 75). As you can see, drip irrigation is the most efficient application method, and sprinklers are the least efficient.

REGIONAL COMPARISONS OF SURFACE WATER AND GROUNDWATER USE

Regionally, surface water withdrawals are greatest in the north central states, and account for more than 60 percent of all withdrawals in many other states (Fig. 10.9). Groundwater withdrawals are greatest in Kansas, followed by Texas and Hawaii. The use of both surface water and groundwater domi-

---

ISSUE 10–1   Palo Verde: Nuclear Power in the Desert

The Palo Verde Nuclear Generating Station (NGS) is located 55 miles (88 ha) west of Phoenix, Arizona. According to the Arizona Nuclear Power Project, the three pressurized water reactors generate enough power (3810 megawatts) to meet the needs of four million people. The plant provides electricity for the entire Southwest and is partially owned by seven utilities representing four states (Arizona, California, Texas, and New Mexico). Construction began in 1976 with all three reactors on line in 1987. Although it may seem like just another nuclear power plant, Palo Verde is quite unique.

All nuclear power plants require some type of cooling water and so are most often located near a source of plentiful and cheap water. Most of the commercial nuclear reactors in this country are located near lakes, major rivers, or on the coast for precisely that reason. Palo Verde is located in the middle of the southwestern desert, where rainfall is less than 20 inches (510 mm) per year. So where does its cooling water come from?

The water used in the reactor and steam cycle in Palo Verde comes from demineralized groundwater, and since this cycle is self-contained, there is little need to provide additional inputs. So the initial use of groundwater in the reactor start-up was acceptable, but the longer term and continuous need for cooling water could not be met by the available groundwater sources. Also, cooling towers (similar to large evaporative coolers) are used to cool water that condenses the steam that is used to drive the turbines, which in turn produce the electricity. The condenser water circulates through underground pipes to the towers, where it is cooled by evaporation and then returned to the plant to

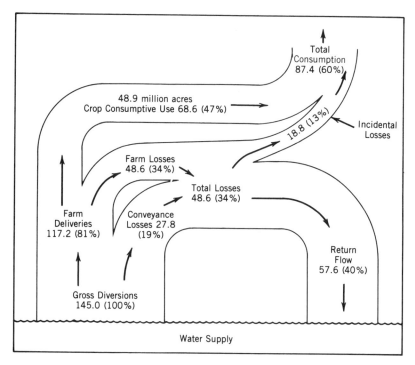

Figure 10.8 Irrigation water budget for the United States and the Caribbean in an average year, 1985. Losses include evaporation and seepage from canals, and percolation from soil. (*Source:* U.S. Department of Agriculture, 1989, p. 76.)

pick up the waste heat and then be recooled. A large, continuous source of water is needed because much water is lost by evaporation in this climate from the cooling towers.

Palo Verde has found a unique source of coolant: sewage effluent from the Phoenix metropolitan area (Fig. 10.17). Each year, 64,000 acre-feet of treated effluent are sent 36 miles (58 km) from two treatment facilities in the metropolitan area to Palo Verde. The effluent is purchased by the operating utility (Arizona Public Service Company) from seven communities in the metropolitan region: Phoenix, Youngstown, Mesa, Tempe, Glendale, Scottsdale, and Tolleson. The communities are paid between $20 and $35 per acre-foot of water supplied. Once the effluent reaches the plant it is further treated and stored in an 80-acre (32-ha) reservoir until it is needed.

This is an extremely innovative use of wastewater. Because of the normal aridity, simply releasing the treated effluent into local rivers would increase pollution problems downstream because of seasonal low flow. On the other hand, the plant could not have been built without a steady and reliable source of cooling water which the effluent provides. The people of the Phoenix metropolitan area are the big winners. They get sufficient energy to provide air conditioning during the hot season, their drinking water supply remains relatively unpolluted from sewage treatment plants, and their municipalities receive some financial compensation for their treated wastewater, thus lowering sewage fees to residents.

TABLE 10.4   Potential Efficiencies and Use of Irrigation Methods

Type	Potential Efficiency (%)	Acreage (Million)
Gravity methods		
Flood		9.0
Level border	90	
Graded	80	
Guide border	70	
Contour ditch	60	
Contour levee	70	
Other Flood	60	
Furrow		18.0
Graded furrow	75	
Corrugations	80	
Subsurface	75	0.4
Pressure methods		
Sprinkle		20.6
Center pivot	82	9.4
Solid set	77	9.4
Wheel/handline	73	6.3
Other	65	3.7
Drip/trickle		1.0
Continuous tape	90	1.0
Point source emitters	90	
Spray emitters	85	

Source: U.S. Department of Agriculture (1989, p. 76).

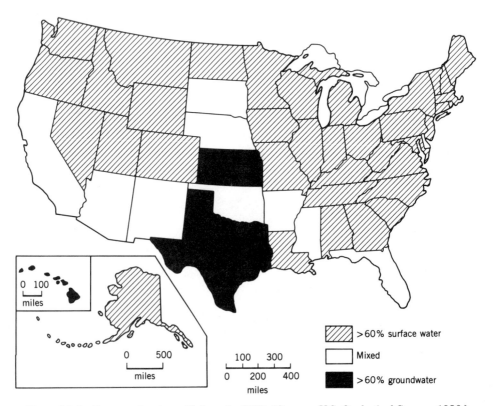

Figure 10.9   Source of water withdrawals, 1982. (*Source:* U.S. Geological Survey, 1986.)

nates the southern tier of states, from California in the west to Florida in the east. Saline water withdrawals, largely for industrial purposes, are locally important in the mid-Atlantic states.

Water withdrawals are greatest in the arid West, where most of the water is used for irrigation. In Idaho, for example, per capita water withdrawals average 19,068 gallons (72,172 liters) per person per day, the highest in the country! This contrasts sharply with Rhode Island residents, who withdraw only 180 gallons (681 liters) per person per day, the lowest in the country (Table 10.5). Consumption patterns are similar, with Idaho, Wyoming, Nebraska, Montana, and Nevada having the highest per capita consumption rates, and Massachusetts, Rhode Island, New Hampshire, Delaware, and Maryland having the lowest.

There are some striking patterns when we look at the functional use of water. For example, industrial use (primarily thermoelectric power generation) accounts for the majority of surface water withdrawals in the eastern half of the United States, whereas irrigation is the dominant use in the West (Fig. 10.10). Most of the irrigation takes place in the more arid parts of the country, particularly the western Great Plains, the intermontane basins west of the Rockies, and California. Much of the water for this irrigation is collected as runoff from mountain areas, but groundwater is also a major source. Because of the arid climate of these areas and the large demands for irrigation water, supplies are short and in many areas groundwater is used faster than it is being replaced. In fact, groundwater depletion due to overpumping for irrigation purposes is particularly severe in Texas, California, Kansas, and Nebraska. In Texas, 72 percent of the total land irrigated uses overpumped groundwater, largely from the Ogallala aquifer. As a result, water tables are falling at the rate of 6 inches (15 cm) per year on most of the state's irrigated lands (Postel, 1989).

The Water Resources Council (1978) predicts that as a result of this shortage, agricultural withdrawals will actually decline by the year 2000, although the efficiency of water use in crop production will increase. The amount of water consumed by agriculture is also expected to increase. Increased efficiency in water use will result from increased control of seepage losses and use of water-conserving systems such as drip irrigation (see Chapter 7).

Domestic use of water is dominant in only two states, Delaware and Rhode Island (Fig. 10.10). When we examine domestic water use more closely, a number of interesting patterns emerge. For example, per capita domestic use of water is lowest in the Northeast and greatest in the West, where water is used for more outdoor purposes such as watering lawns, hosing down sidewalks and driveways, washing cars, and so on. Nevada, Hawaii, and Arizona have the highest per capita rates of domestic water use, averaging 357 gallons (1351 liters), 294 gallons (1113 liters), and 275 gallons (1041 liters) per person per day, respectively (U.S. Geological Survey, 1986). Delaware (20 gallons or 76 liters) Louisiana (81 gallons or 307 liters), and Iowa (110 gallons or 416 liters) have the lowest per capita domestic water use rates in the country.

DEVELOPMENT OF WATER SUPPLIES

METHODS USED TO INCREASE AVAILABLE WATER

As Fig. 10.11 shows, any water supply system must have the following four components: collection system, storage facility, transportation system, and distribution system. Water supply engineers design and construct water systems in a variety of ways, where possible incorporating natural features in one or more of these components. In virtually all cases, the collection system is natural: it is the *drainage basin* of a river or a groundwater aquifer, or some combination of the two. Rivers are particularly efficient concentrators of surface runoff. As a result there is usually little that is done to modify collection systems, although vegetation conversion to increase water yield or improve water quality has been used in many areas. Aquifers are much more dispersed conveyors of water. Water flows toward low points in the water table, and when a well is drilled to pump water out, the local water table is depressed. This causes water to flow toward

TABLE 10.5   Regional Variations in Water Supply and Use

State	Water Source (%)[a] Surface	Ground	Per Capita Withdrawal[b] (Gallons/Day)	Per Capita Consumption[b] (Gallons/Day)
Alabama	97	3	2,825	146
Alaska	77	23	547	87
Arizona	42	58	2,943	1,656
Arkansas	41	59	6,999	1,575
California	60	40	1,859	1,056
Colorado	81	19	5,536	1,384
Connecticut	90	10	418	51
Delaware	41	59	236	19
Florida	49	51	749	246
Georgia	82	18	1,226	183
Hawaii	39	61	1,347	705
Idaho	67	33	19,068	6,250
Illinois	94	6	1,575	52
Indiana	93	7	2,550	126
Iowa	72	28	1,476	100
Kansas	15	85	2,792	1,988
Kentucky	96	4	1,311	79
Louisiana	86	14	2,853	832
Maine	91	9	756	47
Maryland	70	30	261	24
Massachusetts	84	16	436	16
Michigan	96	4	1,620	50
Minnesota	77	23	761	110
Mississippi	48	52	1,150	282
Missouri	93	7	1,403	136
Montana	98	2	13,977	3,431
Nebraska	42	58	7,643	4,841
Nevada	81	19	4,500	2,125
New Hampshire	84	16	413	18
New Jersey	72	28	394	52
New Mexico	53	47	2,993	1,458
New York	90	10	456	34
North Carolina	90	10	1,377	129
North Dakota	91	9	1,991	505
Ohio	93	7	1,297	51
Oklahoma	44	56	562	331
Oregon	84	16	2,554	1,202
Pennsylvania	94	6	1,349	78
Rhode Island	82	18	180	16
South Carolina	96	4	1,986	90
South Dakota	52	48	999	666
Tennessee	96	4	2,178	59
Texas	39	61	984	703
Utah	81	19	3,080	1,985
Vermont	87	13	665	80
Virginia	93	7	1,047	43
Washington	91	9	1,985	702
West Virginia	96	4	2,872	103
Wisconsin	90	10	1,232	66
Wyoming	91	9	11,277	5,532
Total	77	23	2,000	441

Sources: [a]U.S. Geological Survey (1986).
        [b]Conservation Foundation (1987).

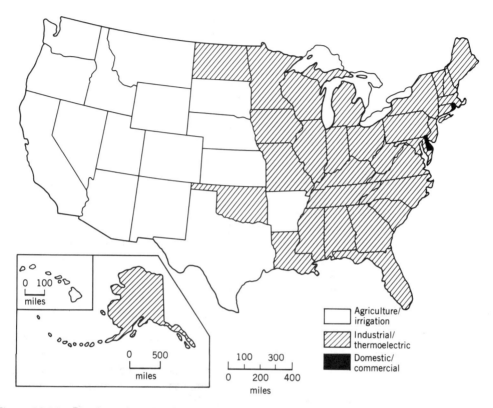

Figure 10.10   Dominant functional surface water use, 1980. (*Source:* U.S. geological survey, 1986.)

the well, which is exactly what is desired. By drilling wells in particularly porous, permeable underground materials, we can tap into aquifers that have a ready supply of available water.

Storage is necessary to smooth out the natural variations in water availability and to save surplus water from high-rainfall periods for later times when water is scarce. Under ideal conditions, a storage facility can allow average withdrawals to equal the long-term average flow and short-term withdrawals can

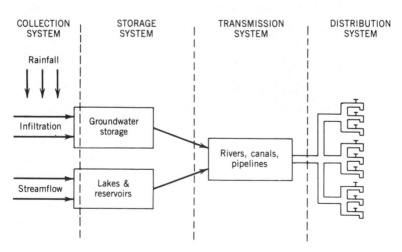

Figure 10.11   Components of a water supply system. The component with the lowest capacity limits the capacity of the entire system.

far exceed average flows. In practice, however, average withdrawals are rarely this large. Storages cannot trap all the water during times of flood, and water must be left for in-stream uses. Nonetheless, short-term withdrawals-for periods of weeks or less-frequently can exceed average inflows in large storages.

Surface water storage is accomplished by constructing dams on rivers and impounding water in artificial lakes behind the dams. The amount of water that can be stored is a function of the shape of the valley and the height of the dam. The ideal dam site is a relatively narrow and deep valley (where the dam is built) with a broad and deep valley just upstream. In addition, the valley that is to be inundated should be underlain by impermeable rocks and be relatively unpopulated, and the land should be of lower long term value than the value of the reservoir replacing it.

There are many locations in the United States that fit these criteria, and most of them have dams in them (see Fig. 10.12). The number of dams and storage volume in the United States increased since the turn of the century. In 1987, there were 2654 reservoirs and controlled natural lakes with a combined storage capacity of 479 million acre-feet (one-half billion m^3). Unfortunately, the rate of construction of reservoirs for municipal and industrial water supplies and for irrigation has not kept pace with increasing populations. In Canada there are many undeveloped dam sites, but most of them are in relatively remote areas and development costs are high. In much of

the Third World, numerous dam sites are still available for development.

Transportation and distribution systems can be of many types, depending mostly on the distance between collection site and use area and the nature of the final use. In many cases transportation distances are so short that the entire system is essentially just a distribution system. These facilities include canals, pipelines, and natural river channels, or any combination of these (Fig. 10.13). The choice of which type of conduit to use depends primarily on terrain, the volumes of water to be carried, the distances involved, and the need to protect against seepage or quality deterioration along the way.

THE ROLE OF WEATHER IN WATER DEVELOPMENT

Because of the variability of water supply and demand, the amount available in any supply system is rarely equal to the demand. Reservoirs smooth out some of the fluctuations, but supply systems are inevitably stressed in time of drought. Thus the supply provided by any particular system fluctuates between plenty and shortage (Fig. 10.14). As population has increased, the demand for water has steadily risen, both on a per capita basis and for regions as a whole. For example, cities have grown in both population and area, and usually develop more centralized water systems to meet the demands of growing populations. If a water supply system is not enlarged to keep pace

Figure 10.12   Ashokan Reservoir, New York, part of the New York City water supply system.

Figure 10.13 The California Aqueduct. This aqueduct carries water from the northern Sierra Nevada mountains to agricultural lands in the Central Valley.

with growing demand, then at some point the supply will be insufficient. The combination of a fluctuating supply with gradually increasing demand results in periods when supply is insufficient, and local water supply crises result (see Issue 10–2).

EXTENT OF WATER RESOURCE DEVELOPMENT

It should be clear by now that, although water supply is constrained by natural factors, water development in the form of engineering works also affects water availability. The extent of water development can be evaluated only relative to what is naturally available, and that in turn is subject to debate, because there are different definitions of what is "available water." One indication of the extent of water use can be gained by comparing withdrawals to natural runoff. In the Mississippi River basin, for example, withdrawals from stream flow are 21 percent of the runoff. In New England, withdrawals are 6 percent of runoff, in the Middle Atlantic states 20 percent, and in California 43 percent. In arid areas, water is used off-stream more than once. In the Colorado River basin, withdrawals from stream flow are 92 percent of runoff, and if we include withdrawals from groundwater, they amount to 136 percent of natural runoff. In the interior Great Basin, freshwater withdrawals are 110 percent of runoff.

Withdrawals can exceed stream flow because not all of the water withdrawn is consumed; some is returned to the stream. Nonetheless, these withdrawals place a heavy demand on water resources, particularly so be-

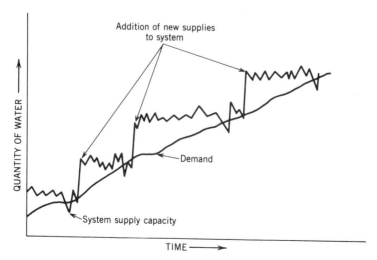

Figure 10.14 Fluctuation in water supply and demand. Demand rises steadily, and crises of supply occur during times of drought. These crises stimulate expansion in the supply system, which lasts a few years, until demand again exceeds supply. (*Source:* Modified from Russell *et al.,* 1970.)

cause they compete with in-stream uses. In the Colorado River basin, for example, a series of power plants at major dams generates about 4 percent of the nation's hydroelectric power, and plants in the Pacific Northwest (mostly in the Columbia River basin) generate almost 50 percent of U.S. hydroelectric power (Water Resources Council, 1978). If water is withdrawn and consumed rather than returned for this in-stream use, energy production will be drastically reduced.

In more densely populated areas of the country, the most important in-stream use is maintenance of water quality. Sufficient flow must be available to dilute and transport sewage effluents and other pollutants, as well as to provide habitat for aquatic life. The U.S. Fish and Wildlife Service estimates the flows necessary to support aquatic habitat and recreation.

They found these flows to be generally 80 to 90 percent of total stream flow in the eastern United States, and 40 to 60 percent of the total flow in most of the western states (Water Resources Council, 1978). Navigation is another important in-stream use that competes with other in- and off-stream uses for the water in our rivers. Depletion of stream flows caused by consumptive off-stream use, particularly irrigation, is a major problem in semiarid and arid portions of the United States (Fig. 10.15).

Groundwater development is also widespread, and in many areas it is severely overextended. Because groundwater storages are so large in relation to inflows, it is possible to withdraw water at rates far in excess of inflows. This is called *overdraft*, or *groundwater mining*.

ISSUE 10–2   New Jersey and You: Thirsty Together

New Jersey is in an area with plentiful rainfall, approximately 45 inches or 115 cm per year. However, twice in the last 20 years, water supply crises have forced state and local governments to require water conservation efforts of both domestic and industrial users. The earlier of these was during the mid-1960s drought on the East Coast, in which rainfall was well below normal over a wide area. After that drought, two major reservoirs were constructed, expanding the storage capacity of the region's water supply systems and protecting it against future occurrences of drought. However, about 15 years later, a minor dry spell put the region's water supply systems in danger again.

A dry summer, autumn, and winter in 1980 resulted in lower than normal reservoir levels statewide in January 1981. At that time the governors of the four states served by the Delaware River (New York, Pennsylvania, New Jersey, and Delaware) imposed a mandatory ban on nonessential water use. This included lawn and garden watering, noncommercial car washing, washing paved surfaces, use of ornamental fountains, nonessential fire hydrant use, and serving water in restaurants. Golf course greens and tees were excepted from this order, which obviously did not have much of an impact in the middle of winter. The ban did, however, prepare the re-

gion's citizens for greater shortages in the spring and summer months ahead.

By mid-February, half of New Jersey's 7.3 million people and much of the state's industry were required to cut consumption by 25 percent, with per capita limits of 50 gallons (190 liters) a day, down from an average use of 80–100 gallons (303–378 liters). Local water companies were to be the enforcers by adding surcharges to the bills of persons exceeding the limit. There was an estimated 40-day supply remaining for the hardest-hit communities in the Hackensack Meadowlands and in the heavily urbanized northeast part of the state. Although reservoir levels in other parts of the state dropped in this period, to 46 percent of capacity in one central New Jersey reservoir, for example, the northeastern reservoirs dropped to below 30 percent of capacity. Flow in the Raritan River, a major water source, was reduced so that more water could be stored in depleted reservoirs. This prompted fears that the remaining river flow would contain dangerously higher concentrations of human and industrial pollutants.

Conservation tips publicized by municipal authorities included such ideas as fewer toilet flushes, not washing dishes with running water, not letting the water run while brushing teeth, and the like. But the drought never reached the

The first effect of groundwater overdraft is declining well levels, often requiring that wells be deepened for withdrawals to continue. In coastal areas, there is usually a boundary between fresh water and salt water in the ground. Salt water is denser, and so is found underneath the fresh water. A decline in the elevation of the fresh water table causes *saltwater intrusion*, an inland movement of the salt/fresh boundary, which contaminates wells and makes them unusable for drinking water. When this happens there is usually no recourse but to close the wells and find alternative sources of water, usually wells farther inland. This problem is particularly acute on the coastal plain of the eastern United States, and in some areas of coastal California (Fig. 10.16). There are also examples of saltwater intrusion into inland aquifers in areas where saline

groundwater underlies fresh water. In some areas, notably coastal Texas, southern Arizona, and central California, groundwater overdrafts are causing *subsidence*, or sinking of the land. In Texas this is contributing to coastal flooding, particularly in suburban Houston, and in Arizona large fissures have opened in the ground.

In the western Great Plains, the most important overdraft problem is in the area underlain by the Ogallala aquifer. This aquifer is a thick, porous layer of sand and gravel that underlies an extensive area from Nebraska to Texas. It contains a large amount of water but has an extremely low recharge rate. Most of this area is too dry for rainfall farming, and groundwater-based irrigation has been rapidly expanding since the 1950s. The rate of withdrawal is enormous, exceeding the recharge

point at which emergency measures such as importing water via tankers, evacuating kidney dialysis patients, closing businesses, and letting buildings burn were required. February brought some rain, and by November of 1981 reservoirs were once again at acceptable levels, although below normal for that time of year. Water rationing remained in effect in the northeastern cities, but was eased with greater rainfall over the following year (Hanley, 1980a, 1980b).

To this day, many New Jersey municipalities have water use restrictions during the summer season (May 15 to September 15). If your house number is even, you can use water for outdoor purposes only on even-numbered days; if you live in an odd-numbered house, you can water your lawn, wash your car, and so on only on odd-numbered days. Conservation of water can help alleviate minor water shortages, but it is never a long-term cure for a water shortage problem. In New Jersey's case, the problem was based on overselling the reservoir water in the Meadowlands area, which had just gone through a period of tremendous growth. Administrators of the several small reservoirs that serve the area had taken on many new customers without expanding the available storage capacity. They were counting on the rain to keep falling and allowed their reservoirs to be depleted to risky, low levels. With several consecutive dry months, the area was soon in trouble. It is clear that the

1980–1981 water shortage was hastened by a minor dry spell, but the real reason for the shortage was that demand was allowed to rise without a concurrent expansion in the capacity of the supply system.

The New Jersey experience is typical of urban and suburban areas everywhere. Droughts are inevitable, and when they occur supply systems are stressed. Governments and the public become aware that new sources of water are needed to avert the next crisis (Ashworth, 1982). This awareness, particularly on the part of the public, is usually necessary before system expansions can be made, because bond issues must be passed by the voters and opposition to projects must be overcome. Within a few months or years, the drought passes, system expansions are completed, and water is again plentiful. Often, this increased supply encourages new development and thus new demands on the water supply. Then, a few years later, the next drought starts the cycle all over again. The important thing to recognize about this process is that water supply droughts such as those that occurred in New Jersey, or in the late 1970s in the West, or the current drought in California are not aberrations. They are a consequence of demand that exceeds the capability of a particular supply system during occasional periods of low precipitation, which will inevitably occur.

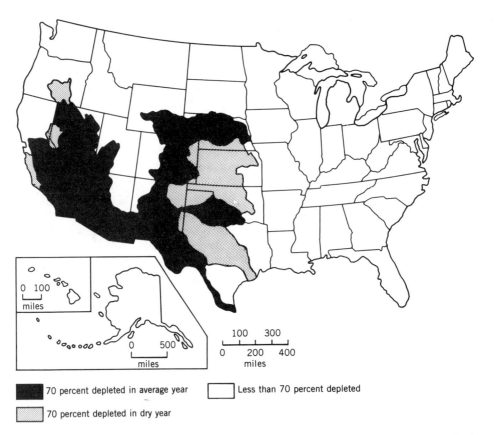

Figure 10.15   Water depletion areas in the United States. (*Source:* U.S. Department of Agriculture, 1989, p. 71.)

Key:
- ■ 70 percent depleted in average year
- □ Less than 70 percent depleted
- ▦ 70 percent depleted in dry year

rate by 100 times in some areas. The Ogallala aquifer initially allowed the rapid development of irrigated agriculture in West Texas, but its depletion will lead to an end of irrigated agriculture in the region and hasten the decline of economic growth (see Issue 10–3). In the Arkansas–White–Red rivers region, which includes much of the Ogallala aquifer, groundwater overdrafts represent over 60 percent of all groundwater withdrawals. Another area of extreme overdraft is the Texas–Gulf region, where overdrafts are 77 percent of all groundwater withdrawals. For the nation as a whole, about 37 percent of all groundwater withdrawals are overdrafts (USDA, 1989).

ENVIRONMENTAL IMPACTS OF WATER RESOURCE DEVELOPMENT

Water resource development has many positive and negative environmental impacts. Some of them occur only in the immediate area of the development; others are felt hundreds of kilometers away. Groundwater withdrawal usually has little impact provided that overdrafts are not made. An important exception to this is that any groundwater extraction lowers the water table, and in wetlands this may seriously affect vegetation and associated ecological communities. Surface water development, on the other hand, usually has quite dramatic effects. The most common of the positive impacts are flood control and creation of recreational facilities. Among the common negative impacts are inundation of land, loss of natural qualities of streams, and increased sedimentation.

Floods cause more property damage in the United States than any other natural hazard, with annual damages averaging $5 billion (USDA, 1989). In 1986, flood damages were more than $6 billion with 208 flood-related fatalities, 80 percent of which were from flash floods (CEQ, 1989). Many different methods

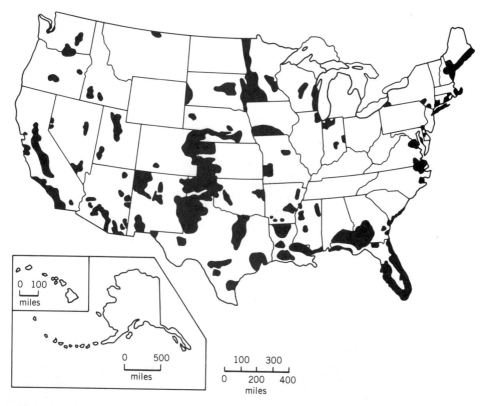

Figure 10.16   Areas where groundwater decline is of state or local concern. (*Source:* U.S. Department of Agriculture, 1989, p. 71.)

are used to reduce these losses, one of the most important being dam construction. Dams control floods by storing runoff during exceptionally high discharge periods and releasing it when flows are low or when it is needed for water supply. Usually dams are built with multiple purposes in mind, primarily for water supply and flood control. These multiple-purpose schemes are more than just water developments, and so flood control is not just a side benefit of water development; it is integral to the planning of a system. Since 1936 the U.S. government has spent about $13 billion on flood control structures that have prevented an estimated $60 billion in damages. An additional benefit of dam and reservoir construction is increased recreational opportunities. These usually include boating, swimming, and camping. Recreation benefits are seldom the primary reasons for constructing a dam, but they often figure importantly in benefit–cost computations for such projects. Recreational use of our waterways has been increasing in

recent decades, and this is expected to continue.

Loss of land is probably the most important of the negative impacts of surface water development. Nearly 20 million acres (8 million ha) of land in the United States are covered with ponded water in reservoirs and regulated lakes. Some of this land was under water before reservoir development, such as that in the river channel itself. Much of it, however, was fertile alluvial land that was cropland, potential cropland, forest, or wetland prior to reservoir filling, and it is permanently lost to those uses today. In many cases this includes land on which towns, roads, and other structures once stood. From 1967 to 1975, 6.7 million acres (2.7 million ha) of land were inundated by water development (Brewer and Boxley, 1981), and a similar pace is likely in the future.

Loss of land is often the most controversial element of water development schemes because it represents a tangible value as well as an emotional attachment for those displaced by the development. For others, loss of the natural qualities of a river or associated wetlands is a major concern. For example, the Glen Canyon Dam in Arizona created Lake Powell, but also inundated an extensive portion of the Colorado River that was almost as spectacular as the Grand Canyon. The famous Tellico Dam in Tennessee was controversial because it modified the habitat of an endangered species of fish (see Chapter 17). But these values are not easily measured, and it is largely a matter of opinion whether a natural river or an engineered reservoir presents a greater environmental amenity. These amenity issues are discussed more fully in Chapter 17.

The effects of reservoirs on sediment movement in streams are another important group of negative impacts. Reservoirs trap sediment carried by streams, so that reservoir capacity decreases through time. For many reservoirs this is a major problem, reducing the usable life of a reservoir to a few decades in some cases. At Imperial Dam on the lower Colorado, sediment is of sufficient importance to justify constructing and maintaining a costly system of sediment traps to clean the water before it enters the reservoir. Sediment trapped in the reservoir is not available to the

---

ISSUE 10–3   The Water Bandits: Three Piece Suits and Cowboy Hats

When questions on the availability and cost of water arise, elected officials in the Southwest often transform into reptilelike creatures with the fangs of a rattlesnake and the changing colors of a chameleon. Water is perhaps the most parochial issue in western politics and can force urbane, socially activist liberals to demand that government get off the backs of the people, while free market conservatives demand more government regulation over natural resources.

Access to and use of both surface water and groundwater has historically been governed by "use it or lose it" water rights laws in states like Arizona, California, Colorado, and Utah. On the basis of water rights granted to riparian property owners at the time of statehood or early land grants by state and federal governments, access to water supplies is generally governed by historic water uses. These water rights can be bought and sold independently of actual land ownership. In addition, the water itself is a commodity subject to sale.

Two basic systems of law govern the allocation of water. *Riparian doctrine* is applied to all states east of the 100th meridian and is derived from English common law. The water is owned and controlled by those who own the riparian land which is defined as the land adjacent to the stream or upon which the stream flows. Riparian landowners are allowed to use the water as long as their use does not substantially reduce the quantity or quality of water available to other riparians. Furthermore, the

rights cannot be lost because of nonuse. In the West, a different system prevails. There water is allocated using a *prior appropriation system* based on a "use it or lose it" principle. Prior appropriation recognizes that the water is a finite resource and allocates the amount of available water to users on a predetermined basis. This protects agriculture and, with the heavy governmental subsidies up until the 1980s, has allowed water prices in the West to remain low.

Since the 1930s, the federal government has been the primary developer of new water supplies in the West. Federal agencies such as the Bureau of Reclamation and the Bureau of Land Management have had significant impact on the western waterscape, ranging from major dam construction to more localized irrigation and canal systems. These large-scale water development projects helped settle the West and brought agriculture to the region. However, the days of large-scale, government-sponsored water projects are over and the West is now entering a new phase in water conflicts: city dwellers versus farmers and ranchers.

Demand for water in the west has shifted from the agricultural sector to the urban one. Because of a virtual halt in new federal water projects, the politics of water are heating up again and pitting farmers and ranchers against city dwellers. Since urbanites are willing and can pay more for water than farmers and ranchers, they are winning the battle over water at the moment. In Arizona, for example, the urban

river below the dam, but in most cases the river still has the capacity to transport sediment. Without its natural sediment load, the river is able to erode into its bed, which results in greater channel erosion below the dam. In most cases this is a relatively minor problem, but it can be significant. In the Grand Canyon of the Colorado, for instance, the combined effects of sediment removal and flow regulation at Glen Canyon Dam have caused erosion of sands from the channel banks, thus restricting areas where boaters can land and camp along the river (Coats, 1984). At the same time, the river is less able to remove large boulders that accumulate in rapids, so that

certain rapids have become more difficult to navigate since the closing of Glen Canyon Dam. When river sediment is not trapped behind dams, it provides sand for beaches in many coastal areas, particularly on the West Coast of the United States. Removal of sediment from rivers prevents it from reaching the beaches, which further aggravates the problems of beach erosion.

In addition to these impacts, many others may occur, including eutrophication of the artificial lakes, changes in water temperatures due to water temperature stratification in reservoirs, seepage, and increased water losses and dissolved solids concentrations as a result

---

areas use twice the amount of water they receive in runoff. In 1980, the state forbade further groundwater drafting in the Phoenix and Tucson regions. Urban development continued unabated, however, as the urban centers merely found other sources of drinking water for their residents. Phoenix, for example, bought 50,000 acres (20, 235 ha) of farms (many in adjacent counties), including their water rights, and pumped the groundwater into the Central Arizona Project canals for use as municipal drinking water. Salt Lake City and St. George, Utah, have bought more than 100,000 acre-feet of water by purchasing shares of canal and ditch companies. To quench their thirst, metropolitan regions in the arid West look to more rural counties and purchase agricultural land to get the water. The water is now worth more than the land itself. A precedent for such water grabs was fictionalized in the movie *Chinatown*, which was based on a real event. Owens Valley, California, is located about 300 miles (483 km) northeast of Los Angeles. Between 1920 and 1950 the city of Los Angeles bought 75 percent of the valley's land and thus its water. The water was then sent by canal to Los Angeles. Some argue that this event helped shape the destiny of Los Angeles to make it one of the country's largest metropolitan regions.

What can be done about the thirsty West? Although some westerners argue for halting development, and sending the new immigrant easterners packing, this is unlikely. Alternative

sources of water, conservation, or new strategies for water allocation must be developed to meet current and projected demands. Marketing water that has already been allocated is now viewed as a substitute for government-subsidized water projects. Water has long been traded among western irrigation districts but now urban centers are vying for some of the action. Speculators and private brokers are now actively involved in water marketing. Western water rights are being purchased at increasing rates by investment firms (who anticipate that their initial investment can only increase in value over time), oil companies who originally purchased the water rights for oil shale development during the 1970s but now realize the value of this water for urban uses, and private developers. Farmers are also being encouraged to sell water as a commodity, not just the rights to the water. In this way, water can be bought and sold like other natural resources such as grain or minerals. However, many states have reacted strongly. Texas, for example, completely outlaws interbasin transfers of water, and New Mexico and Wyoming prohibit out-of-state water transfers, largely to prevent thirsty Californians from taking their water. So while the metropolitan regions of the West increase in population and thirst, their search for water continues. Only time will tell how effective water marketing is in quenching the insatiable demand for water in the West (Steinhart, 1990).

of evaporation. Rivers and water supply systems are so complex and affect so many important natural processes that it is often difficult to predict the many impacts associated with these projects. Such prediction is essential, however, and will continue to be an important environmental issue as more and more water projects are proposed.

At the international level, many of the same impacts are found. For example, the Nile Delta is eroding because of decreased sedimentation caused by the Aswan High Dam (White, 1988). In the Aral Sea, the world's fourth largest lake, water levels are declining so rapidly because of upstream withdrawals for irrigation that the lake is in danger of disappearing (Micklin, 1988). The ecological impacts are already apparent and range from loss of biological productivity to groundwater depression to increased contamination of public drinking water supplies from industrial and agricultural pollutants.

INCREASING WATER AVAILABILITY

INTERBASIN DIVERSIONS

Water problems such as those in the southwestern United States have led to the development of schemes to pipe water enormous distances from areas of surplus to areas of deficit. Already water from northern California is used to supply Los Angeles (Seckler, 1971), and from time to time proposals are discussed to pump water from the Columbia River basin into California. The lower Mississippi has been discussed as a source of water for West Texas. The quest for water in the arid West has a long and colorful history (Reisner, 1986; Gottlieb, 1988) (see Issue 10–3).

One of the largest long-distance water diversion schemes in America is the Central Arizona Project (Hanson, 1982). Although it is not truly an *interbasin transfer,* the project is of the scale and cost typical of such ventures. It was authorized by Congress in 1968 and completed in the mid-1980s. Its main purpose is to take water from the lower Colorado and pump it to the booming urban and agricultural area centered around Phoenix and Tucson. These cities are the heart of one of the

fastest growing urban areas in the country, an area that is also very hot and very dry. Mean annual rainfall in the area is only about 7 inches (175 mm), and mean annual lake evaporation is about 70 inches (1800 mm). Migrants from the North and East are drawn by the sunny climate, but also expect many of the amenities of wetter areas such as lawns and swimming pools. The agriculture of the region has depended primarily on overdrafts of groundwater, but the aquifers are drying up and new sources of water are needed. Nearly half the groundwater withdrawn in the lower Colorado region is overdrawn.

The Central Arizona Project includes an aqueduct to convey water from the Colorado at Parker Dam to the Phoenix region. The water must be pumped over 248 miles (400 km) horizontally and 1969 feet (600 m) vertically. It is to be stored in reservoirs built on the Salt and Gila rivers, and from these it will be distributed to the thirsty cities and farms of the area.

One of the striking features of this project is that it will withdraw water that is already allocated elsewhere. Even without the Central Arizona Project, all the water in the Colorado is used in most years, so that by the time it reaches the Gulf of California it is barely a trickle. This project represents new withdrawals, and so other areas, including Los Angeles, must take less. In a year like 1983, when unusually heavy snows and a rapid melt caught reservoir operators by surprise and caused widespread flooding on the Colorado, this extra withdrawal was feasible. But in average years and droughts, there will not be enough to go around.

In most cases major new long-distance diversions such as these are extremely costly, and pumping costs alone are often prohibitive. In addition, opposition from residents of exporting areas along with environmental considerations are substantial barriers to these projects. Arguments for the projects are usually heard from farmers, landowners, and developers in the areas to receive the water. As a rule, the water users benefit from large public subsidies of these projects and pay only a fraction of the total cost of the water they use. Instead of expanding water use in arid areas, it is usually much cheaper, in both economic and environmental terms, to reduce demand by water conservation, to increase local supplies, or to invest in environmentally sounder means of generating income.

NEW TECHNIQUES FOR EXPANDING WATER SUPPLIES

In addition to the more traditional methods of water supply development by dams, canals, and pumping, several other methods are now being discussed and tested. These include water harvesting, wastewater reclamation, and desalinization.

Water harvesting is not a new idea; it has been practiced for thousands of years. Water harvesting simply means collecting water when it falls as rain, rather than drawing it from rivers or wells. There are many ways to do this, some of them very simple and some relying on advanced technology. In dry areas around the world, especially in Central America, the Near East, and southern Asia, early civilizations had well-developed water-harvesting systems. Techniques included constructing ditches and low berms on hillslopes to catch water and building underground cisterns to store it. Among the modern adaptations of these techniques are corrugated roofs with gutters or ground catchment areas with compacted soil. Stone, log, or vegetation barriers might be used to direct runoff and trap sediment on slopes. In very dry areas, single plants or trees are placed at the lowest point in small catchments so they receive more water. More complex technologies involve clearing vegetation from large areas or converting shrubland to grasses to increase water yield, covering the soil with impervious materials such as wax or asphalt, and constructing large lined catchment basins. Because the water is not filtered by the soil, the runoff is often not of high enough quality for human consumption, but it is of value for cattle and irrigation. Most water-harvesting techniques are best for very local applications, although vegetation conversion is being used on a large scale in parts of Arizona (Johnson and Renwick, 1979).

Wastewater reclamation simply means using dirty water over again instead of returning it to a stream or lake. Often during droughts, people use the "gray water" from baths, dishes, and clothes washing to irrigate gardens and lawns. In most cases the impurities are not harmful to plants, and wastewater contains many nutrients that may even be beneficial (Kourik, 1990a). Reuse of wastewater can satisfy additional demand for water without requiring additional supplies (Issue 10–3) (Fig. 10.17). Israel is the world leader in wastewater reuse, where 95 percent of water used in industry and the home is recovered for use in irrigation (Ambroggi, 1980). Water from municipal sewage systems has been successfully used for irrigation in several areas of the United States, especially Texas and California. It must be partially treated (usually primary treatment is sufficient) to reduce health hazards, and it must not contain substantial amounts of hazardous substances such as metals and toxic organic compounds. Technically it is possible to treat wastewater thoroughly enough to make it suitable for drinking, but as yet this has not become widespread.

The greatest concerns with water reuse in irrigation are public health problems associated with use of wastewater on food crops and possible discharges of polluted waters and the concentration of toxic substances, especially metals, in plant tissues. Another area of concern is pollution of groundwater by percolation of irrigation water that is high in nitrates. These hazards require careful handling of the water, and in some cases restrictions on what crops may be grown, for example, avoiding crops that concentrate metals in edible portions of the plant. However, if carefully managed, wastewater reuse offers considerable potential for providing new supplies of irrigation water in semiarid and arid areas.

Desalinization, or removing salt from seawater or brackish groundwater, is an appealing but costly undertaking. Water must be distilled by boiling and condensing it, and this requires energy. Large-scale plants are expensive to run and maintain, and output is low compared to most conventional water sources. In energy-rich Saudi Arabia, desalinization plants process 40 billion gallons (150 billion liters) of seawater per year (Ambroggi, 1980). However, over the 10 years since beginning desalinization, the country's water demands have risen by 238 billion gallons (900 billion liters). It is unlikely that desalinization will make a significant impact on future water supplies except in very special circumstances. Similarly, there have been some recent attempts to test the feasibility of towing icebergs from the Antarctic to water-poor areas. The amount of water that could be moved practically is very low, and the costs are very high.

WATER CONSERVATION

With any natural resource, problems of insufficient supply can be considered to be problems of excess demand, and this is certainly true for water. Where water is plentiful and cheap, as it is in most of the United States, it is used for a great many activities that are considered excessive in areas of limited water supply or in time of drought.

The role of high demand in water resource problems is most evident in the dry states of the American West and Southwest. The region is dependent on the Colorado River for domestic and agricultural water, and competition for that source is rising with the Sunbelt population boom (Graf, 1985). One example is California's arid Coachella Valley, located about 125 miles (200 km) east of Los Angeles. A mountain-ringed basin, the valley receives an

average of 3 to 5 inches (75 to 125 mm) of rain per year. With water diverted from the surrounding mountains for irrigation, American Indian populations and nineteenth-century white settlers were able to sustain a comfortable living. The mid-twentieth century brought tremendous population growth, rising from an estimated 850 in 1901 to well over 100,000 in the 1980s, not counting seasonal residents and visitors. With this growth has come an immense rise in water use (Renwick, 1984).

The Coachella obtains its water from several sources, including groundwater, some mountain runoff, and water piped in from northern sources and from the Colorado River. These latter two sources provide a reliable supply to the valley, and groundwater supplies are in good shape according to official estimates.

Thus the residents, visitors, and developers have had no qualms about using water freely. There are over 35 golf courses, public and private, which demand huge amounts of water in the 115°F (46°C) summertime heat. Most of the valley's communities are oriented toward green lawns and shade trees, which are very thirsty under desert conditions (Fig. 10.18). New developments and subdivisions,

Figure 10.17 Cooling towers at the Palo Verde Nuclear Plant, Arizona, using metropolitan Phoenix's wastewater as coolant.

Figure 10.18 An irrigated golf course in the desert: Tucson, Arizona.

feeding on the human desire to see deserts transformed into gardens, include condominiums surrounded by moats and a village in the style of Venice, Italy, with lagoons and canals and travel via gondola. One private estate supports a full-scale golf course dotted with twelve small lakes. The Coachella Valley also has a small but profitable agricultural industry that produces dates, grapes, carrots, and other vegetables and fruits. Although residential water demand is rising more rapidly than farming use, irrigation water must be pumped to every field to take advantage of those months when the heat is tolerable to crops.

The Coachella is perhaps an extreme case of high water use in an arid climate, but it does illustrate the enormous demands placed on water resources by a recreation- and irrigation-oriented society. It also highlights the tremendous potential for eliminating "nonessential" uses should water supplies dwindle.

Several techniques are available to managers to encourage conservation. One of the earliest to be widely used is metering, with payment for water based on use. Most American cities today meter almost all water, although New York City is a notable exception. Installation of meters has typically resulted in

reductions in per capita demand of 20 to 40 percent (Baumann and Dworkin, 1978). Pricing systems can also reduce demand. Most cities have either uniform rate charges or decreasing rates. Uniform rates do not vary with volume used, and decreasing rates are highest for small users and lower (per unit of water) for those who use more water. Increasing rate schedules, in which rates increase with amount used, both encourage conservation and more closely reflect the costs of providing water. Such rates can significantly reduce consumption, depending on what price level is set.

Several structural or mechanical means to reduce water use are also available. Water pressure reduction is one of these. If the pressure in a distribution system is reduced, both flow rates through pipes and leakage rates are reduced. Flow regulators and similar devices can be used in homes and commercial establishments. Some are quite simple, including small disks inserted in faucets and shower heads to reduce flow, and bricks, water bottles, or spacers used to reduce the amount of water used in each flush of the toilet. These devices can reduce water usage in the home by 30 to 70 percent. The ultra-low flush (ULF) toilet now being marketed uses 1.6 gallons (6.2 liters) per flush compared to conventional toilets that use between 5 and 8 gallons (19–30 liters) per flush (Kourik, 1990b). Besides conserving water, ULF toilets can save consumers money on water and sewage bills.

Finally, restrictions on use are frequently employed, although generally these are short-term measures enacted during time of shortage rather than permanent measures. Some of the common restrictions are prohibition of car washing, restriction or prohibition of lawn watering or swimming pool filling, and eliminating the automatic service of water at restaurants. Some of these can be quite effective, and in many areas lawn watering restrictions are permanent. Other areas, such as Tucson, employ landscaping restrictions to conserve water, including use of desert plant species rather than humid region species that need more water. Other methods, such as restricting water service in restaurants, are aimed more at generating public awareness of the problem than actually reducing water use in restaurants.

WATER RESOURCES PLANNING

A major shift in water resources planning occurred with the passage of the Water Resources Development Act in 1986. This act, known as WRDA 86, shifts the financial burden of water resources development to states, port authorities, and local communities. In addition, it stipulates that environmental considerations are essential to future planning for water resources. Nonfederal sponsors of proposed projects must now pay a portion of the costs rather than having the federal government pick up the tab. The pork barrel days of federal water projects are thus over. This new cost-sharing provision means that projects have become more realistic in terms of their scope and size. Water resources planning now can be both cost-effective and environmentally sound.

CONCLUSIONS

When we consider all the ways that water consumption can be reduced in our daily lives, the potential demand reduction is great. Most of us could probably be just as comfortable, and accomplish all the things we need to, while using half the water we currently use. Water conservation in industry and commercial establishments is not so simple, but technological and process changes are possible given the economic incentive to institute them. The potential for increased efficiency of manufacturing uses is reflected in the Water Resources Council's projections for water use in the year 2000, discussed earlier. Similarly, there is room for more efficient use of water in agriculture, particularly by installation of drip irrigation systems. A major conservation method as yet underused is the rehabilitation of existing irrigation works, including renovation of reservoirs, canals, and drainage systems. The Food and Agricultural Organization recommends this overhauling as much less costly and of greater return on investment than the construction of new irrigation works.

Water is used in such large quantities that, for a water development plan to be feasible, it must provide water at a relatively low unit cost. In general, techniques that involve advanced technology, very large structures, or extensive public works are expensive. Long-distance pumping is a particularly expensive way to provide water, because in addition to the capital investment, there are substantial energy costs in running pumps. In evaluating the feasibility of water development for irrigation or industrial uses, it can be argued that the goal is really to provide employment and income for people rather than water per se. When the water development being considered is a high-cost project, one should ask whether the money could be better spent in providing jobs that do not depend on water, or in an area where water is more plentiful. For these reasons, most increases in water supply are likely to be derived from more intensive use of surface water and groundwater near their sources, rather than the use of icebergs, seawater, or water in remote polar areas.

Groundwater is still a developable resource for some dry regions, although once it is depleted it is not readily replaced. There are many areas of untapped groundwater resources, especially in the Third World. New groundwater supplies are perhaps a third the cost of water obtained by dam building. Surface water development by dam construction has great potential for increasing supplies, particularly in the Third World. Many potential dam sites have been identified, and these can be developed as long as capital is available and the lost land can be replaced. However, with rising costs and population levels, both increases in supply and better management of demand will be needed to provide adequate and high-quality water to areas in short supply.

REFERENCES AND ADDITIONAL READING

Ambroggi, R.P. 1980. Water. *Sci. Amer.* 243(3): 101–116.

Ashworth, W. 1982. *Nor Any Drop to Drink.* New York: Summit Books.

Baumann, D.D., and Dworkin, D. 1978. *Water Resources for Our Cities.* Resource Paper 78-2. Washington, DC: Association of American Geographers.

Brewer, M.F., and R.F. Boxley. 1981. Agricultural land: Adequacy of acres, concepts, and information. *Amer. J. of Agricultural Econ.* 63: 879–887.

Coats, R. 1984. The Colorado River: River of controversy. *Environment* 26(2): 7–13,36–40.

Conservation Foundation. 1987. *State of the Environment: A View Toward the Nineties.* Washington, DC: Conservation Foundation.

Council on Environmental Quality. 1988. *Environmental Quality, 18th and 19th Annual Reports.* Washington, DC: U.S. Government Printing Office.

———. 1989. *Environmental Trends.* Washington, DC: U.S. Government Printing Office.

Flack, J.E. 1978. Management alternatives for reducing demand. In D. Holtz and S. Sebastian (Eds.), *Municipal Water Systems,* pp. 200–210. Bloomington: Indiana University Press.

Gottlieb, R. 1988. *A Life of Its Own. The Politics and Power of Water.* New York: Harcourt Brace Jovanovich.

Graf, W.L. 1985. *The Colorado River: Instability and Basin Management.* Washington, DC: Association of American Geographers Resource Publications.

Hanley, R. 1980a. Water is franchised trouble in New Jersey. *The New York Times,* October 5. Sec. XI, p. 1.

———. 1980b. Delaware River water supply cut

second time in a month for New York. *The New York Times,* November 20. p. A1.

Hanson, D. 1982. The Colorado complex. *Living Wilderness* 45(157) :27–35.

Johnson, J.F. 1971. *Renovated Waste Water: An Alternative Source of Municipal Water Supply in the U.S.* Research Paper No. 135. Chicago: University of Chicago, Department of Geography.

Johnson, K., and H.L. Renwick. 1979. *Rain and Storm Water Harvesting for Additional Water Supply in Rural Areas.* Unpublished monograph. Nairobi, Kenya: U.N. Environment Programme.

Kourik, R. 1990a. Greywater: Why throw it away? *Garbage* 2(1): 41–45.

———. 1990b. Toilets: Low flush/no flush. *Garbage* 2(1): 16–23.

Luoma, J.R. 1982. Water: Grass-roots opposition stymies Garrison Diversion. *Audubon* 84(2): 114–117.

Matthews, O.P. 1984. *Water Resources, Geography, and Law.* Washington, DC: Association of American Geographers Resource Publications.

Micklin, P. 1988. Desiccation of the Aral Sea: A water management disaster in the Soviet Union. *Science* 241: 1170–1176.

Postel, S. 1989. *Water for Agriculture: Facing the Limits.* Worldwatch Paper #93. Washington, DC: Worldwatch Institute.

Reisner, M. 1986. *Cadillac Desert: The American West and Its Disappearing Water.* New York: Viking Penguin.

Renwick, H.L. 1984. *The Decorated Desert: A Comparative Study of Vegetation Resource Cognition in the Coachella Valley, California.* Unpublished PhD dissertation, Clark University, Worcester, MA.

Russell, C.S., D.G. Arey, and R.W. Kates. 1970. *Drought and Water Supply.* Baltimore: The Johns Hopkins University Press.

Seckler, D. (Ed.). 1971. *California Water: A Study in Resource Management.* Berkeley/Los Angeles: University of California Press.

Steinhart, P. 1990. The water profiteers. *Audubon* 92(2): 38–51.

Strahler, A.N. 1988. *Elements of Physical Geography,* 4th ed. New York: Wiley.

U.S. Department of Agriculture. 1989. *The Second RCA Appraisal: Soil, Water, and Related Resources on Nonfederal Land in the United States, Analysis of Condition and Trends.* Washington, DC: U.S. Government Printing Office.

U.S. Geological Survey. 1986. *National Water Summary 1985—Hydrologic Events and Surface*

Water Resources. USGS Water Supply Paper 2300. Washington, DC: U.S. Government Printing Office.

Water Resources Council. 1978. *The Nation's Water Resources 1975–2000. Volume 1: Summary; Volume 2: Water Quantity, Quality, and Related Land Considerations.* Washington, DC: U.S. Government Printing Office.

White, G.F. 1988. The environmental effects of the high dam at Aswan. *Environment* 30(7): 4–11, 34–40.

TERMS TO KNOW

Aquiclude
Aquifer
Consumptive Use
Desalinization
Drainage Basin
Drought
Evapotranspiration
Groundwater
Groundwater Mining
In-stream Uses
Interbasin Transfer
Nonconsumptive Use
Overdraft
Permeability

Prior Appropriation System
Riparian Doctrine
Saltwater Intrusion
Subsidence
Surface Water
Wastewater Reclamation
Water Harvesting
Water Table
Withdrawal

STUDY QUESTIONS

1. Is groundwater a renewable resource? How does it travel below the ground surface?

2. What are two major ways to evaluate water availability?

3. What are the four components of water supply systems?

4. What are some of the negative and positive environmental impacts of water resource development?

5. Are there significant geographic variations in how water is appropriated (e.g., the West versus the East)?

6. What are some major water conservation methods for industry? for the home?

11

Water Quality: Everybody's Problem

INTRODUCTION

Water pollution is perhaps the most universally recognized form of environmental pollution, and the one about which people have been concerned for the longest period of time. Water is so basic to human health and prosperity that few people in either traditional or industrial societies are unaware of the importance of water quality. The use of natural waterways in waste disposal, combined with our need for clean water, caused it to be the first form of pollution that received widespread government attention, and it continues to be an important political topic. In many parts of the world, water free from disease or harmful chemicals is a scarce commodity. In the wealthier nations the most visible forms of contamination are routinely removed from drinking water, but concern about minute quantities of toxic substances is increasing (see Issue 11–1). And in nearly every populated area, the effects of water pollution on aquatic wildlife are significant.

BASIC PROPERTIES OF WATER

Although water is one of the most common substances on the surface of the earth, it has several remarkable properties. First, it is able to store large amounts of heat. Second, it is an excellent solvent, capable of dissolving large quantities of a wide range of substances. Third, it is relatively inert and able to dissolve substances without reacting with them. Salts, for example, are precipitated as easily as they are dissolved. Water, therefore, is an ideal trans-

porter of other chemicals. Just as this property makes it the basis of life, it also makes water potentially dangerous, especially when it contains unwanted substances or excessive concentrations of normally harmless substances.

Among the many impurities found in natural and polluted waters are all the common elements of the earth's crust and some uncommon ones. Although some of these are found in elemental form, such as oxygen, most are in the form of compounds. Silicon dioxide (SiO_2), salt (NaCl), iron sulfate ($FeSO_4$) and ammonia (NH_4) are among the common *inorganic* impurities. *Organic* (carbon-containing) compounds are usually found at lower dissolved concentrations because they are generally less soluble than other substances. Carbonate (CO_3) is a common organic compound found at relatively high concentrations, but organics are highly varied and include decay products from plant and animal matter, hydrocarbons of natural and human origin, and many other substances. In addition, water contains many living microorganisms such as bacteria and protozoa, and of course larger organisms including insects, water lilies, fish, and giant kelp.

Just as there is a great range of kinds of impurities, the range of concentrations is also large. Impurities are usually measured in parts per thousand (ppt), parts per million (ppm), or parts per billion (ppb). One part per million means that for every million units of water (by weight) there is one unit of the impurity. One part per million is equivalent to one milligram per liter (mg/liter). Seawater contains about 35 ppt of dissolved solids, or 3.5 percent by weight. Some groundwaters and inland lakes in arid regions have natural concentrations of dissolved solids several times greater than this. In humid regions with relatively insoluble bedrock formations, dissolved concentrations in surface waters are generally in the range of 10 to 100 ppm, on the order of 1000 to 100 times less than those in seawater. In the central part of North America, total dissolved solids are typically a few hundred ppm, while some streams in the arid West reach 1000 to 2000 ppm (1 to 2 ppt) during part of the year. Individual ions such as copper or silicon, in contrast, are usually found in concentrations of a few parts per million or less, although there are notable exceptions. Finally, relatively uncommon elements and substances such as exotic organic compounds like chloroform or PCBs are generally found in parts per billion or even parts per trillion.

OVERVIEW OF WATER QUALITY PROBLEMS

Impurities in water come from many different sources, both natural and human, and it is often difficult to separate the two. When we speak of *pollution* or pollutants, we are usually referring to substantial human additions to a stream or lake's load of an impurity or impurities. A polluted stream must be defined relative to its condition unaffected by human activity rather than in absolute terms. Similarly, acceptability of given levels of contamination depends on what we use the water for. For drinking water, absolute levels are important and standards for drinking water are established by governmental and other agencies.

Pollutants come from diverse human-made and natural sources. One way to classify

---

ISSUE 11–1   Problems of an Industrial River: The Rhine

The Rhine River, which rises in the Alps of Switzerland, Austria, and Lichtenstein and flows north about 500 miles (800 km) through Germany, France, and the Netherlands before emptying into the North Sea, has long been a critical commercial lifeline of Western Europe. It has served this densely populated area for centuries, providing water supply, fisheries, transportation, recreation, and waste disposal. In its central reaches it flows in a valley with steep vineyard-covered slopes and picturesque towns that thrive on river-dependent tourism and commerce. Farther north it provides water to the intense industrial areas of northwest Germany and the Netherlands. Barge traffic is continual along almost the entire length; about 125 million tons (114 million tonnes) of goods are carried on it annually. This intensity of use inevitably leads to both pollution and a great need for maintaining high water quality. Not only is the need for management great, but this management is made difficult and complex by the fact that the drainage basin of the Rhine includes eight different countries: the six just mentioned plus Belgium and Luxembourg. Pollution problems have been critical in the Rhine for decades, especially since the post-World War II expansion of

industrial activity along its banks. But recently a series of chemical spills has demonstrated how acute the problem has become.

Several chemical-manufacturing firms have plants near Basel, Switzerland, and in November of 1986 a fire at one of these owned by the Sandoz Corporation resulted in a spill of about 30 tons (27 tonnes) of pesticides, including 440 pounds (200 kg) of mercury, into the river. It was then discovered that hours before the Sandoz fire a nearby plant owned by Ciba-Geigy had released 900 pounds (408 kg) of pesticides into the Rhine. And just a few months later, two separate barge collisions in the German portion of the river resulted in spills of 540 tons (491 tonnes) of nitrogen fertilizer and 10 tons (9 tonnes) of a benzene compound (Hildyarn, 1987).

The many towns along the river that rely on it for their drinking water lost their water supplies, some for weeks. Even after these supplies were restored or replaced, concerns remain. For example, it is unclear whether some of the chemicals may have contaminated groundwater beneath the river. The effects on aquatic life were swift and severe. It is estimated that about 500,000 fish were killed immediately, along with uncounted smaller fauna and plankton that form

pollutant discharges is by point versus non-point sources. A *point source* is a specific location such as a factory or municipal sewage outfall. A *non-point source* is a source that, as far as we know, originates from a large, poorly defined area. Runoff, subsurface flow, and atmospheric sources of water pollution are the primary non-point sources.

Some pollutants, such as iron or suspended particulates, may have very large natural sources, so that human activities only marginally increase concentrations. Other pollutants, such as synthetic pesticides, are only produced by humans. Most common impurities, however, are contributed by both human and natural processes. Therefore, except in extreme cases, human pollution is difficult to define quantitatively. Further, in a complex system such as a drainage basin, a given pollutant may have many different sources, including urban runoff, industrial effluents, municipal sewage, and even atmospheric

precipitation in addition to natural sources. Once in a stream system, pollutants may be removed by deposition or be broken down or combined with other impurities to make new substances, or their concentrations increased by chemical or biological processes. If a known quantity of a substance is put in a waterway, the amount that leaves may be greater or less, depending on the nature of the substances and the processes acting on it. Under these circumstances it is virtually impossible to determine accurately the relative contributions of many sources, or to predict future pollution levels with confidence.

CONVENTIONAL POLLUTANTS AND THEIR SOURCES

The list of substances that are of concern in water quality assessments is long and getting longer every year. In part this increase is the

the basis of the aquatic ecosystem. And the contamination by mercury is likely to remain for years, if not decades, being continually concentrated as it passes up the food chain. Shortly after the spill, scientists found the river to be virtually dead for up to 125 miles (200 km) downstream from Basel. There has been some recovery since, but the long-term effects of the contamination are still being studied.

Although some of the ecological effects of the spill may last for decades, perhaps even more significant are its political effects. The spill came just months after the Chernobyl nuclear accident, and together these helped to stimulate public awareness of environmental problems in Europe. The Green Party's strength grew considerably in 1987 and 1988 in Germany, France, and elsehere, and this growth put pressure on European governments to take positive action to solve the Rhine's problems. This pressure has affected national governments, and the European Community has also stepped up its efforts, particularly toward enforcing stricter standards for ambient water quality and discharge controls.

This pressure has had positive effects, but

even the cooperation brought by membership in the European Community cannot overcome all the problems posed by regulation across international boundaries. There are significant differences among European nations as to how strict environmental regulations should be, and these hamper the establishment of new controls. And not all the countries involved are members of the European Community—Germany, France, and the Netherlands are members but Switzerland is not, and it is difficult for the downstream nations to force controls on Swiss dischargers. Yet another problem lies in regulating practices that may contribute to accidental spills, which are much more difficult to anticipate and prevent through regulations than are everyday, chronic discharges. Given the large number of people and industries using the Rhine, it is unlikely that it will ever be a particularly clean river. But gradually, as more Europeans become aware of the acute environmental problems facing them, and as political integration progresses within Europe, it is likely that controlling pollution of international rivers such as the Rhine will become easier.

result of advances in the analytic capabilities of laboratories and the growth in available water quality data. But still there are so many substances that could be measured in a water sample, and the analyses are so complex and costly, that usually only a few major or index pollutants are determined. Most analyses summarize pollution levels with parameters such as total dissolved solids (TDS) or biochemical oxygen demand (BOD). The following sections present, in general terms, a description of some major classes of pollutants, their sources, human health effects, and effects on aquatic ecology. These categories are somewhat arbitrary and are intended to provide an indication of the diversity of the pollutants found in our waters. The major pollutants, their sources, and environmental effects are shown in Table 11.1.

ORGANISMS

Of the many living things found in natural or polluted waters, only a small fraction can be regarded as important pollutants from a human standpoint. These are the bacteria, viruses, and parasites that cause disease in humans and livestock. The earliest awareness of water pollution as an important human problem came from the recognition that water, particularly drinking water, transmits many diseases. Among the infectious diseases communicated largely through drinking water are cholera, typhoid fever, hepatitis, and dysentery, but many other less known diseases are also transmitted in this manner. Most of these are transmitted through human or animal wastes, hence sewage pollution is their primary source. Many different organisms are potentially dangerous, and only one individual in a large amount of water may be sufficient to cause infections.

The presence of *coliform bacteria* is used as an indicator of the possibility of contamination by infectious organisms. Coliform bacteria live in great numbers in human and animal digestive systems, and their presence indicates the possibility that more dangerous organisms could also inhabit the water. Chlorination of public water supplies has eliminated these diseases from common occurrence in the developed nations, but disease outbreaks

still occur. For example, between 1971 and 1974, 99 outbreaks of waterborne infectious diseases, totaling 16,950 cases, occurred in the United States. (National Research Council, 1977). Between 1981 and 1983, 112 waterborne disease outbreaks occurred from microbiological contaminants like *Giardia lamblia* (U.S. Environmental Protection Agency, 1988). Most of these were intestinal diseases, but four outbreaks of typhoid fever occurred. Major outbreaks of waterborne infectious diseases still occur in less developed nations where public water supplies are not well protected or treated. Many other diseases are transmitted via organisms such as snails or insects that live in water, schistosomiasis and malaria being well-known examples. However, infection results from insect bites, skin contact, and other means rather than ingestion and hence these organisms are not usually considered components of water quality.

PARTICULATE ORGANIC MATTER

Suspended organic particles are the pollutant that places the greatest burden on a stream or lake as a pollution assimilator. Particulate organics are small bits of living or dead and decaying plant and animal matter. They are broken down by bacteria in the water, which use dissolved oxygen in the process. There is no widely used direct measurement for them, but *total suspended particulates* (TSP) and *biochemical oxygen demand* (BOD) are the most often used indicators of the concentration of particulate organics in the water. TSP includes both organic and inorganic matter. BOD indirectly measures organic particulates by measuring the amount of dissolved oxygen that is required to decompose the organic matter. A stream with a high BOD loading will consequently have a low concentration of dissolved oxygen (DO). It is the depletion of oxygen that is primarily responsible for the ecological degradation of rivers and lakes. A second important role of organic particulates is their relation to trace pollutants, both organic and inorganic. Many of these substances travel attached to particles, and so their fate is in part governed by the fate of particulates.

Organic particulates are derived from surface runoff, internal production by algae, agricultural wastes, various industries, especially food processing and paper pulp, and sewage. The relative contributions of these sources vary from one area to another, but historically large point sources have been responsible for the most severe cases of organic particulate pollution. These include feedlots, pulp mills, sewage treatment plants, and other major dischargers. More recently, however, as treatment facilities are installed and upgraded, these sources have been reduced in importance. Since the 1930s to 1950s, when most states enacted pollution control laws, this most noticeable form of pollution has been significantly reduced. Today, with the major point sources under regulation, more attention has been given to diffuse or non-point sources such as urban and agricultural runoff.

INORGANIC PARTICULATES

By weight, *inorganic particulates*, or sediment, are the largest pollutant in our waters. They are measured along with organic particles as total suspended particulates in a water sample and consist of particles of soil and rock that are eroded from the land and from streambeds. Erosion is a natural process, and the movement of sediment through a river system helps to maintain the ecological integrity of that system. However, the accelerated erosion of agricultural lands and erosion associated with urban construction and similar activities have greatly increased the sediment loads of many streams.

For practical purposes, inorganic sediment is chemically inert and thus has little direct effect on the chemical quality of water. Like organic particulates, fine-textured inorganic sediment plays a role in the transport and deposition of trace substances in water, and in this way it can carry pesticides and nutrients from agricultural fields, as well as a wide range of harmful substances contained in urban runoff. Most sediment is easily filtered from water in drinking water treatment plants and thus health hazards associated with sediment pollution are probably minimal.

The major harmful effects of sediment are economic, including damage to turbines and pumps, and reduction in reservoir capacity as sediment is deposited in impoundments. In extreme cases sediment may also reduce stream channel capacity and contribute to flooding. Excessive sediment loads also modify stream habitats and restrict fish reproduction. Some fish are sensitive to chronic high suspended sediment loads, which clog gills, restrict vision, or otherwise interfere with normal activity. There are also a few examples, especially in the western United States, where reduction in sediment loads by reservoir construction has caused detrimental effects downstream, notably erosion in the Grand Canyon and on West Coast beaches.

NUTRIENTS

Although aquatic plants require many different substances for growth, algal growth requires just a few key substances, primarily nitrogen and phosphorus. Nitrogen is available to plants in the form of nitrate (NO_3), nitrite (NO_2), and ammonia (NH_4), while phosphorus is available mostly as phosphate (PO_3) (McCaull and Crossland, 1974). In natural systems, nitrogen is derived primarily from the decay of plant matter. Phosphorus, on the other hand, is made available by weathering of phosphorus-bearing rocks and enters streams either directly in groundwater or surface water or through decay of organic matter. Nitrogen and phosphorus are found in large quantities in sewage, and they enter waterways by the decay of organic particulates and by being dissolved in sewage treatment plant effluent. Runoff from urban and rural areas is also an important source. The close association between intensive agriculture and nitrogen in streams is clearly seen in Fig. 11.1. Water in densely populated areas, such as the mid-Atlantic states, also has high nitrogen concentrations, which is derived from a combination of agricultural and urban sources.

When one or both of these nutrients are the factors limiting algal growth, their introduction stimulates rapid algal growth, also called blooms. The algae then die and decay, releasing still more nutrients and adding to BOD. In swift-flowing rivers this extra BOD loading is a relatively minor problem, but in sluggish rivers and standing bodies of water serious problems can result. One of the effects

TABLE 11.1 Major Water Pollutants, Their Sources, and Effects

Type of Waste	Wastewater Sources	Water Quality Measures	Effects on Water Quality	Effects on Aquatic Life	Effects on Recreation
Disease-carrying agents—human feces, warm-blooded animal feces,	Municipal discharges, watercraft discharges, urban runoff, agricultural runoff, feedlot wastes, combined sewer overflows, industrial discharges	Fecal coliform, fecal streptococcus, other microbes	Health hazard for human consumption and contact	Inedibility of shellfish for humans	Reduced contact recreation
Oxygen-demanding wastes—high concentrations of biodegradable organic matter	Municipal discharges, industrial discharges, combined sewer overflows, watercraft discharges, urban runoff, agricultural runoff, feedlot wastes, natural sources	Biochemical oxygen demand, dissolved oxygen, volatile solid sulfides	Deoxygenation potential for septic conditions	Fish kills	If severe, eliminate recreation
Suspended organic and inorganic material	Mining discharges, municipal discharges, industrial discharges, construction runoff, agricultural runoff, urban runoff, silvicultural runoff, natural sources, combined sewer overflows	Suspended solids, turbidity, biochemical oxygen demand, sulfides	Reduced light penetration, deposition on bottom, benthic deoxygenation	Reduced photosynthesis, changed bottom organism population, reduced fish production, reduced sport fish population, increased nonsport fish population	Reduced game fishing and aesthetic appreciation
Inorganic materials and mineral substances—metals, salts, acids,	Mining discharges, acid mine drainage, industrial discharges, municipal discharges,	pH, acidity alkalinity, dissolved solids, chlorides, sulfates, sodium, specific	Acidity, salination, toxicity of heavy metals, floating oils	Reduced biological productivity, reduced	Reduced recreational use, fishing, aesthetic appreciation

solid matter, other chemicals, oil	combined sewer overflows, urban runoff, oil fields, agricultural runoff, irrigation return flow, natural sources, cooling tower blowdown, transportation spills, coal gasification	metals, toxicity, bioassay, visual (oil) spills		flow, fish kills, reduced production, tainted fish	
Synthetic organic chemicals—dissolved organic material, e.g., detergents, household aids, pesticides	Industrial discharges, urban runoff, municipal discharges, combined sewer overflow, agricultural runoff, silvicultural runoff, transportation spills, mining discharges	Cyanides, phenols, toxicity bioassay	Toxicity of natural organics, biodegradable or persistent synthetic organics	Fish kills, tainted fish, reduced reproduction, skeletal development	Reduced fishing, inedible fish for humans
Nutrients—nitrogen, phosphorus	Municipal discharges, agricultural runoff, combined sewer overflows, industrial discharges, urban runoff, natural sources	Nitrogen, phosphorus	Increased algal growth, dissolved oxygen reduction	Increased production, reduced sport fish population, increased nonsport fish population	Tainted drinking water, reduced fishing and aesthetic appreciation
Radioactive materials	Industrial discharges, mining	Radioactivity	Increased radioactivity	Altered natural rate of genetic mutation	Reduced opportunities for use
Heat	Cooling water discharges, industrial discharges, municipal discharges, cooling tower blowdown	Temperature	Increased temperature, reduced capacity to adsorb oxygen	Fish kills, altered species composition	Possible increased sport fishing by extended season for fish that might otherwise migrate

Source: Council on Environmental Quality (1981).

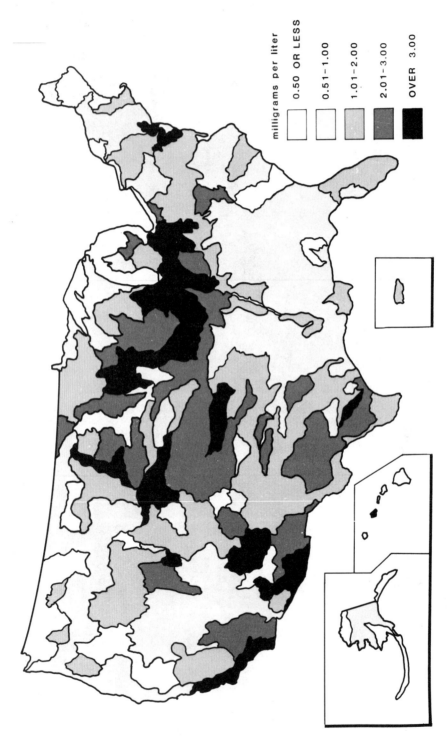

milligrams per liter

0.50 OR LESS

0.51–1.00

1.01–2.00

2.01–3.00

OVER 3.00

Figure 11.1   Total nitrogen levels in U.S. streams. Note the close association between intensive agriculture and nitrogen levels. (*Source:* Water Resources Council, 1978)

of increased nutrients in surface water is *eutrophication*, which is the process whereby a water body ages over geologic time, with the water becoming progressively shallower and nutrient rich. Eutrophic lakes typically support species such as carp and catfish, whereas geologically young *oligotrophic* lakes support pike, sturgeon, whitefish, and other species that require higher oxygen levels and/or cooler temperatures. In summer, lakes commonly develop a stratification, or layering, which prevents mixing of bottom and surface waters. If algal blooms occur, the algae settle to deeper waters, where decay depletes oxygen and deep-water fish suffocate. The absence of oxygen can also cause anaerobic decomposition of organic matter on the bottom, which produces unpleasant odors and may make water unsuitable for drinking, or affect the aesthetic quality of a river or lake.

In drinking water, phosphorus is not a problem because it is an essential nutrient that humans require, and we generally ingest far more in food than in drinking water. Nitrate and nitrite, however, do present health hazards. When ingested in high concentrations, these lead to methemoglobinemia, in which the ability of the blood to carry oxygen is impaired. In addition, ingestion of nitrate or nitrite may lead to the formation of compounds called nitrosamines, some of which have been found to cause cancer in animals, but the carcinogenic potential in humans is unknown.

OTHER DISSOLVED SOLIDS

Dissolved inorganic substances form a major part of the load of most rivers, and they include many different elements and compounds. Most of these are derived from rock weathering and soil leaching, and thus geographic variations in concentrations are often attributable to varying bedrock types. Hardness ($CaCO_3$ and related minerals) is a major indicator of dissolved minerals. Calcium carbonate is a good example of a substance derived from natural sources, primarily from marine sedimentary rocks. In areas of limestone bedrock, such as Florida and many areas of the central United States and Canada, hardness is commonly several hundred milligrams per liter, but in areas of calcium-poor rocks, such as New England and the Canadian Shield, values of 5 to 25 mg/liter are typical. For most trace minerals, regional variations are attributable to natural factors, whereas local "hot spots" are almost always human-made.

There are many different inorganic minerals found in water, and it is impossible to make generalizations about their effects on humans or the environment. Many minerals are essential nutrients in trace quantities, but virtually all have detrimental effects at higher concentrations. Table 11.2 is a list of some of the important major and minor substances found in North American rivers. Major substances tend to be found at the ppm level, and minor substances are generally in ppb.

HEAT

Electric power generation, petroleum refining, and many other industrial processes depend on the production and dissipation of large amounts of thermal energy—heat. For example, typical efficiency levels in electric generation are 32 to 36 percent. This means that about a third of the energy produced at a power plant is converted to electricity, and the other two-thirds must be dissipated as heat, usually in condensing steam. Any industrial process that requires heating and cooling will produce waste heat, and water is the most effective means of dissipating that heat. Depending on the amount of heat discharged and the rate at which it is dispersed by receiving waters, the temperature increase of the water may be as much as 18° to 36°F (10° to 20°C), though usually it is less. Another cause of *thermal pollution* in streams is the removal of vegetation that shades the water. This is particularly severe when an area is deforested. Stream corridors, where shade trees are left along the streambanks, are effective in preventing this.

Heat in water has little direct effect on humans; warm water may be less pleasant to drink but it is no less safe. The primary detrimental effects of thermal pollution are to fish, because most fish have critical temperature ranges required for survival, and these ranges differ among species (McCaull and Crossland, 1974). Spawning and egg development in lake trout, walleye, and northern pike, for example,

TABLE 11.2　Major and Minor Substances in North American Rivers with Typical Concentrations

Major Substance	Concentration (ppm)	Minor Substance	Concentration (ppb)
SiO_2	1–20	Ag	0–1
Fe	0.001–2	Al	10–2500
Mn	0.001–2	B	1–50
Ca	5–500	Ba	10–200
Mg	1–50	Co	0–10
Na	1–300	Cr	0.5–100
K	1–10	Cu	0.5–100
HCO_3	1–500	Mn	0–200
SO_4	5–1000	Ni	0–100
Cl	1–300	Pb	0–100
F	0.01–1	Sr	5–1000
NO_3	1–10	V	0–10
$CaCO_3$	5–1000	Zn	0–300

Source: Modified after Durum (1971).

are inhibited at temperatures above 48°F (9°C). Smallmouth bass and perch will not grow at temperatures above about 84°F (29°C), whereas growth of catfish is possible at temperatures as high as 93°F (34°C). In some cases thermal discharges have benefited commercial fisheries by making otherwise cool water suitable for species that require warmer temperatures, but generally the effects are negative. Equally important is the effect of temperature on dissolved oxygen concentrations. The amount of oxygen that can be dissolved in water decreases with increasing temperature; water a 92°F (33°C) holds only about half the oxygen that water at 32°F (0°C) will hold. At high temperatures, then, increased rates of bacterial activity put more demand on oxygen supplies just when saturation concentrations are low. Many fish kills are caused by a combination of high BOD and high temperatures, particularly in summer.

TOXIC SUBSTANCES AND THEIR SOURCES

SYNTHETIC ORGANICS

Organic compounds in the environment are even more diverse than inorganic substances, as are their sources. Some are of natural origin, primarily by-products of algal or bacterial activity, but those of greatest concern are human-made chemicals that enter waterways in industrial and municipal wastewaters, and from *agricultural* and *urban runoff*. They include herbicides, insecticides, and a wide variety of industrial organic chemicals such as benzene, carbon tetrachloride, polychlorinated biphenyls (PCBs), chloroform, and vinyl chloride. In addition, oils and grease can be included in this category, although they are usually found at higher concentrations than the other compounds.

Trace organics are a major concern because many of them are toxic, carcinogenic, or both. They can be dangerous if present in only parts per billion or parts per trillion, particularly if they are accumulated in tissues or biomagnified in the food chain. Table 11.3 shows some of the compounds that are toxic or known or suspected carcinogens. Adverse health effects may not be observed until many years after exposure, and consequently there is great uncertainty as to what substances are dangerous, and at what levels of exposure. Many more years of intensive research are needed to understand the hazards associated with these substances.

One example of the problem of health hazards of trace organic substances is shown in a study of leukemia in the Boston suburb of Woburn, Massachusetts. The town contains a large toxic waste dump, which is believed to be

TABLE 11.3 Categories of Known or Suspected Organic Chemical Carcinogens Found in Drinking Water

Compound	Highest Observed Concentration in Finished Water (µg/liter)	Unper 95% Confidence Estimate of Lifetime Cancer Risk Per (µg/liter)
Human carcinogen		
Vinyl chloride	10	4.7×10^{-7}
Suspected human carcinogens		
Benzene	10	I.D.[a]
Benzo(a)pyrene	D.[b]	I.D.
Animal carcinogens		
Dieldrin	8	2.6×10^{-4}
Kepone	N.D.[c]	4.4×10^{-5}
Heptachlor	D.	4.2×10^{-5}
Chlordane	0.1	1.8×10^{-5}
DDT	D.	1.2×10^{-5}
Lindane γ-BHC)	0.01	9.3×10^{-6}
β-BHC	D.	4.2×10^{-6}
PCB (Aroclor 1260)	3	3.1×10^{-6}
ETU	N.D.	2.2×10^{-6}
Chloroform	366	1.7×10^{-6}
α-BHC	D.	1.5×10^{-6}
PCNB	N.D.	1.4×10^{-7}
Carbon tetrachloride	5	1.1×10^{-7}
Trichlorethylene	0.5	1.1×10^{-7}
Diphenylhydrazine	1	I.D.
Aldrin	D	I.D.
Suspected animal carcinogens		
Bis(2-chloroethyl) ether	0.42	1.2×10^{-6}
Endrin	0.08	I.D.
Heptachlor epoxide	D.	I.D.

Source: National Research Council (1977).
[a] I.D. = insufficient data to permit a statistical extrapolation of risk.
[b] D. = detected but not quantified.
[c] N.D. = not detected.

a source of contamination for wells in the city's water supply. The wells have been closed since 1979. A study found a significant correlation between leukemia rates and consumption of water from contaminated wells. In a 14-year period, the leukemia rate in Woburn was 2.4 times the national average. There are also indications of a higher incidence of birth defects and other disorders associated with consumption of the water. However, not enough is known about the mechanisms by which consumption of contaminated water causes disease to be sure that the wells were at fault, or to know exactly what chemicals may be to blame.

In the environment, the greatest problems encountered with organic compounds are associated with *biomagnification* of persistent pesticides. These pesticides chemically break down very slowly, and thus they may be passed up the food chain until they reach lethal concentrations. DDT is the most famous of these, because it was very widely used until it was banned in the United States in 1972. Other persistent pesticides banned or restricted in the United States include chlordane, 2,4,5-T (silvex), and dieldrin. Since then concentrations in this country have generally declined, with a corresponding improvement in sensitive indicators such as bird reproduction. However, the American manufacturers of DDT and other banned chemicals have continued to sell them to Third World countries, who in turn apply the pesticides to crops that are then exported back into the United States for consumption. Besides poisoning the environment and the workers in the countries who still receive these chemicals, this "circle of poison" is coming back to endanger American consumers in contaminated fruits and vegetables. Recently, however, the U.S. Congress has drafted legislation that would outlaw the export of banned pesticides (Schneider, 1990).

In surface waters, trace organics are usually diluted such that they are present only in very low concentrations, generally parts per trillion. They are found in higher concentrations in fine-grained sediments in many waterways, with runoff sources being particularly important. In groundwater, dilution is very slow and much higher concentrations have been found than in most surface waters. This is discussed in more detail in a later section entitled Dilution.

METALS

Many metals are toxic to plants and animals at relatively low concentrations and so are a concern in surface water and groundwater. Some are also essential nutrients to certain organisms. Among the metals that are often identified as important toxic pollutants in water are arsenic, barium, cadmium, chromium, cobalt, copper, lead, manganese, mercury, nickel, silver, and zinc. The degree of health hazard associated with these metals depends on whether they are chemically or physically available to organisms. Most metals are relatively insoluble in water and tend to become associated with particulates. Metals bound to particulate matter are easily removed by filtration, and thus are less available to organisms than are dissolved forms. The solubility of most metals in water is affected by pH, with solubility increasing as pH decreases. Acid precipitation may therefore increase problems of metal pollution, as acidic water dissolves metals in soil and sediments and causes them to enter the food chain.

RADIOACTIVITY

Radioactivity, or the emission of particles by decay of certain radioactive substances, is a subject of much public concern today. Ionizing radiation, consisting primarily of alpha, beta, and gamma radiation, is derived from many natural and human-made sources. The rem, or radiation equivalent man, is a unit that describes all ionizing radiation in terms of the biological damage it causes. On the average, Americans receive a dosage of about 100 millirems (0.1 rem) per year from natural sources, and another 80 millirems from artificial sources, primarily diagnostic X rays. The radiation from natural sources comes mostly from cosmic radiation (the sun) and from terrestrial materials (rocks, bricks, and concrete). An average of about 15 to 20 millirems come from radioactive potassium-40 found in bone tissue.

Radioactive substances in water are primarily derived from rock weathering, particularly by groundwater. The greatest amount of radioactivity in water is from potassium-40, but this source is probably only about 1/100 of the amount derived from food sources. However, some substances tend to become concentrated in bone tissues, particularly strontium-90, radium-226, and radium-228. In certain areas, these isotopes occur in groundwater, and if the concentration is high, an increase in the risk of bone cancer is possible. In areas of mining or industrial operations that process rocks with high radionuclide content, local radioactive water pollution may occur. In general, however, surface waters dilute these substances to the extent that concentrations are lower than those found in natural groundwaters.

RELATIVE CONTRIBUTIONS OF DIFFERENT POLLUTION SOURCES

The pollutants discussed in the preceding sections come from many sources, and it is important to examine which sources are quantitatively most important. The relative contributions of point and non-point sources to United States waters are varied. For example, for suspended and dissolved solids, nitrogen, and phosphorus, point sources contribute 10 percent or less of the total loading. For BOD, point sources are somewhat more important, but still non-point sources dominate. Dissolved heavy metals are derived mostly from point sources. Comparable data are not available for trace organic chemicals, but it is likely that pesticides are derived mostly from non-point sources such as urban and agricultural runoff. Point sources are probably important for most industrial chemicals, although these are found frequently in urban runoff. The major causes of stream pollution are non-point sources (65 percent), followed by municipal sources (17 percent) and industry (9 percent) (U.S. EPA, 1988).

FATE OF POLLUTANTS IN SURFACE WATER

Once pollutants are added to rivers and lakes, their *concentrations* and chemical nature change. These changes occur by three major processes: dilution, biochemical decay, and sedimentation.

DILUTION

Dilution is the most important process by which pollutant concentrations are reduced in the environment. Dilution is a simple function of pollution inflow relative to the volume of water in which mixing takes place. In a large river with high discharge, relatively small amounts of pollution are quickly reduced to low concentrations. Conversely, large inputs to small streams will be diluted much less. In lakes, estuaries, and oceans, dilution is often restricted by stratification of the water body. Such layering, caused by cold water underlying warm water, or salt water under fresh water in estuaries, restricts vertical mixing and thus reduces the volume available for dilution.

There are two major problems associated with a dependence on dilution to disperse pollutants. First, dependence on dilution requires that river flow not be depleted by dry spells or consumptive uses. A river may be able to assimilate wastes when flow is high, but at low flow the capacity to dilute pollutants is reduced. When a river is also used as for public water supply and irrigation, which commonly demand the most water when flow is low, there may be acute problems.

Second, some pollutants may be undesirable regardless of their concentrations. This is true for extremely toxic substances such as dioxin, and especially true for substances that are bioconcentrated in the environment. Envi-

ronmentalists have long said "the solution to pollution is prevention, not dilution," and this is certainly true for many substances. Nonetheless, dilution is effective for most pollutants, and it will probably continue to be the most effective and most used method of pollution reduction.

BIOCHEMICAL DECAY

Organic matter, especially particulate matter, is decomposed by organisms in water, particularly bacteria. This *biochemical decay* leads to the release of nutrients that stimulate growth of aquatic plants, which are in turn decomposed by bacteria. This cycle continues until nutrients are removed from the system by dilution or sedimentation and are thus no longer available. A typical pattern observed downstream from a point source such as a sewage outfall is illustrated in Fig. 11.2. This general pattern is essentially the same as the changes observed through time after a sudden influx of organic matter in a standing body of water such as a lake.

Upstream from the pollution source, DO is relatively high, whereas BOD and dissolved and suspended solids are low. The large increase in BOD causes a rapid decline in DO, and there is a corresponding decline in suspended solids as these are decomposed. Dissolved solids decline less rapidly, and their decline takes place more by dilution than decomposition, though both processes occur. Ammonia and phosphate are primary decay products, and their concentrations increase below the outfall. Farther downstream, the concentration of nitrate increases as ammonia is oxidized to nitrate. Dissolved oxygen recovers gradually, partly through contact with air above the stream, but also as algae, stimulated by the increase in nutrients, grow and add oxygen to the water. Finally, even farther downstream, the nutrients are reduced in concentration and the stream returns to its original "clean" condition. Most rivers that flow through urban areas experience a significant DO sag within and below the metropolitan area, but downstream DO recovers. Recovery is usually not complete, however, often because of additional inflows of BOD from other sources along the river.

Two important conclusions can be drawn.

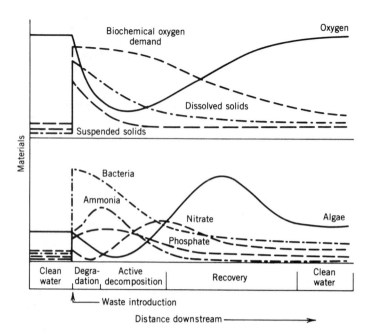

Figure 11.2   Schematic representation of downstream changes in pollution below a sewage outfall. (*Source:* Hynes, 1978.)

First, rivers have an enormous capacity to absorb common organic wastes and cleanse themselves through natural processes within a relatively short distance (or period of time). Second, this assimilation of pollutants is at the expense of dissolved oxygen, which is of course essential to a productive aquatic community. If too much BOD is put in a river, or if successive outfalls are closely spaced, the entire river may be damaged for the duration of the pollution input or longer.

SEDIMENTATION

Sedimentation is the deposition of particles of organic and inorganic particles in water. It is a natural geologic process that occurs in rivers, lakes, and oceans and consists simply of a settling out of particles in areas where flow velocity is low. Large particles eroded by a stream, such as sand and silt are usually deposited near the stream channel, along the banks, or on the floodplain. Smaller particles such as clays and fine organic particles may be deposited in the channel, but more likely they are carried to lakes or estuaries or else left on the floodplain during floods. Some trace substances, both inorganic and organic, have a tendency to

travel attached to particles rather than dissolved, and sedimentation may remove substantial amounts of these pollutants from the water.

In areas that receive large amounts of urban runoff or industrial discharges, contamination levels in sediments can be quite high. Pollutants then accumulate in the mud at the bottom of lakes and along streams. The permanence of this removal from the water is dependent on many factors, including the ability of plants and animals to consume the pollutants and reintroduce them to the environment. In some environments, particularly rivers, contaminated sediments may become resuspended and the contaminants reintroduced to the water. Concern about this possibility recently forced the dredging of large amounts of sediment contaminated with PCBs in the Hudson River. In most cases, however, sedimentation is an effective, if temporary, method of removing pollutants from the water.

GROUNDWATER POLLUTION

Groundwater pollution is probably the most serious water quality problem facing the

United States today. As shown in Chapter 10, groundwater is an essential source of drinking water, and so contamination presents a serious water supply problem. Awareness of the potential magnitude of the problem has only come recently, and there is still much to be learned. In the past, it was generally thought that groundwater was free from contamination by surface sources. But since the late 1970s, concern about toxic chemicals in the environment has prompted much more extensive sampling and analysis of both surface water and groundwater. In many areas, these analyses have shown alarming concentrations of substances such as nitrates, chloride, trichloroethylene, chloroform, benzene, toluene, and carbon tetrachloride. The concentrations are often much greater than those found in surface waters.

VULNERABILITY OF GROUNDWATER TO POLLUTION

As discussed in Chapter 10, groundwater represents a large storage of water that is replaced very slowly. Whereas typical flow velocities for rivers are measured in meters per second, groundwater is likely to flow at rates of meters per day to meters per year. In most cases, flow distances are quite large, and it takes decades to millennia to replace contaminated water in an underground reservoir, if it can be replaced at all. This has two important consequences. First, once an aquifer is contaminated it is lost for an indefinite period of time, except for uses not affected by the contaminants. Second, the contamination being discovered in wells today may result from pollutant discharges that occurred years in the past, and chemicals dumped today may not show up in well water for years to come. Not only are flow rates low, but the purification processes that remove particulates and bacteria are not as effective against human-made chemicals such as chlorinated hydrocarbons. Such chemicals as seep into an aquifer are likely to remain there with little or no dilution or degradation.

SOURCES OF CONTAMINANTS

There are many different sources of groundwater contamination, including municipal and industrial landfills, industrial impoundments, household septic systems, and waste disposal wells. These sources are illustrated in Fig. 11.3. Table 11.4 provides an assessment of the sources of groundwater pollution reported by individual states for 1986. Note that almost half of the states report septic tanks as a major pollution source.

Municipal and industrial landfills are used to dispose of nearly every kind of waste imaginable, most of it relatively harmless but some of it quite dangerous. Industrial landfills may receive much greater volumes of toxic materials, and most of the sites on the Superfund national priority list (sites rated as posing the most immediate threat to human health) are sites in which industrial wastes have been discarded on the ground or in landfills. Municipal landfills, of which there are tens of thousands in the United States, also receive hazardous wastes from household, commercial, and industrial sources, though generally in small quantities (Fig. 11.4). Landfills are often located on whatever land is available, rather than in areas that are geologically suited for waste disposal, and until recently little care has been taken to see that *leachate* (liquid seeping out of the base of a landfill) does not percolate down to an important aquifer.

Industrial impoundments such as storage lagoons and tailings ponds are another important cause of groundwater pollution. Lagoons may be used to temporarily store liquid wastes prior to disposal, reprocessing, or other use (Fig. 11.5). If they are unlined, as most are, liquid wastes can percolate into groundwater. In still other cases, wastes may be intentionally pumped into the ground as a disposal method. In confined, unusable aquifers this can be a safe practice, but leakage may occur. Tailings ponds, or impoundments used to trap mining debris, sometimes cause severe contamination with acids or metals.

Household septic tanks with leach fields are used for sewage disposal in one-quarter of all homes in the United States (U.S. EPA, 1988). Properly designed, constructed, and maintained septic systems are effective water purifiers, returning clean water to the ground and nutrients to the soil. They are generally used when population density is relatively low, such as in rural or low-density suburban areas.

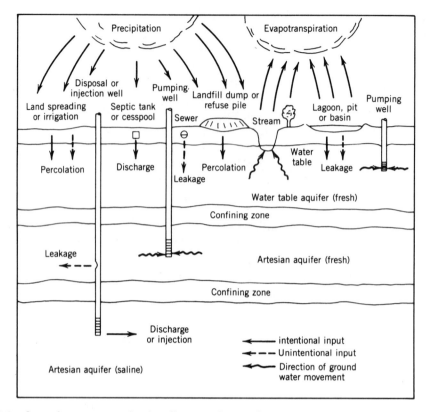

Figure 11.3   Groundwater contamination. Sources of groundwater contamination include septic tanks, landfills, lagoons, and waste disposal wells. (*Source:* U.S. Environmental Protection Agency, 1988.)

TABLE 11.4   Major Sources of Groundwater Contamination

Source	Number of States Reporting Source	Number of States Reporting as Primary Source
Septic tanks	46	9
Underground storage tanks	43	13
Agricultural activities	41	6
On-site landfills	34	5
Surface impoundments	33	2
Municipal landfills	32	1
Abandoned waste sites	29	3
Oil and gas brine pits	22	2
Salt water intrusion	19	4
Other landfills	18	0
Road salting	16	1
Land application of sludge	12	0
Regulated waste sites	12	1
Mining activities	11	1
Underground injection wells	9	0
Construction activities	2	0

Source: U.S. Environmental Protection Agency (1988).

Figure 11.4 A toxic waste lagoon near the Shenandoah River, Virginia. This site is to be cleaned up under the Superfund program.

Figure 11.5 Waste-settling lagoon at a paper mill in Minnesota. Paper manufacturing is a major source of water pollutants.

If they are used at a higher density than is appropriate for the local soil and water conditions, or if they are not properly built and maintained, pollution can result. This may be in the form of either nutrients and bacteria seeping into surface waters or contamination of groundwater, usually with nutrients. Nitrate contamination of groundwater by septic systems is a subject of concern in some areas.

Leaking underground storage tanks are another important source of groundwater pollution. There are approximately 5–6 million underground tanks, and thousands are believed to be leaking (U.S. EPA, 1988). Gasoline stations store gasoline in underground tanks, and where metal tanks have been in the ground for 20 years or more there is a strong possibility of decay and leakage. Often this leakage is at relatively slow rates that go undetected until the contamination is discovered in groundwater.

There is also evidence of widespread contamination of groundwater by agricultural chemicals, including both fertilizers and pesticides. Application of nitrogen fertilizers has increased substantially in recent decades, and today most nitrogen is applied in forms that cause increases in soil nitrate concentrations. Rainfall seeping down through the soil picks up this nitrogen and carries it to the groundwater. One recent study examined data from 1663 agricultural counties in the United States, and found that 474 had 25 percent or more of sampled wells with nitrate levels exceeding 3 mg/liter, and 87 counties had 25 percent or more of sampled wells with greater than the EPA drinking water standard of 10 mg/liter nitrate (Nielsen and Lee, 1987).

Pesticides applied in agricultural operations also reach groundwater. Several pesticides in common use are mobile in soil and groundwater, and there is substantial potential for contamination in many areas. Unfortunately there are few data on pesticides in groundwater because relatively few wells have been tested. Nielsen and Lee (1987) report that 17 pesticides have been found in the groundwater of 23 states; these numbers will certainly rise as more data are compiled.

THE EXTENT OF GROUNDWATER POLLUTION

Groundwater pollution is widespread, but highly variable. The number of wells in the United States is enormous, and only a small fraction of them have been tested for all but the most common impurities (such as hardness, iron, or bacteria). Testing of these wells provides information only about conditions in their immediate vicinity, and often they are not representative of larger areas. Between 1975 and 1985, the EPA found that between 3 and 7 percent of the nation's 40,000 public water supply systems exceeded federal standards for inorganic substances. In 1986, 13 percent of the 58,000 systems did not meet federal standards for 26 pollutants (U.S. EPA, 1988). Perhaps the most troublesome groundwater pollution problems are found in rural areas, where each well serves only a small number of people and water quality testing is minimal. In these cases, not only are tests conducted less frequently than with large municipal systems, but the water is analyzed for fewer potential pollutants. One study of rural water pollution examined 15 inorganic contaminants for which EPA has established drinking water standards. Of these, 14 were detected in concentrations exceeding these standards, and seven (mercury, iron, cadmium, lead, manganese, sodium, and selenium) were found to exceed standards in more than 10 percent of rural households (Table 11.5).

In another survey, the U.S. Geological Survey examined nitrate contamination in groundwater and found that 6 percent of the wells had concentrations exceeding the drinking water standard of 10 ppm (U.S. Geological Survey, 1985). The spatial variations in these concentrations are seen in Fig. 11.6. Concentrations are high in parts of the semiarid West where natural concentrations are higher, in agricultural areas such as the upper Midwest, and in heavily populated states. This survey was not a random one and may overrepresent the magnitude of the problem because it focused on areas with known problems, but it certainly suggests that the problem is a serious one (Conservation Foundation, 1987).

TABLE 11.5 Summary of Inorganic Elements in EPA Rural Water Survey

Element	EPA Drinking Water Standard (PPM)	Percentage of Rural Households Exceeding Standard Nationwide
Mercury	0.002	24.1
Iron	0.3	18.7
Cadmium	0.01	16.8
Lead	0.05	16.6
Manganese	0.05	14.2
Sodium	100	14.2
Selenium	0.01	13.7
Silver	0.05	4.7
Sulfates	250	4.0
Nitrate-N	10.0	2.7
Fluoride	1.4	2.5
Arsenic	0.05	0.8
Barium	1.0	0.3
Magnesium	125	0.1
Chromium	0.05	N.D.[a]

Source: U.S. Environmental Protection Agency (1984).
[a] N.D. = no data.

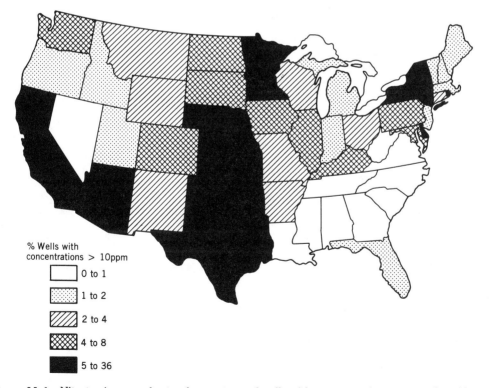

Figure 11.6 Nitrates in groundwater (percentage of wells with concentrations greater than 10 ppm). Results of a study of groundwater contamination show greater numbers of wells exceeding the drinking water standard in agricultural areas of the West and Midwest and urban areas of the Northeast. (*Source:* U.S. Geological Survey, 1985.)

WATER POLLUTION CONTROL

CONTROL METHODS

Because of the many different sources and kinds of water pollution, control is a complex and expensive problem. Wastewater discharged by point sources can be treated by a variety of methods, but non-point sources must be controlled through land management. Sewage treatment methods include primary, secondary, and tertiary techniques. *Primary treatment* consists of removal of solids by sedimentation, flocculation, screening, and similar methods. Primary treatment may remove about 35 percent of BOD, 10 to 20 percent of plant nutrients, and none of the dissolved solids. *Secondary treatment* removes organic matter and nutrients by biological decomposition using methods such as aeration, trickling filters, and activated sludge (Fig. 11.7). It became widely used in the United States during the 1960s. This treatment removes about 90 percent of BOD, 30 to 50 percent of nutrients, and perhaps 5 percent of dissolved solids. *Tertiary methods* have only come into widespread use in the last decade or so, and still only a small proportion of communities have tertiary treatment. There are many methods, and they vary considerably in their effectiveness, but generally they remove 50 to 90 percent of nutrients and dissolved solids. Treatment methods for industrial wastewater are usually specific to the type of wastes being considered. Many industries discharge into municipal sewage systems rather than treat wastes on site, although pretreatment is often required.

Non-point sources are the most difficult to control. In rural areas, they consist primarily of suspended and dissolved solids, nutrients, and pesticides contained in runoff, either dissolved or in particulate form. In agricultural areas, control of overland flow can do much to limit these sources, because soil eroded by water often contains harmful pollutants such as pesticides and nutrients. But, as shown in Chapter 7, such management practices are often difficult to establish or enforce. In urban areas, runoff from streets, parking lots, and similar surfaces usually contains large amounts of suspended solids and BOD as well as many toxic substances. In cities with combined storm and sanitary sewers, runoff is routed through the treatment system, but during storms the treatment plant cannot handle the increased flow, so that sewage and runoff are discharged in an untreated form. The sewage discharge has generally been regarded as the more serious problem, and most cities have converted or are converting to separate sanitary and storm sewer systems. This eliminates the problem of

Figure 11.7   Activated sludge tanks at a sewage treatment plant in Wisconsin.

untreated sewage discharges but does little to solve the problem of urban runoff pollution, as storm water is discharged directly without treatment. In newly developing areas, storage basins can be incorporated into stormwater systems to temporarily or permanently retain runoff, and these may be useful in reducing runoff pollution. But in developed areas the control of urban runoff is usually prohibitively expensive.

GOVERNMENT EFFORTS TO CONTROL POLLUTION

Prior to the early twentieth century, little was done to control water pollution in the United States. Some cities experienced problems of sewage contamination of water supplies, but generally the solution was to simply separate the water intake from the sewage outfall, rather than to treat the sewage. Beginning around 1900 and growing rapidly by the 1940s, wastewater treatment was instituted in the cities. A few states had pollution control laws, and the 1948 Federal Water Pollution Control Act provided impetus for construction of treatment plants. By 1960, however, only about 36 percent of the population served by sewers had wastewater treatment, and this was almost exclusively primary treatment. The remaining 64 percent were served by sewer systems with no treatment at all. In 1961 and 1965, however, new Federal laws greatly increased nationwide efforts at pollution control, mostly by providing funds for construction of treatment plants. By 1970, over 85 million Americans were served by treatment plants, or 52 percent of those with sewer systems (Council on Environmental Quality, 1981). The most ambitious and comprehensive law to date, the Federal Water Pollution Control Act of 1972 and its amendments of 1977, 1980, and 1987, now form the basis of our nationwide pollution control efforts.

Clean Water Act

The Federal Water Pollution Control Act of 1972 (now called the Clean Water Act) established a federal goal of making all waters clean enough to fish and swim in by 1985. It contains provisions for establishment of effluent standards for industries and municipal treatment plants, and for comprehensive local planning to reduce both point and non-point pollution. Municipal plants were required to achieve secondary treatment by 1977 and "best practicable" technology by 1983. Similarly, industries were required to use the best practicable technology by 1977 and the best available technology by 1983. All point dischargers are required to obtain discharge permits under a National Pollutant Discharge Elimination System (NPDES), which was originally administered by EPA, but today some states are taking over the permitting process (Fig. 11.8). Permits allow discharges only within limits established by the permitting agency.

The actual conditions for issuance of permits are primarily determined by the permitting agency, and these conditions have changed with changing public opinion and availability of funds. During the 1970s, for example, the Environmental Protection Agency was relatively rigorous in enforcing compliance with effluent standards, although deadlines for compliance were frequently postponed. During the 1980s, however, standards in some areas have been relaxed, and it is argued that either water quality is already good enough or improved treatment will probably not result in significant improvement of water quality. One example of this administrative modification of the law came in 1982, when the EPA announced that it would no longer require secondary treatment for certain cities (including New York) discharging wastes into coastal waters.

The importance of non-point sources (particularly when major point sources are controlled) is recognized by the Clean Water Act, which requires the establishment of local or regional planning to reduce non-point pollution. Plans vary from one area to another depending on the nature of the sources and local needs. Most plans include provisions for runoff and sediment control at construction sites, as well as guidelines for non-point pollution control in new developments. In some urbanized areas measures such as street sweeping have been instituted. As with the measures for controlling point sources, local plans are subject to modification by the agencies concerned depending on local needs and desires, because of the technical difficulty of controlling non-point

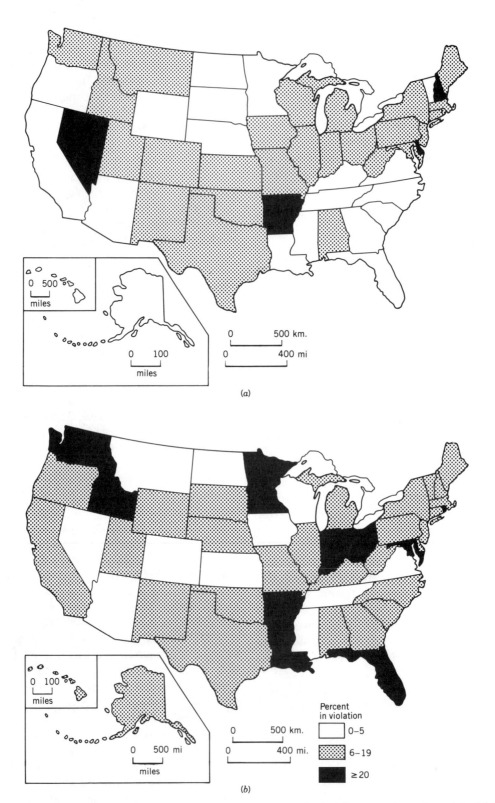

(a)

(b)

Figure 11.8 Measuring compliance toward water quality standards. The percentage of municipal (a) and nonmunicipal (b) discharges in violation of water quality standards based on their NPDES permit. (*Source:* Sapowith and Ridley, 1988.)

pollution. As a result, actual implementation of the guidelines of the federal law has been highly variable from place to place and time to time.

In 1977, the Clean Water Act Amendments were passed, amending earlier legislation. One of the more important aspects of this act was to focus government regulatory efforts on toxic substances rather than on the more conventional pollutants such as BOD or nutrients. Under this law, EPA has established industry-specific effluent limits for many common toxic substances and has developed a system of monitoring certain index contaminants as a means to reduce monitoring costs.

During the 1980s, most of the efforts at water pollution control were led by the states, as the Reagan administration sought to reduce the federal role in this area. The administration of pollutant discharge permit programs was turned over to state regulatory agencies, which in many cases enforce regulations that are more stringent than federal criteria. Efforts at reducing point-source pollution from sewage continued, and many new treatment facilities were built. In 1987 the U.S. Congress overrode a Reagan veto of a bill continuing federal subsidy of these efforts and passed the Water Quality Act.

The Water Quality Act recognizes and reiterates the need for strong regulatory control of non-point sources of toxics and other pollutants. The act continues the effluent standards based on designated use through the NPDES permit process. The legislation also tightens the control on point-source polluters and provides additional money for control of non-point sources through state grants. The Water Quality Act also strengthens the protection of specialized environments like estuaries and wetlands. Finally, the Water Quality Act of 1987 instructs states to establish clean water strategies and assessments of non-point sources of pollution.

The Safe Drinking Water Act

The Safe Drinking Water Act was first passed in 1974 and amended in 1986 in order to establish uniform national drinking water standards. The standards are based on maximum contaminated levels (MCLs) for 26 pollutants. The EPA is in the process of establishing MCLs for another 83 pollutants (U.S. EPA, 1988). Since lead is of primary concern as a contaminant, the Safe Drinking Water Act limits the use of lead solder and lead pipes in new installations and in any repairs to existing public systems. Under the act, local water supply systems must periodically be monitored for contaminants. Enforcement is left up to the individual states.

Bottled water is not included under the provisions of the Safe Drinking Water Act (see Issue 11–2), however, it is regulated by the Food and Drug Administration, which uses the EPA standards. Unfortunately, the FDA performs little testing. Instead, it relies heavily on tests conducted by the bottled water industry.

WATER QUALITY TRENDS

As a result of these and other legislative efforts, water quality has improved in many areas. By 1978, virtually all sewer systems had treatment, with most of these having secondary treatment or better. Water quality violation rates for some pollutants have declined markedly in major rivers. The Cuyahoga River, near Cleveland, Ohio, once notorious for catching fire repeatedly in the 1950s and 1960s, is no longer flammable. Lake Erie, pronounced 'dead' by environmentalists in the 1960s, has shown some signs of improvement. But generally progress has not been as dramatic as was hoped. The regulations were effective in reducing industrial discharges in many areas, and industries made substantial investments in pollution control equipment. Municipal pollution control efforts depended on both local revenues and federal assistance, and often a lack of funds or political disputes delayed treatment plant construction. For example, a 1980 estimate by the EPA indicated that 63 percent of the major municipal treatment facilities were not in compliance with the 1977 deadline for secondary treatment (CEQ, 1980). Difficulties experienced by municipalities in meeting federal requirements have led to some relaxation of the regulations.

Under the 1977 Clean Water Act Amendments, states classified their streams according to the uses they should support, including fish propagation, fish maintenance, drinking, swimming, and boating. A 1986 survey of water quality indicated that in that year, of a total of over 370,000 stream miles assessed, 74 percent had water quality that fully supported the designated uses, 19 percent had quality that partially supported the designated uses, and the water quality in 6 percent of the miles provided no support of the designated uses (U.S. EPA, 1988). Another study also found that between 1972 and 1982, 84 percent of total assessed river miles had maintained existing quality, 13 percent had improved in quality, and quality was degraded in 3 percent (General Accounting Office, 1986).

Throughout the 1980s, construction of improved treatment facilities continued, and this has resulted in locally improved water quality conditions. The total population served by secondary treatment or better is now 127 million, while fewer than 2 million people are still relying on direct discharges of untreated sewage into the nation's lakes and streams (U.S. EPA, 1988). However, although on a per capita basis we are discharging less, the nation is still growing. Improvements in some areas are offset by degradation in formerly less developed areas.

In addition, the overwhelming importance of non-point sources and the difficulty in controlling them are a major barrier to further water quality improvements.

There are some distinct regional differences in water quality. Suspended sediments pose a problem in the Columbia basin due to heavy logging and the eruption of Mt. St. Helens. In the Arkansas and Red rivers region, suspended sediments are derived from agricultural runoff. Road salt, used to deice winter roads, is a major source of total dissolved solids in the Northeast and north-central states. Nitrogen concentrations have increased during the last decade, particularly in those states east of the 100th meridian. This is largely due to increased fertilizer use, feedlot activity, and livestock population density. It is suspected that increased nitrate levels in the Ohio River Basin and the mid-Atlantic states are from atmospheric deposition. Groundwater contamination is more localized but usually consists of dissolved solids, including chloride in the West, and organic substances from detergents, hazardous waste sites, and pesticide use.

ISSUE 11–2   Perrier with a Benzene Chaser

Perrier was the drink of choice for many urban, health-conscious professionals during the 1980s, and the little green bottles came to symbolize elite status. Rather than make their own purified water, many environmental testing labs routinely use Perrier because of its purity in order to gauge local water quality. In January 1990 however, benzene, a known *carcinogen*, was found in the Perrier used by a North Carolina lab. The company was notified, and within a couple of weeks Perrier announced a total recall of 72 million bottles from stores and restaurants in North America. In a check of their Vergeze, France, plant, traces of benzene were found. Benzene occurs naturally in the gases that give Perrier its fizz. Gas filters are used to remove impurities, and someone simply forgot to replace the saturated filters, thus allowing the gas to pass through. In addition, other mineral water brands in the region were also contaminated, leading to

speculation that drought in the region had contributed to the higher concentrations of benzene.

In response to the North Carolina finding, the U.S. Food and Drug Administration (FDA) ordered random testing and 13 bottles were found that had minute amounts of benzene. The FDA concluded that there was very little danger to the public. Drinking two bottles of benzene-tainted Perrier a day would only increase one's lifetime risk of cancer by one in one million. So why all the fuss and why did Perrier recall its product?

North Americans spend $2 billion a year on bottled water. Perrier has about $119 million in U.S. sales per year and the importance of the product's image is crucial to its marketing. By April 1990, Perrier was back on the shelves and in the restaurants. But it may have lost some of its status and market share to other brands and

REFERENCES AND ADDITIONAL READING

Bellafante, G. 1990. Bottled water: Fads and facts. *Garbage* 2(1): 46–50.

Brown, M. 1979. *Laying Waste.* New York: Pantheon.

Camp, T.R., and R.L. Meserve. 1974. *Water and Its Impurities,* 2nd ed. Stroudsburg, PA: Dowden, Hutchinson & Ross.

Conservation Foundation. 1987. *Groundwater Protection.* Washington, DC: Conservation Foundation.

Council on Environmental Quality. 1980. *Environmental Quality 1980.* Washington, DC: U.S. Government Printing Office.

———. 1981. *Environmental Trends.* Washington, DC: U.S. Government Printing Office.

———. 1989. *Environmental Trends.* Washington, DC: U.S. Government Printing Office.

Durum, W.H. 1971. Chemical, physical, and biological characteristics of water resources. In L.L. Ciaccio (Ed.), *Water and Water Pollution Handbook,* Vol. 1, pp. 1–49. New York, Marcel Dekker.

General Accounting Office. 1986. *The Nation's Water: Key Unanswered Questions about the Quality of Rivers and Streams.* Washington, DC: General Accounting Office.

Hallberg, G.R. 1985. *Agricultural Chemicals and Groundwater Quality in Iowa: Status Report 1985.* Ames: Cooperative Extension Service, Iowa State University.

Hildyarn, N. 1987. The Basel disaster and proposition 65. *Ecologist* 17: 3–4.

Hynes, H.B.N. 1978. *The Biology of Polluted Waters.* Liverpool: University of Liverpool Press.

McCaull, J., and J. Crossland. 1974. *Water Pollution.* New York: Harcourt Brace Jovanovich.

National Research Council. 1977. *Drinking Water and Health.* Washington, DC: Superintendent of Documents.

Nielsen, E.G., and L.K. Lee. 1987. *The Magnitude and Costs of Groundwater Contamination from Agricultural Chemicals: A National Perspective.* Washington, DC: USDA, Economic Research Service.

Riviere, J.W. 1989. Threats to the world's water. *Sci. Amer.* 261(3): 80–94.

Sapowith, A., and S. Ridley. 1988. *Surface Water Protection.* Washington, DC: Renew America Project.

Schneider, K. 1990. Senate panel votes to bar export of banned pesticides. *The New York Times,* June 7, p. A16.

plain old seltzer, as the public's concern over toxic substances in drinking water has been heightened.

Unlike public drinking water supplies, bottled water is not tightly regulated. Seltzer and club soda, for example, are filtered, artificially carbonated tap water, and as such are unregulated even by the FDA. Nearly one-third of all bottled water comes from the same surface or groundwater source as public supplies. The Food and Drug Administration requires bottlers to check their source and the final product for about 30 contaminants, but benzene and vinyl chloride are not among those substances tested. In addition, the tests are infrequent (every 1–4 years) and are done by the bottlers themselves. The only regular testing is for bacteria, which is done on a weekly basis. Finally, and most importantly, bottlers are not required to label the source of the water.

The International Bottled Water Association (IBWA) is a trade association of bottlers. The IBWA maintains regulations for its members that are more stringent than those of the FDA and requires that members test for 51 contaminants. They also provide certification, which entails testing for 181 contaminants. In addition, the IBWA sends an independent inspector to bottling plants annually to check records and ensure that the plants are clean and meeting the IBWA standards. In this respect, they provide a better monitor for bottled water purity than the federal government.

So, if you want to drink bottled water and are unsure of the source, the best protection you have is to ascertain whether or not the bottler is a member of the IBWA or has its product certified. If you rely solely on the government to ensure the product's safety, you could be drinking mineral water, club soda, seltzer, or sparkling water with a trace of benzene (Bellafante, 1990).

Silka, L.R., and F.M. Brasier. 1980. *The National Assessment of the Ground Water Contamination Potential of Waste Impoundments.* Washington, DC: U.S. Environmental Protection Agency.

Smith, R.A., R.B. Alexander, and M.G. Wolman. 1987. Water quality trends in the nation's rivers. *Science* 235: 1607–1615.

U.S. Environmental Protection Agency. 1984. *National Statistical Assessment of Rural Water Conditions, Executive Summary.* Washington, DC: U.S. Government Printing Office.

———. 1988. *Environmental Progress and Challenges: EPA's Update.* Washington, DC: U.S. Government Printing Office.

U.S. Geological Survey. 1985. *National Water Summary 1984: Hydrologic Events, Selected Water Quality Trends, and Ground Water Resources.* Washington, DC: U.S. Government Printing Office.

Water Resources Council. 1978. *The Nation's Water Resources, 1975–2000.* Washington, DC: Superintendent of Documents.

Wolman, M.G. 1971. The nation's rivers. *Science* 174: 905–918.

TERMS TO KNOW

Agricultural Runoff
Biochemical Decay
Biochemical Oxygen Demand (BOD)
Biomagnification
Carcinogen
Clean Water Act
Coliform Bacteria
Concentration
Dilution
Dissolved Oxygen
Eutrophication
Inorganic Particulates
Non-point Source
Oligotrophic
Organic Particulates
Point Source
Pollution
Primary Treatment
Radioactivity
Secondary Treatment
Sedimentation
Suspended Particulates
Tertiary Treatment
Thermal Pollution
Urban Runoff

STUDY QUESTIONS

1. What are the main properties of water?

2. List the eight major classes of water pollutants. What are their sources and health effects?

3. What four major processes alter pollutant concentrations once pollutants are added to waterways?

4. Why is groundwater pollution a growing problem?

5. What are the major contaminants of groundwater?

6. What do primary, secondary, and tertiary treatment methods consist of?

7. What is the role of the federal government in protecting water quality?

12

Marine Resources: Common Property Dilemmas

INTRODUCTION

No one nation owns the world's oceans nor controls the resources found in them. The oceans, then, are a *common property resource*. Common property resources cannot be managed by a single individual, nation, or corporation, because without some form of governmental or international regulation to allocate resources among users, individuals have little incentive to preserve or protect resources for future generations (Chapter 2). Historically, those nations who could exploit the world's marine resources, such as oil, fish, whales, and minerals, simply did so.

We tend to think of the earth in terms of land area, yet 71 percent of the earth's surface is covered by water, most of it in the oceans. Virtually all living and nonliving resources are somehow influenced by the oceans.

The living and nonliving resources of the sea have slightly different characteristics than those found on land. First, they are often unseen and thus unmeasurable and uncountable. It is impossible, for example, for a fisheries biologist to know exactly how many fish there are in a given ocean area. It is also difficult to know the size of an oil field in deep water offshore, as exploration technology used on land will not work in the marine environment. Second, the oceans are the ultimate diffuser and therefore the ultimate pollution sink. Oceanic oil pollutants, for example, can travel immense distances, confounding attempts to identify and regulate the polluter.

Finally, despite a number of international treaties, the question of who owns the majority of the oceans and the resources found within them is still unanswered. On land, governments and individuals claim, occupy, and defend areas based on legally binding boundaries using easily recognized geographic features. Ownership of the oceans is less clear and depends on the current use of the ocean area or the political, technological, or military power of a country or private corporation. For example, U.S. companies seeking to mine deep-ocean minerals cannot obtain commercial financing until legal ownership of sections of the deep ocean bottom is established either by international treaty or by unilateral action by the U.S. government. Such disputes are common and resource managers frequently focus on *who* should have access to ocean resources rather than *how* those resources should be allocated and used.

THE WATER PLANET: PHYSICAL PROPERTIES

SALINITY

The physical properties of seawater, the rotation of the earth, and the hydrologic cycle shape the distribution of marine resources and control the ocean's impact on terrestrial ecosystems. Seawater is a solution of materials and salts of nearly constant composition throughout the world. Sea salts, a product of billions of years of terrestrial erosion, contain at least traces of most elements found in the earth's crust. Six elements, however, comprise more than 98 percent of all sea salts (Table 12.1). On the average, a kilogram of seawater

TABLE 12.1   Composition of Dissolved Sea Salts in Seawater

Element	Percentage
Chlorine	55.0
Sulfur	7.7
Sodium	30.6
Magnesium	3.7
Potassium	0.7
Calcium	0.7
Minor elements	1.6
(bromine, carbon, strontium)	
Total	100.0

Source: Gross (1971, p. 57).

contains 35 grams of salt, or 35 parts per thousand (ppt) salt. These salts are dissolved in variable amounts of water and slight differences in the *salinity* of seawater can influence the speed and direction of ocean currents and the vertical mixing of surface and bottom waters.

Salinity change may also have a major impact on the ocean's living resources. For example, it governs the spawning time of oysters and other shellfish on the east coast of the United States and the shrimp migrations in the Gulf of Mexico. Juvenile shrimp can tolerate the wide-ranging salinities (0–25 ppt) found in coastal areas; adult shrimp can only survive in ocean waters of 35 ppt salinity. Thus, the success of the shrimp fishing season is largely dictated by rainfall and freshwater river discharge.

As salinity changes, the density of seawater also changes. Fresh or low-salinity water will float on top of heavier, saltier water to create *stratified estuaries* in coastal areas and *haloclines* in the open ocean. Such *stratification* can complicate efforts to protect shellfish beds and to monitor pollutants, and can even threaten public drinking water supplies. For example, at the mouth of the Delaware River, near Philadelphia, the movement of the so-called salt wedge is dictated by the volume of freshwater flow in the Delaware River. If river flow is low, salty ocean water creeps up Delaware Bay, threatening the city's drinking water intake. Conversely, seasonal high flows of fresh water lower the salinity in the oyster beds downstream of Wilmington,

Delaware, discouraging the spread of oyster parasites and predatory oyster drills. The size and movement of the salt wedge in this partially stratified estuary affects everything from commercial fishing to the drinking water supplies for over 3 million people.

HEAT EXCHANGE

Water temperature and water temperature gradients (*thermoclines*) are other physical aspects of the ocean environment that influence the conservation and management of marine resources. The worldwide distribution of the ocean's surface-water temperature depends on the general supply of heat available from the sun. Surface temperature is highest at the equator and declines northward and southward, toward the poles. Total heat loss from the ocean waters (as opposed to the temperature of the water itself) also declines as one moves away from the equator, but not at the same rate. The difference between a surplus of heat at the equator and relatively little elsewhere results in the global heat-transfer mechanisms (air and water currents) that shape our weather. The oceans, then, can be viewed as a giant weather machine. The major ocean currents in the world are illustrated in Fig. 12.1.

A change in ocean water temperatures can have a worldwide impact. A phenomenon called the Southern Oscillation describes the interannual fluctuation between warm "El Niño" conditions and cold "La Niña" ones (Leetmaa, 1989). In the late fall of each year, a warm current, which local fishermen call "El Niño," develops along the coasts of Ecuador and Peru. At irregular intervals, a much larger ocean warming occurs at the same time of year along the same coast but stretching westward along the equator, two-thirds of the way across the Pacific Ocean. This large-scale warming completely reverses the wind and current systems of the Pacific Ocean, influencing worldwide weather patterns and causing rare winter/spring hurricanes, floods, and droughts. In addition, *El Niño* affects the catch of anchovies off Peru, and a drop in the Pacific coast fish catch has been linked to the 1982–1983 El Niño (Rasmusson and Hall, 1983; Brock, 1984). *La Niña* has the opposite effect in that warm

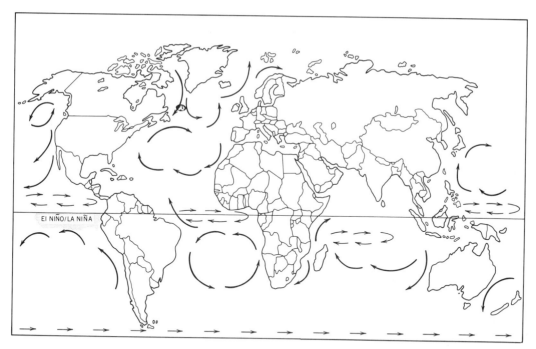

Figure 12.1 Major ocean currents of the world. The large ocean bodies have circular flow patterns, called *gyres*, which are clockwise in the Northern Hemisphere and counterclockwise in the Southern Hemisphere. Superimposed on this pattern are smaller currents, such as the equatorial countercurrents. Periodic disruptions of circulation, labeled El Niño/La Niña, occur in the eastern Pacific.

surface waters are driven westward, thus drawing cold water to the surface in the east.

DISSOLVED OXYGEN

The last important physical feature of the oceans that affects marine conservation and management is *dissolved oxygen*, the total amount of oxygen present within a body of liquid, in this case water. Dissolved oxygen is absolutely essential for aquatic life.

The distribution of dissolved oxygen is controlled by exchanges with the atmosphere, photosynthesis of phytoplankton, and respiration of oxygen-consuming biota. The solubility of a gas such as oxygen is a function of water temperature; the higher the temperature the more dissolved oxygen. The vertical distribution of dissolved oxygen in the oceans is also a function of currents and of photosynthetic activity of phytoplankton in the euphotic zone. Dissolved oxygen levels, then, generally decline with depth. The deep oceans, however, are rarely devoid of oxygen (or *anoxic*), because cold, deep water generally contains

more oxygen than is consumed by the limited populations of animals in deep water. Dissolved oxygen is a key variable in determining the distribution of living resources in the sea and the sensitivity of the oceans to pollutants. For example, many of the fisheries die-offs in the ocean in recent years have been linked to a combination of factors, including weather, currents, and pollution. The pollution stimulates algal growth and creates conditions very similar to the eutrophication processes in shallow lakes. The results are localized anoxic conditions, resulting in massive fish and shellfish kills.

MAPPING THE UNMAPPABLE

One of the keys to managing marine resources is determining where the resources are found and in what quantities. In terrestrial environments, you can see, count, and often map the precise location or habitat of a particular wildlife species or plant. In the ocean, you cannot. Measurement is always indirect and you must rely on limited data and educated guesses.

There are a number of key physical features that tend to influence the distribution of resources, including topography, currents, upwelling areas, salinity gradients, water depth, thermoclines, and prevailing weather conditions. For living resources, mapping these physical features provides data for delineating key habitats of individual species. The fact that many living marine resources tend to concentrate in or near one of these physical features is not coincidental.

HABITAT AND BIOLOGICAL PRODUCTIVITY

MAJOR PRODUCTIVE REGIONS

The biological productivity of the oceans is highly variable and dictated by a combination of bottom topography, salinity, water temperature, sunlight, and currents. We can spatially delimit three major productive regions of the oceans—estuaries, near-shore and continental shelf waters, and the deep ocean. Each of these has a different level of importance to marine fisheries and food resources.

An *estuary* is an enclosed coastal water body that has a direct connection to the sea and a measurable dilution of seawater by fresh water from the land. Estuaries are transition zones where fresh and salt water mix in a shallow environment that is also strongly influenced by tidal currents. Estuaries can be classified as ecotones (see Chapter 4) or transitional areas between two distinct natural systems, terrestrial and marine. Ecotones generally have a greater diversity of species and higher biological productivity than the natural systems on either side. This "edge effect" is especially true in estuaries. The primary productivity of estuaries is 20 times as high as a typical forest (Odum, 1971).

Since phytoplankton and other primary producers serve as the basis for most marine food chains, the majority of fish and shellfish caught for human consumption are dependent on estuaries during at least a portion of their life cycle. A few species are permanent estuarine residents, but the majority of fish species migrate between estuaries and near-shore and continental shelf waters to spawn or feed. Es-

tuaries are also important nursery areas for immature fish and shellfish. In addition, estuaries play a key role in the migration of *anadromous* and *catadromous* fish such as Pacific salmon, the American eel, and the striped bass. Fisheries biologists estimate that 75–90 percent of all fish and shellfish caught by commercial and recreational fishermen in the United States are in one way or another dependent on estuaries.

Near-shore and continental shelf waters are the second geographic division. They encompass a much larger portion of the world's total ocean area (7–8 percent) than estuaries (which occupy 2–3 percent), yet are less biologically productive. They slope from the shoreline out to a depth of approximately 656 feet (200 m) and are affected by geologically recent changes in sea level. The continental shelves are the submerged coastal plains that were above water as late as the last ice age, 10,000 years ago. Often low and marshy in prehistoric times, and subject to repeated burial and changes in pressure as sea level fluctuated, today the continental shelves are a major source of petroleum reserves.

The waters above the continental shelves are also the site of the majority of the world's fisheries. Close to highly productive estuaries, continental shelves are subject to wind-driven and tidal currents and are shallow enough to permit constant mixing of warm surface waters and cool, nutrient-rich bottom waters. The primary productivity of the shelves is approximately double that of the open ocean. One key feature of the continental shelf region is *upwelling*, in which wind-driven surface currents move away from the shoreline and deep, nutrient-rich water is drawn to the surface, creating exceptionally productive areas (Fig. 12.2). Upwelling occurs on a large scale along the western edge of continents and, to a lesser extent, in specific portions of the shelf such as Georges Bank off the coast of Massachusetts. Nearly 99 percent of all fish production occurs in estuaries and continental shelves, and the majority of continental shelf fisheries are concentrated in upwelling regions.

Compared to the continental shelves, the *deep oceans* are a biological desert, even though they encompass 90 percent of the earth's ocean area. They are only half as pro-

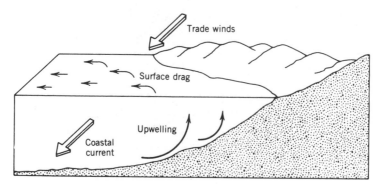

Figure 12.2 Upwelling. This natural event is caused by wind-driven currents that move away from a coastline. Nutrient-laden water is drawn upward to replace the water moved at the surface. Regions of upwelling are generally areas of very productive fisheries.

ductive as continental shelves, with most biological activity concentrated in the euphotic zone, where sunlight penetrates. At present, there are only a few important fisheries found in the deep-ocean, and the most valuable of these is tuna. As coastal nations have claimed the fishery resources of their continental shelves, deep ocean fisheries are becoming increasingly important to nations such as Japan and the Soviet Union, which have relatively little continental shelf area that is under their direct control.

FOOD FROM THE OCEANS

The importance of the ocean as a potential food resource is increasing. In the 1970s, about 9 percent of the protein consumed by the world's population came from marine fish and shellfish. By the year 2000, this figure may rise to as high as 20 percent (Council on Environmental Quality, 1981b). This rising demand for protein and a leveling off of agricultural production in many parts of the world will result in a rapid climb in the world's catch of fish (Fig. 12.3). Nearly 70 percent of all fish caught are eaten by people as fresh or frozen fish; the remaining 30 percent of the catch is reduced to fish meals, which are made into fertilizers, animal feed (primarily chicken feed), or oils that are used in paints and other industrial products (Table 12.2).

Fishery resources are unevenly distributed around the globe in both fresh and salt water, and nearly 90 percent of the total fish catch is in marine waters (Food and Agricul-

tural Organization, 1987). The leading fishing nations in the world are Japan, the USSR, and China (Table 12.3), although these nations do not fish only in their own territorial waters. Regionally, the northern Pacific Ocean is the primary fishing region, followed by the northern Atlantic Ocean and the southern Pacific Ocean. For statistical purposes, the Food and Agricultural Organization (FAO) identifies 19 major marine fishing regions throughout the world. The USSR utilizes all 19 regions, in fact 10 percent of the Soviet catch in 1987 was from the east-central Atlantic Ocean off the coast of western Africa (FAO, 1987). Japan also utilizes all the world's marine fishing areas

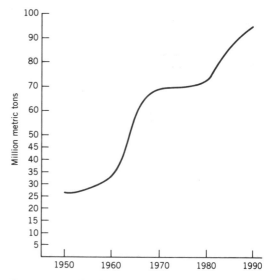

Figure 12.3 World fish catch, 1950–1987. (*Source:* Food and Agricultural Organization, 1987).

TABLE 12.2   World Fishery Catch (Metric Tons)[a]

	1981	1987
Total world catch	74,760,400	92,693,000
Human consumption[b]	70.4	72.4
Fresh	19.4	21.8
Frozen	22.5	23.8
Curing	14.5	14.2
Canning	14.0	12.6
Other[b]	29.6	27.6
Reduction[c]	28.2	26.5
Miscellaneous	1.4	1.1
Total	100.0	100.0

Source: Food and Agricultural Organization (1987, Vol. 65, p. 20).
[a] Excludes whales, seals, mammals, and aquatic plants.
[b] Percentage of total world catch.
[c] Includes reduction to oils and meals.

except the Arctic Ocean. The majority of both the USSR's and Japan's catch originates in the same northwestern Pacific region. The other major fishing countries tend to concentrate their fishing activities in regional waters, although Chile does utilize the southern Atlantic Ocean off the coast of Antarctica, and China also utilizes the western Africa fishing region. Access to fish is therefore a key issue in ocean management, with countries such as the United States using fisheries as a "food weapon" when we disagree with the internal

TABLE 12.3   Leading Fishing Nations, 1987

Country	Metric Tons Caught
Fish, crustaceans, and molluscs	
Japan	11,841,104
Soviet Union	11,159,617
China	9,346,222
United States	5,736,493
Chile	4,814,360
Seaweed	
People's Republic of China	1,196,250
Japan	664,123
Republic of Korea	456,715
Philippines	222,003
Norway	174,109

Source: Food and Agricultural Organization (1987, Vol. 64, p. 97).

politics or political controversies in other nations. Disagreements over marine resources have even resulted in armed conflicts between nations, such as the Malvinas (Falklands) War between Argentina and Great Britain and heated disputes over territory such as Antarctica (see Issue 12–1).

Commercial landings in the United States totaled 2.74 million metric tons in 1986 (CEQ, 1989). The five major species in volume caught were menhaden (the oil is used primarily in industry), salmon, crab, shrimp, and herring. In terms of dollar value, the most important species were shrimp, salmon, crabs, lobsters, and scallops. In 1986, U.S. commercial landings were valued at $2.8 billion.

MARINE MAMMAL HABITAT

The exact population sizes of marine mammals occupying the world's oceans are unknown, although we do have estimates for specific species. Marine mammals include great whales, small whales, dolphins and porpoises, sirenians and otters, and seals and sea lions.

Many factors influence the number of marine mammals in any given region. Often, the best knowledge we have regarding their population is derived from historical data on whaling and harvesting and current information about their reproductive biology, natural mortality, and habitat. In the case of whales, defining habitat is problematic. For example, the distribution of the California gray whale is relatively easy to determine because their breeding areas are limited to several shallow lagoons on the west coast of Mexico and portions of their north–south migration routes follow the edge of the continental shelf along the western coast of North America. Both the lagoons and continental shelf are physical features that can be easily mapped. On the other hand, the distribution of other great whales such as the fin, right, and blue whales is greatly dependent on the concentration of food supplies such as krill and plankton. In turn, the distribution of krill and plankton is dependent on currents and weather conditions, thus making it highly variable. Therefore, mapping the key feeding areas for these species could change from year to year.

ENERGY FROM THE OCEANS

The United States and other nations are becoming increasingly dependent on the oceans for energy production. The share of traditional energy sources such as oil and gas from the offshore areas is growing, and several nontraditional sources of energy from the oceans are under development (Chapter 16).

Approximately 30 percent of the earth's exploitable hydrocarbons are found beneath marine waters, with 90 percent of these unexplored. The majority of the explored oil and gas deposits are found on the continental shelf, near land-based oil and gas reserves. The U.S. outer continental shelf, for example, is roughly 1.8 million square miles (4.7 million km^2) in size. This is comparable to the 1.7 million square miles (4.4 million km^2) of geologically favorable land in the United States that currently supports most domestic oil and gas production. There is a good chance, then, that the offshore regions under U.S. control could produce at least as much oil and gas as is currently produced on land (Halbouty, 1982). A similar pattern can be found worldwide.

In 1986, offshore oil production was 13.5 million barrels per day, slightly down from 1980 levels (World Resources Institute, 1988). The United Kingdom (utilizing North Sea reserves) is the leading offshore oil-producing nation, followed by the United States and Saudi Arabia. Global offshore natural gas production has also increased since 1980, reaching 958.1 million m^3 per day in 1986 (World Resources Institute, 1988). The United States (particularly the Gulf Coast) is the leading offshore natural gas producer, followed by the United Kingdom and Norway.

This rapid growth of offshore oil and gas development depends on the ability to drill for hydrocarbons in ever-deeper water. Early efforts at offshore drilling were simple extensions of land-based techniques in water less than 20 feet (6 m) deep. Advances in drilling technology, semisubmersible drilling-rig designs, offshore pipelines, and other equipment now permit construction of conventional drilling platforms in up to 1000 feet (305 m) of water (Fig. 12.4). In fact, technology for drilling temporary exploratory wells has outstripped the technology for building permanent platforms needed to bring an area into regular production. Exploratory wells have been drilled in up to 5000 feet (1.5 km) of

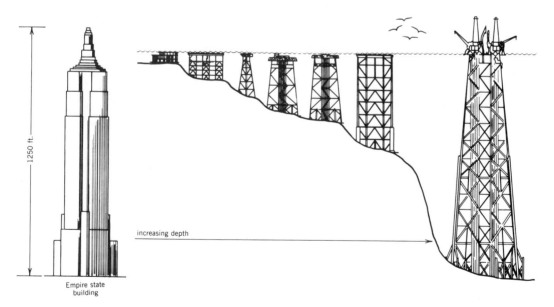

Figure 12.4 Changes in offshore oil drilling technology since 1940. Production oil drilling platforms were installed in 20 ft of water in the 1940s. By 1983, permanent platforms exceeded 1250 ft, approximately the height of the Empire State Building. (*Source:* U.S. Department of the Interior, 1981.)

water, thus opening up large areas of the continental slope and even deep-ocean areas to possible development.

DEEP—SEABED MINERALS

For hundreds of years, sand, gravel, coal, tin, gold, and diamonds have been mined from the sediments beneath shallow-water areas around the world. By the early 1970s, mineral deposits found in the deep ocean became technically and economically exploitable. Many of these mineral deposits contain strategic minerals such as cobalt, which is currently imported by industrial nations, including the United States (see Chapter 15). Of particular interest to the developed nations are manganese nodules. These potato-sized lumps are common features of the seafloor in water from 2.5 to 3.5 miles (4 to 6 km) in depth. The nodules are composed of hydrated oxides of iron and manganese, which often form around a nucleus of shell, rock, or other mate-

rial, just as the pearls that oysters create form around a grain of sand. Manganese nodules are found in all the world's oceans, although the grade (percentage of various metals) and coverage (weight and number per area) vary. The eastern Pacific Ocean several hundred miles south of Hawaii appears to contain exceptionally dense nodule deposits, containing minerals in sufficient quantity to permit commercial exploitation (Knecht, 1982) (Fig. 12.6).

Manganese nodules contain four principal minerals: manganese, nickel, copper, and cobalt. Virtually all cobalt and manganese and 70 percent of all nickel consumed by U.S. industries each year are imported from South Africa, Zaire, Canada, and the Soviet Union. As a result, U.S., Japanese, and European mining companies are interested in gaining access to the billions of tons of deep-seabed minerals that are expected to become available as technology improves.

Exploitation of seabed minerals would require an investment of many millions of dollars. To protect such an investment, mining

---

ISSUE 12–1   Antarctica: Isn't Any Place Pristine Anymore?

Antarctica, the frozen continent, was first discovered in 1772 by James Cook. With its wealth of marine life (fur seals and whales) the marine mammals in Antarctica waters were quickly exploited. In addition to the hunters, explorers came in small numbers to conquer the frozen land and discover the South Pole. Throughout the first half of the twentieth century, Antarctica was relatively immune from the destructive force of people.

In response to mounting pressures and overlapping territorial claims, the Antarctic Treaty of 1959 was signed by 39 nations. This treaty prohibits military activity, bans nuclear weapons, prohibits harming the environment, and promotes cooperative scientific investigation of the polar region. The treaty is complicated by the overlapping territorial claims of seven nations: Argentina, Chile, the United Kingdom, Norway, . Australia, New Zealand, and France. The United States and the Soviet Union have no territorial claims in Antarctica, nor do they recognize any. Since 1959, meetings were held of the signatory nations to discuss current

and future policy regarding Antarctica. Between 1987 and 1989, for example, the signatories developed procedures for environmental impact assessments and a code of conduct for tourism. Why is there such a need?

Antarctica is now suffering from its own popularity as a scientific station and as a tourist attraction. Ever since the International Geophysical Year in 1957, permanent stations have been maintained on the continent. Currently there are about 38 permanent year-round stations, with a total of a few thousand residents. Unfortunately, the residents of these stations have produced tons of garbage, most of which just sits in the frozen environment. Unlike the backcountry hiker, the visitors and scientific expeditions do not pack out what is brought into the continent. In addition to the solid waste generation, parts of the continent are suffering from overcrowding. In the Antarctic Peninsula, for example, there are 13 permanent stations each generating their own hill of garbage (Fig. 12.5). Because of the fragile nature of the environment, these few people tend to have a disproportionate

Figure 12.5 Rubbish dump at the U.S. base at McMurdo Sound, Antarctica.

companies would undoubtedly demand guaranteed and probably exclusive access to this resource. The exploitable fields of seabed nodules, however, are in deep-ocean waters, beyond any single nation's jurisdiction. The interest in seabed mining has prompted a total reevaluation of the concept of ownership of marine resources, resulting in the negotiation of a complex Law of the Sea Treaty, which is discussed later in this chapter. Thus far, the

impact. Most of the plants and animals are confined to the 2 percent of Antarctica that is ice-free for part of the year, which is precisely the area where the heaviest concentration of permanent bases is located.

Oil pollution is also an increasing problem on land and in the sea. At McMurdo Sound, 52,000 gallons (196,820 liters) of fuel leaked in 1989. The waters right off the base are polluted with untreated sewage, heavy metals, and a myriad of other toxic substances. An Argentinian tanker, the *Bahia Paraiso*, ran aground near Palmer Station in 1989, spilling 170,680 gallons (643,450 liters) of jet diesel fuel into the cold waters. A Peruvian tanker, the *Humboldt*, also ran aground a few weeks later, creating an oil slick one-half mile long along the northern coast.

Despite the frozen environment, Antarctica has a wealth of mineral resources. Copper, coal, iron, and other minerals are recoverable in the Transantarctic Mountains, although not with existing technology and economic conditions. Commercial oil and gas deposits are thought to exist below the Ross Sea. In 1988, 20 nations signed the Wellington Convention, which essentially allows mineral exploration or development as long as all treaty participants agree. In 1989, France and Australia withdrew from the agreement, thus effectively destroying (for the moment) any hope of mineral exploration on the continent.

Finally, about 4000 tourists are expected to visit the continent on a yearly basis. They arrive by cruise ship and pay anywhere from $4000 to $10,000 per person for the privilege. To take advantage of the week-long visit, Chilean operators have opened a hotel near their base on the Antarctic Peninsula. These visitors hike in the area, destroying penguin rookeries and other wildlife habitats. Of course, they also leave their litter. Since the Antarctica ecosystem is so fragile, any small disturbance can have disastrous consequences. The destruction by scientific expeditions as well as tourists has been tremendous and the last of the world's truly pristine environments is no more (Lemonick, 1990; Kimball, 1988; Sugden, 1982).

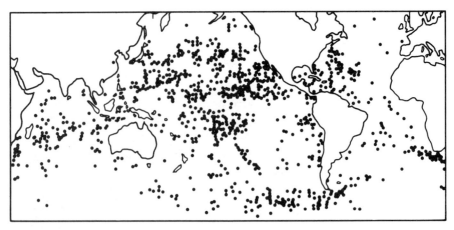

Figure 12.6 Manganese in the oceans. Scientific research vessels have found accumulations of manganese nodules at these locations over the last 100 years. (*Source:* Heath, 1982.)

United States has refused to sign, partly because the treaty limits unrestricted access to manganese nodules. Problems such as boundary disputes, lack of scientific knowledge, huge capital investments required for mining, and the vagaries of the minerals marketplace have all contributed to the lack of development of these seabed resources.

MANAGEMENT OF MARINE RESOURCES

THE CONCEPT OF OWNERSHIP

As discussed earlier in this chapter, the oceans are a common property resource. A classic example of the problems with managing a common property resource is the international regulation of whaling. The introduction of the harpoon gun and steam-powered whaling vessels in the late 1800s, coupled with the advent of the seagoing factory ship in the early twentieth century, revitalized the whaling industry of *Moby Dick* fame. This new technology permitted the exploitation of larger, faster species of whales, such as the blue whale, and the processing of oil, bone, and meat at sea. Several European nations developed fleets of small vessels, called whale catchers, centered around a large factory ship. These fleets caught several different species in both Arctic and Antarctic waters, raising concerns of overfishing as early as 1920. The first international

whaling treaty, signed in 1931, proved ineffective. The *International Whaling Commission* (IWC) was therefore established in 1946, ostensibly to protect and ensure species survival. Currently, 39 countries are members of the IWC.

The wording of the preamble to the 1946 International Convention for the Regulation of Whaling, which created the IWC, is a good example of the difficulty of using a scientifically rational management approach on a common property resource such as whales. The treaty directs that the IWC safeguard for future generations the great natural resources represented by the whale while also increasing the size of whale stocks to bring the population to an "optimal level" to make possible the orderly development of the whaling industry (Bean, 1977). Is the objective of the IWC to protect whales, encourage industry development, or both? Nearly four decades of efforts to manage whales by the IWC indicate that nations generally will seek to protect whales only when it is in their national interest to do so. The 1946 treaty creating the IWC permits member nations to object to and then legally ignore the quotas established by the Commission and its scientific committees. Thus, in 1986 when the IWC formally declared a complete moratorium on all commercial whaling at the urging of the United States and other nonwhaling member nations, Japan and the Soviet Union formally objected and were initially allowed to set their own quotas. In 1987, Norway and the

Soviet Union ceased commercial whaling, as did Japan in 1988. Under the IWC moratorium (which expires in 1991), however, countries can still obtain special permits to harvest whales for subsistence purposes for native populations (Inuit) and for scientific research.

International efforts to protect whales are complicated by the slow reproductive rates of these marine mammals. For example, one of the reasons cited in support of the international whaling conventions was the Pacific bowhead whale. The world catch for this species peaked in the mid-1800s, and the IWC's first act was to ban all further commercial harvest. However, right and bowhead whale populations have not recovered despite 40 years of complete protection. It appears that the slow reproductive rate of these species is responsible for the inability of the small, dispersed populations to grow rapidly.

Given the structure of the IWC, recent whaling follows a pattern of heavy exploitation of one species, leading to a dramatic population decline, and a shift to another species. For example, 11,559 blue whales were caught in 1940, declining to less than 2000 in 1960 and 613 in 1965. The catch of the slightly smaller fin whale peaked at 32,185 in the mid-1950s and dropped to 5057 by 1970. The harvest of the still smaller sei whale was minimal until 1960, when it then rose and subsequently declined (CEQ, 1981a). Similarly, the minke whale catch totaled about 60,000 during the

early 1980s. The status of whale stocks in 1985 is shown in Table 12.4.

There has been an interesting reaction to the failure of international efforts to regulate whales. In 1976, the United States adopted legislation linking the permitted harvest of fish within U.S. waters by foreign nations to their adherence to IWC quotas. Thus, when Japan refused to abide by the IWC's moratorium in 1983, the United States withheld 100,000 metric tons of Japan's 1984 allocation of fish to be caught off Alaska and threatened to limit fishing further if Japan's objections to the IWC were not withdrawn. Several other nations are adopting a similar strategy. In the United States, all marine mammals (whales, porpoises, seals, manatees, and walruses) are protected by legislation. At the international level, however, an agency such as the IWC has no real enforcement powers and must rely on economic sanctions and on the diplomacy of its member nations. Nonwhaling nations such as the United States often cite the need to protect whales as an aesthetic resource. This perception does not carry much weight in whaling nations, such as Japan, Norway, and the Soviet Union, where whales have economic value. Thus, international management of common property resources such as whales often depends on resolving differences over the perceived value of the resource in question (see Issue 12–2). Specific attempts to protect marine mammals are discussed later in this chapter.

TABLE 12.4 Whale Abundance and Catch

Species	Virgin Population[a]	Current Population	Peak Catch	Year of Peak Catch	1980–1985 Catch
Blue	175,000–228,000	8,400–14,000	19,079	1930	0
Humpback	115,000	10,000	5,063	1950	78
Bowhead	30,000–54,700	3,870–7,800	NA[b]	NA	71
Right	100,000–200,000	3,000–4,000	NA	NA	NA
Fin	448,000–548,000	105,000–120,300	32,185	1955	2,015
Sei	256,000	33,800–51,400	25,454	1965	506
Sperm	2,400,000–2,700,000	1,950,000	25,842	1970	5,424
Gray	15,000–20,000	15,000–21,000	NA	NA	650
Minke	140,000	725,000	12,398	1977	59,753

Sources: Brownell, Ralls, and Perrin (1989); Council on Environmental Quality (1982); U.S. Department of Commerce (1985); World Resources Institute (1988).
[a] Estimates of population before harvesting began.
[b] NA = not available.

Figure 12.7   Dolphin entangled in a drift gillnet intended for swordfish. Inadvertent netting of dolphins is a point of conflict between environmentalists and the fishing industry.

ISSUE 12–2   Flipper versus Charlie the Tuna

Many of us regard tuna fish as a staple of our diet. Buy a can of tuna, and you've almost got a meal. Until recently, purchasing a can of tuna also meant that you were paying for porpoise carcasses discarded from the tuna catch.

Schools of tuna often swim below porpoises, which travel in groups near the surface. In the early 1960s, fishing vessels operating out of San Diego began setting their seine nets around the porpoises to get at the tuna. When the tuna were hauled in, hundreds of porpoises suffocated (Fig. 12.7). A 1972 estimate of these by-product kill-ings was 300,000 annually. The most affected species were the spotted and spinner porpoises and the common dolphin (Scheffer, 1977). Why did this rather clever fishing technique generate so much public outrage?

Porpoises, whales, sea otters, seals, and sea cows are mammals. Porpoises are often called dolphins, which can be confusing, as there is also a fish called a dolphin. To many people, the sim-ple fact that porpoises are mammals sets them above other sea creatures. In addition, scientific research on porpoises suggests that they are highly intelligent and possess a complex and subtle language. Thus, although tuna fish fill our stomachs, porpoises provide us with other, less tangible benefits. Many people think that it is wasteful and unethical to kill and discard all those porpoises.

Operators of the tuna seiners are not im-pressed with these arguments. The development of nylon seining nets had helped put the lan-guishing American tuna industry back into com-petition with other tuna sources (Orbach, 1977). When the Marine Mammal Protection Act was passed in 1972, it dictated that porpoise killing had to stop, and soon. From 1973 to 1977, the tuna fishers negotiated with the government, en-vironmentalists, lawyers, and biologists to decide on an allowable annual porpoise quota.

The 1977 quota of 59,050 porpoises was too low for the fishermen, who refused to leave port and threatened to sell their boats to foreign in-vestors. The Carter administration eventually re-sponded by supporting a congressional measure to raise that year's quota to 68,190. The eventual goal was to bring down the quotas, as new tech-niques and equipment were developed to aid in the reduction of porpoise mortality (Scheffer, 1977). From 1978 to 1980, the quotas were 52,000, 42,000, and 31,000. By 1984, the quota was reduced to 20,500. If the annual quota was exceeded for any of the protected porpoise spe-

JURISDICTION: WHO CONTROLS WHAT?

Given the difficulty of managing a common property resource such as whales or fish, it is important to understand where control of marine resources by a single nation stops and where international control begins. Diplomats and international law experts make a distinction between control of ocean space and control over the use of ocean space. Thus, international treaties recognize a 3- to 12-mile-wide (4.8 to 19.3 km) territorial sea along a nation's coastlines as the exclusive territory of that nation. Both ocean space (including bottom sediments) and the use of that space by fishing vessels, navy ships, and oil companies are controlled by the individual nation. Other types of jurisdiction or "ownership" are less clear. Many coastal nations claim control over all fishing resources within 200 miles (322 km) of shore. Yet national control over other activities in this 200-mile area, such as the transit of

military vessels of hostile nations, is not recognized by international law. In some cases, even particular types of fish, such as tuna, do not fall under the jurisdiction of individual coastal nations. In short, the definitions of jurisdiction and ownership of marine resources can vary with the distance from shore and the type of marine activity (Fig. 12.8).

There are three general types of jurisdiction over marine resources that are accepted by most of the world's nations. *Internal waters* include bays, estuaries, and rivers and are under the exclusive control of the coastal nation. In the United States, jurisdiction over the resources found in these internal waters is shared between federal and state governments. Most states and some municipalities control fishing and shellfishing, while the states and the federal government share jurisdiction over water pollution, dredging, and other activities.

The *territorial sea*, a band of open ocean

cies, then the yellowfin tuna fishing associated with that type of porpoise was closed for the year.

A study of incidental porpoise mortality since 1977 indicated that the mortality levels have indeed decreased (Lo, 1983). An important technique for reducing porpoise deaths is to lower the net, once the porpoise and tuna are fully encircled, to a level where the porpoise escape but the tuna do not. This requires considerable skill and experience, especially in heavy seas. The tuna industry has a vested interest in porpoise survival, in that porpoises lead them to tuna and are thus worth more alive than dead.

Public concern over the tuna/porpoise controversy was heightened in 1990. The United States government finally responded by mandating that foreign countries must reduce their kill rate to 1.5 times that of the United States or face an embargo on their catch. The need to enforce these limits for foreign fleets was because of the reflagging of American ships to foreign registries to avoid higher U.S. labor costs and regulations. In 1979, for example, there were 98 large tuna seiners in the United States and by 1989 this had dropped to 30. The public outcry was so great in

early 1990 that three of the leading tuna companies, Star Kist, Bumblebee, and Chicken of the Sea, were forced to no longer purchase tuna caught by seine nets or risk losing sales. To compensate, the companies added 1–3 cents to the price of a can of tuna and now declare it "dolphin free." To their credit, tuna companies are also marketing pet food as dolphin free as well. Since more than 90 percent of the tuna catch can be landed with alternative fishing methods, the industry felt that the public relations benefits of being dolphin free outweighed any loss in tuna catch by the seiners.

There is some irony to the fact that this innovative group of fishermen who developed the seine net were accused of cruelty and lack of concern, because recently the industry has gone to great lengths to return porpoises to the sea. Whether it was a matter of learning how to use new equipment or of heartlessly destroying a valued mammal for profit, these business people saw the situation in strict economic terms, whereas the public saw it in aesthetic and environmental terms. The two sides have been negotiating ever since, although now the public, and the porpoises, are on the winning side.

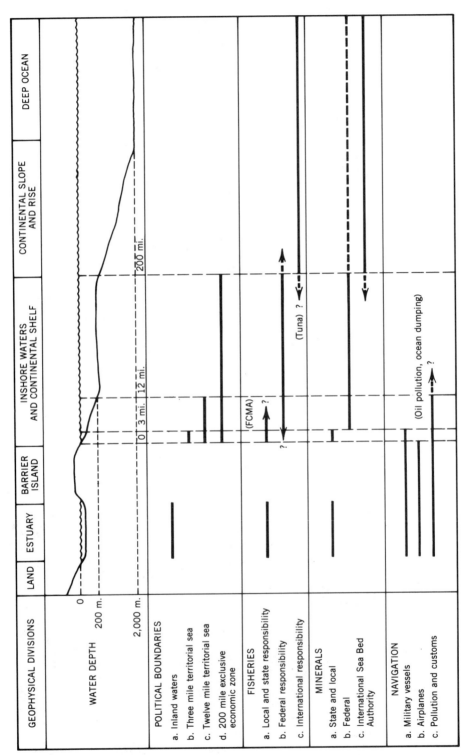

Figure 12.8 U.S. East Coast maritime boundaries. The United States claims jurisdiction over various portions of the sea for different purposes. Dashed lines indicate shared jurisdictions; question marks indicate disputed or ambiguous boundaries.

adjacent to the coast, is measured from a baseline on the shore out to a set distance. The United States currently claims a 3-mile-wide (4.8 km) zone. A few (Liberia, Somalia, Brazil, Argentina, Peru, Ecuador, and Uruguay) even claim a 200-mile-wide (322 km) territorial sea. A coastal nation controls all activities, such as fishing, within its territorial sea—except for the right of "innocent passage" by foreign vessels. A Japanese fishing boat can, for example, pass between the Aleutian Islands off Alaska, without permission from the state or federal government, but it cannot drop nets and proceed to fish. A foreign military vessel may also pass through territorial waters unhindered, as long as it remains outside the internal waters of the coastal nation. Curiously, the right of innocent passage through the territorial sea does not include aircraft. Foreign aircraft must seek permission to enter U.S. air space before moving within 3 miles (4.8 km) of shore. In the United States, the coastal states manage fisheries and oil drilling in the territorial sea, while the federal government patrols and protects it.

The third type of jurisdiction is the 200-mile-wide (322 km) exclusive economic zone that was created by the Law of the Sea Treaty. The *exclusive economic zone (EEZ)* is a special use area where activities such as fishing and oil drilling are controlled by the coastal nation, while other activities are not. In 1946 the United States claimed exclusive jurisdiction over its outer continental shelf, which extends out to a depth of about 660 feet (200 m) of water, to control oil and gas development. In 1976 the United States created a 200-mile-wide Fishery Conservation Zone, claiming control over all fish and shellfish except the highly migratory tuna. Many other nations subsequently adopted this idea and made similar claims. The Law of the Sea Treaty creates a single EEZ that includes fishing and all forms of mineral extraction, no matter what the water depth. Control over other activities in the EEZ is less clear. Some nations (including the United States) claim jurisdiction over ocean dumping and water pollution, and others (excluding the United States) claim jurisdiction over the movements of vessels and oil spills in this zone.

Finally, the *high seas* are those ocean areas that are beyond the jurisdiction of any individual nation (Fig. 12.6). Traditionally, the limits to activities on the high seas are set by international treaties, such as the *Law of the Sea*.

THE LAW OF THE SEA TREATY

There is a long history of confusion over who owns or controls the oceans. There are hundreds of conflicting territorial claims made by coastal nations, many of which either clash with or ignore the international treaties signed in 1958 on territorial seas and the outer continental shelf. There are over 90 independent nations in the world today that did not exist when the 1958 treaties were signed. Many of these nations are landlocked, underdeveloped, or both, and most are ex-colonies with boundaries and economies that were originally designed to benefit only the colonial power.

The combination of maritime boundary problems coupled with the desire of many newly independent countries to allocate or reallocate marine resources led to the negotiations over a new Law of the Sea Treaty. Negotiations started in 1974, with over 160 nations participating, and lasted until 1982, when a final version was approved. A total of 135 nations signed the treaty and are now in the process of ratifying the treaty. The United States refused to sign the treaty because of a disagreement over mining rights for deep-sea manganese nodules (see the following discussion). Other nonsignatory nations include Ecuador, Israel, Peru, the United Kingdom, and Venezuela.

What happens next? The Law of the Sea Treaty is clearly the most far-reaching international agreement ever governing marine resources, yet one of the world's foremost maritime powers has thus far refused to sign or ratify it. The United States claims control over approximately 20 percent of the world's marine fish and shellfish and is one of the world's largest markets for ocean-borne commerce. Can the Law of the Sea Treaty survive without America as an active participant? Can U.S. economic and national defense interests be preserved without signing the treaty? A brief overview of the key elements of the treaty will illustrate the potential conflicts and dilemmas that the United States faces by its refusal to sign.

The Law of the Sea Treaty clarifies boundary claims by establishing internationally agreed-upon limits on the territorial sea, continental shelf, and exclusive economic zone. It establishes a universal 200-mile-wide (322 km) exclusive economic zone, giving the coastal nation exclusive control over exploitable resources, such as fish, oil, and gas. It also preserves the right of free navigation through this zone by foreign ships, airplanes, and submarines.

A universal 12-mile-wide (19.3 km) territorial sea would effectively close off 175 straits or narrow passages through which the majority of shipping travels. The most important of these are the straits of Gibraltar, Dover, Hormuz, and Malacca. The Strait of Gibraltar is 8 nautical miles (15 km) wide and is the major point of access to the Mediterranean Sea. The Dover Strait is the easternmost part of the English Channel and is 17.5 nautical miles (32 km) wide. Virtually all oil imported into northern Europe by ship passes through this narrow portion of the English Channel. The Strait of Hormuz, while only 20.7 nautical miles (38 km) wide, is perhaps the most important in the world. It is located between Iran and Oman in the Persian Gulf. All the oil transported by ship from the Middle East must pass through this vital and strategic strait. The Straits of Malacca (8.4 nautical miles or 16 km wide) lies between the Malay Peninsula and the island of Sumatra. Ship traffic between the Indian and Pacific oceans must use either this strait or others in Indonesian waters. All of Japan's imported oil from the Middle East traverses this strait.

The rights of neighboring nations to regulate traffic, including aircraft, through straits have never been clear. At the insistence of the United States and other nations, the Law of the Sea Treaty creates an internationally recognized right of "transit passage" through straits, permitting unimpeded access as long as ships and aircraft comply with minimal navigational rules. This right-of-transit passage is one of the most significant provisions of the treaty. The industrial nations with large navies insisted on this provision, at the expense of less developed countries, which border most of the straits in question.

The treaty also provides for the regulation of pollution and conservation of living resources, including increased protection of marine mammals. Finally, the treaty allows for the exploitation of deep-seabed minerals but states that these resources constitute the common heritage of humankind. Although the developed nations possess the technology and knowledge of deep-seabed mining, the fruits of this expertise would have to be shared by all nations. In other words, those developed nations would not have exclusive right to the resources, even if they were the only ones with the technology and knowledge to get to them. The United States has refused to sign this treaty because of the deep-seabed mining provisions, which it feels are contrary to the interests and security of all industrialized nations (Kimball, 1983).

DESTROYING MARINE RESOURCES: THE OCEAN AS POLLUTION SINK

The oceans are so large that we often think of them as a place where we can discard the unwanted by-products of civilization. This attitude runs the gamut from passively allowing pollutants in streams and rivers to make their way to the ocean to actively and deliberately burying wastes in the ocean. There are two major sources of marine pollution: accidental oil and hazardous materials spills and ocean dumping.

OIL SPILLS

There have been many major transportation accidents involving oil tankers (Fig. 12.9). The most famous of these include the wrecks of the *Torrey Canyon,* which spilled 700,000 barrels (95,200 tonnes) of oil off the southern coast of England in 1967; the *Argo Merchant,* which spilled 207,200 barrels (28,179 tonnes) off the coast of Massachusetts near Nantucket Island in 1976; the *Amoco Cadiz,* losing 1,628,000 barrels (221,410 tonnes) off the French coast in the English Channel in 1978; the collision in 1979 of the *Atlantic Empress* and the *Aegean Capitan* in the Caribbean, spilling over 1,034,000 barrels (141,071 tonnes) and the recent wreck of the *Exxon Valdez* in 1989, spilling 260,000 barrels (35,374 tonnes) of oil into

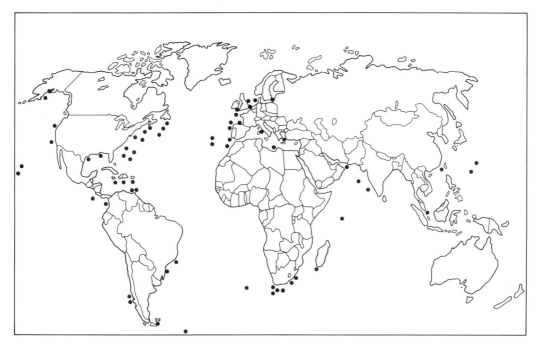

Figure 12.9 Major tanker oil spills, 1962–1989. Each dot represents a spill of over 5000 tons.

Prince William Sound in Alaska (Fig. 12.10). The resulting pollution of the ocean from these spills, including land-based effects, was quite extensive (Fairhall and Jordan, 1980; Winslow, 1978; *Audubon,* 1989).

Tanker accidents account for specific pollution episodes, yet only 12 percent of the total world input of petroleum into the marine environment is a result of these accidents (Farrington, 1985). Oil spills also occur in ports and harbors, from stationary offshore drilling platforms, and through runoff from land-based facilities. In the United States alone there were 10,990 accidents in 1985 in marine waters with 24 million gallons (571,000 barrels) of oil spilled (CEQ, 1988). The majority of these were in inland waters, specifically river channels and ports and harbors (Fig. 12.11). Offshore oil exploration and drilling accounts for less than 5 percent of the total world's oil pollution of the oceans, although at times the local impacts are quite severe. During 1979–1980, over 2.7 million barrels (nearly 367,000 tonnes) of crude oil were spilled in the Gulf of Mexico as a result of the blowout of IXTOC-1, a Mexican-owned oil well in the Bay of Campeche (CEQ, 1981b). The drifting oil spill caused an international dispute when it washed ashore on beaches in Texas, de-

Figure 12.10 Oil spills. Oil spilling from the Exxon Valdez (at left); unspilled oil is being transferred to the ship (at right).

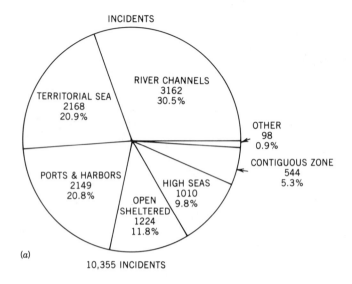

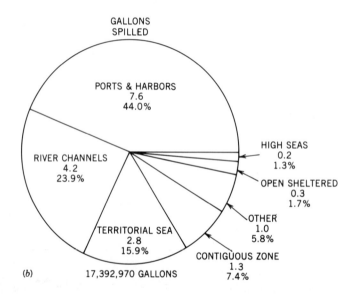

Figure 12.11   Oil spills in U.S. waters. Oil pollution incidents in U.S. waters by location (*a*) and millions of gallons spilled (*b*) for 1984. Although only about 20% of spills occur in ports and harbors, these represent 44% of the oil spilled. (*Source:* U.S. Coast Guard, 1984.)

stroying wildlife and habitat and severely affecting recreational and fishing industries in the region.

HAZARDOUS MATERIALS SPILLS

Transportation of hazardous materials on the high seas is increasing as developed nations seek new disposal options for the by-products of their industrialization. Often, barges of hazardous waste go from port to port seeking entry only to be turned back by the recipient country (see Issue 12–3).

In the United States the number of hazardous materials spills in marine waters has been increasing (Fig. 12.12), although the quantity spilled has been highly variable. In 1975, for example, there were 6 spills involving 51,600 pounds (23.4 metric tons) of materials. In 1984, this number had increased to 196 with more than 3.8 million pounds (1727 metric tons) of materials. Although the majority of

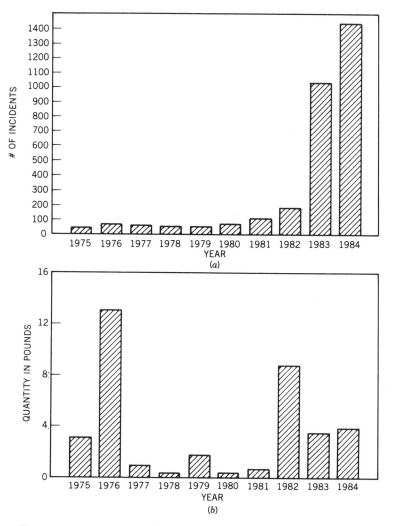

Figure 12.12   Trends (1975–1984) in incidents and quantity of hazardous materials and other substances spilled. The quantity spilled (*b*) is variable from year to year. The number of reported incidents (*a*), on the other hand, has greatly increased. (*Source:* U.S. Coast Guard, 1984.)

these incidents (33 percent) occurred in river channels, the amount spilled in the territorial sea is more significant. In fact, over 90 percent of the 3.8 million pounds of hazardous substances spilled in 1984 were in territorial waters (shoreward to 3 miles or 4.8 km) (U.S. Coast Guard, 1984).

OCEAN DUMPING

Ocean dumping is one of the major contributors to ocean pollution. Ocean dumping includes the disposal of sewage sludge, industrial and solid waste, explosives, demolition

debris, radioactive materials, and dredge spoils (Fig. 12.13).

During the 1960s nearly 8.2 million tons (7.4 million tonnes) of debris were dumped annually into U.S. coastal waters (CEQ, 1982). In addition, 60.5 million tons (54.9 million tonnes) of dredged material were dumped during this time. By 1985, 176 million tons (160 million tonnes) of dredged material were being dumped in coastal waters with an additional 7.4 million tons (6.7 million tonnes) of sewage sludge and industrial waste (U.S. Congress, 1987). By 1986, the amount of sewage sludge was 8.7 million tons (7.9 million tonnes) (U.S.

Figure 12.13 A garbage barge in New York harbor, target of a Greenpeace protest.

ISSUE 12–3   The Karin B.: A Twentieth Century Flying Dutchman

The *Flying Dutchman* was a mythical ship that haunted the waters around the Cape of Good Hope, its appearance a warning of impending disaster. According to the legend, the ship's captain was condemned to sail the waters until Doomsday, unable to make it to port because of blasphemy. As the ship sails unendingly without helmsman, the captain plays dice with the Devil for possession of his soul. The *Flying Dutchman* theme has been used in folklore and literature for centuries in sea chanteys, poetry (most notably by John Boyle O'Reilly), and short stories (Washington Irving's "Rip Van Winkle and the Flying Dutchman"). The legend also provided the basis for Wagner's opera *Der fliegende Höllander.*

The *Flying Dutchman* has many parallels with a modern ship called the *Karin B.* The *Karin B.*, a ship with West German registry, began its ill-fated voyage in June 1988 from Livorno, Italy. Its cargo was 210,000 tons (190,890 tonnes) of toxic waste from two Italian chemical companies and other unknown sources. The ship was destined for Koko, Nigeria, where its cargo was to be deposited in a landfill near a remote Nigerian village. After protests by environmental groups, the Nigerian government refused the cargo and the ship was sent away. The *Karin B.* then docked at Las Palmas in the Canary Islands for a few weeks, moved on to Cadiz, Spain, and then to Plymouth, England, and after a week, the ship sailed to France. At each port, the consignment was refused, and local environmental-ists were outraged. Eventually, the ship returned to Livorno, where its journey had begun four months earlier.

The saga of the *Karin B.* is not unique. Tons of toxic waste are routinely shipped on the high seas. In Western Europe, 22 million tons (20 million tonnes) of hazardous waste are generated every year, with about one-third of it exported primarily to Eastern Europe and Africa. Since landfills are filling up in many of these countries and the costs of incineration are high ($2000 per ton), many of the hazardous waste producers have begun actively exporting the waste to lesser developed countries.

There are two primary reasons for this. As the environmental laws become more stringent in the United States and Western Europe, it is increasingly difficult to find acceptable sites for hazardous waste disposal. It is also cheaper to ship the waste abroad ($20 per ton) than to incinerate locally. The developing countries find it difficult to resist the economic benefits of receiving the waste. If they are paid $20 million for the consignment, for example, and the annual operating budget for the entire country is $40 million, this type of proposition is very appealing, particularly if a debt-burdened host country is not completely informed of the degree of toxicity of the waste. The exporting of hazardous waste from the industrialized nations to the developing world (Africa and Eastern Europe in particular) has become an international controversy.

EPA, 1988). The quantity of municipal sewage sludge dumped in marine waters has increased during the last decade while industrial waste dumping has decreased.

Dredged material, by weight the most significant material currently being dumped in the oceans, accounts for over 90 percent of the waste disposed of in the marine environment. This material comes from the removal of bottom sediments from rivers, harbors, and intercoastal waterways to allow navigation in these water courses. Uncontaminated sediment (or spoil) poses little environmental risk. In the United States, dredged material was traditionally dumped in estuaries and on tidal wetlands. Concern over protecting these productive areas has led to a shift to near-shore and continental shelf dumping of dredged materials, although this varies by region (Table 12.5).

Contaminated sediment that is loaded with toxic materials, such as cadmium, lead, copper, and polychlorinated biphenyls (PCBs), poses another problem. Bottom sediments in many ports and rivers contain high levels of toxic pollutants left over from decades of uncontrolled dumping and pollution. These sediments are usually immobile if undisturbed, but during dredging activities they become suspended in the water. The cost of disposing of such polluted sediments on land is significantly greater than ocean disposal, yet scientific evidence on the safety of various ocean disposal techniques is lacking.

In some parts of the world, sewage sludge

The problems have become so complex that the Organization for Economic Cooperation and Development (OECD) has developed a number of directives for transboundary shipments of hazardous waste. Italy was so embarrassed by the *Karin B.* affair that it unilaterally banned the export of hazardous waste to Third World nations. A European Community (EC) directive allows exports of waste only if the receiving country agrees to accept the waste and if it has the means to dispose of the waste properly. Greece, Belgium, and Denmark enacted the directive immediately. Only after the *Karin B.* tried to unload its cargo in Plymouth, England, did the United Kingdom agree to the directive.

In the United States, the EPA is notified of all transboundary shipments of hazardous waste, and there is also a bilateral agreement with a host country to ensure the safe handling of the waste. Most of the United States hazardous waste that is exported goes to Canada. However, the United States is also guilty of dumping in the Third World. The *Khian Sea* freighter carried 15,000 tons (13,635 tonnes) of toxic ash from Philadelphia's municipal incinerators for two years, going from port to port before finally being illegally dumped in Haiti in 1988.

Because many of the shippers are only interested in making a quick dollar, there is never any guarantee that the waste will end up at its destination. For example, it may be simply dumped into the deep ocean once the ship is in international waters, or dropped in another country with fewer environmental controls. More than 100 countries have signed a 1989 treaty, The Basel Convention on the Control of Transboundary Movements of Hazardous Waste and Their Disposal. The treaty calls for industrial countries to reduce the amount of hazardous waste generated (waste minimization) and to ensure proper packaging and labeling of the waste. It also calls on countries to ensure the safe disposal of any hazardous material, and it prohibits the shipment of hazardous waste to nations who ban it. Radioactive waste is not included in the treaty provisions.

African countries in particular are concerned about the treaty's ramifications and the lack of any enforcement of its provisions. In other words, the treaty is not strong enough to deter nations with stricter environmental statutes from dumping on those with less-stringent ones. The industrialized countries are also concerned, for different reasons, and thus cautious. While agreeing in principle, many nations want to see how the treaty provisions will be implemented before they officially ratify it. Environmentalists are also displeased and believe that the treaty legitimizes commerce in toxic substances and toxic terror (O'Sullivan, 1988; Greenhouse, 1989). Only time will tell. Meanwhile the modern-day equivalents of the *Flying Dutchman* continue to haunt the high seas.

TABLE 12.5   Ocean Dumping

	North Pacific	South Pacific	Gulf Coast	South Atlantic	North Atlantic	Total
Number of municipal dischargers	99	63	113	59	244	578
Number of industrial dischargers	184	112	347	113	576	1332
Quantity dredged (million metric tons/year)	15.7	15.1	118.6	18.2	12.5	180.1
Estuaries	5.4	8.4	91.3	6.1	4.0	115.2
0–3 miles	10.0	4.3	16.4	1.5	2.2	34.4
3 miles plus	0.3	2.4	10.9	10.6	6.3	30.5
Sewage effluent (1982, million gallons/day)	383	1282	522	308	4150	6645

Source: U.S. Congress (1987).

and industrial wastes are a major source of contaminants in the marine environment. Although great efforts have been made to upgrade sewage treatment plants onshore to reduce water pollution, the result has been a higher volume of sewage sludge that needs disposal. In 1972 the U.S. Congress passed the Marine Protection, Research, and Sanctuaries Act, which, among other things, requires a permit for ocean dumping (see the next section). In 1977 the act was amended to encourage land disposal of sewage sludge after December 31, 1981. Ocean disposal of sewage sludge has therefore declined throughout the United States, with the exception of the New York Bight (Swanson and Devine, 1982; Squires, 1983). Boston and Los Angeles are the only other two metropolitan areas to dump sewage in the ocean, although their sludge is partially treated prior to disposal.

The problem of municipal sewage sludge is greatest in the North Atlantic region. New York City, parts of Nassau and Westchester counties, New York, and parts of New Jersey have been routinely dumping sewage sludge 12 miles (19 km) off Sandy Hook at the entrance to New York Harbor in the New York Bight Apex dumpsites (Fig. 12.14). Scientists have identified a 20-square-mile (32 km²) area, locally known as the "dead zone," where there is little or no marine life. A total of 2.4 billion gallons (9 billion liters) of raw and

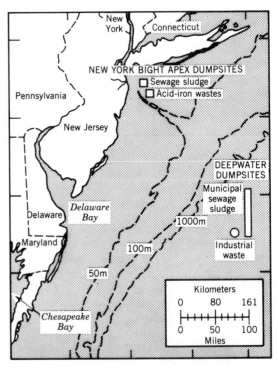

Figure 12.14   Location of municipal sewage sludge and industrial waste dumpsites in the mid-Atlantic Ocean. The New York Bight Apex sites are now closed, but the deepwater sites are still active. (*Source:* U.S. Congress, 1987.)

treated sewage and industrial waste were discharged into the New York Bight daily (Carney, 1984). In 1985, for example, this site (in 80 feet or 24 m of water) received several billion gallons of raw sewage, 7 million tonnes of wet sludge, and 8 million tonnes of dredged materials (U.S. Congress, 1987).

In 1984, the U.S. Environmental Protection Agency ordered New York City and other municipalities to move the dump site 106 miles (171 km) offshore to deep water (7380–9020 feet or 2250–2750 m) beyond the edge of the outer continental shelf (Fig. 12.12). A deepwater industrial dump site is also located in this area. By 1987, New York City was still utilizing the 12-mile site despite its prohibition by the newly amended Clean Water Act, which banned sludge dumping in the New York Bight by December 15, 1987. Fees for ocean dumping continue to rise, going from $200 per ton in 1989 to $400 per ton in 1992 (U.S. Congress, 1987). This does not compare favorably with land disposal (about $20 per ton) or incineration (about $34 per ton).

The economics of sludge disposal forced New York City in 1989 to reach an agreement with the EPA to permanently phase out ocean dumping, although it will continue to dump its 5 million tons (4.5 million tonnes) of waste in the deep-water site until 1991. The costs of ocean disposal coupled with heavy fines from the EPA for not meeting deadlines finally persuaded the city to develop long-term solutions to the sludge problem. The alternative solutions will cost about $700 million and will surely be passed on to the consumer in the form of higher fees for water and sewage for city residents (Lee, 1989). New York City, however, finds these costs tolerable, considering that if they continue to dump until the year 2000, they will be liable for over $1.3 billion in fees and fines for the privilege of dumping their sewage at sea (U.S. Congress, 1987).

Non-point pollution is also a contributor to marine pollution. In coastal areas, the problem results from septic tanks and combined sewer/stormwater systems. Although non-point sources are difficult to measure, officials estimate that they are an even greater threat to the marine environment than are point sources.

Finally, there is one other main contribu-

tor to the pollution of marine waters. The accumulation of nonbiodegradable plastics in the oceans has increased during the last two decades. Originating from land-based activities as well as trash thrown overboard from ships, plastics float on the ocean's surface for decades. The primary effect of plastic is on marine animals. It has been estimated that 100,000 marine mammals die each year by either ingesting the plastic or becoming entangled in it (U.S. Congress, 1987). Many more seabirds meet their fate in this way. The plastic pollution problem of the world's oceans has now become a global concern (Wilber, 1987).

PROTECTING MARINE ECOSYSTEMS

POLLUTION AT SEA

At the national level, there are two primary laws that govern pollution and wastes in the marine environment. The Water Quality Act of 1987 (see Chapter 11) was instrumental in banning sludge dumping in the New York Bight by 1987. The act also provided construction grants for sewage treatment plants and combined sewer/stormwater overflow systems. In addition, the act provided funds for the development of management programs for nonpoint source pollution and the control of toxic pollutants.

The Marine Protection, Research, and Sanctuaries Act (MPRSA) was originally passed in 1972 and was designed to (1) regulate the disposal (dumping and pipeline discharge) of wastes into the marine environment and (2) control the level of pollution in these waters. Marine waters are defined as those waters seaward of the territorial sea (3 miles or 4.8 km). The act restricts the transportation and dumping of wastes in the open ocean and regulates the dumping and discharge of solid waste, sludge, industrial waste, dredged materials, radioactive waste, and biological and chemical warfare agents in marine waters. The act was amended and reauthorized in 1985 and became known as the Ocean Dumping Act.

Because of their common property nature, international efforts to control pollution at sea are also important. The London Dumping Convention of 1972 is the primary international treaty on marine waste disposal and, more importantly, the only one to which the United States is signatory. The treaty has been ratified by 61 nations and prohibits the dumping of "black-listed" substances (organohalogens, mercury, cadmium, plastics, oils, radioactive materials, and biological and chemical warfare agents) in waters seaward of the inner boundary of the territorial sea. The Oslo Convention of 1974 regulates the dumping and incineration of wastes by most European countries, and this treaty applies to Arctic, northern Atlantic, and North Sea waters. Finally, the International Convention for the Prevention of Pollution from Ships 1973, 1978 (referred to as MARPOL 73/78) attempts to reduce pollution from ships, including oil, chemicals, and plastics.

MARINE SANCTUARIES

The Marine Protection, Research, and Sanctuaries Act (1972) also had some preservation elements as well. It designated marine sanctuaries in the oceans and Great Lakes with the intent to preserve or restore these areas for their conservation, recreation, ecological, or aesthetic value. The National Marine Sanctuary Program (administered by the National Oceanic and Atmospheric Administration) was established to designate and manage nationally significant marine areas. Such areas would be classified based on specific criteria, including the representativeness of the marine ecosystems, research potential, recreational or aesthetic values, or uniqueness (historical, geological, ecological, or oceanographic). Sanctuaries range in size from 1 square mile to over 1252 square nautical miles. Although they are managed under multiple-use guidelines, human use is balanced with the maintenance of the health and viability of the ecosystem. The first two sanctuaries included in the program in 1975 were the *U.S.S. Monitor* (off the coast of North Carolina) and Key Largo (off the Florida Keys). The act was amended in 1984, and by 1990, ten units were included in the sanctuary program (Table 12.6).

At the international level, marine protection programs take many forms. There are

TABLE 12.6 Marine Sanctuaries in the United States

Name/Location	Size (square miles)	Criteria for Designation
U.S.S. Monitor Southeast of Cape Hatteras, N.C.	1.0	Historical protection for Civil War vessel
Key Largo South of Miami, FL	100.0	Coral reef and associated reef species
Channel Islands Santa Barbara, CA	1252.0	Habitat protection for marine mammals and seabirds
Looe Key East of Florida Keys, FL	5.0	Submerged Florida reef
Gray's Reef East of Sapelo Island, GA	17.0	Live bottom coral area with associated reef species
Gulf of the Farallones Northwest of San Francisco, CA	948.0	Habitat protection for marine mammals and seabirds
Fagatele Bay Near Tutuila Island, American Samoa	0.25	Deep-water coral terrace, formations unique to Pacific high islands
Cordell Bank West of San Francisco, CA	101.0	Submerged mountaintop, large array of marine species
Flower Garden Banks Southwest of Galveston, TX	175.0	Coral reef with associated reef species
Norfolk Canyon Off VA coast	na[a]	Deep-water submarine canyon with large tree corals

Sources: Council on Environmental Quality (1986); Foster and Archer (1988).
[a] na = not available.

about 1000 coastal and marine protected areas in over 87 countries (World Resources Institute, 1989). The International Union for the Conservation of Nature drafted policy guidelines in 1988 for setting up marine protection programs. As is the case with many resources, protection is determined by the individual country. Some areas are protected in parklike settings where wildlife protection and tourism are stated management objectives, and other marine parks are more preserve-oriented with limited or restricted human use. Australia's Great Barrier Reef Marine Park is the best example of a protected marine resource. It was established in 1975, and the governing authority has the right to regulate and prohibit activities inside the park as well as those activities outside the park that may pollute or otherwise harm the reef ecosystem. The primary purpose of the park is to promote the human use of the park in a manner consistent with the preservation of the ecosystem.

MARINE MAMMAL/ENDANGERED SPECIES PROTECTION

As we have seen, marine mammals are highly mobile species whose territory and range often extend beyond national boundaries, which complicates their management and ultimately their protection. In the United States, marine mammals are protected under the Marine Mammal Protection Act, which was passed in 1972. This legislation is similar to the Endangered Species Act (see Chapter 17) but applies only to marine species. The act places a moratorium on harvesting of these animals in U.S. territorial waters and prohibits the import of animals or animal products except for public display or scientific purposes. Currently, sixteen mammals are listed as endangered and three as threatened.

Multinational agreements on marine mammal protection are limited, however. Over 92 countries have some type of law regarding marine mammals, but only three (New Zealand, the United States, and the Republic of the Seychelles) has comprehensive protection of marine mammals. The Republic of the Seychelles have gone so far as to declare itself a marine mammal sanctuary and thus can legally impose a sentence of up to five years in prison on anyone who kills or harasses a marine mammal. The IWC still has jurisdiction over whaling, with mixed results as we saw earlier in this chapter. Walruses and seals are protected by national and regional treaties, although no comprehensive international agreement exists at this time.

SUMMARY

As a common property resource, the ocean is accessible to all nations. Responsibility for allocation and management of the ocean's vast resources is clouded by lack of certainty surrounding ownership of the resource. International efforts, such as the IWC and the Law of the Sea Treaty, are important steps in recognizing this dilemma and in appreciating the value and wisdom of conserving this resource.

Until recently, the oceans were thought of in superlative terms, capable of providing food, transport, protection, recreation, solitude, and dumping grounds in an apparently unlimited supply. As with other once-"infinite" natural resources, however, the oceans are now an increasingly regulated part of the global village. Marine science research indicates that, like the atmosphere above, the oceans are integrative and interactive: pollutants travel worldwide and the effects of overfishing can be global. However, marine scientists would also be quick to admit that we still have very little understanding of how the oceans operate and their role in climate change. Hence, there is a two-sided battle between, on the one hand, the conservation and political leaders of the world's wealthy nations, who call for research and ocean-use restrictions; and, on the other hand, the emerging countries of the world who are trying to stake a claim to their share of the last great common property resource.

REFERENCES AND ADDITIONAL READING

Audubon. 1989. Wreck of the Exxon Valdez (special issue). *Audubon* 91(5): 74–111.

Bean, M. J. 1977. *The Evolution of National Wildlife Law.* Washington, DC: Council on Environmental Quality.

Brock, R. G. 1984. El Niño and world climate: Piecing together the puzzle. *Environment* 26(3): 14–20,37–39.

Brower, K. 1989. The destruction of the dolphins. *The Atlantic Monthly* 263(1): 35–58.

Brownell, R. L., Jr., K. Ralls, and W. F. Perrin. 1989. The plight of the "forgotten" whales. *Oceanus* 32(1): 5–12.

Carney, L. H. 1984. Ocean dumping: No guidelines. *The New York Times*, May 20, New Jersey Weekly, pp. A1, A4.

Council on Environmental Quality. 1981a. *Environmental Trends*. Washington, DC: U.S. Government Printing Office.

———. 1981b. *The Global 2000 Report to the President*. New York: Penguin Books.

———. 1982. *Environmental Quality 1982, 13th Annual Report*. Washington, DC: U.S. Government Printing Office.

———. 1986. *Environmental Quality, 17th Annual Report*. Washington, DC: U.S. Government Printing Office.

———. 1988. *Environmental Quality, 18th and 19th Annual Reports*. Washingtron, DC: U.S. Government Printing Office.

———. 1989. *Environmental Trends*. Washington, DC: U.S. Government Printing Office.

Fairhall, D. and P. Jordan. 1980. *The Wreck of the Amoco Cadiz*. New York: Stein & Day.

Farrington, J. W. 1985. Oil pollution: A decade of research and monitoring. *Oceanus* 28(3): 3–12.

Food and Agricultural Organization. 1987. *Yearbook of Fishery Statistics: Vol. 52, Catches and Landings; Vol. 53, Fishery Commodities*. Rome: U.N., Food and Agricultural Organization.

Foster, N. M., and J. H. Archer. 1988. The National Marine Sanctuary Program: Policy, education, and research. *Oceanus* 31(1): 5–17.

Greenhouse, S. 1988. Europe's failing effort to exile toxic trash. *The New York Times*, October 16, p. E6.

———. 1989. UN conference supports curbs on exporting of hazardous waste. *The New York Times*, March 23, p. A1.

Gross, M. G. 1971. *Oceanography*, 2nd ed. Columbus, Ohio: Merrill.

Halbouty, M. T. 1982. Petroleum still leader in energy race. *Offshore* 42(7): 49–52.

Heath, G. R. 1982. Manganese nodules: Unanswered questions. *Oceanus* 25(3): 37–41.

Kimball, L. 1983. The Law of the Sea—On the shoals. *Environment* 25(9): 14–20,41–44.

———. 1988. The Antarctic Treaty System. *Oceanus* 31(2): 14–19.

Knecht, R. W. 1982. Deep ocean mining. *Oceanus* 25(3): 3–11.

Lee, F. R. 1989. New York says it will end sea dumping. *The New York Times*, June 24, p. 25.

Leetmaa, A. 1989. The interplay of El Niño and La Niña. *Oceanus* 32(2): 30–35.

Lemonick, M.D. 1990. Antarctica. *Time*, January 15, pp. 56–62.

Lo, N. C. H. 1983. Sample size for estimating dolphin mortality associated with the tuna fishery. *J. Wildlife Management* 47(2): 413–421.

The New York Times. 1980. State of the Union Message, Ronald Reagan, January 24, p. A12.

Odum, E. P. 1971. *Fundamentals of Ecology*. Philadelphia: Saunders.

Orbach, M. K. 1977. *Hunters, Seamen, and Entrepreneurs: The Tuna Seinermen of San Diego*. Berkeley: University of California Press.

O'Sullivan, D.A. 1988. UN Environment Program targets issue of hazardous waste exports. *Chemical and Engineering News*, September 16, pp. 24–27.

Rasmusson, E. M., and J. M. Hall. 1983. El Niño: The great equatorial Pacific Ocean warming event of 1982–1983. *Weatherwise*, August, pp. 166–175.

Scheffer, V. B. 1977. The magnificent mammals: Best 13 most. *Environment* 19(7): 16–20,25–26.

Shabecoff, P. 1989. Huge drifting nets raise fears for an ocean's fish. *The New York Times*, March 21, p. C1.

Squires, D. F. 1983. *The Ocean Dumping Quandary: Waste Disposal in the New York Bight*. Albany: SUNY Press.

Sugden, D. 1982. *Arctic and Antarctic: A Modern Geographical Synthesis*. Totowa, NJ: Barnes & Noble Books.

Swanson, R. L. and C. J. Sinderman. 1979. *Oxygen Depletion and Associated Benthic Mortalities in New York Bight, 1976*. NOAA Professional Paper 11. Washington, DC: U.S. Department of Commerce.

Swanson, R. L., and M. Devine. 1982. Ocean dumping policy. *Environment* 24(5): 14–20.

U.S. Coast Guard. 1984. *Polluting Incidents in and around U.S. Waters 1983 and 1984*. Washington, DC: U.S. Government Printing Office.

U.S. Congress. Office of Technology Assessment. 1987. *Wastes in Marine Environments*. OTA-0-334. Washington, DC: U.S. Government Printing Office.

U.S. Department of Commerce, National Oceanic and Atmospheric Administration, National Marine Fisheries Service. 1985. *Annual Report 1984/85 Marine Mammal Protection Act of 1987.* Washington, DC: U.S. Government Printing Office.

U.S. Environmental Protection Agency. 1988. *Environmental Progress and Challenges: EPA's Update.* EPA 230-07-88-033. Washington, DC: U.S. Government Printing Office.

Wilber, R. J. 1987. Plastic in the North Atlantic. *Oceanus* 30(3): 61–68.

Winslow, R. 1978. *Hard Aground. The Story of the Argo Merchant Oil Spill.* New York: Norton.

World Resources Institute. 1988. *World Resources 1988–89.* New York: Basic Books.

TERMS TO KNOW

Anadromous Fish
Catadromous Fish
Common Property Resource
Continental Shelf
Deep Ocean
Dissolved Oxygen
El Niño/La Niña
Estuary
Euphotic Zone
Exclusive Economic Zone (EEZ)
Halocline
High Seas
Internal Waters
International Whaling Commission (IWC)
Law of the Sea Treaty (UNCLOS III)
Salinity
Stratification
Stratified Estuary
Territorial Sea
Thermocline
Upwelling

STUDY QUESTIONS

1. What is the importance of estuaries to marine fisheries?
2. What are some of the major problems in estimating maximum sustainable yield for a given fishery?
3. Describe some of the major achievements and failures of the International Whaling Commission.
4. Why does the United States refuse to sign the Law of the Sea Treaty?
5. What control does a coastal nation commonly exercise over its internal waters, territorial sea, exclusive economic zone, and the high seas?
6. What waste materials are commonly dumped in the oceans?
7. How effective is the protection provided, internationally and in the United States, for marine mammals?

13

The Air Resource and Urban Air Quality

INTRODUCTION

Although air quality may appear to be a recent issue to many people, some parts of the United States and Europe have been plagued with air pollution problems since the Industrial Revolution. Air pollution is a significant health hazard; acute episodes can cause death while lower, prolonged pollution levels also adversely affect health (National Research Council, 1979; Goldsmith and Friberg, 1977; Lave and Seskin, 1977). Some of the more prolonged air pollution episodes can even be classified as disasters. For example, 20 people died in Donora, Pennsylvania, in 1948, and 4700 people lost their lives in London, England, in 1952 due to thick smog (Elsom, 1987). More recently, nearly 6000 people were treated for "smog poisoning" in Tokyo during a 1970 oxidant and sulfate episode (Goldsmith and Friberg, 1977, p. 476). All of these disasters were the result of a combination of meteorological conditions and excessive emissions of sulfur from coal burning. The situation today is not so dramatic, yet in some parts of the world we find that major pollution episodes require both industry and individuals to curtail their activities on a fairly regular basis.

On a global level, emissions of traditional air pollutants (sulfur dioxide and particulates) continue to rise, particularly in developing countries. Air pollution in many of the world's cities chronically plagues local residents from Auckland to Zagreb. On the basis of one estimate, Shenyang and Xian, in the People's Republic of China, have the highest concentrations of sulfur dioxide and particulates,

respectively, anywhere in the world (World Resources Institute, 1987). More recently, parts of Eastern Europe, particularly Copsa Mica, Romania (Fig. 13.1), and parts of East Germany, Poland, and Czechoslovakia, now head the list of the world's most air polluted regions. Central Europe's air pollution is more dangerous and more widespread than in any other industrialized nation. The scale of pollution is also greater than in developing countries who simply do not have as much industry nor industry that is so geographically concentrated. Mexico City, however, still retains its title as the world's worst air polluted city. Excessive amounts of ozone, lead, and other contaminants spew forth daily from the city's 2.8 million vehicles and 36,000 factories, most with no pollution control equipment (Rohter, 1989). In addition, emissions of carbon monoxide and other so-called greenhouse gases have far-reaching regional and global consequences.

AIR POLLUTION METEOROLOGY

COMPOSITION AND STRUCTURE OF THE ATMOSPHERE

The atmosphere is divided into a number of layers, based on temperature and gaseous content. The *homosphere*, or lower atmosphere, extends from sea level to an altitude of 50 miles (80 km) (Fig. 13.2). It is called the homosphere because the gases are perfectly diffused, so that they act as a single gas. These gases include nitrogen (78 percent), oxygen (21 percent), carbon dioxide (0.03 percent),

Figure 13.1 Copsa Mica, Romania, a city where industrial air pollution contributes to an exceptionally high death rate.

and inert gases, such as argon, neon, helium, and krypton (less than 1 percent).

The homosphere is further divided into the troposphere, stratosphere, and mesosphere. The *troposphere* is the layer in which humans live and extends from sea level to approximately 8—9 miles (13–14 km). In this layer, temperature steadily decreases with altitude, at an average rate of 3.5°F/1000 feet (6.4°C/km). This rate is called the *environmental lapse rate*.

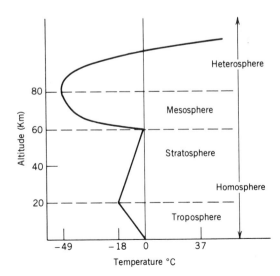

Figure 13.2 Temperature variation with altitude in the atmosphere. Most pollution is found in the troposphere, but some pollutants are carried to the stratosphere.

The next layer is the *stratosphere*. Air temperatures are essentially constant in this layer and then gradually increase with altitude until they reach 32°F (0°C) at an altitude of about 30 miles (50 km). The protective ozone (O_3) layer is located in the stratosphere; this layer serves as a shield in protecting the earth's surface and the troposphere from harmful ultraviolet radiation.

The third layer of the homosphere is the *mesosphere*. Here, temperatures decrease with altitude, reaching a low of −120°F (−83°C) at approximately 50 miles (80 km) altitude.

Air pollutants are not confined to the lower parts of the troposphere. Certain concentrations of contaminants may have disastrous effects at higher altitudes by inducing global changes in climate. Similarly, ozone is considered a pollutant in the troposphere but becomes an essential gas and necessary to protect human health in the stratosphere.

ROLE OF METEOROLOGY AND TOPOGRAPHY

Air pollution problems are the result of two factors: excessive emissions of pollutants and insufficient atmospheric dispersal. The first factor is the reason most cities have pollution problems and most rural areas do not. The second explains much of the variation in pollution problems from one city to another and why some very small cities have pollution problems as severe as those in major metropolitan regions.

Atmospheric dispersal of pollutants depends on air motion, both horizontal and vertical. Horizontal movements, or winds, carry pollutants away from cities. On windy days, the air in most cities is generally cleaner, and on calm days it is dirtier. Horizontal movements also contribute to vertical motions, which play a more direct role in air pollution. Despite the reputation that some cities have for being windy, average wind speeds do not vary much from place to place, and wind speed is not an important factor in explaining spatial variations in pollution.

Vertical movement in the atmosphere and low-pressure systems such as wave cyclones result from wind-generated turbulence and convection. Convection in turn is a result of differential heating of the lower layers of the atmosphere by sunlight, whereby the warmer layers become less dense and therefore rise, while cooler layers sink. Regional circulation patterns, characterized by areas of high and low pressure, can be seen as a larger-scale form of convection. The normal temperature pattern—cooler air at higher elevations—prevails when there is sufficient vertical mixing through the lower atmosphere. Sometimes, however, warmer air overlies cooler air, a condition called a *temperature inversion* (Fig. 13.3). An inversion keeps the atmosphere sta-

ble and thus inhibits vertical motions. Such inversions are the major meteorological factor in most air pollution problems.

Temperature inversions are caused by several different processes, including subsidence, radiation, and advection. A *subsidence inversion* develops when an air mass sinks slowly over a large area, as is common in a high-pressure cell. The atmosphere is compressed as the air mass sinks, and higher layers are warmed more than lower layers, resulting in an inversion. Subsidence inversions are formed over large areas (hundreds of square kilometers), usually at relatively high altitudes, but can occur as low as 1000 meters above the surface. The weather that produces them (slow-moving high-pressure cells) also produces sunny conditions and gentle winds, which contribute to photochemical smog formation and poor dispersal of pollutants. Subsidence inversions are responsible for most of the severe pollution episodes in large cities east of the Rocky Mountains and also contribute to problems in mountainous areas.

Radiation inversions also develop in clear, relatively calm weather, but, unlike subsidence inversions, they are a diurnal phenomenon. On clear nights, the ground radiates heat upward, and the absence of clouds allows this radiation to escape to the upper atmosphere and into space. The result is that the ground cools more than the atmosphere, thus cooling the air near the ground so that it becomes

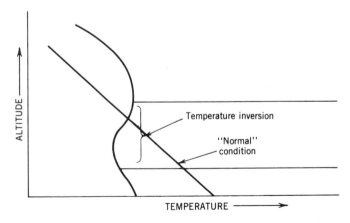

Figure 13.3   Temperature inversions. A temperature inversion consists of a layer in which temperature increases with altitude instead of decreasing. This temperature change prevents vertical circulation through the inverted layer.

cooler than air higher up. Radiation inversions are fairly thin and usually temporary, but cold air drainage can cause them to thicken and thus slow their dispersal in the morning. In hilly or mountainous areas, the dense, cooler air near the ground flows downhill, accumulating in valleys and producing a large pool of cool air. In hilly areas, most cities are situated in the valley bottoms and thus the inversion traps the city's pollutants in the valleys. The pollutants are prevented from dispersing horizontally by the valley walls, and the inversion keeps them from dispersing vertically. Valley inversions, often reinforced by subsidence inversions, are responsible for pollution problems in many cities in western North America, including Denver, Salt Lake City, Albuquerque, and Mexico City.

The third type of inversion, the *advection inversion*, is a problem primarily on the West Coast of the United States, where local winds in the form of sea breezes blow off the Pacific Ocean. Before reaching land, however, they pass over the cold ocean current along the coast of California, and the lower layers of the air are cooled by contact with this water and so become cooler than the air above. These inversions are usually of moderate thickness, from a few hundred meters to 1500 m or more. Los Angeles, San Diego, and, to a lesser extent, the San Francisco Bay area are bordered on the east by mountains that prevent pollutants from being dispersed inland. The particularly severe pollution problems of these cities are essentially the result of the presence of the mountains combined with very persistent advection inversions (Fig. 13.4).

In addition to dispersion, two other aspects of weather are important in understanding air pollution problems. These are sunlight and atmospheric humidity. Sunlight contributes to the formation of photochemical smog, and such smog is therefore more severe on sunny days than on cloudy ones. Cities that have a lot of sunshine have more photochemical smog than do those in cloudy areas. High-altitude cities, such as Denver and most other cities in the Mountain West, have particularly intense sunlight because of the thinner atmosphere, and this is an important factor in their pollution problems. In areas of high sulfur oxide emissions, atmospheric humidity is more of

Figure 13.4 Smog in Los Angeles, California. Per capita emissions in Los Angeles are low, but weather conditions limit dispersal of pollutants.

a problem, because water and oxygen combine with sulfur oxides to form sulfates and sulfuric acid. In areas of high humidity, high sulfur emissions and foggy days can be more dangerous than dry days.

The various combinations of these factors make each metropolitan region's problem different. Some cities suffer mostly from photochemical smog, whereas others have the greatest problems with particulates or carbon monoxide. Some cities have pollution episodes that last only a day or two, and others have much longer episodes. In the Northeast, pollution is usually the most severe in summer and fall, because that is when emissions are highest, as a result of high electrical demand and increased automobile usage, and subsidence inversions most frequent. In the Mountain West, winter is usually the time of the most persistent inversions, and that is when pollution is worst. Within metropolitan regions, local variations in wind direction or speed also contribute to variations in pollution. These regional and local differences in weather conditions are the major factor in explaining differences in pollution problems and the need for local or regional, as well as national and international approaches to air pollution control.

MAJOR POLLUTANTS

Air pollutants can come from both natural and nonnatural sources, with the latter being the most important in the United States. Some natural sources of pollutants include smoke from forest fires, hydrocarbons from coniferous trees and shrubs, dust from a variety of sources, volcanic eruptions, and pollen. At the national level, natural sources are quantitatively significant, even dominant. But in areas of severe pollution problems, human-made (*anthropogenic*) sources are locally much more important.

Anthropogenic sources of air pollutants are either stationary or mobile. *Stationary sources* are site specific and include stack emissions from refineries, smelters, electric power plants, and other manufacturing industries. *Mobile sources* are those that are not site specific. They include automobiles, motorcycles, buses, trucks, airplanes, trains, ships, boats, and off-highway vehicles.

Criteria pollutants are those specific contaminants that adversely affect human health and welfare, for which the U.S. Environmental Protection Agency (EPA) has set *ambient air quality* standards. *Primary standards* are designed to protect human health, and *secondary standards* are designed to protect human welfare (property and vegetation).

PARTICULATE MATTER (PM)

Total suspended particulates or particulate matter include any solid or liquid particles with diameters from 0.03 to 100 microns. Examples of PM include soot, fly ash, dust, pollen, and various chemicals and metals, such as arsenic, cadmium, and lead.

The adverse health effects of particulates include the direct toxicity of some of the metals and chemicals. Other health impacts include aggravation of cardiorespiratory diseases, such as bronchitis and asthma. Suspended particulates also have been linked to lung cancer. Aside from health, some of the negative effects involve the corrosion of metals and the soiling and discoloration of buildings and sculptures. More important, suspended particulates both scatter and absorb sunlight, thus reducing visibility. They also provide nuclei upon which condensation can occur, which increases cloud formation. They can also inhibit photosynthesis in plants.

Suspended particulates are produced primarily by stationary sources, particularly those industries that use coal as a fuel source, such as power plants, steel mills, and fertilizer plants. Construction activities and solid waste disposal (burning) also contribute minor percentages of particulate emissions, as shown in Table 13.1. Natural sources of suspended particulates are volcanic eruptions, forest fires, and wind erosion.

SULFUR DIOXIDE (SO₂)

Sulfur dioxide is a colorless gas with a strong odor. It is highly reactive in the presence of oxygen and moisture and forms sulfuric acid, a corrosive chemical. SO_2 stings the eyes and burns the throat. More important, SO_2 contrib-

TABLE 13.1   Air Pollutant Emissions by Type and Source, 1987 (Million Metric Tons)

Source	CO	SO₂	VOC	PM	NOₓ	Pb
Transportation	40.7	0.9	6.0	1.4	8.4	3.0
Fuel combustion	7.2	16.4	2.3	1.8	10.3	0.5
Industrial processes	4.7	3.1	8.3	2.5	0.6	2.0
Solid waste disposal	1.7	—[a]	0.6	0.3	0.1	2.6
Miscellaneous[b]	7.1	—[a]	2.4[c]	1.0	0.1	—[a]
Total	61.4	20.4	19.6	7.0	19.5	8.1

Source: U.S. Environmental Protection Agency (1989a).
[a] Less than 50,000 metric tons.
[b] Includes forest fires and other uncontrollable burning.
[c] Includes organic solvent use.

utes to respiratory diseases, including bronchitis, emphysema, and asthma; chronic exposures can permanently impair lung functions. SO_2 also corrodes metals, discolors textiles, and speeds the deterioration of building material, especially stone and metals. Perhaps the most significant effect of SO_2 is its role in the formation of acid rain and the resulting damage and decrease in plant growth. This is discussed in Chapter 14.

SO_2 emissions are a direct result of burning sulfur-bearing fossil fuels and smelting sulfur-bearing metal ores. In annual emissions, it is the second-largest pollutant. Certain industrial processes, notably petroleum refining, also contribute SO_2 to the atmosphere. The most significant natural source of SO_2 is volcanic eruptions. The majority of SO_2 emissions in 1987 were from electrical utilities and other stationary fuel-combustion sources (80 percent), followed by industrial plants (15 percent) and transportation (4 percent).

NITROGEN OXIDES (NO$_x$)

Nitrogen oxide emissions include nitrogen monoxide (NO) and nitrogen dioxide (NO_2). Nitrogen dioxide is a reddish-brown gas that aggravates respiratory diseases and increases susceptibility to pneumonia and lung cancer. NO_2 also causes paints and dyes to fade. There are, however, two effects of NO and NO that cause NO_x to be considered a criteria pollutant. The first is its crucial role as an ultraviolet light absorber in the formation of photochemical smog. Second, and perhaps more important, NO_x is a factor in the formation of acid rain.

Nitrogen is usually inert, but it combines with O_2 at high temperatures in internal combustion engines and furnaces to form NO_x. Thus, the primary sources of NO_x are power plants (53 percent) and motor vehicle exhaust (43 percent).

CARBON MONOXIDE (CO)

Carbon monoxide (CO) is a tasteless, odorless, colorless gas. It combines with hemoglobin in the blood, reducing its oxygen-carrying capacity and damaging some of the functions of the central nervous system. In small doses, CO im-

pairs some mental functions as well, resulting in headaches and dizziness. In large doses, especially in enclosed areas, CO causes death.

Most CO pollution results from the incomplete combustion of carbonaceous materials, including fossil fuels. There are some natural sources of CO, such as forest fires and decomposition of organic matter. In 1987, 75 percent of all anthropogenic CO emissions were from transportation (mobile) sources, with an additional 25 percent from stationary sources, including industry, and fuel combustion (Table 13.1). Natural sources of CO equalled 8 percent of the total emissions. CO is the most pervasive of all air pollutants, accounting for slightly less than half of the total emissions by source (Fig. 13.5).

VOLATILE ORGANIC COMPOUNDS (VOCs)

Volatile organic compounds are released through the incomplete combustion of carbon-containing fuels and through the evaporation of fossil fuels from natural gas pipelines, gas tanks, and gas station pumps. Methane, propane, ethylene, and acetylene are some of the specific compounds generically called VOCs. Although many VOCs are suspected carcinogens, their most significant effect on air quality is their role in the formation of photochemical smog.

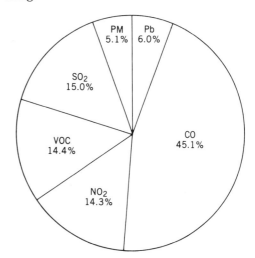

Figure 13.5 Air pollutant emissions in the United States, 1987. By weight, carbon monoxide is the largest human-made emission. (*Source:* U.S. Environmental Protection Agency, 1988a.)

Nearly 69 percent of all anthropogenic VOC emissions are from stationary industrial and fuel-combustion sources, and 31 percent are from mobile transportation sources (Table 13.1). There are some natural sources of VOCs such as coniferous forests, but they are relatively insignificant in their contribution to urban pollution problems.

OZONE (O_3)

Ozone is a photochemical *oxidant* that is the most important component of photochemical smog. In combination with VOCs, NO_x, and sunlight, oxidants comprise the now famous Los Angeles-type smog. In simplified form, the process is this: sunlight causes NO_2 to break down into NO and monatomic oxygen (O). This O atom combines with O_2 to form O_3. In addition, VOCs, O_2, NO, and NO_2 interact to form both ozone and a class of compounds called peroxyacetyl nitrates (PAN), which, like ozone, are harmful photochemical oxidants.

Photochemical oxidants are eye and respiratory irritants, and prolonged exposures result in aggravation of cardiovascular and respiratory illnesses. Other effects include deterioration of rubber, textiles, and paints, and reduced visibility and vegetation growth. Leaves and fruit seem to be the most susceptible to oxidants, the effects of which result not only in injury but also in leaf drop and premature fruit. Since oxidants are produced in chemical reactions in the atmosphere, there is no direct source of emissions other than the sources for VOCs and NO_x. Naturally occurring atmospheric ozone may sometimes contribute significantly to urban smog.

LEAD (Pb)

Lead is a nonferrous, heavy metal that occurs naturally. In the atmosphere, lead occurs in the form of a vapor, dust, or aerosol. Lead acts as a cumulative poison in the human body, causing general weakness and impaired functioning of the central nervous system. Ingestion can lead to severe anemia and even death.

For many years, lead has been added to high-octane gasoline to reduce engine knock. The primary sources of lead in the atmosphere are vehicle exhaust from lead additives in gas-oline, lead mining and smelting, and manufacturing of lead products, such as batteries. Volcanic dust, the major natural source of lead, contributes less than 1 percent of the total emissions. Another source of lead in the air is cigarette smoke.

POLLUTION MONITORING AND TRENDS

LEGISLATIVE MANDATES

The original enabling legislation establishing air pollution control was the Clean Air Act, passed in 1963. Amendments to that legislation, the Air Quality Act of 1967 and the Clean Air Act Amendments of 1970, provided the framework for air resource decisionmaking at both the regional and national levels. The Clean Air Act Amendments of 1970 established standards for ambient air quality for the five major pollutants and also provided timetables for achieving those standards.

The Clean Air Act Amendments of 1977 further refined the monitoring of air pollutants and clarified previous legislation. The 1963, 1967, 1970, and 1977 acts are collectively known as the *Clean Air Act*. The 1977 amendments required standard monitoring of the criteria pollutants and also standardized reporting methods. Under this legislation, the EPA was to review the standards for criteria pollutants and establish deadlines for compliance with the standards. States were to meet the primary standards for SO_2, NO_x, and PM by 1981 and the primary standards for O_3 and CO by 1987.

The Clean Air Act expired in 1982. However, all the rules and regulations in effect at that time are still valid. In 1982 Congress passed a continuing resolution that provides appropriations and legal authority to the EPA to continue the air quality program under the 1977 amendments. In essence this placed the legislation on a hold status while it was debated in Congress. The Reagan administration wanted to relax standards and also to limit provisions for transboundary pollution problems, such as acid rain. In the fall of 1990, Congress finally passed a revision of the Clean Air Act. The new law mandates a 50 percent reduction in sulfur-dioxide emissions to help reduce acid rain. It also requires a phase out of CFCs and other ozone-destroying chemicals in an effort to curtail stratospheric ozone depletion. To help alleviate urban air pollution problems, the new Clean Air Act requires lower vehicular emissions of nitrogen oxides (60 percent reduction) and hydrocarbons (40 percent reduction) and cleaner-burning gasoline, particularly in the country's smoggiest cities. Finally, the 1990 revisions call for a 90 percent reduction in the output of toxic emissions, particularly those 189 known toxic and cancer-causing chemicals.

MONITORING NETWORK AND AIR QUALITY STANDARDS

Under the 1970 amendments, a national network of air quality control regions (AQCRs) was established (Fig. 13.6). Data from each of these regions are stored in a national aerometric data base, and monitoring is actually done on a county level. In 1979, problems with the frequency and accuracy of monitoring data led the EPA to standardize and regulate the monitoring network. State and local monitoring sites were thus incorporated into a national system, with consistent and uniform readings, including frequency, type of pollutant, and placement of monitoring stations (central city versus suburban location). Ambient air quality data are submitted to the EPA's National Aerometric Data Bank (NADB) where trends (10-year and 5-year) in air quality are monitored.

Primary and secondary standards were established under the Clean Air Act for criteria pollutants (Table 13.2). As stipulated by the 1977 amendments, these standards were subject to review and revision prior to the 1982 reauthorization. In July 1987, new standards were promulgated for particulate matter based on size. These smaller particles (designated PM_{10} and so on for sizes less than 10 microns in diameter) cause the most serious health threat since they become lodged in lung tissue and remain in the body for significant lengths of time.

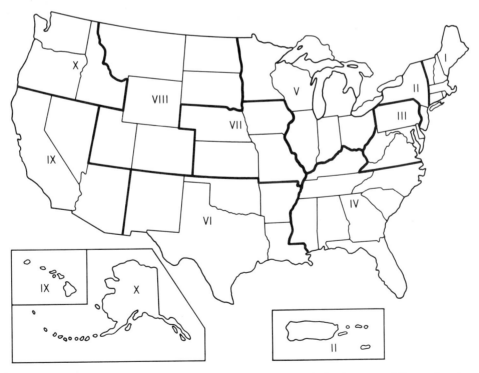

Figure 13.6 Federal Air Pollution Control Regions. (*Source:* U.S. Environmental Protection Agency, 1980.)

TABLE 13.2   National Ambient Air Quality Standards (NAAQS), 1987

Pollutant	Averaging Time	Primary	Secondary
PM_{10}	Annual arithmetic mean	50 $\mu g/m^3$	Same as primary
	24-hour	150 $\mu g/m^3$	Same as primary
SO_2	Annual arithmetic mean	80 $\mu g/m^3$ (0.03 ppm)	N.A.[a]
	24-hour	365 $\mu g/m^3$ (0.14 ppm)	N.A.[a]
	3-hour	N.A.[a]	1300 $\mu g/m^3$ (0.50 ppm)
CO	8-hour	10 $\mu g/m^3$ (9 ppm)	No secondary standard
	1-hour	40 $\mu g/m^3$ (35 ppm)	No secondary standard
NO_2	Annual arithmetic mean	100 $\mu g/m^3$ (0.053 ppm)	Same as primary
O_3	Maximum daily 1-hour average	235 $\mu g/m^3$ (0.12 ppm)	Same as primary
Pb	Maximum quarterly average	1.5 $\mu g/m^3$	Same as primary

Source: U.S. Environmental Protection Agency (1989a).
[a] *Not applicable.*

THE NONDEGRADATION ISSUE

Interesting quirks in the clean air legislation began to emerge in the mid-1970s, and these involved conflicts between economic development and air quality. The intent of the 1970 amendments was to keep clean air clean, while cleaning up dirty air. Primary standards for the criteria pollutants were to have been met by 1975. But there were no provisions or policies for those areas that were already clean in 1970. Industry noticed this and began to relocate into these relatively clean areas. The EPA did not take action on this issue, which became known as Prevention of Significant Deterioration (PSD), until the Sierra Club filed a legal suit over the Kaiparowitz energy facility in southern Utah.

In response to a court order, the EPA established its PSD policy, which effectively limits the extent to which clean air can be degraded by managing economic growth in various regions (National Research Council, 1981). The entire United States was divided into three classes. Class I areas could not have any increases in particulate (PM) or SO_2 levels. All National Parks and National Wilderness Areas were designated mandatory Class I areas, which limits industrial growth in the area. Most of the Class I areas are located in the western half of the country (Fig. 13.7).

Class II areas allow for moderate development and industrial growth. All areas of the country that were not mandatory Class I regions were assigned to this group. The states were then given the opportunity to change this designation to Class I or Class III. Class III areas allow for significant industrial growth and residential development. Changes into Class III areas, however, require environmental impact statements, public hearings, and EPA approval.

There was and still is considerable debate over the PSD program. These debates are particularly acute in the western half of the country, where issues over energy development, industrialization, and pristine areas are hotly contested. Energy developments in the Golden Circle region of the Southwest (Fig. 13.8) illustrate some of the issues in the clean air versus energy development debate. Visibility in the Grand Canyon and other national parks in the region have brought this issue to the public's attention (Rudzitis and Schwartz, 1982; Crawford, 1990). The National Park Service has found that sulfates are the single most important contributor to lowering the visibility in the nation's parks (Conservation Foundation, 1987). In other words, controlling the emissions of sulfur oxides not only reduces acid deposition but would also improve the visibility in the nation's parklands.

TRENDS

Although the United States has had air pollution control measures for more than a decade, the quality of the air has only slightly improved

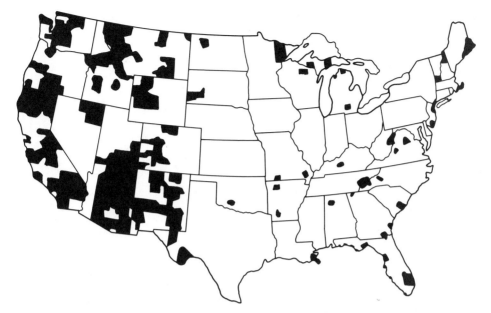

Figure 13.7 Class I counties. These counties have been designated as Class I areas because these areas have the best air quality. Therefore, new industrial growth in these areas has been restricted. (*Source:* U.S. Environmental Protection Agency, 1980.)

during that time. There are 247 AQCRs, with monitoring stations in 3000 counties in the United States (National Commission on Air Quality, 1981). *Emissions data*, for example, are actual estimates on the amount of pollutants released into the air. They illustrate how well the regulations on industrial and vehicular emissions are working. *Ambient data*, in contrast, measure the concentrations of pollutants in the air that are recorded at specific monitoring locations. Using the appropriate health standards, ambient data indicate how close we are to achieving clean air.

Particulate Matter

Total suspended particulate emissions have declined by 23 percent since 1978 (Table 13.3). The slight increase between 1986 and 1987 is the result of increased forest fire activity during the summer of 1987 in the West and Southeast. Although there has been some improvement in emissions from industrial sources due to the installation of control equipment, particulate emissions from mobile sources remain problematic. Emissions standards for diesel automobiles and tailpipe standards for diesel trucks and buses took effect in 1988 and will help to reduce particulate emissions from transportation sources. However,

fugitive sources, such as dust from fields, roads, and construction, account for the disparity between emissions and ambient quality. Despite this, there also has been a 23 percent reduction in ambient particulate levels from 1977 to 1986 (U.S. Environmental Protection Agency, 1989a). In 1982, 345 areas did not achieve particulate standards, and by 1985 this number had dropped to 290 (U.S. EPA, 1989a). Regionally, the highest concentrations are found in the industrial areas of the Midwest and the western section of the country (Fig. 13.9d). Medford, Oregon, had the highest ambient levels (82 $\mu g/m^3$) for 1987 and was closely followed by Yakima, Washington (78 $\mu g/m^3$), and Kansas City (75 $\mu g/m^3$). The arid West continues to show little or no improvement in particulate ambient quality, largely because of wind-blown agricultural dust.

Sulfur Dioxide

SO_2 emissions went down by 17 percent from 1978 to 1987, largely a result of the switch from coal and high-sulfur oil to natural gas and low-sulfur oil. Ambient quality also improved by 35 percent between 1978 and 1987. One factor that may account for the difference between emissions and ambient quality is stack

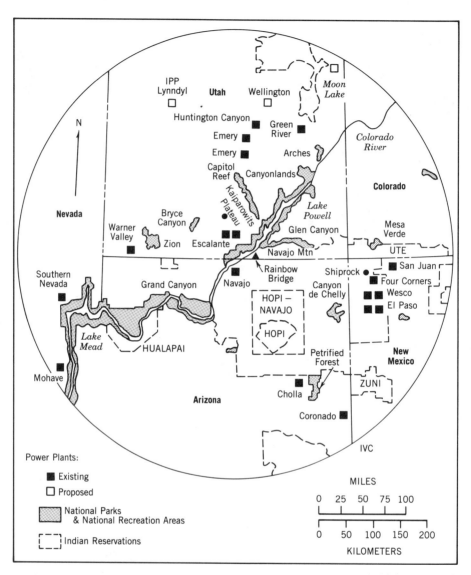

Figure 13.8 National parks and recreation areas, proposed and existing power plants, and Indian reservations in the Golden Circle area of the U.S. Southwest. This is an area of significant natural beauty and recreational use, but it also has large coal reserves. Power plants have been built there to burn the coal and export electricity to urban areas. The result has been a deterioration of air quality. (*Source:* Rudzitis and Schwartz, 1982. Reprinted with permission of the Helen Dwight Reid Educational Foundation. Published by Heldres Publications.

height. The construction of tall stacks by industry in the 1970s dispersed sulfur dioxide emissions far from the local source. The result was that ambient conditions at the local level improved even though emissions increased. The pollutants were simply transported farther downwind to more remote areas. There were 101 nonattainment areas for sulfur dioxide in 1978 and this dropped to 60 in 1985. Despite the overall decline in sulfur dioxide ambient levels, geographically the problem still exists in those areas that burn high-sulfur coal to generate electricity, where nonferrous smelters operate, and where steel and chemical plants and pulp and paper mills predominate, such as in the intermontane West, industrial Midwest, and Maine. During 1987, the 24-hour ambient standard was violated in two metropolitan areas, Pittsburgh, Pennsylvania, and Steubenville–Weirton, Ohio largely as a result of proximity to point sources (industry and fuel-combustion plants).

TABLE 13.3 National Air Pollutant Emissions, 1970–1987 (Million Metric Tons)

Year	PM	SO$_2$	NO$_x$	VOC	CO	Pb
1970	17.9	28.4	17.6	27.2	112.8	
1971	16.8	26.9	18.0	26.3	112.4	
1972	15.4	27.6	19.1	26.7	111.7	
1973	14.4	28.9	19.4	26.3	108.9	
1974	12.6	27.1	19.0	24.7	103.8	
1975	10.6	25.6	18.6	23.2	100.2	
1976	10.0	26.4	19.8	24.2	104.8	
1977	9.2	26.0	20.3	24.4	102.5	141.2
1978	9.1	24.6	21.1	23.5	82.4	127.9
1979	8.9	24.8	21.1	23.5	79.4	108.7
1980	8.5	23.4	20.4	22.3	77.0	70.6
1981	8.0	22.6	20.4	21.0	74.4	55.9
1982	7.1	21.4	19.6	19.7	69.4	54.4
1983	7.1	20.7	19.0	20.4	71.3	46.3
1984	7.4	21.5	19.7	21.5	68.7	40.1
1985	7.0	21.1	19.8	20.2	64.6	21.1
1986	6.8	20.7	19.3	19.3	61.1	8.6
1987	7.0	20.4	19.5	19.6	61.4	8.1

Percentage change						
1970–1987	−61%	−28%	+33%	−28%	−46%	
1978–1987	−23%	−17%	− 8%	−17%	−25%	−94%

Source: Council on Environmental Quality (1982, p. 292); U.S. Environmental Protection Agency, (1989a).

Nitrogen Oxides

Emissions of NO$_x$ have steadily declined since 1978 with a reduction of 8 percent in total emissions, largely because of emissions controls on highway vehicles, a major source. Ambient quality has also improved, except for a slight increase in 1984. Since then, however, ambient levels have continued to decline. Los Angeles–Long Beach, California, is the only area in the country that failed to meet the ambient air quality standard for nitrogen oxides for 1987.

Ozone

Since oxidants are by-products of chemical reactions, there are no direct emissions data for them. Ozone, one type of photochemical oxidant, is formed through a series of complex chemical reactions involving nitrogen oxides and volatile organic compounds in the presence of sunlight. However, we do have emissions data for both precursors: nitrogen oxides (already described) and volatile organic compounds. VOC emissions were down by nearly 17 percent in the period 1978–1987.

Ambient quality in the 1980s both increased and decreased. Higher ozone levels were found in 1983 and were largely attributed to meteorological conditions that favored the formation of ozone. The number of counties where the ozone standard was violated dropped from 607 in 1978 to 368 in 1985. However, 82 metropolitan areas did not meet the ambient standard in 1987 (U.S. EPA, 1989a) (Fig. 13.9c). Los Angeles–Long Beach still has the worst ambient ozone level (0.32 ppm) but is closely followed by other Southern California urban areas (Riverside–San Bernardino and Anaheim). Nationally, nearly 76 million people are exposed to unhealthy levels of ozone yearly (U.S. EPA, 1988a), particularly in Southern California, the Texas Gulf Coast, the Great Lakes, and the Northeast corridor. Although stationary sources do contribute to the problem, EPA efforts focus on auto emissions by stressing motor vehicle inspections and maintenance as control methods. In addition, major life-style changes may be required to significantly reduce ozone levels in some of the nation's harder-hit areas (see Issue 13–1).

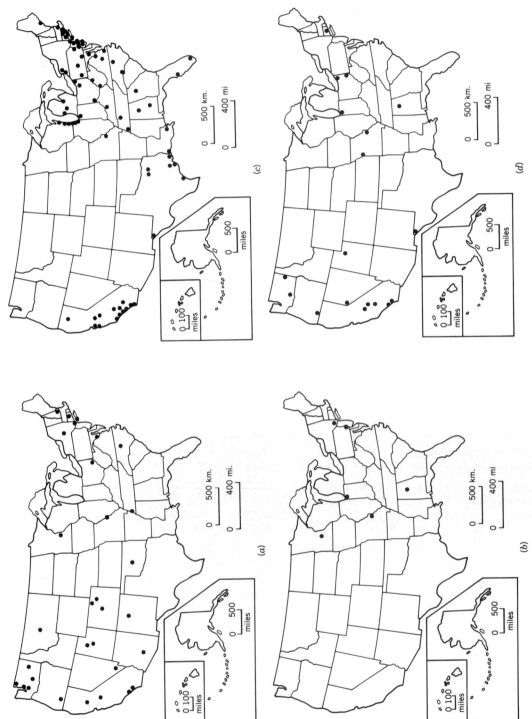

Figure 13.9 Urban air quality. Areas that did not meet the primary air quality standard in 1987 for (*a*) carbon monoxide, (*b*) lead, (*c*) ozone, and (*d*) particulate matter ($> 50 \; \mu g/m^3$ annual arithmetic mean). (*Source:* U.S. Environmental Protection Agency, 1989a.)

Carbon Monoxide

Emissions were down by 25 percent for carbon monoxide from 1978 to 1987 and ambient levels were also reduced by 32 percent during the same period largely because of emissions controls on automobiles. But portions of 142 counties still exceeded the carbon monoxide standard in 1985, a drop from 190 in 1978 (U.S. EPA, 1988a). In 1987, three metropolitan regions (New York, Spokane, Washington, and Steubenville–Weirton, Ohio) had ambient levels 100 percent above the standard. In addition, 29 other metropolitan areas exceeded the CO standard (Fig. 13.9a). Ambient CO levels are also increasing in rapidly growing metropolitan regions with under 200,000 inhabitants, such as Great Falls, Montana, and Yakima, Washington. The primary reason is the failure of autos to meet emissions standards as a result of lax inspection by state regulators and poor maintenance by owners.

Lead

Sources for atmospheric lead include gasoline additives in fuel, nonferrous smelters, and battery plants. Even though unleaded gasoline was introduced in 1975, sales of unleaded gas accounted only for 69 percent of the total gas sales in 1986 (U.S. EPA, 1988a). However, there has been a 94 percent reduction in lead emissions in response to EPA's control efforts to reduce the lead content of gasoline (0.1 g/gallon in 1986), which required the use of unleaded gasoline in new cars (beginning in 1975) and emissions controls on stationary sources. At the same time, there has been a steady decline in ambient lead levels as well. This is a particularly noteworthy achievement in pollution control of mobile sources since the lead standard was first introduced in 1978. Some areas, however, have still not met the ambient standard (Fig. 13.9b). These urban areas are mostly located in the East and their ambient levels are a function of their proximity to nonferrous smelters and other point sources of lead emissions. St. Louis and Birmingham had the highest ambient lead levels in 1987, more than twice the ambient standard. Four other urban areas also exceeded the lead standard including Philadelphia, Minneapolis–St. Paul, Gary–Hammond Indiana, and Orange County, New York.

SPATIAL COMPARISONS OF AIR QUALITY

Before 1978, each state relied on its own air quality monitoring and reporting program. Some states' programs were very good, and others' were nonexistent. As a result, readings were taken at irregular intervals, and reporting was erratic. This made interstate comparisons impossible as there were no mechanisms to compare air quality between New York and Los Angeles, for example. There was also no way to tell which region or city had the dirtiest or cleanest air.

POLLUTION STANDARDS INDEX (PSI)

In an effort to standardize monitoring efforts nationwide, the EPA adopted a uniform air quality index in 1978. This index, the *Pollution Standards Index*, or PSI, is a health-related comparative measure based on the short-term national ambient air quality (NAAQS) primary standards for criteria pollutants.

The PSI translates concentrations of nitrogen dioxide, sulfur dioxide, carbon monoxide, ozone, and particulate matter into a single value, which ranges from 0 to 500 (Table 13.4). When the levels for all five of these pollutants are below NAAQS primary standards, the air is called good or moderately polluted (PSI values 0–99). When ambient concentrations of any of the criteria pollutants exceed their primary standard, the PSI reading is in the 100–500 range depending on the concentration level. PSI values in the range 100–200 are labeled unhealthful. Values from 200 to 300 are called very unhealthful; values in excess of 300 are labeled hazardous.

Public warnings are issued when PSI values rise above the "good air" value of less than 100. An air quality alert is called when PSI values range from 100 to 200; at this time, persons with heart or respiratory ailments should reduce physical exertion. An air pollution warning is given when the PSI ranges from 200 to 300. During a warning elderly and other persons with heart and lung diseases should remain indoors. Industry is also asked to curtail emissions temporarily, until the warning is removed. An air pollution emergency is called when PSI readings exceed 300. Then the general population is advised to refrain from outdoor activities, and persons with heart and lung diseases are advised to remain indoors and minimize their physical activity. Industry and motorists are asked to curb emissions through lower production and less driving, respectively.

In recent years, the PSI has fallen into disuse among air quality control professionals. Although it is often reported in local papers, most air quality districts and metropolitan regions use the ambient quality and emissions data without any specific reference to comparisons throughout the country.

URBAN TRENDS

Overall air quality in metropolitan regions is improving. Selected metropolitan regions had an average number of 72 days of unhealthful air (above 100 on the PSI) in 1978 (Council on Environmental Quality, 1980), down 16 percent from 1972 for the same locations. Although overall quality shows signs of improvement, some metropolitan regions, specifically New York and Los Angeles, still have dangerously polluted air.

Air quality has worsened since 1978 in all of Southern California, which has the worst air quality in the nation. In 1978, Los Angeles had 242 days with PSI levels greater than 100, and by 1981 the count rose to 248. In 1988, ozone levels were three times greater than the ambient standard for almost half of the year. The problem in New York City, on the other hand, is carbon monoxide. CO standards were exceeded on 86 days in 1988, compared to the next highest city, Denver, which had un-

---

ISSUE 13–1   Smog City, U.S.A.

"I love LA" echos the refrain from Randy Newman's popular song about the city of angels. But how much longer will Los Angeles be feeling this if they must begin to wear gas masks before venturing outside in the warm California sun? Los Angeles residents are becoming less enamored of their city as increased air pollution continues to choke not only Los Angeles but all of Southern California and the costs of curbing it escalate.

Smog has been a persistent problem in Southern California since Juan Rodríguez Cabrillo first discovered the Bahia de los Fumos (Bay of Smokes) in 1542. By 1877, air pollution, in the form of dust from the streets, was so bad it prompted one citizen to remark: "It does not allow invalids with lung disease to remain here" (Weaver, 1980,p. 197). By 1944, the term *smog* (*smoke* and *fog*) was coined to describe the brown haze that hung over the Los Angeles basin. With postwar urbanization and industrialization, the now famous Los Angeles smog worsened, and residents began to experience discomfort and adverse health effects. Smog alerts became commonplace and, as early as the 1950s, people were advised to curtail their outdoor physical activities.

Four decades later, the smog problem remains. In March 1989, the South Coast Air Quality Management District (AQMD) finally decided to confront the Southern California icon, the single-passenger automobile. The AQMD developed a 20-year strategy for cleaning up the air by proposing and passing an innovative and far-reaching plan. The three-phase plan covers 13,350 square miles (34,600 km^2) of Southern California and its 12 million inhabitants, as well as their 5.6 million cars and 2 million trucks and other vehicles.

The primary goals of the AQMD strategy are to restructure life in the Los Angeles basin. Restrictions have been placed on everyday activities and ultimately a major change in how cities are organized may transpire before the middle of the next century. The plan has 123 specific actions that involve not only residents but also industry.

Phase I of the plan (1989–1993) places a number of limits on sources of air emissions. Restrictions on car use include the elimination of free parking, a decrease in the number of allowable cars per family, and an increase in registration fees for motorists with more than one car. Emissions standards for diesel engines will be

healthy CO levels on 24 days. Overall, Southern California still has the worst air pollution, prompting a number of innovative solutions to its deteriorating air quality (see Issue 13–1).

AIR QUALITY CONTROL AND PLANNING

ECONOMIC CONSIDERATIONS

In 1985, $73.8 billion was spent in the United States for pollution abatement and control (U.S. Bureau of the Census, 1988, p. 195). Nearly 45 percent of this, or $33.2 billion, was for air quality control alone. Pollution abatement accounted for 94 percent of the expenditures. About $11 billion was spent on abatement for stationary sources of air pollu-

tion, and another $18.6 billion was spent on emissions reductions from cars and trucks. The government (federal, state, and local) spent $500 million (less than 2 percent of all air pollution abatement expenditures). Industry spent nearly $18.8 billion (60 percent) for air pollution abatement, and consumers spent another $10.4 billion (38 percent). Governmental regulation, monitoring, and research cost another $2 billion.

Clean air is a costly business. The National Commission on Air Quality, however, estimates that nearly $6.8 billion would be saved yearly just by achieving current NAAQS goals. These savings could be made by reduction of crop losses, materials, and soiling and increased visibility. In addition, between $4.6 and $51.2 billion could be saved annually in health effects related to air pollution (National

---

tightened. Only radial tires will be available for purchase, as they throw fewer rubber particles into the air. Paints and solvents will be reformulated to decrease emissions. A total ban on gas-powered lawn mowers took effect immediately. Similarly, the American custom of the backyard barbecue is no more. Sales on fuels that require starter fluid are banned, and restaurants that have barbecues are now required to install special vents to trap emissions.

All over the city, businesses and industry are changing. The local dry cleaners must install a combined wash/dry system to reduce emissions when clothes are moved between machines. They must also provide vapor condensers on exhaust vents. Paint shops must switch to water-based paints with fewer solvents. Body shops must now use a lower-pressure spray to reduce the amount of paint in the air. As mentioned previously, all paint, varnishes, and sealants will be reformulated to use less solvents. Bakeries must install afterburners, which unfortunately reduce the efficiency of the ovens, producing a lower-quality baked good. Products in aerosol cans, though not banned, must be reformulated.

Phase II of the plan (1993–1998) calls for

the conversion of 40 percent of the cars and 70 percent of freight vehicles to cleaner fuels such as propane and a 50 percent reduction in emissions from all other consumer and industrial sources. Phase III (1998 and beyond) effectively bans all gasoline vehicles in the region by 2007.

As one might guess, the debate about the AQMD plan is just beginning. Since Southern California already has the toughest air pollution legislation in the country, there was no alternative other than this complete overhaul. Legal challenges and business threats will no doubt fuel the fire over whether or not the costs exceed the benefits. The costs are astounding, around $3 billion annually for Phase I. Opponents claim that the benefits are not nearly that great, and proponents say it must be done to protect the health and welfare of residents. This far-reaching plan is the first of its kind in the nation and will surely serve as a model for other urban areas whose air pollution problems are worsening. A major change in life-style and the pattern of business is occurring in Southern California. Los Angeles has said yes to clean air, but at what cost (Weisman, 1989; Reinhold, 1989; Stevenson, 1989)?

TABLE 13.4 Comparison of Pollution Standards Index (PSI) Values

PSI Value	PM[a]	SO$_2$[a]	CO[b]	O$_3$[c]	NO$_2$[c]	Descriptor
400+	875+	2000+	46.0+	1000+	3000+	Very hazardous
300–399	625–874	1600–1999	34.0–45.9	900–1099	2260–2999	Hazardous
200–299	375–624	800–1599	17.0–33.9	480–899	1130–2259	Very unhealthful
100–199	260–374	365–799	10.0–16.9	240–479	N.R.[e]	Unhealthful
50–99	75[d]–259	80[d]–364	5.0–9.9	120–239	N.R.	Moderate
0–49	0–74	0–79	0–4.9	0–119	N.R.	Good

Source: Council on Environmental Quality (1980, pp. 156–157).

[a] 24 hr, μg/m^3.

[b] 8-hr, μg/m^3.

[c] 1-hr, μg/m^3.

[d] Annual primary NAAQS.

[e] N.R. = no index value reported at concentration levels below those specified by "alert level" criteria.

Commission on Air Quality, 1981). In an era of economic uncertainty, some individuals are still questioning the value of air pollution control programs.

In an attempt to assuage these economic fears, the EPA developed its *bubble approach* to stationary source control. Instead of considering each smokestack as an emitter, which was the previous policy, the EPA now views the entire plant as a point source. Thus, it allows emissions from one smokestack to exceed standards so long as another stack at a different location in the same plant has compensating reductions. As long as the emissions from the entire plant do not exceed the standards, then the plant is not in violation of the Clean Air Act and so is not subject to criminal prosecution. This policy allows the plant to average emissions from all stacks, thus allowing internal decisionmaking about what is most appropriate for the plant. Production levels and expenditures for control equipment are made by the plant management, so long as the total emissions are below federal limits (see Issue 13–2).

CONTROL PROGRAMS

Until recently, it was thought that vehicle exhaust emissions offered the greatest potential for decreasing mobile source contributions to the nonattainment of NAAQS. However, the newest model cars already remove up to 96 percent of the emissions (Levin, 1989a). Real improvements in vehicle emissions will come from a switch from gasoline as a fuel, and from reductions in the number of vehicles and miles driven.

Vehicle exhaust emissions have been federally regulated since 1968 and have become increasingly stricter (Table 13.5). The emissions standards apply only to the newer model year cars and trucks; older models have less stringent controls. One of the problems with emissions control is that many individual car owners tamper with the controls to increase gas mileage, and more and more people are keeping their older model cars rather than buying new cars with the more stringent emissions controls. Increased fuel efficiency is an-

other way to reduce emissions. Smaller, more fuel-efficient cars produce less pollution. During the Reagan era, fuel efficiency standards were rolled back to 26 mpg to ease pressures on US auto makers. The result was that Americans began driving bigger and less fuel-efficient cars, thereby producing more air pollution. In early 1989, the fuel efficiency standard was increased to 27.5 mpg as a result of increased pressure to reduce smog.

State inspection and maintenance programs for vehicles in order to monitor emissions on a yearly basis are one method to control mobile sources. Unfortunately, there are no uniform requirements for such programs, and as a result there is great variation from state to state. California has the strictest state inspection program. In addition to inspections, another alternative to reduce mobile sources is the use of catalytic converters. Catalytic converters are now fitted on all gasoline engines (Fleischaker, 1983). The converter oxidizes unburned gases, thus reducing emissions. It requires more expensive unleaded fuel, and as a result many automobile owners damage the device by using the cheaper leaded fuel. The development of new, cleaner fuels, such as alcohol and methanol, is a potential option. These fuels are not widely available at this time and also have some minor disadvantages. Electric-powered vehicles are another option, particularly for localized commuting, within the downtowns of most American cities.

The most obvious way to reduce vehicle emissions is to force people to drive less. Admittedly, this is a rather impractical solution to the problem, given the increasing number of motor vehicles and trucks on the road. During the last decade, the number of cars and buses increased by 25 percent while the number of trucks using diesel engines increased by 40 percent. Thus, the improved efficiency is more than offset by the increase in diesel-powered vehicles.

Stationary source control involves installing mechanical devices on smokestacks and switching from high-sulfur to low-sulfur fuels. Fitting gasoline pumps with pollution control equipment is another method currently in use to prevent hydrocarbons from escaping at the

TABLE 13.5   Exhaust Emission Standards for Automobiles

Model Year	Standard (g/m³)		
	VOC	CO	NO$_x$
Pre-1968	8.2	90.0	3.4
1968–1971	4.1	34.0	N.A.[a]
1972–1974	3.0	28.0	3.1
1975–1976	1.5	15.0	3.1
1977–1979	1.5	15.0	2.0
1980	0.41	7.0	2.0
1981	0.41	3.4	1.0
1987	0.41	3.4	1.0
1991 (proposed)	0.25	3.4	0.7

Source: National Commission on Air Quality (1981); Renner (1988); Levin (1989a,b).
[a] N.A. = not available.

gas station. There are over 27,000 major stationary sources of air pollution in this country alone. The EPA considers "major" any plant that produces more than 100 tons of pollutants per year. Stack scrubbers, precipitators, and filters are costly capital investments for industry, especially for facilities with old, outdated plants.

For the foregoing reasons, compliance with federal standards is spotty. The EPA estimates that nearly 90 percent of a sample of 6000 major stationary sources were in compliance with federal regulations in 1980. The CEQ notes that these numbers are misleading, however, and should not be used as definitive evidence of widespread compliance. Only 5 percent of the sources were tested for emissions. For the others, compliance was determined by certification of inspection but not by actual measurement of emissions (CEQ, 1980). The industries with the highest noncompliance are iron and steel, with a 13 percent compliance rate, and smelters, with a 46 percent compliance rate.

Unfortunately, there has been no systematic assessment of compliance at the national level since 1980. Reductions in enforcement

---

ISSUE 13–2   Emissions Trading Comes of Age

Although the federal government establishes emissions standards for point and non-point sources, the responsibility for the enforcement of emissions often rests with the state. To comply with Clean Air Act provisions, states develop implementation plans to improve air quality and reduce the number of locales that are in violation of the emissions standards (nonattainment areas).

In 1974, the EPA began to experiment with some economic incentives to reduce air pollution in nonattainment areas rather than imposing regulatory control. This policy is known as *emissions trading*. The purpose of the policy was to improve local air quality by allowing local firms to reduce emissions below allowable limits, for which they would receive "pollution credits" that could be applied elsewhere. The credits can be used by the firm itself to cover other smokestacks at the same site or different sites, or the credits can be traded to other firms, or saved for future use. There are a number of concepts that are important in this policy: offsets, bubbles, netting, and banking.

Offsets were developed in 1976 to reduce the conflict between economic growth and environmental quality. New sources of emissions (smokestacks) can be allowed in a nonattainment area, however, existing emissions must be reduced by an equal or greater amount so that there is no net increase in overall emissions. This can be done by the individual firm or in conjunction with trading credits with another firm in the same area. The bubble concept treats individual point sources of emissions within a firm as a whole. In other words, for the imaginary bubble over the entire plant, combined emissions must be below the existing standards. This means that some sources may exceed the standards while others may be below. The average, however, must be below the legal limits set by state or federal statutes. Netting is an extension of that principle and primarily applies to expansions and modifications of existing firms. Instead of filing for new air emissions permits (and thus being subject to more stringent regulations), firms are allowed to upgrade without the new permits as long as concomitant reductions occur elsewhere in the plant. Again, the total must be below allowable limits. Finally, firms are allowed to "bank" emissions credits for future use. These can be used in anticipation of a proposed expan-

actions as a result of cuts in the federal budget and decentralization of the federal role in air quality control during the Reagan administration obviously do not improve air quality. In 1977 the EPA had 662 enforcement actions,, which increased to 772 in 1979 (CEQ, 1980), and then dropped during the early 1980s. There has also been a concomitant decrease in the federal budget for enforcement and aid to states since 1981. Air pollution control is expensive and requires federal action and support from industry and consumers.

TOXICS IN THE AIR

There are over 70,000 synthetic chemicals available in the world today. Although the effects of immediate (acute) exposures to human health and the environment may be known, scientific information on the effects of lower-level, longer-term exposures is often incomplete or missing. Disasters such as the 1984 release of methyl isocyanate in Bhopal, India, which killed 2000 people, do occur, although not frequently. Perhaps of greater concern are the daily emissions of airborne toxic substances that result in chronic exposures. Unfortunately, we have very little information on the number of deaths attributed to longer-term exposures to toxic chemicals in the air we breathe.

CHRONIC OUTDOOR EMISSIONS

For years, the EPA has been grappling with the problem of air toxics that are emitted from a wide range of mobile and stationary sources, including incinerators, municipal waste sites, plastics and chemical manufacturing plants, and sewage treatment plants. Their first approach was to regulate the source emissions for a small number of toxic pollutants even though hundreds of organic compounds, many with carcinogenic or mutagenic properties, are

sion where the netting principle would come in, or the banked credits can be sold to other firms for potential offsets.

The following example illustrates how the emissions trading works in the real world. E.I. du Pont de Nemours and Company owns the Chambers Works, one of the largest chemical plants in the country. The Chambers Works is located in Deepwater, New Jersey, along the Delaware River south of Philadelphia. In 1977, du Pont realized that impending air pollution control legislation within New Jersey would cost the firm about $15 million to implement. The facility is a major source of volatile organic compounds, with 460 sources of VOCs at the plant, although only a small fraction of them exceed the VOC standard. Du Pont decided to apply the bubble approach to its Deepwater plant, and so overcontrolled its emissions on seven of its largest stacks, which they operated at 99 percent efficiency. Another 119 sources, mostly those involved in petroleum processing and not specific to an individual stack, were controlled with 85 percent efficiency. The result was a reduction in total emissions to 2331 tons per year. Under state law (which is more stringent than federal standards), the du Pont facility was allowed to emit 2489 tons per year. Thus the bubble approach provided a 22 percent reduction in emissions below allowable limits and also saved du Pont $13.5 million in capital costs since it did not have to install expensive new equipment on all of its source emissions in order to meet the state emissions standards for VOCs.

Emissions trading is a good example of promoting cost-effective approaches to pollution control. Unfortunately, the concept has not caught on as anticipated in the early 1970s. Los Angeles and New Jersey actively participate in emissions trading, but other nonattainment areas are slow in accepting this approach. Environmentalists are disappointed because the program is not the panacea that they once thought. To be sure, there are abuses by industry in determining emission reduction credits, and there are problems with the accounting and enforcement mechanisms, but market forces do produce results. Industry has saved $4 billion in control costs since 1976, and emissions have been reduced (Stavins, 1989; Dudek and Palmisano, 1988; Liroff, 1986; Tietenberg, 1985).

routinely emitted into the air. The National Emission Standards for Hazardous Air Pollutants (NESHAP), for example, monitors criteria pollutants and has set emissions standards for eight toxics: asbestos, beryllium, mercury, vinyl chloride, arsenic, radionuclides, benzene, and coke oven emissions. At least 30 chemicals are currently under review for likely inclusion into the NESHAP.

Underlying the current EPA policy was the assumption that emissions are directly related to ambient quality and thus human exposure (Smith, 1988). However, the air toxics problem is complex and requires an integrated approach in managing toxic substances and exposures from a variety of sources and media. As a result, the EPA is now using the total exposure assessment methodology (TEAM) to measure multimedia toxic exposure rather than ambient quality. The largest obstacle to widespread use of this method may be the myriad of environmental laws that restrict an agency's ability to undertake integrated studies of human exposures from different media (air, water, and land).

Under Title III of the Superfund Amendments and Reauthorization Act, industry was required to report on the quantities of toxic emissions for about 320 chemicals. In the first survey, the EPA found that 2.7 billion pounds (1.2 million metric tons) of toxic chemicals were emitted into the air in 1987, significantly more than anyone thought (U.S. EPA, 1989b). Unfortunately, this is a conservative estimate as it excludes those toxic emissions from autos, toxic waste dumps, and, most importantly, those companies that produce less than 75,000 pounds (34.1 metric tons) of toxic materials. The chemical industry is the largest source of toxic emissions, with 946 million pounds (430,000 metric tons) released during 1987. Since only eight toxics are currently regulated, these emissions are quite legal. Texas had the most toxic emissions (238.8 million pounds or 108,000 metric tons), and Nevada the least (0.7 million pounds or 318 metric tons) (Fig. 13.10). When standardized by the size of the state (pounds per square mile), the Northeast (Rhode Island, New Jersey, Connecticut, and Massachusetts) has the most

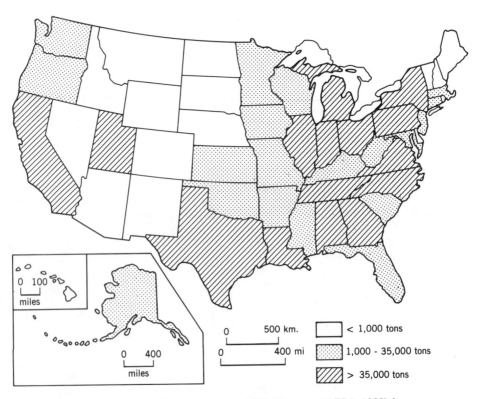

Figure 13.10 Toxic emissions, 1987. (*Source:* USEPA, 1989b.)

toxic emissions, whereas the upper Great Plains and Rocky Mountain states (Montana, Wyoming, South Dakota, New Mexico, and North Dakota) have the least. In 1988, air emissions were down slightly to 2.4 billion pounds (1.09 million metric tons) (Shabecoff, 1990).

ACUTE RELEASES

A related problem of air toxics is the release of acutely toxic substances. These are chemicals that will cause permanent injury and death within minutes to hours of exposure. During the last 25 years, 17 major industrial accidents occurred in the United States that released chemicals in sufficient quantity and with high enough levels of toxicity to potentially kill as many people as were injured in Bhopal, India (Cutter and Solecki, 1989). Luckily, injuries and deaths from acute releases are far lower in this country, although the potential for serious accidents is just as great. Acute releases can occur anywhere and originate from both stationary (sewage treatment plants, municipal swimming pools, and industries) and mobile (truck and train) sources. What separates acute releases from chronic exposures mentioned above is their ability to cause immediate damage to human health, including death, usually from inhaling the substance from a vapor cloud. As a partial response to the Bhopal incident, Congress passed Title III of the Superfund Amendments and Reauthorization Act (SARA), which mandates emergency response planning for these types of incidents (Cutter, 1987). Included within this legislation is a community right-to-know provision that will help local communities plan for these types of emergencies.

INDOOR AIR POLLUTION

Indoor air pollution has become a major health issue in the United States. As houses and buildings become more energy efficient, concentrations of pollutants build up because of lack of ventilation in both the winter and summer. Many people spend as much as 90 percent of their time indoors, and this is particularly dangerous for young children and the elderly. The problems of indoor air pollution have received widespread attention during the last

five years. Potential health effects range from short-term symptoms such as headaches, nausea, and throat irritations, to more long-term health problems like lung disease and even cancer. There are a wide array of pollutants coming from a variety of sources like tobacco smoke, building materials, gas ranges, cleaning agents, and drinking water.

Home

The most serious pollutant in the home is tobacco smoke (especially benzene), followed by radon and particulates from wood-burning stoves. Other sources of pollutants include some consumer products such as paint thinners and wood conditioners. Formaldehyde, often used in furniture, foam insulation, and some wood products, is a major source of volatile organic compounds, and hence the manufacturers recommend use of these products in "well-ventilated areas." Other sources of VOCs are carpet adhesives, latex paint, carpets, and products made from particleboard, such as bookcases.

Workplace and School

Often we hear complaints about "sick buildings" that cause their inhabitants to complain about eye and throat irritations, drowsiness, headaches, and so on. The likely source of many of these ills are elevated pollution levels within the buildings, often caused by the same agents that create elevated levels at home. Heating, ventilating, and air conditioning systems can bring biological contaminants indoors and circulate them throughout buildings, causing allergic reactions to pollen and fungi, as well as promoting more serious bacterial and viral infections. Asbestos, once used widely for insulation and fireproofing, is a known carcinogen. Some of the highest concentrations of asbestos have been found in the nation's schools. In 1986, Congress passed the Asbestos Hazard Emergency Response Act, which required all schools to inspect for asbestos-containing materials and to develop plans to remove them. The role of tobacco smoke in increasing benzene levels, and the increased cancers that result from "passive smoking," has resulted in restrictions on smoking in many public and private buildings and on airplanes.

Radon

Radon is a tasteless, colorless, odorless gas that is a natural by-product of the decay of radium. Radium occurs naturally in many different types of soils and rocks and radon enters buildings through cracks or openings in the foundations or basements. A recent study by the EPA suggests that radon may account for between 5000 and 20,000 lung cancer deaths each year (U.S. EPA, 1988a). The EPA estimates that up to 8 million homes nationwide may have radon levels exceeding 4 picocuries per liter, their indicator of high risk. The radon problem is found everywhere and high-risk areas can be identified using geological maps to identify uranium-rich rocks. Elevated levels of radon were once thought to occur only in winter, but are now found during summer months as buildings remain airtight to keep cool with air conditioning.

Despite the relatively high risk, radon can often be controlled at the individual homeowner level. Once a radon test is done, exposure can be lessened by sealing cracks in the basement, installing home ventilation systems, removing radium-tainted soil, and, if all else fails, relocation. Educational materials and testing kits are often available free of charge from individual state governments. The most comprehensive educational and testing programs are found in Florida, Maine, New Jersey, New York, and Pennsylvania (where the problem was first "discovered" in 1984). New Jersey has the most active educational and testing program, and Pennsylvania offers low-interest loans for home repairs to ameliorate radon exposure (Machado and Ridley, 1988).

SUMMARY

As we have seen, the quality of our air resource has improved in some regions of the country but has worsened in others. Instead of cleaning up pollutants, we often exacerbate the problem by shifting from one pollutant source to another or simply transferring the problem to greater distances. Internationally, the problem of urban air pollution is increasing as many of the world's developing countries become increasingly urbanized.

Cleaning up the air resource is costly and will entail cooperation between industry, government, and citizens. Unless we are willing to don gas masks every time we venture outside, it is essential that we reduce our reliance on the automobile and decrease fossil fuel use. Industry must also do its part by making fuels burn more efficiently and reducing the amount of toxins that are routinely emitted into the air we breathe. Unfortunately, reducing emissions has substantial costs, both for industrial polluters and consumers. While substantial emission reductions have been achieved, further reductions will require substantial capital investments and/or changes in the way we live. It remains to be seen whether we have the political will to force these improvements in air quality.

REFERENCES AND ADDITIONAL READING

Conservation Foundation. 1982. *State of the Environment*. Washington, DC: Conservation Foundation.

——. 1987. *State of the Environment: A View Toward the Nineties*. Washington, DC: Conservation Foundation.

Council on Environmental Quality. 1980. *Environmental Quality, 1980. 11th Annual Report*. Washington, DC: U.S. Government Printing Office.

——. 1981. *Environmental Quality, 1981. 12th Annual Report*. Washington, DC: U.S. Government Printing office.

——. 1982. *Environmental Quality, 1982. 13th Annual Report*. Washington, DC: U.S. Government Printing Office.

Crawford, M. 1990. Scientists battle over Grand Canyon pollution. *Science* 247: 911–912.

Cutter, S.L. 1987. Airborne toxic releases: Are communities prepared? *Environment* 29(6): 12–17, 28–31.

Cutter, S. L., and W.D. Solecki. 1989. The national pattern of airborne toxic releases. *Professional Geographer* 41(2): 149–161.

Dudek, D.J., and J. Palmisano. 1988. Emissions trading: Why is this thoroughbred hobbled? *Columbia J. Environ. Law* 13: 217–256.

Elsom, D. 1987. *Atmospheric Pollution*. Oxford: Basil Blackwell.

Fleischaker, M. L. 1983. Converting the converters: Tampering with cars and the Clean Air Act. *Environment* 25(8): 33–37.

Goldsmith, J. R., and L. T. Friberg. 1977. Effects of air pollution on human health. In Arthur C. Stern (Ed.), *The Effects of Air Pollution*, 3rd ed., Chap. 7, pp. 457–610. New York: Academic Press.

Lave, L. B., and E. P. Seskin. 1977. *Air Pollution and Human Health.* Baltimore: Johns Hopkins Press for Resources for the Future.

Levin, D. P. 1989a. Exhaust of gas engines may be as clean as it can get. *The New York Times*, March 29, p. A1.

———. 1989b. Automakers plea on pollution. *The New York Times*, July 21, p. D1.

Liroff, R.A. 1986. *Reforming Air Pollution Regulation: The Toil and Trouble of EPA's Bubble.* Washington, DC: Resources for the Future.

Machado, S., and S. Ridley. 1988. *Eliminating Indoor Pollution.* Washington, DC: Renew America Project.

Miller, E.W., and R. Miller. 1989. *Environmental Hazards: Air Pollution.* Santa Barbara, CA: ABC-CLIO publishers.

National Commission on Air Quality. 1981. *To Breathe Clean Air.* Washington, DC: U.S. Government Printing Office.

National Research Council. 1979. *Airborne Particles.* Baltimore: University Park Press.

———. 1981. *On Prevention of Significant Deterioration of Air Quality.* Washington, DC: National Academy Press.

Reinhold, R. 1989. Southern California takes steps to curb its urban air pollution. *The New York Times*, March 18, p. A1.

Renner, M. 1988. *Rethinking the Role of the Automobile.* Worldwatch Paper #84. Washington, DC: Worldwatch Institute.

Rohter, L. 1989. Mexico City's filthy air, world's worst, worsens. *The New York Times*, April 12, p. A1.

Rudzitis, G., and J. Schwartz. 1982. The plight of the parklands. *Environment* 24(8): 6–11, 33–38.

Shabecoff, P. 1988. U.S. argues to limit pollutant linked to acid rain. *The New York Times*, November 2, p. A24.

———. 1989. U.S. calls poisoning of air far worse than expected and threat to public. *The New York Times*, March 23, p. B11.

———. 1990. 9% decline in toxic pollution is cited in survey by EPA. *The New York Times*, April 20, p. A11.

Smith, K. R. 1988. Air pollution: Assessing total exposure in the United States. *Environment* 30(8): 10–15, 33–38.

Stavins, R.N. 1989. Harnessing market forces to protect the environment. *Environment* 312(1): 4–7, 28–35.

Stevenson, R.W. 1989. Facing up to a clean-air plan. *The New York Times*, April 3, p. Dl.

Tietenberg, T. 1985. *Emissions Trading: An Exercise in Reforming Pollution Policy.* Washington, DC: Resources for the Future.

U.S. Bureau of the Census. 1988. *Statistical Abstract of the United States, 1988.* Washington, DC: U.S. Government Printing Office.

U.S. Environmental Protection Agency. 1980. *Environmental Outlook.* EPA-600/8-80-003. Washington, DC: U.S. Government Printing Office.

———. 1988a. *Environmental Progress and Challenges: EPA's Update.* EPA-230-07-88-033. Washington, DC: U.S. Government Printing Office.

———. 1988b. *Anthropogenic Emissions Data for the 1985 NAPAP Inventory.* EPA-600/7-88-022. Research Triangle Park, NC: U.S. Environmental Protection Agency.

———. 1989a. *National Air Quality and Emissions Trends Report.* EPA-450/4-89-001. Research Triangle Park, NC: U.S. Environmental Protection Agency.

———. 1989b. *The Toxics Release Inventory: A National Perspective.* EPA-560/4-89-005. Washington, DC: U.S. Government Printing Office.

Weaver, J.D. 1980. *Los Angeles: The Enormous Village 1781–1981.* Santa Barbara, CA: Capra Press.

Weisman, A. 1989. L.A. fights for breath. *The New York Times Magazine*, July 30, pp. 14–17, 30–33, 48.

World Resources Institute. 1987. *World Resources 1987.* New York: Basic Books.

———. 1988. *World Resources 1988–89.* New York: Basic Books.

Zurer, P. S. 1988. Study traces most SO_2 emissions to burning of moderate-sulfur coal. *Chemical and Engineering News*, June 27, pp. 40–41.

TERMS TO KNOW

Advection Inversion
Ambient Air Quality
Anthropogenic
Bubble Approach
Criteria Pollutants
Emissions Trading
Environmental Lapse Rate
Homosphere
Mesosphere
Mobile Sources

Oxidant
Pollution Standards Index (PSI)
Primary Standards
Radiation Inversion
Secondary Standards
Smog
Stationary Sources
Stratosphere
Subsidence Inversion
Temperature Inversion
Troposphere

STUDY QUESTIONS

1. What is an inversion, and how does it affect air pollution?

2. How do sunlight and atmospheric humidity affect air pollution?

3. What are the criteria pollutants? For each one, what are the major emission sources?

4. What emissions cause photochemical smog?

5. What has the government done to prevent air quality deterioration in relatively clean areas? In nonattainment areas?

6. Does your city meet all federal air quality guidelines?

7. Summarize the trends in emissions and ambient concentrations for each of the major pollutants over the last several years. What is the difference among them?

8. Why are toxics in the air of particular concern?

14

Regional and Global Atmospheric Change

INTRODUCTION

Traditionally air pollution has been a local concern, but recently it has taken on a global significance in light of the recent scientific evidence about global warming, climate change, and likely rises in sea level. In addition, the destruction of the protective stratospheric ozone layer by anthropogenic (human) sources of air pollutants has also created international concern about the quality of our air resource. Although the pollutants may have a specific local source, their effects are so widespread that they often transcend national boundaries, hence the term *transboundary pollution*. This chapter highlights a number of these transboundary air pollution issues.

ACID RAIN

Acid rain is a general term that refers to the deposition of acids in rainfall, snow, and dust particles falling from the atmosphere. Although normal rainfall is slightly acidic, air pollution, particularly emissions of sulfur and nitrogen oxides, have greatly increased the acidity of rainfall over wide areas in the last several decades. It is a regional rather than a local consequence of fossil fuel combustion, having been identified as a problem in the eastern United States and Canada and in northern Europe. Acid rain has broad-ranging environmental effects, including damage to vegetation

and structures and reduced surface water quality. It will no doubt continue to be an important environmental issue in industrialized regions of the world for many years.

FORMATION AND EXTENT

Acids are substances that give up a proton (hydrogen nucleus) in a chemical reaction. The acidity of solutions is measured on the pH scale, which gives the negative logarithm of the concentration of hydrogen nuclei in a solution. A pH of 7 is neutral, and numbers less than 7 are increasingly acidic. A pH greater than 7 indicates alkaline conditions. Rainwater is slightly acidic, even under natural conditions. Carbon dioxide dissolves in water to form carbonic acid, a weak acid of about pH 5.6. There are other natural sources of acids in the atmosphere, including sulfur compounds emitted from volcanoes and nitric acids created by lightning passing through the atmosphere. The relative contributions of these other sources to the acidity of rainfall is not known, but the pH of natural rainfall is variable, slightly lower than 5.6, and perhaps as low as 5.0 (Katzenstein, 1981). Acid precipitation, on the other hand, has much lower pH values, commonly in the low 4's and sometimes in the low 3's, about the same as vinegar. A drop of one unit on the logarithmic pH scale represents a tenfold increase in acidity, so these are substantial differences.

Two major pollutants are responsible for the increased acidity of rainfall, sulfur dioxide and nitrogen oxides. Sulfur dioxide (SO_2) combines with oxygen and water in the atmosphere to form sulfuric acid (H_2SO_4). Nitrogen oxides (NO_x) combine with water to form nitric acid (HNO_3). These acids are found in water droplets and on dust particles in the atmosphere, and they are deposited on the ground either in precipitation or in dry dust. The chemical processes that form these acids are not instantaneous; they take from minutes to days to occur, depending on atmospheric conditions (Fig. 14.1).

Sulfur dioxide emissions derive primarily from the combustion of impure fossil fuels, such as coal and fuel oil. In the United States, the areas with the largest sulfur emissions are in the urban industrial areas of the Midwest, particularly the region extending from Illinois to Pennsylvania (Fig. 14.2a). Most of the sulfur emissions are from coal-fired power plants, which are heavily concentrated in the region and account for 70 percent of all the sulfur dioxide emissions nationally (U.S. Environmental Protection Agency, 1988b). These electricity-producing plants burn coal that is much higher in sulfur content than the coal burned in the West. It recently was estimated that

moderate-sulfur coal (which accounts for 40 percent of the total coal burned) is a prime source of emissions, accounting for 49 percent of all sulfur dioxide emissions (Zurer, 1988). In addition, older, smaller electrical utilities emit larger amounts of sulfur dioxide than newer facilities.

In Canada, smelting is a major contributor of sulfur. The world's largest single source of sulfur dioxide emissions is a nickel smelter at Sudbury, Ontario. In Europe, sulfur emissions are greatest in the heavily industrialized regions of Central Europe (Table 14.1).

The pattern for nitrogen oxide emissions is somewhat similar to that for sulfur dioxide (Fig. 14.2b). California, Texas, and Ohio have the highest levels. Again, there is a concentration of emissions in the midwestern states, particularly in Ohio.

The acidity of precipitation in the northeastern United States is mostly attributed to sulfuric acid. The greatest acidity (lowest pH) is found there and in adjacent areas of Canada, downwind from the major sources of sulfur (Fig. 14.3). In the eastern United States, nitric acid is generally a smaller component of acid precipitation than in the West. In Europe, the

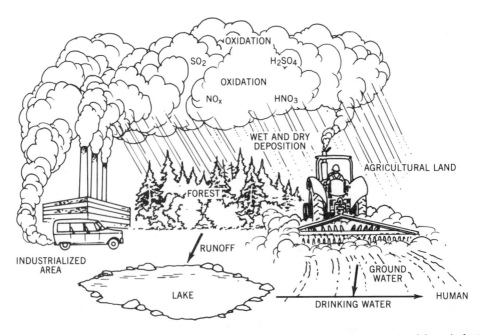

Figure 14.1 Formation and deposition of acid rain. Sulfur and nitrogen oxides emitted from industries, automobiles, and other sources are oxidized in the atmosphere to form nitric and sulfuric acids. These are deposited on the land either in precipitation or in dry dustfall, and affect vegetation, soil, and water quality. (*Source:* U.S. Environmental Protection Agency, 1980.)

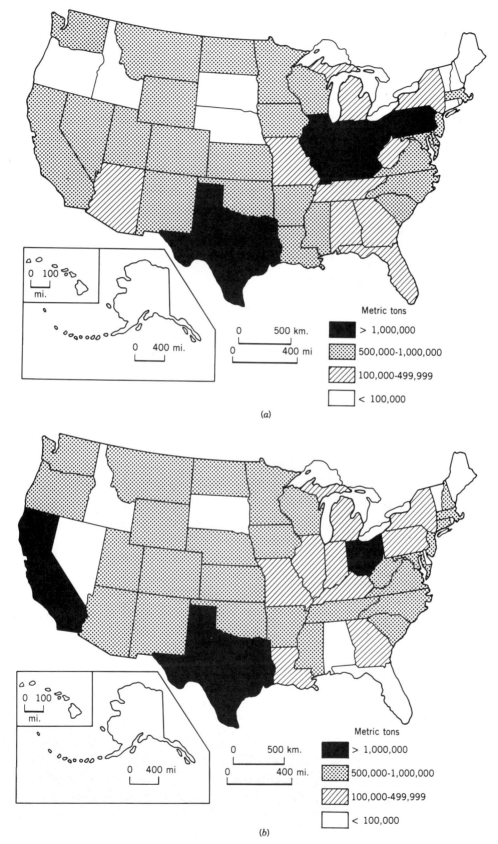

Figure 14.2 Sulfur dioxide and nitrogen oxide emissions that contribute to the formation of acid precipitation. Both Texas and Ohio had high emissions of SO_2 (*a*) and NO_x (*b*) in 1987. SO_2 emissions are greatest in the Midwest. (*Source:* Council on Environmental quality, 1988.)

TABLE 14.1 Sulfur Dioxide Pollution in Europe, 1988

Country	Total Emissions (Thousand Tons)	Total Deposition (Thousand Tons)	Percentage of Emissions Exported	Percentage of Deposition Imported
Austria	62	181	74	91
Czechoslovakia	1400	659	75	47
East Germany	2425	787	75	22
France	760	622	67	59
Italy	1185	513	72	36
Netherlands	145	104	80	72
Norway	37	210	76	96
Poland	2090	1248	68	46
Soviet Union	5150	3201	61	38
Spain	1625	590	72	22
Sweden	110	302	69	89
Switzerland	37	65	81	89
United Kingdom	1890	636	71	15
West Germany	750	628	63	56

Source: French (1990, p. 33).

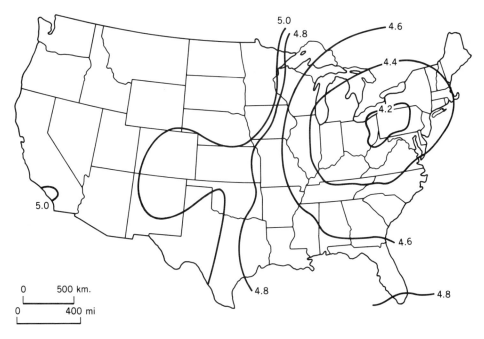

Figure 14.3 The acidity of U.S. precipitation, measured on the pH scale. (*Source:* U.S. Environmental Protection Agency, 1988a; World Resources Institute, 1988.)

greatest acidity of precipitation is concentrated in southern Scandinavia, West Germany, Czechoslovakia, and Poland.

EFFECTS AND DAMAGES

Acid rain has many effects on the environment, most of which are poorly understood at present. The most severe effects are those involving the hydrologic cycle. Acid-neutralizing substances, such as calcium and magnesium compounds, are leached by water as it passes through the ground. In areas of calcium-rich rocks or soil, there are more than enough neutralizing substances to buffer most of the downstream effects of acid precipitation. In areas of more acidic soils or in headwater areas where the water does not pass through much soil or rock before entering streams and lakes, the problem is more severe (Patrick *et al.*, 1981). In the Adirondacks of New York, for example, several high-altitude lakes have become so acidic that most fish cannot survive in the water. In some areas, lime has been added

to lakes in an attempt to buffer the acids, but this has had limited success and is viewed as only a temporary solution to the problem.

A recent study of acidity levels in lakes greater than 10 acres (4 hectares) found extensive damage in six areas. These included lakes in the southwest Adirondacks (39 percent of lakes acidified), the seaboard lowlands of New England (8 percent), Appalachia (10 percent) the Atlantic coastal plain (11 percent), the northern highland lakes in Florida (63 percent), and lakes in Michigan's Upper Peninsula and northern Wisconsin (16 percent) (Stevens, 1990).

In addition to its effects on fish life, acid rain is suspected of contributing to the decline of forests in the United States (Fig. 14.4), Canada, and Europe (Postel, 1984; World Resources Institute, 1987). On Camel's Hump Mountain in Vermont, spruce trees have been dying for several years (Vogelmann, 1982). A drop in the pH tends to make minerals more soluble and thus increases their uptake by plants. Aluminum is of particular concern be-

Figure 14.4   Fraser Firs in decline on Mt. Mitchell, North Carolina.

cause of its toxic effects on plants. Analysis of cores from these trees suggests markedly increased accumulations of aluminum leached from the soil since 1950. Damage to spruce has also been documented in the Adirondacks. The main damage to red spruce, for example, is at 3000–4000 feet (914–1219 m) in the boreal zone of the Green Mountains (Vermont) and the Adirondacks (New York). In West Germany, trees have died over 232 square miles (60,000 ha), and another 14,672 square miles (3.8 million ha) of forests are reported to be severely damaged (French, 1990). In addition, about 35 percent of all European forests are now damaged as a result of acid deposition, approximately 1.9 million square miles (49.6 million ha) (Fig. 14.5) (French, 1990).

There are also concerns about acid rain and its effect on drinking water supplies and human health. Most metals are relatively insoluble in water at near-neutral pH, but as pH decreases, their solubility increases. Aluminum in soils, for example, may be leached out by acid rain and lead to an increase of aluminum concentrations in surface water. Lead, de-

rived from both natural and human sources, is found in lake and stream sediments. As pH decreases, lead concentrations in water may increase. In addition, copper and other metals used in water supply and distribution systems may be dissolved if the water becomes too acidic. Concern with these problems has recently prompted officials in Massachusetts to add lime to Quabbin Reservoir, the major source of water for metropolitan Boston.

Finally, acid rain contributes to the corrosion of building stone and exposed metal, including steel rails, unpainted metal surfaces on bridges and buildings, and so forth (Fig. 14.6). The economic costs of these effects are difficult to estimate, but they are believed to be substantial. The European Community estimates that reductions in sulfur dioxide and nitrogen oxide emissions would cost member nations $4.6–$6.7 billion and $100–$400 million, respectively, per year (World Resources Institute, 1987). Damage estimates resulting from acid rain are spotty and have not been calculated as yet for their effect on crops, forests, human health, or buildings.

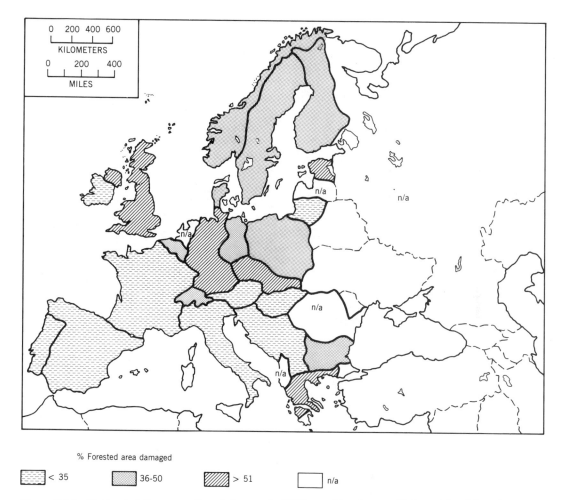

Figure 14.5 Estimated European forest damage in 1988, resulting from acid deposition. More than one half of the forests in the United Kingdom, West Germany, Austria, and Greece have been damaged. (*Source:* French, 1990.)

CONTROL AND MANAGEMENT

Acid rain can be controlled by the same methods used to control sulfur dioxide and nitrogen oxide concentrations in urban areas, including burning low-sulfur fuels, installing sulfur scrubbers, and reducing combustion temperatures. The National Research Council concluded that reductions in emissions will bring proportionate reductions in acid rain (National Research Council, 1983). However, it is virtually impossible to link deposition in one area to emission sources in another because of the large number of sources broadly distributed over vast regions. In addition, NO_x, another component of acid rain, also derives from mobile sources (vehicles).

Control of acid rain is costly. The goal of reducing sulfur dioxide emissions by 8–10 million tons (7.3–9.1 metric tons) during the next five years will cost between $2.1 and $3.6 billion (U.S. Congress, 1986). More ambitious reductions mean an increase in the costs of control. The EPA estimates that to curb emissions that cause acid rain by 50 percent in the United States alone would cost between $16 and $33 billion over the next 20 years (Shabecoff, 1988).

Unfortunately, acid rain is a regional problem that afflicts major industrial areas of North America and Europe. The solutions to the problem must therefore be regional, and this has been one of the primary barriers to reducing acid rain. Another barrier is that it is ex-

Figure 14.6　Destruction of sandstone sculpture caused by air pollution in Germany. The sculpture was installed in 1702; photo (a) was taken in 1908, and photo (b) was taken in 1969.

tremely difficult to detail the exact relationship between emissions and acid deposition because of variations in both time and space (Schwartz, 1989). The geography of acid rain is not precisely known at this time. In the United States, for example, the Clean Air Act was aimed at urban air pollution problems, and its goal was to reduce pollutant concentrations in those areas. One of the techniques used was tall smokestacks, which dispersed the pollutants over a larger area in lower concentrations. This reduced local pollutant concentrations but also helped to spread sulfur and nitrogen oxides over larger areas by placing pollutants into stronger upper winds, thus adding to the acid rain problem at remote locations. Tall stacks (greater than 480 feet or 146 m) are responsible for 56 percent of all point-source sulfur dioxide emissions and 44 percent of the point-source nitrogen oxide emissions nationwide (Table 14.2). Ohio, the leading sulfur dioxide emitter, also leads the nation in sulfur emissions from tall smokestacks (1.8 million pounds or 818 metric tons in 1985) (U.S. EPA, 1988b). If emissions are reduced, acid rain will probably be reduced also, but it is unclear at this time where the benefits will occur.

The U.S. government has been slow to act on the problem. As shown earlier, the cost of controlling emissions is estimated to be on the order of billions of dollars per year, depending on how much control is required. These measures have been resisted by a powerful coal and utility lobby, which have argued that the costs would be too burdensome on consumers and would slow the nation's drive for increased energy self-sufficiency. A panel commissioned by President Reagan reported in mid-1983 that acid rain is indeed a serious problem and that controls would be effective in reducing its effects (National Research Council, 1983). The federal government has taken positive steps in recognizing the problem of acid rain, but it has not taken an active role in reducing emissions. The United States has been working with Canada to solve this transboundary problem, but as of mid-1990 there was no firm commitment to emissions reductions by the United States, which is the necessary first step in the negotiation process.

International agreements will be needed to solve this transnational pollution problem, because some regions cause the pollution and other regions suffer its effects. Persuading one country to pay for cleaning up the environment somewhere else may be difficult. Canada, for example, claims that two-thirds of the sulfur deposited in its eastern provinces comes from the United States and has argued unsuccessfully that the United States should take steps to reduce its emissions. In Europe, more success has been achieved in international ne-

TABLE 14.2 U.S. Sulfur Dioxide Emissions by Stack Height

Stack Height (Feet)	Number of Stacks	Emissions (10^3 Tons)	Emissions as % of Total
<120	13,808	1531.9	7.3
120–240	6,808	2675.6	12.8
241–480	2,101	5090.2	24.3
>480	834	11,676.1	55.7
Total	23,551	20,973.8	100.1

Source: U.S. Environmental Protection Agency (1988b, pp. 5:49).

gotiations, but there are still unresolved claims by the Scandinavian nations that their lakes are being damaged by pollution from France, Britain, Germany, and the Soviet Union.

A November 1988 European Community (EC) directive proposes reducing sulfur dioxide emissions for its member countries by 57 percent of 1980 levels and nitrogen oxide emissions by 30 percent, to be accomplished by 1998. In addition, the amount of reductions will be differentially based on a country's contribution to long-range transboundary pollution problems on the Continent, the level of industrial development, dependence on high-sulfur coal and oil, and the extent of its own antipollution efforts. For example, interim targets for 1993 call for a 40 percent reduction in sulfur dioxide and nitrogen oxide emissions for Belgium, France, Luxembourg, the Nether-

lands, and West Germany, while allowing an increase in emissions for Greece, Ireland, and Portugal (Table 14.3).

In 1987, the protocol to the 1979 convention on Long-Range Transboundary Air Pollution (LRTAP) on the Reduction of Sulphur Emissions or Their Transboundary Fluxes by at Least 30 Percent (referred to as the 30 Percent Club) was ratified by 16 countries. The 30 Percent Club agreed that by 1993 they would reduce sulfur dioxide emissions by at least 30 percent of 1980 levels in order to reduce transboundary pollution problems. By June 1988, 21 countries had signed the treaty, although the largest sulfur dioxide emitters, the United States, the United Kingdom, and Poland, had not. Although the EC directive calls for sulfur dioxide emissions reductions in the United Kingdom, the 1993 target includes

TABLE 14.3 European Community Directive for Sulfur Dioxide Reductions

Country	1980 Baseline (1000 Tons)	1993 Target	1998 Target	2003 Target
		(% Reduction Relative to Baseline)		
Belgium	530	−40	−60	−70
Denmark	323	−34	−56	−67
France	1,910	−40	−60	−70
Greece	303	+ 6	+ 6	+6
Ireland	99	+25	+25	+25
Italy	2,450	−27	−39	−63
Luxembourg	3	−40	−60	−70
Netherlands	299	−40	−60	−70
Portugal	115	+102	+135	+79
Spain	2,290	0	−24	−37
United Kingdom	3,883	−20	−40	−60
West Germany	2,225	−40	−60	−70
Total	14,430	−23	−42	−57

Source: French (1990, p. 34).

only a 20 percent reduction versus the more costly 30 percent in the LRTAP. In addition to the sulfur protocol, negotiations are also under way to limit nitrogen oxide emissions by freezing them at their 1987 levels. This Sofia (Bulgaria) protocol was signed by 24 nations, including the United States (Shabecoff, 1988).

THE GREENHOUSE GASES AND GLOBAL WARMING

THE GREENHOUSE EFFECT

The earth's atmosphere is a partially and differentially transparent medium with respect to energy, and regulates flows of energy between space and the earth's surface. It is highly transparent to the wavelengths of most solar radiation, so sunlight passes through the atmosphere relatively unimpeded. The energy returned to space by the earth has much longer wavelengths than that of sunlight. The atmosphere is only partly transparent to these wavelengths, and much of the outgoing radiation is temporarily trapped in the atmosphere, which keeps the atmosphere warmer than it would otherwise be. Several atmospheric components are responsible for this action, among them methane, ozone, chlorofluorocarbons (CFCs), nitrous oxides, trace gases, and, most important, carbon dioxide. These are collectively known as *greenhouse gases*. The ability of carbon dioxide to allow through shortwave solar radiation but absorb outgoing longwave terrestrial radiation, thus causing atmospheric warming, has been called the *greenhouse effect*. Glass is transparent to shortwave but opaque to longwave energy, which is why a greenhouse heats up on a sunny day. The same principle applies to the atmosphere, with carbon dioxide and the other greenhouse gases taking the place of the glass; and hence the term.

GREENHOUSE GASES

Carbon Dioxide

The amount of heat stored in the atmosphere and its distribution within different layers and regions of the atmosphere play an important role in regulating atmospheric circulation and ultimately climate. The carbon dioxide content of the atmosphere (about 0.03 percent of the atmosphere) has changed considerably throughout the history of the earth. A billion or more years ago, it was probably much higher than today. During the Carboniferous Era, about 280 to 345 million years ago, much of the land surface of the globe was covered with vast swampy forests. The fossil fuels we burn today are derived from carbon taken from the atmosphere and stored in those forests and other ecosystems in the past.

Atmospheric carbon dioxide content also fluctuates on a seasonal basis. In the Northern Hemisphere, the concentration of carbon dioxide varies about 5 ppm within a given year. The maximum occurs in April; as plants photosynthesize and store carbon throughout the summer, the carbon dioxide content steadily decreases. It reaches a minimum in October, then climbs back up as more plant matter decays than grows. The annual cycle shows the close relation between carbon dioxide in the atmosphere and processes at the earth's surface. The global carbon cycle is the biogeochemical cycle that human activity has affected the most. There is reason to believe that this will result in significant climatic changes within the next several decades. If this is true, it will amount to the most profound impact humans have ever had on the global environment and will require substantial adjustments in our use of natural resources.

Since the early nineteenth century, we have steadily increased our extraction and combustion of fossil fuels, returning stored carbon to the atmosphere as carbon dioxide. Not all the carbon dioxide emitted stays in the atmosphere; a substantial amount enters the oceans, and some is stored in living biomass. Since the nineteenth century, the atmospheric content has been steadily increasing (Fig. 14.7). The rate of increase is itself steadily increasing, a result of the exponential growth in fossil fuel use worldwide. In 1880 the average CO_2 concentration was 280 to 300 ppm, and in 1980 it was 340 ppm (Hansen *et al.*, 1981; U.S. EPA, 1983). By 1988, the concentration was 351 ppm (Flavin, 1989). Since 1958, global concentrations of carbon dioxide have risen by 10 percent (U.S. EPA, 1988a).

Not all fuels contribute the same amount

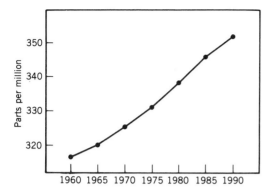

Figure 14.7 Atmospheric concentrations of carbon dioxide. Steady increases in CO$_2$ levels have been observed since 1960. (*Source:* U.S. Environmental Protection Agency, 1983; Flavin, 1989.)

of carbon dioxide when burned. Coal contains about 75 percent more carbon per unit of energy than natural gas, whereas oil contains about 44 percent. Burning oil then releases about 1.5 times the amount of carbon dioxide as natural gas and coal releases twice as much.

In the late 1970s, coal supplied about 29 percent of the world's energy from fossil fuels, but emissions from coal burning were 36 percent of fossil fuel sources. Oil and natural gas supplied about 50 and 15 percent, respectively, of the world's energy from fossil fuels. By 1988, oil only accounted for 33 percent of the world's energy use, followed by coal (27 percent) and natural gas (18 percent). Although fossil fuel combustion rates have been decreasing slightly worldwide, an increase in emissions is expected to continue as a result of the increasing importance of biotic sources of carbon dioxide.

More carbon is currently being released from the biota than is absorbed by it (Woodwell *et al.*, 1978). It is estimated that about 28 percent of the net carbon dioxide emissions come from deforestation and the loss of soil carbon due to soil degradation. Deforestation is the largest source, contributing an estimated 22 percent of total net emissions (Wong, 1978). The future concentration of atmospheric carbon dioxide is difficult to predict and is of course dependent on future rates of fossil fuel use, which are determined by many economic, political, and technological factors. Most estimates, however, predict a doubling of

atmospheric carbon dioxide levels sometime in the twenty-first century.

Methane

Obviously, carbon dioxide is the most important greenhouse gas in contributing about 50 percent of the greenhouse effect. There are other greenhouse gases, however, that also influence the greenhouse effect. Methane (CH$_4$) is responsible for nearly a quarter of the increased warming. Methane also contributes to increased ozone in the stratosphere, which we will discuss later in this chapter. Ambient concentrations of methane have more than doubled in the last 300 years, from 665 to 1675 ppb (Stevens, 1989). The rate of methane increase is 1 percent annually.

Most of the atmospheric methane comes from natural processes, particularly anoxic processes. The natural sources include the decomposition in rice paddies and swamps (46 percent), the action of anaerobic bacteria on plant material in the intestines of ruminants (cows, sheep, and camels) (15 percent), and wood digestion by termites (4 percent). Anthropogenic sources contribute significantly less and include the combustion of fossil fuels (natural gas in particular) (8 percent) and biomass (clearing of forests) (10 percent) and landfills (7 percent).

Nitrous Oxide

Nitrous oxide (N$_2$O) is another greenhouse gas that contributes to the greenhouse effect (about 8 percent). In addition, nitrous oxide acts as a catalyst for stratospheric ozone removal. Nitrous oxide is primarily derived from anthropogenic sources, including the combustion of fossil fuels, the use of nitrogen-rich fertilizer, and deforestation. The rate of increase of nitrous oxide is 0.2 percent per year. The current ambient level is 302 ppb.

Trace Gases

Two other gases are important in the greenhouse effect, but they are less significant than carbon dioxide, methane, and nitrous oxide. Carbon tetrachloride (CCl$_4$) is used as an intermediate to produce CFCs in chemical and pharmaceutical applications and as a grain fumigant. Methyl chloroform (CH$_3$CCl$_3$) is used as an industrial degreaser and as a solvent in paints. Both of these gases also play a small role in the depletion of the ozone layer.

Atmospheric concentrations of trace gases have been increasing at an alarming rate (Table 14.4). Of particular concern is the rapid rise in atmospheric content of the CFCs and the minor trace gases (carbon tetrachloride and methyl chloroform). What is of particular concern is the length of time many of these chemicals remain in the atmosphere, ranging from 8 years (methyl chloroform) to more than 100 (CFCs).

GLOBAL CLIMATE CHANGE: A WARM OR COOL FUTURE?

Increases in atmospheric carbon dioxide cause more rapid plant growth, but some plants respond more dramatically than others. For example, soybeans respond much more than corn, and silver maple responds more than sycamore. These differences may lead to significant agricultural and ecological effects of carbon dioxide, but the most dramatic environmental impacts will probably result from climatic change.

Scientific Uncertainties

There has been considerable debate over the nature of the climatic impact of carbon dioxide emissions. Some have argued that the average temperature of the atmosphere must go up. Others have suggested that there will be an increase in cloudiness and that temperatures will go down as a result. Most predictions of the future effects are based on the use of general

circulation models, which are computerized mathematical models of the circulation of the earth's atmosphere. Because of the enormous number of calculations that would be necessary for absolute accuracy, these models make many simplifying assumptions about the atmosphere that affect the results, but a consensus has emerged (U.S. EPA, 1983).

Given a doubling in the carbon dioxide content of the atmosphere (to about 600 ppm), we can expect an eventual average global temperature increase of a few degrees Celsius with most estimates falling between 3.6° and 10.8° F (2° and 6° C) (Schneider, 1989a). The models also agree that the temperature change will be relatively small in the tropics but as much as several degrees in high-latitude areas. For example, it is anticipated that the average air temperature in the mid-latitudes (North America and Europe) would increase by about 7.2° F (4° C). This means that the number of days that the temperature exceeds 86° F (30° C) in New York would triple (from 15 to 48 days), in Chicago it would more than triple (from 16 to 56 days), and in Los Angeles it would increase fivefold (from 5 to 27 days) (World Resources Institute, 1988).

One of the greatest uncertainties in these predictions is the rate at which the temperature increase will take place. This rate depends on many factors, especially the amount of carbon dioxide emissions, cloud cover, and the mixing characteristics of the ocean. Because of the inherent variability of weather, we have not been able to measure long-term climatic change accurately. Some argue that this lack of

---

TABLE 14.4   Atmospheric Concentrations of Greenhouse Gases, 1975–1986

Year	CO_2 (ppm)	N_2O (ppb)	CH_4 (ppt)	CCl_4 (ppt)	CH_3CCl_3 (ppt)	CFC-11 (ppt)	CFC-12 (ppt)
1975	331.0	291.4	1525	104	70	120	200
1980	338.4	297.6	1639	121	126	179	307
1985	345.7	301.5	1711	130	158	223	384
1986	346.8	305.0	1650	N.A.[a]	N.A.	230	400
Percent change 1975–1986	5	11	11	25	125	86	92
Annual increase (%)	0.5	0.2	1	1	7	5	5

Sources: World Resources Institute (1988); Shea (1988).

[a] N.A. = not available.

detection is evidence that those predicting climate change are wrong. We do know, however, that the effects of increased global temperatures will be felt as regional climate change involving temperature as well as precipitation.

We can also expect rising sea levels as a consequence of global warming, which causes ice cap melting. Most experts conservatively place the rise between 4.5 and 6.6 feet (1.4 and 2 m) (Titus, 1989). The combined effects of these changes will inundate low-lying coastal areas, submerge coastal wetlands, increase coastal erosion, increase flood and storm damage from coastal storms, and increase the salinity of groundwater in low-lying areas, thus threatening drinking water supplies. Bangladesh and Egypt are the most vulnerable countries, where a 7-foot (2-m) rise in sea level would result in a 20 percent reduction in land area in each country. In the United States a similar rise will destroy 50 to 80 percent of our coastal wetlands and between 10 and 28 percent of the land area in Louisiana, Florida, Delaware, Washington DC, Maryland, and New Jersey. Major changes in vegetation and land use will occur and have significant impacts on human society. If the predicted sea level changes are greater than 3 to 7 feet (1 to 2 m), then these effects will be even more pronounced and cover more of the world's low-lying areas.

If we conclude that the world will certainly be warmed by the greenhouse gases, then the next question is the geographic extent of these climatic changes. This is an even more difficult question to answer because of limitations in our knowledge and the lack of computers powerful enough to accurately model such a complex system. One approach is to look at previous periods of earth history with climates different from today's. About 20,000 years ago, for example, the earth was in the depths of an ice age, with glaciers extending as far south as Long Island, New York, on the east coast of North America, and into central Illinois in the Midwest. The circulation and weather patterns that allowed those glaciers to exist were certainly radically different from the present-day climate, yet the average global temperature was only about 5° C (9° F) cooler than today. The change in temperature predicted for the next century is only slightly less than what

occurred during the ice ages, though it is a change to conditions warmer than the present, whereas 20,000 years ago the climate was cooler.

The possible consequences of such climatic changes are imaginable, if unpredictable. Circulation changes might cause today's extreme weather to become the norm 50 years from now. Summers in the midcontinental regions of North America, southern Europe, and Siberia, which are now some of the world's most productive agricultural regions, may become so dry that they will be unable to grow wheat. On the other hand, areas that are now marginal for agriculture may become more favorable. Droughts, floods, and similar problems could become commonplace rather than rare. Significant warming in polar areas might cause rapid melting of some ice caps, producing a global rise in sea level of as much as a few meters. Nearly one-third of the world's population lives within 37 miles (60 km) of the coast, and so any rise in sea level has the potential to inundate many of the world's coastal communities.

Policy Options

The United States is the leading source of carbon dioxide emissions, yet it has been slow to acknowledge the importance of global warming and thus develop a comprehensive climate change strategy. There are, however, several bills in Congress and some provisions of the 1990 Clear Air Act that address carbon dioxide emission reductions. At the international level, concern and political activity is far greater.

In June 1988, a number of nations met in Toronto under the auspices of the United Nations to develop a far-reaching plan to protect the atmosphere. The Intergovernmental Panel on Climate Change recognizes that in order to merely stabilize carbon dioxide levels, a 50–80 percent reduction in carbon dioxide emissions is needed immediately. The panel's goal is to reduce carbon dioxide emissions by 20 percent by 2005 with an equitable distribution of reductions per country. This recommendation is obviously a compromise since many countries wanted an immediate freeze on emissions whereas others oppose restrictions (the United States, Japan, and eastern and central European countries) because they are viewed as too costly.

A Global Warming Treaty was signed by 68 countries who agreed to stabilize emissions of carbon dioxide through reductions in fossil fuel use, but no timetable was set for achieving reductions. The treaty also calls for reductions in the burning of tropical forests. There are three main divisions among countries. Industrial Europe wants to immediately stabilize or reduce carbon dioxide emissions by freezing them at 1988 levels by 2000 and reducing them by 20 percent of the 1988 levels five years later. The Third World countries, notably China and India, are sympathetic to the issue but feel the problem is not of their making. They argue for financial aid from the industrialized nations to compensate for the slower economic growth that they will experience as a result of reduced fossil fuel consumption. Finally, world powers like the United States, USSR, and Japan are taking a cautious approach and calling for more scientific research.

In March 1989, the Hague Declaration called for the creation of an international institution with enforcement powers to carry out the global warming provisions. However, the world's economic and industrial powers did not endorse such an institution. As late as 1990, the United States was still maintaining a cautious approach to any strong reductions in carbon dioxide emissions for itself. It is also reluctant to endorse strong aid packages to assist less fortunate countries in curbing their emissions.

Unfortunately, there are many government skeptics on the issue of global warming. Although scientific uncertainties remain on the magnitude of the change, the irrefutable evidence is that anthropogenic sources of greenhouse gases are fundamentally altering the global climate. Some government policies are attuned to this reality, but most are not.

STRATOSPHERIC OZONE DEPLETION

Another global air pollution problem is the accumulation of *chlorofluorocarbons* in the atmosphere (Forziati *et al.*, 1983). CFCs are a class of synthetic substances that were origi-

nally developed for use in refrigeration. First discovered in 1930, these chemicals became widely used because they are neither toxic nor flammable. Marketed by E.I. du Pont de Nemours & Company under the trademark Freon (CFC-12), these chemicals have amazing versatility and hence many industrial applications. Over time, new chemical formulations were discovered and new applications were found for CFCs. CFC-113, for example, is the fastest-growing member of the family. Its sole use is as a solvent and it is used to clean everything from microchips in computers to your dry-cleaned clothes.

Halons are a related family of compounds that contain bromine, a more potent destroyer of stratospheric ozone. It is speculated that halons cause 20 times the damage to the ozone layer as CFCs. Because of their superb fire-retardant properties, halons (Halon-1211, -1301, -2402) are primarily used in fire extinguishers.

USES OF CHLOROFLUOROCARBONS

CFCs have a variety of uses, although today they are most often used in cooling and foam-blowing. For example, in the United States, 35 percent of all CFCs are used as coolants for refrigeration and air-conditioning, including the air-conditioning in cars (see Issue 14–1). Another 33 percent are used as synthetic rigid foams (insulation, styrofoam ice chests and cups, and fast-food containers) or flexible foams (furniture cushions and foam pillows). The use of CFCs as industrial solvents for cleaning computer microchips and so on accounts for 20 percent of their application. Finally, a mix of uses (fire extinguishers, urethane-soled shoes, and silly string) accounts for the remaining applications (Zurer 1988). The use of CFCs in aerosol sprays was discontinued in the United States in 1979, but they are still used in spray cans in Europe and the developing world. Worldwide, CFCs are primarily used in aerosols (25 percent), rigid foam insulation (19 percent), solvents (19 percent), air-conditioning (12 percent), refrigerants (8 percent), flexible foams (7 percent), and other items (10 percent).

The use of CFCs has increased exponentially, doubling in five to seven years. Peak use was in 1974–1975 and use declined until the mid-1980s when the trend started to reverse. In 1981, 1.3 billion pounds (600,000 metric tons) were produced (World Resources Institute, 1988), and by 1986 this had risen to 1.5 billion pounds (672,000 metric tons) (Zurer, 1988). The primary producers of CFCs are the United States and Western Europe. In America, for example, the market for CFCs increased by more than 30 million pounds (13,600 metric tons) from 1986 to 1988. The total use of CFCs in 1989 was 500 million pounds (225,000 metric tons).

Emissions of CFCs have been steadily increasing since their inception. In 1931, less than 220 million pounds (100 metric tons) were released. By 1976, worldwide CFC emissions peaked at 1.6 billion pounds (707,000 metric tons). A downturn in CFC emissions occurred between 1976 and 1983, but by 1986, CFC emissions were again quite high, averaging 1.5 billion pounds (671,600 metric tons) (World Resources Institute, 1988). The accumulation of CFC in the atmosphere doubled between 1975 and 1985, even though emissions decreased. This helped to highlight the longer-term dangers of CFC use to the atmosphere.

ATMOSPHERIC EFFECTS

CFCs play a role in the troposphere similar to that of carbon dioxide; they absorb longwave radiation and thus enhance the greenhouse effect. Although they are present in much lower concentrations, they are much more effective than carbon dioxide in raising atmospheric temperatures. As their concentrations in the atmosphere increase, they contribute more and more to the greenhouse effect and may eventually have an impact greater than that of the other greenhouse gases (Forziati et al., 1983).

The most significant problem of CFCs is their role in stratospheric ozone depletion. Indeed, one of the properties of CFCs that makes them so useful is that they are chemically inert and therefore very stable. Unfortunately, this also influences their adverse effect on the atmosphere as they remain intact, accumulating rather than breaking down and being removed. The atmospheric lifetime for CFCs, for example, ranges from 76 to 139 years (Table 14.5). This stability allows them to reach the stratosphere, where they are broken down by intense solar radiation, and their components enter into other chemical reactions. One of these reactions results in the reduction of the amount of ozone in the stratosphere. The process is quite simple, but a brief background on its scientific discovery is needed.

In 1985, a group of atmospheric scientists reported a 40 percent reduction in stratospheric ozone during the spring over Antarctica, where they were taking their measurements. Thus the "Antarctic *ozone hole*" was established. During the sunless Antarctic winter (summer in the United States), the air mass is extremely cold; cold enough to freeze water vapor. Polar stratospheric clouds are formed, and chemical reactions on the ice crystals convert chlorine from nonreactive forms to the

TABLE 14.5 Emissions of Ozone-Depleting Chemicals, 1985

Chemical	Emissions (1000 Tons)	Atmospheric Lifetime (Years)	Annual Growth Rate (%)	Contribution to Ozone Depletion (%)
CFC-11	238	76	5	26
CFC-12	412	139	5	45
CFC-113	138	92	13	12
Carbon tetrachloride	66	67	1	8
Methyl chloroform	474	8	7	5
Halon-1301	3	101	N.A.[a]	4
Halon-1211	3	12	23	1

Source: Shea (1988, p. 27).
[a] N.A. = not available.

more reactive hydrogen chloride and chlorine nitrate, which are sensitive to sunlight. As the Southern Hemisphere spring approaches, sunlight appears and releases the chlorine, which starts a chemical chain reaction that transforms ozone (O_3) into oxygen (O_2). The chlorine remains in the stratosphere to initiate many more chain reactions.

In one of the worst years (1987), 50 percent of the ozone over Antarctica was destroyed. Recent evidence indicates that CFC-derived chlorine is also destroying the ozone layer in the Arctic region as well, with 2-8 percent of the stratospheric ozone depleted. With global air circulation patterns, the chlorine could easily be transported to mid-latitudes, and this is what concerns scientists.

Ozone intercepts ultraviolet radiation from the sun, and so one of the results of CFCs in the stratosphere is that more ultraviolet radiation reaches the earth's surface. This radia-

tion is responsible for biological damage to plants and animals. Increased radiation will decrease photosynthesis, water use efficiency, leaf area, and ultimately crop yields by as much as 30 percent (Luoma, 1989). Crops like corn, soybeans, wheat, tomatoes, lettuce, and cotton seem to be the most affected in laboratory studies. Aquatic ecosystems may be most damaged, with estimates suggesting that a 25 percent reduction in ozone would result in a 35 percent reduction in the productivity of these ecosystems and their fish popula-ecosystems and their fish populations.

From a human standpoint, ultraviolet radiation would produce an increase in the number of skin cancers worldwide in the coming years. Every 1 percent decline in ozone is linked to an increase in skin cancers by 4–6 percent (Shea, 1988). There could be 150 million new skin cancers resulting in 3 million deaths in the next 50 years in the United States alone. Some scientists also feel that ul-

---

ISSUE 14–1   Warning! The Air-Conditioning in Your Car Is Now Illegal in Vermont

Automakers are one of the largest users of CFCs in the United States, using about 30,000 tons of CFC-12 a year for air-conditioning in new cars. This represents between 15 and 20 percent of total CFC use in this country. If one examines emissions, 27 percent of CFC emissions are related to car air-conditioning units. Since most new cars sold (about 90 percent) are equipped with air-conditioning, this is a major source for reduction. With the U.S. ratification of the Montreal Protocol, the impacts of CFC reductions in the automobile industry are being felt. The EPA has set restrictions on use and production of CFCs on an industry by industry basis. In July 1989, producers were limited to 1986 production levels (a 15 percent decrease). Further phaseouts occur in 1993 and 1998. Although laudable, many consumers felt that a more drastic reduction was needed, and local action has been taken by individual states and communities who have developed their own CFC bans. One such example is Vermont.

In the spring of 1989, Vermont passed a law that outlawed the sale and registration of new cars (beginning with 1993 models) that contained CFCs in their air-conditioning units. The

bill also mandates CFC recycling and reclamation during repairs on the air-conditioning unit. Hawaii has also enacted CFC restrictions in which CFC-12 must be recycled when car air-conditioning units are serviced. The Hawaii legislation also bans the sale of small cans of refrigerant for home use that contain CFCs. California and other states are considering similar pieces of legislation; in fact there were some 90 bills in 20 states in early 1990. The U.S. Senate also has pending legislation that makes it illegal to sell or export cars with CFCs in the air-conditioning after 1993. How is Detroit responding to all of this?

The immediate reply is, "not well". The automakers have consistently fought the local CFC bans, claiming that while they agree with the dangers of continued CFC use, usable substitutes have not been thoroughly tested and are not available in the quantities they need. There is some truth to this. In addition, the automakers claim that they cannot meet the strict deadlines for the 1993 model year cars that go on sale in the fall of 1992. One new coolant currently being tested is a hydrofluorocarbon, HFC-134a, which can be phased into production in 1993–1994. It

traviolet radiation plays a role in the depression of the human immune system, thus lowering the body's resistance to infections and disease.

MANAGEMENT

In 1974, a group of U.S. scientists postulated that CFCs added chlorine to the stratosphere and through a series of complex chemical reactions reduced the amount of ozone. As a partial response to this concern over "ozone depletion," the United States banned CFCs as aerosol propellants in all nonessential applications (ranging from hair sprays to deodorants to furniture polish). U.S. production of CFCs dropped by 95 percent. Considering that the United States and the European Community account for 84 percent of all CFC output, this was significant. Canada, Sweden, Norway, Denmark, and Finland also banned the use of CFCs as propellants in spray cans. The rest of the EC

was slower to respond and delayed until 1980, when it cut aerosol use by 30 percent of 1976 levels (Conservation Foundation, 1989). As described earlier, the cut in production and use did not significantly alter the amount of CFCs in the atmosphere. With the discovery of the so-called "ozone hole" in 1985 in Antarctica, the theoretical relationship between CFC use and ozone depletion became fact and widely accepted by scientists, policymakers, and the public. The time was ripe for international action.

In 1985, 28 nations participated in the Vienna Convention on the Protection of the Ozone Layer. This meeting was designed as a legal instrument to protect the atmosphere as a resource by reducing the use of CFCs. The conferees were able to agree in principle to protect the atmosphere, but in practical terms they were unable to agree on CFC control. The United States, Canada, and Sweden, for example, wanted an immediate freeze on CFC pro-

is less efficient as a heat exchanger so more of the coolant is required. Now, only 3 pounds of CFC-12 are need for car air-conditioning units. The HFC-134a will require a larger compressor and a new lubricant as well. What this means for Detroit is that the air-conditioning unit will be larger, and thus engines must be re-arranged to accommodate it. Since the space in many engines is already tight, this poses some real design problems for the automakers. Finally, with increased engine sizes (the most likely short-term alternative) we will see a decline in fuel efficiency and thus gas mileage.

The automobile makers are not the only industry to feel the bite of the Montreal Protocol. IBM is a considerable user of CFC-113 for cleaning, around 6000 tons per year. Twenty-two percent of all CFC emissions in the United States are related to the use of CFCs as solvents in the electronics industry. Obviously, other cleaning methods and perhaps less efficient alternatives will be needed.

Last, but not least, "styrowars" have erupted between the food packaging industry and the American consumer. In 1987, McDonald's stopped using CFCs in their foam packaging and

switched to HCFC-22, which is 95 percent less damaging. In late 1990 McDonald's announced its plan to completely eliminate its styrofoam hamburger packaging. Beginning in June 1988 and continuing even today, many communities are now banning the use of CFC-produced food packaging in local retail outlets. Berkeley, California, for example, banned CFC foam packaging in retail stores in 1988 and in 1990 made it mandatory for merchants in the city to stop using foam containers. Suffolk County, New York, banned styrofoam food packaging in schools and local restaurants. These bans are less of a hardship to the packaging industry since less than 2 percent of the CFC consumption in this country is for this purpose. Replacing the CFCs in packaging is easy and there is no difficulty in meeting the production caps imposed by the Montreal Protocol.

Production bans are one approach to curbing CFC use. Local community restrictions on products are another. Ultimately, the most powerful tool is the consumer, who can refuse to purchase the new car with air-conditioning, preferring to cool the car the old-fashioned way: by rolling down the windows (Zurer, 1989).

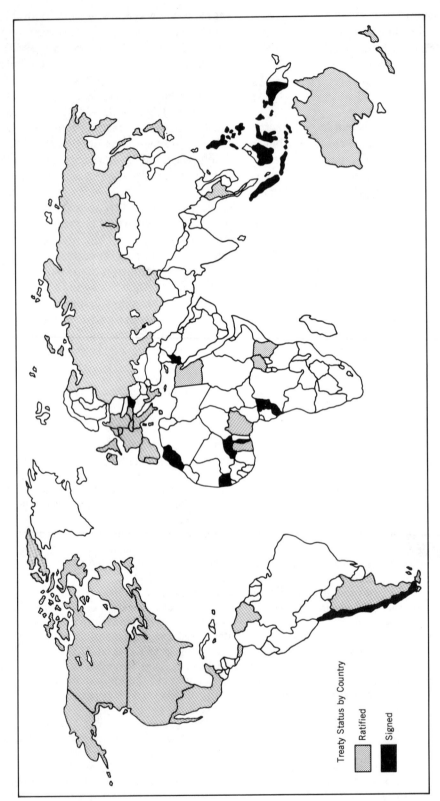

Figure 14.8 Signatory nations to the Montreal Protocol. This treaty calls for reductions in emissions of ozone-depleting substances. (*Source:* Conservation Foundation, 1989.)

Treaty Status by Country

Ratified

Signed

duction and a gradual phaseout. European Community members wanted a freeze in production at existing levels. In early 1986, the Chemical Manufacturers Association, an industry group, supported production limits. Du Pont, the developer of Freon, vowed to find a substitute for CFCs within five years. The industrial race to find suitable CFC substitutes is on as more and more countries either ban or gradually phase out their use.

By 1987, significant international concern had been raised resulting in the passage of the *Montreal Protocol* (officially known as the Montreal Protocol on Substances That Deplete the Ozone Layer). Initially signed by 24 countries (including the United States, Japan, Canada, and the 12-nation European Community), the treaty has now been ratified by a total of 36 countries (Fig. 14.8). The treaty, which became effective January 1, 1989, freezes the production of CFCs by European Community members at mid-1989 levels and calls for 50 percent reductions in emissions globally by 1999. The treaty permits developing countries to increase CFC use for ten more years, while allowing the USSR to continue production through 1990. Finally, the Montreal Protocol limits the use of halons as fire-suppressant chemicals (Table 14.6).

In early 1989, the European Community countries went a step further and agreed to totally eliminate the use of CFCs by the end of the century. The United States agreed with this move, resulting in the total ban of CFC production by 65 percent of the world's producing countries (Whitney, 1989). Despite this effort by industrialized countries, the protocol's goal of halving CFC use by 50 percent at the turn of the century will not be met. Even with 100 percent participation by all countries, chlorine concentrations in the atmosphere will triple by the year 2075 because of the longevity of the chlorine-bearing chemicals. Developing countries are especially important to this global effort because of their growing populations and increased use of CFCs. In 1990, some of the most populous developing countries, such as Brazil, China, India, Indonesia, and South Korea, had still refused to sign the protocol (Fig. 14.8).

TABLE 14.6 Halocarbons Controlled under the Montreal Protocol

Substance	Major Uses
Group 1—Production cuts mandated	
CFC-11	Flexible foam, rigid polyurethane foam, refrigeration, air-conditioning
CFC-12	Rigid polyurethane and rigid nonpolyurethane foam, refrigeration, air-conditioning, aerosols, sterilization, food freezing
CFC-113	Solvent
CFC-114	Rigid nonurethane foam, refrigeration, air-conditioning
CFC-115	Refrigeration, air-conditioning
Group 2—Production freeze mandated	
Halon-1211	Portable fire extinguishers
Halon-1301	Total flooding fire-extinguishing systems
Halon-2402	Fire extinguishers

Source: Zurer (1989, p. 9).

WHERE DO WE GO FROM HERE?

No one knows the geographic extent of the predicted climatic changes, or the exact timing. Most scientists agree that some changes are likely, perhaps within the next several decades. These effects will be slow to come; to prevent them, we would have to act now or, better yet, have acted a few decades ago. For the present, the best that can be done is to become more aware of transboundary pollution problems and the difficulty they pose for environmental management.

Worldwide, both tropospheric and stratospheric pollution levels have worsened and will rise as developing countries become more urban and industrialized. The long-term consequences of altering the earth's atmospheric chemistry are already generating global concern. Tough economic and political action must be undertaken and international cooperation is a must if we are to protect this common property resource for future generations.

REFERENCES AND ADDITIONAL READING

Abrahamson, D.E. (Ed.). 1989. *The Challenge of Global Warming.* Covelo, CA: Island Press.

Bolin, B., R. Doos, J. Jager, and R.A. Warrick (Eds.). 1986. *The Greenhouse Effect,Climatic Change and Ecosystems.* SCOPE 29. New York: Wiley.

Conservation Foundation. 1989. The ozone protocol: A new global diplomacy. *Conservation Foundation Newsletter,* Vol. 4.

Council on Environmental Quality. 1988. *Environmental Quality, 18th and 19th Annual Report.* Washington, DC: U.S. Government Printing Office.

Dovland, H. 1987. Monitoring European transboundary air pollution, *Environment* 29(10): 10–20, 27–29.

Elsom, D. 1987. *Atmospheric Pollution.* Oxford: Basil Blackwell.

Flavin, C. 1989. *Slowing Global Warming: A Worldwide Strategy.* Worldwatch Paper #91. Washington, DC: Worldwatch Institute.

Forziati, H., *et al.* 1983. The chlorofluorocarbon problem. *Resources* 72: 8–9.

French, H. 1990. *Clearing the Air: A Global Agenda.* Worldwatch Paper #94. Washington, DC: Worldwatch Institute.

Hansen, J., *et al.* 1981. Climate impact of increasing atmospheric carbon dioxide. *Science* 213: 957–966.

Jäger, J. 1988. Anticipating climatic change. *Environment* 30(7): 13–15, 30–33.

Katzenstein, A.W. 1981. *An Updated Perspective on Acid Rain.* Washington, DC: Edison Electric Institute.

Luoma, J. 1988. The human cost of acid rain. *Audubon* 90(4): 16–29.

———. 1989. Crop study finds severe ozone damage. *The New York Times,* February 2, p. C4.

National Research Council. 1983. *Acid Deposition: Atmospheric Processes in Eastern North America.* Washington, DC: National Academy Press.

Patrick, R., *et al.* 1981. Acid lakes from natural and anthropogenic causes. *Science* 211: 446–448.

Postel, S. 1984. *Air Pollution, Acid Rain, and the Future of Forests.* Worldwatch Paper #58. Washington, DC: Worldwatch Institute.

Rhodes, S. L., and P. Middleton. 1983. The complex challenge of controlling acid rain. *Environment* 25(4): 6–9, 31–38.

Schneider, S. H. 1989a. The greenhouse effect: Science and policy. *Science* 243: 771–782.

———. 1989b. *Global Warming: Are We Entering the Greenhouse Century?* San Francisco: Sierra Club Books.

Scholle, S. R. 1983. Acid deposition and the materials damage question. *Environment* 25(8): 25–32.

Schwartz, S. E. 1989. Acid deposition: Unraveling a regional phenomena. *Science* 243: 753–770.

Shabecoff, P. 1988. U.S. argues to limit pollutant linked to acid rain. *The New York Times,* November 2, p. A24.

Shea, C. P. 1988. *Protecting Life on Earth: Steps to Save the Ozone Layer.* Worldwatch Paper #87. Washington, DC: Worldwatch Institute.

Stevens, W. K. 1989. Methane from guts of livestock is new focus in global warming. *The New York Times,* November 21, p. C4.

———. 1990. Study of acid rain uncovered a threat of a far wider area. *The New York Times,* January 16, p. C4.

Titus, J.G. 1989. Causes and effects of sea level rise. In D.E. Abrahamson (Ed.), *The Challenge of Global Warming,* pp. 161–195. Covelo, CA: Island Press.

U.S. Congress. 1986. *Curbing Acid Rain: Cost, Budget, and Coal-Market Effects.* Washington, DC: Congressional Budget Office.

U.S. Environmental Protection Agency. 1980. *Acid Rain.* EPA-600-79-036. Washington, DC: U.S. Government Printing Office.

———. 1983. *Can We Delay a Greenhouse Warming?* Washington, DC: U.S. Government Printing Office.

———. 1988a. *Environmental Progress and Challenges: EPA's Update.* EPA-230-07-88-033. Washington, DC: U.S. Environmental Protection Agency.

———. 1988b. *Anthropogenic Emissions Data for the 1985 NAPAP Inventory.* EPA-600/7-88-022. Research Triangle Park, NC: U.S. Environmental Protection Agency.

Vogelmann, H.W. 1982. Catastrophe on Camels Hump. *Natural History* 91(Nov.): 8–14.

Whitney, C. R. 1989. 12 Europe nations to ban chemicals that harm ozone. *The New York Times,* March 3, p. A1.

Wong, C.S. 1978. Atmospheric input of carbon dioxide from burning wood. *Science* 200: 197–200.

Woodwell, G.M., *et al.* 1978. The biota and the world carbon budget. *Science* 199: 141–146.

World Resources Institute. 1987. *World Resources 1987.* New York: Basic Books.

———. 1988. *World Resources 1988–89.* New York: Basic Books.

Zurer, P. 1988. CFC production cuts: EPA rules already under attack. *Chemical and Engineering News,* August 8, p. 4.

————. 1989. Producers, users grapple with realities of CFC phaseout. *Chemical and Engineering News,* July 24, pp. 7–13.

TERMS TO KNOW

Acid Rain
Chlorofluorocarbons (CFCs)
Greenhouse Effect
Greenhouse Gases
Montreal Protocol
Ozone Hole
Transboundary Pollution

STUDY QUESTIONS

1. How can you explain the inconsistencies in U.S. policy with respect to transboundary air pollution issues? On the one hand the government advocates strong controls for CFC use, yet opposes similar controls for emissions of carbon dioxide, sulfur dioxide, and nitrogen oxides.

2. What are the precursors to acid precipitation and what is the geographic extent of the problem?

3. Describe the greenhouse gases and how they contribute to global warming.

4. What are some of the anticipated environmental effects of global warming? What other natural resources will likely be affected? Are these positive effects?

15

Minerals: Finite or Infinite?

INTRODUCTION

In Chapter 1 we stated that resources are defined by their use. They fluctuate in response to changing human evaluations of resources as commodities and our abilities to use them. This is particularly true for minerals. Experts may have knowledge about and the ability to use a given deposit, but more is needed before a substance can be extracted and marketed. Economics and politics cause the status and availability of minerals to fluctuate widely, often much more than other natural resources.

Minerals are defined differently in different contexts. For the purposes of this book, minerals are substances that come from the earth, either from solid rocks or from soils and other deposits. Minerals include fossil fuels, such as coal, oil, and natural gas, but these are discussed separately in Chapter 16. The nonfuel minerals include metal ores, phosphate rock, asbestos, salt, precious stones, clay, gravel, building stone, and similar materials. Minerals are valued for their physical properties, such as strength, malleability, corrosion resistance, electrical conductivity, and insulating or sealing capacity, and they are fundamental to any industrial system. Table 15.1 lists major minerals, some of their uses, and major world producers.

An important feature of mineral resources is that most are traded internationally. Usually a relatively small number of countries dominate production of a particular mineral, and many countries are consumers. A country may have substantial quantities of a mineral available, the capacity to extract it, and the need to use it, but this does not necessarily mean that it will produce the mineral domestically. If sufficient quantities are available on the world market at prices below domestic production costs, then the mineral will be imported. Also, conditions in major producing or consuming nations can significantly affect world markets and have far-flung impacts on the status of mineral resources. We must therefore examine mineral resources on a global scale.

RESERVES AND RESOURCES

Reserves is an important term used to describe the availability of minerals to a production system. Reserves of a mineral are the supplies available for use at the present time. Their location and physical characteristics are known, and they can be extracted using present technology and under prevailing economic conditions. Reserves are a subset of *resources*, which also include deposits that are unavailable for use at present, because of poor geologic knowledge or unfavorable economic or technological conditions, but which might become available in the future. *Unidentified* resources are those that have not yet been discovered; *subeconomic* resources are those that may have been discovered but cannot be extracted at a profit at current prices.

The distinction between reserves and resources is illustrated in Fig. 15.1. The horizontal axis of the diagram represents varying degrees of certainty about the existence or nature of deposits of a particular mineral. The vertical axis represents differing economic values of the deposits, that is, the varying economic profitability of extraction. All deposits of a given mineral are contained symbolically within the boundaries of the diagram.

The boundaries between reserves and other resources in Fig. 15.1 shift over time. Shifts in these boundaries result primarily from three factors: (1) economic conditions; (2) technology of extraction and use; and (3) geologic information. The economic profitability of extraction varies considerably, depending primarily on the price of the commodity. As price goes up, more and more deposits, of lower grade and/or higher cost of extraction, become profitable to extract. Similarly, if price falls, only high-quality or cheaply extracted deposits can be mined at a profit, and the quantity of reserves shrinks. Prices for minerals often fluctuate widely, as discussed in Chapter 2. Fluctuations in the level of production in the economy as a whole affect demand and price for raw materials, and competition between substitutable materials can also cause price variations.

Technology is another factor that is of importance, mainly as it affects the costs of mineral extraction and processing. For example, during the nineteenth and early twentieth centuries, high-quality iron ore was shipped in essentially raw form from Lake Superior ports to steel mills on the lower Great Lakes. In time the high-grade ores were depleted, and transportation costs per unit of steel became prohibitive. The development of a means for concentrating a lower-grade ore, called taconite, into enriched pellets at the mining site reduced transportation costs and allowed renewed mining activities. This technological development made lower-grade ores economically extractable, which they had not been in the past. Technological and social changes can also cause increases in the costs of extraction. Recently environmental regulations have required changes in mining techniques to minimize environmental disruption. These changes have increased the cost of extraction, thus decreasing reserves. Underground mining of coal is another example; stricter safety standards for miners have increased costs of mining coal underground. In some cases this has contributed to the shift from subsurface to surface mining of coal.

Geologic exploration does not directly affect the profitability of extracting minerals but instead brings new deposits to light. If these are extractable at current prices and with

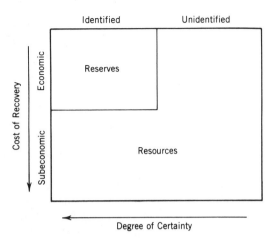

Figure 15.1 Reserves and resources. The boundary between reserves and resources is not fixed. It shifts with new discoveries, price changes, and other technological and socioeconomic factors. (*Source:* Modified from Brobst and Pratt, 1973.)

current technology, they become reserves. Changes in geologic information are generally more important in long-term trends in reserves rather than in the short term. For most minerals there are identified deposits that will last at least a few years, and price fluctuations cause much more variation in reserves than do increases in information. It takes time to acquire new geologic information. Easily located surficial deposits have mostly been identified, and new deposits must be found beneath the surface or in very remote areas. Geologic structures and rock types must be carefully mapped, possible mineral associations checked with geochemical surveys, gravity surveys conducted, and so forth. When a potential deposit is located, it is usually necessary to drill test boreholes and analyze many rock samples before there is any certainty of the nature and extent of a deposit. The sophisticated exploration techniques available today help us to see the subsurface in greater detail more than they significantly speed the process of exploration.

AVAILABILITY OF MAJOR MINERALS

GEOLOGY OF MINERAL DEPOSITS

There are so many different minerals that are of importance, and the geology of their de-

TABLE 15.1 Major Mineral Uses and Producers

Mineral	Major uses	Major producing nations
Antimony	Flame retardants, transportation, batteries	China, Bolivia, South Africa, Mexico
Arsenic	Wood preservatives, agricultural chemicals	France, Sweden, USSR, Chile
Asbestos	Friction products, roofing, pipe, coatings	Several
Barite	Well-drilling fluids, chemicals	China, USSR, Mexico
Bauxite (aluminum)	Packaging, building, transportation, electrical	Australia, Guinea, Jamaica, Brazil
Beryllium	Metal alloys in aerospace and electrical equipment	U.S.A., USSR, Brazil
Bismuth	Pharmaceuticals, chemicals, machinery	Australia, Mexico, Peru, Japan
Boron	Glass, soaps, and detergents	U.S.A., Turkey
Bromine	Fire retardants, petroleum	U.S.A., Israel, USSR
Cadmium	Coating and plating, batteries, pigments	Japan, U.S.A., Canada, Australia
Cesium	Research and development	Canada, Zimbabwe, Namibia
Chromium	Steel alloys	South Africa, USSR
Cobalt	Steel alloys	Zaire, Zambia, USSR, Canada
Columbium	Metal alloys	Brazil, Canada
Copper	Building construction, electrical, machinery	Chile, Canada, U.S.A.
Diamond (industrial)	Machinery, drill bits, abrasives	Zaire, Australia
Diatomite	Filters	U.S.A., Taiwan, France
Feldspar	Ceramics	Italy, U.S.A.
Fluorspar	Metal processing	Mexico, Mongolia, China, USSR
Gallium	Electronics	France, West Germany, Japan
Garnet (industrial)	Abrasives, filters	U.S.A.
Germanium	Infrared optics, fiber optics	Belgium, Luxembourg, U.S.A., China
Gold	Jewelry, electronics	South Africa, Canada, USSR
Graphite	Refractories, lubricants	China, several others
Gypsum	Building materials	U.S.A., Canada, France
Hafnium	Nuclear energy, refractories	France
Helium	Cryogenics, welding	U.S.A.
Ilmenite	Titanium pigments	Australia, Canada, Norway
Indium	Electronics, solder	Japan
Iodine	Animal feeds, catalysts, chemicals	Japan, Chile, USSR
Iron ore	Steel	USSR, Brazil, Australia, China
Kyanite	Refractories	South Africa
Lead	Batteries, fuel additives	Australia, U.S.A., Mexico, China
Lime	Steel furnaces, water treatment, construction	Many
Lithium	Ceramics, aluminum production, lubricants	USSR, Chile, Zimbabwe, China
Magnesium (ore)	Refractories, aerospace	USSR, China, North Korea, Greece
Manganese	Steel alloys	USSR, South Africa, Brazil, Gabon
Mercury	Electrical, chlorine and caustic soda, paints	USSR, Spain, Algeria, Mexico
Molybdenum	Machinery, chemicals, transportation	U.S.A., Chile, Canada

TABLE 15.1 *(Continued)*

Mineral	Major uses	Major producing nations
Nickel	Metal alloys	USSR, Canada
Perlite	Building construction products	U.S.A., Greece
Phosphate rock	Fertilizer	U.S.A., USSR, Morocco
Platinum group	Catalytic converters, electronics, medical	USSR, South Africa
Potash	Fertilizer	USSR, Canada, East Germany
Pumice	Building materials	Italy, Greece
Quartz crystal	Electronics	Brazil, U.S.A.
Rare earths	Petroleum catalysts, metallurgical, ceramics	U.S.A., China, Australia
Rhenium	Petroleum catalysts, electrical	USSR, U.S.A., Chile, Canada
Rutile	Titanium pigments, titanium metal, welding	Australia, Sierra Leone
Scandium	Lasers, lighting	China, U.S.A., USSR
Selenium	Electronics, ceramics	Japan, Canada, U.S.A.
Silicon	Metal alloys	USSR, Norway, U.S.A., Brazil
Silver	Photography, electronics	Mexico, Peru, USSR, Canada
Strontium	Television screens, pyrotechnics	Spain, Turkey, Mexico, Iran, U.K.
Sulfur	Agricultural chemicals, other chemicals	U.S.A., USSR
Talc	Ceramics, refractories, insecticides	Japan, U.S.A.
Tantalum	Electronics, machinery	Brazil, Zaire, Thailand, Australia
Tellurium	Iron and steel, other metals	Japan, U.S.A.
Thallium	Electronics, pharmaceuticals, alloys	Belgium, Luxembourg, Netherlands
Thorium	Nuclear fuel, electrical	India, Norway, U.S.A., Canada
Tin	Electrical, packaging, construction	Malaysia, Brazil, Indonesia
Tungsten	Lamps, other electrical, metalworking	China, USSR
Vanadium	Steel alloys	South Africa, USSR
Yttrium	Television monitors, lasers, alloys, catalysts	Malaysia, China, Australia
Zinc	Metal plating, alloys	Canada, Australia, Peru
Zirconium	Foundry sands, refractories, ceramics	Australia, South Africa, USSR

Source: U.S. Bureau of Mines (1988).

posits is so varied, that it is impossible to describe the specific conditions of all mineral occurrences. However, it is useful to discuss some general principles and examples of some major types of mineral deposits.

Minerals differ greatly in their crustal abundance, that is, in the percentage of the earth's crust that is composed of particular minerals. Iron, for example, composes about 5 percent of the earth's crust, and aluminum about 8 percent (Putnam and Bassett, 1971). Gold, on the other hand, is only about one-billionth of the earth's crust, and copper and zinc are each about one ten-thousandth. These fractions obviously affect the frequency with which we find usable deposits of these elements. Many minerals are valuable because of the particular chemical or molecular structure in which they are found, and the frequency of such occurrences may be high or low. Carbon is a relatively plentiful element, for example, but diamonds, a crystalline form of carbon, are quite rare.

Many minerals, especially metal ores, tend

to be formed by similar geologic processes. For example, if rocks are heavily fractured by stresses in the earth's crust, at high temperatures, then *hydrothermal mineralization* can take place. In this process, various elements dissolved in subsurface water flow below the surface, within the crust. If the chemistry and temperature of the water change in certain ways, then certain minerals are deposited in surrounding rocks, creating concentrations of those minerals. Many valuable ores are created this way and tend to be found near each other in mineralized districts. Mountain building often includes hydrothermal activity, and as a result many of our important mineralized districts are in mountainous areas.

Shields are areas of very old igneous and metamorphic rocks that form the ancient cores of continents, and they are another geologic environment that has yielded large amounts of valuable minerals. In most of the world shields are buried under other rocks, but large surface shield areas occur in Canada, Africa, Australia, and elsewhere. Because of their age, these areas contain different mineral assemblages than do most younger rocks, and many shield areas are very rich in metal ores. Important deposits of iron, nickel, copper, zinc, and other metals are found in the Canadian shield in Ontario and Quebec, for example.

Whereas concentrated metal ores are usually found in metamorphic rocks, there are many areas of sedimentary rocks that yield important minerals. Lead, zinc, and uranium are sometimes found in commercially extractable quantities in sedimentary rocks. Some substances, most notably gold and diamonds, are found in *placer deposits*. These are deposits of sand or gravel in which denser particles have been concentrated by the action of running water. Mining them usually requires excavating large volumes of sediment to recover small quantities of minerals.

Another process that concentrates minerals at the earth's surface is *weathering*, or the gradual breakdown of rocks by mechanical and chemical processes. Weathering can selectively remove some elements while leaving others in the soil. Bauxite, the most important ore of aluminum, is formed in this way in humid tropical environments.

These few examples help to show the range of environments in which minerals are found. Some minerals show up in several different types of deposits, but many are located only in restricted geologic circumstances. Common minerals, such as iron, are found all over the globe, and there is great variability in the quality of those deposits. As a rule, very high grade deposits are relatively rare, but if industry is willing to accept slightly lower grade deposits, there is always more available. This is certainly true for common elements such as iron and aluminum. The United States has little high-quality aluminum ore, and most of our best iron ore has been used. As a result, the United States imports most of its iron and aluminum ore from other countries. But should those foreign sources become too expensive, substantial domestic low-grade deposits are available. Rarer minerals, such as chromium, platinum, molybdenum, and vanadium, are found in commercial concentrations in fairly restricted conditions. Only a few countries dominate world production and marketing for those minerals, and in some cases domestic low-grade deposits are unavailable.

VARIATIONS IN RESERVES AND RESOURCES

Minerals are stock resources, in that the amount available in rocks is finite, thus it is possible to examine how much is in the ground relative to present and projected future demand. But this is not as easy as it might seem for the following reasons. First, the amounts of mineral resources in the ground are extremely large, and the real question is how large the reserves are relative to demand. The amount of a mineral reserve available, however, is very much dependent on price. A doubling in price, for example, may produce a 10- or 100-fold increase in reserves. Price increases also stimulate exploration, which may further increase reserves through new discoveries. In this way minerals act as flow resources rather than stock resources. Second, an increasing number of minerals are recycled and thus are becoming, from the point of view of human production systems, renewable resources. Over 40 percent of U.S. iron and steel supplies are derived from recycled material, and about half the nation's lead consumption is met from recycled material. When the price of minerals rises, so does the economic attraction of recycling, and the contribution of recycled materials will undoubtedly increase in the future. Third, there is a high degree of *substitutability* for most minerals. If we run short of steel, we can often use aluminum. If we run short of aluminum, we can use magnesium or synthetic materials. Substitution may not be possible for all uses of a material, but partial substitution usually alleviates supply problems and keeps the material available for necessary uses. This substitutability is one factor causing demand for minerals to be highly elastic, changing significantly with changes in price.

Taken together, these factors mean that future demands for minerals are difficult to predict and are vulnerable to small changes in prices and technologies. In addition, a distinction must be made between short- and long-term availability. In the long term, we will never "run out" of any minerals. We may find that a particular mineral has become too expensive to justify using it, and, in that sense, it may become unavailable. For groups of minerals, worldwide demand may cause a long-term trend of increasing prices, which would likely reduce demand for those minerals (Brooks and Andrews, 1974). In the short term, however, perhaps over periods of less than 5 to 10 years, sharp fluctuations in mineral prices are common (Fig. 15.2). These fluctuations reflect or cause variations in supply or demand, presenting very real problems when they occur. We often misunderstand the nature of these crises, however. They are not the result of the world running out of a mineral; they are a consequence of the vagaries of the world economic and political system.

WORLD RESERVES AND RESOURCES

In the long run, mineral availability is determined by the level of economic activity, technological changes, and by geologic considerations. Although these factors cannot be predicted with certainty, the current status of reserves relative to demand is indicative of future mineral availability. Table 15.2 is a listing of current world reserves of major minerals in relation to world consumption. Also listed are some of the materials that could be substituted for the mineral in question for some of its major uses. The first column of numbers lists 1987 world production of various minerals. For some minerals the data are incomplete because data from some nations were unavail-

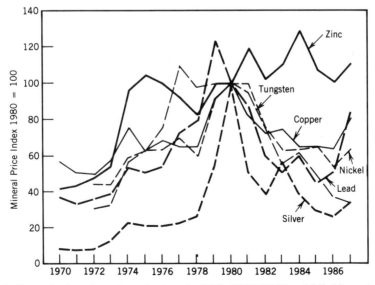

Figure 15.2 Indices of prices for selected minerals, 1970–1987 (1980 = 100). Mineral prices are highly variable; in general, prices for these minerals climbed in the 1970s, but fell dramatically in the early 1980s. (*Source:* U.S. Bureau of Mines, 1989.)

TABLE 15.2   World Reserves and Resources Relative to Demand for Minerals

Mineral	1987 Production[a]	Reserves (years)[b]	Substitutes[c]
Antimony	57.3	73	Several other metals
Arsenic	55.0	18	Synthetic organic chemicals
Asbestos	4.50	24	Glass fiber
Barite	4.26	35	Celestite, ilmenite, iron ores
Bauxite	86,360	252	Clay
Beryllium	0.36	N.A.[d]	Steel, titanium, graphite composites
Bismuth	4.27	21	Several
Boron	1,179	273	Several
Bromine	388	Large	Chlorine, iodine
Cadmium	18.4	29	Zinc, aluminum, tin
Cesium	N.A.	Large	Rubidium
Chromium	10,340	102	Nickel, iron, boron
Cobalt	31.7	109	Nickel, other metals
Columbium	15.0	230	Vanadium, molybdenum, tantalum, titanium
Copper	8,340	41	Aluminum, titanium, steel, optical fiber, plastics
Diamond	0.01	18	Boron, aluminum oxide, silicon carbide
Diatomite	1,814	400	Many
Feldspar	4,263	Large	Nepheline syenite
Fluorspar	4,843	46	Olivine, dolomitic limestone, hydrocarbons, carbon
Gallium	0.05	N.A.	Organic chemicals, silicon, indium phosphide
Garnet	60.8	Large	Diamond, boron, aluminum oxide, silicon carbide
Germanium	0.08	Moderate	Silicon, tellurium, selenium
Gold	1.68	25	Palladium, platinum, silver
Graphite	608	48	Various synthetic materials
Gypsum	88,160	Large	Lime, lumber, cement
Hafnium	0.09	Large	Few
Helium	2.25	Large	Argon, hydrogen
Ilmenite	5,038	76	Rutile
Indium	0.04	39	Silicon, gallium, boron carbide, hafnium
Iodine	13.0	221	Bromine, chlorine
Iron ore	885,227	173	Scrap iron
Kyanite	290	Large	Synthetic mullite, fire clays, alumina
Lead	3,360	22	Plastics, aluminum, tin, iron
Lime	110,501	Large	Limestone, gypsum
Lithium	42.6	Large	Several
Magnesium (ore)	326	Large	Aluminum, zinc
Manganese	23,491	39	None
Mercury	6.00	20	Lithium, zinc air, nickel–cadmium alloys
Molybdenum	81.3	68	Chromium, vanadium, columbium, other metals
Nickel	793	65	Aluminum, steel, plastics
Perlite	1,633	389	Vermiculite, pumice, slag, diatomite
Phosphate rock	144,000	92	None
Platinum group	0.25	226	Tin–lead alloys, gold, silver, titanium
Potash	23,788	244	None
Pumice	10,431	Large	Shale, clay
Quartz crystal	N.A.	Moderate	Synthetic quartz crystals
Rare earths	31.5	1257	Few
Rhenium	0.02	158	Iridium, tin, other metals

TABLE 15.2   *(Continued)*

Mineral	1987 Production[a]	Reserves (years)[b]	Substitutes[c]
Rutile	N.A.	Large	Ilmenite, titaniferous slag, synthetic rutile made from ilmenite
Scandium	N.A.	Large	None in most applications
Selenium	1.17	Moderate	Silicon, cadmium, tellurium, gallium, arsenic
Silicon	2,721	Large	Various metals, germanium
Silver	13.3	18	Aluminum, rhodium, tantalum, stainless steel
Strontium	187	36	Barium
Sulfur	54,500	24	None
Talc	7,856	48	Several
Tantalum	0.22	100	Columbium, aluminum, glass, titanium, other metals
Tellurium	N.A.	Large	Selenium, bismuth, lead, sulfur, germanium
Thallium	0.01	26	Several
Thorium	N.A.	N.A.	Uranium
Tin	163	26	Aluminum, glass, paper, plastic, steel, epoxy resins
Tungsten	41.4	68	Aluminum oxide, titanium carbide, titanium nitride
Vanadium	29.5	145	Columbium, molybdenum, manganese, titanium, tungsten
Yttrium	0.54	1338	Few
Zinc	7,056	21	Aluminum, plastics, magnesium, titanium, zirconium
Zirconium	717	29	Chromite, olivine, staurolite, titanium, tin

Source: U.S. Bureau of Mines (1988).

[a] All figures are estimates, and in many cases data from some countries are not included. Production figures are in thousands of metric tons, except for helium, which is in million cubic feet.

[b] Reserves are shown as a ratio of 1987 reserves to 1987 production. In some cases accurate measures of reserves are unavailable, but qualitative estimates are possible. "Large" means that reserves are probably in excess of 100 times the current annual production. "Moderate" means reserves are probably between 10 and 100 times the current annual production.

[c] Most minerals have several different applications, and substitute materials usually only apply to certain applications.

[d] N.A. indicates data not available.

able, or because proprietary data were withheld. Also, actual consumption may differ from production for some minerals if inventories were depleted or increased. Nonetheless, the figures are reasonably representative of current world conditions. The second column of numbers consists of ratios of 1987 world reserves to 1987 production, as reported by the U.S. Bureau of Mines. These represent the number of years that current reserves would last at 1987 rates of production. The final column in the table lists some of the materials that could be substituted for some of the uses of the minerals if supplies were limited or prices climbed significantly. Substitution is usually possible only for some uses, while for other uses substitution is not currently feasible (see Issue 15–1). Also, in most cases the use of these substitute commodities would result in either increased costs or reduced quality of product, and in some cases new product development would be needed. After all, if these substitutes were suitable under present economic and technological conditions, they would already be in use.

Examination of current reserves indicates that for most minerals, currently identified deposits of economically recoverable materials are sufficient to meet world demand for several decades. If demand increases, as is likely for most minerals, the adequacy of current supplies will be somewhat less. On the other hand, changes in economic and technological conditions, in addition to geologic exploration, will almost certainly result in increases to reserves. Finally, should shortages of any of these minerals develop, higher prices would stimulate substitution of other substances and/or increased recycling, resulting in a reduction of demand. At the world level, then, it seems likely that most of these minerals will continue to be available for the foreseeable future.

This is not to say that there will not be localized, short-duration shortages. As discussed earlier, in many cases a few countries, or a few mines, may dominate world production. For example, four countries control about 70 percent of the world's bauxite production, six countries produce 90 percent of all manganese, 95 percent of platinum group metals are controlled by two countries, and 65 percent of phosphate rock comes from three countries. Closure of a few mines or short-term restric-

tions in trade could easily result in market shortages and dramatic price changes.

One factor that sometimes leads to these short-term supply fluctuations is the *cartels* that artificially control supplies of minerals. The cartels that have been formed, notably those in tin, copper, and bauxite, have been unsuccessful in manipulating world markets (see discussion of OPEC in chapter 16). Their lack of success has been due to several factors. In some cases important producers have refused to join because of political differences with other producers or lack of cooperation with other cartel members. In addition, many countries have large stockpiles of minerals that were accumulated for military uses in times of war, and that are now used to manipulate supplies and prices. Finally, most minerals are simply not in short enough supply nor critical enough to world economies to allow a group of producers to put significant pressure on consuming countries (Netschert, 1981). The result has been a continuation of a relatively unregulated market at the global level.

Issue 15–1   Asbestos and Health

Asbestos is the fibrous form of six minerals: chrysotile, riebeckite, grunerite, actinolite, anthophyllite, and tremolite. When it is mined, asbestos is a dense rock but it easily fragments into fine fibers. Because of its high tensile strength, chemical inertness, and resistance to high temperatures, asbestos is heavily used in manufacturing. For some products like fireproofing materials and brake linings there are no substitutes. Because of its versatility, asbestos was widely used by the construction industry for fireproofing buildings, insulating homes and schools, and insulating electrical wiring and steam pipes in both residential and commercial buildings.

Chrysotile (a fibrous form of serpentine) is mined using an open-pit method in which the rock is crushed to free the fibers. The major world producers of asbestos are Canada (in Quebec province), the USSR (the Urals and Siberia), and South Africa. Domestic production of asbestos has declined since 1973 in response to environmental and economic problems.

Prolonged exposure to the tiny asbestos fi-

bers, which are easily suspended in the atmosphere, results in asbestosis, a lung disorder. Asbestos inhalation also results in the increased incidence of cancer. Asbestosis seldom appears without at least 10 years of exposure and thus the disease is quite prevalent among certain occupations: pipefitters, shipbuilders, and certain construction workers. The U.S. EPA estimates that between 3000 and 12,000 cases of cancer per year are caused by asbestos exposure from 20 or more years ago. In 1964, a study of World War II shipyard workers confirmed the relationship between airborne asbestos exposure and the development of lung disease 20 years later. In 1971, asbestos became the first material to be regulated by OSHA (the Occupational Safety and Health Administration), and by 1986, workplace exposure levels were further reduced to less than 10 percent of their 1976 standard. Johns Manville, one of the leaders in the asbestos industry, was forced into bankruptcy as health-related claims against it mounted. The federal government is also a target of many of the claims

For those Third World nations that are mineral-rich and derive substantial foreign exchange from mineral exports (Zaire, Gabon, Zimbabwe, Malaysia, and Mexico are examples), this situation has thwarted many plans to substantially increase national income through market manipulation.

DOMESTIC RESERVES AND RESOURCES

Although most minerals are essentially global commodities, in that supply and demand are dominated by worldwide markets rather than national policies, it is useful to examine the domestic situation in the United States with respect to mineral supply and consumption. The United States is the largest single consumer of many materials, and conditions here are of considerable importance in the world market. Domestic conditions are sometimes the focus of policy debates relating to strategic material needs or environmental impacts of mining.

Consumption

Table 15.3 summarizes the U.S. mineral situation for selected minerals. The first column of numbers shows U.S. average apparent consumption in the period 1983–1987 as a percentage of 1987 world production. It is necessary to average domestic consumption over several years, because short-term fluctuations in market conditions can dramatically affect use patterns. At the world level, these fluctuations are still present but less dramatic. The second column reports domestic reserves of these minerals divided by domestic consumption. These figures represent the number of years our current reserves would last at current rates of consumption, if that consumption were met exclusively from domestic sources. The final column lists the U.S net import reliance, or the percentage of our consumption that was supplied by imports.

Several important generalizations can be made from these data. First, the United States consumes a substantial portion of world production of many minerals. Typically the United

---

because exposure standards set for World War II shipyards were known to be inadequate at the time.

Although occupational exposures are important, in the early 1980s EPA officials became alarmed at the deterioration of school buildings that were insulated with asbestos, in which friable and crumbling asbestos was visible. They estimated that 15 million school children and 1.4 million school workers were at risk. In 1982, the EPA issued regulations requiring that all public and private schools inspect their buildings for asbestos. Later, the Asbestos School Hazard Abatement Act of 1984 and the Asbestos Hazard Emergency Response Act of 1986 were passed by Congress. These laws require that schools (nursery through college) inspect for asbestos-containing material, and then develop and implement plans to control the risk. The EPA developed training and certification programs to assist in asbestos removal.

Now that the nation's schools are slowly

removing the asbestos, EPA's attention has turned to public and commercial buildings. Asbestos is often used to line steam pipes, and in 1989, an asbestos-lined steam pipe exploded in Manhattan, killing three people and spewing asbestos over an eight-block area in the Gramercy Park neighborhood. Residents were evacuated and many months later were finally allowed to return home after the material had been removed. Con Edison, the New York City utility, acknowledged that there have been at least 16 such incidents since 1973 and the potential for many more (Pitt, 1989). However, there were no established procedures for cleaning asbestos from surfaces such as streets and roofs. So although some progress has been made with asbestos removal, the substance is so pervasive in our lives that it will be years and even decades, and cost of billions of dollars, before we are free of asbestos (Brodeur, 1985; Conservation Foundation, 1987).

TABLE 15.3   U.S. Mineral Consumption, Reserves and Import Reliance

Mineral	1983–1987 consumption, % of world[a]	Domestic reserves (years)[b]	1983–1987 net import reliance[c]
Antimony*	48	2.9	56
Arsenic	34	2.7	84
Asbestos*	4	24	63
Barite	40	16	68
Bauxite*	5	9.6	96
Beryllium*	77	Small	16
Bismuth*	29	7.3	N.A.
Boron	35	250	Net export
Bromine	36	81	Net export
Cadmium*	21	18	62
Cesium	N.A.[d]	N.A.	100
Chromium*	4	Negligible	77
Cobalt*	24	Negligible	91
Columbium*	21	Negligible	100
Copper*	25	27	24
Diamond (industrial)*	107	Negligible	Net export
Diatomite	25	493	Net export
Feldspar	15	Large	Net export
Fluorspar*	12	N.A.	89
Gallium	21	N.A.	N.A.
Garnet	44	170	Net export
Germanium	47	12	N.A.
Gold	6	36	N.A.
Graphite*	6	Very small	100
Gypsum	25	32	38
Hafnium	54	1481	N.A.
Helium	61	168	Net export
Ilmenite	18	14	N.A.
Indium	46	11	N.A.
Iodine*	28	68	N.A.
Iron ore	7	259	28
Kyanite	0	N.A.	Net export
Lead*	34	9.7	18
Lime	13	Large	1
Lithium	6	N.A.	Net export
Magnesium	36	Large	Net export
Manganese*	3	Negligible	99
Mercury*	30	1.9	46
Molybdenum*	22	151	Net export
Nickel*	23	1.5	73.2
Perlite	29	94	5.4
Phosphate rock	25	36	Net export
Platinum group*	36	2.8	90
Potash	17	13	74.4
Pumice	7	Large	47.4
Quartz crystal*	N.A.	Moderate	N.A.
Rare earths	43	366	4.6
Rhenium	29	170	N.A.
Rutile*	N.A.	1.0	N.A.
Selenium	45	23	43
Silicon	18	Large	28.6

TABLE 15.3 *(Continued)*

Mineral	1983–1987 consumption, % of world[a]	Domestic reserves (years)[b]	1983–1987 net import reliance[c]
Silver*	40	5.4	60.8
Strontium	11	Negligible	100
Sulfur	21	13	8
Talc/pyrophyllite*	12	145	0
Tantalum*	N.A.	Negligible	92.2
Tellurium	N.A.	113	N.A.
Thallium	10	22	100
Thorium*	N.A.	2940	N.A.
Tin*	31	0.4	73.2
Tungsten*	19	19	68.2
Vanadium*	14	33	40
Yttrium	5	3320	100
Zinc*	14	21	69
Zirconium	16	32	N.A.

Source: U.S. Bureau of Mines (1988).

[a] Average U.S. apparent consumption, 1983–1987, as a percentage of 1987 world production. Apparent consumption is domestic primary plus secondary production (recycling) plus net imports. All figures are estimates, and in some cases data were incomplete or unavailable.

[b] 1987 U.S. reserves divided by U.S. 1983–1987 apparent consumption.

[c] 1987 U.S. net imports plus adjustments for stock changes, as a percentage of 1987 apparent consumption.

* Mineral commodity in the U.S. Stockpile, in 1982.

[d] N.A.-data not available.

States, with about 6 percent of the world's population, consumes between 10 and 30 percent of world production. This is roughly the same as the proportion of world energy production consumed by Americans and simply reflects the large population, high level of industrialization, and high standard of living in the United States. It is interesting to note that many of the minerals for which our consumption is particularly high are associated with technologically advanced industries like aerospace and electronics. On the other hand, our consumption of iron ore and bauxite is at levels more appropriate to our population.

Second, U.S. domestic reserves of many minerals vary considerably, being virtually nonexistent for some minerals and very large for others. Important minerals for which our domestic reserves are quite small include bauxite, chromium, cobalt, manganese, nickel, and the platinum group metals. The United States has abundant reserves of copper, iron ore, magnesium, molybdenum, rare earths, thorium, vanadium, and numerous other minerals.

Third, the United States is a major trader of minerals and is dependent on imports for such important commodities as bauxite, chromium, cobalt, graphite, iron ore, manganese, tin, tungsten, and zinc. The United States is a net exporter of boron, industrial diamonds, magnesium, phosphate rock, and others. Note that there are some minerals for which there is essentially no domestic production, but for which our import reliance is well below 100 percent. For example, there is no domestic chromium production, but we only imported 77 percent of our needs in 1983–1987. The balance of our consumption was met with recycled chromium. Recycling was also important for iron, aluminum, lead, copper, and tin.

Recent Trends in Production

The peak year of mineral production in the United States was 1979, with about 3 billion tons (2.7 billion tonnes), but by 1986, production was half of that (Fig. 15.3). Most of the production was copper and iron ore (metals), phosphate, sand and gravel, and stone (nonmetals). To produce the 1.5 billion tons (1.4 billion tonnes) of ore in 1986, 909 million (824 million tonnes) tons of mine waste were pro-

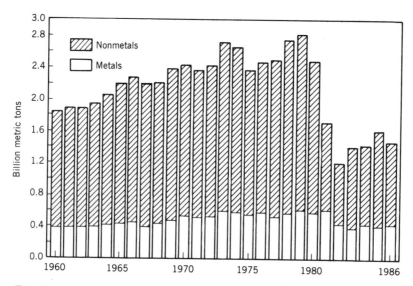

Figure 15.3   Trends in total ore production at domestic mines, 1960–1986. Metal production has been fairly consistent during this period, whereas nonmetal production increased steadily until 1979, and then rapidly declined. (*Source:* Council on Environmental Quality, 1989.)

duced, mostly by the copper, iron, and phosphate mine operators. This waste includes the removal of soil and rock to gain access to the mineral. This waste often represents half of the volume of all the waste generated in the mining operations and is often stored in piles next to the mine site. During the 1970s, the amount of waste increased as more lower-grade copper ore was mined and more phosphate was mined (Fig. 15.4). In comparing metal to nonmetal mining, less waste is generated by nonmetals. Finally, surface mines produced 94 percent of the crude ores mined in 1986 (Council on Environmental Quality, 1989).

STRATEGIC MINERALS AND STOCKPILING

Although effective mineral cartels or other political organizations have yet to significantly restrict supplies of minerals, the possibility of such restriction is a subject of some concern to the United States government. This is particularly true in the case of minerals that are important to military/industrial production and that are imported from nations with unstable or unfriendly governments.

This dependency issue has been recognized for many years. The U.S. government has

therefore defined certain minerals to be of strategic or critical importance to the welfare of the country and has developed policies to prevent shortages. *Strategic minerals* are those essential for defense purposes and for which the United States is totally dependent on foreign sources. Examples of strategic minerals are cobalt, chromium, manganese, and platinum. *Critical minerals* are also necessary for national defense, but the United States can meet some of its demand through domestic sources and supplies from friendly nations. Examples of critical minerals are copper, nickel, and vanadium. It is an interesting quirk of geography that much of the supply of strategic minerals to the United States is from two nations: South Africa and the USSR. Over 30 minerals have been identified as having strategic or critical importance, and these minerals are indicated in Table 15.3 by asterisks. The following examples illustrate that importance.

Chromium is used to harden steel and make it resistant to corrosion. It is an essential component of stainless steel and is used in ball bearings, surgical equipment, mufflers, and tailpipes. It is used in the defense industry in armor plating and weapons and for many parts of piston and jet engines. The leading world producers of chromium are South Africa, the

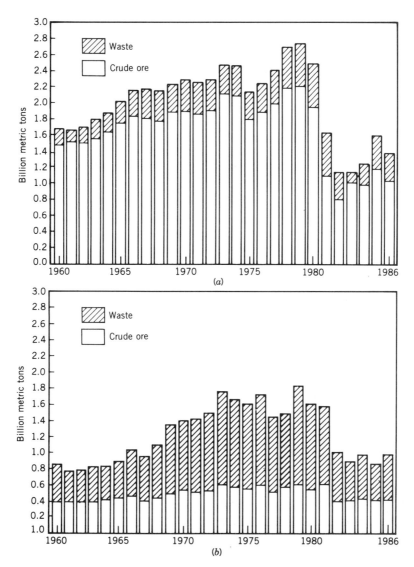

Figure 15.4 Nonmetal and metal ore and waste production at domestic mines, 1960–1986. Less waste (mine spoils) is produced by mining for nonmetal areas (*a*), such as phosphate, sand and gravel, and crushed stone, than for metal ores (*b*), like lead, copper, and iron ore. (*Source:* Council on Environmental Quality, 1989, pp. 4–5.)

USSR, Albania, Zimbabwe, and the Philippines. The United States imports about 80 percent of its chromium, mainly from South Africa, the Philippines, and the USSR.

Cobalt is a metal used in the aerospace industry. It is a high-temperature alloy used in the manufacture of jet engines, cutting tools, magnets, and drill bits. It is also used in electronics equipment, especially in computers, television receivers, and transmitters. The primary producers of cobalt are Zaire, Zambia, Canada, and the USSR. The United States is heavily reliant on imported cobalt, mostly from Zaire and Zambia.

Other strategic minerals are those in the platinum group, which includes six different minerals with similar properties. These metals—platinum, iridium, palladium, oridium, rhodium, and ruthenium—are resistant to corrosion and are used to catalyze chemical reactions. Other applications include catalytic converters in automobiles, petroleum refining, electroplating, electronics, and fertilizer manufacture. The major world producers of platinum group metals are the USSR, South Africa, Canada, and Japan. The United States imports about 90 percent of its platinum, primarily from South Africa, the USSR, and the United Kingdom.

Manganese is essential in steel manufacture and thus has many industrial and military applications. It is added to molten steel to remove oxygen and sulfur, thus hardening the steel. The USSR, South Africa, Brazil, China, and Indonesia are the world's major producers. The USSR and South Africa alone supply about 55 percent of the world's manganese (U.S. Bureau of Mines, 1988). The United States imports most of its manganese from South Africa, Gabon, and Brazil. The presence of large quantities of presently subeconomic manganese in deep-ocean beds was important in the U.S. refusal to sign the Law of the Sea Treaty, as discussed in chapter 12.

Stockpiling, or maintaining large storages of commodities, is one method the United States has chosen to protect itself from restrictions in supplies of strategic minerals. The danger of minerals dependency has been recognized since the turn of the century, but actual stockpiling did not begin until shortly before World War II. In 1949 the U.S. Strategic Stockpile was created to avert shortages of minerals during wartime. The intent was to purchase and store materials in sufficient quantities to meet defense and national security needs for a 3-year period, which is presumably a long enough period of time for alternative supplies to be developed in the event of a cutoff of supply from other nations. Ninety-three substances, not all of them minerals, were on the list. Congress did not appropriate funds for procurement, however, and the stockpile was well below the official goals for many years. Recently procurement has increased, and the stockpile is at or over 100 percent for many materials (Table 15.4). The government occasionally sells some of the material in the stockpile to meet domestic supply needs or to generate revenue to buy more urgently needed materials. It has also occasionally used the stockpile to influence mineral prices through trading or threatening to trade in stockpiled commodities.

Stockpiling is an important policy because it protects a nation from the short-term inter-

TABLE 15.4 Status of National Defense Stockpile Inventory, 1987

Mineral	Percentage of stockpile goals achieved
Aluminum	60
Antimony	101
Bauxite	20
Beryllium group	89
Bismuth	95
Cadmium	54
Chromium	95
Cobalt	62
Columbium	56
Copper	3
Diamond	106
Fluorspar	42
Germanium	0
Iodine	113
Lead	55
Manganese	134
Nickel	19
Platinum group	40
Rutile	40
Tantalum group	40
Tin	415
Tungsten group	143
Vanadium group	8
Zinc	27

Source: U.S. Mineral Management Service (1989).

ruptions of supply and rises in price that minerals are susceptible to. Stockpiling in the United States has historically implied preparedness for war. Of course, it is unlikely that limited regional wars would cut off supplies from all major mineral suppliers, and in the case of all-out world war it is improbable that the United States would exhaust the 3-year supply of industrial minerals. Nonetheless, the strategic stockpiles are very good guarantees against short-term reductions in supplies caused by an industrial collapse or prohibition of trade in one or two countries. From the standpoint of national economic health, it makes sense to guard against such events.

In summary, the market for most minerals is a world market in which a relatively small number of suppliers sell to a large number of customers. In the long term, availability of some minerals is essentially infinite, but for others there will be substantial increases in price, which will lead to conservation, recycling, development of substitute materials, and other means for reducing demand for expensive materials. In the short term, prices fluctuate widely, stimulating changes in sources and uses of minerals, and creating some economic distress in sensitive industries. Even though the production of many minerals is concentrated in a small number of countries, because those nations lack political agreement and depend on exports for foreign exchange, and because of the substitutability of materials, the formation of effective cartels is unlikely. The volatility of mineral prices makes stockpiling useful for insulating national production systems from catastrophic changes in the world market.

ENVIRONMENTAL AND SOCIAL CONSIDERATIONS OF MINING

Mineral extraction has significant environmental and social effects. Individual mines are often very large, as economies of scale are important in maintaining profitability. Few mineral ores are more than 30 percent pure, and some are less than 1 percent pure, thus large quantities of ore must be processed to obtain relatively small amounts of finished product. If the mine is at the surface, such as the open-pit mine shown in Fig. 15.5, the area disrupted can be quite large. In addition, it is often necessary to remove large amounts of undesired rock to get at an ore body, further increasing the area disturbed.

Unused rock and the waste from processing operations must be disposed of (Fig. 15.6), and these materials, called *tailings*, are often processed using large amounts of water and deposited in tailings ponds. These ponds are often themselves quite large. The water pumped from mines after use in extraction or in ore processing is usually of low quality. In many cases it is highly acidic, and it is usually contaminated with the minerals being mined. The resultant pollution of receiving waters is often severe. The huge volume of ore-bearing rock to be processed requires that processing take place near the mine, and thus many mine sites are also locations for smelting or other methods of purifying minerals. Most of these processes produce large emissions of air pol-

Figure 15.5 The Bingham Canyon copper mine in Utah—one of the world's largest open pit mines.

lutants, particularly sulfur oxides and metals. These emissions may be of such quantity as to severely damage vegetation and soils in the surrounding area (Fig. 15.7). Sudbury and Wawa, Ontario; Palmerton, Pennsylvania; and Ducktown, Tennessee, are examples of areas where vegetation destruction is so severe that it is clearly visible on satellite photographs.

Figure 15.6 Spoil piles from hydraulic mining for gold in California.

Figure 15.7 Loss of vegetation caused by emissions from copper mining in Tennessee.

Mine sites are generally dictated by the presence of ore, not by the environmental suitability of the location for a large-scale industrial operation. Many of the mines in the Rockies and Sierra Nevada are in areas of considerable natural beauty, in or near important resort areas. Although long-abandoned mines and ghost towns may be appealing to tourists, modern mines and associated support facilities generally are not.

In addition to environmental effects, mining has many important social and economic effects in the areas where it occurs. Most mining towns are isolated, away from major urban centers, and frequently in mountains. The populations of mining towns are almost entirely dependent on the mines for employment and income. When the mine is operating, they prosper, but when it is not, they become impoverished. Mine operations are governed by the prices of the materials mined, which, as we have shown, tend to fluctuate widely. When demand for a mineral drops, causing a reduction in price, production is usually reduced by closing whole mines rather than reducing production a little at all mines (Fig. 15.8). This is because economies of scale are important in mining, and it is often more economical to

close a mine entirely than to run it at a reduced level. Mining towns thus go through repeated boom and bust cycles, alternating between full employment and extreme unemployment (see Issue 15–2). The toll this takes in the lives of the mine workers and other residents is understandably severe.

CONSERVING MINERALS: REUSE, RECOVERY, RECYCLING

Recycling is the process whereby a material is recovered from the consumer product and then becomes a raw material in the production of a similar or different product. A significant amount of material can be recovered during the manufacture, use, and disposal of goods to decrease our need for raw ores (Table 15.5). Aluminum recycling is a good example. Aluminum cans that are returned to redemption centers are recycled: melted down and used in the manufacture of new aluminum cans and other aluminum products (Fig. 15.9). In 1987, 16 percent of the aluminum consumed was produced from recycled aluminum. Because of its high price and availability, aluminum is consistently recycled and is often the target for

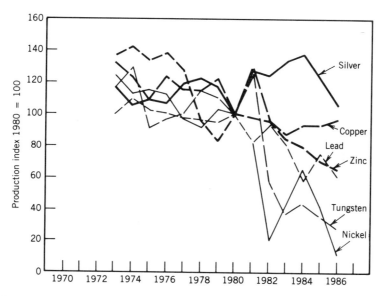

Figure 15.8 Indices of U.S. domestic production for selected minerals (1980 = 100). In general, production levels declined slowly in the 1970s under pressure from foreign sources, and then dropped dramatically in the recession of the early 1980s. (*Source:* U.S. Bureau of Mines, 1989.)

scavengers. Nothing appears to be sacred, as aluminum siding and gutters have been stripped from New York City homes, swing sets from a Miami playground, and even cans from local recycling centers by vandals desperate for money.

TABLE 15.5   Mineral Recycling

Mineral	Recycled obsolete scrap as percentage of apparent consumption, 1987
Aluminum	16
Antimony	42 (1984)
Chromium	25
Cobalt	16
Copper	24
Gold	64
Iron	68
Lead	56
Magnesium	20
Mercury	17
Nickel	26
Platinum group	66
Silver	20
Sulfur	8
Tin	27
Zinc	9

Source: U.S. Bureau of Mines (1988).

The ease with which minerals can be recycled depends on several factors, including the technology of conversion to a desired product, the ease of accumulation of sufficient used material, and the relative costs of manufacture of a good from recycled as opposed to raw materials. This last factor is itself partly affected by differences in quality between products made from raw materials and those made from recycled materials. For most minerals, the cost of converting an ore to pure form is significantly greater than the cost of remanufacture from recycled material, not considering the cost of mining ore and the cost of accumulating recycled materials. This is true not in monetary terms but also applies to energy use and environmental pollution. For example, manufacture of a given amount of aluminum from recycled scrap uses 90 to 95 percent less energy and generates 95 percent less pollution than refining aluminum from bauxite (Chandler, 1983).

Accumulating sufficient material to recycle is the biggest problem, and this depends on the use of the material. One of the biggest uses of lead, for example, is in storage batteries, such as those in automobiles. Old batteries are found at specific locations, primarily automobile junkyards and repair shops. The lead in

Figure 15.9   Recycling aluminum beverage cans saves both materials and large amounts of energy.

Issue 15—2   Living with Boom and Bust

Boom and bust, cycles of rapid growth and catastrophic decline, occur wherever mining dominates a local or regional economy. When national or world production of minerals drops slightly, mines that are marginally profitable close operation, while those with larger profit margins stay open. When prices are high and production increases, new mines open and old ones are reopened. If a mine is located in a remote area, as is often the case, the communities around it depend on the mine for nearly all their income. Most local residents work either for the mine, for businesses that serve the mine, or for businesses that serve the people who work in the mine. As the mine goes, so goes the community.

Both boom and bust are stressful. During boom times, there is usually an increase in population, a shortage of housing, a rise in rents and property values, and a shortage of public services. When immigrants come in large numbers, they bring problems to small towns. Everyday life for the permanent residents is disrupted, shops are more crowded, housing costs rise, and

streets are blocked by construction. Unemployment and crime may also be problems if more immigrants arrive than are hired.

Boom times are certainly not all bad, though, as nearly everyone has a job, property values increase, and business is good. The new money in town brings in new businesses, perhaps a second barber shop, a few gas stations, a discount department store, a bigger supermarket, a few restaurants, and several bars. Those lucky enough to get into business at the right time do very well and may amass small fortunes. Those who came in when the boom was already under way meet stiff competition and high costs, but still manage to earn a living.

Then comes the bust. Maybe competition from cheaper imports is too rough, the higher-grade ore is played out, or the world price may have fallen because of a recession. Maybe new materials are replacing the ore in a few critical industries, or perhaps environmental requirements are making the mine less profitable than one in another state or another country. The

them is valuable enough to warrant recycling, as is much lead used in other ways. As a result, in 1987, 56 percent of the apparent U.S. lead consumption was from recycled materials. Titanium, on the other hand, is primarily used in very dispersed forms. About 90 percent of titanium is used in pigments for paints, and thus it winds up on the walls of houses, buildings, and so forth (Barton, 1979). It would be very difficult to collect used paint in sufficient quantities to recycle the titanium that it contains. Titanium recycling is therefore insignificant.

Over time, the changing use of metals in manufacturing also affects their recycling potential. Until the 1970s, the platinum group metals were recycled with efficiencies around 85 percent (Frosch and Gallopoulos, 1989). However, in the mid-1970s the introduction of catalytic converters for automobiles to reduce exhaust emissions changed the recycling rates. Automotive use of platinum group metals now accounts for most of the permanent consumption of these metals. Although the industrial applications of the platinum group continue to recycle about 85 percent of the metals, poor recycling rates (less than 12 percent) characterize the automotive applications. The reason is quite simple. The poor recycling rates are a function of the limited means for collecting the discarded catalytic converters, which are found in scrap yards along with the discarded automobile. The technology for recycling is known, but the cost of locating, collecting, and emptying all the discarded converters and then transporting the platinum metals for recycling is not profitable for most recovery operations at current prices. If the price of platinum escalates to more than $500 per ounce, then recycling of catalytic converters would become more pronounced.

Accumulation of material for recycling is easiest in industry, where large amounts of material tend to be found in a few locations. In many industrial processes, scrap is generated as part of the manufacturing process, and this is very easily recovered. For example, steel that does not meet specifications is recovered at the steel plant and immediately returned to the production process as a raw material. This

---

actual cause doesn't really matter to those affected, because whatever the cause, it is beyond their control. At any rate, the mine is shut down, and perhaps 40 percent of the town's work force is laid off with 2 weeks' notice and 2 months' severance pay. A few stay on for several months to help with removing the machinery that can be used elsewhere.

Some people leave town immediately, particularly those who had arrived most recently and hadn't established themselves yet. Unemployment compensation and savings keep the rest going for the better part of a year, but eventually that runs out, so most of them leave, too. Those with large debts go bankrupt. Many of the rest can't sell their houses for as much as they owe on the mortgage, and also go bankrupt after the mortgage is foreclosed.

Two years after the mine is closed, the town's population may have dropped by 50 percent. Before the boom, there was one barber shop, three gas stations, and one supermarket, all doing well. Now there are two barber shops, both having trouble making rent payments, one supermarket open and one closed, a closed department store, and six gas stations, only one of which is doing well. Most of the bars that opened during the boom are still there, but now they get more business during the day than at night.

Although the specific town just described is fictional, these things have happened in many towns in the United States, and more than once in most of them. Today, concern about the social impacts of mining is increasing, and many states have taken steps to lessen the blows. Severance taxes, charged to the mining companies when minerals are removed, are often used to pay for improvements in town services and infrastructure during growth times, and for relocation or job training afterward. Mining companies are becoming more willing to contribute to these expenses in their attempts to maintain public good will. These changes will ease the ups and downs to some extent, but they will still occur and recur (Williams, 1979; U. Press of Colorado, 1989).

recycling of so-called new scrap is really just a way of making the manufacturing process more efficient. Recycling of new scrap is not included in the data in Table 15.5.

CONCLUSIONS

Although we often think of minerals as non-renewable resources, we are not going to run out of any of them. Variations in price are far too important in generating new supplies and in controlling demand, to permit geologic considerations alone to determine use. Demand fluctuations occur primarily through substitution, but increased efficiency of use is also important. In the future, recycling, reuse, and recovery will become increasingly important, as higher mineral prices make this source of materials economically more feasible. One of the biggest problems that we face, however, is a shift from mineral-based products to plastics. Many parts of new automobiles, for example, are now made of plastic rather than metals. The same is true for children's toys like trucks and cars. Although some plastic may be recyclable, substituting one nonrenewable resource for another (plastics are made from petroleum) will not solve the problems of diminishing reserves.

REFERENCES AND ADDITIONAL READING

Barton, A.F.M. 1979. *Resource Recovery and Recycling*. New York: Wiley.

Brobst, P.A., and W.P. Pratt, (Eds.). 1973. *United States Mineral Resources*. USGS Professional Paper 820. Washington, DC: U.S. Geological Survey.

Brodeur, P. 1985. *Outrageous Conduct: The Asbestos Industry on Trial*. New York: Pantheon.

Brooks, D.B. and P.W. Andrews. 1974. Mineral resources, economic growth, and world population. *Science* 185: 13–19.

Chandler, W.U. 1983. *Materials Recycling: The Virtue of Necessity*. Worldwatch Paper #56. Washington, DC: Worldwatch Institute.

Conservation Foundation. 1987. *State of the Environment: A View Toward the Nineties*. Washington, DC: Conservation Foundation.

Council on Environmental Quality. 1981. *The Global 2000 Report to the President*. Washington, DC: U.S. Government Printing Office.

———. 1989. *Environmental Trends*. Washington, DC: U.S. Government Printing Office.

DeVore, C. 1981. Strategic minerals: A present danger. *Signal*. January, pp 63–68.

Frosch, R.A., and N.E. Gallopoulos. 1989. Strategies for manufacturing. *Sci. Amer.* 261: 144–152.

Goeller, H.E., and A. Zucker. 1984. Infinite resources: The ultimate strategy. *Science* 223: 456–462.

McKelvey, V.E. 1972. Mineral resource estimates and public policy. *Amer. Sci.* 60: 32–40.

Netschert, B.C. 1981. Dependence on imported non-fuel minerals: The threat of mini-OPECs? *J. Metals*. March, pp. 31–38.

Pitt, D.E. 1989. With asbestos, the law never anticipated the worst. *The New York Times*, September 7, Section 4, p. 24.

Putnam, W.C., and A.B. Bassett. 1971. *Geology*, 2nd ed. New York: Oxford University Press.

Sinclair, J.E., and R. Parker. 1983. *The Strategic Minerals War*. New York: Arlington House.

U.S. Bureau of the Census. 1984. *Statistical Abstract of the United States*. Washington, DC: U.S. Government Printing Office.

U.S. Bureau of Mines. 1988. *Minerals Yearbook*. Washington, DC: U.S. Government Printing Office.

U.S. Congress, Office of Technology Assessment. 1979. *Materials and Energy from Municipal Waste*. Washington, DC: U.S. Government Printing Office.

U.S. Geological Survey. 1975. *Mineral Resource Perspectives, 1975*. USGS Professional Paper 940. Washington, DC: U.S. Geological Survey.

U.S. Mineral Management Service. 1989. *Mineral Commodities Summary 1989*. Washington, DC: U.S. Government Printing Office.

University Press of Colorado, 1989. *Boomtown Blues: Colorado Oil Shale 1885–1985*. Boulder: University Press of Colorado.

Williams, R.N. 1979. A tiny town battles a mining giant. *The New York Times Magazine*, March 4, page 17.

TERMS TO KNOW

Cartel
Critical minerals
Hydrothermal mineralization
Placer deposit

Recycling
Reuse
Stockpiling
Strategic minerals
Subeconomic resource
Substitutability
Tailings
Unidentified resource
Weathering

STUDY QUESTIONS

1. What are three reasons for the shifting boundary between reserves and other resources?

2. In which environments do minerals tend to be located?

3. How can minerals be both stock and flow resources?

4. Have mining cartels been successful in controlling access to their products? Why or why not?

5. President Carter felt that the support of human rights was more important than obtaining strategic minerals. Presidents Reagan and Bush seem to hold the opposite opinion. What does each position imply for foreign and domestic policy?

6. How do conflicts arise between mining and other uses of the same land? Name some environmental impacts of mining.

16

INTRODUCTION

Of all demands placed on our world's natural resource base, the need for energy is perhaps the most far-reaching and basic. Energy provides heat for living and cooking, is used for lighting and refrigeration, and turns motors and wheels that power machines and move people and goods. Whether the energy is nuclear-generated electricity lighting an office building or wood burned in a cooking stove, everyone depends on it daily for physical health and economic prosperity.

Since 1970 the world has experienced dramatic shifts in the availability and price of energy commodities, particularly petroleum. The Arab oil embargo of 1973–1974 and the Iranian revolution of 1978–1979 triggered shortages of oil in much of the world and sharp increases in the prices of fuel oil, gasoline, chemicals, and other petroleum-derived products. Energy policy was a critical issue in many nations, and people came to view natural resources in a different way, seeing them as immediately exhaustible instead of indefinitely renewable. Since the early 1980s that situation has been dramatically reversed, and we once again enjoy low energy prices. In 1988 the real (inflation-adjusted) retail price of gasoline was lower than at any other time since World War II, and yet the underlying realities of a limited resource base and growing demand that precipitated the energy crises of the 1970s have not disappeared. The 1990 confrontation over Iraq's occupation of Kuwait again drove up oil prices, and made the importance of oil in world politics and economics clear.

Energy exists in many different forms and is used for many purposes. Energy includes the kinetic energy of a speeding train or of the wind, the radiant energy of the sun or of a warm building, and the stored energy of water in a reservoir above a hydroelectric plant or in fossil fuels. This chapter is primarily concerned with those forms of energy that are used to do work in the production of goods and services, and that form the basis of our national and world economies. It will examine the complex nature of energy: where it comes from, how it is used, and why it is such a significant subject in our lives when as recently as the early 1970s it was taken for granted.

ENERGY IN THE MODERN WORLD

EFFICIENCY

Efficiency of energy use can be measured in terms of economic gain per unit of energy expended. Throughout much of recent U.S. history, energy has been plentiful enough so that we did not consider efficiency of energy use in most of our economic decisions. Today, however, we are very conscious of the contrasting patterns of energy use and efficiency between different nations and economic systems.

Traditional agricultural economies produce goods and services at a relatively low level, using virtually no energy except that provided by the sun through heat and photosynthesis. In contrast, mechanized agriculture uses large amounts of nonrenewable fossil fuel in every step of the production system from building the tractor to manufacturing fertilizer and fueling farm machinery. This system produces much more food per unit of human labor, but much less per unit of energy input.

The best indicator of energy efficiency is a comparison of per capita gross national product (GNP) with per capita energy consumption (Fig. 16.1). As a rule, the higher the GNP

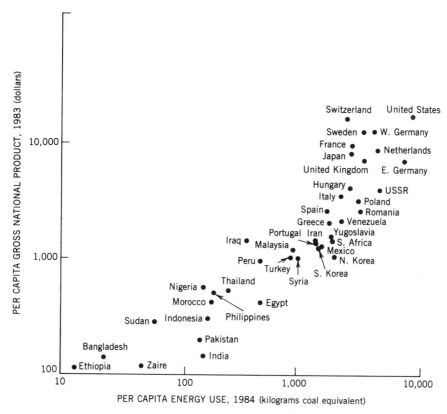

Figure 16.1 Per capita GNP and energy consumption. This comparison is an indicator of energy efficiency at the national level. In general, the higher the GNP per capita (as in countries like the United States, Canada, and West Germany), the higher their consumption of energy. (*Source:* Data from U.S. Bureau of the Census, 1989.)

per capita, the higher the energy consumption, and vice versa. A nation with a higher income can spend more money on machines and raw materials to increase production and quality of life. This in turn leads to more energy consumption, which if expended in production leads to more income. The more industrialized nations consume much more energy per capita than less industrialized nations. The United States, for example, with about 6 percent of the world's population, consumes 23 percent of the world's energy, whereas China, with 25 percent of the world's population, consumes only 6 percent of the world's energy. Furthermore, there are great variations in energy efficiency among industrialized nations. Most of the Western European nations, for example, use less energy per unit of economic return than the United States. This is because energy prices have been much higher there for a long time, and Europeans have adjusted by driving

smaller cars, driving shorter distances, heating buildings to lower temperatures, and so on.

FIRST AND SECOND LAWS OF THERMODYNAMICS REVISITED

In Chapter 4, we reviewed the laws of thermodynamics. Those laws are just as important in discussing energy resources as in describing energy transfers in ecosystems. We know that energy cannot be lost, but merely processing it does little good. Energy is only valuable because of its ability to do work or generate power. Thermodynamic principles can be important considerations when selecting energy sources and allocating them to various uses (Commoner, 1977). For example, if low-intensity energy is used for purposes to which it is best suited, then thermodynamically more costly energy can be spared for uses that need it most. An example of this would be using solar energy for space heating, which frees up electricity for such uses as air-conditioning or driving motors. Similarly, methods of capturing waste energy from some processes and using it for other purposes, for example, capturing waste heat from electricity generation to heat buildings, are considerably more efficient than allowing that waste heat to escape unused. Increased overall efficiency depends on techniques such as these.

TRENDS IN U.S. CONSUMPTION

In 1950, U.S. consumption of energy was slightly over 30 *quads* (quadrillion British Thermal Units, or BTUs) (Fig. 16.2 and Table 16.1). It steadily increased at a rate of about 3.5 percent annually, reaching 74.3 quads in 1973. At this time, the pattern of steady growth changed, largely as the result of a sharp increase in energy prices, relative scarcities of oil, a slowing economy, and changes in consumers' attitudes. Energy consumption declined in 1974 and 1975, before increasing again in 1976 as energy prices leveled off and even declined a little. Consumption rose until 1979, when a second wave of price increases and shortages again drove consumption down. By 1980 many of the conservation measures

TABLE 16.1   Energy Equivalents

One quadrillion BTUs (quad) equal:
- 50 million metric tons of coal production
- 66 million metric tons of oven-dried hardwood
- 1 trillion cubic feet of dry natural gas
- 170 million barrels of crude oil
- 470 thousand barrels of crude oil per day for a year
- 293 billion kilowatt-hours of electricity converted to heat
- 27 days of petroleum imports to the United States
- 26 days of gasoline usage for American motor vehicles
- 28 hours of world energy consumption in 1986

Source: Council on Environmental Quality (1989, p.11).

taken to reduce energy consumption (smaller engines in smaller cars, use of energy-efficient lighting and heating systems in buildings, and so on), were beginning to have significant impacts on consumption patterns, and consumption continued to decline through 1983. These were also years of relatively little economic growth, and when the economy began to grow rapidly in the mid-1980s, consumption again increased, and it increased steadily from 1984 through 1988, reaching 79.9 quads in 1988.

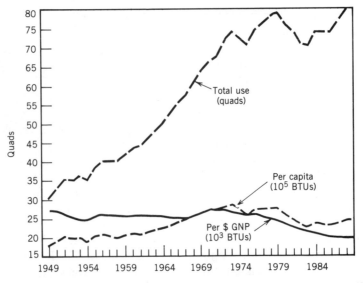

Figure 16.2   U.S. energy consumption, 1949–1988. Total use is shown in quads, or 10^{15} BTUs, per year. Per capita consumption is shown in 10^5 BTUs per year. Also shown is energy use in 10^3 BTUs per dollar of GNP, an indicator of energy-use efficiency. (*Source:* EIA, 1989.)

SHIFTS IN FUEL TYPE

In addition to changes in overall consumption, there have been some dramatic changes in the sources of energy consumed (Fig. 16.3). For example, in 1950 the leading sources of energy were petroleum (13.3 quads) and coal (12.4 quads). Ten years later, petroleum consumption was still first, but natural gas had replaced coal as the second most consumed resource. This pattern continued until 1972, when natural gas consumption reached its peak of 22.7 quads. Natural gas consumption declined steadily until the early 1980s, when it leveled off at about 16 to 18 quads. Consumption of coal has increased steadily since the early 1960s, and in 1986 it passed natural gas; coal is once again our second most important source of energy.

Consumption patterns for petroleum have followed the patterns of total consumption. Oil consumption increased steadily to 1973, and after a brief decline in 1974 and 1975, climbed to a peak of 37.1 quads in 1979. It declined sharply in the early 1980s, but rose again in the late 1980s, reaching 34.0 quads in 1988.

The use of nuclear power rose steadily from the first commercial generation in 1957 to 1978, when a mixture of weak demand and technical/environmental problems temporarily reduced nuclear power generation. Nuclear power use has increased since 1980, reaching 5.68 quads in 1988. Production of hydropower has always been relatively small and has not grown significantly since the early 1970s.

The United States is dependent on imports for a significant portion of its energy consumption. Since the early 1970s, net imports have been between about 10 and 15 percent of total energy consumption. Most of these imports have been of petroleum, and since 1970 imported oil has accounted for between 20 and 45 percent of total oil consumption. The contribution of imports has varied considerably, reaching a peak in the late 1970s, decreasing sharply in the early 1980s, and rising again since 1985.

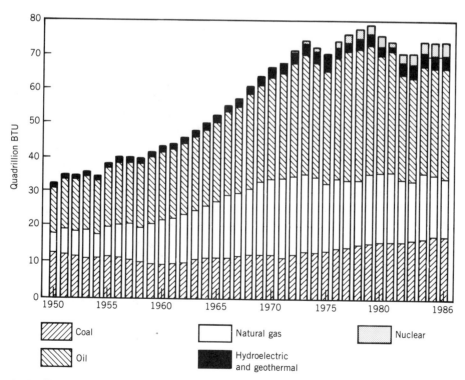

Figure 16.3 Domestic energy consumption by source, 1950–1986. Energy consumption peaked in the late 1970s, declined a little during the early 1980s, and began an upward trend during the late 1980s. (*Source:* Council on Environmental Quality, 1989, p. 15.)

CONSUMPTION BY SECTOR

The use of primary energy sources (petroleum, natural gas, coal, nuclear, hydro, and geothermal) to generate electricity (a secondary energy source) has increased sharply since 1950. In 1951, for example, electric utilities were responsible for only about 14 percent of all energy consumption in the United States; by 1988 that figure had reached 36 percent. Of course much of the energy consumed by the electric utilities is lost as waste heat and not available to residential and commercial, transportation, or industrial uses. Of all energy consumption, the industrial sector's share is the greatest (30.0 quads in 1988), followed by the residential and commercial (29.1 quads) and transportation (21.9 quads) sectors.

In the following sections we will discuss each of the major energy sources available to us today and likely to be available in the near future. In the last part of this chapter, we will examine some of the alternatives available to the United States and the world, as an expanding population struggles to sustain economic growth while not exceeding the available supplies of energy.

OIL AND NATURAL GAS

Oil and natural gas are the most versatile energy sources in use today. They are used in every sector of economic activity at both world and national levels, and as a result fluctuations in their availability and price control much of the world's economic activity. Oil is a major factor in international politics, and concern about domestic oil production has had significant impacts on other natural resources in the United States. The complex issues affecting oil availability and price are often clouded with ideology and partisan politics.

GEOLOGY

Oil and *natural gas* are produced by the accumulation of organic matter in sedimentary rocks and the later alteration of that organic matter by the heat of burial in the earth's crust. Oil and gas are both composed of hydrocarbons, but they differ in their boiling temperatures. Oil is liquid in the ground, but gas is not. Oil and gas usually occur together, but sometimes they can become separated if gas migrates through a rock that is not permeable enough for oil to flow. Crude oil may contain natural gas in solution, and gas sometimes contains liquid petroleum. Because they occur together and are readily substitutable in most end uses, they are discussed together.

Sediments rich in organic matter are relatively common, but the geologic circumstances necessary to accumulate oil or gas in commercially useful quantities are not. For this to occur there must be a reservoir rock that is permeable enough for oil to flow through. Oil is less dense than water, and it is forced upward by density differences as well as pressures in the earth's crust. Another requirement is a trap, in which a reservoir rock is overlain by an impermeable rock that prevents the oil from escaping to the surface. Many different kinds of traps exist, and exploration geologists usually look for such structures in their initial searches for oil. Accumulations of oil, or fields, vary considerably in size, with the numbers of fields inversely related to their size. There are very few giant fields. The largest known field is the Ghawar in Saudia Arabia (about 75 billion barrels), although there are indications of a field approaching this size in Mexico. Oil also comes in many different forms, and the quality of crude oil depends on the mix of different hydrocarbons in the oil. *Crude oil* with a high proportion of high-boiling-point hydrocarbons is called heavy oil. Tar and asphalt are major components of heavy oil. Light oil is rich in hydrocarbons with low boiling points, such as naphtha and kerosene. The proportion of various hydrocarbons affects both the ease of extraction and the price of the crude oil. Natural gas is made up of several different gases, including methane, propane, and butane.

LOCATION OF KNOWN RESERVES

Oil-bearing formations are found all over the world, but the largest deposits are concentrated in a few areas. Locations of U.S. oil resources are shown in Fig. 16.4. In 1988 world oil reserves were 889.5 billion barrels (Energy Information Administration, 1989a), and over 60 percent of these reserves were in the Mid-

Figure 16.4   Natural gas and petroleum fields. Considerable supplies of oil and natural gas are located in the outer continental shelf waters of the Gulf of Mexico and Southern California. (*Source:* Council on Environmental Quality, 1989.)

dle East. Thirteen nations had reserves exceeding 10 billion barrels: Saudi Arabia (19.0 percent of world total), Iraq (11.2 percent) United Arab Emirates (11.0 percent), Kuwait (10.6 percent), Iran (10.4 percent), USSR (6.6 percent), Venezuela (6.3 percent), Mexico (5.5 percent), United States (3.1 percent), Libya (2.4 percent), China (2.2 percent), Nigeria (1.8 percent), and Norway (1.7 percent). These 13 nations together have over 91 percent of the world reserves.

World natural gas reserves were 3798 trillion cubic feet (108 trillion m³). The USSR led in natural gas reserves with 38.2 percent of the world total, followed by Iran (12.9 percent), United Arab Emirates (5.4 percent), United States (4.9 percent), Qatar (4.1 percent), and Saudi Arabia (3.8 percent). It should be recognized that much of the world is poorly explored, and new discoveries in these areas can be expected in the future, but well-explored areas such as the United States are not expected to increase their reserves substantially.

HISTORY OF EXPLOITATION

The first commercial oil well in the United States was drilled in 1859, but rapid growth in oil production and consumption did not come until the early twentieth century. At that time the major oil fields of Texas, Oklahoma, and California began to be developed, and simultaneously the automobile became popular as a means of transportation. The use of oil grew exponentially until the middle of the twentieth century, and as more oil was discovered and produced, refining and distribution capacity increased and more uses were found for it. There were shortages during World War I, and during World War II gasoline was rationed. Throughout this period, the real price of oil in the United States (adjusted for inflation) steadily declined, reaching a low in the late 1960s. Oil and gas replaced coal as the primary fuels for heating and transportation in the middle of this century.

Recent trends in the U.S. oil industry are shown in Fig. 16.5. By the mid-1950s, domestic

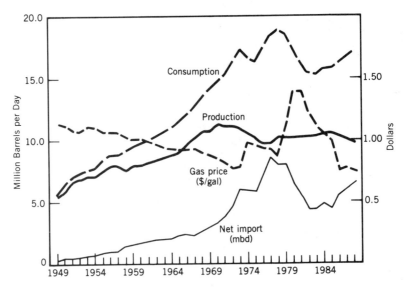

Figure 16.5　Trends in U.S. petroleum production and consumption, 1949–1988. The retail price of gasoline in constant dollars declined steadily, with the exception of sudden increases in 1973 and 1979–1980. These price rises stimulated immediate drop in consumption and growth in production in the early 1980s. (*Source:* EIA, 1989.)

oil began to get harder to find, and exploration in other regions of the world picked up. Domestic exploration, as measured by numbers of wells drilled, peaked in 1956 and has not reached that level since, although by other measures exploration in 1981 was higher than ever before. American oil companies in the 1950s and 1960s placed more emphasis on exploration abroad, particularly in South America and the Middle East. Those areas held large untapped fields that could be developed more cheaply than the smaller fields in the United States, and even considering transportation costs this oil was cheaper than domestic oil.

As a result of this exploitation of foreign oil, in the early 1970s the United States found itself a major importer of oil, with imports amounting to about 25 percent of consumption. Domestic oil production peaked in 1970, and natural gas production peaked in 1974. Domestic demand has continued to climb, and the difference is made up by imports. In 1981, 53 percent of our oil consumption was supplied by domestic production, with 47 percent supplied by imports. However, the dramatic price increases that accompanied the oil shortages of the 1970s stimulated conservation, and by 1981 demand began to be reduced. This was

partly a result of the cumulative effect of conservation measures such as reduction in size of automobiles, but it was also caused by the economic recession of 1981–1983. At the same time, domestic production was spurred by high prices, and supply increased. Similar trends occurred in other countries and a worldwide surplus developed, with inventories at high levels and demand low. Oil prices peaked in 1981, and declined through the 1980s to levels about one-third that of the 1981 peak (in constant dollars). Our current consumption of oil in the United States is about 6.3 billion barrels per year, and world consumption is about 23 billion barrels per year. U.S. natural gas consumption is about 18 trillion cubic feet (510 billion m^3), and world consumption is about 63 trillion cubic feet (1.8 trillion m^3).

END USES

Petroleum and natural gas replaced coal as the primary heating fuel in the middle of this century. Today, oil supplies about 42 percent of U.S. energy demand, and natural gas another 23 percent. Most of the oil (62 percent) is consumed in the transportation sector in the form of gasoline and diesel fuel for automobiles and trucks and in aviation fuels. The industrial sector accounts for about 25 percent of U.S. oil consumption. Industry consumes oil not only for heating, but also for manufacturing petroleum-based products such as synthetic fibers, pesticides, and fertilizers. Four percent of the oil is consumed by electric utilities, and the remaining 8 percent is used in residential and commercial space heating (EIA, 1989a). About 55 percent of American households heat with natural gas or liquefied gas, and 14 percent are heated with oil.

HOW MUCH IS LEFT?

The oil shortages of the 1970s, like those of earlier years, generated much discussion about how much oil is available and how long it is likely to be before we run out. First, it should be recognized that, as with nonfuel minerals, we will never run out of oil. Rather, it will become so expensive that we will replace it with other sources, or we will reduce our demand for it. Nonetheless it is worthwhile to investigate just when oil and natural gas are going to become so hard to find and recover that the price must rise substantially, for at that time we will effectively cease to use these fuels for all but the most essential uses.

There are two basic approaches to estimating how much oil we are likely to produce in the future: the geologic estimate and the performance-based estimate. The *geologic estimate* examines how much oil is in the ground in technically recoverable quantities, without regard to the larger economic forces affecting exploration and production. Most geologic estimates classify sedimentary basins with regard to petroleum-producing potential and use the well-known basins to extrapolate to the quantities likely to exist in poorly known areas. Thus these are estimates of how much oil (or gas) is likely to be in an area, without regard to whether we have the desire or ability (other than technical ability) to get it out.

Performance-based estimates examine the pattern of exploration and production through time, considering all the economic forces that determine whether or not an oil company supplies oil and whether or not a consumer buys it. This technique was pioneered by M.K. Hubbert, who argued that for any stock resource there is a pattern of exponential growth in use of that resource, until the amount used begins to approach the approximate amount in the earth. Then production will level off and decline exponentially (Fig. 16.6). The decline is related as much to the fact that substitute commodities are found and adopted as it is to actual difficulty in obtaining supplies. Hubbert used this method to calculate the total amount of oil likely to be produced in the United States.

Over the years many estimates have been made of the ultimately recoverable petroleum resources in the world. Recent world estimates are generally in the range of 2000 to 5000 billion barrels, with most of them clustering nearer the low end of that range. About 650 billion barrels have already been used as of 1988. If there are 1500 billion barrels remain-

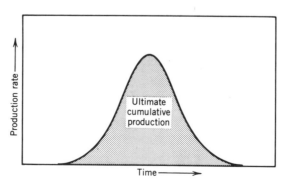

Figure 16.6 Performance-based estimates of oil recoverability. In oil production, a pattern of exponential growth first occurs. Production levels off when the amount used approaches the amount naturally found in the earth. This is followed by an exponential decline in production and use. (*Source:* Hubbert, 1969.)

ing, these will last about 60 years at current rates of consumption. If there are 4500 billion barrels remaining, we have 180 years to go. The world consumption rate is rising, however, and the total life of the resource is likely to be somewhat shorter. In the United States, estimates of ultimately recoverable oil range from about 250 to 600 billion barrels, of which about 160 had been used and 30 were proved reserves in 1988 (Exxon, 1982; EIA, 1989a). Geologic estimates are generally higher than performance-based estimates.

A refinement of Hubbert's performance-based method was used to estimate when we will stop finding oil in the United States (Hall and Cleveland, 1981). It is based on yield of oil per effort expended in looking for it. Both yield and effort are expressed in barrels of oil per foot of exploratory well drilled, and it is argued that we will stop looking for oil when it costs as much (in oil) to explore and produce as we are likely to find. As oil gets harder and harder to find, the yield per foot of well drilled decreases. This yield fluctuates with changing conditions in the industry, but generally it has declined steadily. Hall and Cleveland estimate that for existing oil regions in the United States, we will stop finding oil sometime around the turn of the century or shortly after. If we consider unexplored areas, such as some deep-water offshore areas, this may extend exploration and production a few years. Estimates for gas are similar to those for oil, with gas lasting a few years longer.

Thus the performance-based estimates, which probably more accurately reflect the true behavior of the U.S. oil industry, suggest that we have only 15 to 25 years before we stop finding domestic oil. After that we may have a few years to draw down existing reserves, but not many. It seems very likely, therefore, that the United States will cease to be a significant producer of oil and gas in the first few decades of the next century.

But on the world level there are too many uncertainties to effectively apply performance-based estimates of remaining oil. There are many areas of the world that are relatively poorly explored, especially offshore areas, and throughout the history of oil exploration and use, estimates of the amount of oil that will be found have been consistently low, with estimates rising as more and more areas

are explored. There has also been a tendency to predict much faster rises in consumption than have in fact occurred. Thus estimates of the length of time until we stop using oil, or until a particular nation exhausts its resources, have continually been revised upward, and optimists have tended to be more accurate predictors than pessimists.

ENVIRONMENTAL CONSIDERATIONS

The most significant environmental concerns about petroleum involve the transportation, refining, and burning of oil and natural gas. Because of the geographic locations of the major world producers and consumers, crude oil must be moved by ship (supertanker, tanker, or barge), pipeline, tank truck, or tank car. This is predominantly high seas traffic, with shipments of oil from the producing nations in the Middle East to European and North American markets. As a result of shipping these massive amounts so frequently, accidents are likely to happen—and they do. Pollution of the oceans from tanker accidents has both local and global impacts (see Chapter 12). Another environmental concern is the refining and burning of petroleum, which releases hydrocarbons and carbon dioxide to the atmosphere. This was discussed in Chapter 13.

Finally, a number of land-based problems are involved in petroleum production and natural gas storage. The withdrawal of both oil and natural gas has caused ground subsidence in such places as Long Beach, California, and Houston, Texas. Another problem with natural gas involves the transportation of *liquid natural gas* (LNG) by tanker and its storage and support at land-based facilities. Large volumes of volatile gas are vulnerable to fires of potentially disastrous proportions. As yet, the fires that have occurred have been less devastating than feared, but the possibility of monumental conflagrations has caused concern over the location of LNG facilities near urban areas.

COAL

Coal is the most abundant fossil fuel in the world, with reserves far exceeding those of oil or natural gas. The United States is particularly well supplied with coal, with one-fourth of the world's reserves. Coal is also a dirty fuel, and the environmental impacts associated with its extraction and combustion are a matter of considerable concern.

GEOLOGY

Coal is the partially decomposed and consolidated remains of plants, that were deposited in ancient swamps and lagoons. The original material was modified by heat and the weight of overlying materials from the original plant matter to a substance that is much harder, drier, and chemically different. The degree to which modification of coal has occurred varies greatly from one deposit to another, so that there are several different kinds, or *ranks*, of coal (Table 16.2). The least modified form is *peat*, which has a very high moisture content and which is being deposited in many areas today. In order, the remaining ranks of coal are *lignite*, *subbituminous*, *bituminous*, and finally *anthracite*, which is the most completely converted rank. Typical moisture contents vary from over 40 percent for lignite to less than 10 percent for anthracite. As moisture content is reduced and hydrogen is lost, the heat content per unit weight increases. In addition to rank, ash and *sulfur contents* are important to the value of coal deposits. Ash is primarily derived from mineral sediments deposited along with the plants. In some areas ash content may be very high, but generally coal with ash greater than 15 percent is uneconomic. Sulfur accumulates in most sediments deposited in swampy conditions, and in coal sulfur contents typically vary from less than 1 percent to more than 3 percent.

LOCATION OF RESERVES

Coal is found throughout the world, but the greatest quantities are in the United States, the USSR, China, Australia, western Europe, and South Africa. Bituminous coal is the most abundant type of coal found in the United States. The largest bituminous regions are in the Appalachian Mountains in the East and in sections of the Midwest, particularly Illinois, Iowa, and Missouri (Fig. 16.7). There are also bituminous deposits throughout the Rocky Mountains and in northern Alaska. Anthracite deposits are quite localized and are found in eastern Pennsylvania and in the Appalachian regions of West Virginia and Virginia. Subbituminous deposits are found throughout the Rocky Mountain region. Lignite deposits are found in North and South Dakota and Montana. Although coal is found virtually everywhere in the United States, the ease and the economics of its extraction vary as we shall see in the next section.

EXTRACTION

Coal is mined in three ways: underground, in surface strips, and with augurs. In the nineteenth and early twentieth centuries, most coal mining took place in the eastern United States, where most of the coal seams are in hilly areas and many are steeply inclined relative to the surface. In such situations most of the coal is well below the surface, and underground mining is necessary. *Underground mining* involves drilling, blasting, or otherwise excavating tunnels and chambers underground from which coal is removed and transported to the surface. Much of the coal must be left behind to support overlying rocks, and

TABLE 16.2 Sulfur Content of U.S. Coal Reserves and Resources (Percent)

Rank	Sulfur content		
	Low (0–1%)	Medium (1–3%)	High (>3%)
Anthracite	97	3	—
Bituminous	30	27	43
Subbituminous	100	—	—
Lignite	91	9	—
All	65	15	20

Source: Brobst and Pratt (1973).

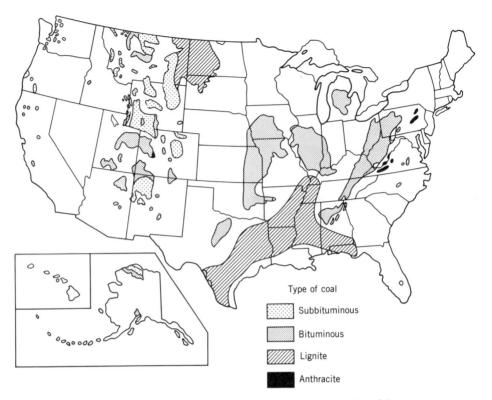

Figure 16.7 Coal resources in the United States. Anthracite deposits are found in eastern Pennsylvania and the Appalachian region of Virginia and West Virginia. Bituminous deposits are found throughout the United States, whereas lignite deposits are largely confined to the West. (*Source: Council on Environmental Quality, 1989.*)

generally no more than 50 percent of the coal is removed. Underground mining is the most dangerous form of mining, indeed it is one of the most dangerous occupations in the world. The greatest hazards are from explosions of methane gas, which is an important component of many coal deposits, and from rock bursts that result from removal of pressure on rocks deep underground.

Strip-mining or *surface mining* is conducted in areas where the coal is near the surface (Fig. 16.8). The *overburden*, or rock and soil overlying the coal, is first removed, and then the coal is removed. In areas of relatively flat terrain where the coal seams are horizontal, strip-mining can remove about 90 percent of the coal from a large area and is thus much more efficient than underground mining. In hilly areas, coal outcrops along hillsides are sometimes mined by stripping, leaving deeper coal unmined. Alternatively, coal in such areas may be mined by *auguring*, in which a large

Figure 16.8 Area strip mining of coal in Missouri. The active face is along the left; areas to the right are being graded prior to reclamation.

augur or drill bores into a coal seam, removing the coal in the process.

Until recently most coal mined in the United States was mined underground in the East. In the last two decades, strip-mining has grown substantially, especially in the West. In 1974, surface mining surpassed underground mining, and as of 1981 over 60 percent of U.S. coal was surface mined (EIA, 1989a).

END USES

The rapid expansion of coal use came with the Industrial Revolution in the eighteenth and nineteenth centuries, when it was the primary energy source for industrial production and rail transportation. In urban areas of Europe and eastern North America it was also a major fuel for home heating in the nineteenth and continuing into the twentieth centuries. Early in this century, however, oil production began to grow rapidly in the United States, particularly with the growth of automobile transportation, and coal was displaced. Those areas that had used much coal for home heating began to shift to oil to avoid the smoke and odors of coal use. After World War II most American railroads replaced steam locomotives with diesel, and coal use continued to decline. The decline ended in the United States in the 1960s, when rapid growth of electric energy use increased the demand for new power plants. Coal is an excellent fuel for high-bulk uses such as in boilers, and today it supplies over 55 percent of the electricity generated in the United States.

Very little coal is used today for home heating in the United States, but it still is used in industry, primarily in producing iron and steel. In steelmaking, coal is first converted to coke by driving off water and volatile matter through destructive distillation, and then it is burned in blast furnaces. Industrial use currently amounts to about 13 percent of U.S. coal use, with electric utilities using over 85 percent (EIA, 1989a).

Since the energy crises of the 1970s, U.S. coal production has risen dramatically, and in 1988 it was 959 million tons. Of this, 95 million tons were exported, mostly to Western Europe, Canada, and Japan. In 1900, coal contributed about 70 percent of U.S. energy supplies, but today its contribution is much lower. In the last 30 years its contribution has varied from 40 percent in 1951 to a low of 22 percent in 1971. Today it contributes about 30 percent of total U.S. energy production.

HOW MUCH IS THERE?

Coal is so abundant in the United States that normally we only discuss reserves, without considering undiscovered or subeconomic resources. Most of the economically recoverable deposits have probably already been discovered because the cost of recovery is primarily determined by depth below the surface, with shallow deposits being most easily recovered. Most of the shallow bedrock in the United States is well explored, and there is little point in looking for deeper coal, with a 1984 U.S. recoverable reserves estimate of 291 billion short tons (265 billion tonnes), about 300 times our current annual production.

On a global basis, recoverable reserves are about 1000 billion tons (910 billion tonnes), which is 250 times the annual world production of about 5 billion tons (4.5 billion tonnes). Most of the reserves are in only a few nations, which also dominate world production. In 1984 seven countries held over 90 percent of world recoverable coal reserves, including the United States with 28.5 percent, the USSR (26.5 percent), China (10.7 percent), Australia (7.1 percent), West Germany (6.4 percent), South Africa (6.3 percent), and Poland (4.6 percent) (EIA, 1989a). Thus there is plenty of coal to meet both U.S. and world demands for at least several decades if not hundreds of years. This is true even if we consider increasing per capita energy consumption and conversion from oil and natural gas to coal for some uses. The major concerns with coal are not ones of supply, but rather of the environmental impact of greatly expanded coal use (Perry, 1983).

ENVIRONMENTAL CONSIDERATIONS

Coal mining and combustion are the most destructive methods in use today for obtaining energy. The environmental impacts are many and far-reaching. Mining impacts include destruction of land underlain by coal, and water pollution. Combustion impacts include acid precipitation and increasing atmospheric carbon dioxide (see Chapter 14).

Underground mining has two major environmental effects: acid drainage and subsidence. *Acid drainage* results from air and water coming in contact with sulfur-bearing rocks and coal. The sulfur is oxidized to sulfuric acid, and groundwater flow carries this acid to streams. This is a particularly severe problem in mining regions of the Appalachians, where some streams have become too acidic to support fish life. Acidity of streams also has effects on the solution of metals in water, making it less suitable for human consumption. *Subsidence* is the sinking of the land as underground voids collapse. It results in structural damage to buildings overlying mined areas and is widespread in Pennsylvania and other underground mining areas.

Strip-mining is generally much more disruptive of the land than underground mining. Overburden must be removed, and so the soil and topography of the area underlain by coal are completely altered in the mining process. While the mine is in operation and until the land is reclaimed, the overburden is exposed to air and rain, resulting in accelerated runoff and oxidation of newly exposed rocks. Runoff from spoils piles results in increased sediment loads of streams, oxidation of sulfur-rich rocks leads to the formation of sulfuric acid, and runoff water from these areas is usually very acidic. These problems are particularly severe in areas of steep slopes, where runoff and erosion are more rapid. In addition, steeply sloping spoils piles are sometimes prone to landsliding.

In 1977, Congress passed the Surface Mining Reclamation and Control Act, which requires reclamation on surface mined lands. Since passage of that act, surface mines are required to remove topsoil separately from lower overburden layers and to store it during mining. After mining is completed, the overburden is replaced with topsoil above it, and the land must be graded to its approximate original contour. Finally, the land must be replanted with vegetation similar to that present before mining. The Act also places a tax on surface mining activities that is used to pay for reclamation of areas mined and aban-

doned before 1977. As of 1965 there were about 3.2 billion acres (1.3 billion ha) disturbed by strip-mining in the United States. Of these, 41 percent were coal mine areas, and another 26 percent were sand and gravel quarries. In 1965 only 34 percent of these disturbed lands were reclaimed, and much of these were reclaimed by nature. Today, 47 percent of all disturbed lands—75 percent of bituminous regions and 14.4 percent of anthracite and peat regions—are reclaimed.

In addition to these problems, coal combustion is a major cause of acid precipitation. Of U.S. coal reserves, about 20 percent is high-sulfur coal, 15 percent is medium-sulfur coal, and 65 percent is low-sulfur coal. Eastern coal is generally higher in sulfur than that west of the Mississippi River, which is unfortunate because the East is generally more susceptible to problems of acid precipitation than the West. Sulfur can be removed from coal before or during combustion, or it can be removed from flue gases after combustion. Some of the techniques for reducing sulfur emissions are discussed in Chapter 14. Although costly, these do offer the possibility of maintaining or increasing coal use while reducing sulfur emissions and, consequently, acid precipitation.

Carbon dioxide emissions, on the other hand, are not controllable. CO_2 is produced as the end product of efficient combustion, and there is no known way to prevent this. As stated in Chapter 14, coal produces proportionately more CO_2 than oil and natural gas, and if coal combustion is increased then CO_2 emissions will increase. The nature of the environmental impact of those emissions is still open to question, but if we intend to prevent CO_2 buildup in the atmosphere then there is no alternative but to reduce coal combustion.

SYNFUELS

Synfuels (synthetic fuels) are liquid or gaseous fossil fuels that are manufactured from other fuels that are not usable as found in the earth. There are many different kinds, but the most promising ones are gasified coal, tar sands, and shale oil. In some cases the technology to convert these substances to usable fuels has been available for several decades, and in other cases it is yet to be commercially developed. For example, in several European countries, oil shale extraction and coal gasification were major energy sources earlier in this century. But these energy sources have been replaced by conventional oil and gas, because of the ease of extraction and shipment and less severe environmental impacts. As liquid petroleum resources dwindle, however, synfuels will attract more interest because they rely on raw materials that are much more plentiful than the oil they may replace.

GEOLOGY, TECHNOLOGY, AND LOCATION

Coal gasification or *liquefaction* means the conversion of coal to a gas or liquid that can be transported via pipeline and burned much as we burn conventional fuels today. Coal is of course plentiful, and one of the major barriers to expanded use of coal is that it is difficult to transport relative to liquids and gases, and it is inappropriate for such uses as internal combustion engines or cooking stoves. Several different gasification techniques are available, but most involve the addition of hydrogen to the carbon in coal to make hydrocarbons. In some processes the volatile hydrocarbons in coal are used as a source of hydrogen, and in others water (in the form of steam) is used. The most common gasification processes make gas that has a lower heat content than conventional fuels, though it can be further processed into high-quality gas and liquid fuels. Coal gasification is most easily carried out in above ground facilities, but there is potential for development of below ground, or *in situ*, technologies. The technology of coal gasification and liquefaction is fairly well known, but as yet it is not economically competitive with conventional oil and gas.

Tar sands are deposits of sand that are high in heavy oil, or tar, content. This tar is too viscous to be pumped from the ground as oil is, but if it is heated it will liquefy and can then be pumped and refined much as heavy crude oil is refined. The sands are generally mined from the ground and then heated, using steam to extract the oil. Most of the tar sand deposits in the United States are either inaccessible because of depth below the surface or are in seams that are too thin to mine. In Alberta,

Canada, however, there are extensive areas of tar sands near or at the surface that are being commercially mined today. Tar sands currently supply more than 8 percent of Canada's oil, and by 1990 this share is expected to reach 20 percent (EIA,1982).

Shale oil is not true oil, rather it is a waxy hydrocarbon called *kerogen* that is found in shale, a fine-textured sedimentary rock. Shale oil is extracted, or retorted, by first crushing and then heating the rock. This liquefies the kerogen, which seeps out of the rock and can then be piped away. Kerogen can be refined into most of the fuels that are produced from conventional crude oil. Shale oil has been produced intermittently on an experimental basis for several decades, but as yet there has been no full-scale commercial production. Most of the experiments have been conducted in above ground facilities, but *in situ* methods are also available. In either above ground or *in situ* retorting, the crushed shale is heated by igniting it. Some of the kerogen in the shale burns, but some is released. Recovery is fairly low, ranging from about 20 percent to 50 percent in most cases.

Most of our high-quality oil shale is located in a few areas in three western states: Colorado, Wyoming, and Utah. There are also some lower-grade deposits in the East, including Tennessee and Michigan. The western oil shale region is a sparsely populated, semiarid rangeland. The richest layers of the shale are located about 700 to 3500 feet (215 to 1000 m) below the surface, except along deep river valleys where the rocks are exposed in the valley walls. For the kerogen to be extracted, either very large areas must be strip-mined or a substantial portion of the retorting must be done underground.

HOW MUCH IS THERE?

One of the most attractive aspects of synfuels is that the raw materials are available in vast quantities. At present rates of extraction, the United States has an ample supply of coal, so clearly we could expand the use of coal for other purposes without jeopardizing its availability in the near future. In addition, if *in situ* methods of coal gasification or liquefaction prove to be economic, then deep deposits of coal could become exploitable. The United States has somewhat fewer tar sand resources, which contain 30 to 40 billion barrels of oil (Canby and Blair, 1981). In Canada, tar sand resources are much greater, perhaps 1000 billion barrels, mostly in Alberta. U.S. domestic oil shale resources are enormous, in excess of 2000 billion barrels, or enough to supply our entire present domestic oil consumption for nearly 100 years.

ENVIRONMENTAL AND ECONOMIC ASPECTS

None of these synfuels can be extracted without significant environmental impacts. All the impacts associated with mining coal also apply to coal gasification—unless the conversion is made underground. If liquid or gaseous coal fuels are to replace oil, then our use of coal must increase, and so must the area affected by mining. The processing also requires large amounts of water, and this is scarce in many of our western coal regions. Gasified or liquefied coal probably would be cleaned of most sulfur in processing, and so sulfur emissions are not likely to be a major barrier to the use of these fuels. However, use of coal in any form, particularly one for which energy is lost in conversion, means that there will be substantial emissions of carbon dioxide.

There are several environmental problems associated with extraction of shale oil. First, to obtain a substantial amount of oil, large areas must be mined. If strip-mining is used, then all the problems associated with strip-mining of other minerals must be considered. Even with *in situ* retorting, about 25 percent of the volume of the rock must be removed to make room for retorting.

Second, retorting involves burning kerogen under conditions not conducive to clean combustion. This combustion produces emissions of hydrocarbons, carbon monoxide, and particulates. The areas where retorting would take place are areas of high air quality, and retorting would almost certainly cause some deterioration.

Third, retorting will use substantial amounts of water in an area already short of supply. Paradoxically, mining will also produce large amounts of brackish water pumped from

the ground to dewater the mines. This water is high in dissolved solids, and disposal may prove difficult.

Finally, the social impacts of development are significant. Large numbers of workers are needed for construction and operation of these facilities, and most of them will come from elsewhere. Populations of some of the towns near the planned developments will soar, with associated stresses on infrastructure and native populations. After construction is completed, employment is expected to drop, causing a decline in local economic conditions. This boom and bust cycle is well known to most mining areas, and the disruption it causes is an important part of the impact of mineral development.

Economic conditions are also a barrier to the extraction of shale oil. Commercial interest began during the oil shortages in the 1920s, but to date there has been no successful commercial-scale extraction. This is due to the relatively low price of conventional fuels, uncertainties about the extraction technology, and, more recently, environmental concerns. Most of the work in the area has been done either directly by the government or with major subsidies. The first major attempt at stimulating development was made during the 1960s, when leases were offered by the government, but no private concerns were then willing to attempt development. Then in 1969 new leases were offered, and this time four of six tracts offered were successfully bid. Two of these were later abandoned, and development work began in the early 1970s on two tracts in northwestern Colorado.

At first the plans were to strip-mine these lands and retort the shale aboveground, but later the companies involved switched to *in situ* methods. During the 1970s environmental studies were conducted, and problems emerged concerning whether the proposed plants could meet air quality regulations. These questions were eventually resolved when the state of Colorado agreed to downgrade its air quality classification for the region, and development proceeded rapidly from 1978 to 1980. However, tests of the retorting technology were not as successful as hoped, and when world oil prices dropped in 1981 and 1982 the projects were suspended. Over the decades there have been times when the industry thought that extraction was commercially feasible, only to find a few years later that substantially higher oil prices were necessary for profitability. When or whether extraction will become economic remains to be seen.

Tar sands are perhaps the least environmentally destructive of these synfuels. They are chemically similar to oil and can be refined in much the same ways that oil is refined. The major negative environmental impacts are those associated with strip-mining, and in that sense they are no worse than coal. But because they are refined and thus burn cleaner than coal, their air pollution impacts are not as severe.

NUCLEAR POWER

The first self-sustaining nuclear reaction took place in December 1942 at the University of Chicago. Although the first applications of nuclear energy were in weapons, atomic power was also used for peaceful purposes after World War II. Although the dichotomy between weapons applications and energy production still exists today, we will discuss only the commercial aspects of nuclear energy.

The first commercial use of nuclear power was to generate electricity in 1957 in Shippingport, Pennsylvania. Westinghouse Electric, in conjunction with the Atomic Energy Commission (now the Nuclear Regulatory Commission and Department of Energy), opened the first full-scale nuclear electrical power plant to be operated by a public utility. At 60 megawatts, the plant was small by today's standards. Nuclear generation of electricity has grown steadily since then, and in 1988 nuclear power supplied nearly 20 percent of U.S. electricity and 7.1 percent of total energy consumption. On a worldwide basis, nuclear energy production was 5.4 percent of total energy production in 1987 (EIA, 1989a).

NUCLEAR FUEL CYCLE

Nuclear power is based on the *fission* process, in which the nuclei of heavy atoms of enriched uranium-235 or plutonium-239 (the latter a by-product of the fission process) are split into lighter elements, thereby releasing energy in a chain reaction. The energy thus released is used to heat water into steam. The steam is then used to drive a turbine, which turns an electric generator.

The nuclear fuel cycle consists of eight stages (Fig. 16.9). Unlike some of the more conventional fuel sources, which can be used with a minimum of processing, nuclear power requires several processing steps with transportation linkages between them. Uranium is the primary fuel for nuclear power plants. Most U.S. uranium resources are found in the Rocky Mountain states and are mined by both open-pit and underground techniques. Nearly two-thirds of the uranium is mined in New Mexico and Wyoming. Of the naturally occurring *uranium*, which is a mixture of the isotopes ^{235}U and ^{238}U, less than 1 percent, that is, only the ^{235}U, is highly fissionable. Thus most of the uranium ore must be enriched and/or converted to make it sustain the fission process. Once mined, the uranium ore is milled to produce a purer concentrate called yellowcake. Yellowcake is about 85 percent natural uranium oxide (U_3O_8).

The third stage in the fuel cycle is the chemical purification and conversion of the yellowcake to uranium hexafluoride (UF_6). In the United States, the conversion is carried out at facilities in Metropolis, Illinois; Sequoyah, Oklahoma; Apollo, Pennsylvania; and Barnwell, South Carolina. The conversion process prepares the uranium for enrichment, the next stage in the fuel cycle.

At the enrichment plant the concentration of ^{235}U is increased from 0.7 percent to about 4 percent, to meet the requirements of the reactors. All the enrichment facilities in the United States are government-owned and are located in only three areas—Oak Ridge, Tennessee; Paducah, Kentucky; and Portsmouth, Ohio. Once the UF_6 has been enriched, it is ready to be made into fuel rods. The UF_6 is converted into uranium dioxide (UO_2), which is then formed into small pellets and placed in alloy tubes. These tubes are then made into fuel rods and assembled into bundles, called fuel rod assemblies. The fuel fabrication process is carried out at five locations in the United States. The fuel rod assemblies are then shipped to individual reactors, where they are used to produce electricity.

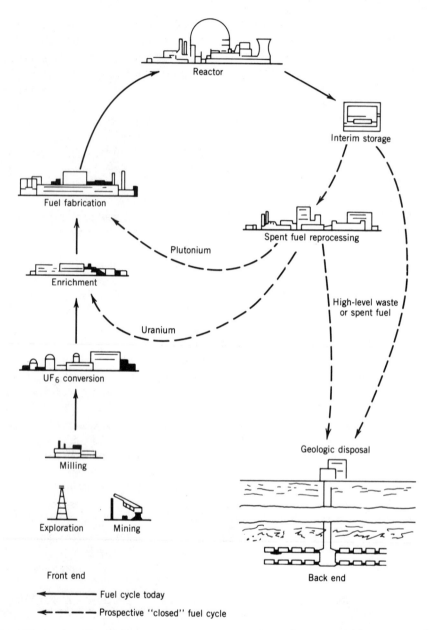

Reactor

Interim storage

Fuel fabrication

Spent fuel reprocessing

Plutonium

High-level waste
or spent fuel

Enrichment

Uranium

UF_6 conversion

Geologic disposal

Milling

Exploration   Mining

Front end

Back end

◀—————— Fuel cycle today

◀— — — — Prospective "closed" fuel cycle

Figure 16.9 The nuclear fuel cycle. At each stage in the cycle, nuclear material is transported varying distances from mining regions to conversion and enrichment facilities, fabrication plants, and nuclear reactors. After use, spent fuel is reprocessed and/or disposed of. (*Source:* Council on Environmental Quality, 1981.)

Spent fuel is removed from the reactor core and stored on site for several months to permit the levels of radioactivity to decline. Optimally, the spent fuel is then shipped to a reprocessing plant, where the unused portions of uranium and plutonium are separated from the fission wastes. The unused uranium is recycled back to the enrichment plant, and the

unused plutonium is refabricated into new fuel pellets. There are currently no fuel reprocessing plants in the United States; as a result, spent fuel is stored at the reactor site.

The last stage in the nuclear fuel cycle is disposal of the radioactive waste. Low-level wastes (only half of which are generated by nuclear power plants) are buried in metal or concrete containers at 22 sites around the country. Since the start of the commercial reactor program, over 106 million cubic feet (3 million m^3) of low-level waste have been buried. High-level waste is stored either at the nuclear power plant or at three temporary locations—Richland, Washington; Idaho Falls, Idaho; and Aiken, South Carolina. A permanent disposal facility is proposed for a site at Yucca Mountain, Nevada, and site investigations are under way. The project has been plagued with technical and management problems, however, and it is unlikely that a permanent high-level waste storage facility will be available in the United States before about 2010.

POWER PLANTS

There are four basic types of reactors now in use worldwide, but most of the reactors in the United States are classified as *light-water reactors* (Fig. 16.10), which means that ordinary water is used as the cooling agent. In one type of light-water reactor, the boiling-water reactor, water is circulated through the reactor vessel, which contains the fuel rods, where the water boils and produces steam, which is then piped to the turbine. In a pressurized-water reactor, another type of light-water reactor, water is kept at high pressure to prevent it from boiling in the reactor vessel. The high-pressure water is then pumped through the core, and the superheated water exchanges heat in a secondary water/steam loop.

The second basic type of reactor is the *high-temperature gas-cooled reactor*. Helium gas is used as the coolant, transferring the heat from the core to the steam generator. There is only one reactor of this type in the United States—the Fort St. Vrain plant just outside of Denver, Colorado.

The third type of reactor is the *heavy-water reactor*. This system uses heavy water (water containing a higher than usual proportion of deuterium) as the moderator of the fission process. Regular water passes through the core and carries heat to the secondary water/steam loop. Heavy-water reactors are not used in the United States but they dominate the Canadian reactor program (the

Figure 16.10   Power plant using a pressurized water reactor, Three Mile Island, Pennsylvania. The reactor experienced a loss-of-coolant accident in 1979.

CANDU system). Canada is also a large exporter of the CANDU technology and of the heavy water that is manufactured at the Bruce Nuclear Generating Station on Lake Huron.

The fourth type of reactor is the *liquid-metal fast-breeder reactor*, in which fissionable material is surrounded by nonfissionable material (^{238}U) in the core. Sodium is used as the moderating substance and heat exchanger. During the fission process, some of the nonfissionable material is converted to fissionable ^{239}Pu. The reactor produces more fuel than it consumes, hence the name breeder reactor. There are no breeder reactors in the United States, although they have been used in other countries for some time.

Nuclear power is used only to generate electricity. In 1988 it produced 19.5 percent of the total U.S. generation of electricity, about 527 billion kilowatt-hours. Production of electricity using nuclear power increased substantially during the 1980s as plants under construction since the 1970s were completed and began operation.

This growth in the U.S. nuclear industry has recently ended, because in the 1970s nuclear power became much more expensive than other heat sources used to generate electricity. Most plants under construction in the 1970s have been completed, but no new plants have been ordered since 1978. Rising concerns about safety at nuclear reactors were spurred by accidents at Three Mile Island, in Pennsylvania in 1979 and at Chernobyl in the Soviet Union in 1986. In the United States today (as in much of the world), nuclear power is not economically feasible without government subsidies, and in many areas it is politically unacceptable. This political force was demonstrated clearly in New York and California in 1989. In New York, after a long battle over evacuation plans in the event of an accident, the Shoreham nuclear power plant on Long Island was prevented by the state from beginning full-power generation and plans are under way to dismantle the plant. And in a referendum in California, voters decided to shut down the Rancho Seco plant, which had been plagued with technical problems and was believed vulnerable to damage in the event of an earthquake. In New Hampshire, however, the controversial Seabrook plant came on line after more than a decade of debate.

Because very few additional plants will be operating, U.S. generation capacity will not increase substantially in the 1990s. In 1988 the total U.S. nuclear generating capacity was about 95 gigawatts; this number is not expected to increase by more than about 10 percent before at least 2005 (EIA, 1989b). It remains to be seen whether confidence in nuclear energy will be restored and growth will continue, or whether we are today reaching the peak of nuclear energy generation. If nuclear energy is to become viable again, it will almost certainly require the development of new, safer technology that will restore public confidence in this energy source. Otherwise, the high costs of overcoming political opposition and meeting safety requirements will continue to make construction of nuclear plants prohibitively expensive.

In other parts of the world similar problems have arisen, though not everywhere. In much of western Europe, public concern about reactor safety increased dramatically after the Chernobyl incident (see Issue 16–1). In 1989, the British government acknowledged that its nuclear industry (which generates about 20 percent of that nation's electricity) was not economic in comparison to conventional generation technology and abandoned plans for any additional power plants. France, however, which has had a very aggressive nuclear program since the 1950s, generates 70 percent of its electricity from nuclear power. France has remained firm in its commitment to this energy source.

One potential positive factor regarding the future of nuclear power is public concern over air pollution. In many parts of the world, particularly North America and Europe, there is also concern about both the greenhouse effect and acid rain. Coal is the primary alternative to nuclear power in these areas, and coal-fired electric plants are major sources of CO_2, NO_x, and sulfur. Nuclear energy is seen as relatively clean from an environmental perspective, and it offers the potential to increase electric generation capacity without contributing to global warming or acid rain, although long-term waste storage remains a problem.

HOW MUCH URANIUM IS LEFT?

The United States has substantial uranium resources, although extraction costs are high relative to those in other countries. Because of these costs we currently import approximately half of our uranium needs. For the foreseeable future, there is not expected to be any significant shortage of uranium, because fuel costs are small in comparison to other costs of operating nuclear reactors, and price increases for fuel would substantially increase the amount of reserves available in the United States.

ENVIRONMENTAL AND HEALTH ASPECTS

The primary concern about the use of nuclear energy is the potential for human exposures to radioactivity, resulting in *somatic* and *genetic damage*. Accidental releases of radioactivity occur at all stages in the fuel cycle, from the mining of uranium, which produces radon gas, to occupational exposures in fabricating fuel rods, to accidental releases at nuclear power plants. Releases of radioactivity can also occur as a result of sabotage and simple mishandling of materials. There is considerable debate on the effects of low levels of exposure to ionizing radiation.

There are also other environmental considerations at each of the stages in the fuel cycle. Land disturbance and radioactive mine tailings are the primary impacts of mining and milling. In the production of power, waste heat is produced, causing thermal pollution. This occurs, of course, with any type of steam-powered electricity plant. The most important environmental aspects of nuclear power production involve the accidental release of airborne or waterborne radioactivity (Fig. 16.11). For example, in the Chernobyl incident radioactive fallout was spread over much of Europe, resulting in levels of contamination high enough to prevent the consumption of numerous food products produced in contaminated areas for at least several years following the accident (Hohenemser *et al.* 1986; Hohenemser and Renn, 1988). These safety issues cause great public concern about the use of nuclear energy on a large scale. The technology is hazardous, and the future extent of nuclear energy production will be a function of the risks that society is willing to tolerate in exchange for additional electric power.

RENEWABLE ENERGY

There are several renewable sources of energy available today, and many more will probably become available in the future. *Renewable energy* is a term used to describe energy sources that are either continuously available, like heat and light from the sun, or those that are replaced relatively rapidly and therefore can only be temporarily depleted, like wood. Renewable energy sources are quite varied, being in the form of radiant energy (the sun), chemical energy (biomass), potential energy (water stored in reservoirs), and kinetic energy (wind). Some, like wood fuel, have been used for thousands of years, some are relatively recent developments (hydroelectric generation), and some are likely to be used in the future (ocean thermal energy conversion, or OTEC).

Although many different technologies are available for renewable energy sources, there are a few that are likely to be most important in the next few decades. Some of these will be types in which energy is produced in large, concentrated facilities (as most of our electricity is produced today). For purposes of this discussion, we will call these centralized facilities. In other cases, energy production will most likely be in a large number of small facilities, like the photovoltaic cells that are used to power satellites, calculators, and remote communications facilities. We will call these decentralized renewables.

CENTRALIZED RENEWABLES

Centralized renewables are those that are used in large, concentrated facilities such as electric generating stations. They require large capital investments in single facilities, and most are used to generate electricity that is fed into the same grids that transport energy generated from fossil fuels or nuclear power. The primary centralized renewable energy sources in use today are hydroelectric generation, geothermal energy, tidal power, and biomass. The most promising technologies for future centralized renewable power include OTEC, low-temperature geothermal, and large-scale solar power facilities.

Decentralized renewables are energy sources that will probably be of greatest importance in small facilities not connected to large-scale energy systems. The most impor-

tant of these is solar thermal energy for space or water heating. Other important decentralized energy sources for the future include photovoltaics and wind.

Hydroelectric Power

From both economic and environmental considerations, *hydroelectric power* is probably

---

Issue 16–1   Chernobyl: "The Structure of Nature Has Been Deranged"

Although nuclear energy is very useful and reported accidents are rare, both perhaps are not so rare or harmless as we are led to believe. The problem is that the results of a single accident can be disastrous for so many for a very long period of time. On April 26, 1986, a nuclear reactor in the small Soviet town of Chernobyl experienced a temporary loss of its cooling water, and the resulting fire spread radioactive contaminants around the globe. If you managed to find your way to a vast swath of land around Chernobyl, this is the ominous scene that would have greeted you (Werner 1990).

Driving toward Chernobyl, three hours north of Kiev, the sky is lightly overcast, the air is not too cold. Spring is coming, you think, and you check the roadside trees for buds. That's strange—most of the trees are brown, brittle, dead. No, there's a live pine—green, but huge! It looms above the dead ones all around. There are some more pretty green pines, but they're so tiny! Fully formed, mature in shape, but only a foot high! That bunch there is dead. No, wait—I need a closer look. I'll turn off on this side road to check. Yes, I was right—they're living, breathing pine trees, but they're rusty orange in color. And, come to think of it, if spring is here, where are the birds? This place is so dead quiet—only a tractor in the distance. And why is this road barred with a barbed-wire fence? I can see a village further along. The houses are all falling apart and the yards are overgrown—did I just see someone, walking along that street? I guess this sign here with the skull and crossbones means business....

When the Soviet authorities finally acknowledged that the Chernobyl incident was major, they evacuated all the children of the immediate area, because young bodies are more vulnerable to the effects of fallout. It was too late for many. When they returned from their unexpected summer "vacation," many children were already ill

with leukemia, thyroid cancer, and other radiation-induced diseases. Irina, who lives 9 miles (15 km) from the reactor, was a slim three-year-old in 1986. In 1990 she is obese from chemotherapy and her parents keep her alive with regular blood transfusions. She is one of the thousands of Soviet children with Chernobyl-related cancer.

The Soviet authorities are paying a heavy price for their long-term policy of insisting that they can handle their own problems without help from the outside. In 1986 the Soviet government maintained that they could easily handle this local problem, that only 200 people had been contaminated, and life and farming would soon return. Word is finally getting out via the scientific journals that reality is much worse than the official statements. In addition, reporters have risked their health to explore this forbidden zone, to discover the human side of the numbing statistics. Today, several years later, the picture is a little clearer.

Farmers cannot consume their own produce. Cereals, milk, and meat are shipped to Kiev, where they are diluted with clean food at a ratio of 10:1, and then disappear into distant markets. Residents have crept back into the forbidden zones, because there is nowhere else for them to go. They are unwitting guinea pigs in a study of the long-term effects of living in a radiation-contaminated environment. The soil, the water, and the produce of their gardens and of the forest, are full of cesium-137, strontium-90, and plutonium. They live in the "dead zone," the area within 19 miles (30 km) of the reactor. Only reactor and repair workers are allowed through this innermost barbed-wire barrier. Three undamaged reactors at the plant are still supplying power, and the shift is three days in the zone, followed by a week off. Shifts are much briefer— a few minutes of exposure—for those working to

the best source of electricity available to us today. Hydroelectric power is generated by impounding water in a location where a substantial vertical drop is available, such as near a waterfall or in a steeply sloping portion of a river valley, and passing the water through turbines that drive generators. Water power has of course been used for several centuries to drive various industrial facilities, but only in the last 100 or so years has it been used to generate electricity. In that time many large dams have been built, and today about 8 percent of U.S. electricity, or 3 percent of total U.S. energy consumption, is supplied by hydroelectric power. Some of the major generating facilities in North America include those at Niagara Falls, in the Tennessee Valley, the Colorado River, the Columbia River, and on several riv-

---

entomb the damaged reactor in something more permanent than concrete.

A Soviet map of contaminated areas issued in July 1989 eventually found its way to the public and illustrates a problem far more vast than had previously been admitted. Hundreds of villages, over a much wider area than that officially designated, were contaminated at levels above 60 curies per square kilometer, a massive dose to live with on a daily basis. Milk was found to be radioactive at 530 locations, and several hundred times the "normal" number of livestock were being born deformed, and over two million people were significantly contaminated (Werner, 1990).

The effects of Chernobyl were felt internationally, and we still do not know the full impact of the drifting fallout on downwind areas in Eastern Europe, the British Isles, and Scandinavia, where the Lapps' lives have been changed forever. Their reindeer, consuming contaminated lichens, are no longer permitted in livestock markets. In parts of Wales, England, and Scotland, heavy rainstorms occurring just as the cloud of fallout was passing overhead brought contamination to upland areas. Four years later, sheep from these areas still must be screened before being allowed in the market. Two hundred and fifty farmers—perhaps 50 percent of north Wales' total—are affected, and a half million sheep have had their lives prolonged because their bodies contain unsafe levels of radiation. When sheep are brought down from pastures in contaminated hills, their radiation levels decrease by one-half about every three weeks. These sheep are specially marked and are tested regularly until the levels reached are deemed safe for human consumption (Atherton and Atherton, 1990).

Unfortunately, the contaminated areas are not very well defined. The initial testing was hap-

hazard, and it is now emerging that some uncontaminated areas are actually defined as contaminated—and vice versa—suggesting that some quantities of unsafe meat, milk, and cheese may have reached consumers. The numbers of sheep deformities have also risen enormously.

With emergencies come technological breakthroughs, and it is now possible to detect irradiated areas from a helicopter equipped with radiation sensors. The maps resulting from this and from research on soils and runoff indicate that the cesium is becoming more environmentally active. The cesium is no longer simply lying on the vegetation but is weathering into the soil to be absorbed more efficiently by grass, the sheep's major food supply. The gradual loss of radiation in livestock in north Wales and other areas has leveled off and may begin to climb once more. North Wales farmers are unable to farm under these conditions; government compensation, where available, is no solace. Many are suggesting that north Wales' hot spots should become a nature reserve instead of a farming area. Throughout the United Kingdom, 757 farms on 400,000 acres (160,000 ha) are affected by restrictions (Ghazi, 1990).

Chernobyl is not the first Soviet nuclear disaster; a 1958 explosion at a research plant in the Ural Mountains was treated as top secret, but the empty towns, restricted access, and informal death counts tell the story. Apparently, the 1979 accident at Pennsylvania's Three Mile Island power plant had no lethal or widespread effects; we can only hope that our government and power companies are being honest in this assessment. A lot of capital and national defense concerns are tied up in our use of nuclear energy, and authorities tend to downplay negative effects to protect their political and economic interests.

Figure 16.11   Workers monitoring radiation levels on vehicles near the Chernobyl power plant, USSR.

ers in Ontario and Quebec that drain north into Hudson Bay.

These facilities are all located at sites that offer the greatest potential for hydroelectric generation, namely, large volumes of available water, good dam sites, and in some cases low population density. At these sites the cost of generating electricity is quite low in comparison to other methods. There is of course a rather large capital cost involved in dam construction and land acquisition, but once this is paid for the operating costs are extremely low. Most of the large dams in North America have been built either by governments or with large government subsidies, and this has contributed to the low cost of hydroelectric power in many areas. In the northwestern United States, for example, electricity prices are substantially lower than in the rest of the country because of the large contribution of hydroelectric power generated at federally built dams along the Columbia River and its tributaries.

Unfortunately, there is relatively little potential for expansion of hydroelectric gener-

ation in the United States. Most of the best dam sites are already in use, and those that are not are generally not available because of commitment of the river valleys to other uses, such as agriculture or wilderness preservation. There may be some opportunity for increasing hydroelectric generation at smaller dams, and there are a few examples of existing dams that had been unused until recently, when higher energy prices made hydroelectric power generation on a small scale more feasible. In New England, for example, there are hundreds of dams that were constructed for hydroelectric power or industrial uses in the past, but that are no longer in use. In Canada, there is considerable potential for increased hydroelectric generation. Canada already exports substantial amounts of electricity to the United States, primarily from Quebec to New York. This trade is facilitated partly because the peak demand for electricity in Quebec occurs in winter, whereas the peak in most of the United States is in summer. Several additional dam sites are available in northern Quebec to increase this production, although capital costs, transmission distances, and opposition from native populations are significant barriers.

Although hydroelectric generation is probably the cleanest source of electricity we have, it is not without its environmental problems. One of these is of course the loss of the land and aquatic habitat that is submerged when a reservoir is filled. The construction of dams and subsequent regulation of flow patterns may also have adverse effects on stream channels and aquatic life downstream. There have been problems of erosion in the Grand Canyon, for example, as a result of the construction of Glen Canyon Dam upstream. In arid areas, such as the Colorado basin, reservoirs contribute to evaporative water losses by increasing water surface areas. Many valleys contain fertile agricultural land, and reservoir development has been a significant contributor to loss of agricultural land in the United States. There may also be effects on water quality as a result of impoundment, as nutrient-laden water stimulates algal blooms, leading to eutrophication. Several other adverse effects have occurred at various locations too numerous to describe here. In spite of these effects, however, our existing hydroelectric facilities are important energy sources, and they cause only minor environmental problems. Construction of new facilities, however, is a much more contentious issue, as they almost always require the loss of some other valued resource.

Geothermal

Geothermal energy is derived from the internal heat of the earth. The core of the earth is hot, and this heat is convected and conducted outward toward the surface. In many parts of the earth's crust, sufficiently large amounts of heat are delivered to the surface to make the use of that heat feasible. Geothermal energy is used in many parts of the world today, for space and water heating, for industrial processing, and for electricity generation.

There are three major types of geothermal resources: hydrothermal, geopressurized, and dry rock. Hydrothermal resources occur in locations where there is a source of heat relatively near the surface, and the overlying rocks are fractured enough to allow water to circu-

late. In addition, the water must be trapped in the ground to prevent heat from escaping rapidly to the surface. This results in the formation of hot springs and geysers. If this steam or hot water can be tapped, it can be used to generate electricity or heat buildings. Geopressurized resources are deeper pockets of water trapped in sedimentary formations in much the way as oil and gas are trapped. Hot dry rock is simply rock in areas of high heat flow, but without large quantities of water contained in the rock. To tap this heat, the rocks must be fractured and wells drilled so that water can be injected into the rocks to draw the heat out. At present, geopressurized and hot dry rock resources are not in use, but hot dry rock offers considerable potential for development in the future.

Only one facility in the United States is currently generating electricity from geothermal energy—The Geysers, in California. It presently produces about 1000 megawatts at peak output, or about the same as a large conventional power plant. The output from this plant amounts to less than 0.2 percent of total U.S. electricity generation. One possibility for increased geothermal production is in the development of hot dry rock facilities. There are numerous areas of the United States, mostly in the West, where subsurface temperatures are particularly high. The economics of such ventures are still uncertain, however, and it is unlikely that geothermal energy will make large contributions to total electric generation in the near future.

Other Centralized Renewables

In addition to hydroelectric and geothermal power, there are a few technologies that offer limited potential for future development. One of these is combustion of biomass, primarily solid wastes. Garbage consists largely of combustible organic materials, and heat from this combustion can be used directly for industrial processes or for generating electricity. Such combustion is often called *resource recovery*. At present there are several dozen operating resource recovery plants in the United States that use solid waste as fuels, with most of these producing steam for industrial processes. In a few cases wood or agricultural wastes are used for fuel, but in most plants municipal wastes are burned. The major incentive for this at the present time is the high cost of disposal of solid waste rather than the value of the steam produced, and the disposers pay to have the fuel burned rather than the plants buying fuel. At present, combustion of wood and municipal solid waste and the production of alcohol from sugar and grain provide approximately 3.5 percent of the nation's energy needs, with alcohol being the largest part of this total (U.S. Department of Energy, 1987; 1989a).

Another centralized renewable energy source is tidal power. Tidal fluctuations produce strong currents in coastal embayments, and these currents can be harnessed to produce electricity. A large tidal range is required, and a dam must be constructed across the bay to create the hydraulic head necessary to drive turbines. Power can be generated only during a portion of the tidal cycle, and diurnal or semi-diurnal tidal fluctuations do not always correspond to the fluctuations in demand. Thus, tidal power can be viewed only as a supplement to other sources of energy. At present, there is one tidal power plant in operation in France.

Large-scale solar thermal and photovoltaic collectors, plants that harness wave energy, and large-scale wind-powered generating facilities have also been proposed. There has been relatively little activity in these areas in the 1980s because of low costs of conventional energy and weak growth in demand for electricity. If prices rise significantly in the future these methods may again be considered. Centralized renewable sources in general will probably continue to provide only small portions of our total energy supply, with only biomass (primarily municipal solid waste) and hydroelectric generation making a large contribution to total electricity generation. New power generation from all centralized renewable sources together will probably not contribute more than a few percent of the total U.S. energy supply for a few decades.

DECENTRALIZED RENEWABLES

Solar energy offers enormous potential for heating buildings and water, and thereby replacing more conventional energy sources such as fossil fuels and electricity. Solar energy

is plentiful, though not uniformly available in space and time. The technology is reasonably well developed and is economically feasible in most of the United States. The major barrier to its use at present is capital costs.

Solar energy reaches the earth's surface in the form of radiant energy, and it is converted to heat when sunlight is absorbed on an exposed surface. The amount of radiant energy received varies with the time of day, season, weather conditions, and location on earth (Fig. 16.12). For example, there is no sunlight at night, and during cloudy weather, sunlight is less intense, though it is still present. Seasonality influences the length of day, so that there are fewer hours of daylight in winter than in summer. Also, the angle of the sun changes during the year, reducing the intensity of solar radiation per unit of horizontal surface area in the winter. Because of these large fluctuations in solar energy availability, only a few places in the United States can rely on solar energy as a single consistent source. In other regions, backup energy systems are required.

Solar energy is often discussed in terms of passive and active technologies. *Passive solar* heating and cooling involves neither mechanical devices nor the production and storage of electricity. Passive solar employs proper design of structures, building materials that insulate or store energy, correct orientation of structures, and careful landscaping to provide heating and cooling. A house with many windows on the southern exposure allows for maximum sun during the winter. Planting deciduous trees on the south side of the house protects it from the hot summer sun's rays, yet allows the sunlight to penetrate during the winter months, when the trees have dropped their leaves. The use of adobe as a building material and the design of houses with shaded arcades and small windows, such as those of Spanish-style haciendas in the Southwest, are other examples of passive approaches to solar heating and cooling.

Active solar systems use mechanical devices to collect and store solar radiation for heating and cooling. The solar collector is the basic unit of a solar space heating system and can vary greatly in size and complexity. The simplest type of collector consists of a flat plate, painted black for maximum absorption,

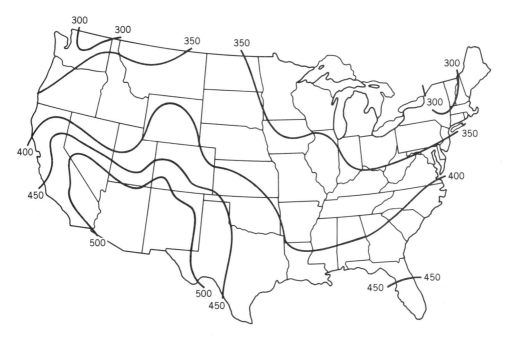

Figure 16.12 Annual mean daily solar radiation. Areas such as the Southwest receive an average of over 500 langleys of solar radiation daily, providing a stable source of solar energy for heating and cooling. The Northeast and Southeast must have backup energy systems because of fluctuations in mean levels of solar radiation. (*Source:* U.S. Weather Service, 1965.)

encased in an insulated, glass-covered box. The plate absorbs light, while the glass impedes energy loss, so that temperatures rise to about 200°F (93°C). This heat is then used to warm rooms and water as air moves across the black plate or water circulates through a pipe attached to the plate. Higher temperatures (up to 1000°F or 538°C) are obtained by concentrating the light with one or more curved mirrors, which rotate along with the sun's movement across the sky. Temperatures of up to 4000°F (2205°C) can be attained by focusing a bank of mirrors on a central point, such as a tower containing a water boiler for operating a steam turbine.

The amount of solar energy received by a collector varies with the time of day, season, and weather. These variations, plus obstructions by trees and buildings, still allow for the use of solar energy for space heating. The heating and hot water needs of a one- or two-story building can be met by using available roof surfaces, southern walls, and other areas for the installation of collectors.

The use of solar collectors nationwide rose substantially in the late 1970s and early 1980s,

but slowly in the late 1980s. Low-temperature collectors are used almost exclusively for swimming pool heating. Medium-temperature collectors are used both for space heating and cooling and for domestic water heating. Regionally, there are more collectors in use in the western, high-sunshine states than in the East, but advocates maintain that solar collectors are capable of a quick return on investment even in the cloudiest of climates.

One of the more promising solar technologies for the future is *photovoltaic cells*. These are thin silicon wafers that convert sunlight directly to electricity. When first produced in the 1950s they were extremely expensive, but with rapid growth in production technologies and concurrent increases in demand, the prices have fallen dramatically in the past decade (Flavin, 1983). In 1982 the capital cost of purchasing solar cells was about $10 per peak watt, which is too expensive to be used in large-scale generation. There are many applications for these cells today, however, primarily in running small machines such as weather recorders in remote locations. Further price reductions may greatly expand the usefulness of photovoltaic cells (Fig. 16.13), and it is possible that they could be used for some domestic purposes in the next few decades (see Issue 16–2).

One of the main challenges in solar energy technology is the development of storage devices for use at night, on cloudy days, and in cooler seasons. Fuel cells offer some promise of alleviating this problem. Fuel cells operate by passing electricity through a salty solution, splitting water into hydrogen and oxygen. These can later be recombined to produce electricity. One of the important advantages of fuel cells is their high efficiency, but at present they are too expensive for ordinary applications.

Although many reports claim that solar energy is the way of the future, many obstacles will have to be overcome before it makes a truly significant contribution to our energy supplies. The most important economic barriers to residential heating and cooling are the high capital costs and relatively long payback period for an investment. This is particularly troublesome for retrofitting, and less so for new installations. As a result of the slowdown in solar energy installation in the mid-1980s, substantial infrastructure in the form of manufacturers, dealers, and installers was lost, and the economics of solar energy will have to improve substantially before there is another wave of installation of these systems.

Figure 16.13 Photovoltaic cells generating electricity for lighting a road sign in New Mexico.

WIND POWER

Windmills have been used worldwide since ancient times. We perhaps know them best in the United States as a symbol of the nineteenth-century farm, where wind energy was converted to mechanical energy to pump water from the farm well. Although windmills have largely been replaced with other pumping devices, the windmill is again feasible as a method of generating electricity. The industry is small but has considerable potential. Growth in this area was encouraged by a 1978 federal law requiring public utilities to purchase electric power offered to them by small generating companies. The price is determined by the avoidance costs of producing equivalent amounts of energy by conventional sources.

The first utility company to incorporate windmill-generated power into its power grid was Southern California Edison Company in 1980. A privately financed 200-foot-tall wind turbine was installed in the desert near Palm Springs, California, that is capable of generating enough electricity for about a thousand homes. The blades are driven by reliable winds, which average 17 mph with gusts up to 40 mph. The amount of electricity generated by this turbine is equivalent to an annual saving of about 10,000 barrels of oil. Another example is the Wind Farm project operated by Pacific Gas & Electric in the Altamont Pass area in northern California. The 407 windmills there are each turning out 50 kilowatts.

In the late 1970s and early 1980s, the U.S. Department of Energy put millions of dollars into developing prototype wind machines that were rated from 200 to 2500 kilowatts at peak power output. The largest of these has a blade span of 300 ft. Early 1980s projections estimated that wind energy would provide 2 to 4 percent of our electricity by 2000, but lower oil prices in the middle and late 1980s slowed development of this and other alternative sources.

Windpower is recognized as the first renewable energy source since hydroelectricity to move beyond government sponsorship and into control by traditional public utilities (Fig. 16.14). Its application to large-scale electricity generation holds fewer uncertainties than

Figure 16.14 A wind energy-generating facility at Altamont Pass, California.

other renewable sources. Wind power is also more easily integrated into existing utility power grids, which are necessary to provide backup power when wind velocities are low.

ENERGY CONSERVATION

Energy conservation has been our largest single source of "new energy" in the 1980s. Conservation in this sense simply means using less or using what you have with more efficiency. As we have seen earlier in this chapter, energy consumption in the United States peaked at 79 quads in 1979 and declined until 1983; it has since risen back to 1979 levels. But the total output of goods and services in 1989 was much higher than in 1979, and this increased output represents the benefits of conservation.

If we consider *energy efficiency* in terms of the value of industrial output per unit of energy input, then our energy efficiency has increased substantially. In the mid-1970s, the total energy consumed (in production and end use) per constant dollar was about 10,500 BTU; in 1985 the figure had declined to about 9000 BTU. In 1985 our industrial output was about 20 percent higher than in 1975, but this was produced with about 7 percent less

energy. In other words, increased efficiency (conservation) in the industrial sector produced about 5 quads of energy per year in 1985 relative to 1975.

Energy conservation develops in stages. In the first stage, less fuel does less work; for example, people drive more slowly and reduce heat and light use. In the second stage, less fuel is used to do the same amount of work. This requires minor design and investment decisions, but not major overhaul of facilities or reorientation of an industry. Finally, less fuel is used to do more work. This provides the greatest savings, yet it requires investment in applied research efforts to be effective. This applied research requires substantial technological innovations and usually takes at least several years to realize.

In the late 1970s and 1980s all of these stages were seen in certain sectors of the economy. Using automobiles as an example, in the mid-1970s consumers and auto manufacturers responded to higher gasoline prices by shifting from larger to smaller cars, smaller engines, and manual transmissions. Consumers also responded by driving less: miles per vehicle decreased over 4 percent and total motor fuel consumption dropped by 9 percent between 1978 and 1982. By the mid-1980s most people were driving much more fuel-efficient cars. In 1976 the average fuel consumption by U.S. cars was 12.1 miles per gallon; by 1987 this had increased by 25 percent to 15.1 miles per gallon. In 1985 more people were driving more cars more miles per car, but using less fuel than had been consumed in 1978. But in the late 1980s low gasoline prices led consumers to demand larger engines and faster cars, and total motor fuel consumption rose substantially, mirroring trends of the late 1960s.

ENERGY ALTERNATIVES

There is a high degree of substitutability between the various sources of energy, and a wide range of alternatives exist for aggregate energy supply and demand in the future. The choices of which sources of energy to use more and which less, and which to use for heating and which to use for electricity, are important policy decisions with far-reaching impacts. At the present time the U.S. government is relying primarily on market forces to determine our national energy policy. The result has been that, in an era of plentiful oil and slow economic growth (the early 1980s), energy use patterns have been relatively static. If war in the Persian Gulf Region should cause a return to energy shortage and rapidly rising energy prices such as in the 1970s, we would probably suffer the same fate as was suffered then, that is, severe economic shock. The shortages that occurred in the 1970s were small in comparison to the potential changes in energy supply and demand that could be achieved in a decade or two. The crises of the 1970s were precipitated by shortages of as little as 5 percent, and yet we can foresee variations in supply of oil and other energy sources, or variations in demand, of several tens of percent by the year 2010. Clearly, then, there is much room to alter

---

Issue 16–2   If Photovoltaic Technology Is So Great, Why Aren't We Using It?

Photovoltaic cells are thought by many to be the most promising new energy technology for the near future. They are simple devices that convert sunlight into electricity and consist of layers of semiconducting material that produce an electric current when intense light strikes the cell. At present these cells are capable of converting a little over 20 percent of the incoming sunlight to electric energy, but efficiencies of about 30 percent are anticipated in the future (Hubbard, 1989). Photovoltaic cells have been in use for decades in a number of applications. They provide the electric power for most space satellites and a variety of industrial and consumer electronic devices, including solar-powered hand calculators. But photovoltaic cells are expensive in relation to the amount of electricity they generate, and so as yet they have not been used in ordinary large-scale or large-power applications. Since the 1970s oil crises and associated energy price increases, they have become more attractive.

In 1973, the National Science Foundation kicked off a national research and development program to make photovoltaics into a competitively priced source of energy, and experts now anticipate that photovoltaic power can displace other sources of electricity—worldwide—by the 2090s. What needs to happen, soon, for this prediction to come true in your children's lifetimes?

- Cost of photovoltaic-generated power: Ten years of research have seen a 40-fold drop in the cost of photovoltaic-generated power, to a price equivalent to the peak-time costs of our present power sources. However, the director of the Solar Energy Research Institute, H.M. Hubbard, suggests that if we add the environmental costs of our conventional power sources (air and water pollution, mining impacts, and so on), then photovoltaic and coal-fired plants are already comparable in price.

The cost of power generation via individual residential rooftop-mounted, fixed flat-plate power systems is technically less expensive than the massively scaled photovoltaic landscapes of the future. However, it is also a much less profitable venture for utility companies. For residential units to become appealing, many adjustments will have to be made in the way electricity is currently marketed. Government policy, utility rate setting, and state regulations on financing of homeowner power generation will all have to change if home-based photovoltaics are to become appealing enough to attract power company support.

- Space requirements: One of the major problems with photovoltaic solar arrays is the massive amount of land area they require: on the order of five to ten times that needed for coal-fired or nuclear power plants. However, Hubbard suggests that if we take into account the hidden land use costs of coal and nuclear—mining, transportation, and waste disposal—then once again photovoltaic-generated power uses about the same amount of space as our present-day, mainstream power sources. Moreover, with photovoltaics, land uses can be combined: roadside rights-of-way and rooftops become potential photovoltaic power-grid sites.

our energy production and consumption patterns to adapt to changing times.

Several studies have projected the energy supplies available to the United States in the year 2000 and beyond, and they are instructive as to the range of alternatives available. For example, the National Academy of Sciences in 1978 made a series of projections of energy supply and demand for the year 2010 (CONAES, 1978). They constructed a series of four scenarios regarding government policy, ranging from policy that vigorously encouraged conservation to no policy change from 1978. On the basis of these scenarios, they predicted that total U.S. energy consuption in 2010 could be as low as 58 quads (as compared to 71 in 1975) if very strong conservation measures were instituted, or as high as 136 quads if there were no change in policy. They also predicted that in some sectors conservation (and a resulting decline in consumption) offered considerable potential, such as energy use in

---

- Grid interfacing: Envisioning a photovoltaic-powered United States in the future, we see a mix of centralized photovoltaic arrays and dispersed, smaller setups, in size all the way down to that of a single rooftop. Technical and safety problems abound in integrating these differing scales into a single power system. In addition, the arrival of cloud cover over one part of the network could disrupt power delivery gridwide, which leads to the following main limitation on photovoltaic power use.

- Lack of low-cost energy storage: Right now, photovoltaic-generated electricity is usable only as it is produced, during daylight hours. Research into developing ways to store photovoltaic power until it is needed is presently the most intensive and highly speculative. Among the big contenders are lead-acid battery storage, pumped hydroelectric power, and compressed air storage. Future dreams include electrically generated hydrogen production and superconducting magnetic energy storage.

Photovoltaic technology needs only one to two years to bring a large (1000 megawatt) power plant on line, so when the economic and social time is ripe, the world can move rapidly into photovoltaic power. At present there are thousands of stand-alone units across the world, there are 20 larger systems in use in Europe, and a half dozen projects of significant size are under way in the United States. Although these are largely experimental projects cosponsored by government and private funds, they point the way to a time when photovoltaics will be at least a part of the world's power supply, and perhaps the dominant source.

Of course, it is still early enough in the development of this technology for us to have some leeway in deciding whether or not we want it to be the premier power producer a hundred years from now. We have learned enough from the adverse environmental impacts of coal, oil, and nuclear to be able to predict where the big problems may come with photovoltaic power.

For one thing, the confident statements that photovoltaics are cleaner may not take into account the pollution associated with the production of photovoltaic cells. Many of the materials involved are toxic and create substantial workplace health problems, and large-scale production might involve significant quantities of toxic by-products.

As for space requirements, can we really afford to spend five to ten times the space used for conventional sources for photovoltaic panel arrays? Certainly if photovoltaic power were to replace other power generators and their land uses, we could manage, but is such a scenario realistic? Surely, photovoltaic power will gradually be integrated into a system with other power sources, thus enabling our oil and gas supplies to last longer. With photovoltaic power systems filling up empty spaces in addition to our present power plant land uses, would we really be willing to accept the aesthetic and crowding consequences?

Before we embrace any energy system as the "wave of the future" it is best to anticipate and plan for the adverse effects. That way some as yet unknown impact of photovoltaic power does not take us by surprise.

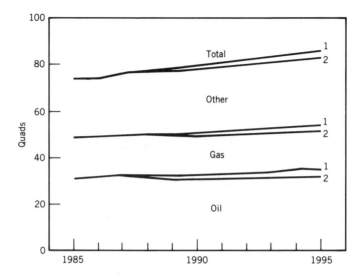

Figure 16.15   U.S. Department of Energy projection of total U.S. energy consumption to 1995, in quads (10^{15} BTUs). Two different projections are made based on different oil price assumptions, with higher prices causing lower consumption. (*Source:* DOE, 1987.)

buildings. In other sectors, such as industry, even under the most aggressive conservation policies, energy use was expected to rise. Concerning the sources of that energy, they saw the greatest increases being in the use of coal, with smaller increases in the use of other fuels.

Those projections were made in 1978, and since that time the range of possible conditions in the year 2010 has narrowed. The basic projections appear to be sound, however, and we are on a trend that would result in total energy consumption in 2010 near the middle of the 1978 projections. In a 1987 study, the U.S. Department of Energy projected total energy use in the United States in 1995 to range between 81 and 83 quads, depending on oil price trends in the early 1990s (U.S. DOE, 1987) (Fig. 16.15), and in 1988 the DOE predicted energy use in 2010 to range between 87 and 111 quads, depending on implementation of conservation measures then part of DOE programs (Wilbanks, 1988). The DOE projections are regarded as conservative, and so the range of outcomes is necessarily less than predicted by the National Academy of Sciences in 1978. But these ranges show that there is considerable flexibility in our choice of energy futures, depending primarily on how much we pay for energy and how much we are willing to conserve.

REFERENCES AND ADDITIONAL READINGS

Atherton, C., and D. Atherton. 1990. Disaster that fell with the rain on a bleak hill. *Guardian*, April 27, p. 25.

Brobst, P.A., and W.P. Pratt (Eds.). 1973. *United States Mineral Resources.* USGS Professional Paper 820. Washington, DC: U.S. Geological Survey.

Burnett, W.M., and S.D. Ban. 1989. Changing prospects for natural gas in the United States. *Science* 244: 305–310.

Calzonetti, F.J., and M.S. Eckert. 1981. *Finding a Place for Energy.* Washington, DC: Association of American Geographers Resource Publication.

Canby, T.Y., and J. Blair. 1981. *Synfuels: Fill er up! With What?* National Geographic Special Report, pp. 974–995. Washington, DC: National Geographic Society.

Commoner, B. 1977. *The Poverty of Power.* New York: Bantam Books.

Committee on Nuclear and Alternative Energy Sources (CONAES). 1978. U.S. energy demand: Some low energy futures. *Science* 200: 142–152.

Cook, E. 1978. *Energy: The Ultimate Resource.* Washington, DC: Association of American Geographers Resource Publication.

Council on Environmental Quality. 1989. *Envi-*

romental Trends. Washington, DC: U.S. Government Printing Office.

Energy Information Administration. 1982. *1981 Annual Report to Congress,* Vols. 1 and 2. *Washington, DC*: U.S. Government Printing Office.

————. 1989a. *Annual Energy Review, 1988.* Washington, DC: Energy Information Administration.

————. 1989b. *Commercial Nuclear Power 1989: Prospects for the United States and the World.* Washington, DC: Energy Information Administration.

Exxon Corporation. 1982. *How Much Oil and Gas?* New York: Exxon Corporation.

Flavin, C. 1983. Photovoltaics: International competition for the sun. *Environment* 25(3): 7.

Flavin, C., and A.B. Durning. 1988. *Building on Success: The Age of Energy Efficiency.* Worldwatch Paper #82. Washington, DC: Worldwatch Institute.

Ghazi, P. 1990. Chernobyl fallout may affect British farmland for decades. *Sunday Observer,* April 29, p. 9.

Gibbons, J.H., P.D. Blair, and H.L. Gwin. 1989. Strategies for energy use. *Sci. Amer.* 261(3):136–143.

Hall, C.S., and C.J. Cleveland. 1981. Petroleum drilling and production in the U.S., yield per effort and net energy analysis. *Science* 211: 576–579.

Heiken, G., *et al.* 1981. Hot dry rock geothermal energy. *Amer. Sci.* 69: 400–407.

Hohenemser, C., M. Deicher, A. Ernst, H. Hofsass, G. Linder, and E. Recknagel. 1986. Chernobyl: An early report. *Environment* 28(5): 6–13, 30–43.

Hohenemser, C., and O. Renn. 1988. Shifting public perceptions of nuclear risk: Chernobyl's other legacy. *Environment* 30(3): 4–11, 40–45.

Hubbard, H.M. 1989. Photovoltaics today and tomorrow. *Science* 244: 297–304.

Hubbert, M.K. 1969. Energy resources. In *NAS, 1969, Resources and Man,* pp. 157–242. San Francisco: W.H. Freeman.

Landsberg, H.H. 1982. Relaxed energy outlook masks continuing uncertainties. *Science* 218: 973–974.

Lovins, A.B. 1977. *Soft Energy Paths.* New York: Harper Colophon Books.

Pasqualetti, M.J., and K.D. Pijawka (Eds.). 1984. *Nuclear Power: Assessing and Managing Hazardous Technology.* Boulder, CO: Westview Press.

Perry, H. 1983. Coal in the United States: A status report. *Science* 222: 377–384.

Sawyer, S.W. 1986. *Renewable Energy: Progress, Prospects.* Washington, DC: Association of American Geographers.

Shea, C.P. 1988. *Renewable Energy: Today's Contribution Tomorrow's Promise.* Worldwatch Paper #81. Washington, DC: Worldwatch Institute.

Smith, B.P. 1978. Power from yesterday's dams. *Environment* 20(9): 16–20.

Taylor, J.J. 1989. Improved and safer nuclear power. *Science* 244: 318–325.

U.S. Congress, Office of Technology Assessment. 1980a. *An Assessment of Oil Shale Technologies. Vol. II: A History and Analysis of the Federal Prototype Oil Shale Leasing Program.* OTA-M-119. Washington, DC: U.S. Government Printing Office.

————. 1980b. *World Petroleum Availability 1980–2000.* OGA-TM-E-5. Washington, DC: U.S. Government Printing Office.

U.S. Department of Energy. 1987. *Energy Security.* Washington, DC: U.S. Department of Energy.

U.S. Weather Service, 1965. *Climatic Atlas of the United States.* Washington, DC: U.S. Government Printing Office.

Werner, C. 1990. Life in a land without birds. *Guardian,* April 27, p. 25.

Wilbanks, T.J. 1988. The impacts of energy development and use. In H. deBlij (Ed.), *Earth '88: Changing Geographic Perspectives,* pp. 96–114. Washington, DC: National Geographic Society.

TERMS TO KNOW

Acid Mine Drainage
Active Solar Power
Anthracite
Auguring
Bituminous Coal
BTU (British Thermal Unit)
Coal Gasification
Coal Rank
Crude Oil
Energy Conservation
Energy Efficiency
Fission
Genetic Damage
Geologic Estimate of Recoverable Oil
Geothermal Energy
Heavy-Water Reactor
High-Temperature Gas-Cooled Reactor
Hydroelectric Power

Kerogen
Light-Water Reactor
Lignite
Liquefaction
Liquid-Metal Fast-Breeder Reactor
Liquid Natural Gas (LNG)
Natural Gas
Oil
Overburden
Passive Solar Power
Peat
Performance-Based Estimate of Recoverable Oil
Photovoltaic Cell
Quad
Renewable Energy
Resource Recovery
Shale Oil
Somatic Damage
Spent Fuel
Strip or Surface Mining
Subbituminous Coal
Subsidence
Sulfur Content
Synfuels
Tar Sands
Underground Mining
Uranium

STUDY QUESTIONS

1. What is the significance of the changing patterns of energy use, by fuel type and economic sector?

2. Describe the different methods of calculating how much oil is left. What is the importance of the choice of method?

3. Will we ever run out of oil? Why or why not?

4. Describe some of the environmental concerns about the use of coal, oil, natural gas, synfuels, hydroelectric, and nuclear power.

5. What are the pros and cons of underground versus surface mining of coal?

6. What are synfuels, and what are the major substances involved?

7. Describe the stages and linkages in the nuclear fuel cycle.

8. What is the difference between centralized renewable energy and decentralized renewable energy? Which forms of renewable energy are likely to be most important in the near future?

INTRODUCTION

"Once a resource, always a resource"? Not at all true. As discussed in Chapter 1, the list of available resources is not carved in stone. When technological, societal, and economic conditions change, so do those things that we see as useful and valuable. For example, during the eighteenth century, European preferences for hats made of beaver fur had a profound effect on the value of beaver pelts and on the numbers of North American beaver. Overhunted near settlements, the beaver became an endangered species in these areas. The desire to find more beaver pelts was the engine that drove much of the westward exploration through the lake and river country of the Canadian–U.S. borderlands. Today, however, beaver pelts are no longer worth their weight in gold: they are a resource that few of us value. Beavers are mostly left alone, except where their dam-building interferes with our road-building and use of inland waterways.

Other species are today in the same position the beaver once held: both valued and endangered. However, our methods of harvesting and eradication have become much more efficient than in the days of Canadian voyagers, so many species are very quickly approaching the brink and falling over the edge into extinction, and many are wiped out before we even know of their existence and possible value.

In this chapter, we examine the shifting makeup of resources by looking at those portions of the natural world that were not highly valued until very recently, or that may be valued in the near future. The values of many of these *potential* and *amenity* resources are still being debated. How can we set a value for

something that has shown no evidence of being useful beyond the promises made by its promoters? This question is especially pertinent to the preservation of plant and animal species and to evaluating the potential recreational use of urban landfill areas.

Another problem in defining and evaluating resources is the notion of beauty (Fig. 17.1). Questions of aesthetics were once the realm of philosophers, but today costly decisions are made on the basis of economic versus amenity evaluations of a contested resource. That is, one group of people will evaluate the potential development of a ski resort in a remote area according to its economic value. It might create jobs, stimulate local investment, and improve the lives of some consumers. Others evaluate the ski resort from an amenities viewpoint, asking if the resort or the untouched wilderness would better contribute to the world's beauty, ecological stability, or spiritual happiness.

Aesthetic and spiritual qualities are very difficult to quantify, yet resource use pressures demand realistic, practical evaluations. As you read about the value of intangibles, ask yourself: What is the economic value of habitat and species preservation? How important is a beautiful environment? What kinds of recreation are necessary for the happiness and well-being of the public?

HABITAT AND
SPECIES CONSERVATION

For thousands of years, the human race has been altering animal and plant species and the places they inhabit or *habitats*, and some life-

Figure 17.1 Grand Teton National Park, Wyoming. This national park has natural beauty in a landscape with both high economic and amenity value.

forms have been obliterated. The European lion was extinct by A.D. 80; wolves vanished along with Europe's forest cover. In the United States, the American bison or buffalo, whose vast herds impeded agricultural settlement and held up trains for hours, was almost wiped out in the second half of the nineteenth century. Today, the American bison lives in protected refuge areas. The passenger pigeon suffered a more drastic fate. In 1810 the estimated total passenger pigeon population was about 5 billion. During most of the nineteenth century, killing these birds for food or sport was easy, as they could be shot down in the hundreds by aiming into their roosting places at night or by firing at random as they flew overhead. The passenger pigeon was extinct by 1899, and the last one died in the Cincinnati, Ohio, zoo in 1914. Other lost species include the eastern elk, gone since the 1880s; the plains wolf (1920s); and going or gone are the ivory-billed woodpecker and Bachman's warbler (Fig. 17.2) (Council on Environmental Quality, 1989).

The human role is not always one of destruction; often we are responsible for the swift spread of species to new areas. It is esti-mated, for example, that one-eighth of California's plant species are exotic species, that is, imported from other places (Ornduff, 1974). The suburbs offer a very comfortable habitat for deer, coyote, squirrel, and raccoon. The white-tailed deer population had dropped to 500,000 in 1900; with control over hunting, their numbers have risen to at least 13 million, at least as many as when Europeans first arrived.

Concern has been mounting in the Western world since at least the nineteenth century regarding the negative effects of species endangerment. George Perkins Marsh, as discussed in Chapter 3, was a scientist concerned with the impact of rapid settlement on North America, and he drew his lessons of warning about our New World future from Old World landscapes, like those of the denuded, eroded slopes around the Mediterranean Sea.

Since the late 1960s the cry has really been heard regarding the destruction and alteration of habitats and species. Researchers and naturalists such as Eckholm (1978), Campbell (1980), and Ehrlich and Ehrlich (1970, 1981) were among the first to raise the worrying thought that when forests are

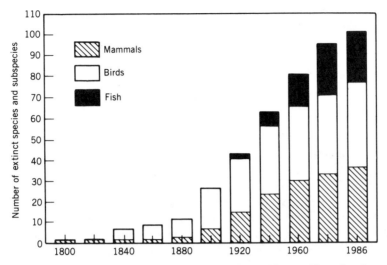

Figure 17.2 Extinction of animal groups, 1800–1986, in the United States. There has been a substantial rise in known species extinctions since World War II in this country. (*Source:* Council on Environmental Quality, 1989.)

clear-cut, when meadows are paved, when rivers become sewers, we are destroying species with potential value—both economic and amenity value. These researchers maintained that species and habitat destruction have reached epidemic proportions worldwide. At a 1981 conference on genetic diversity, sponsored by the U.S. Department of State and the U.S. Agency for International Development, researchers predicted that by A.D. 2000, a million additional species of all types would become extinct (Wolkomir, 1983).

By the late 1980s, concern over species destruction—and the implications for life on earth—was no longer confined to gloom and doom debates on college campuses and in government offices. Newspapers, magazines, and the electronic media were pelting the public with statistics about the destruction of the world's rainforests and the killing of elephants and other much-adored species (Allman, 1988; Linden, 1989). Scientists once estimated that the total number of species on the earth lay somewhere between 3 and 10 million. New research in the world's tropical forests suggests that we have grossly underestimated this number. Wilson (1989) estimates that science has put an official name to about 1.4 million species, but that there may be as many as 30 million species in all!

Wilson also estimates that the world's

rainforests are being cut down at a rate of 1 percent per year, and that 55 percent of the total has already been cleared. Using very conservative estimates of a total of two million species in the remaining forested areas, he suggests that we are losing from 4000 to 6000 species a year to extinction in our tropical forests alone; this is 10,000 times the natural rate of extinction, that is, the rate before human beings appeared on the scene (Wilson, 1989). It is also estimated that at current rates, the world's tropical forests will be gone in 50 years (Table 17.1) (Watkins, 1989).

The effects of this *biocide,* or destruction of species, are several. Ecosystems are under-

TABLE 17.1 Number of Species Lost to Extinction for Every Four Square Miles of Tropical Forest Cut Down[a]

Flowering plants	1500
Trees	750
Mammals	125
Birds	400
Reptiles	100
Amphibians	60
Butterflies	150

[a] The number of insect species is unknown, although one estimate suggests that there are 42,000 insect species for every 2.5 acres of tropical rainforest (Watkins, 1989).

mined when plant and animal species are destroyed or when they move into new areas. The possibility of using as yet untried species for food, fuel, fiber, or medicine disappears when they are eradicated. Human appreciation and understanding of nature are also diminished by species and habitat loss. Many people question the right of human beings to deny other species the right to exist. Most profoundly, even from a completely selfish, *homocentric* point of view, it is feared that removal of even a few species from the web of life could cause a chain reaction, leading to widespread ecological disaster. One early warning of this possibility was the introduction of sea lampreys to the Great Lakes when the St. Lawrence Seaway was first opened. The sea lampreys killed off lake trout, the natural predators of alewives, which caused a population boom for alewives. As a result, the alewife population shot beyond available food supplies, and for years dead alewives in the hundreds were washed up on Great Lakes beaches (Ragotzkie, 1974).

Many people in favor of resource development and exploitation feel that the situation is hardly so dire as this suggests. They point out the long record of human destruction and alteration of species and habitats, stressing that this is not a recent phenomenon and implying that the world has yet to suffer much from these losses. It has even been stated that there are so many plant and animal species worldwide that the loss of a few thousand should not seriously affect potential resource development. In addition, it is felt that the economic benefits derived at the cost of occasional species and habitat destruction outweigh the benefits to their artificial preservation for the enjoyment of a few nature lovers. These questions and arguments are not easily resolved, because they involve unknown consequences in an unpredictable future.

BIOLOGICAL DIVERSITY

Biological diversity refers to both the genetic variability among individuals of a species and the abundance of individuals within a species. Wide variations in genetic traits increase the likelihood that at least some individuals of a given species will survive environmental change. The number of different species and the abundance of individuals in that species are also indicators of biological diversity in a particular ecosystem. The most ecologically diverse environments are the tropical forests, where there is a much greater abundance of plant and animal species than in any other single biome.

Species *extinction* is a fundamental threat to biological diversity. The death of an individual represents the loss of an organism capable of reproducing the same form as other individuals in the species. The death of individuals is a natural process. By contrast, the death of an entire species is an irreversible process in which both the basic form and the reproductive potential are lost. The contribution of the species to the vitality of the planet is also lost. Species extinctions can be natural, but humans can accelerate the process.

Human activities often result in the reduction of biological diversity through the destruction and simplification of natural habitats. Urban sprawl leads to an increase in the amount of asphalt and concrete at the expense of fields, forests, marshlands, and other valuable habitats. Modern farming and forest cultivation result in single-crop patterns over broad areas, maintained by chemicals that destroy unwanted species. These practices endanger the genetic and ecological diversity of plant and animal communities. These extinctions are taking place worldwide, but the numbers of extinctions are greatest in tropical areas, particularly in tropical rainforests.

ETHICS AND ECONOMICS

Should endangered species be preserved or simply allowed to become extinct? At one extreme is the view that it is the fault of human beings that many plant and animal species are on the verge of dying out and that it is thus our responsibility to keep them alive at any cost. Supporters of this position maintain that the aggressive, environmentally destructive nature of technologically advanced societies has led to the extinction and near-extinction of many species. This ethical argument centers on the rights of nonhuman entities merely to exist, regardless of any usefulness to humans. Ehrenfeld (1981) argues that all living things have a right to coexist on the planet. Humans, possessing the power to destroy and alter plant and animal species, should exercise stewardship in preserving plant and animal species. This nonhomocentric view represents only one of the arguments for preserving biological diversity.

Another intriguing and controversial idea is that the earth itself (or *her*self, according to some) is a single living, breathing organism, named Gaia. The *Gaia Hypothesis* (see Chapter 1), named for the ancient Greek earth mother goddess, suggests that the earth can regulate its own biosphere, and that if we push her too far, with pollution and large-scale alteration of nature, then she will push back—in ways destructive to human beings, but restorative for the biosphere. Thus, suggest proponents, it behooves us to learn to live with Gaia:

> *We must try to regain the spirit of the ancient Greeks, once again comprehending the earth as a living creature and contriving the modern equivalent of the worship of Gaia. We must try to learn that she is, in every real sense, sacred, and that there is therefore a holy way to confront her and her works, a way of awe and admiration and respect and veneration that simply will not permit despoliation and abuse.* (Sale, 1985, pp. 41–42)

Many, however, feel that the Gaia approach is somewhat extreme, as extreme as those at the other end of the spectrum who continue to support the Darwinian view of "survival of the fittest." The Darwinians maintain that species should be allowed to die because they have been unable to compete successfully with humans and other species; furthermore we should feel no guilt about species extinction because it is a natural process, and we should not have to keep rare species alive at great cost to human society.

Certainly, keeping rare plants and animals alive costs a lot and is sometimes of debatable merit. Florida's dusky sparrow is a good illustration. During the 1970s the U.S. government spent over $2.5 million to buy 6.25 acres (2.5 ha) on Florida's east coast to create the St. John's River Refuge for the dusky sparrows. By 1981, there were five male sparrows living in a large cage (for their own safety), and a sixth male was believed to be alive in the wild. There were no known females in existence. How did this highly artificial situation develop?

The sparrows' original island habitat had been flooded to control mosquitos around Cape Canaveral. Fires and drainage of marshes had further destroyed the birds' nesting and living area. Scientists proposed that the males be allowed to mate with a close relative, the Scott's seaside sparrow; after five generations, the offspring would be nearly full-blooded dusky sparrows. The suggestion was turned down in 1980, when the U.S. Fish and Wildlife Service decided that this hybrid sparrow would not meet the requirements of the Endangered Species Act. The agency instead gave a "pension" of $9200 per sparrow to care for them until their death.

The last surviving member, Orange Band, an aging male with gout, died in June of 1988 in luxurious captivity. Using new techniques, his keepers studied his genetic makeup and found that he and the other duskies were not really a separate subspecies after all—at the genetic level, they were identical to the common seaside sparrow that lives in abundance along the Atlantic. The scientists suggest that nineteenth-century taxonomic classifications should be updated with twenty-first-century biotechnology when species are being kept alive at great cost, to make absolutely sure that these organisms are definitely entitled to their own separate grouping. Before he died, Orange Band was the father of two near-pure "duskies," who were released into the wild to prosper with their genetically identical relatives along the beach (Wilford, 1989).

This is an extreme example, but what are the alternatives if a species is found to be unique and in danger? Who can play God, deciding which species should survive and which need not?

Animal Species: Victims of a Crowded World

The claims of animals on food and space repeatedly come into conflict with a rapidly expanding human population and, more often than not, the animal loses (Fig. 17.3). For ex-

Figure 17.3   Bison in Wind Cave National Park, South Dakota. Populations of American Bison were reduced dramatically as the Great Plains were settled in the 19th century.

ample, in 1900, there were an estimated 100,000 tigers worldwide. Today, there are only 4000 to 5000. One subspecies, the Bali tiger, is extinct; the Caspian tiger probably is extinct. There are a few Javan and Chinese tigers in the wild, several hundred Sumatran, 250 Siberian, and perhaps 2000 each of the Indochinese and Bengal tigers. This extreme drop over such a short period can be attributed to hunting and to loss of habitat to human uses. The ethical argument centers on animals' rights to their own territory (Regan and Singer, 1976; Shepard, 1978). In Nepal's Royal Chitawan National Park, the Bengal tigers, outfitted with radio collars, are tracked to learn about their habits and requirements. The hope is that the animals can be accommodated and their future made secure and stable. The park is not large, however, and on one occasion a young tiger, evidently wanting his own territory, wandered out of the park into a village and killed a man before being captured and removed to a zoo (Jackson, 1978).

Another example is that of the black rhinoceros of Africa, whose population is dropping rapidly because of poaching—from 65,000 in 1970 to less than 4000 today. The animals are killed simply to obtain their horns, which are sold for thousands of dollars each and used as daggers and aphrodisiacs in Asia and the Middle East. In Namibia, wildlife au-

thorities are actually dehorning the animals to save their lives! In Zimbabwe, it's a war—poachers are shot and sometimes killed by wildlife authorities (Knox, 1989; Perlez, 1989; Rees, 1988). These are international examples in which the situation is exacerbated by human population pressures on insufficient and marginal lands: when a family is pushed off their land to make way for a wildlife preserve, it is no wonder that they may be tempted to turn to poaching.

However, human population pressures are having an enormous impact on nonhuman species in North America as well. For example, the black bear was once a resident of New Jersey, but it long ago almost disappeared from the state in the face of hunting pressure and incompatibility with increased human populations. In 1983 there were an estimated 80 to 100 bears in northern New Jersey (Carney, 1983). In 1982, the State Department of Environmental Protection's Bureau of Wildlife Management announced an experimental program to reintroduce the black bear to areas of New Jersey's Pine Barrens. The bureau argued that, if managed carefully, bears could coexist with human beings in this relatively unpopulated area. Local residents by and large did not agree. They felt that the age of the bear in New Jersey was and should remain history.

The struggle for space and food between

humans and bears is a part of daily life in the western United States, where bears become too devoted to human garbage and must be removed by helicopter to wilder areas. Unfortunately, even this measure is decreasingly effective, as more and more wilderness hikers penetrate remote bear country in search of solitude. In the early 1980s it was feared that grizzly bears could not coexist with humans even in the 9600 square miles (24,900 km^2) of rugged habitat that make up the Yellowstone ecosystem. There were an estimated 170–180 grizzlies present in 1985. In their search for food, the animals move out of areas classified as "preserved and protected" into "multiple-use" areas, where the chance of a face-off with humans is much greater. Today, based on a partial survey, it is probable that the grizzly population in the Yellowstone region is increasing at a rate of about two bears each year. This is due to careful management and perhaps to more careful counting methods (U.S. Fish and Wildlife Service, 1988a).

Grizzlies are prospering in some other remote regions. In fact the great and terrible *Ursus arctos* has been so effectively protected in northwestern Montana that the Interagency Grizzly Bear Committee is locally "delisting" this species from its present endangered status. However, elsewhere within its range the grizzly continues to struggle for survival. For example, eleven grizzlies in the Selkirk Mountains of Idaho were radio-collared in 1984 so that experts could monitor their whereabouts and needs; five of the eleven have since been illegally shot and killed. To help the grizzly population recovery efforts in Montana's Cabinet Mountains, two young female grizzlies were introduced to the area in late summer of 1989, along with a public relations program that included a brochure, slide program, and question-and-answer session so that nearby human beings would be fully informed as to these developments (U.S. Fish and Wildlife Service, 1989a).

Currently, over 800 faunal species around the world are officially listed as either *endangered* or *threatened* (Table 17.2). The majority of these are mammals and birds, such as the leopard, gray wolf, piping plover, and roseate tern. In the United States, the species in the most trouble—nearest *extinction*—are birds, fishes, and clams. Some of these are the bald eagle, California condor, American crocodile, Gila trout, ocelot, and Ozark big-eared bat.

Aside from the ethical arguments for animal species preservation, economic arguments can also be made. There are direct human medical benefits from animal products for medical purposes such as anticancer agents and antibiotics. Bee venom, for example, has been used to relieve arthritis. The venom of the Malayan pit viper is used as an anticoagulant to prevent blood clots and to lessen the

TABLE 17.2   Endangered Species Listed in the United States and Internationally

Category	Endangered		Threatened	
	U.S.	Foreign Only	U.S.	Foreign Only
Mammals	53	244	8	22
Birds	76	145	11	0
Reptiles	15	59	17	14
Amphibians	6	8	5	0
Fishes	51	11	33	0
Snails	3	1	6	0
Clams	36	2	1	0
Crustaceans	8	0	2	0
Insects	11	1	7	0
Arachnids	3	0	0	0
Plants	173	1	57	2
Total	435	472	147	38

Source: U.S. Fish and Wildlife Service (1990).

danger of heart attack (Ehrlich and Ehrlich, 1981). Cytarbine, or cytosine arabinoside, which is derived from a sponge, has antiviral properties that make it useful in the treatment of leukemia and against herpes infections (Ruggieri, 1976). Animals also have economic importance as a source of protein for human populations.

Even when a species is protected from extinction, zoologists worry about the consequences of inbreeding among the relatively few surviving members. A small group of animals is not enough for a breeding population. Within a few generations of inbreeding, negative recessive traits may become prevalent, and the species can even die out, a victim of its own genetic weaknesses. For example, some of California's rare Tule elk have short lower jaws, which makes eating difficult. This may be the result of breeding within the small group of animals that biologists used to establish the herd. Therefore, researchers advocate a more sophisticated use of genetics when attempting to reestablish species. Today, for example, "embryo banks" preserve the frozen genes of some vanishing species. Another solution, of course, is to use more animals for the initial breeding population, however, there is just not enough room in wildlife refuges to maintain larger populations. Fewer than 5 percent of the world's preserves have the space for a genetically diverse breeding population of large wild mammals. It is probable that, in a crowded world, species survival will depend on human genetic technology (Wolkomir, 1983).

Plant Species: Short-Term Decisions Can Mean Long-Term Losses

The world's plant species are disappearing at an increasing rate. The loss of this diversity and richness has become a major environmental issue, tying together humanity's food supply, health, and scientific research. Newly discovered species are an important potential resource, but once extinct, they are lost to scientific and other uses. In Africa, an average of more than 200 new plant species are collected by scientists annually. South America is even less well known to Western science; a 1970s expedition to the Panama–Colombia border found that one in every five of the spe-

cies collected was previously unknown to science (Eckholm, 1978).

Of all naturally occurring species, plant and animal, it is estimated that humans have found uses for less than one-tenth of 1 percent of the total. The enormous majority are untested and unknown regarding their potential beneficial uses. It is known that at least 75,000 species of plants have edible parts, yet the world today relies almost entirely on about twenty plant species for its food supply, mostly wheat, rice, millet, and rye. At present, food production is keeping pace with population growth, and probably can do so into the foreseeable future, although the politics involved in food distribution are so complex that many thousands starve to death annually. It seems like a good idea to reexamine some of the 7000 plant species that humans have used for food during our occupancy of the earth and to conduct research on newly discovered plant species with promising value.

When complex ecosystems are destroyed to obtain timber and to make way for cities and agriculture, little consideration is given to the potential aesthetic or economic value of the species being eliminated. Of the aproximately 20,000 to 30,000 plant species and varieties native to the United States, one-tenth are endangered, rare, threatened, or in an uncertain state (Schwartz, 1988). As of 1989, only 213 of these species are listed as protected under the Endangered Species Act.

Once again, short-term human uses come first. The main causes of plant species extinction are agriculture, urbanization, air and water pollution, strip-mining, industry, and overcollection by hobbyists and commercial interests. Fifty species of native American plants have become extinct in recent years.

Why does the protection of plant species matter? For one thing, plant extinctions can be even more disruptive to ecosystems than animal extinctions. When a plant species is eliminated, either locally or globally, the species that directly or indirectly rely on it, including insects, higher animals, and other plants, can be adversely affected. For example, a now-extinct shrub may have been a source of food for a browsing animal, a source of shelter for birds and insects, and protective cover for smaller plant species. Also, for the sake of human scientific knowledge alone, biologists feel that plant species should be preserved and protected. More pragmatically, many disappearing plant species could well be of considerable economic and social value.

In recent years, researchers have looked at the possibility that previously unused or even despised plant species could be used for food, fiber, and medicine. Mesquite, a weedy nuisance on western cattle ranges, is promoted by researchers as a potential world food source. It produces abundant annual crops of a highly nutritious bean, once a staple for the region's Native Americans. Mesquite wood has become popular as a fuel in gourmet cooking, commanding a high price in some urban markets. Another recent discovery—recent to modern science, at least—is the buffalo gourd, used for at least 9000 years by the Native Americans. This widespread wild plant provides vegetable oil, protein, and starch of high quality and thrives on very little water (Kazarian, 1981). Since humans depend on a narrow range of crop species for food, the discovery of new food resources is very important. The Central American amaranthus produces seeds that contain a high-quality protein that could be of use to protein-deficient human societies. Eelgrasses, grown in salt water, offer a potential substitute for grains in some heavily populated seacoast areas.

Historically, Indian tribes in what is now the southwestern United States and northern Mexico made use of some 450 wild plants. Anthropologists Felger and Nabhan (1978) suggest that many of these desert-adapted species could be of value to modern society. Guayule is a shrub grown in northern Mexico and Texas. Before 1910 it supplied 10 percent of the world's rubber (Ehrlich and Ehrlich, 1981); the latex in the guayule shrub is very similar to that in the rubber tree. Jojoba, a shrub related to boxwood, has seeds that contain a liquid wax. This wax, which makes up as much as 60 percent of the jojoba bean's weight, can be used for lubricating metal parts and other purposes once served by sperm whale oil, the use of which is now outlawed. Another seemingly unlikely possibility for development is the all-American goldenrod, whose leaves

contain up to 12 percent natural rubber. It is easy to grow, can be mowed and baled, and resprouts without annual sowing. *Euphorbia lathyrius*, a desert shrub, might yield 10–20 barrels of crude oil per acre if cultivated (Wilford, 1980; Johnson and Hinman, 1980; Broad, 1978). Clearly, these are just a few of the thousands of potentially useful plant species, that make a strong economic argument for preserving not only rare but also abundant species.

As these new species move into the mainstream of production and consumption, we may find in 50 years that the list of major global crops will have changed considerably, especially if the predicted global warming takes place. New crops will have to be developed to take over from wheat if the great United States and USSR grain-growing regions become too dry, as some climate-change scenarios suggest (Brown *et al.*, 1988; Crosson and Rosenberg, 1989; Wilson, 1989). A 13-organization network of agricultural research establishments, the Consultative Group on International Agricultural Research, or CGIAR, has been formed to promote the development of new crops and agricultural techniques worldwide (Table 17.3).

Many of our most valuable medicines are derived from plants. Vincristine, discovered in the mid-1950s, is an alkaloid found in a Madagascar periwinkle. The chemical causes a decrease in white-blood-cell counts and has been used to fight cancer and cancerlike diseases. Quinine, an alkaloid in *Cinchona* bark, was used to treat malaria until synthetic quinine was developed in the 1930s. Digitalis, from foxglove, is widely used to treat chronic heart failure by stimulating the heart to pump more blood and use less energy. A number of well-known pain killers, including morphine and codeine, are derivatives of the opium poppy (Ehrlich and Ehrlich, 1981).

In northern California, a ranching family worked hard to eradicate a locally unique form of locoweed because it contained poisons that killed their grazing sheep. Luckily, a few plants escaped extermination and may be the basis of a new anticancer drug. The locoweeds of the American West are all endangered, and this particular form, the Humboldt milk vetch (*As-*

TABLE 17.3 **The Centers and Purposes of the Consultative Group on International Agricultural Research (CGIAR) System**[a]

Centro Internacional de Agricultura Tropical (1966), Cali, Colombia
Improve production of beans, cassava, rice, and beef in the tropics of the Western Hemisphere

Centro Internacional de la Papa (1971), Lima, Peru
Improve the potato in the Andes and develop new varieties for lower tropics

Centro Internacional del Mejoramiento de Maiz y Trigo (1943), Mexico City, Mexico
Improve maize, wheat, barley, and triticale

International Board for Plant Genetic Resources (1974), Rome, Italy
Promote an international network of genetic resources (germ plasm) centers

International Center for Agricultural Research in the Dry Areas (1977), Aleppo, Syria
Focus on rainfed agriculture in arid and semiarid regions in North Africa and West Asia

International Crops Research Institute for the Semi-Arid Tropics (1972), Andhra Pradesh, India
Improve quantity and reliability of food production in the semiarid tropics

International Food Policy Research Institute (1974), Washington, D.C., U.S.A.
Address issues arising from governmental and international agency intervention in national, regional, and global food problems

International Institute of Tropical Agriculture (1967), Ibadan, Nigeria
Responsible for improvement of worldwide cowpea, yam, cocoyam, and sweet potato, and for cassava, rice, maize, and beans, among others

International Laboratory for Research on Animal Disease (1974), Nairobi, Kenya
Help develop controls for trypanosomiasis (transmitted by the tsetse fly) and theileirosis (transmitted by ticks)

International Livestock Centre for Africa (1974), Addis Ababa, Ethiopia
Conduct research and development on improved livestock production and marketing systems, train livestock specialists, and gather documentation for livestock industry

International Rice Research Institute (1960), Los Banos, Philippines
Select and breed improved rice varieties and maintain a germ-plasm collection bank

International Service for National Agricultural Research (1980), The Hague, The Netherlands
Strengthen national agricultural research systems

West Africa Development Association (1971), Monrovia, Liberia
Promote self-sufficiency in rice in West Africa and improve varieties suitable for the area's agroclimate and socioeconomic conditions

Source: Crosson and Rosenberg (1989, p. 134).
[a] Years in parentheses indicate year of establishment.

tragalus agnicidus, the "lamb-killer"), was believed to be extinct since 1954, when the Tosten family yanked out the last one from their 3000-acre (1200 ha) ranch. However, in 1988 a team of botanists from the California Native Plant Society found a few young plants in a newly cleared area. The National Institutes of Health (NIH) in Washington have done research that suggests that the locoweed's toxins, like those of many poisons, may be of medical value when diluted. The young Humboldt milk vetch plants are now carefully nurtured, as the NIH requires eight pounds of the plant in order to begin research (Shabecoff, 1989).

About 40 laboratories in the United States and Great Britain are conducting genetic research on an unprepossessing garden weed, the thale-cress (*Arabidopsis*). Although of no value in itself, thale-cress has several characteristics that will help scientists both understand and manipulate the genetic material of valuable plant species. Thale-cress is a fast grower, so that new generations can be grown quickly, leading to quick genetic changes and faster research results; its DNA is minuscule—making it a sort of Model T Ford of the plant world—so that its genetic makeup can be relatively easily pinpointed. Once scientists understand how thale-cress "works," they can extrapolate to other species, especially its close relatives in the cabbage family. The eventual goal of this multimillion-dollar work will be the ability to move individual genes, including human ones, from species to species in order to increase crop and medical value. Plants may one day yield insulin, human growth hormone, and blood-clotting agents based on the research now being done on thale-cress (McKie, 1990).

Humans depend on only a few dozen plant species for food. A substantial loss of any one of these crops in a given year would almost certainly lead to widespread human starvation. How might such a loss occur? Modern agricultural technology has led to greater uniformity in the world's crops. The seed sown in a field is genetically uniform, minimizing irregularities in the mature crop and making the plants easy to harvest by machine. Unfortunately, a genetically uniform crop also means that the individual plants are all equally vulnerable to attack from pests and diseases. If such a crop is exclusively planted over a wide geographic area, the food supply of an entire region could be drastically reduced in a very short period of time. In Salina, Kansas, researchers at the Land Institute are working on these problems from a novel perspective. They see present-day agribusiness as disruptive to the soil and to water supply and argue that a sustainable agriculture is possible by developing farm fields that imitate the native prairie. Working with native prairie species that today's farmers regard as weeds, these researchers hope to make the

native perennials into major food crops that can be harvested year after year with little plowing and with no use of herbicides and pesticides. The resulting fields would be a complex mixture of several productive food crops that are difficult to harvest but that are environmentally and ecologically healthy (Luoma, 1989).

Crop species are also endangered by a decrease in their genetic diversity and by the disappearance of wild relatives. It is therefore necessary to maintain germ-plasm banks of the wild relatives of our principal crops. Agricultural experts can interbreed the positive characteristics of these plants, such as resistance to particular diseases, with the high productivity of the crop plants. In the event of an ecological disaster that eradicated the entire crop, we would have a well-preserved, genetically less vulnerable replacement to fall back on. The likelihood of such a large-scale disaster is exceedingly small, however, because experts have learned to provide seed with greater built-in diversity, following a near disastrous failure of the America corn crop in the early 1970s (National Academy of Sciences, 1982). Modern crop plants are very sophisticated genetic packages.

Germ-plasm banks are also a refuge of last resort for threatened plant species. Even if the plant dies out, its genetic makeup is preserved in case of a need to revive the species. Unfortunately, this is impossible for the great numbers of species eradicated by the clearing of tropical rainforests, which are not catalogued or noted by the scientific community, much less collected and preserved.

A clearinghouse for germ-plasm collection and research is the National Plant Germplasm System, managed by the U.S. Department of Agriculture. It has over 400,000 accessions, and new ones are added at a rate of 7000 to 15,000 a year. The NPGS collects, preserves, evaluates, and distributes U.S. and international plant germ-plasm resources. In addition, 19 U.S. botanical gardens have formed a network called the Center for Plant Conservation. When a rare plant's habitat is destroyed, a number of the plants are moved to these protected gardens. A self-perpetuating 50-plant collection of each species is then grown in the belief that this number of plants will hold most of a species' possible genetic variations. In addition, seeds of each species are stored in freezers, and a few are thawed every five years and tested for continuing germination viability (Schwartz, 1988).

PROTECTION OF SPECIES: RECENT LEGISLATION

The United States has taken an active role in the protection of species. The most comprehensive piece of legislation, regulating protection of all species of flora and fauna, is the Endangered Species Act (ESA), passed in 1973. The act has four main provisions:

1. The Department of the Interior is responsible for identifying nonmarine species in imminent danger of extinction and for naming these endangered species, and should actively pursue the preservation of these species. Those species with rapidly declining populations but not in imminent danger of extinction are classified as threatened species and are provided with the protection necessary to prevent further decline in numbers. The National Marine Fisheries Service (NMFS) of the Department of Commerce is responsible for marine species.

2. The act makes it illegal to capture, kill, sell,

ISSUE 17–1   The God Committee: The Story of the Snail Darter and Tellico Dam

Once upon a time there was a three-inch fish known as the snail darter, which became geographically isolated as the last glacial period ended. This species (*Percinia tanasi*), a member of the perch family, found itself a home in what became the Little Tennessee River, in what is now Tennessee. The snail darter was not much to look at, had no real redeeming social value, was not edible, and had no economic potential. It simply existed.

The Tennessee Valley Authority (TVA) had been constructing dams in the entire Tennessee River valley for decades, and the Tellico Dam project was simply another contribution to their hydroelectric network. The project was initiated in the late 1960s, ostensibly as a combined power, water supply, and irrigation project.

Local residents were against the dam from the very first. They felt the dam would destroy as much farmland as it would bring into production downstream. They also claimed that much of the land to be inundated by the reservoir was sacred Cherokee land and had archaeological significance. With the aid of a Washington, D.C., group, the Environmental Defense Fund, the residents filed the first legal action to halt construction of the dam in 1968. The initial lawsuit failed, and many others followed, none of them successful.

In 1973 ichthyologist David Etnier discovered the three-inch fish and named it the snail darter, as it fed exclusively on snails. Because of its small population and its apparent geographic isolation from others of its species, efforts were

made to get the snail darter designated as an endangered species under the newly passed Endangered Species Act. The U.S. Fish and Wildlife Service listed the snail darter as endangered in 1974, after a lengthy review and comment period. The TVA fought hard against the listing, while simultaneously accelerating work on the project. The local residents filed suit to halt construction, arguing that completion of the dam and the filling of the reservoir would completely destroy the habitat of the snail darter. The district court agreed that the snail darter was threatened by the dam but declined to halt the project, which was now 80 percent completed. In early 1977, the district court decision was overturned by a circuit court of appeals, and the case went to the U.S. Supreme Court. The Supreme Court decided in favor of the snail darter (*Hill* vs. *TVA*, 1978), but in its written opinion asked Congress to modify or amend the Endangered Species Act of 1973 to allow exemptions. The Court felt that the act did not allow any flexibility within the executive branch nor did it allow broad judicial review on such matters; they believed the act was too clear-cut.

The story does not end here. By 1978 the Endangered Species Act was up for reauthorization by the Congress. With the Supreme Court opinion in mind, members of Congress put forth a number of proposals, ranging from completely doing away with it, to clarifying some of the terms used, to the establishment of a committee to review possible exemptions. This

transport, buy, possess, import, or export any species on the endangered or threatened list.

3. The act also requires the Departments of the Interior and Commerce to delineate the habitats of endangered and threatened species and to map these critical habitats, which are a prerequisite for species survival.

4. The act forbids any private, state, or federal concern from destroying critical habitats as a result of dam-building, highway construction, housing developments, or other projects supported in whole or part by federal monies.

The Endangered Species Act was amended in 1978, after the snail darter controversy threatened completion of the Tellico Dam in Tennessee (Fig. 17.4) (see Issue 17–1). The amendments required closer consultation between the Office of Endangered Species, the Fish and Wildlife Service, the Department of the Interior, the National Oceanographic and Atmospheric Administration, and sponsors of capital improvement projects to avoid long and costly disputes over the fates of both the endangered species and the construction project. The amendments also allowed some exceptions to comprehensive species protection. Specifically, a major project can go ahead if it can be shown clearly that

---

group, dubbed the God Committee, would rule on whether or not a specific species could be extinguished. It would receive counsel from an endangered species review board, which would first review the specific issues and technical aspects to ascertain whether the Fish and Wildlife Service had done a proper job of listing the species as threatened or endangered in the first place. This information would be passed on to the God Committee, which would ultimately decide the fate of the species under scrutiny.

One of the first cases reviewed by the committee was the Tellico project. The committee found that continued agricultural production without the dam would be twice what was expected after the completion of the project. Furthermore, statistical analyses of the dam's predicted electricity output showed it would be produced at a deficit. The committee could not condone such an unnecessary and inefficient project and thus ruled in favor of the snail darter. The Tellico project was finished—or was it?

The halting of this $120 million pork-barrel project did not go over well with the dam's proponents, particularly congresspersons and senators from Tennessee. After numerous legislative attempts had failed to exempt the project from the Endangered Species Act, proponents attached an amendment to a $10 billion water projects appropriations bill. The amendment exempted the Tellico project from any and all laws that would prevent its successful completion. President Carter could not veto the bill without

subjecting many people in the country to harm and placing the welfare of the country in jeopardy. Minutes after the bill was signed, the reservoir began filling up.

Before the dam gates closed, however, some of the snail darters were transported to a new home. Unfortunately, the Fish and Wildlife Service accidentally killed between 20 and 30 percent of the population in the relocation process by using pesticide-contaminated nets. The survivors reproduced, however, and in 1983 the snail darter's status was downgraded from endangered to threatened, and by 1984 it was no longer threatened.

The significance of the snail darter lies not in its ecological contributions to science, but rather in its raising fundamental questions regarding the rights of species to simply exist. As noted biologists Paul and Anne Ehrlich state:

A Tellico Dam will eventually be found for every population and species of non-human organism, and there will always be developers, politicians, and just plain people to argue that short-range economic values must take precedence over other values. For they do not understand that their own fates are intertwined with the Snail Darters of our planet. They are unaware of how much they would indeed miss these little fishes. (Ehrlich and Ehrlich, 1981, p. 13)

Figure 17.4   The Tellico Dam, Tennessee.

the benefits of the project outweigh and over-shadow the species preservation issue. Excep-tions to the ESA can be granted by six high-ranking (cabinet and subcabinet) officials and one representative of the state affected. Envi-ronmentalists have named this group the God Committee.

When it came into office in 1981, the Reagan administration was not kind to the en-dangered species legislation. The Secretary of the Interior resisted the inclusion of new spe-cies on the endangered and threatened lists, even though the Fish and Wildlife Service had identified 2000 species that were eligible for listing. Amendments to the ESA in October 1982 stated that the Department of the Inte-rior would consider only biological factors, not habitat destruction, in evaluating a species for listing. This resulted in a precipitous drop in the number of species considered for pro-tection (Bean, 1983).

Nonetheless, in the summer of 1988 the U.S. Senate renewed the Endangered Species Act by the largest margin ever, largely because of a rising outcry of public opinion against the environmental destruction encouraged by the Reagan administration (Pope, 1988). The

newly strengthened act includes increased funding, a commitment to cooperate with state-level programs, increased protection for listed plants, monitoring of list candidates, and recovery efforts (U.S. Fish and Wildlife Ser-vice, 1988b).

Just as terrestrial species are protected by the ESA, the Marine Mammal Protection Act (MMPA) covers marine species. It was passed in 1972, partly in response to pressures from environmentalists and resource managers. The MMPA preempted state authority over marine mammals offshore and called for a moratorium on hunting marine mammals in U.S. territorial waters and on importing such catches to the United States. The act was needed for protection of various species of marine mammals, but even more important is its protection of individual population stocks (Bean, 1977). These mammals include mana-tees, polar bears, walruses, sea and marine ot-ters, and dugongs. The Fish and Wildlife Ser-vice manages the populations of these animals and enforces a moratorium on the taking and importing of them, alive or dead. Any proposals for offshore oil or mineral exploration must take the impact on these species into consideration; walruses are now protected from use by the Inuit (Native Americans of northern Alaska), who have traditionally used the fur and other parts of walruses, sea otter, and polar bear. The Fish and Wildlife Service is also involved in communication, education, and negotiation concerning the future of marine mammals with other countries, including the USSR, Pakistan, and Egypt (U.S. Department of the Interior, 1986).

Internationally, efforts are also being made to protect species. Early attempts at regulating commercial whaling in the face of declining stocks led to the formation of the International Whaling Commission (IWC) in 1946. The IWC was to promote the conservation of whales by establishing quotas on the levels of the commercial whale catch. As discussed in Chapter 12, although the idea is a good one, there are no enforcement mechanisms other than persuasion. Because of this lax enforcement, whalers and some whaling nations, notably Japan and the Soviet Union, routinely ignore the biological harvest quotas set by the IWC.

The Convention on International Trade in Endangered Species of Wild Fauna and Flora, or CITES, regulates and controls commerce in endangered species and other species threatened by overharvest. The treaty negotiations began in 1973, with representatives from 80 countries. It had been ratified by 102 countries, including the United States, as of June 1989 (U.S. Fish and Wildlife Service, 1989b). CITES prohibits international trade in the 600 most endangered species and their products and requires export licenses for another 200 species and their products. Enforcement is left up to the individual treaty nations and varies according to national motivation, economics, and ability. As a result, trade in endangered species has increased, despite the efforts of CITES.

Most of the traded species originate in developing countries and are imported to markets in developed nations. The illegal wildlife trade is often as lucrative as illegal drug trafficking, but without the risks. Products made of ivory and rhino horn and furs from South American ocelots and jaguars and from North American lynxes, bobcats, otters, and wolves are all protected under CITES, but the trade continues. Collectors of rare birds and animals,

such as the South American macaw or the Asian cockatoo, pay up to $8000 for one of these endangered species, thus providing a market for the illegal trade (Ehrlich and Ehrlich, 1981). Do you have handbags, shoes, or coats made from the hides of any of these animals? Unless you obtained them prior to the passage of the 1973 legislation, you are in violation not only of the CITES treaty but also of the Endangered Species Act, and you are therefore subject to criminal prosecution.

The most notorious example of poaching is the insatiable demand for elephant-tusk ivory and the impact this demand has had on the African elephant, *Loxodonta africana*. In 1979 there were 1.5 million of these majestic beasts; today that number stands at 550,000 to 700,000, and it is estimated that a hunter can kill 200 to 300 of these animals daily. The countries that ratified the CITES treaty have all agreed to a certain legal quota of elephant ivory; however, it is estimated that 80 percent or more of ivory harvesting and trade takes place illegally. In June of 1989, the United States announced a total ban on the importation of any African ivory, even via indirect routes such as Hong Kong. A number of African countries have also called for a total ban on the international ivory trade; and in Kenya, the message was made clear in a dramatic pyre of fire that consumed tons of confiscated ivory (U.S. Fish and Wildlife Service, 1989b). In Europe, a treaty for the protection of wildlife has been signed by 20 nations and by the European Community. This treaty, the Convention on the Conservation of European Wildlife and Natural Habitats, became binding on its members in June of 1982 (Council of Europe, 1983).

HABITAT PROTECTION

Another method of protecting species is to protect their habitats, those areas best suited to species' needs. Habitat protection has a long history in the United States, and Theodore Roosevelt was the first President to propose the establishment of national wildlife refuges. During his presidency, the first national wildlife refuge was established in 1903 at Pelican Island, Florida, for herons and egrets. This was the beginning of the National Wildlife Refuge

System, which is currently managed by the Fish and Wildlife Service of the U.S. Department of the Interior. The system provides sanctuaries for endangered and threatened species of plants and animals (Fig. 17.5).

The National Wildlife Refuge System has a total of 445 units. Unfortunately, many of these refuges are severely polluted, to the extent that birds nesting in them are producing deformed or stillborn offspring. The most notorious of these is the Kesterson NWR in California, which has become a collecting basin for the chemically laden runoff from surrounding farmlands. Instead of refuges, Kesterson and at least ten other refuges have become lethal traps (Table 17.4) (Wilderness Society, 1989b).

The federal government is not the only agency in the United States involved in the protection of wildlife habitat. There are many wildlife refuges in the form of state game preserves, and also many private and public interest organizations, such as the Nature Conservancy, the Trust for Public Lands, and the Izaak Walton League, that purchase critical habitat lands and preserve them from encroachment.

An estimated 2 percent of the world's land surface is under some form of protection from development. To amplify and broaden protection internationally, the United Nations Educational, Scientific, and Cultural Organization (UNESCO) has established the Biosphere Reserve Program. The number of *biosphere reserves* worldwide has risen rapidly since the early 1970s, with the main objectives of conserving diverse and complete biotic communities, safeguarding genetic diversity for evolutionary and economic purposes, educating the public and training people in conservation, and providing areas for ecological and environmental research. In 1989 there were 269 biosphere reserves in 70 countries, with two-thirds found in developing nations. To qualify as a biosphere reserve, an area must have outstanding, unusual, and complete ecosystems, with accompanying harmonious traditional human land uses. A reserve consists of a largely undisturbed core area surrounded by one or more buffer zones of human occupancy. Scientific research and training are carried on between the core and buffer zones, and local communities are encouraged to involve themselves in this approach to the preservation of older human and natural ecosystems (Fig. 17.6a). At present, certain biomes such as mountains are well represented in the reserve system, whereas others, including tropical, subtropical, warm-arid, and intermediate areas, have very little protection (Batisse, 1982; Emory, 1989; U.S. Man and the Biosphere Program, 1988).

One United States biosphere reserve is the Pinelands National Reserve (PNR) of New Jersey, which was designated a U.S. National Reserve in 1978 and made part of the international network in 1983. The PNR is also part of the U.S. Experimental Ecological Reserve network. What makes the Pinelands so ecologically valuable?

Often known as the Pine Barrens, this distinctive area covers about 990,000 acres (400,000 ha) of sandy soils on the coast and inland in south-central New Jersey (Fig. 17.6b). Threatened on all sides and from within by accelerated development, the Pine Barrens supports a wide variety of plant and animal life in upland, aquatic, and wetland environments, including 39 species of mammals, 59 species of reptiles and amphibians, 91 species of fish, 299 species of birds, and over 800 different kinds of vascular plants. Of the 580 native plant species, 71 are in jeopardy. Over a hundred of these are at the northern or southern limits of their geographic range, creating a unique and irreplaceable mix of species (Good and Good, 1984). The area was long used by Native American tribes, but human population numbers remained low until recent decades. However, pressure has grown to develop the Pine Barrens for residential, retirement, recreational, military, and commercial purposes. The layers of national and international protection will do a lot to ensure the continued integrity of this largely intact natural area.

HABITAT AND SPECIES PRESERVATION: CRITICAL ISSUES

Species extinction is, of course, a natural process. Over a span of millions of years, a species may develop, flourish, then slowly die out. Human beings, for example, will one day

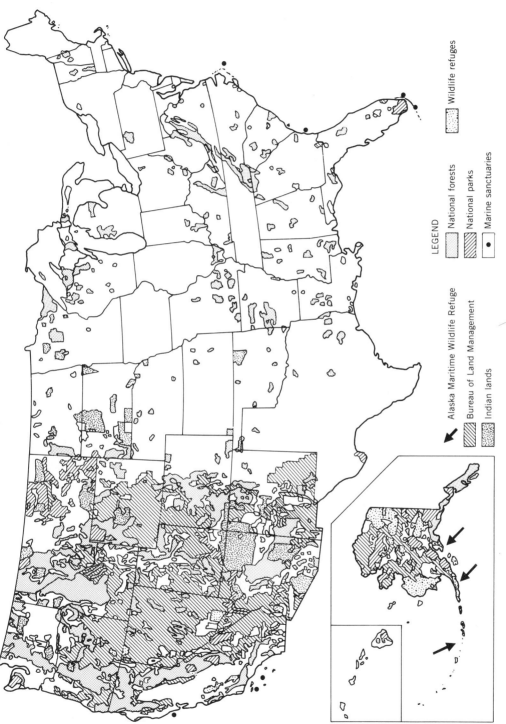

Figure 17.5 Public lands in the United States. Not all of these lands are completely protected from over-exploitation. Some are managed for preservation goals, others for conservation goals. (*Source:* Council on Environmental Quality, 1989.)

LEGEND

- National forests
- National parks
- Marine sanctuaries
- Wildlife refuges

- Alaska Maritime Wildlife Refuge
- Bureau of Land Management
- Indian lands

TABLE 17.4 Contaminant Issues of Concern on National Wildlife Refuges, 1986[a]

Evidence indicates the need for corrective action (9)

Industrial wastes (DDT, PCBs), agricultural drainwater (selenium, other trace elements), military activities (nerve gas, mustard gas, dioxin, plutonium, DDT), waste dumps (asbestos), asbestos insulation (refuge buildings)

Evidence indicates the need for in-depth monitoring and analysis of impacts (26)

Municipal/industrial/military wastes and discharges (PCBs, trace metals), agricultural drainwater (agrichemicals, selenium, arsenic, mercury, boron, other trace metals), waste dumps (heavy metals, mercury, pesticides, cyanide, nutrients, petroleum, other landfill effluents), mining activities (mercury, arsenic, other trace elements), cattle feedlots (nutrients)

Circumstantial evidence indicates a priority need for additional reconnaissance monitoring (43)

Agricultural drainwater (agrichemicals, trace elements, nutrients, toxic chemicals, metals, pesticides, selenium), industrial dumps and discharges (petroleum by-products, mercury, heavy metals, chemicals, trace elements), buried drums (agrichemicals, PCBs, fuel, unknown contents), mining activities (cyanide, placer mining), oil and gas activities

Source: Council on Environmental Quality (1989).
[a] Number in parentheses indicates the number of refuges affected.

become extinct. The question is whether our own demise will be sudden, in the aftermath of war or some other human-made cataclysm, or a gradual and drawn-out process, taking millions of years. It may be that our decline as a species has already begun. A nonhuman archaeologist may one day piece together the strange history of *Homo sapiens.*

One of the most serious problems with present-day species extinctions is that so many of them are not natural or gradual. Plant and animal species that seemed to be in equilibrium have been wiped out in a hundred years or less because human beings tampered with their habitats and other necessities of life. The United States could one day be symbolized by an extinct species. The bald eagle has come very close to extinction, though recent reports suggest a modest comeback over the years since the pesticide DDT was banned.

In keeping with the systems theme that underlies this book, there is another point to be made. As species become extinct, they make way for possible new species that could take advantage of changing environmental conditions. Thus, much as we worry about the eradication of present-day species, so should we be keeping an eye on the conditions we are creating for the development of new ones. It is probable that new species can take advantage of the lands that now lie waste. If only a few species, however, can utilize barren soil, toxic wastes, and dirty water, the richness of the world's ecosystems will be diminished. Such an impoverished biota could set the stage for severe environmental disturbances, and the world would be a much less interesting place.

RECREATION RESOURCES

Humans are recreators—we love to play (Fig. 17.7). Over the past several decades, the United States has seen increases in both the time and money available for both indoor and outdoor recreation. This trend shows no sign of slowing down; some futurists suggest that, with increased automation, North Americans will have more time for play than for work (Fig. 17.8).

As our capacity to play grows, so do the pressures on available outdoor recreational resources. There is a continuing, growing demand for the development of new recreational activities and areas. Places that were of little recreational value in the past, such as the western deserts, are increasingly crowded with people working hard at play. Recreation is simultaneously an economic and an amenity resource. Those who administer and develop a recreational activity or area earn money from it, and those who pay to use the resource enjoy the amenities associated with it. Unfortunately, there is often conflict between con-

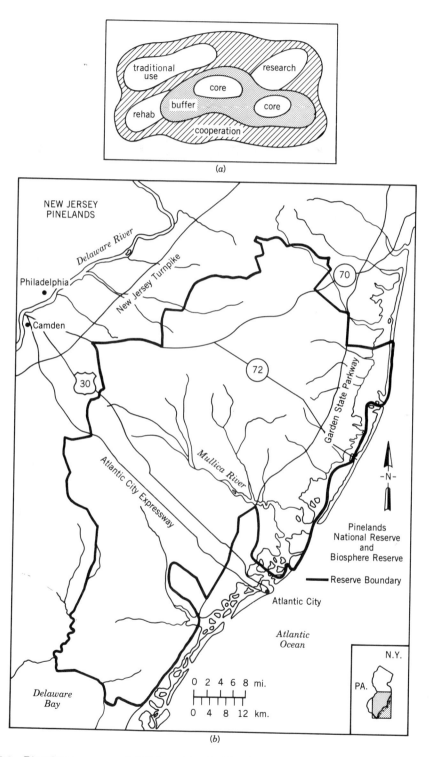

Figure 17.6 Biosphere reserves. (a) Schematic of a biosphere reserve, with core, buffer, research, rehabilitation, and cooperation zones. (*Source:* U.S. MAB, 1988.) (b) The Pinelands National Reserve in New Jersey, a part of the International Biosphere Reserve Programme. (*Source:* Good and Good, 1984.)

Figure 17.7 Cross-country skiing is one of many increasing popular outdoor recreational sports in the United States.

sumers over how best to use a recreational resource.

Recreation covers such a wide range of activities that it would be impossible to discuss all of them adequately. Instead, we will limit ourselves to outdoor recreation in naturalistic settings. Recreational use of the land has expanded manyfold since the first European settlements in North America, and it now constitutes a major economic part of American land use.

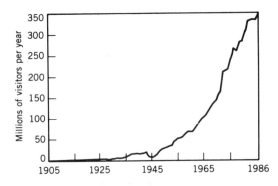

Figure 17.8 Public use of national parks, 1905–1986. As leisure time has increased since the early part of this century, so have the number of Americans visiting the nation's national parks. (*Source:* Council on Environmental Quality, 1989.)

BRINGING THE OUTDOORS TO THE CITY: URBAN PARKS

Even the earliest and hardest working European settlers found time for outdoor recreation: they traveled to mineral spas in search of waters to cure illness and maintain good health. It was not until the mid-nineteenth century, however, that the resort gained popularity, with the development of coastal resorts in the East and West. What we today regard as outdoor recreation did not really become popular until the nineteenth century, when the populations of large U.S. cities began to expand with newly arrived European immigrants. In the mid-nineteenth century, New York City had only 117 acres (47 ha) of developed open green space, but the countryside was just a few miles distant. In the period between 1850 and 1880, several of the city's greatest parks were built in the spirit of democracy; parks for all the people, rich and poor alike. Central Park, designed by Frederick Law Olmstead, is one of the most carefully designed "natural" landscapes in the world. It was a place of rubbish heaps, gullies, and squatter settlement in the 1840s: 20 years later, it had been made into 830 acres (336 ha) of vistas, paths, lakes, and pastoral open space.

The nineteenth-century parks of New

York City were generally not intended for heavy use. Central Park was intended to recreate the country in the city, a place for contemplation and quiet relaxation. In direct opposition to this ideal, the "Playground Movement" of the same era advocated strenuous play for children and adults as a way of removing the stresses of urban life. Many parks were built for both types of use. By the early twentieth century, the area of American urban parks had increased enormously. Cleveland had 94 acres (38 ha) in 1880 and 1480 acres (600 ha) by 1905; Los Angeles had 6 acres (2.4 ha) in 1880 and 3700 acres (1500 ha) in 1905; New York City, the pioneer, had 3700 acres (1500 ha) in 1880 and 24,700 acres (10,000 ha) by 1926 (Schmitt, 1969; Huth, 1957; Quinlan, 1980). Today, our fifty largest cities have a total of over 338,000 acres (137,000 ha) of parks. New York's Central Park and San Francisco's Golden Gate Park are among the best known.

THE NATIONAL PARKS MOVEMENT

In the late nineteenth century U.S. cities became congested and many urban dwellers looked westward for solace and solitude. The first national park, the 2-million-acre (800,000 ha) Yellowstone National Park in Wyoming, was established in 1872. In 1916, Stephen Mather, a Sierra Club member and borax magnate, was named the first director of the U.S. National Park Service (NPS) under the Department of the Interior. Mather and his assistant, lawyer Horace Albright, brought a tough pragmatism to the job, enabling the NPS to expand in the face of anticonservationist economic interests.

The NPS was created with a twofold purpose: to preserve nature and to make nature accessible to the American public. As interest in outdoor recreation has grown over the past decades, a conflict has developed between these two purposes.

The first areas selected for inclusion in the national parks program adhered to traditional European landscape values and were of guaranteed economic worthlessness. After Yellowstone, the Yosemite, Sequoia, and General Grant national parks were established by Congress beginning in 1890. They possessed beautiful valleys, tumbling waterfalls, magnificent trees, and other spectacles. Members of Congress were very cautious in agreeing to the demands for parks made by John Muir (see Chapter 3) and other preservationists. They required ample proof that these parks could not be used for some economic purpose: indeed, Congress usually retained the right to mineral prospecting and timbering when establishing a park's existence.

In 1906 Congressman John F. Lacey of Iowa introduced legislation, which later became the American Antiquities Act, for the preservation of objects of cultural and historical interest on government lands. Lacey had famous historical buildings in mind, and today a wide array of national historic sites and battlefields are included as national monuments and parks. In addition, President Theodore Roosevelt used Lacey's act to speed up the preservation of spectacular scenic areas. Roosevelt was empowered to make all national monument choices, and in 1906 he made national monuments of Devil's Tower in Wyoming, Petrified Forest and Montezuma Castle, both in Arizona, and El Morro (Inscription Rock) in New Mexico. Most dramatically, he stretched the definition of national monument to include 800,000 acres (325,000 ha) around the Grand Canyon in Arizona and 600,000 acres (240,000 ha) around Mount Olympus in Washington.

Tourism in the national parks was at first largely for wealthier people who could afford long, leisurely trips by train and the accommodations in romantic park lodges and hotels. The Yosemite Valley railroad was opened in 1907, and by 1915 about 30,000 visitors arrived annually by car and train. The widespread use of the automobile very quickly took the lead: one auto visited Yellowstone in 1915; by 1919 about 10,000 cars had brought people to Yellowstone. Auto camping was popular with middle-class Americans from the 1920s onward.

National park visitations rose from 3 million in 1929 to 12 million in 1940. By the 1950s, population pressures on the parks caused conservationists to wonder whether the protection of nature could long continue to coexist with the recreational demand. Starting in 1955, a 10-year expansion plan for the parks brought widened roads, more visitor centers, and increased overnight accommodations. Visitation more than tripled between 1955 and 1974, from 14 million to 46 million in the parks alone. Visitors to national monuments rose from 5 million to 17 million during the same period.

Today, the National Park System is a complex mixture of tiny and huge, rural and urban, historical and primeval units (see Table 17.5 and Fig. 17.4). As American attitudes toward nature and recreation have changed, so has the NPS moved to accommodate the new trends as best it could in the face of an often hostile Congress and President.

For example, the 1960s and 1970s saw the creation of a number of National Seashore and National Recreation Areas (NRAs) for urban populations to enjoy. By preserving these areas, the NPS was able to provide recreational opportunities for people who could not travel to more remote national parks. At the same time, the NPS hoped to take some recreational pressure off the overwhelmed ecosystems of Yosemite and other popular parks. The first two NRAs were Golden Gate NRA, in San Fran-cisco, and Gateway NRA, along the coastal margins of metropolitan New York. Later additions included Point Reyes National Seashore, in northern California, Cuyahoga Valley NRA, in Cleveland, and Lowell National Historical Park, in Massachusetts (Fig. 17.9).

Since 1960 more than 130 units have been added to the National Park System. To be eligible for inclusion, an area must have national significance. Areas can be added to the NPS system only by an act of Congress or by an Executive Order. In 1978 nearly 45 million acres (18 million ha) were added to the National Park System, almost doubling its size. Most of these additions were Alaskan lands involving changes from national monument to national park status. Since 1979 there have been few additions to the system.

Today, the NPS administers over 76 million acres (31 million ha) in 343 different units. These units range from national parks and seashores, to trails, to urban and historic parks. Small as the rate of new additions to the system has been since 1980, there has been a continuing rise in visitors to units of the Na-

TABLE 17.5   The National Park System

Type of Area	Number of Areas	Federal Acreage	Visits (Millions)
National parks	49	45,875,126	56.6
National historic parks	26	94,815	29.5
National monuments	78	4,626,647	23.5
National military parks	9	33,099	4.5
National battlefields	11	9,358	2.1
National battlefield parks	3	7,449	1.7
National battlefield site	1	1	N.A.[a]
National historic sites	64	16,454	10.6
National memorials	25	7,865	20.1
National seashores	10	476,215	18.5
Parkways	4	159,648	39.3
National lakeshores	4	143,282	3.4
National rivers	12	237,137	3.6
National capital parks	1	6,469	8.1
Parks, other	10	31,953	8.0
National recreation areas	17	3,338,848	56.5
National trails	3	91,103	N.A.
National preserves	12	20,899,872	.1
National Mall	1	146	N.A.
White House	1	18	1.1
Other	2	N.A.	N.A.

Source: Council on Environmental Quality (1989).

[a] N.A. = not available.

Figure 17.9 Visitors to preserved industrial buildings in Lowell National Historic Park, Massachusetts.

tional Park System. In 1960, for example, 79.2 million people visited 176 units (CEQ, 1982). By 1970 this had increased to 172 million people visiting 235 units, and by 1980 the figure was 300 million people visiting 277 units (CEQ, 1982). In one year alone, 1980–1981, visitations to the national parks rose by 29.6 million. In 1986 the national parks saw 365 million visitors, a rise of over 285 million since 1960.

This increased demand has made some units overcrowded, polluted, and severely degraded. The most popular national parks (Table 17.6) bear the brunt of the assault. Because

of its dual mission—conserving resources and making them available for public use and enjoyment—the NPS often finds itself in the center of controversy concerning its management plans. One particular issue involves the impact of very heavy use. The challenge for the future is for the NPS to provide recreational opportunities for those who visit the parks while minimizing environmental degradation due to the visitors themselves.

MULTIPLE-USE AND SPECIAL-PURPOSE LANDS

Wild and Scenic Rivers

In 1968, Congress established the National Wild and Scenic Rivers System to preserve free-flowing rivers as a balance to future dam and reservoir development. The system is designed to protect recreational river use at three different levels of development. *Wild rivers* are inaccessible to motorized vehicles and have undeveloped shorelines. *Scenic rivers* are accessible by motorized traffic at certain points and sustain some development along their shorelines. *Recreational rivers* are easily reached, usually well developed, and are heavily used. The formal rationale for inclusion in the system is that a river or river

TABLE 17.6 Visits at Selected National Parks, 1987

National Park	Visits (Millions)
Acadia	4.3
Glacier	1.7
Grand Canyon	3.5
Grand Teton	1.5
Great Smoky Mountain	10.2
Olympic	2.8
Rocky Mountain	2.5
Yellowstone	2.6
Yosemite	3.2
Zion	1.8

Source: Council on Environmental Quality (1989).

segment must have one or more outstanding scenic, recreational, geologic, fish and wildlife, historic, cultural, or similar values. The Secretary of the Interior, in consultation with state governors and others, has the power to designate rivers or river segments as wild and scenic.

Originally, the Wild and Scenic Rivers System consisted of 8 river segments in 7 states, for a total of about 800 miles (1280 km). As of 1988 there were 161 rivers and river segments in 23 states, for a total of almost 7223 miles (11,650 km) (CEQ, 1982; *Wilderness,* 1987). Almost half of the total river mileage is in Alaska, with 26 rivers in the system. The longest river in the system is a 400-mile (640 km) stretch of the upper Mississippi in Minnesota, with Alaska's Fortymile River second at 396 miles (634 km) (Fig. 17.10).

A variety of state and federal agencies, among the latter the Departments of the Interior and Agriculture, administer the separate segments in the lower 48 states. Management plans have been individually tailored to maintain each river or segment in its present condition.

Wilderness

Wilderness has always been special to North Americans (Nash, 1982). Although the meaning of the term wilderness has changed over the centuries, it still connotes a sense of wildness, a sense of humans against nature. It is estimated that worldwide one-third of the land surface is wilderness today (Olson 1990). In

the United States, many wilderness advocates, such as John Muir, Aldo Leopold, Robert Marshall, and Howard Zahniser, argued long and hard for the permanent establishment of wilderness areas that would be protected from all encroachment of civilization. Preservation of wilderness was a concern as early as 1840, but it was not until 1964 that the concept was formalized by the passage of the Wilderness Act.

The purpose of the Wilderness Act was to secure lands for protection and preservation and to administer these lands for use and enjoyment as wilderness. Management of these lands was meant to leave them unimpaired for future use, that is, they were to be managed as wilderness areas. Within the legislation is a definition of wilderness that specifies which lands can be considered for inclusion under the Wilderness Act. The definition includes the following:

1. The area should be affected by the forces of nature only, and human impact should be unnoticeable;

2. The area should possess outstanding opportunities for solitude and primitive recreation;

3. The area should have at least 5000 acres of land or be of sufficient size to make preservation practicable; and

4. The area should contain ecological, geologic, or other features of scientific, educational, scenic, or cultural value.

Under the Wilderness Act, the federal agencies that manage public lands (the Forest Service, the National Park Service, the Fish and Wildlife Service, and the Bureau of Land Management) were asked to review lands under their jurisdiction for possible inclusion in the system. Immediately after passage of the Wilderness Act, 54 areas, encompassing 9.14 million acres (3.7 million ha), were preserved (CEQ, 1982). Most of these lands were in the western states, under the jurisdiction of the U.S. Forest Service. As part of the Wilderness Act, all federal land managers were also asked to undertake periodic reviews of lands for potential inclusion, and the NPS and the FWS

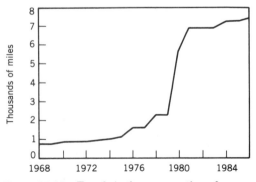

Figure 17.10 Trends in the preservation of American wild and scenic rivers, 1968–1986. More than half of the total river mileage is in Alaska. (*Source:* Council on Environmental Quality, 1989.)

were specifically asked to review lands over a 10-year period.

The definition of wilderness in the original legislation automatically excluded eastern wild lands that showed some evidence of human impact (early forestry by settlers, remnant roads, and so on) and that were smaller than the 5000-acre limit. In response to this, the Eastern Wilderness Act was passed in 1974, adding 16 new areas to the system. Under this legislation, the Forest Service was required to undertake a 5-year review of its lands for potential inclusion.

By 1980 nearly 79.8 million acres (32.3 million ha) had been preserved in wilderness status in 257 areas. The vast majority of the new additions from 1974 to 1980 were Alaskan lands. Nine out of the ten largest wilderness areas, ranging in size from 2.1 to 8.7 million acres (850,000 to 3.5 million ha), are in Alaska. In 1984, another 8.6 million acres (3.48 million ha) were signed into law as wilderness, and another 2 million acres (810,000 ha) in 1988, bringing the total to over 90 million acres (36.4 million ha) (Frampton, 1988; Wilderness Society, 1989a) (Fig. 17.11).

Most of the wilderness areas include alpine and arctic environments; in response to this, pressure was put on the Bureau of Land Management to accelerate its review process of desert and semidesert lands. The Federal Land Policy and Management Act, passed in 1976, codified the role of the BLM and directed the agency to inventory lands for potential inclusion. The BLM review process has been controversial, and a number of legal challenges have been made.

The Wilderness Preservation System in the United States has added many new areas in the last two decades. Environmentalists continue to push for more areas and argue for the need to preserve America's wilderness heritage (see Issue 17–2). In 1988, on the 25th anniversary of passage of the Wilderness Act, the president of the Wilderness Society called for the preservation of another 100 million acres (40 million ha) (Frampton, 1988).

CONFLICTS OVER RECREATIONAL RESOURCES

Because we are individuals, our definition of recreation varies from one person to another. As a result of these differences, conflicts often arise between individuals or groups of individuals who want to use the same area for different recreational purposes. For years there has been conflict between people who want to sail on small recreational lakes and those who want to use power boats. In trying to accommodate these different recreational demands, some state agencies have gone so far as to segregate sailing and power boats, either by specifying different uses on different lakes, or

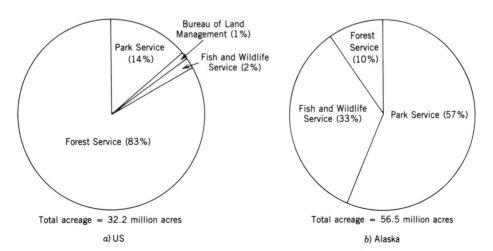

Total acreage = 32.2 million acres

a) US

Total acreage = 56.5 million acres

b) Alaska

Figure 17.11 Federal ownership of land classified as wilderness in 1986. The Forest Service controls most of the wilderness land in the conterminus United States. In Alaska, the Park Service administers the majority of the wilderness lands. (*Source:* Council on Environmental Quality, 1989.)

on the same lake on alternate days, for example, Mondays for sailing, Tuesdays for power boats.

Another example is the rivalry between off-road vehicle (ORV) enthusiasts and non-motorized recreationists. Those who like to make noise, go fast, and stir up a lot of dust are anathema to those who go outdoors in search of solitude. ORV enthusiasts are well organized and adamant about what they want, however. As the editor of an Idaho-based ORV newspaper says, "We don't hate environmentalists, we're just sick of them taking our rights." His organization's motto: "Preserving our natural resources for the public instead of from the public." To protect their access to the great out-of-doors, ORV lobbyists have managed to defeat wilderness designation for millions of acres in Montana and California. Also in California, millions of dollars of the state's gasoline taxes are now spent annually on the purchase of acreage for State Vehicular Recreation Areas (Dagget, 1989).

The tension between users is often local-

ISSUE 17–2   The Values of Caves

For many people, caves are a normal feature of the landscape, and for others, caves are as unusual and alien as the moon itself (Fig. 17.12). In those karst areas of the country where the geologic conditions are right—thick layers of water-soluble limestone, often overlain with a more resistant layer such as sandstone—caves are as common as dandelions. The United States' most famous cave system is also the world's largest known cave, the over 300-mile-long labyrinth known as the Mammoth–Flint Ridge system in Kentucky. Carlsbad Caverns in New Mexico are equally spectacular, with vast underground chambers and avenues, all carved by the chemical and physical action of water on limestone.

In the United States, caves are found mostly along the Appalachian Highlands from Vermont to Alabama and within the interior plateaus between Missouri, Kentucky, and Alabama. Some states such as West Virginia and Texas have over 2000 caves each; and though less abundant, caves in the West are among the country's most spectacular. A rough estimate of the number of caves in America is around 30,000, but this doesn't include the many thousands that still lie undiscovered. The underground world, in the United States and globally, remains one of the few frontiers for the explorer in an increasingly crowded world.

This, then, is an amenity value of caves: the thrill of discovery, for those unclaustrophobic persons who do not fear the dark and who enjoy being wet and dirty for hours or days on end. What are other reasons for placing a positive value, perhaps even legal protection, on the country's caves? After all, caves can be a nuisance. To the livestock farmer, caves are traps for unwary cows and are valued mostly as places to dump trash. To highway builders, caves have to be pumped full of concrete so that they will not collapse under the weight of new roadways. For residents of Florida, sinkholes have sucked up homes and cars, and landowners generally are nervous about the legal implications of cavers becoming lost or injured while underground (except in cave diving, deaths are a rarity).

Geographers George Huppert and Betty Wheeler (1986) argue that caves should be protected as wilderness under the 1964 Wilderness Act, and they support this with a compilation of the values of caves:

- Scientific and historic value: Caves are either fossil (no longer being carved) or active (still subject to new development) and serve as underground ecological, evolutionary, and mineralogical laboratories. Their varied life-forms are largely unknown and contribute to global diversity and to our potential resource base. As home to early humans, caves hold clues to ancient times. When caves are destroyed by overuse and pollution, the remaining protected caves become more valuable.

- Recreational value: Call them spelunkers, speleologists, or cavers, there are over 6000 members of the National Speleological Society and uncounted others who benefit from the self-testing, discipline, and camaraderie of explora-

ized, but the mediation of these competing demands often falls to the governmental agency that manages the land. In some cases, BLM managers and NPS personnel, in addition to their other responsibilities, must enforce the laws and police these recreational areas. Recreational disputes will no doubt continue to be a problem, particularly in the face of declining recreational space and increasing demand. The management of recreational resources includes not only resource management but people management as well.

VISUAL RESOURCES

Human beings, if given a choice, would no doubt prefer to live in a beautiful environment rather than an ugly one. They would prefer to gaze upon beautiful landscapes. Beautiful can be defined in many ways, and this can lead to conflict over the appearance of our environment. One hundred or more years ago, the suburbanization of the North American landscape had not yet begun; the continent was

---

tion, contemplation, and discovery to be found in caves.

- Aesthetic and religious value: Mammoth Caves and Carlsbad Caverns National Parks are among the United States' most frequently visited parks. The millions of annual visitors come—and return numerous times—to experience the otherworldly beauty and mystery of the vast halls extending out of sight, the sparkling and weird formations, and the strangeness of feeling comfortable under such conditions! Awe is an endangered emotion nowadays, to be protected wherever it is felt.

In addition, water management experts are realizing that cave systems are of central value to the health of our country's groundwater supply. In karst regions, many villages, towns, and rural residents obtain their water from underground rivers, streams, and pools, with surface water being scarce. Unfortunately, these excellent water resources are easily polluted, and the pollutants can travel a long way with destructive results. The soil and rock in karst regions are very porous, and sewage, gasoline, and other domestic and industrial pollutants quickly find paths to underground waterways. The town of Horse Cave, Kentucky, has in this way polluted its own water supply to the extent that it is unusable. In southern Indiana, a cave system has been inundated with sewage. The local sewage treatment plant overflowed during a wet season and inundated an otherwise pristine set of pools and passageways: today they are still beautiful, but disturbance of the mud and water raises odors, and

cave biota have been considerably reduced. These local examples are repeated throughout the United States' and the world's rapidly urbanizing and industrializing karst regions (Huppert et al., 1988), and vast systems such as Mammoth Cave are threatened by uncontrollable plumes of pollution entering from unknown and numerous aboveground sources.

In 1988, the U.S. Congress passed into law the Federal Cave Resources Protection Act, the first law to specifically provide protection to caves located under federal lands. Although it is of limited benefit to caves located under private, local, and state-owned lands, this law sends a signal that caves, once feared as entrances to an infernal underworld, are now a valued natural resource. The 1988 act specifies that only "significant" caves will be protected, but this is a workable compromise to supporters who spent 6 years lobbying for passage.

Exactly how will U.S. caves benefit from this legislation? No preexisting environmental legislation specifically mentioned caves, so that any previous attempt to control their overuse and abuse was easily countered by pro-industry and development interests. Now, more than 4200 caves may be protected by this law, which will put teeth into the Audubon Society, Wilderness Society, National Speleological Society, and other groups' efforts to save and protect caves for their many positive values. These include their mineral formations, unique life-forms and habitat, archaeological remains, and historic, hydrologic, recreational, and wilderness values (Huppert and Thorn, 1989; Bishop and Huppert, 1990).

Figure 17.12   Luray Caverns, a show cave in Virginia.

made up of vast rural expanses and relatively small and discrete urban places. The past century's expansion of populations outward from the cities has produced a new landscape that is a hodgepodge of rural and urban elements. Rapid changes in technology, the development of an automobile-oriented life-style, changing tastes, and increased pressures to develop rural areas have all contributed to changes in our appreciation of landscapes. There is therefore greater disagreement today than in the past over what constitutes an attractive visual environment.

DEFINING VISUAL QUALITY

One of the biggest problems in discussing visual resources is the determination and definition of beauty. What is a beautiful landscape? Visual evaluations are based on aesthetic standards, which in turn are a function of the social, moral, and ecological values of the group making the evaluation. These judgments are then applied to the environment, be it a landscape, city, or town. There is no uniform definition or measure of beauty, or conversely, ugliness. To ruin the visual aspects of a landscape is to create *visual blight*. Blight varies by culture, region, individual personality, experience, and type of land, town, city, or sea-

scape. What is acceptable to one individual may be blight to another. Beauty is still in the eye of the beholder.

Lewis, Lowenthal, and Tuan discuss visual blight in America in their 1973 essay. These three geographers, concerned with the plight of America's landscape, sought to discuss the meaning, history, and causes of visual blight. They found that visual blight went beyond such easily defined examples as litter and billboards along roadways. It was found everywhere in the United States and was worst in cities where most people lived, along roads where most people traveled, and along approaches to resorts where most people recreated.

CAUSES OF VISUAL BLIGHT

How and why do landscapes become blighted? There are a great number of reasons, and we will mention just a few. First, we degrade the visual quality of landscapes out of habit, because it is easier to toss that gum wrapper out of the car along the highway than to place it in a trash receptacle that is emptied later. Have you ever thought why neon, plastic, and a quarter acre of blacktop are needed to sell gasoline, fried chicken, or hamburgers?

Another contributory factor in blight is economic: blight is financially profitable. There are many industries, such as land developing, outdoor advertising, and other roadside industries, that create blight in the process of making money. These industries are spinoffs from the automobile subculture, which has greatly influenced the transformation of the landscape.

Finally, landscapes are blighted because our political institutions rarely provide reliable mechanisms to prevent blight. This laissez faire attitude toward landscapes has let blight become so prevalent that it is almost unnoticeable. Zoning or legislating against blight often leads to court challenges in support of individuals' and communities' rights.

CONSERVING VISUAL QUALITY

Strategies to conserve visual quality include legal action that prohibits the intrusion of unsightly businesses, the preservation of historic places, the restoration of places, and the protection of unspoiled environments, such as wilderness. To take action to conserve visual resources, however, we must first be willing to agree on a definition of beauty. This involves some legal and ethical questions about the determination and regulation of aesthetics. Some recent court cases have decided that the state or federal government has no business making ethical judgments about beauty and that this burden should be placed squarely on the local community.

Conflicts are bound to arise, especially when there is not a consensus within the local community about what is visually acceptable. Communities such as Williamsburg, Virginia, or Annapolis, Maryland, are exceptions, as they have architectural standards aimed at preserving their historical character. Aesthetic standards often divide communities and occasionally result in legal challenges to local zoning ordinances.

REGULATING ROADSIDE BLIGHT IN AMERICA

One of the most well-known attempts at regulating visual quality involves outdoor advertising along America's highways and byways. Outdoor advertising includes on-premise signs that advertise services or commodities available on that parcel of private property and off-premise advertising that occurs primarily in the form of billboards.

Billboards have been around as long as there has been automobile traffic. In the late 1950s, roadside America became so unsightly that a number of national legislative attempts were made to get the nation to clean up along the highways. The Federal Aid Highway Act of 1958 established a national policy regulating placement and maintenance of outdoor advertising displays within 600 feet of the right-of-way of the U.S. Interstate Highway System. Displays had to conform to standards of size, number, and location. There was no provision for the active enforcement of the policy.

Partly as a result of Lady Bird Johnson's attempts to beautify America, a strong outdoor advertising regulation bill was passed. The Federal Highway Beautification Act of 1965 was designed to control advertising within 1000 feet (305 m) of the nearest edge of the pavement along the interstate system and along federally aided primary roads. No federal aid for highway construction or maintenance would be given to states that did not control outdoor advertising. The only billboards permissible along the roadway were directional in nature or for traffic control. The act also required that all nonconforming billboards be removed and that the costs of the removal be shared by the federal government and the states. Unfortunately, this program has not been successful, leading some to comment that the Highway Beautification Act is the environmental movement's greatest failure (Floyd and Shedd, 1979).

Litter is another problem that has impaired the visual quality of American roadscapes. Gum wrappers, pull-tabs, and plastic containers can be found along most American roadways, river walks, and play areas. One million tons of litter are picked up each year along our highways. Aside from improved personal habits, the most effective litter control strategies are educational and punitive. Fines up to $500 for littering are not uncommon. Campaigns, such as those sponsored by Keep America Beautiful, Inc., constantly remind us that litter has its place (in the trash can). Smokey the Bear reminds us that "Every litter bit hurts," and Woodsy the Owl cries, "Give a hoot, don't pollute."

SUMMARY

It is possible that today's landfills will be tomorrow's valued fuel sources. Stranger things have happened, as resources have shifted in value over the centuries. We have made no attempt to examine the entire range of potential resources, because that is impossible. How can we discuss the value of substances as yet unrecognized as having value?

Certainly, the question of what is beauty in the out-of-doors has changed considerably over the centuries. Once only cities were considered beautiful, and now, for millions of Americans, only wilderness is beautiful. Once billboards were indicators of progress and prosperity, like the city; now they simply block the view. Once wolves were reviled as monsters; now they are symbols of an unspoiled, golden past.

This chapter has shown that new resources are constantly coming into existence, within the dictates of politics, economics, and cultural backgrounds. The resource base is neither static nor unresponsive. In fact, over your lifetime, you will undoubtedly see a shift to a very different mix of resources than we have today.

REFERENCES AND ADDITIONAL READING

Allman, W.F. 1988. Planet earth, how it works, how to fix it. *U.S. News and World Report* 105(17), October 31, pp. 56–68.

Batisse, M. 1982. The biosphere reserve: A tool for environmental conservation and management. *Environ. Conservation* 9(2): 101–111.

Bean, M.J. 1977. *The Evolution of Natural Wildlife Law*. Washington, DC: Council on Environmental Quality.

————. 1983. Endangered species: The illusion of stewardship. *National Parks*, July/August, pp. 20–21.

Bishop, S.G. and G.N. Huppert, 1990. Taking wilderness underground. In D.W. Lime (Ed.), *Managing America's Enduring Wildlife Resource*. Minnesota Extension Service: St. Paul.

Broad, W.J. 1978. Boon or boondoggle: Bygone U.S. rubber shrub is bouncing back. *Science* 202: 410–411.

Brown, L.R., *et al.* 1988. Earth's vital signs. *The Futurist*, July/August, pp. 13–20.

Campbell, F.T. 1980. Conserving our wild plant heritage. *Environment* 22(9): 14–20.

Carney, L. 1983. New Jersey environment. *The New York Times*, January 16, XI, p. 14.

Council of Europe. 1983. Wildlife protection: Ensuring observance through the Council Of Europe. *Environ. Conservation* 10(2): 167–168.

Council on Environmental Quality. 1982. *Environmental Quality, 1982: 13th Annual Report*. Washington, DC: U.S. Government Printing Office.

————. 1989. *Environmental Trends*. Washington, DC: U.S. Government Printing Office.

Crosson, P.D., and N.J. Rosenberg. 1989. Strategies for agriculture. *Sci. Amer.* 261(3): 128–135.

Dagget, D. 1989. An old foe with new tricks. *Sierra* 74(1), January/February, pp. 30–32.

Eckholm, E. 1978. *Disappearing Species: The Social Challenge*. Worldwatch Paper #22. Washington, DC: Worldwatch Institute.

Ehrenfeld, D.W. 1981. *The Arrogance of Humanism*. Oxford: Oxford University Press.

Ehrlich, P., and A. Ehrlich. 1970. *Population, Resources, and Environment: Issues in Human Ecology*. San Francisco: W.H. Freeman.

————. 1981. *Extinction: The Causes and Consequences of the Disappearance of Species*. New York: Ballantine Books.

Emory, J. 1989. Where the sky was born. *Wilderness* 52(185), Summer, pp. 55–57.

Felger, R.S., and G. Nabhan. 1978. Agroecosystem diversity: A model from the Sonoran Desert. In N. Gonzalez (Ed.), *Social and Technological Management in Dry Lands—Past and Present, Indigenous and Imposed*. AAAS Selected Symposium 10. Boulder, CO: Westview Press.

Floyd, C.F., and P.J. Shedd. 1979. *Highway Beautification: The Environmental Movement's Greatest Failure*. Boulder, CO: Westview Press.

Frampton, G.T. 1988. Wilderness Act, 25 years. *Wilderness* 52(183), Winter, p. 2.

Good, R.E., and N.F. Good. 1984. The Pinelands National Reserve: An ecosystem approach to management. *Bioscience* 34: 169–173.

Huppert, G.N., and J.B. Thorn. 1989. Federal cave protection in the U.S.: The Federal Cave Resources Protection Act of 1988. In *Proceedings, 10th International Congress of Speleology, 13–20 August, Budapest, Hungary*. Pub. in Budapest by the Organizational Commission, 10th International Congress of Speleology.

Huppert, G.N., and B.J. Wheeler. 1986. Underground wilderness: Can the concept work? In *Proceedings, 1985 National Wilderness Research Conference Current Research*. General Technical Report INT-212. Ogden, UT: USDA Forest Service Intermontane Research Station.

Huppert, G.N., B.J. Wheeler, E.C. Alexander, and R.S. Adams. 1988. Agricultural land use and ground water quality in the Coldwater Cave groundwater basin, Upper Iowa River karst region, U.S.A. Part I. In *Resource Management in Limestone Landscapes: International Perspectives. Proceedings, IGU Study Group, Man's Impact on Karst*. Special Publication No. 2. Canberra: Department of Geography and Oceanography, Australian Defense Force Academy.

Huser, V. 1983. Riding the current—Our wild and scenic rivers system. *National Parks* 57(11/12): 20–25.

Huth, H. 1957. *Nature and the American*. Berkeley: University of California Press.

Jackson, P. 1978. Scientists hunt the Bengal tiger—But only in order to trace and save it. *Smithsonian* 9(5): 28–37.

Johnson, J.D., and C.W. Hinman. 1980. Oils and rubber from arid land plants. *Science* 208: 460–464.

Kazarian, R. 1981. Plant scientists get closer to developing buffalo gourd as a commercial food-source. *Environ. Conservation* 8(1): 66.

Knox, M.L. 1989. Horns of a dilemma. *Sierra* 74(6), November/December, pp. 58–67.

Lewis, P.F., D. Lowenthal, and Y. Tuan. 1973. *Visual Blight in America.* Resource Paper No. 23. Washington, DC: Association of American Geographers.

Linden, E. 1989. Playing with fire. *Time,* September 18, pp. 76–85.

Luoma, J.R. 1989. Prophet of the prairie. *Audubon* 91(6): 54–60.

McKie, R. 1990. Little weed may be key to revolution in agriculture. *Observer,* April 29, p. 3.

Nash, R. 1982. *Wilderness and the American Mind,* rev. ed. New Haven, CT: Yale University Press.

———. 1989. *The Rights of Nature.* Madison: University of Wisconsin Press.

National Academy of Sciences. 1982. *Genetic Vulnerability of Major Crops.* Washington, DC: National Academy of Sciences.

The New York Times. 1981. Efforts in Florida provide little hope to save the dusky sparrow. *The New York Times,* January 19. p. A18.

Norton, B.G. (Ed.). 1986. *The Preservation of Species—The Value of Biological Diversity.* Princeton, NJ: Princeton University Press.

Olson, R.K. 1990. Wilderness international: The new horizon. *Wilderness* 54(90), Fall, pp. 14–20.

Ornduff, R. 1974. *Introduction to California Plant Life.* Berkeley/Los Angeles: University of California Press.

Perlez, J. 1989. Namibia cuts rhino's horns to thwart poachers. *The New York Times,* July 11, pp. A1.

Pope, C. 1988. The politics of plunder. *Sierra* 73(6), November/December, pp. 49–55.

Quinlan, A. 1980. New York City park system stands as a battered remnant of its past. *The New York Times,* October 13, p. B1.

Ragotzkie, R.A. 1974. The Great Lakes rediscovered. *Amer. Sci.* 62: 454–464.

Rees, M.D. 1988. Undercover investigation breaks rhino horn trafficking ring. *Endangered Species Technical Bulletin* XIII(11–12): 6–7.

Regan, T., and P. Singer, 1976. *Animal Rights and Human Obligations.* Englewood Cliffs, NJ: Prentice–Hall.

Report of the President's Commission. 1987. *Americans Outdoors: The Legacy, the Challenge.* Washington, DC: Island Press.

Ruggieri, G.D. 1976. Drugs from the sea. *Science* 194: 491–497.

Runte, A. 1979. *National Parks—The American Experience.* Lincoln: University of Nebraska Press.

Sale, K. 1985. *Dwellers in the Land, the Bioregional Vision.* San Francisco: Sierra Club Books.

Schmitt, P.J. 1969. *Back to Nature: The Arcadian Myth in Urban America.* New York: Oxford University Press.

Schwartz, A. 1988. Banking on seeds to avert extinction. *Audubon* 90(1): 22–27.

Shabecoff, P. 1989. Once scorned and nearly extinct, toxic plant is protected. *The New York Times,* July 25. p. C4.

Shepard, P. 1978. *Thinking Animals.* New York: Viking.

U.S. Department of the Interior. 1986. *Administration of the Marine Mammal Protection Act of 1972, January 1, 1985 to December 31, 1985.* Washington, DC: U.S. Fish and Wildlife Service.

U.S. Fish and Wildlife Service. 1982. *Endangered and Threatened Wildlife and Plants.* Washington, DC: U.S. Government Printing Office.

———. 1988a. Region 6 report. *Endangered Species Technical Bulletin* XIII(8): 8.

———. 1988b. Congress reauthorizes and strengthens the Endangered Species Act. *Endangered Species Technical Bulletin* XIII(11–12): 1, 11.

———. 1989a. Region 6 report. *Endangered Species Technical Bulletin* XIV(5): 10–11.

———. 1989b. U.S. bans ivory imports. *Endangered Species Technical Bulletin* XIV(6): 1, 6–8.

———. 1990. *Box score of listings and recovery plans. Endangered Species Technical Bulletin* XV(6): 8.

U.S. Man and the Biosphere Program. 1988. Biosphere reserves: What, where and why? *Focus* 39(1): 17–19.

Watkins, T.H. 1989. The tropical equation. *Wilderness* 52(183), Winter, p. 19.

Wilderness Society. 1985. Areas of critical environmental concern. *Wilderness* 48(169), Winter, p. 44.

———. 1987. Gallery: Fountainheads. *Wilderness* 51(178), Fall, p. 28.

———. 1989a. Introduction: The vision continues. *Wilderness* 52(184), Spring, pp. 4–11.

———. 1989b. Society lists ten most endangered refuges. *Wilderness* 52(183), Winter, pp. 3–4.

Wilford, J.N. 1980. Agriculture meets the desert on its own terms. *The New York Times,* January 15, p. C1.

———. 1989. Fallen breed of sparrows isn't so rare. *The New York Times,* February 8, p. D25.

Wilson, E.O. (Ed.). 1988. *Biodiversity.* Washington, DC: National Academy Press.

———. 1989. Threats to biodiversity. *Sci. Amer.* 261(3): 108–117.

Wolkomir, R. 1983. Draining the gene pool. *National Wildlife* 21(6): 25–28.

TERMS TO KNOW

Amenity Resource
Biocide
Biological Diversity
Biosphere Reserves
Endangered
Extinction
Gaia Hypothesis
Habitat
Homocentric
Potential Resource
Recreational River
Scenic River
Species
Threatened
Visual Blight
Wild River

STUDY QUESTIONS

1. How can a species be both valued and endangered?

2. What is the economic value of habitat and species preservation?

3. How important is a beautiful environment?

4. How many species exist in the world? How many are lost annually?

5. How is extinction a threat to biological diversity?

6. Should endangered species be preserved, or allowed to become extinct?

7. How many plant species are estimated to have edible parts, and how many do we rely on for the bulk of the world's food supply?

8. How does conflict arise over use of a recreation resource? Are there examples in your local area?

9. How have the two primary missions of the U.S. Park Service conflicted?

10. Why do we value wilderness? visual quality?

Preparing for the Future: Information Gathering, Planning, and Action

INTRODUCTION

Humankind has always wanted to know what the future would bring. For thousands of years people have visited sages, seers, and oracles, seeking information about what would happen in one year or one hundred. Generals needed to know the outcome of the next day's battle, an investor was interested in the fate of his money, and farmers worried over what the weather would be like that season. Today we have predictive tools based on mathematical and scientific principles that we like to believe are more accurate than dreams, visions, and teacup leaves.

The United States government began to use formal forecasting in 1929, when President Hoover created a Presidential Research Committee on Social Trends. Formal forecasting has since become an invaluable tool in business and governmental planning. Based on the collection and objective analysis of correct social and economic data, forecasting predicts the future by extrapolating, or extending, known and measured trends to some future date (see Issue 18–1).

In the decades after World War II, the growing sophistication of computers and programming made increasingly complex forecasts possible. Planners could easily extrapolate a dozen trends instead of laboriously plotting out two or three. Computer programming also made it possible to quantitatively examine the interactions among different trends. Eventually, forecasters were able to calculate the effects that trends and situations have on one another under a variety of conditions. Thus researchers could present different versions of the future based on different starting assumptions and operating conditions (Fig. 18.1).

These comprehensive, broad-based *forecasts*, or *models*, have come into particular favor since the early 1970s. Researchers and planners in most fields of study during this period have favored a viewpoint that emphasizes the interrelatedness or interdependence of most aspects of our existence. This viewpoint has been integrated with computerized model-building to produce global models of the future that extrapolate the intricate interactions between human choices, population growth, climate change, food supply, the natural environment, and energy consumption.

MODEL-BUILDING: STRENGTHS AND WEAKNESSES

The word model usually implies a simplified version of an object such as a train or car. A global model is an attempt to recreate the entire earth system, including its physical, social, and technological subsystems. Because of the immensity and complexity of the task, these

ISSUE 18–1   Science Fiction as Forecast

Global models of the future are not solely limited to computer modeling of statistical data; rather, they have a long tradition within the literary world, in the form of science fiction. A separate but related genre is environmental fiction, which is based on the environmental sciences and uses current environmental problems as the basis for stories. Normally, environmental fiction novels are set in the near future (A.D. 2000 or earlier), as opposed to science fiction, which is often based in the far-distant future. As environmental concerns became more pervasive in the 1970s and 1980s, so did the number of fiction works focusing on the conservation of natural resources.

A few examples of environmental fiction show that these novels forecast future environmental trends just as well as do the global models. Even before Paul Ehrlich's nonfiction *The Population Bomb* was published in 1970, overpopulation was a popular topic with science fiction writers. Anthony Burgess' *The Wanting Seed* (1962, Norton) describes the problems of overpopulation. The story is set in England and describes a "Malthusian comedy" in which prevailing population policies favor homosexuality. Zoe Fairbairns' *Benefits* (1979, Avon) describes the consequences of population control in a society that is plagued by an antifeminist backlash. The government begins paying benefits to women to lure them into the traditional roles of mothers and housewives, but social engineers then exploit the program by restricting reproduction to the most desirable women. Another novel of a sexist society with reproductive restrictions is Margaret Atwood's *The Handmaid's Tale* (1988).

The disruption of ecosystems by humans is another theme often found in environmental fiction. Attempts to control nature backfire, with the inevitable disastrous effects. In *Cachalot* (1980, Ballantine), Alan Dean Foster uses the pollution of the terrestrial ecosystem as the backdrop for a battle for species survival. In this case, the species that survives is the whale, which eventually rules the world. Frank Herbert's *The Green Brain* (1966, Ace) tells the tale of rapid tropical deforestation. Insect populations suffer and eventually revolt against the human despoilers, driving them out of the tropics. Kate Wilhelm's *Where Late the Sweet Birds Sang* (1976, Harper & Row) is a classic story of the effects of ecosystem disruption, mixed with human cloning.

Natural resource extraction and allocation is another theme of environmental fiction. The allocation of water resources shapes the politics of survival in John Nichols' 1974 *The Milagro Beanfield War* (Ballantine). David Hagberg's *Heartland* (1983, Tor) centers on American grain and Soviet attempts to control the world grain market by purchasing surplus grains from Canada, Argentina, and the United States. The novel's theme is that control of the world's grain equals control of the world. Marilyn Harris' *The Portent* (1981, Jove) tells the story of nature fighting back in retaliation for exploitation of mineral resources. A new molybdenum mine has opened in western Colorado, and nature—personified—is angered by this assault, striking back through earthquakes, avalanches, floods, and even blizzards in August. *Texas on the Rocks* (1986, Del Rey) by Daniel de la Cruz tells the story of catastrophic drought in the United States in 2008 and Ripley Forte's attempt to haul icebergs from Antarctica to the Republic of Texas to then sell to the United States.

Antinuclear sentiments and nuclear waste provide topics for a number of novels. In Paul Theroux's *O-Zone* (1986, Ivy), nuclear waste has contaminated many civilized areas and society is polarized into rich urban dwellers and poor aliens who live outside the heavily fortified cities in the radioactive territories. A nuclear power plant accident provides the setting for Alexander Sidhar's *The Dorset Disaster* (1980, Stonesong Press), and Frederik Pohl's *Chernobyl* (1987, Bantam) illustrates how nuclear fact is far stranger than fiction.

Perhaps the works of environmental fiction that are closest to global models are those involving survival of societies in the future. As early as 1949, George R. Stewart, in *Earth Abides* (Random House), wrote about the survival of society in northern California after epidemics virtually wipe out the U.S. population. The most apocalyptic of these future-societies novels are Ernest Callenbach's *Ecotopia* and *Ecotopia Emerging*, written in 1975 and 1981

(Bantam). *Ecotopia* describes the isolated nation-state of Ecotopia (western California, Oregon, and Washington), which seceded from the United States in the near future. The novel, which takes place in 1999, is narrated by a reporter from the United States who is sent to observe this new society. The reporter's findings sound familiar to those aware of E.F. Schumacher's "small is beautiful" concept. Ecotopia has weaned itself from a petroleum-based economy to one based on decentralized, renewable resources. Bicycles are the main form of transportation, urban places are decentralized and livable, recycling is continuous, and the society has a healthy respect for nature.

In *Ecotopia Emerging,* Callenbach describes how Ecotopia came to be. By the 1980s, the United States was moving toward economic and ecological suicide, with the military–industrial complex holding power, backed by the ultraconservative right. Government protection of the environment and the workplace had been destroyed. In 1986 residents of the Pacific Northwest and northern California opposing this trend began to revolt. They created a new nation, Ecotopia, which was determined to shape its own evolutionary destiny. One of the most chilling novels is Whitley Streiber and James Kunetka's *Nature's End* (1986, Warner). Set in 2025, the story centers on the cumulative impacts of human manipulation of the environment and the pollution that resulted. The protagonists crusade to alter current policy before total environmental collapse occurs.

Finally, dozens of science fiction novels and stories have speculated on the state of the world following nuclear war. At one end of the spectrum are tales in which only small and specific areas are damaged, as in Eugene Burdick and Harvey Wheeler's 1962 *Fail Safe* (McGraw–Hill), in which Moscow and New York are annihilated. Moving toward a picture of total devastation is John Wyndham's *The Chrysalids* (1955, Penguin). He depicts farming communities in temperate-zone Labrador, one to two thousand years after war's end. South of Labrador are the fearsome Fringes and Badlands, the territory of mutants. What was once the northeastern United States is known only as the Black Coasts, and South America is reputedly a "sinful" place, where mutants are allowed to live beyond birth. The societal role of mutants is also the main theme of Walter M. Miller's *A Canticle for Leibowitz* (1959, Lippincott) and of Aldous Huxley's *Ape and Essence* (1948, Harper & Brothers).

One example of future resource availability is provided by Steve Wilson in his 1976 *The Lost Traveller* (St. Martins), in which the U.S. West Coast, spared from much nuclear damage, is run by Hells Angels and university professors. The feudal southern states produce oil, essential to the Angels' motorcycle-based economy. *Warday* by Whitley Streiber and James Kunetka (1984, Warner) tells the tale of two survivors as they journey across the postnuclear landscape of America. Set 60 years after the nuclear destruction, *Fiskadoro* by Denis Johnson (1985, Knopf) describes postnuclear culture and society in the Florida Keys. Russell Hoban's *Riddley Walker* (1980, Summit) is a portrait of a postnuclear fuedal society in England that is slowly piecing together the earlier civilization through its now fractured language.

All–female cities surrounded by wilderness occupied exclusively by males provide the scene for Pamela Sargent's *The Shore of Women* (1987, Crown). This postnuclear novel takes a feminist look at male–female relationships in this new society. A comedic interpretation is offered by Stefano Benni in *Terra!* (1985, Pantheon). As six nuclear wars have left the Earth in a state of nuclear winter, the futurescape of Earth has reverted to a subterranean funhouse of decadence centered in Paris, where 200-year-old Mick Jagger and Paul McCartney are global industrialists, pornorobots are available, and video games kill.

Does any of this sound familiar? Who is to say whether the computer-generated models of the global future are any better or any worse than these fictionalized accounts? Environmental fiction and science fiction give us another glimpse at what the future may bring based on current trends. Only time will tell which approach is the most insightful.

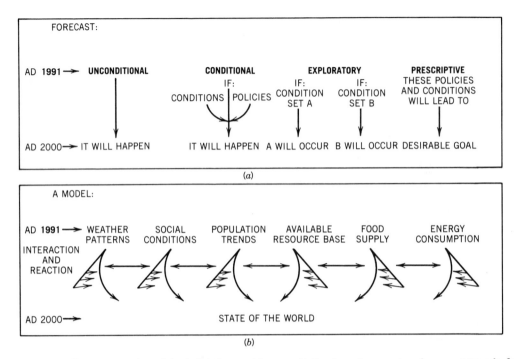

Figure 18.1   Forecasts and models. (*a*) A forecast is a prediction based on past and present trends. It may include certain conditions, such as government policies. (*b*) A model is an integrated representation of many different aspects of a system, which can be used to predict the future.

subsystems and relationships are often simplified into general assumptions and equations suitable for computer programming. Critics of global modeling point out that these simplifications may render a model's prediction useless. Thus a basic question for modelers is how close to reality a model has to be to produce useful results. Let us look at this in more detail.

One of the main appeals of global modeling as opposed to the simpler forecasting is a model's apparent closer resemblance to "real life." This is because of the model's greater complexity, which is in turn due to computer-based abilities to juggle a huge number of variables, conditions, and equations. As model-makers refine and improve their tools, they struggle toward a closer and closer approximation of actual conditions. This requires accurate data and an understanding of how the world works, both of which are perhaps ultimately unattainable, in an absolute sense. This understanding must furthermore be stated in statistical and mathematical terms if it is to be part of the computer model's data base.

Some aspects of the world's resource base are relatively easy to quantify, for example, the

amount of corn harvested on 50 acres (20 ha) under a certain set of climatic and technological conditions. Resource use issues related to human behavior and to changes in public attitude are much more difficult to measure. For example, 25 years ago forecasts on energy use predicted that the U.S. energy supplies would eventually come mainly from nuclear power plants. This prediction has not come true, because of subsequent developments, including weak demand and rising costs of construction due to federal safety requirements instituted after the accident at Three Mile Island, due to increased efficiency of energy use in automobiles, appliances, and so forth, and lastly due to falling demand. People are simply using less as the costs increase. None of these factors was predicted by forecasters a quarter of a century ago, who saw a glowing future for nuclear energy.

Modelers with an understanding of ecosystems behavior have worked to incorporate cycles and other normal ecosystem changes into models. The applicability of these natural-systems components to predictive models of human affairs has yet to be seen, as a longer time span is needed to test their value. The model of a single simple ecosystem may incorporate enough input, output, and feedback data to approximate reality. A model of all the world's millions of ecosystems and all the interactions among them is doomed to failure, because of the limited capacity of computers and huge gaps in our knowledge about world patterns. Models are thus reduced to simplification and approximation, which may severely limit their precision as predictive and decisionmaking tools.

Global models of the 1970s, such as *Limits to Growth* (Meadows *et al.*, 1972), World Integrated Model (Mesarovic and Pestel, 1974), Latin American World Model (Herrera *et al.*, 1976), United Nations Input–Output Model (Leontief *et al.*, 1977), and the Global 2000 Report (Council on Environmental Quality, 1981), were very influential. These models brought awareness to both the scientific world and the general public of environmental pressures resulting from population growth and pollution. Furthermore, these models signaled the interconnected, even global nature of such problems (Fig. 18.2).

However, these models provided predictions only, because the environmental data were not accurate and because the models themselves were not nearly sophisticated enough to simulate real-world environmental complexities. In order to solve—not just talk about—today's environmental problems for tomorrow's world, geographers and other environmental scientists are developing better and more comprehensive and accurate data-collection methods and models that are multilayered and multidimensional to match the complexity of the problems that must be tackled.

GREENHOUSE EFFECT MODELS: LIMITS TO FACT

Several greenhouse effect models of today come much closer to simulating reality than did their 1970s ancestors. However, this does not mean that scientists are willing to state with any certainty whether or not the greenhouse effect has already begun, or if it ever will. It may be that it will take as many years for

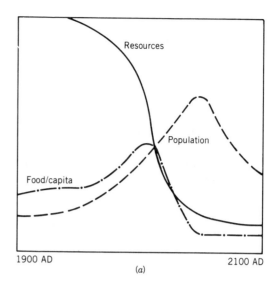

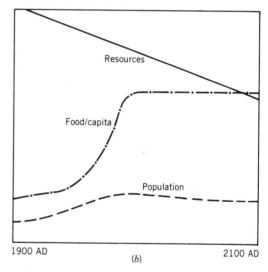

Figure 18.2 Results of the Limits to Growth Model. (*a*) These curves are based on simple extrapolation of present trends into the future. (*b*) These curves are based on early achievement of stability in population and resource use. (*Source:* U.S. Congress, 1982.)

the models to be developed and run as it will take the real world to decide for itself whether or not it is undergoing a greenhouse effect. The scientific method requires absolute proof for a scientist to state a fact with certainty. In the climate modeling game, those few scientists who are willing to state with certainty their opinions about the greenhouse effect are regarded by some as irresponsible, unscientific, and downright villainous (see Issue 18–2).

Two of the new-generation models are those being developed at the National Center for Atmospheric Research (NCAR) by Warren Washington and Gerald Meehl and at the Geophysical Fluid Dynamics Laboratory (GFDL) by Syukuro Manabe and colleagues. In addition, three other U.S. and British *general circulation models*, or GCMs, are regarded as state-of-the-art and are run on the latest generation of supercomputers when time and budget allow (Kerr, 1989).

These new models are far more flexible than those of past decades. For example, earlier models could provide only a single-time output. All relevant climate data available would be entered, along with a doubled amount of greenhouse gases, and the completed program would produce the greenhouse effect results for a single future year. By contrast, these new models simulate the gradual effects of real-world, real-time accumulation of greenhouse gases with an ever-changing computer output. Unfortunately, this artificial real-world activity may not produce results soon enough to be useful. The problem is complex, and modeling of effects on regional-level circulation patterns may not be possible before they actually happen (Kerr, 1989).

Of those simulations that have been run to date, the carefully hedged results make predictions for climate change that have some

---

ISSUE 18–2   How Much Scientific Proof Should a Policymaker Need?

For a scientist to be confident of her results, the facts have to be in. This is essential to the successful use of the scientific method, which is a philosophic approach to understanding the natural world based on objective observation and data-keeping of real-world phenomena. The scientific method, as a product of Western culture, has dominated the direction of human life for 300 years, and its high success rate at problem solving guarantees that many more years will pass before it is superseded by any other approach to understanding the world we see around us.

However, a chink in the armor may have been found. Many people who are concerned with environmental issues feel that the scientific method is inadequate to the task of taking immediate action to solve the world-altering problems that they see looming over us. As discussed in Chapter 1, ecology, a scientific approach to the study of interactions in nature, has taken on the emotional, spiritual heat of a mission to save a planet in danger of death. As scientific ecologists continue with careful data collection and observation, their less objective acquaintances are charging forward, crying that the world is a single organism whose life must be saved with emergency action, which needs to be taken immediately.

It is only natural and reasonable that the cool, lucid scientists would be alarmed at this emotion-laden hijacking of their research. They are quick to back away when one announces that he has enough data, enough careful observation, and that he is ready to join the call for emergency action now. This is what has happened with regard to the greenhouse effect.

James Hansen has earned his scientific credentials. He is a climate modeler and director of the National Aeronautic and Space Administration's Goddard Institute of Space Studies. He is well-published, well-funded, a preeminent researcher, and the key to his success has been careful adherence to the scientific method.

In 1988, however, Hansen did something that no other top-level climate modeler has been willing to do. On national television, testifying at a congressional hearing in Washington, Hansen announced that the greenhouse effect was here, now. The implications of such a statement are profound. If the greenhouse effect is here, then we can no longer question the basic validity of the predictions made over the past two to three decades. We should be doing something about it, to lessen the impact on climate, agriculture, economic systems, and society, and these actions should be taken globally.

Hansen's colleagues immediately undercut his unequivocal statement, because they felt he had gone beyond his data and come to a conclusion on the basis of inadequate proof. They announced that his methods, his research, his models, and his confidence in his results were all faulty. Scientists are also prone to worry when one of their number becomes popular; they fear that objectivity cannot survive in the bright glare

similarities to and some differences from the older models. For example, all the models suggest a future in which the world warms up, with the land warming more rapidly than the oceans. The new models suggest that a greater warming at higher latitudes, as indicated by the earlier model generation, may not be so significant in the twenty-first century after all.

The NCAR model also brings in new complexities: a near-future in which the lower atmosphere becomes warmer over the land masses of North America and Europe while cooling over the ocean areas of the North Atlantic and Pacific. This modeling result has recently been backed up by real-world data.

However, the GFDL model has set off some alarms, suggesting that as the Northern Hemisphere warms up, the Southern Hemisphere will become cooler, probably as a result of oceanic cooling around Antarctica. The alarm here is not so much about these possible climatic trends, but instead that scientists' modeling of the world's oceans is woefully inadequate. If the models are only realistic for a portion of the earth–atmosphere system, then errors in one part of the model can make results from other parts meaningless. At present we have relatively little information about the behavior of the oceans, and the oceanic segments of the models are a barrier to further improvement.

---

of publicity. Also, there is often a kind of snobbish belief among scientists that if the public can understand it, it is not worth knowing. All of these factors have worked to put Hansen in the strange position of being both the main greenhouse spokesperson to U.S. policymakers and something of an outcast among the scientists he is supposed to represent.

What, exactly, did Hansen say? In his own words:

> I said three things. The first was that I believed the earth was getting warmer and I could say that with 99% confidence. The second was that with a high degree of confidence we could associate the warming and the greenhouse effect. The third was that in our climate model, by the late 1980s and early 1990s, there's already a noticeable increase in the frequency of drought . . . the one thing that has the greatest impact on my thinking is the increase in atmospheric carbon dioxide from 280 ppm in the 19th century to its present 350 ppm. It's just inconceivable that is not affecting our climate. There's no model that would not say it's affecting it right now. (Kerr, 1989)

And what, exactly, do Hansen's critics find at fault in these statements? One, that "99% confidence" is too high: a 30-year warming trend is not proof that the earth is getting warmer. Two, no prominent researcher will agree with Hansen

that this warming trend is a signal that the greenhouse effect has begun. And three, scientists feel that Hansen's models are not good enough to accurately simulate changes in climate variability should the greenhouse effect in fact arrive.

Who are we to believe? How long does the public wait until the scientific method produces results that even the most stringent scientific mind will agree is proof positive that a greenhouse effect is or is not taking place? The problem here is that the scientific method is not up to the task of policymaking and action. We need to know well ahead of time if a greenhouse effect is developing so that we can radically alter our way of life around the globe to lessen the greenhouse's negative effects. If, however, we don't learn of its presence until it is upon us, we will be able to do very little in the way of mitigation. Do we act now, based on the observations of a scientist who says the evidence is sufficient, or do we wait another 20 years until there is widespread agreement in the scientific community?

Most scientists involved in the problem probably believe, privately, that the greenhouse warming is here (Kerr, 1989). But even when expressing a gut reaction, these scientists would hedge with the word "probably." To do otherwise is to risk headlines and quotes in newspapers, and condemnation from the more conservative scientific establishment. But the question is clear: What do we do when the need to know outstrips our ability to know?

DATA COLLECTION AND MANAGEMENT

The problems of inadequate understanding of the oceans are in large part a result of inadequate data. Similar problems plague other world-scale models. These problems are being approached on several fronts, including new data-collection programs and development of means to integrate and manage the data once it is collected.

New data-collection programs have been established to focus on critical problem areas, including stratospheric ozone depletion, tropical deforestation, and physical oceanography. Most of these programs are being undertaken by individual nations, although agencies such as the World Meteorological Organization, UNESCO, and the United Nations Environment Programme are playing important roles in coordinating global data-collection efforts.

Among the most important data for global environmental management are those collected from satellites. Satellite, or remotely sensed, data are gathered by orbiting satellites that sense radiation from the earth in several important wavelengths. For example, most weather satellites sense either visible light or infrared radiation of the dominant wavelengths emitted by the atmosphere. These allow determination of cloud temperature and sea-surface or ground temperature in areas that are cloud-free. Most satellites designed for terrestrial applications operate in the visible and near-infrared wavelengths and sense reflected sunlight. These wavelengths have been shown to be very useful for mapping land cover, vegetation, soil moisture, and similar features.

Recently new satellites have been developed, most notably the French SPOT system first launched in 1986 and the U.S. Landsat 6 and 7 systems to be launched in the early 1990s. These systems sense the radiation from small areas called pixels, and pixels are assembled into larger images. Unlike previous satellite systems that had pixels 30 m square or larger, the newer SPOT and Landsat systems have pixels as small as 10 to 15 m across. This greatly increases their ability to distinguish relatively small features such as roads and buildings, or small agricultural plots. The satellites pass over a given area as often as once every several days, making frequent updates of changing surface characteristics possible. The increased data-collection capabilities of these new satellites have the potential for helping in the management of large- and small-scale environmental resources. But the amount of data generated is large, and analysis of these data is itself a major task.

GEOGRAPHIC INFORMATION SYSTEMS

Just as the growth of computer speed and capability has made development of world models possible, so has it enhanced our ability to store and manipulate data about the world. Data-handling technology is obviously critical in the efforts to understand the world, both through integrative world models and through regional or local analyses of natural resource systems (Mounsey and Tomlinson, 1988).

A new type of computer software is being created to help in the management and integration of global environmental data: *Geographic Information Systems* (GISs). GISs are essentially computerized data bases in which the information is stored according to location on the earth's surface. In addition to storing data, GISs have the capability to organize and manipulate a variety of data in a spatial context, thus allowing users to see relations between environmental variables in space and time.

Most GISs organize data as a series of layers of information about a region (Fig. 18.3). For example, one layer might contain topographic data, another soils, another vegetation, and so forth. These layers themselves may be quite complex, for example, vegetation information may include a wide variety of data regarding species, coverage, productivity, and so forth. Data layers can include anything that can be shown on a map: demographic and economic features, transportation networks, political organization, natural resources, and so on.

In a GIS, data in a single layer can be manipulated: for example, data about spot elevations can be made into a contoured topo-

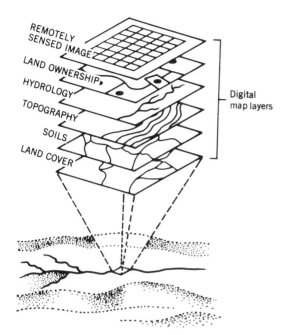

REMOTELY SENSED IMAGE

LAND OWNERSHIP

HYDROLOGY

TOPOGRAPHY

SOILS

LAND COVER

Digital map layers

Figure 18.3 The structure of a geographic information system.

graphic map. New data layers can be created, such as using a map of road networks to create a new map showing road distances to a city. But the real power of a GIS comes from the ability to combine layers to show relations between different features of the earth's surface. For example, suppose production of a particular crop required certain conditions of rainfall, elevation, and soil characteristics. Each of these variables would be stored separately, but the GIS would combine them to make a new map showing those areas having the particular rainfall, elevation, and soils specified by the user (Jessup and Carey, 1989).

Another important aspect of GISs, and a related type of software called image processors, is their ability to use the enormous amounts of information about earth resources that are gathered by satellites. When satellite imagery was first made available in the 1970s much of the data interpretation was heavily dependent on detailed ground-level information, and the computer requirements of these large data bases made large-scale analyses difficult. But larger, faster computers and advanced software have recently made satellite data much more valuable. Such capabilities have made possible very rapid and frequent

determination of the locations and extent of tropical deforestation in the Amazon, for example. Data on vegetation cover such as this can in turn serve as an input to global climate models examining the greenhouse effect.

CONCLUSIONS: MODELS AND SYSTEMS

As we have emphasized throughout this book, environmental problems are not simple. They involve interactions among many different features of the environment, and we therefore find that systems thinking is a useful way to study and understand them. The climate system is an excellent example of this: it includes the oceans, the land surface (with its vegetal layer), and several layers of the atmosphere. The modeler attempting to simulate the world's climate must break it down into these components, and also divide the earth's surface into latitude and longitude zones, each with different characteristics. The modeler treats the earth as a system and represents each component of that system with various equations and rules that interact with each other in the model.

Throughout this book we have also stressed the fact that human and environmental systems interact. It is not sufficient to analyze the earth's climate as only a physical system—we must also recognize that the CO_2 and other substances affecting the climate are emitted from power plants, forests, automobiles, and other things created and/or managed by humans. And of course the physical environmental systems of climate and CO_2 themselves affect human systems.

The Limits to Growth Model and others like it included some features of the world's socioeconomic functions, but human-controlled institutions, such as governments, are probably more difficult to quantify than physical systems, and prediction of their future behavior is certainly more difficult. It is unlikely that computer models will ever be able to effectively incorporate such human systems in their representations of the earth, but such models can be very useful as educational devices. Their educational functions include helping the world's people become aware of what futures may be possible, so that they may then choose to influence their governments and other decisionmakers to change the way they manage the earth's resources. The Limits to Growth Model certainly played this role in the early 1970s, and the various general circulation models are helping make the world aware of global warming today.

REFERENCES AND ADDITIONAL READING

Council on Environmental Quality. 1981. *The Global 2000 Report to the President*. New York: Viking Penguin.

Herrera, A.O., 1974. *Proceedings of the 2d IIASA Global Modelling Conference*. Berlin: International Institute of Applied Systems Analysis.

Herrera, A.O., *et al*. 1976. *Catastrophe or New Society? A Latin American World Model*. Ottawa, Ontario, Canada: International Development Research Center.

Jessup, S.P. and E. Cary. 1989. Geographic information systems: What and how. *Focus* 32(2) Summer, pp. 10–12.

Kahn, H., and J. Simon. 1984. *The Resourceful Earth*. New York: Basil Blackwell.

Kahn, H., and A. Wiener. 1967. *The Year 2000: A Framework for Speculation on the Next Thirty-Three Years*. New York: Morrow.

Kerr, R.A. 1989. Hansen vs. the real world on the greenhouse threat. *Science* 244: 1041–1043.

Leontief, W., A. Carter, and P. Petri. 1977. *The Future of the World Economy: A United Nations Study*. New York: Oxford University Press.

Liverman, D. 1989. Evaluating global models. *J. Environ. Management* 29: 215–235.

Meadows, D.H., *et al*. 1972. *The Limits to Growth*. New York: Universe Books.

Mesarovic, M., and E. Pestel. 1974. *Mankind at the Turning Point*. New York: Dutton.

Mounsey, H., and R.F. Tomlinson (Eds.). 1988. *Building Databases for Global Science*. London: Taylor & Francis.

U.S. Congress, Office of Technology Assessment. 1982. *Global Models, World Futures, and Public Policy: A Critique*. Washington, DC: Superintendent of Documents.

TERMS TO KNOW

Forecast
General Circulation Model
Geographic Information System
Limits to Growth
Model

STUDY QUESTIONS

1. What is the difference between a forecast and a model?

2. How have global models changed since their inception in the 1970s?

3. Do you think that global models are better than crystal balls at predicting the future?

4. Who do you think is acting more responsibly, James Hansen for saying the greenhouse effect is here and we must act, or his colleagues who refuse to venture an opinion until they have more data?

5. List the good and bad aspects of the first generations of global models.

6. How can geographic information systems contribute to solving regional and global environmental problems?

Epilogue

Throughout the writing of this book, we have attempted to present a balanced analysis of environmental issues. If parts are not completely balanced, at least we have undertaken to touch on a diversity of opinions. Here, we diverge from this textbook style and present an epilogue containing three personal pieces about the conservation of natural resources. Unlike the rest of the book, each is written by only one person, without the compromises required by joint authorship. They represent our less objective sides—after all, resource use and development is a matter of opinion as much as a matter of fact.

WHAT IS THE MOST PRESSING ENVIRONMENTAL PROBLEM FACING US TODAY?

William H. Renwick

Before answering this question, I feel it is important to put environmental problems in perspective. Presumably, the ultimate goal of environmentalists is the betterment of the human condition, through proper management of environmental resources. But as we stated in the introduction to this book, resources are created and defined by both human and environmental factors. In order to better the human material condition, it is necessary to consider both the physical characteristics of natural resources and the ways in which we convert these raw materials into food, clothing, shelter, and the various other physical requirements of a comfortable existence.

It is my view that although certain aspects of the natural environment are very important to the ultimate well-being of human beings, the social or cultural aspects of our resource use systems are much more critical in determining the quality of life. These social/cultural aspects include the creation and selection of various technologies for converting the raw materials of natural resources into things usable by humans, and the social and economic systems used to allocate and distribute resources and goods to people. I believe this because in my interpretation most of the major cases of large-scale human suffering can be attributable primarily (if not entirely) to human causes, and because hardships caused by the many environmental problems we have discussed are minor, even trivial, by comparison.

To someone who has just finished reading this book, or to a dedicated environmentalist, this may seem heretical, but a few examples will help illustrate the point. First, most major modern and historical episodes of widespread death and/or suffering are directly attributable to aggression by one group against another, either explicit in the case of most wars, or indirect in the case of the eradication of native populations in the New World. There have been periods of severe population reduction by nonhuman agents, most notably the plagues in Europe in the Middle Ages. The causes of these tragedies were certainly complex, and included environmental factors such as fluctuations in host animal populations. But few modern diseases cause human suffering of the scale caused by direct human action. The occurrences of famine in much of the Third World are essentially attributable to economic/political causes. Yes, the famines occur as a result of crop failures that are triggered by unfavorable weather and similar causes, and yes, rapidly rising populations have stressed the ability of the environment to supply us with food and water. But virtually all experts on Third World food problems agree that if domestic and international political and economic conditions were different, these famines would not occur. Some would argue that more agricultural technology must be transferred from rich nations to poor ones, while others argue that the colonial status of the poor nations, today or in the past, is the cause of their economic problems. But very few would argue that the physical limits of the environment's productivity have been reached.

The other side of the issue is to consider the severity of the natural resource problems facing us today. As examples I will mention urban/industrial pollution and soil erosion. Pollution today is certainly a problem, and we all regret the fouling of water and air that is most acute in major urban areas. But in most of the industrialized world, this pollution has been going on for a long time—150 years or more. The major problem of water pollution, the contamination of potable water supplies with disease-causing organisms, has been all but solved by a combination of effluent treatment and chlorination. The most visible and acute forms of air pollution that caused severe health problems in past decades have also been much reduced. We are concerned about toxic substances in water and the health effects of low concentrations of various substances, but at the present time there is little evidence that health problems from these sources will be significant in comparison to those caused by poor diet, smoking, or other individual habits. With regard to soil erosion, there are many areas of the world where this has been going on at high rates for decades or even centuries. When economic conditions have allowed substituting other inputs to agriculture such as fertilizers and improved seeds, yields have increased dramatically, obscuring any effect of soil erosion on production.

Human-induced climatic change presents an interesting case. Predictions made in the late 1980s include a wide range of possible dire consequences, including sea level rise, droughts and floods, with associated death and destruction, crop failures, and so forth. Some people are suggesting that radical reductions in CO_2 output are necessary to avert these

tragedies, and propose various measures to stop tropical deforestation, reduce automobile use, reduce combustion of fossil fuels by electric power plants, and so on. If we assume that these measures could actually stabilize CO_2 emissions at something near current levels, then global warming would be greatly slowed but not stopped. Would that not be a good thing?

Consider the social, economic, and political upheavals this would involve. Use of electricity would have to be seriously curtailed, with major adverse economic effects, including cost increases, unemployment, and probably chronic recession. People in poor countries would be prohibited from increasing agricultural production by opening up new lands, thus limiting their options to increasingly intensive cultivation of existing lands and so slowing any improvement in diet. And either economic development that involved greater use of fossil fuels by poor countries would have to be prevented, or such use by rich nations would have to be seriously reduced. Given the political realities of the world today, and the tendency for voters and politicians alike to be much more concerned about self-interest and short-term rather than long-term problems, measures such as these are very unlikely.

On the other hand, what if the greenhouse warming is allowed to take place, and the predictions prove true? Sea level rise will be a problem in rich countries, but not an insurmountable one. We have the capability to build dikes a few meters high around coastal areas and pump water out of lowlands—the Dutch provide a good model for this. It would be a more difficult problem in poor countries. Bangladesh, much of which is within a few meters of sea level, would probably suffer the most. Agricultural problems caused by unfavorable weather would be most acute in the higher-latitude countries that are best able to cope with them. But the history of North America and Europe over the past few decades makes it quite clear that farmers adjust regularly to market stresses and changes in policy that are much more dramatic than any weather fluctuations that are likely to occur as a result of global warming. Again the rich countries have the capital and technology to deal with the problem, and poorer nations would probably suffer more. So what is the real problem—climatic change or poverty?

Having said all this, it is important to recognize that there are environmental problems that require considerable attention. Air and water pollution are becoming worse in much of the world, especially in poor countries. The extent of the problem in Eastern Europe has recently become known in the West, and perhaps we will also begin to think about the situation in the more densely populated parts of the Third World. Land degradation by soil erosion and depletion of nutrients also continues to stress the food production system. And finally, even though I do not think that global warming is in itself something we should concentrate our efforts on, there would certainly be significant benefits in the improvement of air quality and preservation of species that would result from curtailing fossil fuel use and tropical deforestation.

Even though the many problems discussed in this book are environmental problems, their solutions are political and economic. Given sufficient capital, poor land can be made to produce high yields, clean water can be made available, or energy supplied or conserved without significant decline in standard of living. This has been demonstrated clearly in the wealthy nations. What is needed in the Third World are the economic resources and political power to make the necessary investments and return the proceeds of those investments to the land and people that need it most. Only when the economic and political changes that would make this possible come about will significant progress be made in solving environmental problems.

RESOURCES AND ENVIRONMENTAL DEGRADATION: LEAN YEARS, MEAN YEARS

Susan L. Cutter

As should be patently obvious by now, the use of natural resources is a political and economic issue. Access to and allocation of resources are controlled by economic and political powers. Resource scarcity, in this context, can be viewed as the lack of access to resources. It arises from the inequities in the supply of a particular resource, usually as a consequence of some natural or human calamity that temporarily decreases the supply or affects the distribution. These calamities can be natural hazards, such as frost or drought, or they can be human-induced hazards, such as armed conflict. All have the potential to disrupt the supply of a particular resource for short or long periods of time. Because we live in the global village, disruptions in one part of the world have serious repercussions all over.

With increasing inequities between the less developed and more developed countries, between resource-rich and resource-poor nations, and between urban places and rural hinterlands, the potential for conflict is enhanced. Not all conflict is resolved militarily, but increasingly force is required. The conflict between Iran and Iraq and Iraq's occupation of Kuwait are good examples of the effect of armed conflict on global resource dependencies. Over half of the world's oil comes from the Persian Gulf region, and more than 50 percent of Japan's oil supply is from that region. The importance of these resources is such that the world was united in opposition to Iraq's actions, an unusual situation in international politics.

The ability of the world's nation-states to reduce environmental degradation of the commons (air and oceans) will also lead to conflict, particularly between the industrialized and polluting nations and the less industrialized ones. Why should developing nations accept carbon dioxide emissions reductions to meet the requirements of a global warming treaty when they are not to blame in the first place? Conversely, why should the industrialized nations pay for the costs of tropical deforestation? These forests belong to the equatorial nations and shouldn't they be allowed to exploit their own resources for the benefit of their society?

Although there is a certain amount of global harmony at the moment, as resources become more scarce, population increases, and degradation of our air, water, and land continues at its accelerating pace, I worry that our global citizenship will degenerate and "resource wars" will increase in frequency. The haves must reduce their standard of living to give more to the have-nots. While this may result in a decrease in the poverty gap between nations, it certainly won't alleviate economic inequities within nations assuming that it could be accomplished in the first place. Leaner and meaner years may lie ahead as nations cope with these social, environmental, and economic inequities.

The picture is complicated by the addition of multinational corporations and resource cartels who increasingly influence domestic and international politics. One only has to look at the cocaine trade to assess its international importance and the potential disruption it has caused in American society (the importing nation) and in Colombia (the exporting nation). More often than not, decisions on the rate of exploitation of natural resources are being made not by governments but by corporations operating under very different political and economic constraints. Loss of control over production leads to a lower return on investment, which is one reason why multinational corporations are opposed to the nationalization of resources. The power of multinationals coupled with the increased militancy of Third World nations makes the prospects of resource conflicts very real. If the two banded together to protect their interests, perhaps a new map of the world might ensue. We never thought democratization in Eastern Europe would succeed in our lifetime, so why not? We may see a new nation called North America, a political entity controlled by Exxon, Cargill, and Weyerhauser. The Pacific Rim (i.e., Japan) would become the mightiest nation in the world because of its healthy economy. De Beers, known previously as white South Africa, could exercise control over such strategic resources as platinum and diamonds and sell to the highest bidder regardless of race or political ideology. Andean South America, another nation, might be totally dependent on one export crop resulting in a toxic landscape laced with chemicals. All this just to keep up with the North American demand for illegal drugs. Although this scenario may seem a little far-fetched, some would argue that this futuristic vision is already present.

WILL IT BE LIKE THIS?

Hilary Lambert Renwick

Eileen had always been a happy woman, but lately she suspected that Mother Nature was out to get her. Today was New Year's Eve, 2005, but she didn't feel like celebrating. Her memories of childhood in the 1980s made the new century pale by comparison.

She gazed out the back door of her home at the once-beautiful oceanfront view. Nowadays the sight simply filled her with fear. She had placed a meterstick in the shallow water that covered what was once her backyard, and she was pretty sure the water had risen a millimeter over the past week. Her friends said she was imagining things, but she took the eventual consequences a lot more seriously than they did: the submergence of the beautiful shore cottage she'd been given by her grandparents. Her parents had taken early retirement when they reached fifty and had moved north with her grandparents to the Canadian Warmbelt some years previously. The weather was still uneven along the St. Lawrence River, but Mom and Dad's videocalls were full of excitement when yet another warming trend month was announced. They had made a bet on the global warming, and won.

Eileen, on the other hand, had finally decided that sentiment had overruled sense when she'd chosen to make a year-round home out of the site of so many childhood memories. The problem had begun to intrude about two years ago, when her husband Tom noticed that their dock was nearly submerged at high tide. It being so gradual, she hadn't noticed; but Tom's eyes were those of a visitor. He was on home leave from the United Business Ventures space station, where he was business manager of the Planetary Prospecting Project. So they'd raised the dock, but the water had kept pace and she hadn't had the energy to get the dock raised again this past summer. Now seawater slapped across its surface and was beginning to seep into their septic system. Eileen's six-year-old daughter swore the drinking water was salty. Eileen didn't want to know. Lately she felt safe only when she and the two kids boarded the 7 A.M. strato-bullet to Outer Glasgow, where she worked in the World Waste Watch monitoring center, after dropping the kids off at the regional International School. It was a two-hour commute each way, but considering where her husband worked, she didn't complain.

Eileen's job in the Information Flow subcenter was so interesting that she had little time to be depressed about the implications. Her team was working on the synthesis and interpretation of the pioneering collection work of the late 1990s. This massive research effort had resulted in the collection of all known information on the location and makeup of all toxic waste dumps, spills, accidents, and storage areas, on land and sea. Her group had developed a global model to help in predicting both the localized and large-scale effects of this waste on the biosphere. One of their frequent tasks was to announce their predictions of the poisoning of water supplies, fishing areas, and agricultural acreages as the long-buried toxics worked their way through the ground and along the ocean's currents.

Occasionally Eileen was interviewed for the Global News Service, when she would try to give a low-key answer to a reporter asking if a toxic chemical were to blame for the latest outbreak of Industrial Disease Syndrome in southern Africa. She was thankful that she didn't work for the Precipitation Watch group. They had a lot to answer for, what with the failure of crops worldwide, year after year. They had no simple answers either. They had to explain everything in terms of the combined effects of acid precipitation, ozone depletion, and CO_2 buildup, not to mention the climatic backlash caused by the melting ice caps. Global Newsviewers were uncomfortable with complicated answers. They wanted food on the table, and they wanted an end to the massive forced migrations of starved people. The world's cities were sprawling, wretched places, with their accompanying AIDS-decimated quarantine zones. All the trade and immigration barriers that a series of conservative United States administrations had erected were not enough to keep the unhappy flow at bay.

As well paid as Eileen and her husband were, she still had found it a struggle to get a nice feast together for tonight's New Year's Eve party. There had been no flour for sale for two weeks, while the government developed an emergency rationing plan; nonstop rain the previous summer had wiped out the wheat crop across the nation after a two-year recovery from the 2001 to 2003 Climatic Disaster years. So the table was a little light on pastries. Good thing she'd taken the grape shortage seriously and put up two cases of dandelion and elderberry wine. It would be a merry party, the first in a while, since the beer and liquor industries had laid off hundreds of thousands of workers when most governments had seized their grain stocks for food.

Through her work, Eileen had been able to order some meat for the holiday season, so that she and the kids had a hamburger stew for Christmas dinner. She'd saved a kilo for tonight, however, and with a discreet addition of soybean concentrate, she'd produced a handsome pot of meatballs. She hoped her generosity would not be interpreted as showing off. Friends were bringing other homemade goodies from locally collected wild crops. There had been a big newspaper article last week on Holiday Meals from Your Roadside Larder.

Tony and Tara ran in from the front yard, for once not needing to be reminded that their ultraviolet exposure time was up. It was a system that needed getting used to, but they dutifully watched the ozone-depletion readings every morning on the weather report and followed the guidelines. At least Eileen had managed to locate a reliable water-supply company, Alaskan Pure. She suspected that the water was actually from the Appalachians, but as long as it was well above the minimum on the toxicity standards, she didn't complain. The water tank needed cleaning, though. But she'd think about that in the New Year.

Could this be your life in 2005? Well paid, an interesting job, but somehow things just aren't what they used to be, and the necessities of life hard to come by?

Glossary

Absolute scarcity A condition when there is not enough of a resource in existence to satisfy demand for it.

Acid mine drainage Water leaving a surface or underground mine enriched in acid, usually sulfuric acid.

Acid rain The deposition of acids, either in precipitation or through dry dustfall, on the land surface.

Active solar power Solar energy gathered by a device that collects this energy and mechanically distributes it to where it is needed.

Advection inversion A temperature inversion caused by warm air passing over a cool surface.

Age structure The relative proportions of a population in different age classes.

Agribusiness Large-scale, organized production of food, farm machinery, and supplies as well as the storage, sale, and distribution of farm commodities, for profit.

Agricultural runoff Water leaving areas of agricultural land use, usually enriched in nutrients, sediment, and agricultural chemicals.

Ambient air quality The chemical characteristics of air as it exists in the environment; measures pollutant concentrations.

Amenity resource A resource valued for nonmonetary characteristics, such as its beauty or uniqueness.

Amenity value The nonmonetary, intangible value of a good or service.

Anadromous fish Fish that breed in fresh water but spend most of their adult lives in salt water. Examples are salmon and striped bass.

Animal unit month The amount of forage needed to support a certain number of grazing animals for one month.

Anoxic Water without dissolved oxygen.

Anthracite The highest rank of coal, most modified from its original plant form.

Anthropogenic Of human origin, such as carbon dioxide emitted by fossil fuel combustion.

Aquiclude An impermeable layer that confines an aquifer, preventing the water in it from moving upward or downward into adjacent strata. Shale and some igneous rocks often form aquicludes.

Aquifer A geologic unit containing groundwater. An underground reservoir made up of porous material capable of holding substantial quantities of water.

Arable land Land that is capable of being cultivated and supporting agricultural production.

Arroyo A deep, steep-sided gully found in semiarid areas, particularly in the southwestern United States.

Augur mining A coal-mining technique using a screw that extracts coal as it is drilled into a deposit.

Baby boom A period from 1945 to the mid-1960s in which the average fertility rate in the United States was over 3 children per woman.

Benefit–cost analysis A process of quantitatively evaluating all the positive and negative aspects of a particular action in order to reach a rational decision regarding that action.

Bioaccumulation The tendency for a pollutant to accumulate in the tissues of plants or animals.

Biochemical decay Breakdown of pollutants in water through the action of bacteria.

Biochemical oxygen demand (BOD) The amount of oxygen used in oxidation of substances in a given water sample. Measured in milligrams per liter over a specific time period.

Biocide Willful destruction of living things.

Biogeochemical cycle The movement of a particular material through an ecosystem over long periods of time.

Biological diversity The range or number of species or subspecies found in a particular area.

Biomagnification An increase in the concentration of a pollutant as it is passed up the food chain, caused by a tendency for animals to accumulate the pollutant in their tissues.

Biomass The total amount of living or formerly

living matter in a given area, measured as dry weight.

Biomass harvesting A forest harvest technique in which whole trees are chipped and used as fuel.

Biome A major ecological region within which plant and animal communities are similar in general characteristics and in their relations to the physical environment.

Bioregion A geographic area defined by ecological characteristics. A bioregion should include an area of relatively homogeneous ecological characteristics, or a specific assemblage of ecological communities. Similar to biome, but may refer to a smaller area with more specific characteristics.

Biosphere The worldwide system within which all life functions; composed of smaller systems including the atmosphere, hydrosphere, and lithosphere.

Biosphere resources Resources associated with living organisms.

Biotic potential The maximum rate of population growth resulting if all females in a population breed as often as possible and all individuals survive past their reproductive periods.

Birth rate The number of babies born per year per 1,000 population.

Bituminous coal A rank of coal below anthracite, characterized by a high degree of conversion from the original plant matter and a high heat content per unit weight.

BLM The U.S. Bureau of Land Management, located in the Department of the Interior, established in 1946 to administer federal lands not reserved for military, park, national forest, or other special uses.

Boreal forest A biome dominated by coniferous forests and found in relatively high altitudes or latitudes, almost exclusively in the Northern Hemisphere.

British Thermal Unit (BTU) The amount of energy required to raise the temperature of one pound of water one degree Fahrenheit at or near 39.2°F.

Bubble approach An approach to air pollution emissions control that allows a plant to consider emissions from several sources as combined emissions from the plant.

Carcinogen A substance that causes cancer.

Carrying capacity The maximum number of organisms in one species that can be supported in a particular environmental setting.

Cartel A consortium of producers of a single product who agree to limit production to keep the price of the product high.

Catadromous fish Fish that breed in salt water but live most of their adult lives in fresh water. The American eel is an example.

Centralized energy An energy conversion technology in which the key conversion (such as combustion of coal to create electricity) is made at a large scale at a single site (such as a power plant).

Chaparral A subtropical drought-resistant and fire-prone shrubby vegetation associated with Mediterranean-type climates.

Chlorofluorocarbons(CFCs) A group of substances that are compounds of chlorine, fluorine, and carbon. They are widely used in refrigeration and many industrial processes, and may contribute to deterioration of stratospheric ozone.

Clean Water Act The name given to a series of water quality improvement laws and their amendments passed in the United States beginning in 1964.

Clear-cutting A forest harvest technique in which all trees in a particular area are cut, regardless of species or size.

Coal gasification A chemical process converting coal to a gas that can then be used in place of natural gas.

Cohort A group of individuals of similar age.

Coliform bacteria Bacteria of the species *Escherichia coli*, commonly occurring in the digestive tracts of animals. Used as an indicator of the potential for disease-causing organisms in water.

Common property resource Resource such as air, oceans, or sunshine that is in theory owned by everyone but in practice utilized by a few. The question of regulation arises to prevent or lessen resource abuse.

Community A collection of organisms occupying a specific geographic area.

Concentration In the context of air or water quality, the amount of a substance per unit (weight or volume) of air or water.

Conservation The wise use or careful management of resources to attain the maximum possible social benefits from them.

Conservation tillage An agricultural system

using tillage techniques designed to reduce soil erosion and overland flow. Most conservation tillage techniques involve less manipulation of the soil than conventional techniques, leaving more plant matter on the soil surface.

Consumptive use   Water use that results in water being evaporated rather than returned to surface water or groundwater after use.

Continental shelf   Area of the seafloor, averaging less than 650 feet (200 m) deep, that generally was exposed at times of lower sea level in the past.

Contour plowing   A soil conservation technique involving plowing parallel to the contour, across a slope rather than up and down it.

Cost-effectiveness analysis   An analysis of all the costs involved in taking a specified action to determine the most efficient way to carry out the chosen action.

Cowboy economics   An approach to resource economics that is based on short-term and immediate gains without regard for long-term or external effects of that resource use.

Criteria pollutants   Air pollutants, including carbon monoxide, hydrocarbons, lead, oxidants, particulates, nitrogen oxides, and sulfur oxides, for which maximum permissible concentrations in ambient air are established.

Critical mineral   A mineral necessary for defense of the United States and available partly in America and/or partly from friendly nations.

Crop rotation   A soil conservation technique involving changing crops grown on a given parcel of land from year to year. Crop rotations may include fallow periods.

Cropland   Land in which crops are regularly planted and harvested. Includes land in fallow or pasture as part of a regular rotation system.

Crown fire   An intense forest fire that consumes the tops of trees as well as lower strata of vegetation.

Crude oil   Unrefined petroleum as it is extracted from the ground; it is liquid at normal ambient temperatures.

Death rate   The number of deaths per year per 1,000 population.

Decentralized energy source   An energy conversion system characterized by numerous small-scale facilities located at or near the end-use site. Photovoltaic cells are an example.

Decreaser   A plant species in a range community that declines in importance as a result

of grazing pressure. Usually decreasers are the most palatable to the grazing animals.

Deep ocean   Ocean areas seaward of the continental shelf.

Deforestation   Any process of replacement of forest vegetation with other types.

Demographic transition   The process by which a human population goes through a sigmoidal growth pattern, including an early phase of high birth and death rates, an intermediate phase of high birth rates but low death rates, and a later phase of low birth and death rates.

Desalination   Artificial removal of salt from water, such as by distillation or reverse osmosis.

Desert   A biome characterized by plants and animals adapted to extreme moisture scarcity.

Desertification   A process of land becoming more desertlike as a result of human-induced devegetation and related soil deterioration, sometimes aggravated by drought.

Dilution   In water quality, a reduction in pollutant concentration caused by mixing with water with a lower concentration of the substance.

Dissolved oxygen   Oxygen found in dissolved form in water.

Dissolved solids   Substances normally solid at ambient temperatures but dissolved into ionic form in water.

Diversification   The trend in many large corporations toward ownership of a wide array of companies producing unrelated goods and services.

Domesticate   A species that has been bred for specific characteristics that humans value, thereby rendering the species dependent on humans for its continued survival.

Doubling time   The length of time needed for a population to double in size. It is a function of the growth rate.

Drainage basin   An area bounded by drainage divides and defined with respect to a point along a stream. All the runoff generated within the area must pass the point along the stream; runoff generated outside the basin will not pass that point.

Drip irrigation   A method involving small pipes placed at the base of plants delivering water slowly to the plant roots.

Drought   A period of time with unusually low precipitation.

Dry farming   Agricultural production in climatically marginal lands without the use of irrigation.

Ecology   The study of the interrelationships between living organisms and the living and nonliving components and processes that make up their environment.

Ecosystem   The collection of all living organisms in a geographic area together with all living and nonliving things they interact with.

Ecotone   A transitional zone between two adjacent ecosystems.

El Niño/La Niña   A transient, periodic warming of the equatorial eastern Pacific Ocean, associated with fisheries depletion and large-scale climatic fluctuations.

Emissions trading   A procedure in air quality regulation by which one polluter can acquire permission to discharge pollutants formerly discharged by another discharger that has ceased emitting pollutants.

Endangered species   A species in imminent danger of extinction.

Energy budget   An accounting of all energy inputs and outputs for a system.

Energy conservation   Using energy resources in such a way as to minimize energy consumption in relation to benefits gained.

Energy efficiency   The amount of utility, either work performed or income generated, gained per unit of an energy resource.

Environmental cognition   The mental process of making sense of the world that each of us inhabits.

Environmental lapse rate   The average rate at which temperature declines with increasing altitude in the troposphere.

Environmental refugee   A person fleeing a natural or human-caused environmental disaster.

Environmental resistance   Factors such as food supply, weather, disease, and predators that keep a population below its biotic potential.

Erosion   Removal of soil by running water or wind.

Erosivity   The ability of rainfall to cause erosion. Erosivity is a function of rainfall intensity and drop size.

Estuary   A semienclosed water body, open to the sea, in which seawater is significantly diluted by fresh water from the land.

Euphotic zone   The upper portion of the sea, in which sunlight is intense enough to allow plant growth.

Eutrophication   The process by which lakes become increasingly nutrient rich and shallow. It is a natural process that is accelerated by water pollution.

Evapotranspiration   The process by which liquid water is conveyed to the atmosphere as water vapor, including water use by plants.

Exclusive economic zone   A zone of the oceans over which a particular nation has claims or exclusive control of certain economic activities, such as fishing.

Exploitation   Use of a resource at the maximum profitable short-term rate, without regard for long-term resource quality or availability.

Externality   A cost outside of the production and marketing that produces it.

Extinction   The process by which a species ceases to exist.

Farmland   Land that is part of farm units, including cropland, pasture, small woodlots, and areas used for small farm roads and buildings.

Feedback   An information transmission that produces a circular flow of information in a system.

Fertility rate   The average number of children that women in a given population bear in their reproductive years.

Fertilizer   A substance added to the soil to improve plant growth. The most commonly used fertilizers are those containing large amounts of nitrogen, potassium, and phosphorus.

Fire frequency   The average number of fires per unit time at a given location.

First law of thermodynamics   The law of conservation of energy, which states that energy is neither created nor destroyed, but merely transformed from one state to another or converted to or from matter.

Fission   A process of splitting heavy atoms of uranium or plutonium into lighter elements, thereby releasing energy.

Fixed costs   Costs of operating a business that do not vary with the rate of output of goods and services.

Flood irrigation   A means of irrigation whereby entire fields are occasionally inundated.

Flow resource   A resource that is simultaneously used and replaced. Perpetual and renewable resources are flow resources.

Food chain　A linear path that food energy takes in passing from producer to consumers to decomposers in an ecosystem.

Food web　A complex, interlocking set of pathways that food energy takes in passing from producer to consumers to decomposers in an ecosystem.

Forecast　A prediction of the future based on actual or assumed past, present,or future conditions. Forecasts may be unconditional, conditional, exploratory, or prescriptive.

Furrow irrigation　A type of irrigation in which water is allowed to flow along the furrows (troughs) between rows of crops.

Fusion　The combination of two hydrogen atoms to create a helium atom, yielding energy.

Gaia hypothesis　A view of earth history that emphasizes the earth's tendency to maintain a balance or equilibrium of natural systems.

Genetic damage　Damage to individual cell tissues resulting in changes that are passed along to offspring in chromosomes.

General circulation model　A computerized representation of the earth's atmospheric and oceanic circulation system used to simulate weather and climate.

General Systems Theory　A way of looking at the world or any part of it as an interacting set of parts.

Geographic Information System (GIS)　A computer data base and data manipulation system designed to use geographically organized data.

Geologic estimate of resource　An estimate of the amount of a mineral resource in the earth based on information about the concentration and distribution of that mineral in rocks, without regard for the economics of extraction.

Geothermal energy　Energy extracted from heat contained in rocks near the earth's surface.

Grassland　A biome dominated by grasses. Most grasslands have semiarid climates.

Green Revolution　A variety of agricultural systems developed for application in Third World countries, involving the introduction of improved seed varieties, fertilizers, and irrigation systems.

Greenhouse effect　The tendency of the atmosphere to be transparent to shortwave solar radiation but opaque to longwave terrestrial radiation, leading to a warming of the atmosphere.

Greenhouse gases　Substances that are transparent to short-wave (solar) radiation but absorb long-wave (terrestrial) radiation and thus contribute to warming of the atmosphere. Carbon dioxide, ozone, chlorofluorocarbons, and methane are important greenhouse gases.

Ground fire　A forest fire that only burns at ground level, consuming litter and downed trees but not live standing trees.

Groundwater　Water below the ground surface, derived from the percolation of rainfall and seepage from surface water.

Groundwater mining　See Overdraft.

Guest worker　A person allowed in a country on a temporary basis in order to increase the available labor force in that country.

Gully　A steep-walled stream channel incised in the soil by accelerated erosion.

Habitat　Land that provides living-space and sustenance for plants and animals.

Halocline　A marked change in salinity at a particular depth in the ocean or an estuary; it signals the boundary between two layers of water.

Hardwoods　Trees with particularly dense wood; primarily broad-leafed trees.

Heavy-water reactor　A nuclear fission reactor using deuterium-enriched water to moderate the fission reaction.

High seas　Areas of the oceans beyond legal control of any nation.

High-temperature gas-cooled reactor　A nuclear fission reactor using helium gas to transfer heat from the core to a steam generator.

Homestead Act　A law passed in 1862 providing 160 acres of federal land free to settlers.

Homocentric　A view of nature that only considers human, rather than plant or animal, needs.

Homosphere　The lower portion of the earth's atmosphere, characterized by relatively uniform gaseous composition. Consists of the troposphere, the stratosphere, and the mesosphere.

Horizon　A layer in the soil with distinctive textural, mineralogical, chemical, and/or structural characteristics.

Hydroelectric power　Electricity generated by passage of runoff-derived water through a turbine, usually at a dam.

Hydrothermal mineralization　A process of concentration of metallic ores caused by high-temperature geochemical processes in underground waters.

Illegal immigrant　A person who enters and lives in a country in violation of that country's laws.

Incommensurables　Effects of a given action

that can, with some effort, be given monetary value.

Increaser A range plant species that is present in a range ecosystem prior to grazing and that increases in numbers or coverage as a result of grazing.

Incrementalism A type of decisionmaking strategy that reacts to short-term imperfections in existing policies rather than establishing long-term future goals. Decisions are made on a sequential basis and do not radically depart from existing policy.

Infiltration capacity The maximum rate at which a soil can absorb water.

Inorganic Describes a chemical substance that does not contain carbon.

Input Energy, matter, or information entering a system.

In-stream uses Uses of water that do not require it to be removed from a stream or lake. They include such things as shipping, swimming, and waste disposal.

Intangible A good, service, or effect of an action that cannot be assigned monetary value.

Integrated pest management A pest control technique that relies on combinations of crop rotation, biological controls, and pesticides.

Interbasin transfer A movement of water from one drainage basin to another, such as from the east side of the Rocky Mountains into the west-flowing Colorado River.

Internal waters Waters under the exclusive control of a coastal nation, including bays, estuaries, and rivers.

International Whaling Commission An organization set up under the International Convention for the Regulation of Whaling, in 1946, to regulate the whaling industry.

Invader A range plant species not present in a given area before grazing, but enters the area as a result of the ecological changes caused by grazing.

Irrigation The artificial application of water to a crop or pasture beyond that supplied by direct precipitation.

Kerogen A waxy hydrocarbon found in oil shale.

Land Capability Classification System A scheme used by the U.S. Soil Conservation Service for assessing and classifying productivity of land units.

Landfill An updated form of a dump, in which waste is deposited in layers and covered with earth.

Law of entropy The second law of thermodynamics. Entropy is a measure of disorder in a system.

Law of the Sea Treaty A treaty largely negotiated in the 1970s establishing jurisdiction over marine resources in coastal and deep-sea areas.

Leachate Water seeping from the bottom of a layer of ground and containing substances derived from that layer. Usually applied to landfills and other contamination sources.

Light-water reactor A type of nuclear power plant that uses ordinary water as the cooling medium.

Lignite A rank of coal characterized by a relatively low degree of modification of plant matter.

Limits to Growth A world model developed in the 1970s by a group called the Club of Rome; it predicted resource scarcity if world population and resource use growth continued.

Liquefaction Conversion of coal into a liquid hydrocarbon that can be transported by pipeline and burned as a liquid.

Liquid-metal fast-breeder reactor A nuclear fission reactor moderated and cooled by liquid sodium, and used to convert nonfissionable material such as uranium-238 to fissionable material such as plutonium-239.

Liquid natural gas (LNG) Natural gaseous hydrocarbons that are pressurized and cooled in order to be stored and/or transported in liquid form.

Maximum sustainable yield The largest average harvest of a species that can be indefinitely sustained under existing environmental conditions .

Mesosphere Layer of the atmosphere between 30 and 50 miles (50 and 80 km) in altitude, characterized by decreasing temperatures with increasing altitude.

Mined-land reclamation The return of land disturbed by mining to a more productive condition, usually a use similar to that existing before mining took place.

Minimum tillage A soil and water conservation technique that leaves the crop residue or stubble on the surface rather than plowing it under to minimize the number of times a field is tilled. Weeds are controlled by herbicides.

Mining Act   An act passed in 1872 providing free access to minerals on federal lands.

Mixed cropping   An agricultural system in which several different crops are grown in close proximity, in a rotation system, or both.

Mobile sources   Sources of air pollution that move, such as automobiles, boats, trains, and aircraft.

Model   A representation of the real world that can be used to help understand or predict the operation of that world.

Monoculture   An agricultural system in which a sole crop is grown repeatedly over a large area.

Monopoly   Control of access to a good or service by a single entity.

Montreal Protocol   An agreement signed in Montreal in 1987 in which signatory nations consented to limit production and consumption of ozone-damaging chemicals.

Multinational Corporation   A business entity that operates in many nations, and is not wholly subject to the laws of any one nation.

Multiple use   The use of lands for as many different purposes as possible in order to gain maximum benefit from them.

Multiple Use Sustained Yield Act   A law passed in 1960 establishing the principles of multiple use and sustained yield as guidelines for management of the national forests.

Municipal solid waste   Mixed solid waste derived primarily from residential and commercial sources.

National Forest Management Act   An act, passed in 1976, establishing operating principles and administrative divisions for the U.S. Forest Service.

Natural gas   Gaseous hydrocarbons extracted from subterranean reservoirs that hold gas at normal ambient temperatures.

Natural increase   In demography, the net change in population without regard to migration. It is the birth rate less the death rate, and can be positive or negative.

Natural resource   Something that is useful to humans and exists independent of human activity.

Neo-Malthusianism   Modern advocates of Thomas Malthus's ideas; those who advocate birth control to avert overpopulation, and who see overpopulation as ultimately leading to widespread malnourishment and famine.

NEPA   The National Environmental Policy Act, signed on Jan. 1 1970, which established

nationwide environmental goals and provided for preparation of Environmental Impact Statements to ensure compliance with those goals.

Neutral stuff   Something that exists but at present meets no known human material or non-material needs.

Non-point source   A pollution source that is diffuse, such as urban runoff.

Nonrenewable or stock resources   Resources that exist in finite quantity and are not replaced in nature.

Oil   Hydrocarbons found in the earth, liquid at normal ambient temperatures.

Oligopolistic competition   A process in which a small group controls access to a good or service by agreeing on a single price or by restricting access to these commodities.

Oligotrophic   Describes lakes that are relatively deep and nutrient poor. Opposite of eutrophic.

Organic   Refers to substances containing carbon.

Output   Energy, matter, or information leaving a system.

Overburden   Rock and soil that lie above coal or other mineral deposits and that must be removed to strip-mine the coal.

Overdraft, or groundwater mining   Withdrawal of groundwater in excess of the replacement rate over a long period of time.

Overgrazing   Grazing by a number of animals exceeding the carrying capacity of a given parcel of land.

Overland flow   Water flowing on the soil surface and unchannelized. Usually derived from precipitation that has not infiltrated.

Oxidants   A group of air pollutants that are strong oxidizing agents. Ozone and peroxyacetylnitrate are among the more important oxidants.

Ozone hole   A semi-permanent depletion in stratospheric ozone concentration over a polar region. Most prominent over the South Pole.

Parent material   The mineral matter from which soil is formed.

Particulate   In water or air quality matters, a solid contaminant.

Passive solar power   The collection of solar energy as heat at the end-use site, without any mechanical redistribution or storage of the energy.

Pastoral nomad   A person who herds animals

from place to place with no permanent settlement.

Pastoralist   A person whose livelihood is based on grazing animals.

Pasture   In U.S. terminology, land on which the natural vegetation is not grass, but which is used primarily for grazing.

Peat   The accumulated remains of plants, found in swampy or cool, humid areas. The initial material from which coal may be formed; may be dried and used for fuel.

Performance-based resource estimate   An estimate of the quantity of a mineral deposit available in the earth based primarily on the ability of prevailing technology to extract the mineral under existing and probable future economic conditions.

Permafrost   Ground below 0°C all year round.

Permeability   A measure of the rate at which water will flow into or through soil or rocks.

Perpetual resources   Resources that exist in perpetual supply, no matter how much they are used. Solar energy is an example.

Pesticide   A general term used to refer to a chemical used to control harmful organisms such as insects, fungi, rodents, worms, and bacteria. Insecticides, fungicides, and rodenticides are kinds of pesticides.

Photosynthesis   The formation of carbohydrates from carbon dioxide and water, utilizing light as energy.

Photovoltaic cell   A semiconductor-based device used to convert sunlight directly to electricity.

Placer deposit   A deposit of a mineral formed by concentration of heavy minerals in flowing water, such as by a stream or waves.

Point source   A pollution source that has a precise, identifiable location, such as a pipe or smokestack.

Polluter pays principle, or residuals tax   A means of shifting the cost of pollution from the community to the polluter, usually in the form of a tax.

Pollution   Human additions of undesirable substances to the environment.

Pollution Standards Index (PSI)   An index of air quality that is a combined measure of the health effects of several pollutants.

Population dynamics   The study of the rapidity and causes of population change.

Population pyramid   A graphic representation of the number or portion of males and females in each of several age categories in a population.

Potential evapotranspiration   The amount of water that could be evaporated or transpired if it were available.

Potential resource   A portion of the natural or human environment that is not today considered of value, but that one day may gain value as a result of technological, cognitive, or economic developments.

Preservation   The nonuse of resources. Limited resource development for the purpose of saving resources for the future.

Primary standards   Air pollution standards designed to protect human health.

Primary treatment   Sewage treatment consisting of removal of solids by sedimentation, flocculation, screening, or similar methods.

Principle of limiting factors   Whatever factor (nutrient, water, sunlight, etc.) is in shortest supply will limit the growth and development of an organism or a community.

Prior appropriation   A doctrine of water ownership in which the first productive user of water establishes the right to the water indefinitely. The primary water-ownership doctrine in the western United States.

Privatization   The transfer of government-owned resources, such as national forests, to private ownership and/or management.

Proxy value   A price applied to a commodity that has no established market value.

Quad   A measure of energy use, equal to one quadrillion (1,000,000,000,000,000) BTUs.

Radiation inversion   A temperature inversion caused by radiational cooling of air close to the ground.

Radioactivity   The emission of particles by decay of atoms of certain substances.

Railroad Acts   A series of acts passed in the 1850s and 1860s granting large amounts of land to railroad companies as a subsidy to railway construction and stimulant to settlement of western lands.

Range condition   As defined by the U.S. Forest Service, an estimate of the degree to which the present vegetation and ground cover depart from that which is presumed to be the natural potential (or climax) for the site.

Rangeland   Land that provides or is capable of providing forage for grazing animals.

RARE I and II   Two phases of Roadless Area

Review and Evaluation, conducted by the Forest Service in the 1970s, to evaluate wilderness qualities on its lands and designate areas for protection.

Recreational river A designation applied by the U.S. Deptartment of the Interior to rivers that are easily reached, usually developed, and heavily used.

Recycling Reprocessing of a used product for reuse in a similar or different form.

Relative scarcity Short supply of a resource in one or more areas due to inadequate or disrupted distribution.

Renewable energy Energy resources that are produced naturally as fast as they are consumed, such as solar, wind, and hydroelectric power.

Renewable resource A resource that can be depleted but will be replenished by natural processes. Forests and fisheries are examples.

Replacement cost The cost of replacing a resource that is used.

Replacement level The number of births that will replace a population at the same size, without reduction or rise. Also called Zero Population Growth.

Reserve In the context of mineral resources, a deposit of known location and quality that is economically extractable at the present time.

Residuals management An approach to production of goods and services that includes accounting of waste products associated with both production and consumption phases.

Resource Something that is useful to humans.

Resource recovery Separation of garbage into recyclable components such as metal, glass, and heat from incineration.

Respiration Oxidation of food that releases oxygen, water, and energy, which are dissipated in the biosphere.

Reuse Repeated use of a product without reprocessing or remanufacture.

Rill A small channel created by soil erosion and small enough to be obliterated by plowing.

Riparian areas Lands adjacent to and subject to flooding by streams.

Riparian Rights A doctrine of water ownership in which those whose land adjoins a stream have right to use the water in the stream. The primary water-ownership doctrine in the eastern U.S.

Ruminant One of a group of grazing animals including cattle, bison, sheep, goat, which have digestive systems particularly adapted to grasses.

Sagebrush Rebels An informal, politically conservative, group that in the early 1980s attempted to reduce government controls over use of federal lands in the western United States. Interior Secretary James Watt was prominent in this group.

Sahel A semiarid east–west swath across Africa, environmentally transitional between the Sahara Desert (to the north) and equatorial rainforests (to the south), in which recent desertification and drought have been particularly severe.

Salinity The concentration of mineral salts in water. The average salinity of the oceans is about 35 parts per thousand.

Saltwater intrusion Movement of salt water into aquifers formerly occupied by fresh water as a result of groundwater withdrawal in coastal areas.

Satisficing A decisionmaking strategy that seeks a course of action that is good enough but not necessarily perfect. A few alternatives are compared and the best course of action is chosen from this limited range of options.

Savanna Tropical or subtropical semiarid grassland with scattered trees.

Scenic river A designation applied by the U.S. Department of the Interior to rivers with strong amenity value that are accessible at certain points by motor vehicles and sustain some development along their shorelines.

Secondary standard An air quality standard designed to protect human welfare (property, vegetation, etc.) as opposed to health.

Secondary treatment Sewage treatment that removes organic matter and nutrients by biological decomposition using such methods as trickling filters, aeration, and activated sludge.

Sedentarization Permanent settlement of once nomadic people.

Sedimentation Deposition of solid particles by settling in a water body.

Selective cutting A timber harvesting technique in which only trees of specified size and/or species are taken, leaving other trees.

Separate impacts Effects of a system's activity that can be measured separately.

Shadow price An artificial monetary value applied to those resources for which a simple price tag is not easy to calculate, e.g., wilderness, habitat.

Shale oil A petroleumlike substance, kerogen, found in high concentrations in some shale rocks.

Shelterwood cutting   A two-phase timber harvesting technique in which not all trees are taken in the first phase so that some trees may provide shelter for young seedlings; when these are established the remaining older trees are cut.

Sigmoidal growth curve   An S-shaped pattern of population growth, including a phase of accelerating growth followed by decelerating growth and finally population stability.

Social cost   The cost of producing a good or service, plus its cost to humans in terms of pollution and other negative socioenvironmental effects.

Softwoods   Timber species with relatively low-density wood; primarily needle-leaf trees.

Soil   A porous layer of mineral and organic matter at the earth's surface, formed as a result of the action of chemical and biological processes on rocks over a period of time.

Soil erodibility   A measure of the inherent susceptibility of a soil to erosion, without regard to topography, vegetation cover, management, or weather conditions.

Soil fertility   The ability of a soil to supply essential nutrients to plants.

Soil structure   The way in which individual soil particles form aggregates, particularly the shapes and arrangement of such aggregates. Especially important to soil hydrologic characteristics.

Soil texture   The mix of different sizes of particles in a soil.

Solid waste   Refuse materials primarily composed of solids at normal ambient temperatures.

Somatic damage   Nonhereditary damage to individual cell tissues from radiation.

Species   A group of organisms with similar genetic and morphologic characteristics, that are capable of interbreeding.

Spent fuel   Nuclear material that is no longer capable of sustaining the fission process.

Sprinkler irrigation   Irrigation by pumping water under pressure through nozzles and spraying it over the land.

Stationary source   A pollution source that does not move, such as a smokestack.

Stock resource   See Nonrenewable resource.

Stockpiling   Amassing amounts of some substance well beyond present need in anticipation of a shortage of that substance.

Strategic mineral   A mineral needed for the defense of the United States, yet available only from other nations.

Stratification   A layering of a water body caused by differences in water density. Stratification is commonly caused by temperature or salinity differences.

Stratified estuary   An arm of the sea in which fresh water from the land overlies denser salt water.

Stratosphere   Layer of the atmosphere between 3 and 30 miles (5 and 50 km) in altitude, characterized by increasing temperature with altitude.

Stress management   A decisionmaking strategy that is reactive in nature. Once a resource issue becomes critical, then policy is determined to cope with the immediate problem without any consideration of long-term implications of such a policy.

Strip cropping   A soil conservation technique in which parallel strips of land are planted in different crops.

Strip-mining or surface mining   Extraction of a mineral from the ground by excavation at the ground surface.

Stubble mulch   A soil covering composed of the unused stalks of crop plants.

Subbituminous coal   A rank of coal intermediate between lignite and bituminous coal.

Subeconomic resource   A resource that at present is unavailable for use because of high cost of extraction.

Subsidence   Sinking of the land surface caused by removal of water, oil, or minerals from beneath the surface.

Subsidence inversion   A temperature inversion caused by differential warming of a sinking air mass. Upper portions of the mass are warmed more than lower portions, causing the inversion.

Substitutability   The degree to which one material can be substituted for another in end uses.

Sulfur content   The amount of sulfur found in coal. Combustion of coal with a high sulfur content results in emissions of sulfur oxides, which contribute to acid precipitation.

Surface fire   A moderate-intensity forest fire in which low-level vegetation, such as shrubs, is consumed along with some of the surfaces (bark) of trees, but the crowns of trees are not consumed and trees survive.

Surface water   Water and ice found in rivers,

lakes, swamps, and other aboveground water bodies.

Suspended particulates In reference to air quality, solid or liquid particles with diameters from 0.03 to 100 microns. In water quality, solid particles transported in suspension.

Sustainability Economic growth with environmental responsibility; economic activity that could be carried on indefinitely without resource depletion.

Sustainable agriculture An agricultural system that is dependent solely on renewable resources and that maintains the soil in a condition so that it will continue to be productive indefinitely.

Sustained yield Management of renewable resources conducted in such a way as to allow a constant rate of harvest indefinitely.

Synergistic impacts Effects of a system's activity that are different from the individual effects of component parts of the system.

Synfuel A contraction of synthetic fuel. Liquid or gaseous fossil fuel manufactured from other fuels that are less useful as found in nature.

System An entity consisting of a set of parts that work together to form a whole. The human body, a transportation network, and the earth are all systems.

Tailings Solid waste products derived from mineral extraction and/or refinement.

Tar sand Sandy deposits containing heavy oil or tar; the sand must be heated to extract the oil.

Taylor Grazing Act An act passed in 1934 closing most public lands to homesteading, and establishing controls on grazing use of federal lands.

Temperate forest A biome characterized primarily by deciduous broad-leaved trees.

Temperature inversion A condition in the atmosphere in which warm air overlies cool air. Inversions restrict vertical air circulation.

Terracing A soil and water conservation technique consisting of ridges on the contour, or level areas constructed on a slope.

Territorial sea A band of open ocean adjacent to the coast, over which the coastal nation has control. It is generally either 3 or 12 miles (4.8 or 19.4 km) wide.

Tertiary treatment Any of a wide range of advanced sewage treatment processes aimed at removing substances not removed by primary or secondary treatment.

Thermal pollution Heat added by humans to a water body or to the air.

Thermocline A zone in a water body in which temperature declines rapidly with increasing depth. Vertical water circulation is limited by the presence of a thermocline.

Threatened species A species that is not endangered but has a rapidly declining population.

Throughput tax, or disposal charge A fee paid by a producer on materials that go into the production of polluting products. The fee reflects the social cost of the pollution.

Timber Culture Act An act passed in 1873 providing free access to timber on federal lands.

Toxic substance A substance that causes disease or death when organisms are exposed to it in very low quantities.

Transboundary pollution Transport of pollutants (particularly air pollutants) across national or state boundaries.

Trophic level One of the steps in a food chain.

Tropical rainforest A biome composed primarily of evergreen broad-leaved trees growing in tropical areas of high rainfall throughout most of the year.

Troposphere The lowest layer of the atmosphere, below about 9 miles (15 km) in altitude, characterized by decreasing temperature with increasing altitude.

Tundra A biome found in arctic and subarctic regions consisting of a dense growth of lichens, mosses, and herbs.

Underground mining A mineral extraction technique consisting of subsurface excavation with minimal disturbance of the ground surface.

Unidentified resource A mineral resource assumed to be present within known geologic districts, but not yet specifically located or characterized in detail.

Universal Soil Loss Equation A statistical technique developed by the U.S. Department of Agriculture for predicting the average erosion rate by rainfall under a variety of climatic, soil, topographic, and management conditions.

Upwelling An upward movement of seawater that usually occurs near the margins of oceans.

Uranium An element, two isotopes of which (^{235}U and ^{238}U) are important in atomic energy production.

Urban runoff Runoff derived from urban areas,

usually containing relatively high concentrations of pollutants. Also called urban stormwater.

Variable costs   Costs of production that vary with the rate of output.

Visual blight   Modification of a landscape that is visually undesirable.

Wastewater reclamation   Any process in which waste water is put to use, such as for cooling or irrigation, with or without treatment.

Water harvesting   Any of several techniques for increasing the amount of runoff derived from a land area.

Water holding capacity   The ability of the soil to retain or store water.

Water table   The upper limit of groundwater or of the saturated zone.

Weathering   The breakdown of rocks into smaller particles and/or new chemical substances as a result of exposure to water and air at the earth's surface.

Wild river   A designation applied by the U.S. Department of the Interior to rivers with strong amenity value and that are inaccessible by motorized vehicles and have undeveloped shorelines.

Willingness to pay   A method of determining proxy value of a resource by asking how much users of that resource would be willing to pay to use or not use it.

Windbreak   A line of trees or shrubs planted perpendicular to the prevailing winds, designed to reduce wind velocities and thus reduce wind erosion.

Withdrawal   The removal of water from surface water or groundwater.

Zero population growth   A term applied to the fertility rate needed to attain a stable population over a long period of time.

Zoning   A system of land use management in which land is classified according to permitted uses.

Index